Academic Reading

Academic Reading

SIXTH EDITION

Kathleen T. McWhorter

NIAGARA COUNTY COMMUNITY COLLEGE

PEARSON
Longman

New York   San Francisco   Boston
London   Toronto   Sydney   Tokyo   Singapore   Madrid
Mexico City   Munich   Paris   Cape Town   Hong Kong   Montreal

Acquisitions Editor: Melanie Craig
Development Editor: Gillian Cook
Senior Supplements Editor: Donna Campion
Media Supplements Editor: Jenna Egan
Marketing Manager: Thomas DeMarco
Production Manager: Bob Ginsberg
Project Coordination, Text Design, and Electronic Page Makeup: Thompson Steele, Inc.
Cover Design Manager/Cover Designer: John Callahan
Cover Illustration: Courtesy of iStockphoto
Photo Researcher: Anita Dickhuth
Senior Manufacturing Buyer: Alfred C. Dorsey
Printer and Binder: Von Hoffman/Owensville
Cover Printer: Coral Graphic Services

For permission to use copyrighted material, grateful acknowledgment is made to the copyright holders on pp. 503–508, which are hereby made part of this copyright page.

Library of Congress Cataloging-in-Publication Data

McWhorter, Kathleen T.
  Academic reading / Kathleen T. McWhorter. -- 6th ed.
    p. cm.
  ISBN 0-321-36479-1
  1. Reading (Higher education). 2. Study skills. 3. Reading comprehension. I. Title.
LB2395.3.M37 2006
428.4071'1--dc22   2006013358

Visit us at www.ablongman.com/mcwhorter

ISBN 0-321-36479-1

12345678910—VHO—09 08 07 06

Brief Contents

Detailed Contents

* This chapter is available online at www.ablongman.com/mcwhorter

Directions for Accessing Online Chapter
1. Type in URL http://www.ablongman.com/mcwhorter
2. Click on cover of text
3. Click on link to Online Chapter

Preface

Each academic discipline has its own subject matter, approach, and methodology. Consequently, reading assignments in each discipline require unique sets of reading skills and strategies. Many students who possess adequate general reading skills have not learned to adapt them to the demands of different academic disciplines. *Academic Reading,* Sixth Edition, is a unique text that focuses on these important discipline-specific reading skills.

■ Approach

Although many texts teach general reading skills, few of them show students how to apply, modify, and adapt their skills to accommodate the unique features and requirements of various academic disciplines. This text provides a complete review of comprehension and vocabulary skills and general textbook reading strategies; then it discusses ways to apply these strategies to six major academic disciplines. Professors in each academic discipline contributed to and evaluated each of the academic discipline chapters.

Academic Reading, Sixth Edition, uses several current, effective methodologies to develop reading skills:

- **Active Reading** For many students, reading is a passive assimilation process: their goal is to acquire as many facts and as much information as possible. The active reading approach used in *Academic Reading* encourages students to interact with the text by predicting, questioning, and evaluating ideas.
- **Levels of Thinking** Using Bloom's taxonomy of cognitive skills (updated by Anderson) as a framework, this book shows students how to apply higher-order thinking skills to their course work.
- **Metacomprehension** Metacomprehension is the reader's awareness of his or her own comprehension processes. Mature and proficient readers exert a great deal of cognitive control over their reading: they analyze reading tasks, select appropriate reading strategies, and monitor the effectiveness of those strategies. This text guides students in developing these metacomprehensive strategies.
- **Academic Thought Patterns** The text describes six common academic thought patterns that are used in various disciplines to organize and structure ideas. Four additional patterns are also discussed. These patterns, presented as organizing schemata, are used to establish order, consistency, and predictability within academic disciplines.

- **Writing as Learning** Although most students regard writing as a means of communication, few are accustomed to using it as a reading aid to help them organize information, focus ideas, recognize relationships, or generate new ideas. This text introduces writing as a vehicle for learning. Techniques such as underlining, outlining, note taking, and cognitive mapping are approached as learning strategies.
- **Learning Style** Not all students learn in the same way. To help students discover their unique learning preferences, the text includes a Learning Style Questionnaire and offers students suggestions for adapting their study methods to suit their learning style characteristics.

■ Discipline-specific Reading Skills

With the fundamental skills in place, college students are able to develop a diverse repertoire of reading strategies and to select and alternate among them. Professors from each of the academic disciplines worked as consultants during the writing of the book. A new set of specialists was used to develop a revision plan for the sixth edition. These consultant teams offered suggestions for both skill coverage and methodology. Some of the discipline-specific reading skills included are the following:

In the Social Sciences

- understanding theories in the social sciences
- reading research reports
- making comparisons and applications

In Business

- reading models
- reviewing case studies
- studying organization charts and flowcharts
- approaching supplemental readings

In the Humanities and the Arts

- understanding figurative language
- reading poetry and short stories
- working with literary criticism
- studying visual elements in art

In Mathematics

- understanding mathematical language
- reading sample problems
- verbalizing processes
- reading graphics
- approaching word problems

In the Natural Sciences

- previewing before reading
- understanding scientific approaches
- studying sample problems
- learning terminology and notation

In Technical and Applied Fields

- reading illustrations and drawings
- using visualization
- reading technical manuals
- employing problem-solving strategies
- benefiting from practicum experiences

Each chapter in Part 4 includes a list of Web sites relevant to the discipline. These lists will help students find reliable academic sources to consult for research and reading in the field.

■ Content Overview

Academic Reading, Sixth Edition, is organized into four units. Chapters within each unit are interchangeable, allowing the instructor to adapt the material to a variety of instructional sequences.

Part 1, Fundamental Reading Strategies, presents fundamental reading strategies that provide the foundation for the remainder of the text. Chapter 1 introduces the key concepts of active reading and comprehension monitoring, and includes a learning style analysis. Chapter 2 presents fundamental comprehension skills and integrates the concept of adjusting reading rate to meet comprehension demands. Chapter 3 discusses vocabulary: contextual aids, structural analysis, and specialized terminology.

Part 2, Critical Reading Strategies, teaches students to interpret and evaluate what they read. Chapter 4 concentrates on evaluating the author's message and includes topics such as making inferences, distinguishing between fact and opinion, and analyzing the writer's tone. In Chapter 5 students learn to analyze the author's technique; topics include evaluating generalizations and assumptions, understanding connotative meanings, and recognizing manipulative language. Reading and evaluating arguments, both inductive and deductive, and identifying errors in logical reasoning are the focus of Chapter 6.

Part 3, Academic Reading Strategies, teaches students how to recognize patterns of general academic thought, learn from textbooks, use writing to learn, read graphics and visuals, and read online sources.

Part 4, Strategies for Specific Disciplines, consists of six chapters, each of which focuses on reading strategies for a specific discipline: social sciences, business, the humanities and arts, mathematics, the natural sciences, and technical fields. Each chapter describes unique characteristics of the discipline, specialized reading techniques, predominant thought patterns, and methods for adapting study techniques.

Online Chapter: Reading Research, Reference, and Collateral Assignments provides students strategies for reading and evaluating research and reference material commonly used in college courses.

■ Special Features

The following features enhance the text's effectiveness:

- Learning Objectives   Each chapter begins with a brief list of objectives that establishes the chapter's focus and provides students with purposes for reading. The objectives can also be used as a way to review and check retention after reading the chapter.
- Discipline Overviews   The text provides an introduction to six major academic disciplines. It acquaints the student with the basic subject matter and the basic approach used in those disciplines. For example, the text explains and discusses
  - why social science is a "science."
  - how business focuses on organization and management.
  - literature as a focus on ideas.
  - why mathematics is a sequential thinking process.
  - how the sciences focus on explanations of natural phenomena.
  - the importance of application and performance in technical fields.

- **Curriculum-Specific Web Sites**   Each chapter in Part 4 contains a list of useful academic Web sites that students can visit to initiate reading or research within a discipline. The list is divided into four categories: Directories/Web Guides, Journals/Indexes/Databases, References, and Government Resources.
- **Multimedia Activities**   Each chapter contains two Web activities that reinforce the skills taught in the chapter.
- **Self-test Chapter Summaries**   Each chapter includes a question and answer summary intended to help students review and consolidate chapter content through self-testing.
- **Reading Selections**   Each chapter concludes with one or more reading selections from a college textbook or related academic source to reinforce the skills and strategies presented in the chapter. Each reading is accompanied by a vocabulary review exercise, comprehension questions, critical thinking questions, and an exercise on applying learning/study strategies.
- **Paired Readings**   Eight sets of paired readings are included in the text. Each pair provides two viewpoints on a given topic and encourages students to integrate ideas and synthesize sources. Questions are included to guide students in applying critical thinking skills to make connections between the ideas and approaches of the readings.
- **Academic Applications**   Exercises labeled "Academic Application" require students to apply their reading skills to textbook or course materials from their other college courses.
- **Exercises for Collaborative Learning**   Additional exercises designated "Collaborative Learning" provide structured activities in which students can learn from one another as they analyze and apply skills introduced in the chapter.

■ Changes in the Sixth Edition

Numerous changes and additions have been made in the sixth edition. Many of the changes stemmed from the disciplinary review process. College professors from the disciplines represented in Chapters 12 through 17 were asked to review the text in general and to devote specific attention to the content of the chapter that discusses their academic discipline.

- **NEW Second Color.**   Color is used throughout the text to highlight headings, exercises, test-taking tips, self-check summaries, and other chapter features to make text navigation simpler and the text more visually appealing.

- REVISED Part 4. Chapters 12 through 17 have been revised and updated based on feedback from a panel of reviewers who provided information on current trends and innovations in their fields, new examples and problems to illustrate types of content material students will be expected to read, and relevant Web sites for research.
- NEW Section on Allied Health Fields. Due to the growing emphasis on allied health careers, a new section has been added to Chapter 17 that covers reading, learning, and studying in the allied health fields.
- NEW "A Professor Talks About . . ." Sections. A new feature has been added to Part 4 that provides quotations from the review panel members that highlight the usefulness and appropriateness of the chapter content relevant to their field. The professors also offer personal advice to students taking courses in their discipline on how to successfully read and study in their field.
- REVISED Academic Success Section. The study tips, previously included in the Appendix, have been moved to the front of the book, allowing students to access them more easily. A new section on Balancing School and Work has been added and the section on using the computer as a study aid has been updated and expanded.
- NEW "A Student Talks About . . ." Section. This new feature includes a photo of the student, brief biographical information, and a quotation explaining how he or she has successfully used one of the specific study skills addressed in the Academic Success section.
- NEW Think About It! Each chapter opens with a stimulating photograph linked to an assignment that ties the image into the chapter content. These openers immediately engage students while demonstrating the link between real-life experiences and chapter content.
- ONLINE CHAPTER: Reading Research, Reference, and Collateral Assignments. This online chapter provides students strategies for reading and evaluating research and reference material commonly used in college courses. Techniques include skimming and scanning, note taking, evaluating sources, and synthesizing and comparing sources.
- NEW Readings. Fourteen new end-of-chapter reading selections have been chosen to provide current, up-to-date coverage of a wide range of academic fields including stem-cell research, information privacy and security, the ivory trade, and racial profiling. Numerous in-chapter textbook excerpts have also been replaced or updated.
- NEW Self-test Summaries. The chapter summaries have been revised to use a question and answer format, making them interactive and easy to use for study and review.
- REVISED Chapter Sequence. The chapter on using writing to learn (formerly Chapter 11) has been moved to follow Chapter 8: Learning from Textbooks.

■ Book-Specific Ancillary Materials

The Instructor's Manual

The Instructor's Manual provides numerous suggestions for using the text, including how to structure the course and how to approach each section of the book. The Instructor's Manual also contains a complete answer key for the text and a set of overhead projection transparency masters (ISBN 0-321-41497-7).

Assessment Package/Test Bank

An assessment package/test bank accompanies the text. It contains two sets of multiple-choice chapter review quizzes that measure students' knowledge of chapter content. It also contains a set of mastery tests that measure students' ability to apply concepts, principles, and techniques taught in the chapter. The mastery tests simulate actual academic situations, assignments, and course materials and are designed to be self-scoring if the instructor so desires (ISBN 0-321-41496-9).

PowerPoint Slides

A series of PowerPoint slides for each chapter can be downloaded free from the Longman Web site at http://www.ablongman.com.

McWhorter Companion Website

A dedicated Web site to accompany the McWhorter reading and study skills series is available to instructors and students. This Web site includes study tips, electronically scored quizzes, Internet activities and links, and more. Please visit the site at http://www.ablongman.com/mcwhorter.

In addition to these book-specific supplements, many other skills-based supplements and testing packages are available for both instructors and students. All these supplements are available either at no additional cost or at greatly reduced prices.

■ The Longman Developmental Reading Package

Longman is pleased to offer a variety of support materials to help make teaching reading easier on teachers and to help students excel in their coursework. Many of our student supplements are available free or at a greatly reduced price when packaged with *Academic Reading,* Sixth Edition. Contact your local Longman sales representative for more information on pricing and how to create a package.

Support Materials for Reading Instructors

Printed Test Bank for Developmental Reading (Instructor / ISBN 0-321-08596-5)
Offers more than 3,000 questions in all areas of reading, including vocabulary, main idea, supporting details, patterns of organization, critical thinking, analytical reasoning, inference, point of view, visual aids, and textbook reading. (Electronic version also available)

Electronic Test Bank for Developmental Reading (Instructor / CD ISBN 0-321-08179-X)
Offers more than 3,000 questions in all areas of reading, including vocabulary, main idea, supporting details, patterns of organization, critical thinking, analytical reasoning, inference, point of view, visual aids, and textbook reading. Instructors simply choose questions, then print out the completed test for distribution or offer the test online.

The Longman Guide to Classroom Management (Instructor / ISBN 0-321-09246-5)
This guide is designed as a helpful resource for instructors who have classroom management problems. It includes helpful strategies for dealing with disruptive students in the classroom and the "do's and don'ts" of discipline.

The Longman Guide to Community Service-Learning in the English Classroom and Beyond (Instructor / ISBN 0-321-12749-8)
Written by Elizabeth Rodriguez Kessler of California State University—Northridge, this monograph provides a definition and history of service-learning, as well as an overview of how service-learning can be integrated effectively into the college classroom.

The Longman Instructor's Planner (Instructor / ISBN 0-321-09247-3)
This planner includes weekly and monthly calendars, student attendance and grading rosters, space for contact information, Web references, an almanac, and blank pages for notes.

For Students

Vocabulary Skills Study Cards (Student / ISBN 0-321-31802-1)
Colorful, affordable, and packed with useful information, Longman's Vocabulary Study Card is a concise, eight-page reference guide to developing key vocabulary skills, such as learning to recognize context clues, reading a dictionary entry, and recognizing key root words, suffixes, and prefixes. Laminated for durability, this Study Card can be kept for years to come and pulled out whenever students need a quick review.

Reading Skills Study Card (Student / ISBN 0-321-33833-2)
Colorful, affordable, and packed with useful information, Longman's Reading Skills Study Card is a concise, eight-page reference guide to help students develop basic reading skills, such as concept skills, structural skills, language skills, and reasoning skills. Laminated for durability, this Study Card can be kept for years to come and pulled out whenever students need a quick review.

The Longman Textbook Reader, Revised Edition (with answers Student / ISBN 0-321-11895-2 or without answers Student / ISBN 0-321-12223-2)
Offers five complete chapters from our textbooks: computer science, biology, psychology, communications, and business. Each chapter includes additional comprehension quizzes, critical thinking questions, and group activities.

The Longman Reader's Portfolio and Student Planner (Student / ISBN 0-321-29610-9)
This unique supplement provides students with a space to plan, think about, and present their work. The portfolio includes a diagnostic area (including a learning-style questionnaire), a working area (including calendars, vocabulary logs, reading response sheets, book club tips, and other valuable materials), a display area (including a progress chart, a final table of contents, and a final assessment), as well as a daily planner for students including daily, weekly, and monthly calendars.

The Longman Reader's Journal, by Kathleen T. McWhorter (Student / ISBN 0-321-08843-3)
The first journal for readers, *The Longman Reader's Journal* offers a place for students to record their reactions to and questions about any reading.

The Longman Planner (Student / ISBN 0-321-04573-4)
Ideal for organizing a busy college life! Included are hour-by-hour schedules, monthly and weekly calendars, an address book, and an almanac of tips and useful information.

10 Practices of Highly Effective Students (Student / ISBN 0-205-30769-8)
This study skills supplement includes topics such as time management, test taking, reading critically, stress, and motivation.

***Newsweek* Discount Subscription Coupon (12 weeks) (Student / ISBN 0-321-08895-6)**
Newsweek gets students reading, writing, and thinking about what's going on in the world around them. The price of the subscription is added to the

cost of the book. Instructors receive weekly lesson plans, quizzes, and curriculum guides as well as a complimentary *Newsweek* subscription. The price of the subscription is 59 cents per issue (a total of $7.08 for the subscription). *Package item only.*

Interactive Guide to *Newsweek* (Student / ISBN 0-321-05528-4)

Available with the 12-week subscription to *Newsweek,* this guide serves as a workbook for students who are using the magazine.

Research Navigator Guide for English, H. Eric Branscomb and Linda R. Barr (Student / ISBN 0-321-20277-5)

Designed to teach students how to conduct high-quality online research and to document it properly, *Research Navigator* guides provide discipline-specific academic resources, in addition to helpful tips on the writing process, online research, and finding and citing valid sources. *Research Navigator* guides include an access code to Research Navigator™, providing access to thousands of academic journals and periodicals, the New York Times Search by Subject Archive, Link Library, Library Guides, and more.

Penguin Discount Novel Program

In cooperation with Penguin Putnam, Inc., Longman is proud to offer a variety of Penguin paperbacks at a significant discount when packaged with any Longman title. Excellent additions to any developmental reading course, Penguin titles give students the opportunity to explore contemporary and classical fiction and drama. The available titles include works by authors as diverse as Toni Morrison, Julia Alvarez, Mary Shelley, and Shakespeare. To review the complete list of titles available, visit the Longman-Penguin-Putnam Web site at www.ablongman.com/penguin.

Oxford American College Dictionary (Student / ISBN 0399144153)

Drawing on Oxford's unparalleled language resources, including a 200-million-word database, this college dictionary contains more than 175,000 entries and more than 1000 illustrations, including line drawings, photographs, and maps. *Available at a significant discount when packaged with a Longman textbook—only $15.*

The New American Webster Handy College Dictionary (Student / ISBN 0-451-18166-2)

A paperback reference text with more than 100,000 entries.

Multimedia Offerings

Interested in incorporating online materials into your course? Longman is happy to help. Our regional technology specialists provide training on all of our multimedia offerings.

MyReadingLab (www.myreadinglab.com)

This exciting new Web site houses all the media tools any developmental English student will need to improve his or her reading and study skills, and all in one easy-to-use place. Resources for reading and study skills include:

- **Reading Roadtrip 5.0 Web Site.** The best-selling reading software available, Reading Roadtrip takes students on a tour of 16 cities and landmarks throughout the United States, with each of the 16 modules corresponding to a reading or study skill. The topics include main idea, vocabulary, understanding patterns of organization, thinking critically, reading rate, note taking and highlighting, graphics and visual aids, and more. Students can begin their trip by taking a brand-new diagnostics test that provides immediate feedback, guiding them to specific modules for additional help with reading skills. New version 5.0 includes a brand-new design, a new Pioneer Level (fourth- to sixth-grade level), and new readings.
- **Longman Vocabulary Web Site.** The Longman Vocabulary Web site component of MySkillsLab features hundreds of exercises in ten topic areas to strengthen vocabulary skills. Students will also benefit from "100 Words That All High School Graduates Should Know," a useful resource that provides definitions for each of the words on this list, vocabulary flashcards, and audio clips to help facilitate pronunciation skills.
- **Longman Study Skills Web Site.** This site offers hundreds of review strategies for college success, time and stress management skills, study strategies, and more. Students can take a variety of assessment tests to learn about their organizational skills and learning styles, with follow-up quizzes to reinforce the strategies they have learned.
- **Research Navigator.** In addition to providing valuable help to any college student on how to conduct high-quality online research and to document it properly, Research Navigator provides access to thousands of academic journals and periodicals (including the New York Times Archive), allowing reading students to practice with authentic readings from college-level primary sources.

■ State-Specific Supplements

For Florida Adopters

Thinking Through the Test: A Study Guide for the Florida College Basic Skills Exit Test, by D. J. Henry

FOR FLORIDA ADOPTIONS ONLY. This workbook helps students strengthen their reading skills in preparation for the Florida College Basic Skills Exit Test. It features both diagnostic tests to help assess areas that may need improvement and exit tests to help test skill mastery. Detailed explanatory answers have been provided for almost all of the questions. *Package item only—not available for sale.*

Available Versions:

Thinking Through the Test, A Study Guide for the Florida College Basic Skills Exit Tests: Reading and Writing, Third Edition (ISBN 0-321-38740-6)

Thinking Through the Test, A Study Guide for the Florida College Basic Skills Exit Tests: Reading and Writing, w/Answers, Third Edition (ISBN 0-321-38739-2)

Thinking Through the Test, A Study Guide for the Florida College Basic Skills Exit Tests: Reading, Third Edition (ISBN 0-321-38738-4)

Thinking Through the Test, A Study Guide for the Florida College Basic Skills Exit Tests: Reading, w/Answers, Third Edition (ISBN 0-321-38737-6)

Reading Skills Summary for the Florida State Exit Exam, by D. J. Henry (Student / ISBN 0-321-08478-0)

FOR FLORIDA ADOPTIONS ONLY. An excellent study tool for students preparing to take Florida College Basic Skills Exit Test for Reading, this laminated reading grid summarizes all the skills tested on the Exit Exam. *Package item only—not available for sale.*

CLAST Test Package, Fourth Edition (Instructor / Print ISBN 0-321-01950-4)

These two, 40-item objective tests evaluate students' readiness for the Florida CLAST exams. Strategies for teaching CLAST preparedness are included.

For Texas Adopters

The Longman THEA Study Guide, by Jeannette Harris (Student / ISBN 0-321-27240-0)

Created specifically for students in Texas, this study guide includes straightforward explanations and numerous practice exercises to help students prepare for the reading and writing sections of THEA Test. *Package item only—not available for sale.*

TASP Test Package, Third Edition (Instructor / Print ISBN 0–321–01959–8)
These 12 practice pre-tests and post-tests assess the same reading and writing skills covered in the Texas TASP examination.

For New York / CUNY Adopters

Preparing for the CUNY-ACT Reading and Writing Test, edited by Patricia Licklider (Student / ISBN 0–321–19608–2)
This booklet, prepared by reading and writing faculty from across the CUNY system, is designed to help students prepare for the CUNY-ACT exit test. It includes test-taking tips, reading passages, typical exam questions, and sample writing prompts to help students become familiar with each portion of the test.

■ Acknowledgments

I wish to acknowledge the contributions of my colleagues and reviewers who have provided valuable advice and suggestions for this and previous editions of *Academic Reading*.

Academic Discipline Reviewers

Reviewers for Current Edition

Allied Health: Professor Bradley Foley, Nursing Program, Minneapolis Community and Technical College
Business: Professor John Ribezzo, Department of Business, Community College of Rhode Island
Humanities and Arts: Professor Pat Mathias, Department of English, Itasca Community College; Professor Thomas Hayes, Department of English, John Carroll University
Mathematics: Professor Jerry Muir, Department of Mathematics, University of Scranton
Natural Sciences: Professor William Straits, Department of Science Education, California State University, Long Beach
Social Sciences: Professor Bob Schwegler, College Writing Program, University of Rhode Island
Technical and Applied Fields: Professor Jim White, Dean of Technical Engineering, Industrial and Engineering Technology Division, Central Carolina Technical College

Reviewers for Previous Editions

Biology: Professor Jan Pechenik, Department of Biology, Tufts University; Professor Dave Baker, Delta College
Business: Professor Andrew Szilagyi, College of Business Administration, University of Houston; Professor Ernest T. Fitzgerald, Department of Business, Delgado Community College

History: Professor Barbara Klemm, Department of Social Sciences, Broward Community College; Professor Richard Marius, Professor Emeritus, Harvard University

Literature: Professor Victor Uszerowicz, Department of English and Communication, Miami-Dade Community College

Mathematics: Professor Paul Perdew, Department of Mathematics, University of Scranton; Professor Marvin L. Bittinger, Department of Mathematics, Indiana University–Purdue University; Professor Diana Hestwood, Minneapolis Community and Technical College

Physics: Professor Bill Leonard, Department of Physics, Univeristy of Massachusetts

Sociology: Professor J. Ross Eshleman, Wayne State University

Technology: Professor Thomas Athey, California State Technical College; Professor Josephine Brankey, New York Technical College

Visual Arts: Professor Jannette Morales, Department of Visual Arts and Technology, San Antonio College

■ Reading Specialist Reviewers

Betty Andrews-Tobias, Suffolk Community College; Pamela Bourgeois, California State University, Northridge; Greta Buck, Pima Community College; Janice Buchner, Suffolk County Community College; Terry Bullock, University of Cincinnati; Marilyn Burke, Austin Community College; Steve Cohen, Norwalk Community Technical College; Diane Cole, Pensacola Junior College; Janet Curtis, Fullerton College; Pat D'Allessio, Dutchess Community College; Susan Deese, University of New Mexico; Cathlene Denny, St. Johns River Community College; Marty Frailey, Pima Community College; Helen Gilbart, St. Petersburg Junior College; Ed Gill, Indiana Vocational Technical College; Lori Grimm, Pima Community College; Jon Hanson, Sacramento City College; Brian Holmes, San Jose State University; Peter Incarderone, New Jersey City University; Jenny Joczik, College of Charleston; Denise Josten, St. Louis Community College; Sandra Keith, St. Cloud State University; Kathleen Kiefer, Colorado State University; Terry Kozek, Housatonic Community College; Linda W. Larou, Dutchess Community College; Beverly Lipper, Dutchess Community College; Alice Mackey, Missouri Western State College; Monique Manning, Brookhaven College; Donna Mayes, Blue Ridge Community College; Gail Moore, York Technical College; David Murphy, Waubonsee Community College; Karen Nelson, Craven Community College; Michael Newman, Hunter College; Michelle Peterson, Santa Barbara City College; Karen Samson, Chicago State University; Nancy E. Smith, Florida Community College at Jacksonville; Betsy Tobias, Suffolk County Community College; Katherine Wellington, Metropolitan State University; Michaeline Wideman, University of Cincinnati; Mary Wolting, Indiana University–Purdue University; Kimberley Zernechel, Minneapolis Community and Technical College; Lawrence Ziewaz, Michigan State University.

I am particularly indebted to Gillian Cook, my development editor, for her most valuable advice and guidance. She has contributed knowledge, creativity, and energy, as well as practicality. I also wish to thank Melanie Craig, Acquisitions Editor, for her support in developing the revision plan and overseeing its implementation.

KATHLEEN T. McWHORTER

The McWhorter Reading and Study Skills Series

Kathleen T. McWhorter has written numerous textbooks for reading and study skills courses. All the McWhorter books emphasize research-proven techniques for active learning, critical thinking and metacognition, writing to learn, and learning styles, and provide detailed coverage of new online contexts for reading.

Academic Reading combines six chapters on reading in the disciplines—the social sciences, business, the humanities and arts, mathematics, the natural sciences, and the technical and applied fields—with coverage of reading comprehension and critical thinking. Fundamental reading strategies, including how to read arguments, and academic reading strategies, such as how to read research and collateral assignments, provide a strong basis for the discipline-specific reading strategies. This text is designed for use in the third reading course, or in a college-level reading course.

College Reading and Study Skills presents the basic techniques for college success, including time management, analysis of learning style, active reading, and note taking. The text offers strategies for strengthening literal and critical comprehension, improving vocabulary skills, and developing reading flexibility. Students also discover methods for reading and learning from textbook assignments, including outlining and summarizing, and for taking exams.

Efficient and Flexible Reading teaches students how to vary their approach to written texts based on the material and their purpose for reading. In addition to instruction in literal and critical comprehension skills, vocabulary, and study skills, *Efficient and Flexible Reading* teaches students how to identify text structures and thought patterns for more efficient learning. Emphasizing reading as an active thinking process, the text (designed for use in the second reading course) presents systems for monitoring concentration, comprehension, and recall.

Essential Reading Skills, designed for use in the first reading course, is the most basic of the McWhorter texts. Focusing on the essential reading skills of vocabulary development, main idea, details, and patterns of organization (with a brief introduction to critical reading), this text features a programmed approach of instruction, example, and practice, followed by a series of review and mastery tests on each reading skill.

Guide to College Reading is designed for use in the first reading course, focusing on the key areas of reading comprehension, vocabulary improvement, and textbook reading. *Guide to College Reading* provides instruction in the basics—main idea, vocabulary building, supporting details, and patterns of organization. Extensive skill practice and four mastery tests in each chapter provide ample practice in the basic reading skills. Additional readings at the end of the text provide more exercises and applications.

Reading Across the Disciplines improves college students' reading and thinking skills through brief skill instruction and extensive practice structured around readings in various academic disciplines. *Reading Across the Disciplines* is organized into three parts. Part One, "Reading and Thinking in College," presents a brief skill introduction (in handbook format) introducing students to essential vocabulary, comprehension, critical reading, and reading rate skills. Part Two, "Selections from Academic Disciplines," has twelve chapters, each containing four readings representative of a different academic discipline. Part Three, "Textbook Chapter Readings," contains two complete textbook chapters that enable students to practice skills on longer pieces of writing.

Study and Critical Thinking Skills in College integrates the study and critical thinking skills students need to achieve college success. Active learning strategies and techniques that develop students' proficiency in interacting with text and lecture material are presented, along with three chapters on test-taking strategies. Students learn how they can take charge of their college careers, establish goals, and manage their time, in addition to how to take notes in class, study specialized vocabulary, and organize and synthesize content from lectures and reading. For use in study skills, freshman orientation, or academic success courses.

Academic Success

Studying and applying the following tips will help you be successful in college.

■ Planning and Organization

Veronica Evans–Johnson
Durham Technical College, Durham, NC

Veronica has been attending Durham Tech since 2000, first as a part-time student and recently as a full-time student where she is successfully working toward an associate's degree in business administration. She plans to transfer to Central University and prepare for a career in business administration.

Planning and Organizing:

"I take care of my family first in the evenings. Then I go to my room, close the door, and don't take calls. My family knows not to bother me. I have a laptop and I take it everywhere with me so if I have some free time I can get some (school) work done."

Becoming a successful student requires planning and organization. Here are a few suggestions for ensuring your success:

1. **Organize a place to study.** Select a quiet, comfortable location and study in the same place each day. Be sure to have all your materials (paper, pens, etc.) at hand.

2. **Use a pocket calendar to record exams and due dates for papers.**

3. **Carry a small notebook for recording daily assignments for each course.** Check it each evening before you begin to study.

4. **Get to know someone in each class.** You might enjoy having someone to talk to. Also, in case you miss a class, you will have someone from whom you can get the assignment and borrow notes.

5. **Attend all classes, whether or not the instructor takes attendance.** Studies show that successful students attend class regularly, whereas students who do not are unsuccessful.

6. **Get to know your instructors.** Use your instructors' office hours to talk about exams or assignments, ask questions, and discuss ideas for papers.

■ Keeping a Learning Journal

Ted Sawchuck
Maryland University, College Park, MD

Ted is a sophomore at Maryland University, where he is studying for a bachelor's degree in journalism. He is also a general assignment reporter for the college newspaper *The Diamondback.*

Keeping a Learning Journal:

"Learning journals are a great help to me. To do them on paper, organize your information using different note-books, different sections in the same notebook, or colored tape flags to make it easier to find and review the information later. A steno pad or spiral-bound notebook is useful for jotting down quick notes in class. Write in bullet points to jog your memory when rereading. By the time you've finished with the information, you've processed it once in class, written it in bullet points in your journal, and categorized it. This process increases the number of times you interact with the material, which helps when you need to recall the information.

"If you have a laptop or don't mind jotting and transferring, using a blog for a learning journal is a newer option that offers easier search and archiving options. It's also available anywhere you have Internet access. To organize posts, you can use post categories, available from some blog service providers. When making a new post, you'll be asked to categorize it. As long as your categories are consistent (easier if they're kept simple), you'll be able to review all posts in any category with just one click from your blog's front page. This makes reviewing your information easier, which means you'll be more likely to do so."

As you begin college, you will encounter many new ideas and meet many new people from whom you will discover new ways of looking at and doing things. You also will begin to explore many new academic fields. A learning journal can be helpful in sorting out your thoughts, ideas, impressions, and reactions. Here are some suggestions for a learning journal:

1. **Keep a journal for each of your most challenging courses.** Many students use a separate spiral or steno notebook or notebook section for each course.

2. **Date your entries, and reference them to particular chapters or assignments.** Some students find it helpful to record the amount of time spent on each assignment, as well.

3. **Express your reactions to the course in general.** Record your feelings about the overall course content and what you like and do not like about the course. Include ideas that interest you and that you would like to explore further.

4. **Record your impressions about specific assignments.** Include problems you encountered with particular assignments or unique features of them.

5. **Analyze reading and study techniques you have tried.** Include both those that worked and those that did not work (and why).

6. **Include new ideas for learning.** Write down changes you made in using various study approaches, and record any new ideas you have encountered for studying the course material.

FIGURE A-1   Sample Learning Journal: Criminal Justice

> _Paraphrasing_   It is difficult not to use the same words. I was unable to find a paraphrase for some of the technical terms. I learned the material very well, though, because I spent so much time thinking about it.
>
> _Self-testing_   Our instructor suggested that we test ourselves as a way of preparing for the next exam. This was very helpful and helped me to focus on important parts of each chapter. I'm going to keep the questions I wrote and use them while studying for the final exam, too.
>
> _SQ3R_   I learned this method in a study skills class. This was really effective, and I improved on it by highlighting the answer I found to the question I asked. This helped to focus my reading. Asking and answering the question out loud also helped since I'm an auditory learner. I also drew maps and diagrams and I reread them out loud.

7. **Enter your reactions to and analysis of exams.** Right after you take an exam, you may have a different impression than when it is returned to you. Comparing these impressions can be useful in improving your exam-taking skills.

8. **Use your journal entries as sources for writing assignments.** They offer excellent starting points for choosing topics of papers and contain information for developing those topics.

A sample learning journal is shown in Figure A-1. It was written by a student taking a criminal justice course.

■ Procrastination

Rachel Goodman
West Chester University, West Chester, PA

Rachel successfully completed her associate's degree at Middlesex County College in May 2005 and has transferred to West Chester University in Pennsylvania where she is enrolled in the Elementary Education program. She plans to become an elementary school English teacher.

Dealing with Procrastination:

"Last semester I waited to the last day to write a 5–6 page research paper on obesity. I was up till 2 in the morning, had three hours sleep, and got up early to finish it. It was one of the most miserable days and nights I've had. I've learned that waiting till the last minute is miserable. This semester, I do long assignments over a few days and it's easier that way. I can concentrate better. I do study guides, a few questions each night, and it sticks with me. I learn more."

When your work load increases, it is tempting to put things off. Here are some suggestions to help you overcome or control procrastination:

1. **Clear your desk.** Move everything from your desk except materials for the task at hand. With nothing else in front of you, you are more likely to start working and less likely to be distracted from your task while working.

2. **Give yourself five minutes to start.** If you are having difficulty beginning a task, tell yourself that you will work on it for just five minutes. Often, once you start working, your motivation and interest will build, and you will want to continue working.

3. **Divide the task into manageable parts.** Complicated tasks are often difficult to start because they seem so long and unmanageable. Before beginning such tasks, spend a few minutes organizing and planning. Divide each task into parts, and list what you need to do and in what order.

4. **Start somewhere, no matter where.** If you are having difficulty getting started, do something rather than sit and stare, regardless of how trivial it may seem. If you are having trouble writing a paper from rough draft notes, for example, start by recopying the notes. Suddenly, you will find yourself rearranging and rephrasing them, and you will be well on your way toward writing a draft.

5. **Recognize when you need more information.** Sometimes, procrastination is a signal that you lack skills or information. You may be avoiding a task because you are not sure how to do it. You may not understand why you use a certain procedure to solve a type of math problem, for example, so you feel reluctant to do math homework. Or selecting a term paper topic may be difficult if you are not certain of the purpose or expected length of the paper. Overcome such stumbling blocks by discussing them with classmates or with your professor.

■ Managing Your Study Time

Christina Ebbert
University of Arkansas, Fayetteville, AR

Christina is a married, 31-year-old mother of three. She is attending college full time with the goal of attaining a degree in nursing.

Time Management:

"Scheduling is hard. I have to drop the little guy at daycare, drop the other two at school, and then pick them up at the end of the day. Once a week I set time aside time to work in the library. I do my homework when the kids do theirs. I do one class each day so I have time to study in the morning or after the kids go to bed. If you're as dedicated as I am you're going to succeed."

As college students, many of you struggle to divide your time among classes, study, job responsibilities, and friends and family. Effective planning and time management are essential for you to maintain a workable balance. Here are a few suggestions for managing your study time effectively:

1. **Develop a weekly study plan.** Allocate time for reading, reviewing, doing homework, and studying for exams. Select several specific times each week for working on each of your courses. A sample weekly plan is shown in Figure A-2 (p. 6).

2. **As a rule of thumb, reserve two study hours for each hour you spend in class.**

3. **Use peak periods of concentration.** Everyone has high and low periods of concentration and attention. First, determine when these occur for you; then reserve peak times for intensive study and use less efficient times for more routine tasks such as recopying an assignment or collecting information in the library.

4. **Study difficult subjects first.** While it is tempting to get easy tasks and short little assignments out of the way first, do not give in to this approach. When you start studying, your mind is fresh and alert and you are at your peak of concentration. This is the time you are best equipped to handle difficult subjects.

5. **Schedule study for a particular course close to the time when you attend class.** Plan to study the evening before the class meets and soon after the class meeting. For example, if a class meets on Tuesday morning, plan to study Monday evening and Tuesday afternoon or evening. By studying close to class time, you will find it easier to relate class lectures and discussions to what you are reading and studying, to see connections, and to reinforce your learning.

6. **Include short breaks in your study time.** Take a break before you begin studying each new subject. Your mind needs time to refocus so that you can switch from one set of facts, problems, and issues to another. You should also take short breaks when you are working on just one assignment for a long period of time. A 10-minute break after 50 to 60 minutes of study is reasonable.

■ Balancing School and Work

Robert Badillo
Middlesex County College, Edison, NJ

Robert is a junior at Middlesex County College and is working toward a bachelor's degree in graphic arts.

Finding a Balance:

"Don't overwork yourself. Not everyone's a superhero. I was working full time and taking a full course load. It was too difficult and I was beginning to mess up. I couldn't get the work done and my grades were suffering. I decided to take fewer classes. It used to be stressful but now it's a lot easier. I schedule a day at work so I just have work, and I have all my classes together on the same days. When it comes down to it you've got to decide the best way it has to be for you."

FIGURE A-2   Sample Weekly Schedule

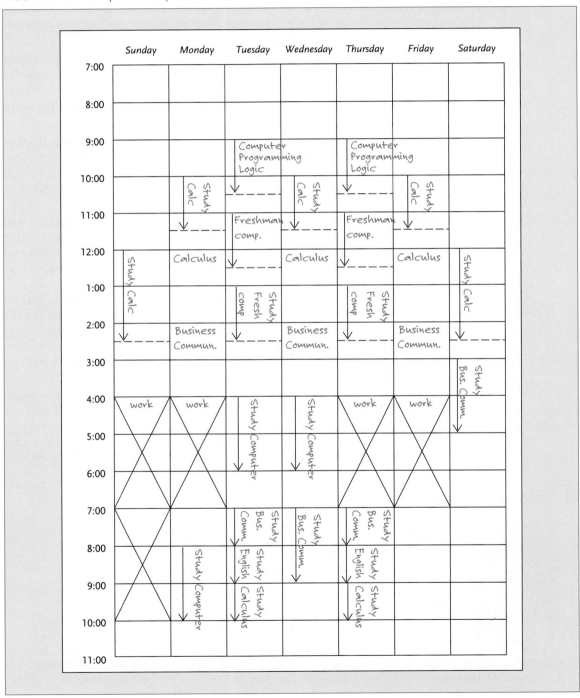

Many students find they must juggle school responsibilities with their part-time job commitments. Still others must make time for household and/or family responsibilities, as well. Use the following suggestions to help you keep your life running smoothly and efficiently:

1. **Try to choose flexible jobs.** Try to find an employer that is flexible about your work hours. Offer to work unpopular days or times in exchange for fewer hours during busy weeks, such as final exams.

2. **Consider travel time.** Be sure you don't waste too much valuable time traveling from campus to a job.

3. **Build a compact class schedule.** In future semesters, select a class schedule that is compact and convenient, without too many hours between classes. This will free up larger blocks of time for work and study.

4. **Make a schedule to reflect your priorities.** Don't try to fit college into your old weekly schedule before you started college; succeeding in college takes too much time for this to work well. You will need to reserve plenty of time for reading, writing, and studying.

5. **Make a household schedule.** Just as you have planned a weekly study schedule, develop a weekly household schedule. Instead of hoping that all jobs will get done, plan when you or a family member will tackle each. Designate specific times for laundry, shopping, errands, and so forth.

6. **Increase your efficiency by doing things at off-peak times.** Don't go to the grocery store or laundromat on a busy Saturday morning; instead, choose a weekday early morning or later evening.

7. **Use weekends for study.** Try to take care of work and household responsibilities during the week by "sandwiching" them between each other. For instance, you could run a load of laundry while washing your car. This will free up larger blocks of time on the weekend for study.

8. **Consider remaining on or returning to campus to study.** If your house or dorm is too distracting a place to concentrate, try studying at the college library or at a local public library. Once you are away from home, you will tend to forget job worries, as well.

■ Working with Classmates: Group Projects

Doug Mello
Modesto Junior College, Modesto, CA

Doug is currently a student at Modesto Junior College. He plans to transfer to a university and earn a bachelor of science degree in engineering.

Study Groups:

"I try to put together study groups for all my classes. I always try to hook up with someone in my class to work on homework, even if it's just to call and talk about what we're doing in class. I put together a study group for a really difficult math class. There were 45 people in the class and only 20 passed; everyone in my study group but one passed."

Many assignments and class activities involve working with a small group of classmates. For example, a sociology instructor might divide the class into groups and ask each group to brainstorm solutions to the economic or social problems of the elderly. Group presentations may be required in a business course, or groups in your American history class might be asked to research a topic.

Group projects are intended to enable students to learn from one another by viewing each other's thinking processes and by evaluating each other's ideas and approaches. Use the following suggestions to help your group function effectively:

1. **Select alert, energetic classmates if you are permitted to choose group members.**

2. **Be an active, responsible participant.** Accept your share of the work and expect others to do the same. Approach the activity with a serious attitude, rather than joking or complaining about the assignment. This will establish a serious tone and cut down on wasted time.

3. **Make sure your group has a leader.** Because organization and direction are essential for productivity, every group needs a leader. Unless some other competent group member immediately assumes leadership, take a leadership role. While leadership may require more work, you will be in control. As the group's leader, you will need to direct the group in analyzing the assignment, organizing a plan of action, distributing work assignments, planning, and if the project is long term, establishing deadlines.

4. **Suggest that specific tasks be assigned to each group member and that the group agree upon task deadlines.**

5. **Take advantage of individual strengths and weaknesses.** For instance, a person who seems indifferent or is easily distracted should not be assigned the task of recording the group's findings. The most organized, outgoing member might be assigned the task of making an oral report to the class.

If your group is not functioning effectively or if one or more members are not doing their share, take action. Communicate directly, but try not to alienate or anger group members.

■ Taking Lecture Notes

Ryan Vidaurri
Sam Houston State University, Huntsville, TX

Ryan is currently a junior at Sam Houston State University in Huntsville, Texas. He is pursuing a bachelor's degree in history and, as an active member of the ROTC, plans on a career in the military after graduation.

Taking Lecture Notes:

"Usually when a teacher's doing a lecture I try to follow along as closely as possible in the textbook. Before a class I try and read everything we're going to cover. If I can keep up with the teacher I highlight in the (text) book which (topics) she's covering. If I can't keep up I make notes in a notepad. Often in my history class the teacher speaks from personal knowledge and research which is not in the textbook so I write it down. Usually I just hit the key notes off the board."

In many courses, your instructor will lecture, and you will need to take accurate notes for study and review. Use the following suggestions to take effective notes:

1. **Read the textbook material on which the lecture will be based before attending the lecture.**
2. **Listen carefully to the lecturer's opening comments.** They often reveal the purpose, focus, or organization of the lecture.
3. **Focus on ideas, not facts.** Do not try to record everything the lecturer says.
4. **Discover the thought pattern(s) on which the lecture is based.**
5. **Record the main ideas and enough details and examples so that the ideas will make sense later.**
6. **Record the organization of the lecture.** Use an indentation system to show the relative importance of ideas.
7. **Leave plenty of blank space as you take notes.** You may want to fill in missed or additional information later.
8. **Use an abbreviation system.** Abbreviate commonly used words (psy = psychology, w/ = with, etc.) to save time.
9. **Review your notes as soon as possible after the lecture, filling in missing or additional information.** This review will also help you remember the lecture.
10. **Consider your learning style.** Use the suggestions in Figure A-3 to adapt your note-taking strategies to suit your learning style.

FIGURE A-3   Adapting Note Taking to Your Learning Style

LEARNING CHARACTERISTIC	NOTE-TAKING STRATEGY
Auditory	Take advantage of your advantage! Take thorough and complete notes.
Visual	Work on note-taking skills; practice by tape-recording a lecture; analyze and review your notes.
Creative	Annotate your notes, recording impressions, reactions, spin-off ideas, related ideas.
Pragmatic	Reorganize notes during editing. Pay attention to the lecturer's organization.
Social	Review and edit notes with a classmate. Compare notes with others.
Independent	Choose seating close to the instructor; avoid distracting groups of students.
Applied	Think of applications (record as annotations). Write questions in the margin about applications.
Conceptual	Discover idea relationships. Watch for patterns.
Spatial	Add diagrams, maps during editing.
Verbal	Record the lecturer's diagrams, drawings—but translate into words during editing.

■ Learning Strategies

Jeremy Tyler
Prairie State College, Chicago Heights, IL

Jeremy is a sophomore at Prairie State College and has a work-study job in the computer writing lab. He plans to pursue a degree in law.

Learning Strategies:

"In my biology class I made up the sentence 'King Philip cried out for goodness sake' (an acrostic) in order to remember the different classifications of the animal kingdom. The first letter of each word is the first letter of the different levels of classification in the right order: kingdom, phylum, class, order, family, genus, and species. I was reading a book where they used the abbreviation (acronym) ROY G BIV to help you remember the order colors come out of a prism: red, orange, yellow, green, blue, indigo, and violet."

For each of your courses, you will need to learn many facts, ideas, and concepts. Use the following suggestions to learn most efficiently:

1. **Apply the principle of spaced study.** It is more effective to space, or spread out, study sessions than to study in one or two large blocks of time.

2. **Use immediate review.** As soon as you finish reading or studying, take a few minutes to look back through the material, recalling key points and rereading notes or summaries. If you review immediately after study, you will increase the amount you remember.

3. **Review frequently.** In order to retain information over time, it is necessary to review periodically. Although you are learning new material each week, reserve time to reread notes, underlining, and chapter summaries of previously covered material.

4. **Associate new information with previously learned information.** Call to mind what you already know about a topic before you begin to read or study.

5. **Use numerous sensory channels by incorporating writing, speaking, and listening into your study.** For example, consider tape-recording and playing back your history notes or writing a summary sheet of key formulas for a math course.

■ Managing Stress

Corrine Roberts
Modesto Junior College, Modesto, CA

Corinne is married and the mother of three children. She is currently working and taking classes at Modesto Junior College. She plans to transfer to a university in her junior year.

Keeping a Perspective on Stress:

"There's a point in every semester where I begin to cry. You just have to remember tomorrow is round the corner. You either die with it or keep going. Think about whether this will make a big difference in the future. And it will, economically, for my family."

FIGURE A–4

STRESS QUESTIONNAIRE

Respond to each of the following statements by checking "Yes," "No," or "Sometimes" in the boxes provided and then adding up the total for each column.

	Yes	*No*	*Sometimes*
1. I feel as if I don't have enough time in a week to get everything done.	☐	☐	☐
2. Having at least one healthy meal per day at which I can sit down and relax is unusual.	☐	☐	☐
3. I have more conflicts and disagreements with friends than I used to.	☐	☐	☐
4. I seem to get colds and other minor illnesses (headaches, upset stomachs) more frequently.	☐	☐	☐
5. I find myself confused or listless more than usual.	☐	☐	☐
6. My usual level of physical activity or exercise has decreased.	☐	☐	☐
7. I seldom get six to eight hours of sleep at night.	☐	☐	☐
8. I seldom find time to do some fun things each week.	☐	☐	☐
9. I find myself unable to meet deadlines and am losing track of details (appointments, chores, promises to friends, and so on).	☐	☐	☐
10. I am more short-tempered or more impatient than I used to be.	☐	☐	☐
Total	____	____	____

If you answered "Yes" to more than two or three items or "Sometimes" to more than five or six items, you may be experiencing more stress than you realize. Evaluate the pattern of your responses. Look at the questions to which you answered "Yes" or "Sometimes." Some questions deal with physical habits; others focus on organizational skills. By checking your answers, you will get an idea of your own stress indicators.

College is a new and challenging experience, and new and challenging experiences tend to produce stress. Consequently, stress is a common problem that many college students face. Try the Stress Questionnaire shown in Figure A-4 to assess your level of stress.

How to Reduce Stress

1. **Eliminate stressors.** Identify possible sources of stress, and work toward eliminating them. If a part-time job is stressful, for instance, quit or find another that is less stressful. If a math course is creating stress, take action: go to the learning lab or math lab for assistance, or inquire about tutoring.

2. **Establish a daily routine.** To eliminate daily hassles and make daily tasks as simple as possible, establish a daily routine. A routine eliminates the

need to make numerous small decisions, thereby giving you a sense of "smooth sailing."

3. **Accentuate your accomplishments.** When you feel pressured, stop and review what you have already accomplished that day and that week. This review will give you confidence that you can handle the work load. A positive attitude goes a long way in overcoming stress.

4. **Eat nutritious meals.**

5. **Get physical exercise.** Exercise often releases tension, promotes a general feeling of wellness, and improves self-concept. Many students report that as little as 30 minutes of exercise produces immediate relaxation and helps them to place daily events in perspective.

6. **Get adequate amounts of sleep.**

7. **Seek knowledgeable advice.** If stress becomes an insurmountable problem, seek assistance from the student counseling center. The office may offer workshops in stress-reduction techniques such as relaxation or biofeedback training.

8. **Get involved with campus activities.** Some students become so involved with their course work that they do little else but study or worry about studying. In fact, they feel guilty or stressed when they are not studying. Be sure to allow some time in each day to relax and have fun. Campus activities provide a valuable means of releasing tension and taking your mind off your work.

■ Using a Computer as a Study and Learning Aid

Gentry Carlson
Itasca Community College, Grand Rapids, MN

Gentry is working toward two associate's degrees—one in natural resources and one in geographical information systems. When he graduates, he plans to transfer to Bemidji University, earn bachelor's and master's degrees there, and pursue a career in natural resources or high school or junior college teaching.

Information Resources:

"In my writing class I did a paper on a geographical information systems subject. My instructor set up a day for the college librarian to come in and talk about good Web sites to go to, and which ones are dependable and which ones aren't. The librarian said look for .gov, or .edu in the site name because those sites should be reliable. It was amazing to me as I didn't know all that stuff was available. So next year I'll know where to go for research papers."

Computers are good for so much more than word processing, Web browsing, and instant messaging. If you don't have a computer or access to one, every school has at least one lab for student use. These tips are useful to anyone with computer access, but better suited to students who already key in some or all of their notes:

1. **Use a computer to organize notes from textbook reading.** As you take notes on a reading, your notes tend to follow the organization of the text. At times it is useful to reorganize and rearrange your notes. For example, you may want to pull together information on a certain topic that is spread throughout one or more chapters. Once your notes are entered into a computer file, you can use the cut and paste function to rearrange and reorganize your notes or outlines easily without rewriting.

2. **Use a computer to organize lecture notes.** Lecture notes are recorded by hand as you listen to the lecture, unless you are using a laptop. Keying your notes into a computer file is a means of editing and reviewing, as well as reorganizing. Re-keying handwritten notes is a great way to review. Once the notes are keyed, you've then heard the information, written it, and keyed it. This gives you several repetitions, and you will be more comfortable and familiar with material.

3. **Save your notes into one document for each class session.** This makes pre-class review much easier and is especially useful when preparing for cumulative exams. After you finish the class, having an electronic copy of the notes will allow you to quickly review for related classes.

4. **Use a computer to integrate text and lecture notes.** The computer offers an ideal solution to the problem of how to integrate notes you have taken from your textbook and those you have taken in class. The cut and paste function allows you to move sections of your lecture notes to corresponding sections in your notes from your text.

5. **Use a computer to create lists of new terminology for each of your courses.** The computer's word processing capabilities allow you to group similar terms, organize them by chapter, or sort them into "know" and "don't know" files. A biology student, for example, grouped terms together into the following categories: energy and life, cells, biological processes, reproduction, biological systems, brain and behavior, and environmental issues.

6. **Communicate with classmates.** Use instant messages, Facebook, and other social networking tools to make and further relationships with classmates. You can share study sheets, quiz each other, or share practice tests you create. Use caution, however, about the amount of information you list on these sites—the Internet is a big place.

7. **Avoid distractions.** Make sure your computer isn't distracting more than it's helping. Instant messages, pop-up windows, music, downloaded video, and games are all barriers to efficient work. Set your messaging program to

display an away message to avoid interruptions. On Windows XP, right-click the desktop, go to Arrange Icons By, and unclick Show Desktop Icons to clear your desktop entirely.

8. **Protect your files.** Use anti-spyware programs like Ad-Aware and Spybot: Search and Destroy to remove the detritus that comes with using the Internet these days. Both programs make it easy to download and install updates, an essential part of keeping your computer free of malicious code. A clean computer runs faster, handles more programs running at once, and requires less rebooting, all things that keep it from getting in your way during work.

C H A P T E R

1

Strategies for Active Reading

LEARNING OBJECTIVES

✦ To understand how reading contributes to college success

✦ To assess your learning style

✦ To build your concentration skills

✦ To develop multilevel thinking skills

✦ To learn to preview and predict before reading

✦ To develop questions to guide your reading

✦ To check your comprehension

Think About It!

The students in this photograph are successful college students. They have achieved their goals and are looking forward to successful careers. What skills did they use to become successful?

When college graduates are asked to name the ingredients of college success, they often say:

"Knowing how to study."
"You have to like school."
"Hard work!"
"Time to study!"
"Motivation!"

Students seldom mention reading as an essential skill, and yet reading is a hidden factor in college success. When you think of college, you may think of attending classes and labs, completing assignments, studying for and taking exams, and writing papers. A closer look, however, reveals that reading is an important part of each of these activities.

Reading stays "behind the scenes" because instructors rarely evaluate it directly. Grades are based on outcomes, that is, how well you express your ideas in papers or how well you do on exams. Yet reading is the primary means by which you acquire your ideas and gather information.

Throughout this text, you will learn numerous ways to use reading as a tool for college success.

■ Reading and Academic Success

Reading involves much more than moving your eyes across lines of print, more than recognizing words, and more than reading sentences. **Reading is thinking.** It is an active process of identifying important ideas and comparing, evaluating, and applying them.

Have you ever gone to a ballgame and watched the fans? Most do not sit and watch passively. Instead, they direct the plays, criticize the calls, encourage the players, and reprimand the coach. They care enough to get actively engaged with the game. Just like interested fans, active readers get involved. They question, challenge, and criticize, as well as understand. Table 1-1 contrasts the active strategies of successful readers with the passive ones of less successful readers.

Throughout the remainder of this chapter, you will discover specific strategies for becoming a more active learner. Not all strategies will work for everyone. Experiment to discover those that work for you.

EXERCISE 1-1 *Consider each of the following reading assignments. Discuss different ways in which you could get actively involved with them.*

1. Reading two poems by e.e. cummings for a literature class.
2. Reviewing procedures for your next biology lab.
3. Taking notes on an article in *Time* magazine assigned by your political science instructor.

EXERCISE 1-2 *Write a list of active reading strategies you already use. Add to your list several new strategies that you intend to begin using. Compare your list with a classmate's.*

_____

_____

_____

TABLE 1-1   Active Versus Passive Reading

ACTIVE READERS . . .	PASSIVE READERS . . .
Tailor their reading to suit each assignment.	Read all assignments the same way.
Analyze the purpose of an assignment.	Read an assignment *because* it was assigned.
Adjust their speed to suit their purpose.	Read everything at the same speed.
Question ideas in the assignment.	Accept whatever is in print as true.
Compare and connect textbook material with lecture content.	Study lecture notes and textbook separately.
Skim headings to find out what an assignment is about before beginning to read.	Check the length of an assignment and then begin reading.
Make sure they understand what they are reading as they go along.	Read until the assignment is completed.
Read with pencil in hand, highlighting, jotting notes, and marking key vocabulary.	Simply read.
Develop personalized strategies that are particularly effective.	Follow routine, standard methods.

■ Assessing Your Learning Style

Textbook reading assignments are central to many college classes. Your instructors make daily or weekly assignments and expect you to read the material, learn it, and pass tests on it. Textbook assignments often form the basis of class lectures and discussions. An important part of many college classes, then, consists of completing reading assignments.

Reading and understanding an assignment, however, does not mean you have learned the material. You need to do more than read to learn the content. What else should you do? The answer is not simple.

People differ in how they learn and the methods and strategies they use to learn. These differences can be explained by what is known as *learning style*. Your learning style can begin to explain why some courses are easier for you than others and why you learn better from one instructor than another. Learning style also can explain why certain assignments are easy for you and other learning tasks are difficult.

The following brief Learning Style Questionnaire will help you analyze how you learn and show you how to develop an action plan for learning what you read. Complete and score the questionnaire before continuing with this section.

Learning Style Questionnaire

DIRECTIONS: Each item presents two choices. Select the alternative that best describes you. In cases in which neither choice suits you, select the one that is closer to your preference. Write the letter of your choice in the blank to the left of each item.

PART ONE

_____ 1. I would prefer to follow a set of
   a. oral directions.
   b. written directions.

_____ 2. I would prefer to
   a. attend a lecture given by a famous psychologist.
   b. read an article written by the psychologist.

_____ 3. When I am introduced to someone, it is easier for me to remember the person's
   a. name.
   b. face.

_____ 4. I find it easier to learn new information using
   a. language (words).
   b. images (pictures).

_____ 5. I prefer classes in which the instructor
   a. lectures and answers questions.
   b. uses films and videos.

_____ 6. To follow current events, I would prefer to
   a. listen to the news on the radio.
   b. read the newspaper.

_____ 7. To learn how to operate a fax machine, I would prefer to
   a. listen to a friend's explanation.
   b. watch a demonstration.

PART TWO

_____ 8. I prefer to
   a. work with facts and details.
   b. construct theories and ideas.

_____ 9. I would prefer a job that involves
   a. following specific instructions.
   b. reading, writing, and analyzing.

_____ 10. I prefer to
   a. solve math problems using a formula.
   b. discover why the formula works.

_____ 11. I would prefer to write a term paper explaining
   a. how a process works.
   b. a theory.

_____ 12. I prefer tasks that require me to
   a. follow careful, detailed instructions.

   b. use reasoning and critical analysis.

_____ 13. For a criminal justice course, I would prefer to
   a. discover how and when a law can be used.
   b. learn how and why it became law.

_____ 14. To learn more about the operation of a high-speed computer printer, I would prefer to
   a. work with several types of printers.
   b. understand the principles on which they operate.

PART THREE

_____ 15. To solve a math problem, I would prefer to
  a. draw or visualize the problem.
  b. study a sample problem and use it as a model.

_____ 16. To best remember something, I
  a. create a mental picture.
  b. write it down.

_____ 17. Assembling a bicycle from a diagram would be
  a. easy.
  b. challenging.

_____ 18. I prefer classes in which I
  a. handle equipment or work with models.
  b. participate in a class discussion.

_____ 19. To understand and remember how a machine works, I would
  a. draw a diagram.
  b. write notes.

_____ 20. I enjoy
  a. drawing or working with my hands.
  b. speaking, writing, and listening.

_____ 21. If I were trying to locate an office on an unfamiliar campus, I would prefer
  a. a map.
  b. written directions.

PART FOUR

_____ 22. For a grade in biology lab, I would prefer to
  a. work with a lab partner.
  b. work alone.

_____ 23. When faced with a difficult personal problem, I prefer to
  a. discuss it with others.
  b. resolve it myself.

_____ 24. Many instructors could improve their classes by
  a. including more discussion and group activities.
  b. allowing students to work on their own more frequently.

_____ 25. When listening to a lecturer or speaker, I respond more to the
  a. person presenting the idea.
  b. ideas themselves.

_____ 26. When on a team project, I prefer to
  a. work with several team members.
  b. divide the tasks and complete those assigned to me.

_____ 27. I prefer to shop and do errands
  a. with friends.
  b. by myself.

_____ 28. A job in a busy office is
  a. more appealing than working alone.
  b. less appealing than working alone.

PART FIVE

_____ 29. To make decisions, I rely on
  a. my experiences and gut feelings.
  b. facts and objective data.

_____ 30. To complete a task, I
  a. can use whatever is available to get the job done.
  b. must have everything I need at hand.

_____ 31. I prefer to express my ideas and feelings through
a. music, song, or poetry.
b. direct, concise language.

_____ 32. I prefer instructors who
a. allow students to be guided by their own interests.
b. make their expectations clear and explicit.

_____ 33. I tend to
a. challenge and question what I hear and read.
b. accept what I hear and read.

_____ 34. I prefer
a. essay exams.
b. objective exams.

_____ 35. In completing an assignment, I prefer to
a. figure out my own approach.
b. be told exactly what to do.

To score your questionnaire, record the total number of a's you selected and the total number of b's for each part of the questionnaire. Record your totals in the scoring grid provided below.

SCORING GRID

Part	Total # of Choice "a"	Total # of Choice "b"
One	_____ Auditory	_____ Visual
Two	_____ Applied	_____ Conceptual
Three	_____ Spatial	_____ Verbal
Four	_____ Social	_____ Independent
Five	_____ Creative	_____ Pragmatic

Now, circle your higher score for each part of the questionnaire. The word below the score you circled indicates a strength in your learning style. The next section explains how to interpret your scores.

Interpreting Your Scores

Each of the five parts of the questionnaire identifies one aspect of your learning style. These five aspects are explained below.

Part One: Auditory or Visual Learners   This score indicates whether you learn more effectively by listening (auditory) or by seeing (visual). If your auditory score is higher than your visual score, you tend to learn more easily by hearing than by reading. A higher visual score suggests strengths with visual modes of learning such as reading, studying pictures, reading diagrams, and so forth.

Part Two: Applied or Conceptual Learners   This score describes the types of learning tasks and learning situations you instinctively prefer and find easiest to handle. If you are an applied learner, you prefer tasks that involve real objects and situations. Therefore, practical, real-life examples are ideal for you. If you are a conceptual learner, you prefer to work with language and ideas; you tend to rely less on practical applications for understanding than applied learners.

Part Three: Spatial or Verbal Learners   This score reveals your ability to work with spatial relationships. Spatial learners can visualize or mentally "see" how things work or how they are positioned in space. Their strengths may include drawing, assembling, or repairing things. Verbal or nonspatial learners lack skills in positioning things in space. Instead, they rely on verbal or language skills.

Part Four: Social or Independent Learners   This score reveals whether you like to work alone or with others. If you are a social learner, you prefer to work with others—such as classmates and instructors—closely and directly. You tend to be people-oriented and enjoy personal interaction. If you are an independent learner, you tend to be self-directed or self-motivated as well as goal-oriented.

Part Five: Creative or Pragmatic Learners   This score describes the approach you prefer to take toward learning tasks. Creative learners are imaginative and innovative. They prefer to learn through discovery or experimentation. They are comfortable taking risks and following hunches. Pragmatic learners are practical, logical, and systematic. They seek order and are comfortable following rules.

If you disagree with any part of the Learning Style Questionnaire, go with your own instincts, rather than the questionnaire results. Think of the questionnaire as just a quick assessment, but trust your self-knowledge.

Using Learning Style Effectively

Now that you have completed the Learning Style Questionnaire and know more about *how* you learn, you are ready to develop an action plan for learning what you read. Suppose you have discovered that you are an auditory learner. You still have to read your assignments, which is a visual task. To learn the assignment, however, you should translate the material into an auditory form. For example, you could repeat aloud, using your own words, information that you want to remember, or you could tape-record key information and play it back. If you are a social learner, you could work with a classmate, the two of you testing each other out loud. Such activities not only shift the presentation of ideas from visual to auditory form but also give you practice in using internal dialogue (see p. 39).

Table 1-2 (p. 22) lists the different types of learning styles and offers suggestions for how students who exhibit each style might learn most effectively from a reading assignment. You can use this table to build an action plan for more effective learning.

1. Circle the five aspects of learning style in which you received the highest scores on the Learning Style Questionnaire. Disregard the others.
2. Read through the suggestions that apply to you.

TABLE 1-2   Learning Styles and Reading/Learning Strategies

IF YOUR LEARNING STYLE IS . . .	THEN THE READING/ LEARNING STRATEGIES TO USE ARE . . .	IF YOUR LEARNING STYLE IS . . .	THEN THE READING/ LEARNING STRATEGIES TO USE ARE . . .
Auditory	• Discuss/study with friends. • Talk aloud when studying. • Tape-record self-testing questions and answers.	Verbal	• Translate diagrams and drawings into language. • Record steps, processes, and procedures in words. • Write summaries. • Write your interpretation next to textbook drawings, maps, and graphics.
Visual	• Draw diagrams, charts, and/or tables. • Try to visualize events. • Use films and videos. • Use computer-assisted instruction when available.	Social	• Form study groups. • Find a study partner. • Interact with the instructor. • Work with a tutor.
Applied	• Think of practical situations to which learning applies. • Associate ideas with their application. • Use case studies, examples, and applications to cue your learning.	Independent	• Use computer-assisted instruction. • Purchase review workbooks or study guides when available.
Conceptual	• Organize materials. • Use outlining. • Focus on organizational patterns.	Creative	• Ask and answer questions. • Record your own ideas in the margins of textbooks.
Spatial	• Use mapping. • Use outlining. • Draw diagrams; make charts and sketches. • Use visualization.	Pragmatic	• Study in an organized environment. • Write lists of steps, procedures, and processes. • Paraphrase difficult materials.

3. Place a checkmark in front of suggestions that you think will work for you. Choose at least one for each of your five learning styles.

4. List the suggestions that you chose below.

a. _____

b. _____

c. _____

d. _____

e. _____

The next step is to experiment with these techniques, one at a time. Use one technique for a while, and then move to the next. Continue using the techniques that seem to work, and work on revising or modifying those that do not. Do not hesitate to experiment with other techniques listed in the table. You may find other techniques that work well for you.

Overcoming Limitations

You should also work on developing learning styles in which you are weak because your learning style is not fixed or unchanging. You can improve areas in which you scored lower. Even though you may be weak in auditory learning, for example, many of your professors will lecture and expect you to take notes. If you work on improving your listening and note-taking skills, you can learn to handle lectures more effectively. Make a conscious effort at improving areas of weakness as well as taking advantage of your strengths.

■ Building Your Concentration

Concentration is the ability to focus on the task at hand. Most students find that by improving their concentration, they can reduce their reading time. Building your concentration is a three-part process: eliminating distractions, focusing your attention, and assessing your concentration.

Eliminating Distractions

Activities going on around you can break your concentration. A dog barking, a radio playing, and an overheard conversation are examples of distractions. The first step in improving your concentration is to eliminate distractions. Use the following suggestions in eliminating distractions:

1. **Choose a place conducive to reading.** The spot you select should be as free of distractions and interruptions as possible. If your home or dorm is too busy or noisy, you will be distracted. Study in a quiet place such as student lounge areas or library study areas. Find a place you can associate with studying so that you are ready to concentrate as soon as you sit down. Although your TV chair or your bed may look like a perfect place to study, you already associate them with relaxation and sleep. If you read and work at the same desk or study carrel regularly, you will find that when you sit down you will feel ready to concentrate, and distractions will be less bothersome.

2. **Notice your physical state.** If you are tired, you will have trouble concentrating. If you are hungry, your thoughts will drift toward food. If you feel sluggish and inactive, you may not be able to focus on your work. Try to schedule reading or studying at times when your physical needs are not likely to interfere. If you find that you are hungry, tired, or sluggish while reading, stop and take a break, have a snack, or get up and walk around. If you are physically or mentally exhausted, you may need to stop and find a better time to complete the assignment.

3. **Have necessary materials available.** When you sit down to work, be sure that you have all the needed materials. Surrounding yourself with these

tools helps to create a psychological readiness for reading and eliminates the distraction created by breaking off your work to find a book or pen.

4. **Choose your peak periods of attention.** The time of day or night when you read also influences how easy or difficult it is to shut out distractions. You have a natural time limit for how long you can successfully attend to a task; this is your **attention span.** People experience peaks and valleys in their attention spans. Some people are very alert in the early morning, whereas others find they are most focused at midday or in the early evening. To make concentration easier, try to read during the peaks of your attention span. Choose the times of day when you are most alert and when it is easiest to keep your mind on what you are doing. If you are not aware of your own peaks of attention, analyze your reading effectiveness. Over a period of several days, keep track of when you read and study and how much you accomplish each time. Then look for a pattern.

5. **Keep a list of distractions.** Often, as you are reading or studying, you will be distracted by thoughts of something you must remember to do. If you have a dental appointment scheduled for the next afternoon, you will find that a reminder occasionally flashes through your mind. To help overcome these distractions, keep a list of them. Use a sheet of paper to jot down these mental reminders as they occur. You will find that writing them down on paper temporarily eliminates reminders from your conscious memory.

Focusing Your Attention

Focusing your attention means directing all mental activity to what you are reading. To help focus your attention on the material you are reading, try the following.

1. **Set goals.** Achieving your goals is positive and rewarding; it feels good to accomplish what you set out to do. Before each study or reading session, set specific goals and time limits. Divide large assignments into smaller parts to give yourself the best chance to achieve your goals. Concentrating on these goals and time limits will help you avoid distractions; your attention will remain on your reading. One student set the following reading goals for herself for one evening of study.

Reread Psych lecture notes	15 min.
Read first half Chapter 10—Psych	90 min.
Review Chapter 9—Accounting	30 min.
Read short story—English	30 min.

2. **Reward yourself.** Meeting goals within a time limit is a reward in itself. Other rewards could include watching TV, snacking, or making phone calls. Use these activities as rewards by arranging them to follow periods of reading and studying. For example, you might call a friend after you finish

your math problems, or you could plan to rewrite your English composition before watching a favorite TV program.

3. **Begin by reviewing previously read material.** Reviewing the preceding assignment will direct your attention to today's work and help you make the "mental switch" from your preceding activity to what you are doing now.

4. **Write and underline as you read.** It is easy to let your mind wander while reading, especially if you find the material dull or boring. One way to solve this problem is to involve yourself in your reading by writing or underlining the important ideas in each section. Make marginal notes, and jot down questions. These activities force you to think: to identify important ideas, to see how they are related, and to evaluate their worth and importance. Refer to Chapters 2 and 4–6 for specific suggestions on each of these techniques.

5. **Approach assignments critically.** Be an active reader. Instead of simply trying to take in large amounts of information, read critically. Seek ideas you question or disagree with. Look for points of view, opinions, and unsupported statements. Try to predict how the author's train of thought is developing. Make connections with what you already know about the subject, with what you have read before, and with what the instructor has said in class. If you can maintain an active, critical point of view, you will minimize distractions.

Assessing Your Concentration

Once you are aware of your concentration level and can recognize when your focus is fading, you can take action to control and improve your concentration. Begin by keeping track, for a half-hour or so, of how many times your mind wanders. Use a piece of paper to make a tally of distractions as they occur. Each time you think about something other than what you are reading, make a mark on the paper. You probably will be surprised at how many times your concentration was broken during the time you were keeping count. Work on decreasing the tally; use this method once a week or so as a check on your concentration. After reading, analyze your performance. Why did you lose your concentration? Was it an external distraction? Did an idea in the text trigger your memory of a related idea? Look for patterns: At what time of day are you most easily distracted? Where are you studying when many distractions occur? What are you studying? Adjust your reading habits to decrease distractions and improve concentration.

EXERCISE 1-3

LEARNING COLLABORATIVELY

Make a list of common distractions and problems that interfere with your concentration. Next to each item, note how you can overcome it. Discuss with classmates or your instructor any items for which you have no remedy.

_____

_____

_____

_____

EXERCISE 1-4 | *Discuss how each student might improve his or her concentration in the following situations.*

1. A student cannot concentrate because of frequent interruptions by his two preschool children.
2. A student says she cannot concentrate because she is obsessed with a conflict she is having with her parents.
3. A student says he cannot read sociology for longer than a half-hour because he becomes restless and bored.

■ Developing Levels of Thinking

Throughout your educational career, your primary task is to **understand** and **recall** information. Consequently, you may not be prepared when your instructors ask you to **apply, analyze, synthesize,** and **evaluate** information.

Table 1-3 describes a hierarchy, or progression, of thinking skills. It was developed by Benjamin Bloom in 1956 and revised by Anderson (2000) and remains widely used among educators in many academic disciplines. You will notice that the progression moves from basic literal understanding to more complex skills that involve synthesis and evaluation.

When they write exams, most college instructors assume that you can operate at each of these levels. Table 1-4 shows a few items from an exam for a course in interpersonal communication. Note how the items demand different levels of thinking. You do not need to identify the level of thinking that a particular assignment or test item requires. However, you should be able to think and work at each of these levels.

TABLE 1-3   Levels of Thinking

LEVEL	EXAMPLES
Remembering: recalling information; repeating information with no changes	Recalling dates; memorizing definitions
Understanding: understanding ideas; using rules and following directions	Explaining a law; recognizing what is important
Applying: applying knowledge to a new situation	Using knowledge of formulas to solve a new physics problem
Analyzing: seeing relationships; breaking information into parts; analyzing how things work	Comparing two poems by the same author
Evaluating: making judgments; assessing the worth of information	Evaluating the effectiveness or value of an argument opposing the death penalty
Creating: putting ideas and information together in a unique way; creating something new	Designing a new computer program

TABLE 1–4   Level of Thinking Required

TEST ITEM	LEVEL OF THINKING REQUIRED
Define nonverbal communication.	Remembering
Explain how nonverbal communication works.	Understanding
Describe three instances in which you have observed nonverbal communication.	Applying
Study the two pictures projected on the screen in the front of the classroom, and compare the nonverbal messages sent in each.	Analyzing
Evaluate an essay whose major premise is "Nonverbal communication skills should be taught formally as part of the educational process."	Evaluating
Construct, for an international student visiting your hometown, a set of guidelines that will enable him or her to understand local nonverbal communication.	Creating

The following passage is taken from a psychology textbook chapter on memory and learning. Read the passage, and study the list that follows.

Some of the oldest data in psychology tell us that retrieval will be improved if practice (encoding) is spread out over time, with rest intervals spaced in between. . . . In fact, this experiment, first performed in 1946, provides such reliable results that it is commonly used as a student project in psychology classes. The task is to write the letters of the alphabet, upside down and from right to left. (If you think that sounds easy, give it a try.)

Subjects are given the opportunity to practice the task under four conditions. The *massed-practice* group works with no breaks between trials. The three *distributed-practice* groups receive the same amount of practice, but get rest intervals interspersed between each 1-minute trial. One group gets a 3- to 5-second break between trials, a second group receives a 30-second rest, and a third group gets a 45-second break between trials.

Subjects in all four groups begin at about the same (poor) level of performance. After 20 minutes of practice, the performance of all the groups shows improvement, but by far, the massed practice (no rest) group does the poorest, and the 45-second rest group does the best.

The conclusion from years of research is that almost without exception, *distributed practice is superior to massed practice.* There are exceptions, however. Some tasks may suffer from having rest intervals inserted in practice time. In general, whenever you must keep track of many things at the same time, you should mass your practice until you have finished whatever you are working on. If, for example, you are working on a complex math problem, you should work it through until you find a solution, whether it's time for a rest break or not. And of course, you should not break up your practice in such a way as to disrupt the meaningfulness of the material you are studying.

—Gerow, *Psychology: An Introduction,* pp. 217–18

Below you can see how you might use each level of thinking to understand and evaluate this passage on memory and learning.

Remembering	How was the experiment designed?
Understanding	What did the experiment show about learning?
Applying	How can I use distributed practice to plan my study time tonight?
Analyzing	Why is distributed practice more effective?
Evaluating	How effective is distributed practice?
Creating	What kind of experiment could I design to test what types of tasks benefit most (and which least) from distributed practice?

As mentioned earlier, professors use these levels of thinking in writing exams. An effective way to prepare for an exam, then, is to be sure you have thought about the test material at each level. Do this by predicting possible test questions at each level.

EXERCISE 1-5   *Read the following excerpt from an interpersonal communications textbook. Demonstrate your ability to think at various levels by answering the questions that follow.*

A **friendship relationship** is one marked by very close association, contact, or familiarity. Usually a warm friendship has developed as a result of a long association, but this is not always the case. Sometimes friendship develops suddenly. Friendship relationships are very personal or private, and they are often characterized by different types of communication.

People seek friendship relationships for many reasons. These reasons may operate singly or in conjunction with each other. Many overlap. In some situations, with some people, one of these reasons may sustain a relationship, whereas in others, several are likely to operate. The more needs that are fulfilled in a relationship, the more solid the foundation upon which the relationship rests. You seek friendship relationships to fulfill six basic needs: for enjoyment, security, affection, self-esteem, freedom, and equality. They are not necessarily ranked here in order of importance.

Enjoyment is an important, perhaps the most important, need that friendships fulfill. Simply put, friends enjoy each other's company. The "What do you want to do?" syndrome ("I don't know, what do you want to do?") often occurs because neither friend really cares. Just enjoying being together is enough; *doing* something (anything!) is secondary. . . .

Affection relates to a sense of belonging. This could encompass sexual gratification, but does not need to. Affection suggests a moderate feeling toward or emotional attachment to another person. When you feel tender attachment for others or pleasure in being with them, you are experiencing affection. Abraham Maslow labels this "belonging and love needs," placing this need among the basic or essential needs after "psychological" and "safety" needs.

Self-esteem is felt when you are recognized or appreciated by others. Sometimes being with someone enhances your status. Also, if other people attribute a joint identity to your relationship with another person, this may also increase your self-esteem. Self-esteem is affected because such a high premium is often placed on dating and "going steady." Maslow places self-esteem needs only one step higher than affection—as slightly less essential and more optional.

—Weaver, *Understanding Interpersonal Communication,* pp. 423–26

Remembering and Understanding

1. Define a friendship relationship.
2. List the six basic needs that friendship relationships fulfill.
3. Explain the meaning of the term *self-esteem.*

Applying

4. Name a person with whom you have a friendship that fulfills your need for self-esteem.

Analyzing

5. Think of a long-standing friendship. Analyze that friendship by identifying the needs it fulfills.

Evaluating

6. Do you agree with the author's statement that a high premium often is placed on dating? Why or why not?

Creating

7. The author states that the six basic needs are not necessarily ranked in order of importance. On the basis of your experience with friendships, list these needs in order of importance to you.

EXERCISE 1-6

Select a one- or two-page section from one of your textbooks. Read the section, and then write questions that might be asked to test your thinking at each level.

_____

_____

_____

_____

_____

_____

_____

■ Previewing and Predicting

Previewing and predicting are skills that will help you to think beyond the basic levels of knowledge and comprehension. **Previewing** is a means of familiarizing yourself with the content and organization of an assignment *before* you read it.

Think of previewing as getting a "sneak preview" of what a chapter or reading will be about. You can then read the material more easily and more rapidly.

How to Preview Textbook Assignments

Use the following steps to become familiar with a textbook chapter's content and organization:

1. **Read the chapter title.** The title indicates the topic of the article or chapter; the subtitle suggests the specific focus of, or approach to, the topic.

2. **Read the introduction or the first paragraph.** The introduction or first paragraph serves as a lead-in to the chapter by establishing the overall subject and suggesting how it will be developed.

3. **Read each boldface (dark print) heading.** Headings label the contents of each section and announce the major topic of the section.

4. **Read the first sentence under each major heading.** The first sentence often states the central thought of the section. If the first sentence seems introductory, read the last sentence; often, this sentence states or restates the central thought.

5. **Note any typographical aids.** Italics are used to emphasize important terminology and definitions by distinguishing them from the rest of the passage. Material that is numbered 1, 2, 3; lettered a, b, c; or presented in list form is also of special importance.

6. **Note any graphic aids.** Graphs, charts, photographs, and tables often suggest what is important in the chapter. Be sure to read the captions of photographs and the legends on graphs, charts, or tables.

7. **Read the last paragraph or summary.** This provides a condensed view of the chapter by outlining its key points.

8. **Quickly read any end-of-article or end-of-chapter material.** This might include references, study questions, discussion questions, chapter outlines, or vocabulary lists. If there are study questions, read them through quickly because they tell you what is important to remember in the chapter. If a vocabulary list is included, skim through it to identify the terms you will be learning as you read.

A section of a speech communication textbook chapter discussing purposes of listening is reprinted here to illustrate how previewing is done. The portions to focus on when previewing are shaded. Read only those portions. After you have finished, test how well your previewing worked by answering the questions in Exercise 1-7 on page 32.

PURPOSES OF LISTENING

Speakers' motivations for speechmaking vary from situation to situation just as listeners' purposes for paying attention vary. Researchers have identified five types of listening (each serving a different purpose): (a) appreciative, (b) discriminative, (c) therapeutic, (d) comprehension, and (e) critical.

Appreciative Listening

Appreciative listening focuses on something other than the primary message. People who are principally concerned with participating in the experience are appreciative listeners. Some listeners enjoy seeing a famous speaker. Other listeners enjoy the art of good public speaking, pleasing vocal modulation, clever uses of language, impressive phraseology, and the skillful use of supporting materials. Still other listeners simply like to attend special occasions such as inaugurations, dedications, and graduations.

Discriminative Listening

Discriminative listening requires listeners to draw conclusions from the way a message is presented rather than from what is said. In discriminative listening, people seek to understand what the speaker really thinks, believes, or feels. You're engaging in discriminative listening when you draw conclusions about how angry your parents are with you, based not on what they say, but on how they say it. Journalists listening to the way that a message is presented often second-guess the attitudes of national leaders on foreign policy. Performers, of course, can convey emotions such as anger or exhilaration to audiences through their delivery alone. In each of these examples, an important dimension of listening is based on relatively sophisticated inferences drawn from—rather than found in—messages.

Therapeutic Listening

Therapeutic listening is intended to provide emotional support to the speaker. It is more typical of interpersonal than public communication—the therapeutic listener acts as a sounding board for a speaker attempting to talk through a problem, work out a difficult situation, or express deep emotions. Sometimes, however, therapeutic listening occurs in public speaking situations such as when a sports star apologizes for unprofessional behavior, a religious convert describes a soul-saving experience, or a classmate reviews a personal problem and thanks friends for their help in solving it. In therapeutic listening, special social bonding occurs between speaker and listener. Consider the communication of joy that occurs when listeners react to someone who wants to tell others about a new relationship, a new baby, a promotion at work, or an award at school.

Listening for Comprehension

Listening for comprehension occurs when the listener wants to gain additional information or insights provided by the speaker. This is probably the form of listening with which you are most familiar. When you listen to radio or TV news programs, to classroom lectures on the four principal causes of World War II, or to an orientation official previewing your school's new registration process, you're listening to understand—to comprehend information, ideas, and processes.

Critical Listening

Critical listening requires listeners to both interpret and evaluate the message. The most sophisticated kind of listening is critical listening. It demands that auditors go beyond understanding the message to interpreting it, judging its strengths and weaknesses, and assigning it some value. You'll practice this sort of listening in your class. You may also use critical listening as you evaluate commercials, political campaign speeches, advice from career counselors, or arguments offered by controversial talk show guests. When you listen critically, you decide to accept or reject ideas. You may also resolve to act or delay action on the message. . . .

The variety of listening purposes has serious implications for both listeners and speakers. Appreciative listeners are highly selective, watching for metaphors, responding to speaking tones, and searching out memorable phrasings. At the other extreme, critical listeners work hard to catch relevant details, to judge the soundness of competing arguments and to rationally decide whether to accept ideas. Therapeutic listeners decide when to positively reinforce speakers through applause or other signs of approval, and those listening for comprehension distinguish between important and unimportant information. Finally, discriminative listeners search for clues to unspoken ideas or feelings that are relevant to themselves. As you think about your own listening purposes, you'll find yourself adapting your listening behavior to the speaking situation more carefully.

—Gronbeck et al., *Principles of Speech Communication,* pp. 38–39

EXERCISE 1-7

Without referring to the passage, answer each of the following true-false questions.

_____ 1. Discriminative listening requires listeners to pay attention to how the message is presented rather than to the message itself.

_____ 2. The purpose of therapeutic listening is to provide support for the speaker.

_____ 3. The purpose of listening for comprehension is to acquire information.

_____ 4. In appreciative listening, the listener focuses on the primary message.

_____ 5. Depending on their purpose, listeners pay attention to different parts of a message.

You probably were able to answer all (or most) of the questions correctly. Previewing, then, does provide you with a great deal of information. If you were to return to the passage from the speech communication textbook and read the entire section, you would find it easier to do than if you had not previewed.

When you preview an assignment, use the following hints to get the most out of it:

- Assess the difficulty of the material.
- Discover how it is organized.
- Identify the overall subject.
- Establish what type of material it is (for example, practical, research report, historical background, or case study).
- Look for logical breaking points where you might divide the assignment into portions, perhaps reserving a portion for a later study session.
- Identify points at which you might stop and review.
- Look for connections between the assignment and class lectures.

Previewing Nontextbook Material

With nontextbook material, you may have to make changes in how you preview. Many articles, essays, and reference books do not have the same features as textbook chapters. They may lack headings or clearly identifiable introductions and summaries. The following hints will help you to preview materials of this sort.

- **Pay close attention to the title;** it may make a statement about the theme or key focus of the article.
- **Identify the author and source of the material.** This information may provide clues about the article's content or focus.
- **Read the first paragraph carefully, searching for a statement of purpose or theme.**
- **If there are no headings, read the first sentence of each paragraph.** The first sentence of the paragraph is often the topic sentence that states the main idea of the paragraph. By reading first sentences, you will encounter most of the key ideas in the article.
- **Pay close attention to the last paragraph.** It probably will not provide a summary, but it usually serves as a conclusion to the article.

Why Previewing Is Effective

Previewing helps you to make decisions about how you will approach the material. On the basis of what you discover about the assignment's organization and content, you can select the reading and study strategies that will be most effective.

Previewing puts your mind in gear and helps you start thinking about the subject.

Also, previewing gives you a mental outline of the chapter's content. It enables you to see how ideas are connected, and, since you know where the author is headed, your reading will be easier than if you had not previewed. Previewing, however, is never a substitute for careful, thorough reading.

EXERCISE 1–8

Select a textbook chapter that you have not read and preview it using the procedure described in this section. When you have finished, answer the following questions.

1. What is its overall subject?
2. What topics (aspects of the subject) does the chapter discuss? List as many as you can recall.
3. How difficult do you expect the chapter to be?
4. How is the subject approached? In other words, is the material practical, theoretical, historical, research oriented, or procedural?
5. How can you apply this material in your class?

Activating Background Knowledge

After previewing your assignment, you should take a moment to think about what you already know about the topic. Whatever the topic, you probably know *something* about it: this is your background knowledge. For example, a student was about to read an article titled "Growing Urban Problems" for a sociology class. His first thought was that he knew very little about urban problems because he lived in a rural area. But when he thought of a recent trip to a nearby city, he remembered seeing homeless people and crowded conditions. This recollection helped him remember reading about drug problems, drive-by shootings, and muggings.

Activating your background knowledge aids your reading in three ways. First, it makes reading easier because you have already thought about the topic. Second, the material is easier to remember because you can connect the new information with what you already know. Third, topics become more interesting if you can link them to your own experiences. Here are some techniques to help you activate your background knowledge:

- **Ask questions, and try to answer them.** If a chapter in your biology textbook titled "Human Diseases" contains headings such as "Infectious Diseases," "Sexually Transmitted Diseases," "Cancer," and "Vascular Diseases," you might ask and try to answer such questions as the following: What kinds of infectious diseases have I seen? What caused them? What do I know about preventing cancer and other diseases?
- **Draw on your own experience.** If a chapter in your business textbook is titled "Advertising: Its Purpose and Design," you might think of several ads you have seen and analyze the purpose of each and how it was constructed.
- **Brainstorm.** Write down everything that comes to mind about the topic. Suppose you're about to read a chapter in your sociology textbook on domestic violence. You might list types of violence—child abuse, rape, and so on. You might write questions such as "What causes child abuse?" and "How can it be prevented?" Alternatively, you might list incidents of domestic violence you have heard or read about. Any of these approaches will help to make the topic interesting.

EXERCISE 1-9

Assume you have just previewed a chapter in your psychology text on psychological disorders. Discover what you already know about psychological disorders by using each of the techniques suggested previously. Then answer the questions that follow.

1. Did you discover you knew more about psychological disorders than you initially thought?
2. Which technique worked best? Why?

Making Predictions

We make predictions about many tasks before we undertake them. We predict how long it will take to drive to a shopping mall, how much dinner will cost at a new restaurant, how long a party will last, or how difficult an exam will be. Prediction helps us organize our time and cope with new situations.

Prediction is an important part of active reading as well. It enables you to approach the material systematically. Also, it helps you to read actively because you continually accept or reject your predictions. As you preview, you can predict the development of ideas, the organization of the material, and the author's conclusions. For example, for her philosophy class, a student began to preview an essay titled "Do Computers Have a Right to Life?" From the title, she predicted that the essay would discuss the topic of artificial intelligence: whether computers can "think." Then, as she read the essay, she discovered that this prediction was correct.

When you make predictions, you draw on your background knowledge and experience, making connections between what you already know about the subject and the clues you pick up through previewing. Now, predict the topic and/or point of view of each of the following articles:

"Dangerous Myths About Nuclear Energy"

"Where Darwin Went Wrong on Evolution"

"Why I Am Not a Christian"

Did you predict that the first article would favor the use of nuclear energy, that the second would hold that evolutionary theory is incorrect, and that the third would be concerned with religious beliefs?

In textbook chapters, the boldface headings serve as section "titles" and also are helpful in predicting content and organization. Considered together, chapter headings often suggest the development of ideas through the chapter. For instance, the following headings appeared in a sociology text chapter titled "Energy and the Environment":

The Limits of Fossil Fuels

Nuclear Power: High Promises, Grave Dangers

Conservation: The Hidden "Energy Source"

Solar Power: An Emerging Role

These headings reveal the author's approach to energy resources. We can predict that the chapter will describe the supply of fossil fuels as finite and nuclear power as dangerous; conservation and solar energy will be offered as viable alternatives.

EXERCISE 1-10 *Predict the subject and/or point of view of each of the following essays or articles.*

1. "Reality as Presented by Television News"
2. "TV Violence—The Shocking New Threat to Society"
3. "Professional Sports: Necessary Violence"

EXERCISE 1-11 *Turn to the table of contents in one of your textbooks. Study the headings for two or three chapters you have not read. Predict the organization or focus of each chapter. Explain which words in the headings helped you make your prediction.*

_____

_____

_____

■ Developing Guide Questions

Have you ever read an entire page or more and forgotten everything you read? Have you found yourself going from paragraph to paragraph without really thinking about what the writer is saying? Because you are not looking for anything in particular as you read, you do not notice or remember anything specific.

Reading should be a purposeful activity. You should have a reason for reading each piece of material that you pick up. Before you begin reading any article, selection, or chapter, you should know what you want to find out. Your purpose will vary with the situation. For example, you might read a magazine article on child abuse for the purpose of learning more about the general nature and extent of the problem. On the other hand, if you were doing a research paper for a sociology course on the topic of child abuse, your purpose might be quite specific. You would be looking for facts and figures about the causes, effects, and extent of child abuse so you could use this information in your paper.

The easiest way to make certain you are reading purposefully is to use guide questions. These are specific questions that guide or direct your attention to what is important in each chapter section you are reading. Guide questions are most useful in developing the knowledge and comprehension levels of thinking.

One of the easiest ways to make up guide questions is to turn the chapter title and headings into questions that you will try to answer as you read. Jot them down in the margin of your text, next to each heading, until you get in the habit of forming them. Later, you can form the questions mentally. For instance, for a chapter from a sociology text titled "Methods of Studying Society," you could ask, "What are the methods of studying society?" Then, as you read the chapter, you could look for and underline the answer. Here are three other examples of questions you might ask:

Chapter Title:	"Nine Principles of Communication"
Question:	What are the nine principles of communication?
Essay Title:	"The Real Way to Prevent Nuclear War"
Questions:	How does the essayist think nuclear war can be prevented?
	Are these preventive measures realistic and practical?
Chapter Heading:	"Theories of Color Vision"
Questions:	What are the theories of color vision?
	How do they differ?

Avoid asking guide questions that have one-word answers or that require recall of details. "How," "what," and "why" questions generally are more useful than those beginning with "who," "when," and "where."

EXERCISE 1-12   *Write at least one guide question for each of the following headings that appeared in a criminology textbook.*

Headings	Questions
Technology and Criminal Justice	_____
Criminalistics: Past, Present, and Future	_____
The Justice System Today	_____

Cybercrime: The New White-Collar
  Crime   _____

Rules of Terrorism   _____

Controlling Terrorism   _____

Technology and Individual Rights _____

EXERCISE 1-13   *Select a chapter from one of your textbooks, and write guide questions for each major heading.*

_____

_____

_____

_____

■ Checking Your Comprehension

You maintain an awareness or "check" on how well you are performing many of your daily activities. In sports such as racquetball, tennis, and bowling, you know if you are playing a poor game; you actually keep score and deliberately try to correct errors and improve your performance. When preparing a favorite food, you often taste as you cook to be sure the recipe will taste the way you want it. When you wash your car, you check to be sure that you have not missed any spots.

A similar type of checking should occur as you read. You need to "keep score" of how effectively you are comprehending and reacting to content. Because reading is a mental process, it is more difficult to check than is bowling or cooking. You may understand certain ideas you read and be confused by others.

Recognizing Comprehension Signals

What happens when you read material you can understand easily? Does it seem that everything "clicks"? Do ideas seem to fit together and make sense? Is that "click" noticeably absent at other times?

Read each of the following excerpts. As you read, be alert to how well you understand each one.

EXCERPT 1

As you well know, all you have to do to reveal anger is change the way you talk: you may talk louder, faster, and more articulately than usual. You can say exactly the same thing in a fit of anger as in a state of delight and change your meaning by how you say it. You can say "I hate you" to sound angry, teasing, or cruel. Vocal cues are what is lost when your words are written down. The term often used to refer to this quality is paralanguage. As noted before, it includes all the nonlan-

TABLE 1-5 Comprehension Signals	
POSITIVE SIGNALS	**NEGATIVE SIGNALS**
You feel comfortable and have some knowledge about the topic.	The topic is unfamiliar, yet the author assumes you understand it.
You recognize most words or can figure them out from context.	Many words are unfamiliar.
You can express the main ideas in your own words.	You must reread the main ideas and use the author's language to explain them.
You understand why the material was assigned.	You do not know why the material was assigned and cannot explain why it is important.
You read at a regular, comfortable pace.	You often slow down or reread.
You are able to make connections between ideas.	You are unable to detect relationships; the organization is not apparent.
You are able to see where the author is leading.	You feel as if you are struggling to stay with the author and are unable to predict what will follow.
You understand what is important.	Nothing (or everything) seems important.

guage means of vocal expression, such as rate, pitch, and tone. It includes, therefore, what occurs beyond or in addition to the words you speak.

—Weaver, *Understanding Interpersonal Communication,* pp. 226–27

EXCERPT 2

Large-quantity waste generators and SQGs must comply with the RCRA regulations, including obtaining an EPA identification (EPA ID) number, proper handling of the waste transport, manifesting the waste (discussed in the next section), and proper record keeping and reporting. Conditionally exempt SQGs do not require EPA ID numbers. Appropriate transport handling requires suitable packaging to prevent leakage and labeling of the packaged waste to identify its characteristics and dangers.

—Nathanson, *Basic Environmental Technology,* p. 351

Did you feel comfortable and confident as you read Excerpt 1? Did the ideas seem to lead from one to another and make sense? How did you feel while reading Excerpt 2? Probably you found it difficult and felt confused. Unfamiliar terms were used, and you could not follow the flow of ideas, so the whole passage did not make sense.

Table 1-5 lists and compares common signals to assist you in checking your comprehension. Not all the signals appear at the same time, and not all the signals work for everyone. As you study the list, identify those positive signals you sensed as you read the first excerpt about paralanguage. Then identify the negative signals you sensed when reading the excerpt about waste generators.

EXERCISE 1-14   *Select and read a three- to four-page section of a chapter in one of your textbooks. Be alert for positive and negative comprehension signals as you read. After reading the section, answer the following questions.*

1. How would you rate your overall comprehension? What positive signals did you sense? Did you feel any negative signals?
2. Where was your comprehension strongest?
3. Did you feel at any time that you had lost, or were about to lose, comprehension? If so, go back to that part now. What made it difficult to read?

Checking Techniques

At times, signals of poor comprehension do not come through clearly enough. In fact, you may think you understand what you have read until you are questioned in class or take an exam. Only then do you discover that your comprehension is incomplete. Alternatively, you may find that you comprehend material on a factual level, but you cannot apply, analyze, synthesize, or evaluate what you read. Use the following checking techniques to determine whether you really understand what you read.

1. **Use your guide questions.** Earlier in this chapter, you learned how to form guide questions from the boldface headings in your text. Use those questions to check your comprehension while reading. When you finish a boldface-headed section, take a moment to recall your guide questions and answer them mentally or on paper. Your ability to answer your questions will indicate your level of comprehension.

2. **Ask yourself thought-provoking questions.** To be certain that your comprehension is complete and that you are not recalling only superficial factual information, ask yourself questions that require you to think about content. Try to focus on the higher-level thinking skills: application, analysis, synthesis, and evaluation. Here are a few examples:

   - Can I apply this information to a real-life situation?
   - How does this reading assignment fit with the topics of this week's class lectures?
   - How does this material fit with what I already know about the topic?
   - Can I identify a principle that this material illustrates?

3. **Use internal dialogue.** Internal dialogue—mentally talking to yourself—is another excellent way to check your reading and learning. Rephrase, in your own words, the message the author is communicating. If you cannot express the ideas in your own words, your understanding is probably incomplete. The following examples of internal dialogue illustrate how the technique is used:

   You are reading an essay that argues convincingly that capital punishment does not stop crime. As you finish reading each stage of the argument, you rephrase it in your own words.

   While reading a section in a math textbook, you mentally outline the steps to follow in solving a sample problem.

   As you finish each boldface section in an anthropology chapter, you summarize the key points in your own words.

This chapter has shown you several active reading techniques, but each takes time and initially may slow you down. Considering all the competing pressures you face, you may be wondering whether you can afford the time to experiment with these techniques. However, each of these techniques will save you time in the long run. You will learn more while you are reading and will have to spend less time after reading to learn the material.

EXERCISE 1-15

Choose a section from one of your own textbooks. Read it, and check your comprehension by using both guide questions and thought-provoking questions. List your questions on a sheet of paper. List the positive and negative comprehension signals you noted as you read.

EXERCISE 1-16

Select another section from one of your textbooks and experiment with the technique of internal dialogue to check your comprehension. On a sheet of paper, describe the technique you used and evaluate its effectiveness.

Self-Test Summary

1. Why is active reading important for success in college?	Reading is the primary way in which students acquire ideas and gather information.
2. How is active reading different from passive reading?	Active readers analyze an assignment, determine its purpose, and tailor their reading accordingly. Passive readers read only what is assigned. Active readers make notes as they read and make sure they understand what they are reading. Passive readers read everything at the same pace and in the same way, not making the distinction between what is relevant to the information they are getting in class and what is not.
3. People have different learning styles. Why is it important to understand what your learning style is?	A person's learning style can make certain classes or assignments easy and others more difficult. Understanding how you learn can help you form an action plan and develop strategies for tackling the subjects and assignments that are difficult for you.
4. What are some of the things you can do to focus your attention on what you are reading?	Set goals, reward yourself, review previously read material, write notes and underline as you read, and read critically.
5. How can you assess your concentration and what can you do to improve it?	Concentration can be assessed by keeping track of every time your mind wanders and analyzing what happened each of these times to distract you. To improve your concentration, look for patterns and make adjustments to when, where, and how you study.
6. What are the six stages involved in active reading?	Remembering, understanding, applying, analyzing, evaluating, and creating
7. Why is previewing important?	Previewing helps you become familiar with the chapter's content and organization and enables you to make predictions.
8. What are guide questions?	Specific questions that direct your attention to what is important in each chapter or section you read
9. How can you check your comprehension?	Use guide questions, ask thought-provoking questions, and use internal dialogue.

PSYCHOLOGY

Factors Affecting Interpersonal Attraction

Josh R. Gerow

Prereading Question

Think of a person to whom you are attracted. Why are you attracted to him or her?

1   Now let's look at some empirical evidence related to attraction. What determines whom you will be attracted to? What factors tend to provide the rewards, or the positive reward/cost ratios, that serve as the basis for strong relationships? Here we'll describe four common principles related to interpersonal attraction.

Reciprocity

2   Our first principle is perhaps the most obvious one. Not surprisingly, we tend to value and like people who like and value us (Backman & Secord, 1959; Curtis & Miller, 1986). Remember that we've already noted, in our discussion of operant conditioning, that the attention of others often can be a powerful reinforcer. This is particularly true if the attention is positive, supportive, and affectionate. Research indicates that the value of someone else caring for us is particularly

Proximity leads to liking, which is why teenagers who go to the same school are likely to form friendships.

powerful when that someone initially seemed to have neutral or even negative attitudes toward us (Aronson & Linder, 1965). That is, we are most attracted to people who like us now, but who didn't originally. The logic here is related to attribution. If someone we meet for the first time expresses nothing but positive feelings and attitudes toward us, we are likely to attribute their reaction internally to the way the person is—rather shallow and the sort who just likes everybody. But if someone at first were to express neutral, or even slightly negative, feelings toward us and then were to become more and more positive, we might have a different, more positive view of their ability to judge others.

Proximity

3   Our second principle suggests that physical closeness, or proximity, tends to produce attraction. Sociologists, as well as your own personal experience, will tell you that people tend to establish friendships (and romances) with others with whom they have grown up, worked, or gone to school. Similarly, social-psychological studies consistently have found that residents of apartments or dormitories tend to become friends with those other residents living closest to them (Festinger et al., 1950). Being around others gives us the opportunity to discover just who can provide those interpersonal rewards we seek in friendship.

4

There may be another social-psychological phenomenon at work here called the **mere exposure phenomenon.** Research, pioneered by Robert Zajonc (1968), has shown with a variety of stimuli that liking tends to increase with repeated exposure to stimuli. Examples of this phenomenon are abundant in everyday life. Have you ever bought a CD that you have not heard previously, assuming that you will like it because you have liked all the other CDs this performer made? The first time you listen to your new CD, however, your reaction may be lukewarm at best, and you may be disappointed in your purchase. Not wanting to feel that you've wasted your money, you play the CD a few more times over the next several days. What often happens is that soon you realize that you like this CD after all. The mere exposure effect has occurred, and this commonly happens in our formation of attitudes about other people as well. Apparently, familiarity is apt to breed attraction, not contempt. I also have to add that although there seems to be ample evidence that the mere exposure phenomenon is real, there remains considerable disagreement about *why* familiarity and repeated interactions breed attraction (e.g., Birnbaum & Mellers, 1979; Kunst-Wilson & Zajonc, 1980).

Physical Attractiveness

5

Our physical appearance is one personal characteristic that we cannot easily hide. It is always on display in social situations, and it communicates something about us. People are aware of the role of appearance in nonverbal, interpersonal communication and may spend hours each week doing whatever can be done to improve the way they look.

6

The power of physical attractiveness in the context of dating has been demonstrated experimentally in a classic study directed by Elaine Walster (Walster et al., 1966). University of Minnesota freshmen completed a number of psychological tests as part of an orientation program. The students were then randomly matched for dates to an orientation dance, during which they took a break and evaluated their assigned partners. This study allowed researchers the possibility of uncovering intricate, complex, and subtle facts about interpersonal attraction, such as which personality traits might tend to mesh in such a way as to produce attraction. As it turned out, none of these complex factors, so carefully controlled for, was important. The effect of physical attractiveness was so powerful that it wiped out all other effects. For both men and women, the more physically attractive their date, the more they liked the person and the more they wanted to go out again with that individual.

7

Numerous studies of physical attractiveness followed this one. Some of these studies simply gave subjects a chance to pick a date from a group of several potential partners (usually using descriptions and pictures). Not surprisingly, subjects almost invariably selected the most attractive person available to be their date (Reis et al., 1980).

8

You may have noticed, however, that in real life we seldom have the opportunity to request a date without at least the possibility of being turned down. When experimental studies began to build in the possibility of rejection, an interesting effect emerged: Subjects stopped picking the most attractive candidate and started selecting partners whose level of physical attractiveness was more similar to their own. This behavior has been called the **matching phenomenon,** and it is an effect that has been verified by naturalistic observation studies (Walster & Walster, 1969).

Similarity

9

There is a large body of research on the relationship between similarity and attraction, but the findings are consistent, and we can summarize them briefly. Much of this research has been done by Donn Byrne and his colleagues (e.g., Byrne, 1971). It indicates that there is a strong positive relationship between attraction and the proportion of attitudes held in common. Simply put, the more similar another person is to you, the more you will tend to like that person (Buss, 1985; Davis, 1985; Rubin, 1973). Sensibly, we also tend to be repelled, or put off, by persons we believe to be dissimilar to us (Rosenbaum, 1986).

10   Perhaps you know a happily married couple for whom this sweeping conclusion does not seem to fit. At least some of their behaviors seem to be quite dissimilar, almost opposite. Perhaps the wife appears to be the one who makes most of the decisions while the husband simply seems to follow orders. It may very well be the case, however, that this apparent lack of similarity in behavior exists only on the surface. There may be an important similarity that makes for a successful marriage here: Both have the same idea of what a marriage should be like—wives decide and husbands obey. In such a case, the observed differences in behavior are reflecting a powerful similarity in the view of the roles of married couples.

—Gerow, *Psychology: An Introduction,* pp. 654–56

Writing About the Reading

CHECKING YOUR VOCABULARY

1. For each of the words listed below, use context; prefixes, roots, and suffixes (see Chapter 3); and/or a dictionary to write a brief definition or synonym of the word as it is used in the reading.

   a. empirical (para. 1) _____

   b. reciprocity (para. 2) _____

   c. proximity (para. 3) _____

   d. phenomenon (para. 4) _____

   e. invariably (para. 7) _____

   f. dissimilar (para. 9) _____

2. Underline new, specialized terms introduced in the reading.

CHECKING YOUR COMPREHENSION

1. Write a list of guide questions useful in reading and reviewing this reading.
2. Check your level of comprehension. What positive or negative signals did you sense?
3. What are the four principles discussed in this reading?
4. Explain the mere exposure phenomenon.
5. Explain the matching phenomenon.

THINKING CRITICALLY

1. Think of someone to whom you are attracted. Which of the principles of attraction can account for your attraction?
2. Can you think of other factors not discussed in this reading that may account for interpersonal attraction?

3. Describe an instance in which you experienced the mere exposure phenomenon.

4. Have you observed or experienced the matching phenomenon? If so, describe the situation in which it occurred.

LEARNING/STUDY STRATEGY

For each of the four principles of attraction, the author describes one or more experiments that are related to the principle. To review this research, complete the study chart below.

Principle	Author(s)	Summary of Findings
1. Reciprocity		
2. Proximity		
3. Physical attractiveness		
4. Similarity		

ADDITIONAL PRACTICE

MULTIMEDIA ACTIVITIES

1. **Index of Learning Styles Questionnaire**

   http://www.engr.ncsu.edu/learningstyles/ilsweb.html

   Try another learning style assessment at this site from North Carolina State University. Compare your results with those from the assessment in this book. How do online tests differ from those on paper? Which do you prefer? Is this a result of your learning style?

2. **Improving Your Concentration**

   http://www.k-state.edu/counseling/topics/career/concentr.html

   Kansas State University offers some interesting ideas to keep your mind from wandering, being distracted, and much more. Try some of these techniques, and keep track of what works for you. In what other areas of your life could these ideas be useful? Discuss with your friends the potential benefits of techniques such as meditation, yoga, and acupuncture.

MYREADINGLAB

If your instructor has asked you to use Reading Road Trip, be sure to visit the "Bourbon Street, New Orleans" module for multimedia tutorials, exercises, and tests on Active Reading Strategies.

2 Fundamental Comprehension Skills

LEARNING OBJECTIVES

✦ To identify what is important in a chapter

✦ To learn how to vary your reading rate

✦ To learn how to read selectively

Think About It!

Study the photo above. Write a sentence explaining what is happening.

The photo gives a general idea: two Nobel prize winners, Barry J. Marshall and J. Robin Warren exchange a high five to celebrate their shared prize in medicine. However, you would need to do further research to find out the details of their achievements, the reasons why they received their awards, and so forth. When you study a paragraph, essay, or textbook chapter, you also start with general ideas. Then you try to look for and examine the information that supports these general ideas.

This chapter presents techniques that enable you to read better and more efficiently. There are no easy tricks to becoming a faster reader; textbook reading must always be relatively slow and deliberate. However, if you can learn to locate what is important and then find essential supporting details, your reading will be smoother and faster. You will find, too, that you will learn more as you read, which will enable you to accomplish more as you study and review. The key to success when you are faced with large amounts of reading, then, is selectivity: sorting out what is important and focusing your attention on it.

■ Locating Main Ideas and Supporting Details

Not all sentences within a paragraph are equally important. In fact, there are three levels of importance:

Most important: the main idea

Less important: primary supporting details

Least important: secondary supporting details

As you read a paragraph, you should be sorting ideas according to their relative importance and paying more attention to some than to others. Here, you will learn how to identify these levels of importance as well as how ideas fit and work together in a paragraph.

Finding the Main Idea

A **paragraph** can be defined as a group of related ideas. The sentences are related to one another and all are about the same person, place, thing, or idea. The common subject or idea is called the **topic**—what the focus of the entire paragraph is about. As you read the following paragraph, you will see that its topic is elections.

Americans elect more people to office than almost any other society. Each even year, when most elections occur, more than 500,000 public officials are elected to school boards, city councils, county offices, state legislatures, state executive positions, the House of Representatives and the Senate, and of course, every fourth year, the presidency. By contrast with other countries, our elections are drawn-out affairs. Campaigns for even the most local office can be protracted over two or three months and cost a considerable amount of money. Presidential campaigns, including the primary season, last for at least ten months, with some candidates beginning to seek support many months and, as noted earlier, even years before the election.

—Baradat, *Understanding American Democracy*, p. 163

Each sentence of this paragraph discusses or describes elections. To identify the topic of a paragraph, then, ask yourself: *"What or who is the paragraph about?"*

The **main idea** of a paragraph is what the author wants you to know about the topic. It is the broadest, most important idea that the writer develops throughout the paragraph. The entire paragraph explains, develops, and supports this main idea. A question that will guide you in finding the main idea is, *"What key point is the author making about the topic?"* In the paragraph above, the writer's main idea is that elections in America are more numerous and more drawn out than in other countries.

Topic Sentence

Often, but not always, one sentence expresses the main idea. This sentence is called the **topic sentence.**

To find the topic sentence, search for the one general sentence that explains what the writer wants you to know about the topic. A topic sentence is a broad, general statement; the remaining sentences of the paragraph provide details about or explain the topic sentence.

In the following paragraph, the topic is stereotypes. Read the paragraph to find out what the writer wants you to know about this topic. Look for one sentence that states this.

> In everyday life, we use a variety of **stereotypes**, which are *static and oversimplified ideas about a group or social category,* that strongly influence our expectations and behaviors. In American society, there are stereotypes of women, men, jocks, the elderly, racial and ethnic minorities, college students, and countless other groups and social categories. When people are identified as belonging to a particular category, we assume they possess particular traits, and we act accordingly. Thus many people believe that redheads should be approached with caution, for they have hot tempers and can "explode at any time." By the same measure, negative stereotypes influence our interactions with racial and ethnic groups. If Scots are believed to be cheap, Italians passionate, and African Americans violent, in the early stages of interaction people will respond to them as if they possess these and other traits associated with their group, whether or not they have them.
>
> —Thompson and Hickey, *Society in Focus,* p. 131

The paragraph opens with a statement and then proceeds to explain it by citing examples. The first sentence of the paragraph functions as a topic sentence, stating the paragraph's main point: Stereotypes exert strong influences on people's expectations and behaviors.

The topic sentence can be located anywhere in the paragraph. However, there are several positions where it is most likely to be found.

Topic Sentence First   Most often, the topic sentence is placed first in the paragraph. In this type of paragraph, the author first states his or her main point and then explains it.

> *There is some evidence that colors affect you physiologically.* For example, when subjects are exposed to red light, respiratory movements increase; exposure to blue decreases respiratory movements. Similarly, eye blinks increase in frequency when eyes are exposed to red light and decrease when exposed to blue. This seems consistent with intuitive feelings about blue being more soothing and red being more arousing. After changing a school's walls from orange and white to blue, the blood pressure of the students decreased while their academic performance improved.
>
> —DeVito, *Human Communication,* p. 182

Here, the writer first states that there is evidence of the physiological effects of colors. The rest of the paragraph presents that evidence.

Topic Sentence Last   The second most likely place for a topic sentence to appear is last in the paragraph. When using this arrangement, a writer leads up to the main point and then directly states it at the end.

> Is there a relationship between aspects of one's personality and that person's state of physical health? Can psychological evaluations of an individual be used to predict physical as well as psychological disorders? Is there such a thing as a disease-prone personality? *Our response is very tentative, and the data are not all supportive, but for the moment we can say yes, there does seem to be a positive correlation between some personality variables and physical health.*
>
> —Gerow, *Psychology: An Introduction,* p. 700

In this paragraph, the author ponders the relationship between personality and health and concludes with the paragraph's main point: that they are related.

Topic Sentence in the Middle   If it is placed neither first nor last, then the topic sentence appears somewhere in the middle of the paragraph. In this arrangement, the sentences before the topic sentence lead up to or introduce the main idea. Those that follow the main idea explain or describe it.

> There are 1,500 species of bacteria and approximately 8,500 species of birds. The carrot family alone has about 3,500 species, and there are 15,000 known species of wild orchids. *Clearly, the task of separating various living things into their proper groups is not an easy task.* Within the insect family, the problem becomes even more complex. For example, there are about 300,000 species of beetles. In fact, certain species are disappearing from the earth before we can even identify and classify them.
>
> —Wallace, *Biology: The World of Life,* p. 283

In this paragraph, the author first gives several examples of living things for which there are numerous species. Then he states his main point: Separating living things into species is not an easy task. The remainder of the paragraph offers an additional example and provides further information.

Topic Sentence First and Last   Occasionally, the main idea is stated at the beginning of a paragraph and again at the end, or elsewhere in the paragraph. Writers may use this organization to emphasize an important idea or to explain an idea that needs clarification. At other times, the first and last sentences together express the paragraph's main idea.

Many elderly people have trouble getting the care and treatment they need for their ailments. Most hospitals, designed to handle injuries and acute illness that are common to the young, do not have the facilities or personnel to treat the chronic degenerative diseases of the elderly. Many doctors are also ill-prepared to deal with such problems. As Fred Cottrell points out, "There is a widespread feeling among the aged that most doctors are not interested in them and are reluctant to treat people who are as little likely to contribute to the future as the aged are reputed to." *Even with the help of Medicare, the elderly in the United States often have a difficult time getting the health care that they need.*

—Coleman and Cressey, *Social Problems,* p. 277

The first and last sentences together explain that many elderly people in the United States have difficulty obtaining needed health care.

EXERCISE 2-1   *Underline the topic sentence(s) of each of the following paragraphs.*

PARAGRAPH 1

People of nearly every culture have given names to patterns in the sky. The pattern that the Greeks named Orion, the hunter, was seen as a supreme warrior called *Shen* by the ancient Chinese. Hindus in ancient India also saw a warrior, called *Skanda,* who rode a peacock as the general of a great celestial army. The three stars of Orion's belt were seen as three fisherman in a canoe by Aborigines of northern Australia. As seen from southern California, these three stars climb almost straight up into the sky as they rise in the east, which may explain why the Chemehuevi Indians of the California desert saw them as a line of three sure-footed mountain sheep. These are but a few of the many names, each accompanied by a rich folklore, given to the pattern of stars that we call Orion.

—Bennett et al., *The Cosmic Perspective,* p. 28

PARAGRAPH 2

Language consists of a large number of *symbols.* The symbols that constitute language are commonly referred to as words—labels that we have assigned to concepts, or our mental representations. When we use the word *chair* as a symbol, we don't use it to label just one specific instance of a chair. We use the word as a symbol to represent our concept of chairs. As symbols, words need not stand for real things in the real world. We have words to describe objects or events that cannot be perceived, such as *ghost* or, for that matter, *mind.* With language we can communicate about owls and pussycats in teacups and a four-dimensional, time-warped hyperspace. Words stand for cognitions, or concepts, and we have a great number of them.

—Gerow, *Psychology: An Introduction,* p. 250

PARAGRAPH 3

Body mass is made up of protoplasm, extracellular fluid, bone, and adipose tissue (body fat). One way to determine the amount of adipose tissue is to measure the whole-body density. After the on-land mass of the body is determined, the underwater body mass is obtained by submerging the person in water. Since water helps support the body by giving it buoyancy, the apparent body mass is less in water. A higher percentage of body fat will make a person more buoyant, causing the underwater mass to be even lower. This occurs because fat has a lower density than the rest of the body.

—Timberlake, *Chemistry: An Introduction to General, Organic, and Biological Chemistry,* p. 30

PARAGRAPH 4

Early biologists who studied reflexes, kineses, taxes, and fixed action patterns assumed that these responses are inherited, unlearned, and common to all members of a species. They clearly depend on internal and external factors, but until recently, instinct and learning were considered distinct aspects of behavior. However, in some very clever experiments, Jack Hailman of the University of Wisconsin showed that certain stereotyped behavior patterns require subtle forms of experience for their development. In other words, at least some of the behavior normally called instinct is partly learned.

—Mix et al., *Biology, The Network of Life,* p. 532

PARAGRAPH 5

The poorest 20 percent of the elderly, who are primarily unmarried women, minorities, and the physically impared, possess only 5.5 percent of all of the elderly's resources, whereas the wealthiest 20 percent own 46 percent of the total (Crystal and Shea, 1990). Reitrement or loss of work due to ill health, decreased physical abilities, or other age-related factors can be economically devastating. While it is a myth that the vast majority of the elderly are poor, those over age 65 have a lower median income than all other adult categores between ages 25 and 64, and elderly members of African American, Hispanic, and other minority groups fare far worse than elderly white Americans (church et al., 1988; Census Bureau News, 2003). Sixty-two percent of persons over age 65 in this country receive over half their income from Social Security, which is the only source of income for many elderly Americans (Church et al., 1988). In short, the public perception that inequality narrows after age 65 in numbers is inaccurate, and for the aged, even more than for other age cohort, it is true that the rich get richer and the poor get poorer.

— Thompson and Hickey, *Society in Focus,* p. 35

Finding an Implied Main Idea

Although most paragraphs do have a topic sentence, some do not. Such paragraphs contain only details or specifics that, taken together, point to the main idea. The main idea, then, is implied but not directly stated. In such paragraphs, you must infer, or reason out, the main idea. This is a process of adding up the details and deciding what they mean together or what main idea they all support or explain. Use the following steps to grasp implied main ideas:

- Identify the topic by asking yourself, "What is the one thing the author is discussing throughout the paragraph?"

- Decide what the writer wants you to know about the topic. Look at each detail and decide what larger idea each explains.
- Express this idea in your own words.

Here is a sample paragraph; use the preceding steps to identify the main idea.

> As recently as 20 years ago, textbooks on child psychology seldom devoted more than a few paragraphs to the behaviors of the neonate—the newborn through the first 2 weeks of life. It seemed as if the neonate did not do much worth writing about. Today, most child psychology texts devote substantially more space to discussing the abilities of newborns. It is unlikely that over the past 20 years neonates have gotten smarter or more able. Rather, psychologists have. They have devised new and clever ways of measuring the abilities and capacities of neonates.
> —Gerow, *Psychology: An Introduction,* p. 319

The topic of this paragraph is the neonate. The author's main point is that coverage of neonates in psychology texts has increased as psychologists have learned more about them.

EXERCISE 2-2

Read the following section from an ecology textbook and underline the topic sentence in each paragraph. Monitor your comprehension and list positive or negative comprehension signals (see Chapter 1, p. 38) you received while reading. Compare your list with those of other students in the class.

LIVING THINGS ARE BOTH COMPLEX AND ORGANIZED

Life on Earth consists of a hierarchy of structures. Each level is based on the one below it and provides the foundation for the one above it. All of life is built on a chemical foundation of substances called elements, each of which is a unique type of *matter.* An atom is the smallest particle of an element that retains the properties of that element. For example, a diamond is made of the element carbon. The smallest possible unit of the diamond is an individual carbon atom; any further division would produce isolated subatomic particles that would no longer be carbon. Atoms may combine in specific ways to form assemblies called molecules; for example, one carbon atom can combine with two oxygen atoms to form a molecule of carbon dioxide. Although many simple molecules form spontaneously, only living things manufacture extremely large and complex molecules. The bodies of living things are composed primarily of complex molecules. The molecules of life are called organic molecules, meaning that they contain a framework of carbon, to which at least some hydrogen is bound. Although the chemical arrangement and interaction of atoms and molecules form the building blocks of life, the quality of life itself emerges on the level of the cell. Just as an atom is the smallest unit of an element, so the cell is the smallest unit of life. The differences between a living cell and a conglomeration of chemicals illustrate some of the emergent properties of life.

All cells contain genes, units of heredity that provide the information needed to control the life of the cell: subcellular structures called organelles, miniature chemical factories that use the information in the genes and keep the cell alive;

and a plasma membrane, a thin sheet surrounding the cell that both encloses the cytoplasm (the organelles and the watery medium surrounding them) and separates the cell from the outside world. Some life-forms, mostly microscopic, consist of just one cell, but larger life-forms are composed of many cells, each with a specialized function. In multicellular life-forms, related cells combine to form tissues, which perform a particular function. For example, nervous tissue is composed of nerve cells and a variety of supporting cells. Various tissue types combine to form a structural unit called an organ (for example, the brain, which contains nervous tissue, connective tissue, and blood). A group of several organs that collectively perform a single function is called an organ system; for example, the brain, spinal cord, sense organs, and nerves form the nervous system. All the organ systems functioning cooperatively make up an individual living thing, the organism.

Broader levels of organization reach beyond individual organisms. A group of very similar, potentially interbreeding organisms constitutes a species. Members of the same species that live in a given area are considered a population. Populations of several species living and interacting in the same area form a community. A community and its nonliving environment—including land, water, and atmosphere— constitute an ecosystem. Finally, the entire surface region of Earth inhabited by living things (and including its nonliving components) is called the biosphere.

—Audesirk, et al., *Biology: Life on Earth,* pp. 2, 4

Positive signals: _____

_____

_____

Negative signals: _____

_____

_____

EXERCISE 2-3

Select a two- to three-page excerpt from one of your textbooks and underline the topic sentence of each paragraph.

Recognizing Primary and Secondary Details

Supporting details are those facts, reasons, examples, or statistics that prove or explain the main idea of a paragraph. Though all the details in a paragraph support the main idea, not all details are equally important. As you read, try to identify and pay attention to the most important, primary details. These primary details directly explain the main idea. Secondary, less important details may provide additional information, offer an example, or further explain one of the primary details. You might visualize the structure of a paragraph as follows:

```
MAIN IDEA
    Primary detail
        Secondary detail
        Secondary detail
    Primary detail
        Secondary detail
    Primary detail
```

Read the following paragraph. The topic is boxed, the main idea is double-underlined, and primary details are single-underlined.

<u><u>Our data on the kinds of people who are more likely to read magazines are better than our data on the number who do.</u></u> Surveys show, not surprisingly, that the amount of [magazine reading] is <u>highly correlated with education.</u> The more educated people are, the more time they are likely to spend reading magazines. We also know that <u>women tend to read magazines more than men do.</u> This is shown by various kinds of data, including the fact that magazines that appeal primarily to women outsell magazines that appeal primarily to men. There is <u>little evidence that the sexual revolution has erased the clear distinctions between men's and women's tastes in magazines.</u> Men are more likely than women to read magazines that cover news on business and finance, mechanics and science, sports, outdoor life, and those that include photographs of women in various states of undress. Men also have a higher probability of reading the general newsmagazines. Women, on the other hand, are more likely to read magazines with useful household information (recipes, home decor, child care, and gardening) or fashion and beauty information.

—Becker, *Discovering Mass Communication*, p. 159

This paragraph begins with a topic sentence. The primary details present what is known about magazine readership patterns, and the secondary details further explain and offer examples of these patterns.

To determine the importance of a particular detail, decide whether it directly explains the main idea or explains or provides further information about one of the primary details.

EXERCISE 2-4

Read the following excerpt from a psychology textbook. For each paragraph, draw a box around the topic sentence and underline the primary details. What types of details did the author provide? When you have finished, evaluate your comprehension by using internal dialogue (see Chapter 1, p. 39) to summarize the key points of the excerpt in your own words.

STRESSORS ANCIENT AND MODERN

Early humans survived mortal dangers by responding quickly and decisively to potentially lethal attacks by predators or hostile tribes, and some of the ways we respond to stressors in modern times are the result of their evolutionary legacy. Modern life, of course, adds some new dangers: demanding jobs, financial worries, and computer crashes. Most recently we have faced the stressors of international terrorism. Yet, while we are exposed to new stressors, our stress response reflects the body's millennia-old ability to become quickly aroused to meet emergencies. So, when the power company threatens to cut off your power or your boss criticizes your work, your muscles may tighten, your hormones may surge, and you may feel an urge to flee or fight. Unfortunately, these old remedies don't work as well with the new problems.

Some of the problems of our ancestors, however, are still with us—including war, famine, flood, fire, earthquake, and hurricane, to name a few. We will begin our survey of the human stress response by grouping these ancient and devastating maladies under the heading of *catastrophe.* But we will see that certain distinctive behavior patterns emerge under all sources of stress.

CATASTROPHE

Stress in the extreme can accompany catastrophic events. Anyone caught in a war, hurricane, fire, flood, or earthquake may suddenly lose loved ones and a lifetime of possessions. What is not always obvious, however, is that our response to a catastrophic experience can also have a devastating effect on our physical and mental health.

Psychologists have learned much about stress from people who have undergone catastrophic losses and traumas (Baum, 1990). One such opportunity to understand how people respond to extreme ordeals presented itself just as the 1989 World Series was about to begin at San Francisco's Candlestick Park. As spectators settled into their seats, the entire stadium started to shake violently, the lights went out, and the scoreboard turned black. Sixty thousand fans fell silent. They had just experienced a major earthquake. Elsewhere in the city, fires erupted, a bridge collapsed, highways were crushed—and people were dying.

One week after the quake, a team of research psychologists began interviewing approximately 800 people chosen randomly from the San Francisco area and from several comparison cities some distance away. Subjects completed a ten-minute phone survey about their thoughts, social behavior, and health. For the next year, these same subjects were interviewed again every few weeks.

These surveys revealed a pattern: The lives of people who had been through the quake revolved around the disaster for about a month. After this period, the obsessive thoughts about the quake rather abruptly moved out of the center of consciousness. At about the same time, people reported an increase in other stress-related symptoms, such as earthquake dreams and troubled relationships. Most of these symptoms diminished during the ensuing one or two months, although as many as 20% of San Francisco area residents remained distressed about the quake a year later (Pennebaker & Harber, 1991).

In general, researchers have found that the psychological responses to disasters, such as the San Francisco quake, tend to occur in five stages (see Cohen & Ahearn, 1980):

- First, there comes a period of shock, confusion, and even *psychic numbness,* during which people cannot fully comprehend what has happened. This period may last only a few moments, or it can linger several days.

- In the next phase, people engage in *automatic action*. They respond to the disaster with little awareness of their actions and later show poor recall of these experiences. However, the numbness of the first stage may, under some conditions, linger and paralyze victims into dangerous inaction. For example, when an earthquake shattered the city of Kobe, Japan, in January 1995, the citizens' shock and lack of preparedness prevented timely rescues. This delay in automatic action was later blamed for many of the almost 6,000 related deaths.
- In the third stage, people often have a sense of great accomplishment and *communal effort*. Also in this phase, they may feel weary and are aware that they are using up their reserves of energy. This phase builds on automatic action, but without conscious planning and collaboration people may lose hope and take no initiative in rebuilding their lives.
- During the fourth phase, people often experience a *letdown;* their energy is depleted, and they finally comprehend and feel the impact of the tragedy emotionally. For example, in recent years victims of hurricane damage have felt frustrated and abandoned when, weeks after natural disasters occurred, the rest of the country appeared to forget their continuing state of emergency.
- An extended final period of *recovery* follows, as people adapt to the changes brought about by the disaster. A flood may leave a small town so changed that some businesses are permanently shut down, while others move in and change the appearance and social activity of the postflood community.

In the wake of catastrophic experiences, we formulate accounts, or stories, that explain what happened and what it means. These accounts are an important part of efforts to explain ourselves to each other. Forming and transmitting such accounts may even reflect a more general human need to tell our stories and be understood by those close to us (Harvey, 1996; Harvey et al., 1990). We especially like to tell of surprising and/or unpleasant experiences (Holtzworth-Munroe & Jacobson, 1985). An important part of working through the pain of loss is formulating an account and confiding it to others (Weber & Harvey, 1994b).

The stress response under catastrophic conditions has a physical side, as well. This was reflected in the health records of people living in Othello, Washington, which was covered by a blanket of gray volcanic ash during the eruption of Mount Saint Helens in 1980. During the six months just after the eruption, these people had a nearly 200% increase in stress-related disorders. The death rate for the period also jumped by 19% (Adams & Adams, 1984). In general, people who undergo any sort of trauma become more susceptible to physical illness. We will look more closely at the physical basis for this response to stress in the second section of this chapter. Significantly, however, research shows that those who discuss the experience in detail with others suffer fewer health problems (Pennebaker, 1990; Pennebaker & Harber, 1993; Pennebaker et al., 1989).

—Zimbards, et al., *Psychology: Core Concepts,* pp. 381–84

■ Adjusting Your Rate to Meet Comprehension Demands

Do you read the newspaper in the same way and at the same speed at which you read a biology textbook? Do you read an essay for your English class in the same way and at the same speed at which you read a mystery novel? Surprisingly, many people do.

If you are an efficient reader, however, you read the newspaper more quickly and in a different way than you read a biology textbook. Usually, the newspaper is easier to read, and you have a different purpose for reading it. Efficient readers adapt their speed and comprehension levels to suit the material.

To adapt your rate, you need to decide how you will read a given item. How you will read depends on why you are reading and how much you need to remember. A number of variables work together. To read efficiently, you must create a balance among these factors each time you read.

Rate and comprehension are the two main factors that you must keep in balance; as your reading rate increases, your comprehension may decrease. Your goal is to achieve a balance that suits the nature of the material and your purpose for reading it. The following steps will help you learn to vary your reading rate:

1. **Assess the text's difficulty.** Factors such as difficulty of the language, length, and organization all affect text difficulty. Usually, longer or poorly organized material is more difficult to read than shorter or well-organized material. Numerous typographical aids (italics, headings, etc.) can make material easier to read. As you preview an assignment, notice these features and estimate how difficult the material will be to read. There is no rule to use in adjusting your speed to compensate for differing degrees of difficulty. Instead, use your judgment to adjust your reading rate and style to the material.

2. **Assess your familiarity with and interest in the subject.** Your knowledge of and interest in a subject influence how fast you can read. Material you are interested in or that you know something about will be easier for you to read, and you can increase your speed.

3. **Define your purpose.** The reason you are reading an assignment should influence how you read it. Different situations demand different levels of comprehension and recall. For example, you can read an article in *Time* magazine assigned as a supplementary reading in sociology faster than you can read your sociology text because the magazine assignment does not require as high a level of recall and analysis.

4. **Decide what, if any, follow-up activity is required.** Will you have to pass a multiple-choice exam on the content? Will you be participating in a class discussion? Will you summarize the information in a short paper? The activities that follow your reading determine, in part, the level of comprehension that is required. Passing an exam requires a very high level of reading comprehension, whereas preparing for a class discussion requires a more moderate level of comprehension or retention.

Table 2-1 shows the level of comprehension required for various types of material and gives approximate reading rates appropriate for each level.

TABLE 2–1   Levels of Comprehension

DESIRED LEVEL OF COMPREHENSION	TYPE OF MATERIAL	PURPOSE IN READING	RANGE OF READING RATES
Complete, 100%	Poetry, legal documents, argumentative writing	Analysis, criticism, evaluation	Under 200 wpm
High, 80–100%	Textbooks, manuals, research documents	High comprehension recall for exams, writing research reports, following directions	200–300 wpm
Moderate, 60–80%	Novels, paperbacks, newspapers, magazines	Entertainment enjoyment, general information	300–500 wpm
Selective, below 60%	Reference materials, catalogues, magazines	Overview of material, location of specific facts, review of previously read material	600–800 wpm

EXERCISE 2–5

For each of the following situations, define your purpose and indicate the level of comprehension that seems appropriate.

1. Reading the end-of-chapter discussion questions in a business marketing text as part of your chapter preview.

   Purpose: _____

   Comprehension level: _____

2. Reading a critical essay that analyzes a Shakespearean sonnet you are studying in a literature class.

   Purpose: _____

   Comprehension level: _____

3. Reading an encyclopedia entry on poverty to narrow down a term paper assignment to a manageable topic.

   Purpose: _____

   Comprehension level: _____

4. Reading a newspaper article on a recent incident in the Middle East for your political science class.

   Purpose: _____

   Comprehension level: _____

5. Reading an excerpt from a historical novel set in the Civil War period for your American history class.

   Purpose: _____

   Comprehension level: _____

Measure Your Reading Rate

To verify that you are adjusting your reading rate to suit the material and your purpose for reading, measure your reading rate in a variety of situations and make comparisons. The following is an easy method of estimating your reading rate on whatever material you are reading.

1. **After you have chosen a passage in a book or article, count the total number of words in any three lines.** Divide that total by 3. Round to the nearest whole number. This will give you the average number of words per line.

2. **Count the number of lines in the article or passage** (or on one page if it is longer than one page). Multiply the number of words per line by the total number of lines. This will give you a fairly accurate estimate of the total number of words.

3. **As you read, time yourself.** Record the hour, minute, and second of your starting time (for example, 4:20:00). Start reading when the second hand of the clock reaches 12. Record your finishing time. Subtract your starting time from your finishing time.

4. **Divide the total reading time into the total number of words.** To do this, round the number of seconds to the nearest quarter of a minute and then divide. For example, if your total reading time was 3 minutes and 12 seconds, round it off to $3\frac{1}{4}$ or 3.25 minutes and then divide. Your answer will be your words-per-minute (wpm) score.

Example:

Total number of words on 3 lines: 23

Divide by 3 and round: $23 \div 3 = 7\frac{2}{3} = 8$

Total number of lines in article: 120

Multiply number of words per line by number of lines:

$8 \times 120 = 960$ (total words)

Subtract starting time from finishing time:

$$\begin{array}{r} 1:13:28 \\ - \underline{1:05:00} \\ 8:28 \end{array}$$

Round to nearest quarter minute: 8.25 minutes

Divide time into total number of words:

$960 \div 8.25 = 116 +$ a fraction (your wpm score)

EXERCISE 2-6

Measure how effectively you adjust your reading rate by reading each of the following materials for the purpose stated. Fill in your reading rate in the space provided, and then compare your results with those given in Table 2-1.

1. Material: A legal document (insurance policy, financial aid statement, credit card agreement)

   Purpose: Complete understanding

   Rate: _____

2. Material: A three-page assignment in one of your textbooks

   Purpose: High comprehension; recall for an exam

   Rate: _____

3. Material: An article in a favorite magazine

   Purpose: Moderate comprehension; entertainment

   Rate: _____

Reading Selectively to Improve Your Reading Efficiency

As part of learning how to adjust your reading rate, you should accept the idea that there is nothing sacred about the printed word. Many students erroneously believe that anything that appears in print must be true, valuable, and worth reading. Actually, the importance and value of printed information are affected by whether you need to learn it and whether you can use it in a practical way. Depending on the kind of material and your purpose for reading it, many times you may need to read only some parts and may skip over others. You might read selectively when:

1. **You are searching for specific information.** If you are looking up the date of a historical event in your history text, you skip over everything in the chapter except the exact passage that contains the information. This technique of skipping everything except the specific information for which you are looking is called *scanning.*

2. **A high level of comprehension is not needed.** If you are not trying to remember a major portion of the facts and details, then you might concentrate on reading only main ideas. This method of reading only main ideas is called *skimming.*

3. **You are familiar with what you are reading.** In a college chemistry course, for example, you might find that the first few chapters of your text are basic if you have already studied high school chemistry. You could afford to skip basic definitions and the explanations and examples of principles that you already know. Do not, however, decide to skip an entire chapter or even large sections within it; there just may be some new information included. You may find that more exact and detailed definitions are given or that a new approach is taken toward a particular topic.

4. **The material does not match your purpose in reading.** Suppose that, in making an assignment in your physics text, your instructor told you to concentrate only on theories, laws, and principles presented in the chapter. As you begin reading the chapter, you find that the first topic discussed is Newton's law of motion, but the chapter also contains a biogra-

phical sketch of Newton giving detailed information about his life. Because your purpose in reading the chapter is to focus on theories, laws, and principles, it would be appropriate to skip over much of the biographical information.

5. **The writer's style allows you to skip information (portions).** Some writers include many examples of a particular concept or principle. If, after reading two or three examples, you are sure that you understand the idea being explained, quickly glance at the remaining examples. Unless they present a new aspect or different point of view, skip over them. Other writers provide detailed background information before leading into a discussion of the intended topic. If a chapter starts out by summarizing information that was covered in a chapter you just read last week, it is not necessary to read this information again carefully unless you feel you need to review.

EXERCISE 2-7

The following items suggest different reading situations and describe the material to be read. For each item, decide whether you should (a) read the material completely, (b) read parts and skip other parts, or (c) skip most of the material.

1. Your computer science instructor has just returned a test on a chapter of your textbook. She indicates that the class's overall performance on this test was poor and suggests that the chapter be reviewed. You received a grade of 77 on the test. How should you reread this chapter?
2. You have just attended English class, where your instructor discussed Shakespeare's *Richard III*. During his discussion, he made numerous references to Machiavelli's *The Prince*. You have never read this second work but think it's important to know something about it. How would you read it?
3. You are doing research for a sociology term paper on world trends in gender inequality. You are looking for information and statistics on recent income and employment trends. You have located several books from the 1960s on the topic of gender inequality in the United States. How would you read these books?
4. Your American history instructor has assigned each student to read a historical novel for the purpose of getting a realistic picture of what life was like and how people lived during a certain period. As you are reading, you come to a detailed two-page description of decorative glass making in Sandwich, Massachusetts. How should you read these two pages?
5. Your zoology professor has assigned a number of brief outside readings along with the chapters in your regular textbook. He has put them on reserve in the college library for the use of all his classes. This is the only place where they can be used. He did not say whether you would be tested on these readings. How would you read them?

Self-Test Summary

1. What is a paragraph?	A paragraph is a group of related ideas.
2. What is meant by the "main idea"?	The main idea is the most important idea expressed in the paragraph; it is the idea which the remainder of the paragraph explains or supports.
3. What is a primary supporting detail?	A primary supporting detail provides information that backs up the main idea.
4. What is a secondary supporting detail?	A secondary detail provides further explanation of the main idea or of one of the primary details.
5. What is a topic sentence?	A topic sentence is a broad statement that expresses the main idea.
6. What is an implied main idea?	An implied main idea is one that is suggested, but not directly stated.
7. What position can a topic sentence have in a paragraph?	The topic sentence can be the first, last, middle, or first and last sentence in a paragraph.
8. Why should you vary your reading rate?	You should vary your reading rate to suit the material and your purpose for reading it.
9. Why is measuring your reading rate a good thing to do?	Measuring your reading rate can help you assess whether you are reading at the proper rate for good comprehension.
10. When is it appropriate to read selectively?	It is appropriate to read selectively when you are reading for only main ideas, a specific fact, or the answer to a question; when you are very familiar with the material; when the material does not match with your purpose; and when the style or type of material is conducive to skipping information.

SOCIOLOGY

Diversity in U.S. Families

James M. Henslin

Prereading Questions

1. Is there any such thing as a typical American family?
2. What different types of family structure have you encountered?

1   It is important to note that there is no such thing as *the* American family. Rather, family life varies widely throughout the United States. The significance of social class, noted earlier, will continue to be evident as we examine diversity in U.S. families.

African American Families

2   Note that the heading reads African American *families,* not *the* African American family. There is no such thing as *the* African American family any more than there is *the* white family or *the* Latino family. The primary distinction is not between African Americans and other groups, but between social classes. Because African Americans who are members of the upper class follow class interests—preservation of privilege and family fortune—they are especially concerned about the family background of those whom their children marry (Gatewood 1990). To them, marriage is viewed as a merger of family lines. Children of this class marry later than children of other classes.

3   Middle-class African American families focus on achievement and respectability. Both husband and wife are likely to work outside the home. A central concern is that their children

There is no such thing as the African American family, any more than there is the Native American, Asian American, Latino, or Irish American family. Rather, each racial-ethnic group has different types of families, with the primary determinant being social class. This African American family is observing Kwanzaa, a relatively new festival, that celebrates African heritage.

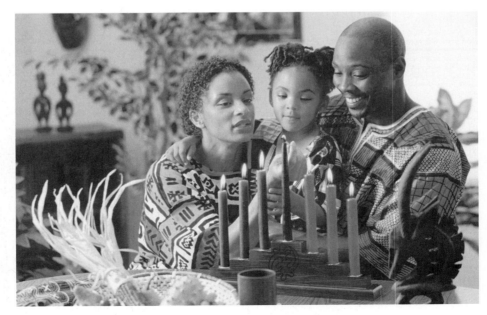

go to college, get good jobs, and marry well—that is, marry people like themselves, respectable and hardworking, who want to get ahead in school and pursue a successful career.

4   African American families in poverty face all the problems that cluster around poverty (Wilson 1987, 1996; Anderson 2001). Because the men are likely to have few skills and to be unemployed, it is difficult for them to fulfill the cultural roles of husband and father. Consequently, these families are likely to be headed by a woman and to have a high rate of births to single women. Divorce and desertion are also more common than among other classes. Sharing scarce resources and "stretching kinship" are primary survival mechanisms. That is, people who have helped out in hard times are considered brothers, sisters, or cousins to whom one owes obligations as though they were blood relatives (Stack 1974). Sociologists use the term *fictive kin* to refer to this stretching of kinship.

5   From Figure A, you can see that, compared with other groups, African American families are the least likely to be headed by married couples and the most likely to be headed by women. Because of a *marriage squeeze*—an imbalance in the sex ratio, in this instance fewer unmarried men per 1,000 unmarried women—African American women are more likely than other racial-ethnic groups to marry men who are less educated than themselves (South 1991).

Latino Families

6   As Figure A shows (p. 64), the proportion of Latino families headed by married couples and women falls in between that of whites and that of African Americans. The effects of social class on families, which I just sketched, also apply to Latinos. In addition, families differ by country of origin. Families from Cuba, for example, are more likely to be headed by a married couple than are families from Puerto Rico (*Statistical Abstract* 2000: Table 45).

7   What really distinguishes Latino families, however, is culture—especially the Spanish language, the Roman Catholic religion, and a strong family orientation coupled with a disapproval of divorce. Although there is some debate among the experts, another char-

Although there is no such thing as the Latino family in general, Latinos place high emphasis on extended family relationships.

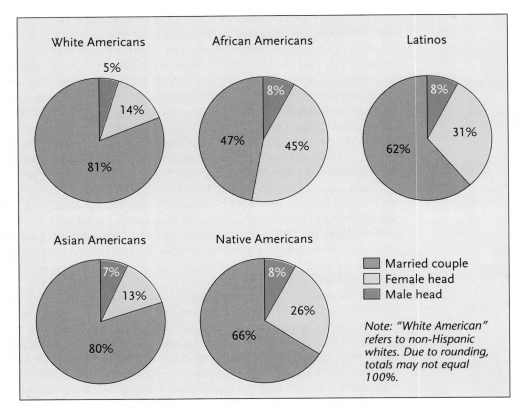

FIGURE A   Family Structure: The percentage of U.S. Households Headed by Men, Women, and Married Couples
Source: *Statistical Abstract 2000: Tables 41, 42, 44, 45*

acteristic seems to be machismo—an emphasis on male strength and dominance. In Chicano families (those originating from Mexico), the husband-father plays a stronger role than in either white or African American families (Vega 1990). Machismo apparently decreases with each generation in the United States (Hurtado et al. 1992; Wood 2001). The wife-mother, however, generally makes most of the day-to-day decisions for the family and does the routine disciplining of the children. She is usually more family centered than her husband, displaying more warmth and affection for her children.

8   Generalizations have limits, of course, and as with other ethnic groups, individual Latino families vary considerably from one to another (Baca Zinn 1994; Carrasquillo 1994).

Asian American Families

9   As you can see from Figure A, the structure of Asian American families is almost identical to that of white families. Apart from this broad characteristic, because Asian Americans come from twenty countries, their family life varies considerably, reflecting their many cultures. In addition, as with Latino families, the more recent their immigration, the more closely their family life reflects the family life of their country of origin (Kibria 1993; Glenn 1994).

To search for the Native American family would be fruitless. There are rural, urban, single-parent, extended, nuclear, rich, poor, traditional, and assimilated Native American families, to name just a few. Shown here is an Apache family in Whiteriver, Arizona.

10   Despite such differences, sociologist Bob Suzuki (1985), who studied Chinese American and Japanese American families, identified several distinctive characteristics. Although Asian Americans have adopted the nuclear family, they have retained Confucian values that provide a distinct framework for family life: humanism, collectivity, self-discipline, hierarchy, respect for the elderly, moderation, and obligation. Obligation means that each individual owes respect to other family members and is responsible for never bringing shame on the family. Asian Americans tend to be more permissive than Anglos in child rearing and more likely to use shame and guilt rather than physical punishment to control their children's behavior.

Native American Families

11   Perhaps the single most significant issue that Native American families face is whether to follow traditional values or to assimilate into the dominant culture (Yellowbird and Snipp 1994; Garrett 1999). This primary distinction creates vast differences among families. The traditionals speak native languages and emphasize distinctive Native American values and beliefs. Those that have assimilated into the broader culture do not.

12   Figure A depicts the structure of Native American families. You can see how close it is to that of Latinos. In general, Native American parents are permissive with their children and avoid physical punishment. Elders play a much more active role in their children's families than they do in most U.S. families: They not only provide child care, but also they teach and discipline children. Like others, Native American families differ by social class.

In Sum

13   From this brief review, you can see that race-ethnicity signifies little for understanding family life. Rather, social class and culture hold the keys. The more resources a family has, the more it assumes the characteristics of a middle-class nuclear family. Compared with the poor, middle-class families have fewer children and fewer unmarried mothers, and place greater emphasis on educational achievement and deferred gratification.

Writing About the Reading
CHECKING YOUR VOCABULARY

1. For each of the words listed below, use context, prefixes, roots, and suffixes (see Chapter 3), and/or a dictionary to write a brief definition or synonym of the word as it is used in the reading.

   a. diversity (para. 1)_____

   b. preservation (para. 2) _____

   c. merger (para. 2) _____

   d. respectability (para. 3) _____

   e. cultural (para. 4) _____

   f. machismo (para. 7)_____

   g. nuclear family (para. 10) _____

   h. permissive (para. 10)_____

   i. assimilate (para. 11) _____

2. Underline new, specialized terms introduced in the reading (see Chapter 3).

CHECKING YOUR COMPREHENSION

1. What is more important than race and ethnicity in understanding family life?
2. What is the primary interest of the upper class?
3. What is a "marriage squeeze"?
4. In what ways are Native American and Asian American families similar?
5. Which racial/ethnic group is least likely to be headed by a married couple?
6. Which family structure varies least from racial/ethnic group to racial/ethnic group (refer to Figure A)?
7. Which group has the most similar structure to white (non-Hispanic) American families?

THINKING CRITICALLY

1. Why is there no such thing as *the* African American family?

2. Explain the meaning of *fictive kin*. Give examples of fictive kin in families you know.
3. Discuss possible reasons why machismo decreases with each generation in the United States.
4. Respect for family members is important in Asian American families. Discuss whether respect for elderly family members exists among families you know.
5. Discuss the pros and cons of a racial/ethnic group being assimilated into the dominant culture. What is gained? What is lost?

LEARNING/STUDY STRATEGY

Assume that this reading was assigned as a topic for class discussion by your sociology instructor. Reread and annotate the reading in preparation for the class discussion.

ADDITIONAL PRACTICE

MULTIMEDIA ACTIVITIES

1. **What Is a Topic Sentence?**

   http://www.cerritos.edu/reading/topic1.html

   Review how to locate the topic sentence of a paragraph with these tips and exercises from Cerritos College. Pay attention to the way you speak. Do you use topic sentences? Try putting more of them into your conversations and see if you are expressing yourself more clearly.

2. **Effective Reading Tutorial**

   http://www.jcu.edu.au/studying/services/studyskills/effreading/index.html

   Try this online module for improving your reading rate and comprehension from James Cook University in Australia.

MYREADINGLAB

If your instructor has asked you to use Reading Road Trip, be sure to visit the "The Maine Woods" and "The St. Louis Arch" modules for multimedia tutorials, exercises, and tests on Main Idea and Supporting Details.

3 Essential Vocabulary Skills

LEARNING OBJECTIVES

✦ To learn techniques for vocabulary development

✦ To develop skill in using context clues

✦ To use word parts to expand your vocabulary

✦ To use word mapping

✦ To handle technical and specialized vocabulary

Think About It!

Study the photograph above. It is interesting and engaging because it reveals a great deal of information about the woman. Your vocabulary is like a photograph—it can be lively, interesting, and descriptive and convey a great deal of information, or it can be dull, uninteresting, and convey minimal information.

Your vocabulary can be one of your strongest academic assets or one of your worst liabilities. Language is the primary vehicle of thought, expression, and communication. Vocabulary is the basic unit of language. If your vocabulary is limited, your potential for self-expression, effective communication, and adequate comprehension of oral or printed materials also is limited. Conversely, a strong vocabulary can have both immediate (academic) and long-term (career) effects.

◼ Techniques for Vocabulary Development

Here are some basic techniques for vocabulary development that can produce immediate results.

Be Selective

An unabridged (most nearly complete) dictionary lists approximately 300,000 words. Be realistic: you'll never learn them all. Your first task, then, is to decide what to learn—that is, to be selective. Some words are more useful to you than others, depending on several factors—the most important being your college major and your career goals. If you are a business administration major and plan to get a job with a major corporation, your working vocabulary should be much different than if you are a biology major planning a career in genetic research.

Use What You Already Know

You may believe that you have one vocabulary and that it is either weak or strong. Actually, you have four different vocabulary levels: reading, writing, listening, and speaking. Although they share a common core of basic, functional words, these levels range widely in both size and content. For example, there are words that you recognize and understand as you read but that you never use in your own writing. Similarly, there are words that you understand when you listen to them but that you do not use when you speak. Probably your listening and reading vocabularies are larger than your speaking and writing vocabularies. In other words, you already know a large number of words, but many of them you do not use. Here are a few examples of words you may know but probably don't use:

conform	contour
congeal	contrite
congenial	cosmic
congenital	cosmopolitan
contort	cosmos

When strengthening your vocabulary, a good place to start is to experiment with words you already know but don't use regularly.

Use New Words You Have Learned

Make a point of using one new word each day, both in speaking and in writing.

Regardless of how much time you spend looking up and recording words, you probably will remember only those that you use fairly soon after you learn them. Forgetting occurs extremely rapidly after learning unless you take action to apply what you have learned.

Acquire the Necessary Tools

To develop a strong vocabulary, you must acquire the necessary tools. These include a dictionary and a thesaurus, as well as access to subject area dictionaries.

Buy a Dictionary   Students commonly ask, "Which dictionary should I buy?" There are several types of dictionaries, each with its own purpose. A pocket or paperback dictionary is an inexpensive, shortened version of a standard desk dictionary. It is small enough to carry with you and costs around $10. Although a pocket dictionary is convenient, its use is also limited. A desk dictionary is more extensive. A pocket edition lists about 50,000 to 60,000 words, whereas a standard desk edition lists up to 150,000 words. Also, the desk edition provides much more information about each word it lists. Desk dictionaries are usually hardbound and cost more than $25. Figure 3-1 is a comparison of entries from a pocket and a collegiate desk dictionary.

Several standard dictionaries are available in both desk and paperback editions. These include *Random House Dictionary of the English Language, Merriam-Webster's Collegiate Dictionary,* and *The American Heritage Dictionary of the English Language.* A third type of dictionary, the unabridged dictionary, is found in the reference section of the library. The unabridged edition provides the most nearly complete information on each word in the English language.

FIGURE 3-1   Comparison of Pocket and Collegiate Dictionaries

Pocket Dictionary	*Collegiate Dictionary*
di•lem′ma (di-lem′ə) *n.* a choice between alternatives equally undesirable.	di-lem-ma (dĭ-lĕm′ə) *n.* **1.** A situation that requires a choice between options that are or seem equally unfavorable or mutually exclusive. **2.** *Usage Problem.* A problem that seems to defy a satisfactory solution. **3.** *Logic.* An argument that presents an antagonist with a choice of two or more alternatives, each of which contradicts the original contention and is conclusive. [Late Latin, from Greek *dilemma,* ambiguous proposition : *di-,* two; see DI-¹ + *lēmma,* proposition; see *LEMMA*] — dil′em-mat′ic (dĭl′ə-mat′ĭk) *adj.*
	USAGE NOTE: In its primary sense *dilemma* denotes a situation in which a choice must be made between alternative courses of action or argument. Although citational evidence attests to widespread use of the term meaning simply "problem" or "predicament" and involving no issue of choice, 74 percent of the Usage Panel rejected the sentence *Juvenile drug abuse is the great dilemma of the 1980's.* • It is sometimes claimed that because the *di-* in *dilemma* comes from a Greek prefix meaning "two," the word should be used only when exactly two choices are involved. But 64 percent of the Usage Panel accepts its use for choices among three or more options in the example *Ph.D. students who haven't completed their dissertations by the time their fellowships expire face a difficult dilemma; whether to take out loans to support themselves, to try to work part-time at both a job and their research, or to give up on the degree entirely.*

SOURCE: *The New American Webster Handy College Dictionary* (left) and *The American Heritage Dictionary of the English Language* (right)

You should buy a pocket dictionary to carry with you regularly. Use it to check unfamiliar words or unusual spellings. Also, you should purchase a collegiate edition desk dictionary. It is not necessary to have the most up-to-date edition; a used dictionary is just as good and costs considerably less.

A desk dictionary provides complete and varied meanings of words as well as information on word origin and structure. It also contains useful reference information, such as tables of weights and measures, metric equivalents, lists of abbreviations, lists of signs and symbols, a punctuation guide, and information about the mechanics of English and of manuscript form. Biographical and geographical guides also may be included.

If you have difficulty with spelling, a misspeller's dictionary is another valuable reference. It can help you locate correct spellings easily. Two commonly used online misspeller's dictionaries are *Webster's New World Misspeller's Dictionary* and *How to Spell It: A Handbook of Commonly Misspelled Words.*

Several desk dictionaries are available online. Two of the most widely used are Merriam-Webster (http://www.m-w.com) and American Heritage (http://yourdictionary.com/index.shtml). Both of these sites feature an audio component that allows you to hear how a word is pronounced.

Use a Thesaurus   A thesaurus is a dictionary of synonyms that groups together words with similar meanings. This type of dictionary is useful for locating a precise descriptive word to fit a particular situation. For example, suppose you are looking for a more precise term for the boldface expression in the following sentence in a term paper you are writing:

> Whether men and women react differently to similar situations is often **talked about** in popular magazine articles.

FIGURE 3-2   Thesaurus Entry

12   discuss, debate, reason, deliberate, deliberate upon, exchange views *or* opinions, talk, talk over, hash over <nonformal>, talk of *or* about, rap <nonformal>, comment upon, reason about, discourse about, consider, treat, dissertate on, handle, deal with, take up, go into, examine, investigate, talk out, analyze, sift, study, canvass, review, pass under review, controvert, ventilate, air, thresh out, reason the point, consider pro and con; kick *or* knock around <nonformal>

Source: *Roget's International Thesaurus*

Figure 3-2 shows a thesaurus entry for the phrase *talk about.* Right away, you can identify a number of words that are more specific than the phrase *talked about.* The next step is to choose a word from the entry that most closely suggests the meaning you wish to convey. Words such as *debate* and *discuss* would be appropriate. The easiest way to do this is to substitute various choices in your sentence to see which works best; check the dictionary if you are not sure of a word's exact meaning. Many students misuse the thesaurus by choosing words that do not fit the context. Use a word only when you are familiar with all its shades of meaning. Remember, a misused word is often a more serious error than a wordy or an imprecise expression.

The most widely used thesaurus originally was compiled by Peter Mark Roget and is known today as *Roget's Thesaurus*; it is readily available in an inexpensive paperback edition.

EXERCISE 3-1

Use a thesaurus to find a more specific or descriptive word to replace the underlined word in each of the following sentences. Revise the sentence, if necessary.

1. The jury made the <u>right</u> decision on the sexual discrimination case.
2. The videotape on the rights of victims shown in my criminal justice class was <u>dull</u>.
3. After completing three exams in one day, Joe seemed <u>tired</u>.
4. Dr. Rodriguez is a <u>good</u> teacher.
5. My friends thought the biology exam was <u>hard</u>.

Use Subject Area Dictionaries

Many academic fields have specialized dictionaries that list most of the important words used in that discipline. These dictionaries give specialized meanings for words and suggest how and when to use the words. For the field of nursing, for instance, there is *Taber's Cyclopedic Medical Dictionary*. Other subject area dictionaries include Henderson's *Dictionary of Biological Terms*, *The New Grove Dictionary of Music and Musicians*, and *A Dictionary of Economics and Business*.

Find out whether there are subject area dictionaries for the disciplines you are studying. Many such dictionaries are available only in hardback and are likely to be expensive; however, students often find them worth the initial investment. Most libraries have reference copies of many specialized dictionaries.

EXERCISE 3-2

For each of the courses you are taking, find out whether there is a subject area dictionary available. If so, record its title.

Use a System for Learning Vocabulary

One of the most practical systems for expanding your vocabulary is the index card system. It works like this:

1. **Whenever you hear or read a new word that you want to learn, jot it down in the margin of your notes or mark it in the material you are reading.**

2. **Later, write each word on the front of an index card.** Then look up the meaning of each word, and write it on the back. You also might record a phonetic key for the word's pronunciation, if it is a difficult one, or a sample sentence in which the word is used. Sample index cards are shown in Figure 3-3 on the next page.

3. **Whenever you have a few spare minutes, go through your pack of index cards.** For each card, look at the word on the front and try to recall its meaning on the back. Then check the back of the card to see whether

FIGURE 3-3 Sample Index Cards

Front	Back

nonprosequitur	judgment entered against a plaintiff who fails to appear in court to prosecute his/her suit
diffraction	the bending of waves around a barrier

you were correct. If you were unable to recall the meaning or if you confused it with another word, retest yourself. Shuffle the cards after each use.

4. **After you have gone through your pack of cards several times, sort the cards into two piles, separating the words you know from those you have not learned.** Then, putting the known words aside, concentrate on the words still to be learned.

5. **Once you have mastered all the words, periodically review them to refresh your memory and to keep the words current in your mind.**

6. **Once you have learned the words, use them in your speech and/or writing and evaluate how effectively you have used them.** This step is perhaps the most important of all, because it moves you from the knowledge and comprehension levels of thinking to the application and evaluation levels (see Chapter 1).

This system is effective for several reasons. First, you can accomplish it in your spare time; you can even review your cards while you wait for a bus. Second, the system enables you to spend time learning what you do not know rather than wasting time studying what you already have learned. Finally, the system overcomes a major problem that exists in learning information that appears in list form. When the material is in a fixed order, you tend to learn it in that order and may be unable to recall the items when they appear in isolation or out of order. Shuffling the cards enables you to scramble the order of the words and avoid this problem.

EXERCISE 3-3

Over the next week, prepare a set of 15 to 20 index cards for new words used by your professor or introduced in your textbook. Include only words you feel you could use in your own speech or writing.

■ Using Context Clues

Although a dictionary is invaluable, it is not practical to look up every new word you encounter. An alternative is to reason out the meaning of an unfamiliar word by using clues in the sentence or paragraph. Read the following paragraph, from which several words have been deleted. Fill them in after you have read the paragraph through once.

> Karl Marx (1818–1883) was born _____ Germany. _____ father, a lawyer, and his _____ were both descended from long lines of rabbis. Marx _____ college and planned _____ practice law, but after becoming involved with a radical antireligious _____, he decided to devote his _____ to philosophy.
>
> —Eshleman et al., *Sociology, An Introduction,* pp. 34–35

Certainly, you had no trouble filling in the missing words. You were able to do this because the paragraph contained enough information or clues about what was missing. Now imagine that instead of blanks, the paragraph contained several unfamiliar words. Often, you can "fill in" the meaning of the unknown words by using clues contained in the paragraph. Use these clues to determine the meanings of the boldface words in the following passage:

> The condition most feared among governments as a cause of war is power **asymmetry**—that is, an unfavorable tilt in the distribution of power. There is widespread conviction that whatever other **impetuses** to war may be present, a careful equilibration of power between **antagonists** will tend to prevent war, while a disequilibrium will invite aggression. . . .
>
> —Jones, *The Logic of International Relations,* p. 379

Although you may not have been able to define exactly words such as *asymmetry, impetuses,* and *antagonists,* you were probably able to make a reasonable guess about their meanings. You used the clues contained in the context (surrounding words and phrases) to arrive at the meaning.

Types of Context Clues

Now, let's look at various types of context clues. Each clue requires analysis of the word's context and the ideas that context contains.

Definition or Synonym   Frequently, a writer gives a brief definition or synonym for a word, usually in the same sentence as the word being defined. The definition may be the key idea of the sentence, as in the following examples:

Ethology is the study of the behavior of animals in their natural settings.

At other times, the definition or synonym may be set apart from the key idea of the sentence through the use of commas, dashes, or parentheses.

> Experimental biology includes the study of learning, behavior, memory, perception, and **psychology** (biological bases of behavior).

> Most societies are **patriarchal**—males exert dominant power and authority.

You will find this type of clue used in most introductory college textbooks, especially in the first several chapters in which the "course language" is introduced.

Example Clues   Writers include examples to clarify or illustrate important concepts and ideas. If you are unfamiliar with a word or concept, often you can figure it out by studying the example.

> The use of **nonverbal communication,** such as a smile or gesture, usually reduces the risk of misinterpretation.

From the examples, *smile* and *gesture,* you know that nonverbal communication refers to "body language"—physical movements and facial expressions. Here are two other sentences that contain example clues:

> Collecting **demographic data** on potential consumers, including age, marital status, residency, and income, is an essential part of market research.

> Salary increases, promotions, privileges, and praise are forms of **extrinsic** rewards that motivate behavior.

You may have noticed that the examples in these sentences are signaled by certain words and phrases. *Such as* and *including* are used here. Other common signals are *for instance, to illustrate,* and *for example.*

Contrast Clues   Sometimes, you can determine the meaning of an unknown word from a word or phrase in the context that has an opposite meaning. Note, in the following sentence, how a word opposite in meaning from the boldface word provides a clue to its meaning.

> Despite their seemingly **altruistic** actions, large corporations are self-interested institutions that exist to make profits.

Although you may not know the meaning of *altruistic,* you know it means the opposite of self-interested. The word *despite* suggests this. *Altruistic,* then, means "interested in the welfare of others." Here are two additional sentences containing contrast clues:

> Studies of crowd behavior suggest that people in a crowd lose their personalities and act **impulsively,** rather than making reasoned decisions.

> Polytheism, the worship of more than one god, is common throughout India; however, **monotheism** is the most familiar religion to Americans.

Each of these examples contains a word or phrase that indicates that an opposite or contrasting situation exists. Two such signals that were used in the examples are *rather than* and *however.* Other signal words that also show a contrasting idea include *but, despite, rather, while, yet,* and *nevertheless.*

Inference Clues   Many times, you can figure out the meaning of a word you do not know by using logical reasoning or by drawing on your own knowledge and experience. From the information given in the context, you can infer the meaning of a word you are not familiar with, as in the following sentence:

> Confucius had a **pervasive** influence on all aspects of Chinese life, so much so that every county in China built a temple to him.

If every county in China built a temple to Confucius, you can imagine that his influence was widespread. You can infer, then, that *pervasive* means "spread throughout."

Similarly, in the following example, the general sense of the context provides clues to the meaning of the word.

> In wind instruments such as the trumpet, sound is **emitted** directly by the vibrations of air columns in the instrument.

In this sentence, *emitted* means "sent out."

Sometimes your knowledge and experience can help you figure out an unknown word. Consider, for instance, the following sentence:

> To **simulate** the weightless environment of outer space, astronauts are placed in a specially designed room.

Here, *simulate* means "to give the appearance of."

Limitations of Context Clues

Although context clues generally are useful, they do not always work. There will be words for which the context provides no clues. Also, you should recognize that context clues give you only a general sense of what the word means—not its exact or complete definition. If you've figured a word out from context clues and you feel it is worth learning, mark it and later check its complete meaning in a dictionary.

A final limitation of context is that it suggests the meaning of the word only as it is used in a particular context. Words have multiple meanings; the meaning you infer from a single context gives you only a limited understanding of the word.

EXERCISE 3-4   *Use context clues to determine the meaning of each boldface word. Write a brief definition or synonym in the space provided.*

1. People who practice **totemism,** the worship of plants, animals, or objects as gods, usually select for worship objects that are important to the community.

   _____

2. The tone of **percussion** instruments, such as drums and cymbals, depends in part on the geometry of the surface area.

   _____

3. A cult may recruit followers through **deception**; potential followers may not be told what the cult involves or what will be expected of them.

_____

4. **Euthanasia**, sometimes called mercy killing, is a controversial issue among the families of terminally ill patients.

_____

5. Establishing a buying **motive**, such as hunger, safety, or prestige, is important in developing an advertising plan for a new product.

_____

6. Our **paleolithic** ancestors relied on their own body power and the controlled use of fire to get things done. In later Stone Age societies, people used animals for muscle power.

_____

7. Information, as well as rumors and gossip, is quickly spread through the office **grapevine**, although it is not recognized as an official channel of communication.

_____

8. New hourly employees in the firm are **accountable** to the training director, who, in turn, is accountable to the director of personnel.

_____

9. In one culture, a man may be **ostracized** for having more than one wife, whereas in other cultures, a man with many wives is an admired and respected part of the group.

_____

10. **Homogeneous** groups, such as classes made up entirely of teenagers, social organizations of high-IQ people, and country clubs of wealthy families, have particular roles and functions in our society.

_____

EXERCISE 3-5

Working with a classmate, use context clues to determine the meaning of each word in boldface print in the following passage. Write a brief definition or synonym in the space provided.

ORGANIZATION OF RELIGION

Religious associations take the form of cult, sect, or church depending upon their degree of institutionalization and level of formality. **Cults** represent the most loosely structured and unconventional forms of organization. They consist of small numbers of persons who band together in order to express a new religious cause—a cause often at great **variance** from that of established religion. In Roman times Christians were members of a cult. Today **adherents** of the Reverend Moon's Unification Church—"Moonies"—can be considered [members of] a cult.

Most cults dissipate after a short period of time. They are held together only as long as their charismatic leaders are able to mobilize the loyalty and passion of followers. In order to remain viable, then, religious groups must move to another level of organization: They take the form of either sect or church.

A **sect** is a small religious association that generally appeals to poor, propertyless, or otherwise marginal members of society. As in the case of a cult, the sect frequently supports a cause that places its membership at odds with established religious organizations. Unlike cults, sects usually **emerge** out of established religious orders. Also unlike cults, sects perpetuate themselves over time by developing a loose structure usually consisting of a part-time minister from the congregation who leads a highly involved membership in a number of emotionally charged services. The recent "Born Again" movement in Protestantism is a case in point. On television weekly, the various "Born Again" groups gained enormous popularity in the early and mid-1980s but found themselves **tottering** after the highly publicized scandals of Jim and Tammy Bakker and Jimmy Swaggert in the latter part of the decade.

The most highly structured and conventional religious organization is known as the church. Unlike a sect, a church draws membership from the cultural and economic mainstream of a society. Thus the religious beliefs and rituals of a church generally reflect an acceptance of the **prevailing** social order. Also unlike a sect, a church typically **engages** a specialized and full-time minister (or rabbi) who leads the congregation and socializes new members in religious beliefs and rituals.

—Levin and Spates, *Starting Sociology,* pp. 251–52

1. _____
2. _____
3. _____
4. _____
5. _____
6. _____
7. _____
8. _____

■ Learning Word Parts: The Multiplier Effect

Suppose you want to learn 50 new words. For each word you learn, your vocabulary increases by one word; if you learn all 50, then you've increased your vocabulary by 50 words. The vocabulary of the average young adult is 30,000 words. Adding 50 words is equal to a 0.17 percent increase—negligible at best.

You may be thinking, "There must be a better way," and fortunately, there is. If you learn word parts—prefixes, roots, and suffixes (beginnings, middles, and endings of words)—instead of single words, your vocabulary will multiply geometrically rather than increase by one word at a time.

Learning word parts, then, produces a multiplier effect. A single prefix can unlock the meaning of 50 or more words. Think of the prefix *inter-*. Once you learn that it means "between," you can define many new words. Here are a few examples:

intercede	interscholastic
interconnect	intersperse
interracial	interstellar
interrelate	intertribal
interrupt	intervene

Similarly, knowledge of a single root unlocks numerous word meanings. For instance, knowing that the root *spec* means "to look or see" enables you to understand words such as:

inspect	retrospect
inspector	retrospection
introspection	spectator
introspective	speculate
perspective	speculation

Learning word parts is a much more efficient means of building vocabulary than learning single words. The following sections list common prefixes, roots, and suffixes and provide practice in learning them. Before you begin to learn specific word parts, study the following guidelines:

1. **In most cases, a word is built on at least one root.**
2. **Words can have more than one prefix, root, or suffix.**
   a. Words can be made up of two or more roots (geo-logy).
   b. Some words have two prefixes (in-sub-ordination).
   c. Some words have two suffixes (beauti-ful-ly).
3. **Words do not always have both a prefix and a suffix.**
   a. Some words have neither a prefix nor a suffix (read).
   b. Others have a suffix but no prefix (read-ing).
   c. Others have a prefix but no suffix (pre-read).
4. **Roots may change in spelling as they are combined with suffixes (arid, arable).**
5. **Sometimes, you may identify a group of letters as a prefix or root but find that it does not carry the meaning of the prefix or root.** For example, in the word *internal,* the letters *i-n-t-e-r* should not be confused with the prefix *inter-*, which means "between." Similarly, the letters *m-i-s* in the word *missile* are part of the root and are not the prefix mis-, which means "wrong or bad."

Prefixes

Prefixes appear at the beginning of many English words and alter the meaning of the root to which they are connected. Table 3-1 groups 36 common prefixes according to meaning.

Learning word parts is particularly useful for science courses. Many scientific words are built from a common core of prefixes, roots, and suffixes. Chapter 16 offers several examples on page 460.

TABLE 3–1 Common Prefixes		
PREFIX	**MEANING**	**EXAMPLE**
Amount or Number		
bi-	two	bimonthly
deci-	ten	decimal
centi-	hundred	centigrade
equi-	equal	equidistant
micro-	small	microscope
milli-	thousand	milligram
mono-	one	monocle
multi-	many	multipurpose
poly-	many	polygon
semi-	half	semicircle
tri-	three	triangle
uni-	one	unicycle
Negative		
a-	not	asymmetrical
anti-	against	antiwar
contra-	against, opposite	contradict
dis-	apart, away, not	disagree
in-/il-/ir-/im-	not	illogical
mis-	wrongly	misunderstood
non-	not	nonfiction
un-	not	unpopular
pseudo-	false	pseudoscientific
Direction, Location, or Placement		
circum-	around	circumference
com-/col-/con-	with, together	compile
de-	away, from	depart
ex-/extra-	from, out of, former	ex-wife
hyper-	over, excessive	hyperactive
inter-	between	interpersonal
intro-/intra-	within, into, in	introduction
post-	after	posttest
pre-	before	premarital
re-	back, again	review
retro-	backward	retrospect
sub-	under, below	submarine
super-	above, extra	supercharge
tele-	far	telescope
trans-	across, over	transcontinental

EXERCISE 3-6

Using the list of common prefixes in Table 3-1 write the meaning of each of the following boldface words. If you are unfamiliar with the root, check its meaning in a dictionary.

1. a **multinational** corporation _____

2. **antisocial** behavior _____

3. **inefficient** study habits _____

4. **postglacial** period _____

5. **unspecialized** training _____

6. housing **subdivision** _____

7. **redefine** one's goals _____

8. a **semifinalist** _____

9. **retroactive** policies _____

10. a sudden **transformation** _____

EXERCISE 3-7

Select two classmates and, working as a team, record as many words as you can that begin with one of the following prefixes. Compare your findings with those of other classroom teams.

1. pre-
2. de-
3. mis-

Roots

Roots carry the basic or core meaning of a word. Hundreds of root words are used to build words in the English language. Table 3-2 (p. 82) lists 30 of the most common and most useful roots.

EXERCISE 3-8

Use the list of common roots in Table 3-2 to determine the meanings of the following boldface words. Write a brief definition or synonym of each, checking a dictionary if necessary.

1. **bioethical** issues _____

2. **terrestrial** life _____

3. to **desensitize** _____

4. to study **astronomy** _____

5. **synchronize** your watches _____

6. **visualize** the problem _____

7. a religious **missionary** _____

8. **biographical** data _____

9. a **geology** course _____

10. **pathological** behavior _____

TABLE 3–2   Common Roots

ROOT	MEANING	EXAMPLE
aud/audit	hear	audible
aster/astro	star	astronaut
bio	life	biology
cap	take, seize	captive
chron(o)	time	chronology
corp	body	corpse
cred	believe	incredible
dict/dic	tell, say	predict
duc/duct	lead	introduce
fact/fac	make, do	factory
graph	write	telegraph
geo	earth	geophysics
log/logo/logy	study, thought	psychology
mit/miss	send	dismiss
mort/mor	die, death	immortal
path	feeling	sympathy
phono	sound, voice	telephone
photo	light	photosensitive
port	carry	transport
scop	see	microscope
scrib/script	write	inscription
sen/sent	feel	insensitive
spec/spic/spect	look, see	retrospect
tend/tent/tens	stretch or strain	tension
terr/terre	land, earth	territory
theo	god	theology
ven/vent	come	convention
vert/vers	turn	invert
vis/vid	see	invisible
voc	call	vocation

Suffixes

Suffixes are word endings that often change the part of speech of a word. For example, adding the suffix -*y* to the noun *cloud* produces the adjective *cloudy*. Accompanying the change in part of speech is a shift in meaning.

Often, several different words can be formed from a single root word with the addition of different suffixes. Some examples follow:

Root: class

root + suffix = class-ify, class-ification, class-ic

Root: right

root + suffix = right-ly, right-ful, right-ist, right-eous

TABLE 3-3   Common Suffixes

SUFFIX	EXAMPLE
State, Condition, or Quality	
-able	touchable
-ance	assistance
-ation	confrontation
-ence	reference
-ible	tangible
-ion	discussion
-ity	superiority
-ive	permissive
-ment	amazement
-ness	kindness
-ous	jealous
-ty	loyalty
-y	creamy
"One Who"	
-ee	tutee
-eer	engineer
-er	teacher
-ist	activist
-or	advisor
Pertaining to or Referring to	
-al	autumnal
-ship	friendship
-hood	brotherhood
-ward	homeward

If you know the meaning of the root word and the ways in which different suffixes affect the meaning of the root word, you will be able to understand a word's meaning when a suffix is added. A list of common suffixes and their meanings appears in Table 3-3.

EXERCISE 3-9

For each of the words listed, add a suffix so that the word will complete the sentence. Write the new word in the space provided.

1. *behavior*

   _____ therapy attempts to change habits and illnesses by altering people's responses to stimuli.

2. *atom*

   Uranium, when bombarded with neutrons, explodes and produces a heat reaction known as _____ energy.

3. *advertise*

   One important purpose of an _____ is to inform potential customers about the service or product and familiarize the public with the brand name.

4. *uniform*

The _____ of a law requires that it must be applied to all relevant groups without bias.

5. *evolution*

Darwin's theory of natural selection tied the survival of a species to its _____ fitness—its ability to survive and reproduce.

6. *compete*

When food sources are not large enough to support all the organisms in a habitat, environmental _____ occurs.

7. *religion*

During the Age of Reason in American history, _____ revivals swept the nation.

8. *perform*

Perhaps an administrator's most important duty is establishing conditions conducive to high employee motivation, which results in better job _____.

9. *effective*

A critical factor in evaluating a piece of literature or art is its _____—how strongly and clearly the artist's message has been conveyed to the audience.

10. *theory*

_____ have spent decades studying the theory of relativity.

EXERCISE 3-10

Use your knowledge of context clues and word parts to determine the meaning of each boldface word. On a separate sheet of paper, write a brief definition of each word that fits its use in the sentence.

1. GLOBAL TECHNOLOGY

The advancement of technology is a **global** issue. The United States has been known as a world leader in the advancement of technology. To remain **competitive,** however, global research and development strategies must respond to changes in transportation, communication, information technology, and **merged** national markets. Intellectual capital is the critical resource in the global economy. The ability to **generate,** access, and rapidly use new knowledge and **convert** it (technology transfer) into marketable quality products and processes is the key to competitive advantage.

The **diffusion** of technological capabilities and expansion of the technically trained work force worldwide have strengthened the competitive position of industrialized countries and **enabled** many more to enter the marketplace. As a result, **dominance** by the United States in nearly all high-tech markets is being challenged.

In many countries, government-sponsored programs have reduced the costs and risks associated with technological development by **assuring** long-term financial commitment. Airbus Industries, for example, is a cross-national European consortium that has developed and produced airplanes through support of its partner companies in the form of repayable loans.

—Kinnear et al., *Principles of Marketing,* pp. 57–58

2. LINGUISTIC ANTHROPOLOGY

While all organisms have some way of communicating, and some animals, such as porpoises and chimpanzees, have highly developed means of communicating, humans have evolved a unique and extremely complex system. Without it, human culture as we know it would be impossible. The field of **linguistic anthropology** focuses on this aspect of human life. It is, in turn, divided into a number of **subfields.**

Descriptive linguistics deals with how languages are constructed and how the various parts (sound and grammar) are **interrelated** to form coherent systems of communication. Historical linguistics concerns the **evolution** of language—how languages grow and change. Sociolinguistics studies the relationship between language and social factors, such as class, ethnicity, age, and gender. Finally, a topic of interest to many anthropological linguists is language and culture, which examines the ways that language affects how we think and, *conversely,* how our beliefs and values might influence our linguistic patterns.

—Howard, *Contemporary Cultural Anthropology,* pp. 12–13

■ Using Word Mapping to Expand Your Vocabulary

Word mapping is a visual method for expanding your vocabulary. It involves examining a word in detail by considering its meanings, synonyms (words similar in meaning), antonyms (words opposite in meaning), part(s) of speech, word parts, and usages. A word map is a form of word study. By the time you have completed the map, you will find that you have learned the word and are ready to use it in your speech and writing. On page 86 is a sample map for the word *extension.*
Use the following steps to complete a word map:

1. **Write the sentence containing the word at the top of the map.**
2. **Look the word up in your dictionary.** Figure out which meaning fits the context of the sentence and write it in the box labeled "Meaning (as used in context)."
3. **In the "Part of speech" box, write in the word's part(s) of speech as used in context.**
4. **Study the dictionary entry to discover other meanings of the word.** Write them on the map in the box labeled "Other meanings."
5. **Find or think of two synonyms (words similar in meaning), and write them in the "Synonyms" box.** You might need a thesaurus for this.
6. **Analyze the word's parts and identify any prefixes, roots, or suffixes.** Write each word part and its meaning in the space provided.
7. **At the bottom of the map write two sentences using the word.**

8. **In the box labeled "Other," include any other interesting information about the word.** You might include antonyms, restrictive meanings, or word history.

Word Map

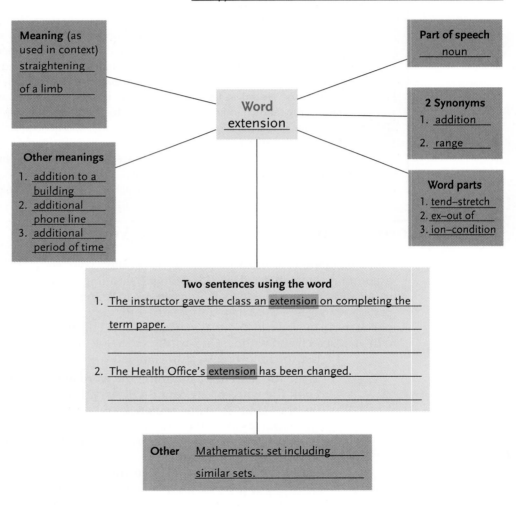

Original sentence using the word   Full extension of the leg is necessary in order for the

therapy to be effective.

Meaning (as used in context)
straightening

of a limb

Other meanings
1. addition to a
   building
2. additional
   phone line
3. additional
   period of time

Word
extension

Part of speech
noun

2 Synonyms
1. addition
2. range

Word parts
1. tend–stretch
2. ex–out of
3. ion–condition

Two sentences using the word
1. The instructor gave the class an extension on completing the
   term paper.

2. The Health Office's extension has been changed.

Other   Mathematics: set including
similar sets.

EXERCISE 3–11   *Using a dictionary, complete the word map on page 87 for a new word you are learning in one of your other courses.*

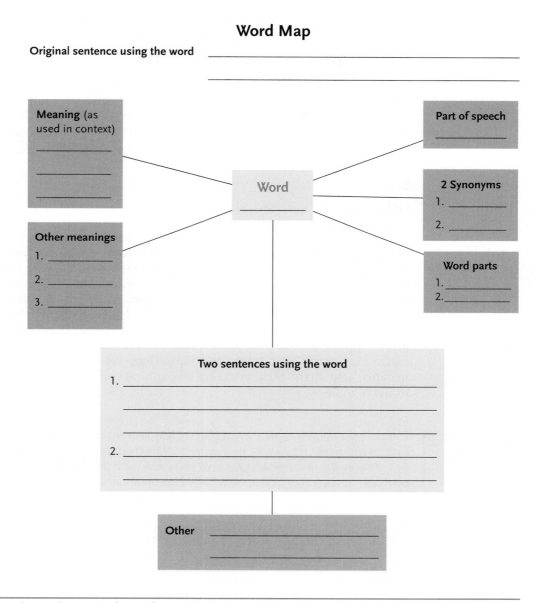

Word Map

Original sentence using the word _____

Meaning (as used in context)
_____
_____
_____

Part of speech
_____

Word
_____

2 Synonyms
1. _____
2. _____

Other meanings
1. _____
2. _____
3. _____

Word parts
1. _____
2. _____

Two sentences using the word
1. _____
   _____
   _____
2. _____
   _____

Other _____
          _____

■ Learning Specialized and Scientific Vocabulary

You probably have noticed that each sport and hobby has its own language—a specialized set of words with specific meanings. Baseball players and fans talk about no-hitters, home runs, errors, and runs batted in. Each academic discipline, too, has its own set of specialized words. These terms enable specialists to give accurate and concise descriptions of events, principles, concepts, problems, and occurrences.

One of the first tasks that you face in a new course is to learn its specialized language. This task is especially important in introductory courses where the subject is new and unfamiliar to you. In an introductory computer science course, for instance, you often start by learning how a computer functions. From that point, many new terms are introduced: *bit, byte, field, numeric characters, character positions, statements, coding, format,* and so forth.

In science courses, new terminology is especially important. Hundreds of new scientific terms are introduced in each course. For specific suggestions on learning scientific terminology, refer to Chapter 17, pages 486, 495.

Specialized Terminology in Class Lectures

Often, the first few class lectures in a course are devoted to acquainting students with the nature and scope of the field and to introducing its specialized language. Many instructors devote considerable time to presenting the language of the course carefully and explicitly. Be sure to record each new term accurately for later review and study. Good lecturers give you clues to what terms and definitions are important to record. Some instructors make a habit of writing new words on the chalkboard; others may speak very slowly so that you can record definitions. Still other instructors may repeat a word and its definition several times or offer several variations of the word's meaning. As a part of your note-taking system, develop a consistent way of easily identifying new terms and definitions recorded in your notes. For instance, you might circle or draw a box around each new term or write "def." in the margin.

EXERCISE 3-12

Estimate the number of new terms that each of your instructors introduced during the first several weeks for each of your courses. Now check the accuracy of your estimates by reviewing the first two weeks of your class notes and the first several chapters of the textbook for each course you are taking. How many new terms and definitions were included for each course? Most students underestimate. Did you?

Specialized Terminology in Textbooks

The first few chapters in a textbook are generally introductory, too. They are written to familiarize you with the subject and acquaint you with its specialized language. In one economics textbook, 34 new terms were introduced in the first two chapters (40 pages). In the first two chapters (28 pages) of a chemistry book, 56 specialized words were introduced.

Textbook authors use various means to emphasize new terminology. In some texts, new vocabulary is printed in italics, boldface type, or colored print. Other texts indicate new terms in the margin of each page. Still the most common means of emphasis, however, is the "New Terminology" or "Vocabulary" list that appears at the beginning or end of each chapter. Many texts also include a glossary of key terms at the back of the book.

EXERCISE 3-13

Review the first chapter from two of your texts and then answer the following questions.

1. How many new terms are introduced in each?
2. If your texts contain glossaries, are all of these new terms listed?
3. Are most new words technical terms, or are they words in everyday use to which a specialized meaning is attached?
4. How does each textbook author call your attention to these new terms?

Learning Core Prefixes, Roots, and Suffixes

Terminology in a particular academic discipline often uses a core of common prefixes, roots, and suffixes. For example, in the field of human anatomy and physiology, the prefix *endo-* means "inner" and the root *derma* refers to "skin." Thus, the word endoderm refers to the inner layer of cells in the skin. Numerous other words are formed by using the root *derma* in conjunction with a suffix.

As you are learning new terminology for each course, make a point of noticing recurring prefixes, roots, and suffixes. Compile a list of these word parts and their meanings, along with several examples of each one. A partial sample list for anthropology follows.

	MEANINGS	EXAMPLES
Prefixes		
bi-	two	bipedalism
anti-	against	antibody
poly-	many	polygyny
Roots		
terra	earth, ground	territory
gene	unit of chromosomes	genotype
anthropo	human	anthropoid
Suffixes		
-us	one who	Australopithecus
-cene	era or epoch	Pleistocene
-cide	killing of	infanticide

EXERCISE 3-14

For one of your courses, identify five commonly used prefixes, roots, and suffixes. If you have difficulty, review the glossary of the text to discover commonly used word parts.

Developing a Course Master File

For each course you are taking, set up a master file that includes new terminology to be learned and a list of essential prefixes, roots, and suffixes. Also include a list of frequently used signs, abbreviations, and symbols and their meanings.

In the sciences, numerous symbols are used in formulas. You'll save time and avoid frequent interruptions if you learn these symbols right away rather than having to refer to the text to translate each sign or symbol. Your course master file can be a big help in this effort.

An abbreviated version of a course master file for a course in American politics is shown in Figure 3-4.

Because each course is different, your course master file will change for each course you are taking. Check with the Learning Lab or Academic Skills Center at your college; it may offer lists of common prefixes and roots.

FIGURE 3–4   Sample Course Master File

New Terminology

Cabinet	Group of presidential advisors made up of the attorney general and the secretaries who head government departments.
Deficit	An excess of government expenditures over federal revenues.
Bill	A proposed law that must be passed by Congress and signed by the president to become a law.

Prefixes, Roots, Suffixes

Prefix	*Meaning*	*Example*
anti-	against	antitrust
bi-	two	bicameral
sub-	under	subgovernments

Root	*Meaning*	*Example*
pol	political	policy
employ	to provide work	unemployment
pluri	many	pluralist

Suffix	*Meaning*	*Example*
-ism	a quality, doctrine, theory, or principle	capitalism
-ive	state, condition, or quality	progressive
-al	referring to	presidential

Abbreviations

CIA	Central Intelligence Agency
PAC	political action committee
FTC	Federal Trade Commission
CPI	Consumer Price Index
FEC	Federal Election Committee

EXERCISE 3-15

Begin preparing a master file for one of your courses. Using both your text and your lecture notes, begin with the first chapter and list new terms, prefixes, roots, and suffixes, as well as symbols and abbreviations.

Self-Test Summary

1. What are some basic tools for vocabulary development?	Vocabulary development tools are pocket and collegiate dictionaries, thesauruses, subject area dictionaries, and an index card system.
2. What is the difference between a dictionary and a thesaurus?	A dictionary is a nearly complete listing of words and their definitions. A thesaurus is a dictionary of synonyms that groups together words with similar meanings.
3. List the four most common types of context clues.	Types of context clues are definition or synonym, example, contrast, and inference.
4. Name three common word parts and explain where each appears and what it does.	A prefix appears at the beginning of a word and alters the meaning of the root to which it is connected. A root carries the basic or core meaning of a word. A suffix appears at the end of a word and often changes the part of speech of that word.
5. What is a word map?	A word map is a visual method of word study involving examination of meanings, parts of speech, synonyms, and usages.
6. How can you master specialized terminology?	You can master specialized terminology by using subject area dictionaries; learning core prefixes, roots, and suffixes; and keeping a course master file.

INTERPERSONAL COMMUNICATION

What Words Can and Cannot Do

Richard L. Weaver, III

Prereading Questions

1. Do people always understand what you are saying?
2. Why does miscommunication occur?

1   If we see a series of stones lying across a stream, we know they will help us get to the other side. But our experience with such stones tells us that some of the stones may be loose or covered with slime and could cause us to slip. Like these stones, words can help us to reach our goals, or they can cause us to stumble and fall. Let's look at some characteristics of language that affect our interpersonal communication.

2   When we talk to people, we often assume too quickly that we are being understood. If we tell people we are going to put on some music, we probably don't think about whether they are expecting to hear the kind of music we intend to play—we just turn it on. But think about the word *music* and how many different interpretations there are of it. (See Figure A.)

3   We depend on context and on nonverbal cues to give us the meaning of words. If we say we are going to put on some music, our friends may be able to predict from knowing our taste and from nonverbal cues (our mood) what we might play. But they have a good

FIGURE A   One word may have many different interpretations.

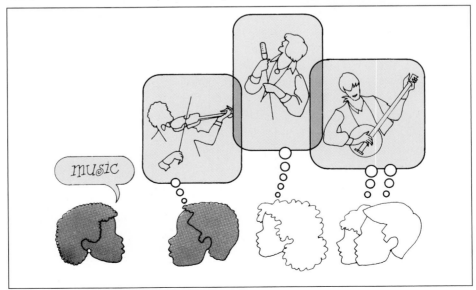

chance of being wrong. In our daily conversation, we use about 2,000 words. Of those 2,000, the 500 we use most often have more than 14,000 dictionary definitions. Think of the possibilities for confusion! The problem of figuring out what a person means by a certain word is compounded by the fact that even dictionary meanings change, and new words are constantly being added to the language.

4   **Denotative meanings.** *The* **denotative meaning** *of a word is its dictionary definition.* Dictionaries provide alternatives; we still must choose from those alternatives. The choice of what is "appropriate" or "inappropriate" is left to the user.

5   Some words have relatively stable meanings. If several people were to define a particular word special to their discipline, they would probably use about the same definition—an agreed-upon interpretation. To lawyers, the word *estoppel* has one precise, denotative meaning. Doctors would probably agree upon the definition of *myocardial infarction*. People in many disciplines depend on certain words having precise, unchanging meanings in order to carry on their work. There is little likelihood of confusion with denotative meanings because there is a direct relationship between the word and what it describes. Connotative meanings, on the other hand, depend a lot more than denotative meanings on our subjective thought processes. (See Figure B on page 94.)

6   **Connotative meanings.** *The* **connotative meaning** *of a word is the associations and overtones people bring to it.* Dictionary definitions would probably not help our friends predict the kind of music we would play or what we mean by "music." But their experience with us and with music will give them a clue as to what we mean. If "music" connotes the same thing to us and to our friends, there's less chance of misunderstanding.

7   When we hear a word, the thoughts and feelings we have about that word and about the person using it determine what that word ultimately means to us. This is the word's *connotative* meaning. Connotative meanings change with our experience. Just as we experience something different in every second of life that we live, so does everyone else. And no two of these experiences are identical! It's no wonder there are infinitely many connotations for every word we use. Figure B illustrates the process through which words may accumulate their connotative meanings.

8   If a word creates pretty much the same reaction in a majority of people, the word is said to have a general connotation. Actually, the more general the connotation of a word, the more likely that meaning will become the dictionary meaning because most people will agree on what that word represents. The more general the connotation of a word, the less likely people are to misunderstand it.

Consider This

The belief that sitting down and talking will ensure mutual understanding and solve problems is based on the assumption that we can say what we mean, and that what we say will be understood as we mean it.

—Tannen, *That's Not What I Meant!* p. 124

FIGURE B   Connotative meanings may depend a great deal on the perceiver's experience.

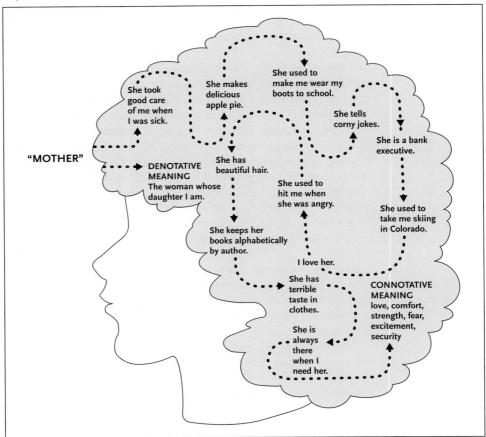

9   Problems in interpersonal communication increase as we use words with many connotative meanings. Because these meanings are so tied to the particular feelings, thoughts, and ideas of other people, we have a bigger chance of being misunderstood when we use them. On the other hand, richly connotative words give our language power. Note, for example, the differences between the following lists of words:

freedom	book
justice	piano
love	tree
liberty	teacher
music	fire

The words in the left column have many connotations; the words in the right column are more strictly denotative. "The teacher put the book on the piano" is an unambiguous statement. The sentence, "The love of freedom burns like a white flame in all of us" can be interpreted in numerous ways.

10   What does all this have to do with our use of words? First, we should recognize that words evoke sometimes unpredictable reactions in others. We should try to anticipate the reactions of others to our words as much as we can. For example, if we are talking to an art major, we may cause confusion or even produce a hostile response if we use the psychology-major jargon we have picked up. If we anticipate this negative reaction, we'll leave the jargon in the psychology classroom.

11   Second, most words have both denotative and connotative meanings, and we should recognize that these meanings vary from person to person. People will react to words according to the meaning *they* give them. An effective communicator tries to recognize different reactions and to adapt to them. Remember as you communicate that meanings do *not* reside in the words themselves. *Meanings are in the minds of the people who use and hear the words. That is the essence of the transactional view of communication.*

—Weaver, *Understanding Interpersonal Communication*, pp. 230–33

Writing About the Reading
CHECKING YOUR VOCABULARY

1. For each of the words listed below, use context; prefixes, roots, and suffixes (see Chapter 3); and/or a dictionary to write a brief definition or synonym of the word as it is used in the reading.

   a. nonverbal (para. 3) _____

   b. denotative (para. 4) _____

   c. connotative (para. 6) _____

   d. unambiguous (para. 9) _____

   e. jargon (para. 10) _____

   f. transactional (para. 11) _____

2. Underline new, specialized terms introduced in the reading.
3. Draw a word map of one of the words in the reading.

CHECKING YOUR COMPREHENSION

1. Explain the differences between denotative and connotative meanings.
2. Why do professions use words with agreed-upon denotative meanings?
3. According to this author, what are the causes of miscommunication?

THINKING CRITICALLY

1. Make a list of words with numerous connotations.
2. Give an example of a word whose connotative meaning changes with the speaker's experience.

3. International students often have difficulty understanding the connotations of English words. Why?
4. This reading focuses on miscommunication in speech. Do similar miscommunications occur in reading and writing? If so, do they stem from the same causes?
5. Do you think more or fewer misunderstandings occur in reading and writing than in speaking? Justify your answer.
6. Are there other causes of miscommunication not discussed in the reading? If so, what are they?

LEARNING/STUDY STRATEGY

Summarize the most important information in this reading.

ADDITIONAL PRACTICE

MULTIMEDIA ACTIVITIES

1. **Commonly Misused Words**

   http://www.cmu.edu/styleguide/trickywords.html#misused

   Be on the lookout for the easy-to-confuse words listed here by Carnegie Mellon University. Which words would you add to this list? Which words surprised you? Write a paragraph on the importance of proper usage. Why does it matter if people know what you mean?

2. **A Word A Day**

   http://www.wordsmith.org/awad/index.html

   Sign up to receive a word a day in your e-mail or read a newsletter about words at this interesting site for language lovers. Use the new words in your writing and speech.

MYREADINGLAB

If your instructor has asked you to use Reading Road Trip, be sure to visit the Library of Congress module for multimedia tutorials, exercises, and tests.

CHAPTER

Evaluating the Author's Message

LEARNING OBJECTIVES

◆ To make inferences and understand implied meanings

◆ To assess the author's credentials

◆ To distinguish between fact and opinion

◆ To identify the author's purpose

◆ To evaluate the data and evidence

◆ To analyze the author's tone

◆ To annotate as you read

◆ To synthesize your ideas

The advertisement above appears in a business textbook titled *Consumer Behavior.* The ad is for a brand of Brazilian pet food. Using your reasoning skills, predict what point this advertisement makes.

Although the message is not stated, it is clear. It is a popular belief that pets and their owners come to resemble one another. In the business textbook, the authors go on to explain that pets become a part of our extended selves.

In college you will be reading many kinds of print and electronic material in which you have to reason out the author's message as you did for this advertisement. You will be reading research articles, essays, critiques, reports, and analyses. Your instructors expect you to be able to do much more than understand and remember the basic content. They often demand that you read critically—interpreting, evaluating, and reacting to assigned readings. To meet these expectations, you'll need to make solid inferences, recognize the author's tone, annotate as you read, and analyze and evaluate what you have read.

■ Make Inferences as You Read

So far, we have been concerned primarily with the literal meanings of writing. You have been shown techniques to help you to understand what the author says and retain the literal, factual content. However, you often need to go beyond what authors *say* and to be concerned with what they *mean*. Look at the photograph shown in Figure 4-1, which appeared in a psychology textbook. What do you think is happening here? Where is it happening? What are the feelings of the participants?

To answer these questions, you had to use any information you could get from the photo and make guesses based on it. You used the information at hand—the facial expressions, body language, clothing, other objects, and locale—to predict the author's message. This reasoning process is called "making an inference."

Inferences from the Given Facts

An inference is a reasoned guess about what you don't know made on the basis of what you do know. Inferences are common in our everyday lives. When you enter an expressway and see a long, slow-moving line of traffic, you might predict that there is an accident or roadwork ahead. When you see a puddle of water under the kitchen sink, you can infer that you have a plumbing problem. The inferences you make may not always be correct, even though you base them on the available information. The water under the sink might have been the result of a spill. The traffic you encountered on the expressway might be normal for that time of day, but you didn't know it because you aren't normally on the road then. An inference is only the best guess you can make in a situation, given the information you have.

EXERCISE 4-1

Study the photograph shown in Figure 4-1, and make inferences to answer the following questions.

FIGURE 4–1

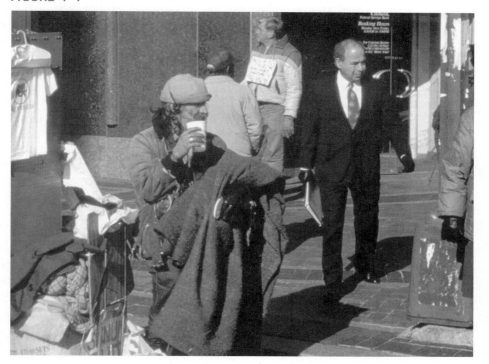

1. What is happening in the photograph? _____

_____

_____

2. List the evidence shown in the photograph that supports your answer to
   Question 1. _____

_____

_____

3. This photograph was included in a sociology textbook chapter that discusses economic stratification (levels) in the United States. What does this
   photograph contribute to chapter content? _____

_____

_____

Inferences from Written Material

When you read the material associated with your college courses, you frequently need to make inferences. Writers do not always present their ideas

directly. Instead, they often leave it to you to add up and think beyond the facts they present. You are expected to reason out, or infer, the meaning an author intended (but did not say) on the basis of what he or she did say. In a sense, the inferences you make act as bridges between what is said and what is not said but is meant.

There are several reasons why textbook authors and other writers require you to make inferences. Often, information is left out because it would make the message too long or would divert you from the central point. Sometimes an author assumes the readers know enough to fill in the omitted ideas. Other times, the writer believes that you will get more meaning or enjoyment from engaging in the thought process required to make an inference. Finally, some writers leave out pertinent information in order to make it easier to influence you to draw a desired conclusion, especially if you might have challenged the details had they been included. You can see, then, that making solid inferences is an important first step toward reading critically.

How to Make Inferences

Each inference you make depends on the situation, the facts provided, and your own knowledge and experience. Here are a few guidelines to help you see beyond the factual level and make solid inferences.

Know the Literal Meaning   Be sure you have a firm grasp of the literal meaning. You must understand the stated ideas and facts before you can move to higher levels of thinking, which include inference making. You should recognize the topic, main idea, key details, and organizational pattern of each paragraph you have read.

Notice Details   As you are reading, pay particular attention to details that are unusual or stand out. Often, such details will offer you clues to help you make inferences. Ask yourself:

- What is unusual or striking about this piece of information?
- Why is it included here?

Read the following excerpt, which is taken from a business marketing textbook, and mark details that are unusual or striking.

MARKETING IN ACTION

Dressing Up the Basics in Idaho

In almost any grocery store across the United States, consumers can purchase ten pounds of Idaho-grown potatoes for less than $5.00. Despite this fact, Rolland Jones Potatoes, Incorporated, has been extremely successful selling a "baker's dozen" of Idaho potatoes for $18.95. The potatoes are wrapped in a decorative box that uses Easter grass.

The Baker's Dozen of Idaho potatoes is only one example of a growing phenomenon. Laura Hobbs, marketing specialist for the Idaho Department of Agriculture, reports that more than 200 Idaho farms produce specialty or value-added products. These goods typically consist of basic farm commodities that have been "dressed-up" with packaging. Consumers can choose from these products: microwave pop-corn that comes on the cob and pops right off the cob, a bag of complete chili ingredients that makers claim won't cause embarrassing side-effects, and choco-late-covered "Couch Potato Chips."

Idaho farmers are supported by two groups, the Idaho Specialty Foods Association and Buy Idaho, whose goals are to help producers market and promote unique items. With the help of the groups, Idaho farmers are getting quite savvy. The marketers have discovered, for example, that packaging certain items together can increase their attractiveness. Hagerman's Rose Creek Winery found that sales of its wines soared when they were packaged in gift baskets with jars of Sun Valley brand mustard.

According to Hobbs, consumers attracted to the unique packaging provide a market for an endless variety of products, all of which are standard commodities transformed into new products through packaging. The value added through the unique packaging also provides opportunities to charge prices in ranges far above the prices of standard products—like $18.95 for 12 potatoes!

—adapted from Kinnear et al., *Principles of Marketing,* p. 301

Did you mark details such as the price of $18.95 for potatoes, corn that pops right off the cob, and chocolate-covered potato chips?

Add Up the Facts   Consider all of the facts taken together. To help you do this, ask yourself such questions as the following:

- What is the writer trying to suggest with this set of facts?
- What do all these facts and ideas seem to point toward or add up to?
- Why did the author include these facts and details?

Making an inference is somewhat like assembling a complicated jigsaw puzzle, in which you try to make all the pieces fit together to form a recognizable picture. Answering these questions will require you to add together all the individual pieces of information, which will enable you to arrive at an inference.

When you add up the facts in the article "Dressing Up the Basics in Idaho," you realize that the writer is suggesting that people are willing to pay much more than a product is worth if it is specially packaged.

Be Alert to Clues   Writers often provide you with numerous hints that can point you toward accurate inferences. An awareness of word choices, details included (and omitted), ideas emphasized, and direct commentary can help you determine a textbook author's attitude toward the topic at hand. In the foregoing excerpt, the authors offer clues that reveal their attitude toward increased prices for special packaging. Terms such as *dressed-up* and the excla-mation point at the end of the last sentence suggest that the authors realize that the products mentioned are not worth their price.

In addition to these clues, writers of fiction also provide hints in their descriptions of characters and actions and through the conversations of their characters.

Consider the Author's Purpose   Also study the author's purpose for writing. If an author's purpose is to convince you to purchase a particular product, as in an advertisement, as you begin reading you already have a clear idea of the types of inferences the writer hopes you will make. For instance, here is a magazine ad for a stereo system:

> If you're in the market for true surround sound, a prematched system is a good way to get it. The components in our system are built for each other by our audio engineers. You can be assured of high performance and sound quality.

Verify Your Inference   Once you have made an inference, check that it is accurate. Look back at the stated facts to be sure that you have sufficient evidence to support the inference. Also, be certain that you have not overlooked other equally plausible or more plausible inferences that could be drawn from the same set of facts.

EXERCISE 4-2

Read each of the following statements and the sentences that follow. Place a check-mark in front of each sentence that is a reasonable inference that can be made from the statement.

1. Political candidates must now include the Internet in their campaign plans.

    _____ a. Political candidates may host online chats to assess voter opinion.

    _____ b. Informal debates between candidates may be conducted online.

    _____ c. Internet campaigning will drastically increase overall campaign expenditures.

    _____ d. Television campaigning is likely to remain the same.

2. Half of the public education classrooms in the United States are now hooked up to the Internet.

    _____ a. Children are more computer literate than their parents.

    _____ b. Many students now have access to current world news and happenings.

    _____ c. Books are no longer considered the sole source of information on a subject.

    _____ d. Teachers have become better teachers now that they have Internet access.

3. The Internet can make doctors more efficient through the use of new software and databases that make patient diagnosis more accurate.

    _____ a. The cost of in-person medical care is likely to decrease.

    _____ b. Doctors may be able to identify patients with serious illness sooner.

    _____ c. Doctors are likely to pay less attention to their patients' descriptions of symptoms.

    _____ d. Information on the symptoms and treatment of rare illnesses is more readily available.

EXERCISE 4-3

Read the following paragraph. A number of statements follow it; each statement is an inference. Label each inference as either:

PA—Probably accurate—there is substantial evidence in the paragraph to support the statement.

IE—Insufficient evidence—there is little or no evidence in the paragraph to support the statement.

> While working for a wholesale firm, traveling to country stores by horse and buggy, Aaron Montgomery Ward conceived the idea of selling directly to country people by mail. He opened his business in 1872 with a one-page list of items that cost one dollar each. People could later order goods through a distributed catalog and the store would ship the merchandise cash on delivery (COD). The idea was slow to catch on because people were suspicious of a strange name. However, in 1875 Ward announced the startling policy of "satisfaction guaranteed or your money back." Contrasting with the former retailing principle of caveat emptor (Latin for "buyer beware"), this policy set off a boom in Ward's business.
>
> —Frings, *Fashion: From Concepts to Consumer,* p. 11

_____ 1. Aaron Ward had experience in sales before he began his own business.

_____ 2. Country people were targeted because they did not have access to stores in cities.

_____ 3. Ward's mistake was to give every item on the list the same price.

_____ 4. Other stores in operation at the time did not offer money back guarantees.

_____ 5. Other mail order business quickly followed Ward's success.

EXERCISE 4-4

Read the following passages, and then answer the questions. The answers are not directly stated in the passage; you will have to make inferences in order to answer them.

PASSAGE A "IS LAUGHTER THE BEST MEDICINE?"

Lucy went to the hospital to visit Emma, a neighbor who had broken her hip. The first thing Lucy saw when the elevator door opened at the third floor was a clown, with an enormous orange nose, dancing down the hall, pushing a colorfully decorated cart. The clown stopped in front of Lucy, bowed, and then somersaulted to the nurses' station. A cluster of patients cheered. Most of them were in wheelchairs or on crutches. Upon asking for directions, Lucy learned that Emma was in the "humor room," where the film *Blazing Saddles* was about to start.

Since writer Norman Cousins's widely publicized recovery from a debilitating and usually incurable disease of the connective tissue, humor has gained new respectability in hospital wards around the country. Cousins, the long-time editor of the *Saturday Review,* with the cooperation of his physician, supplemented his regular medical therapy with a steady diet of Marx brothers movies and *Candid Camera* film clips. Although he never claimed that laughter alone effected his cure, Cousins is best remembered for his passionate support of the notion that, if negative emotions can cause distress, then humor and positive emotions can enhance the healing process (Cousins, 1979, 1989).

—Zimbardo and Gerrig, *Psychology and Life,* p. 501

1. What is the purpose of the story about Lucy and Emma?
2. What is a "humor room"?
3. What type of movie is *Blazing Saddles?*
4. Answer the question asked in the title.

PASSAGE B "OPRAH WINFREY—A WOMAN FOR ALL SEASONS"

Oprah Winfrey—actress, talk-show host, and businesswoman—epitomizes the opportunities for America's women entrepreneurs. From welfare child to multimillionaire, Ms. Winfrey—resourceful, assertive, always self-assured, and yet unpretentious—has climbed the socioeconomic ladder by turning apparent failure into opportunities and then capitalizing on them.

With no playmates, Oprah entertained herself by "playacting" with objects such as corncob dolls, chickens, and cows. Her grandmother, a harsh disciplinarian, taught Oprah to read by age 2½, and as a result of speaking at a rural church, her oratory talents began to emerge.

At age 6, Winfrey was sent to live with her mother and two half-brothers in a Milwaukee ghetto. While in Milwaukee, Winfrey, known as "the Little Speaker," was often invited to recite poetry at social gatherings, and her speaking skills continued to develop. At age 12, during a visit to her father in Nashville, she was paid $500 for a speech she gave to a church. It was then that she prophetically announced what she wanted to do for a living: "get paid to talk."

Her mother, working as a maid and drawing available welfare to make ends meet, left Oprah with little or no parental supervision and eventually sent her to live with her father in Nashville. There Oprah found the stability and discipline she so desperately needed. "My father saved my life," Winfrey reminisces. Her father—like her grandmother—a strict disciplinarian, obsessed with properly educating his daughter, forced her to memorize 20 new vocabulary words a week and turn in a weekly book report. His guidance and her hard work soon paid off, as she began to excel in school and other areas.

—Mosley et al., *Management: Leadership in Action,* p. 555

1. What is the author's attitude toward Winfrey?
2. What is the author's attitude toward strict discipline for children?
3. Is the author optimistic about business opportunities for women? How do you know?
4. What factors contributed to Winfrey's success?

■ Assess the Author's Qualifications

Not everything that appears in print is accurate and competently reported. Also, there are varying levels of expertise within a field. Consequently, you must assess whether the material you are reading is written by an expert in the field who can knowledgeably and accurately discuss the topic. For example, a sociologist who has studied the criminal justice system is not necessarily an expert on problems of immigrant populations. A scientist who specializes in genetics cannot write authoritatively about the greenhouse effect. In some materials, the author's credentials are footnoted or summarized at the end of the work. In journal articles, the author's college or university affiliation is often included. Authors also may establish their expertise or experience in the field within the material itself.

EXERCISE 4-5   *Read each statement and place a checkmark next to the individual who would seem to be the best authority on the subject.*

1. One simple way to improve your diet is to put away the salt shaker.

    _____ a. Paula Weigel, registered dietician and nutritionist

    _____ b. John Mishler, life-long dieter

    _____ c. Maria Sanchez, columnist for *Food and Wine* magazine

2. The Dalai Lama is one of the great spiritual leaders of our time.

    _____ a. Richard Gere, film actor and follower of Buddhism

    _____ b. Alice Kohler, college student majoring in religion

    _____ c. Joseph Campbell, author and scholar of religion and mythology

3. Genetic engineering has enhanced both the quality and quantity of many crops, including soybeans, rice, and corn.

    _____ a. Craig Stinson, stockbroker

    _____ b. Andrew Burnette, television news reporter in the Midwest

    _____ c. Charlotte Corbeille, professor of agriculture at Iowa State University

EXERCISE 4-6

Working together with a classmate, discuss and identify who (title or job description) would be considered a qualified expert on each of the following topics.

1. the side effects of a prescription drug
2. building code laws for an apartment building
3. controlling test anxiety
4. immigration laws
5. influence of television violence on children

■ Distinguish Between Fact and Opinion

Facts are statements that can be tested as true or false—they are verifiable pieces of information. *Opinions* are statements that express feelings, attitudes, or beliefs that are neither true nor false. Here are a few examples of each.

Facts

Birthrates declined from 1960 to 1979.

The proportion of married women in the work force has steadily increased in the past 40 years.

Opinions

A drastic change is soon to occur in family structure.

Parenthood is the most rewarding human experience.

There is also what is known as expert opinion or testimony—the opinion of an authority. Ralph Nader represents expert opinion on consumer rights, for example. Here are a few examples of expert opinions.

Bill Gates, Chairman and Chief Software Architect, Microsoft Corporation	"Right now, we're only scratching the surface of what computing technology can do."
David Satcher, former U.S. Surgeon General	"The prevalence of overweight and obesity has nearly doubled among children and adolescents since 1980. It is also increasing in both genders and among all population groups of adults."
Sir Edmund Hillary, one of the first two men to climb Mt. Everest	"Other mountains have more technically difficult routes than Everest, but none have that last 800 feet of extreme height."

Textbook authors, too, offer expert opinions, especially when they interpret events, summarize research, or evaluate trends. In the following paragraph, the author of a sociology textbook on marriage and the family interprets recent studies on sexuality.

> Recent studies of the history of sexuality in Western society have revealed that dramatic changes have taken place in beliefs and behavior. Among the most striking contrasts with our own times are the acceptance of bisexuality among men in ancient times and the disapproval of sexual pleasure in marriage for many centuries of the Christian era. The new studies also reveal that the sexual culture of any particular place and time is a complex mixture of expressive and repressive codes.
>
> —Skolnick, *The Intimate Environment,* p. 224

Some authors are careful to signal the reader when they are presenting an opinion. Watch for words and phrases such as:

apparently	this suggests	in my view	one explanation is
presumably	possibly	it is likely that	according to
in my opinion	it is believed	seemingly	

Here is an example:

> Among the many moons of Saturn is Titan, Saturn's only large moon and the second-largest in the solar system. Titan's hazy and cloudy atmosphere hides its surface, so we do not know whether Titan is geologically active. However, given its relatively large size and icy composition, it seems likely that Titan has a rich geological history.
>
> —Bennett et al., *The Cosmic Perspective,* pp. 311–12

As you read a work, it is essential to distinguish between fact and opinion. Factual statements from reliable sources can be accepted and used in drawing conclusions, building arguments, and supporting ideas. Opinions, however, are one person's point of view that you are free to accept or reject.

EXERCISE 4–7

Read each of the following statements and identify whether it sounds like fact (F), opinion (O), or expert opinion (EO).

_____ 1. Most Americans feel strongly about the gun control issue.

_____ 2. Mosquitoes can transmit a disease known as encephalitis.

_____ 3. By 2009, more than 800 million people will use the Internet.

_____ 4. Marine biologists use the Internet in researching and identifying plant and animal species.

_____ 5. Computer users often feel guilty and blame themselves when their computer fails or performs an illegal operation.

_____ 6. Borders is the biggest music retailer on the Internet.

_____ 7. James Gleick, a well-known author who writes about technology, notes that networked digital devices set the pace of change in the computer field.

_____ 8. An increasing number of private citizens have their own Web sites.

_____ 9. Personal Web sites give people a sense of power and importance.

_____ 10. Capron, an author of a textbook on computers, says Internet traffic jams can be expected, creating slow response times in sending and receiving messages.

EXERCISE 4–8

Read each of the following statements. In each, underline the word or phrase that suggests that the author is offering an informed opinion.

1. According to recent studies, infants who use pacifiers may experience delays in their speech development.
2. The candidate lost the election apparently because voters disapproved of her negative campaigning tactics.
3. In my opinion, the Tour de France is the most demanding athletic event in the world.
4. One explanation for the elementary school's declining enrollment is an aging population in the area.
5. It is likely that the drought will continue through the summer.

EXERCISE 4–9

Each of the following paragraphs contains both fact and opinion. Read each paragraph and label each sentence as fact or opinion.

PARAGRAPH 1

1 Harriet Tubman was born a slave in Maryland in 1820 and escaped to Philadelphia in 1849. 2 Her own escape presumably required tremendous courage,

but that was just the beginning. 3 Through her work on the Underground Railroad, Harriet Tubman led more than 300 slaves to freedom. 4 During the Civil War, Tubman continued her efforts toward the abolition of slavery by working as a nurse and a spy for the Union forces. 5 Today, Americans of all races consider Harriet Tubman one of the most heroic figures in our country's history.

Sentences: 1. _____ 2. _____ 3. _____ 4. _____ 5. _____

PARAGRAPH 2

1 Smokeless tobacco is used by approximately 5 million U.S. adults, most of whom are young males. 2 One explanation for the popularity of smokeless tobacco among young men is that they are emulating professional athletes who chew tobacco or use snuff. 3 In any major league baseball game, more than a few players with chewing tobacco bulging in their cheeks apparently believe the myth that smokeless tobacco is less harmful than cigarettes. 4 In reality, smokeless tobacco contains 10 times the amount of cancer-producing substances found in cigarettes and 100 times more than the Food and Drug Administration allows in foods and other substances used by the public. 5 Smokeless tobacco has been banned from minor-league baseball, a move that should be extended to all professional sports to help discourage the use of smokeless tobacco products.

Sentences: 1. _____ 2. _____ 3. _____ 4. _____ 5. _____

PARAGRAPH 3

1 Managed care plans have agreements with certain physicians, hospitals, and health care providers to give a range of services to plan members at a reduced cost. 2 There are three basic types of managed care plans: health maintenance organizations (HMOs), point-of-service plans (POS), and preferred provider organizations (PPO). 3 The PPO, in my opinion, is the best type of managed care plan because it merges the best features of traditional health insurance and HMOs. 4 As in traditional plans, participants in a PPO pay premiums, deductibles, and co-payments, but the co-pay under a PPO is lower (10 percent or less compared to the 20 percent co-pay under a traditional plan). 5 The best part of a PPO, though, is its flexibility: participants may choose their physicians and services from a list of preferred providers, or they may go outside the plan for care if they wish.

Sentences: 1. _____ 2. _____ 3. _____ 4. _____ 5. _____

■ Identify the Author's Purpose

Writers have many different reasons or purposes for writing. Read the following statements and try to decide why each was written:

1. Acute coronary syndromes are caused by a decrease or interruption of blood flow to the muscular tissue of the heart.

2. The new *Slumber-Rest* adjustable bed features a patented coil system and a triple-thick mattress for night after night of deep, refreshing sleep. And

with any *Slumber-Rest* bed purchased before January 1, you'll receive two luxurious down pillows.

3. A bad workman quarrels with his tools.

4. If your car engine is overheating, turn on the heater immediately. Pull over to the side of the road and open the hood as soon as possible.

5. Never open an e-mail attachment from an address you do not recognize. It could contain a virus.

Statement 1 was written to give information, 2 to persuade you to buy a bed, 3 to stimulate thought, 4 to explain how to handle an overheated car engine, and 5 to give advice.

In each of the examples, the writer's purpose was fairly clear, as it will be in most textbooks (to present information), newspaper articles (to communicate daily events), and reference books (to compile facts). However, in many other types of writing, authors have varied, sometimes less obvious, purposes. In these cases, an author's purpose must be inferred.

Often a writer's purpose is to express an opinion indirectly. Or the writer may want to encourage the reader to think about a particular issue or problem. Writers achieve their purposes by manipulating and controlling what they say and how they say it. The author's style and intended audience often reveal his or her purpose.

Writers have unique characteristics that distinguish their writing from that of others. One author may use many examples; another may use few. One author may use relatively short sentences; another may use long, complicated ones. The characteristics that make a writer unique are known as **style.** By changing style, writers can create different effects.

Writers may vary their styles to suit their intended audiences. A writer may write for a general-interest audience (anyone who is interested in the subject but is not considered an expert). Most newspapers and periodicals, such as *U.S. News & World Report* and *Newsweek,* appeal to a general-interest audience. On the other hand, a writer may have a particular interest group in mind. A writer may write for attorneys in the *ABA Journal* or for golf enthusiasts in *Golf Digest* or for antique collectors in the *World of Antiques.* A writer may also target his or her writing for an audience with particular political, moral, or religious attitudes. Articles in the *New Republic* often appeal to a particular political viewpoint, whereas the *Catholic Digest* appeals to a specific religious group.

Depending on the group of people for whom the author is writing, he or she will change the level of language, choice of words, and method of presentation. One step toward identifying an author's purpose, then, is to ask yourself the question, "Who is the intended audience?" Also ask yourself, "Why did the author write this?" In academic reading, you will most often find that the author's purpose is either to inform (present information) or to persuade. For example, an essay on state aid to private colleges may present information on current levels of funding, it may argue for an increased or decreased level of funding, or it may address both topics. Knowing the author's primary purpose will alert you to the type of critical questions you should ask.

EXERCISE 4-10 *Based on the title of each of the following essays, predict whether the author's purpose is to inform or persuade.*

1. Changing habits: How shopping online is different
2. I got straight A's, but I wasn't happy.
3. Animals can't speak: We must speak for them!
4. Guns don't kill people; people kill people.
5. What the Bible says about the end of the world

EXERCISE 4-11 *Read each of the following statements and decide for whom each was written. Write a sentence that describes the intended audience.*

1. Autumn is the best time of year to plant most trees, shrubs, and perennials. The warm days and cool nights of fall are ideal for root systems to develop, resulting in healthy, hardy plants.

   _____

2. Learning to play a musical instrument can have many rewards for your children. They will develop confidence as a result of successful individual study, and if they choose to play in a band or orchestra, their interpersonal skills and social awareness will be enhanced through their participation in a group. Most important, they will develop a satisfying, lifelong leisure activity.

   _____

3. In the second season of the Women's United Soccer Association, the Carolina Courage defeated Mia Hamm and the Washington Freedom for the WUSA championship. Hamm continues to reign as the leading international scorer in women's soccer history.

   _____

4. For a refreshingly healthy way to quench your thirst, try Pauley's Parrot Juice. Pauley has cleverly combined the juice of pears and carrots to create natural, nutritious, and uniquely delicious Parrot Juice. And while you're quenching your thirst, remember that one-third of all proceeds from Pauley's Parrot Juice goes to conservation efforts in the Amazon rainforest.

   _____

5. When you are choosing a dog, it is important to identify a breed that matches your lifestyle. An apartment with a balcony may lend itself well to smaller breeds that do not require a great deal of outdoor exercise, whereas a house on acreage will provide a larger and more physically demanding dog with the space it needs.

   _____

■ Evaluate the Data and Evidence

Many writers who express their opinions, state viewpoints, or make generalizations provide data or evidence to support their ideas. Your task as a critical reader is to weigh and evaluate the quality of this evidence. You must examine the evidence and assess its adequacy. You should be concerned with two factors: the type of evidence being presented and the relevance of that evidence. Various types of evidence include:

- **personal experience or observation.**
- **statistical data.**
- **examples, descriptions of particular events, or illustrative situations.**
- **analogies (comparisons with similar situations).**
- **historical documentation.**
- **experimental evidence.**

Each type of evidence must be weighed in relation to the statement it supports. Acceptable evidence should directly, clearly, and indisputably support the case or issue in question.

EXERCISE 4-12   *Study the photograph shown above. Place a checkmark in front of those statements that seem reasonable based on the evidence shown in the photograph.*

_____   1. The soldier is an American.

_____   2. The soldier is greet a close friend or relative.

_____   3. The soldier has been deployed in Iraq.

_____   4. The soldier is happy.

_____   5. The photo was taken in a public place, like an airport.

_____   6. The soldier will probably be re-deployed.

EXERCISE 4–13   *For each of the following statements, discuss the type or types of evidence that you would need in order to support and evaluate the statement.*

1. Individuals must accept primary responsibility for the health and safety of their babies.
2. Apologizing is often seen as a sign of weakness, especially among men.
3. There has been a steady increase in illegal immigration over the past 50 years.
4. More college women than college men agree that abortions should be legal.
5. Car advertisements sell fantasy experiences, not means of transportation.

■ Analyze the Writer's Tone

Suppose you are a customer service manager and a customer has complained about the assembly instructions for a computer workstation your company sells. You need to write a letter responding to the customer's complaints. You also need to send an e-mail message to the customer support department describing the problem. Would the two messages sound the same? Probably not. The letter to the customer would be friendly, polite, and accommodating, attempting to build goodwill and restore confidence in the company. The message to the customer support would be straightforward, direct, and factual. It would describe the problem and emphasize its seriousness. Each message, then, would have a different tone.

Tone refers to how a writer sounds to readers and how the writer feels about his or her topic. Recognizing an author's tone will help you interpret and evaluate his or her message. Tone also helps to suggest the author's purpose. Tone is revealed primarily thorough word choice and stylistic features such as sentence patterns and length. Tone, then, can reveal feelings. A writer can communicate surprise, disapproval, hate, disgust, admiration, gratitude, or amusement, for example.

Read the following statement, paying attention to the author's tone:

"Although hazing is considered a time-honored tradition at many fraternities, any activity centered around the senseless humiliation of individuals and the reckless consumption of alcohol has no place on a college campus."

Here the author's disapproval is apparent. Through choice of words such as *humiliation* and *reckless,* as well as choice of detail, she makes the tone obvious. Here are a few examples of different tones. How does each make you feel?

- **Instructive**—"Before you begin any knitting project, always check your gauge. Using the yarn and needles called for in the instructions, knit a two-inch swatch and then compare it with the scale given in the pattern. By making adjustments before beginning the project, you can avoid problems later on."
- **Sympathetic**—"After the whales had beached themselves for a third time, the exhausted volunteers abandoned their rescue efforts and looked on grimly while the dying whales were euthanized."
- **Persuasive**—"Many frequent flyer programs allow you to donate points to charity. Your frequent flyer points may be used to help people with life-threatening medical conditions travel by plane to obtain the treatment they need, or to transport emergency relief personnel to the site of natural disasters, or simply to enable seriously ill children and their families to enjoy a trip to Disney World."
- **Humorous**—"A boy can run like a deer, swim like a fish, climb like a squirrel, balk like a mule, bellow like a bull, eat like a pig, or act like a jackass, according to climate conditions. A boy is a piece of skin stretched over an appetite. However, he eats only when he is awake. Boys imitate their Dads in spite of all efforts to teach them good manners." (former President Herbert Hoover; source: www.hooverassoc.org)
- **Nostalgic**—"The handwritten letter is a vanishing art. Although the convenience of e-mail can't be beat, when someone sits down with pen and paper to write a good, old-fashioned letter, it reminds us of a simpler, more thoughtful time."

Tone can also be used to help establish a relationship between writer and reader. Through tone a writer can establish a sense of a shared communication with the reader, drawing them together. Or a writer may establish a distance from the reader, keeping them apart. In the excerpts that follow, notice how in the first passage a formality, or distance, is evident, and in the second, how a familiarity and friendliness are created.

PASSAGE 1

Meditation, which focuses awareness on a single stimulus, generally brings a subjective sense of well-being and relaxation, along with such physiological changes as decreased heart and respiratory rates and shifting EEG patterns of brain activity. There are three main types of meditation: concentrative, in which the meditator's focuses on one chosen image or word; opening-up, in which the mediator's surroundings become part of the meditation; and mindfulness, in which the meditator focuses on whatever is most prominent at the moment.

—Kosslyn and Rosenberg, *Psychology: The Brain, the Person, the World,* p. 162

PASSAGE 2

To begin evaluating a poem, first try to understand your own subjective response—don't pretend it doesn't exist. Admit, at least to yourself, whether the poem delights, moves, bores, or annoys you. Then try to determine what the poem seems designed to make you think and feel. Does it belong to some identifiable form or genre? (Is it, for instance, a love sonnet, narrative ballad, satire, or elegy?) How does its performance stack up against the expectations it creates? Considering those questions will give you some larger sense of perspective from which to evaluate the poem.

—Kennedy and Gioia, *Literature*, 2d edition, p. 789

To identify a writer's tone, pay particular attention to the words he or she uses, particularly their connotative meanings. Ask yourself: "How does the author feel about his or her subject and how is it revealed?" It is sometimes difficult to find the right word to describe a writer's tone. Table 4-1 list words that are often used to describe the tone of a piece of writing.

| EXERCISE 4-14 |

Read each of the following statements, paying particular attention to the tone. Then write a sentence that describes the tone. Prove your point by listing some of the words that reveal the author's feelings.

1. I could not believe my ears when the boy who bagged my groceries demanded a tip!
2. The spectacular house known as "Falling Waters" illustrates Frank Lloyd Wright's unparalleled genius as an architect.
3. It rained steadily all day, ruining our plans to go out on the boat.
4. The penalty for creating and launching a computer virus should include a personal apology to every single person whose computer was affected by the virus, and each apology should be typed—without errors!—on a manual typewriter.
5. When you are backpacking, you can reduce the risk of back injury by adjusting your pack so that most of its weight is on your hip belt rather than your shoulder straps.

TABLE 4-1   Words Frequently Used to Describe Tone

abstract	condemning	formal	joyful	reverent
absurd	condescending	frustrated	loving	righteous
amused	cynical	gentle	malicious	sarcastic
angry	depressing	grim	melancholic	satiric
apathetic	detached	hateful	mocking	sensational
arrogant	disapproving	humorous	nostalgic	serious
assertive	distressed	impassioned	objective	solemn
awestruck	docile	incredulous	obsequious	sympathetic
bitter	earnest	indignant	optimistic	tragic
caustic	excited	indirect	outraged	uncomfortable
celebratory	fanciful	informative	pathetic	vindictive
cheerful	farcical	intimate	persuasive	worried
comic	flippant	ironic	pessimistic	
compassionate	forgiving	irreverent	playful	

The following brief excerpt is taken from an article titled "Trash Troubles" that appeared in the periodical The World and I, *in November 1998. Using the guidelines you have learned in this chapter for evaluating the writer's message, answer the questions that follow.*

TRASH TROUBLES

Our accumulating piles of solid waste threaten to ruin our environment, pointing to the urgent need for not only better disposal methods but also strategies to lower the rate of waste generation.

As our ship surges forward, we notice a mound jutting up ahead, directly in our path. Like an iceberg, a much larger mass is hidden beneath the surface. If we keep running the vessel at current speed, we may have a major problem on our hands.

No, this not the Titanic. The ship we're on is our consumer-goods-dependent lifestyle that creates as much as a ton of solid waste per person each year. And the peak ahead is but the tip of a massive "wasteberg" that is 95 percent hidden from view: For every ton of trash we generate, there is an underlying loss of another 19 tons of industrial, agricultural, mining, and transportation wastes, building up into a mound that threatens to shatter our future.

The wasteberg entails a formidable economic and environmental challenge. For most local governments, solid waste management ranks behind only schools and highways as the major budget item. Improperly managed solid waste eats up dollars while polluting water supplies, threatening neighborhoods, and squandering natural resources.

So how is this odyssey progressing? Are we about to capsize on the wasteberg and drown, or can we successfully circumnavigate the threat? Better yet, can we shrink the wasteberg?

Circumnavigating the Wasteberg

The simplest way to steer around the wasteberg is to try to isolate wastes from their surrounding environment. This has been the major approach worldwide—solid waste management has usually meant solid waste disposal. Around the world, many nations have chosen incineration as the preferred way to dispose of solid waste. This is particularly the case where landfill sites are scarce. Japan, for example, has around 2,800 municipal incinerators that reduce solid wastes to ashes. In the United States, though, incineration has fallen strongly out of favor. Despite significant improvements in the technology, concerns that the incineration process may release toxic pollutants such as dioxins have brought this once-popular technology to near-obsolescence.

Shrinking the Wasteberg

For every pound of trash that goes into the waste basket, another 19 are released elsewhere in the environment—in forms ranging from industrial byproducts to fertilizer runoff to wasted energy. Thus if we reduce our generation of solid waste, the "leverage effect" is enormous: Each ton of trash kept out of the dump means that 19 tons of waste, along with related environmental impacts and the dollar cost of producing it, are avoided.

There are three major approaches to narrowing the waste stream: reducing, redesigning, and recycling. All require vigorous participation by both producers and consumers.

Reducing. Producers reduce waste through offering products that are less wasteful. Consumers reduce waste by using less of the product and using materials longer.

Redesigning. Producers offer alternative products that have a lower environmental impact than traditional ones, while continuing to meet given needs.

Recycling. Producers make reusable products, utilizing waste materials in manufacturing these goods. Consumers reuse the products and collect the materials to recycle out of the waste stream and back to the producers.

—Purcell, "Trash Troubles" in *The World and I*, p. 190

1. The author, Arthur H. Purcell, is the founder and director of the Resource Policy Institute, the author of *The Waste Watchers*, and a commentator for National Public Radio's "Marketplace." Evaluate his authority to discuss this topic.
2. Is the article primarily fact, opinion, or expert opinion? Support your answer with examples.
3. What is the author's purpose?
4. Evaluate the types and adequacy of the evidence the author provides.
5. Describe the author's tone.

EXERCISE 4-16   *Working with another classmate, review the reading "Factors Affecting Interpersonal Attraction," which appears on page 41 in Chapter 1, and answer questions 2 through 5 from Exercise 4-15.*

■ Annotate as You Read

An important part of reading critically is to react to the author's ideas. You may agree, disagree, question, challenge, or seek further information, for example. To do so, begin by writing down your reactions while and after you read. Then, once you have finished, review your notes and evaluate the writer's ideas.

If you were reading the classified ads in a newspaper in search of an apartment to rent, you probably would mark certain ads. Then, when you phoned for more information, you might make notes about each apartment. These notes would be useful in deciding which apartments were worth visiting.

Similarly, in other types of reading, making notes—*annotating*—is a useful strategy. Annotating is a means of keeping track of your impressions, ideas, reactions, and questions as you read. Reviewing your annotations will help you form a final impression of the work. If a writing assignment accompanies the reading, your annotations will serve as an excellent source of ideas for a paper. This reading strategy is discussed in more detail in Chapter 9.

There are no fixed rules about how or what to annotate. In general, try to mark or note any ideas about the work that come to mind as you read or reread. Underline or highlight within the work and use the margins to write your notes. Your annotations might include:

- questions.
- opinions.
- strong pieces of evidence.
- key points.
- ideas with which you disagree.
- good or poor supporting data or examples.
- inconsistencies.
- key terms or definitions.
- contrasting points of view.
- key arguments.
- words with strong connotations.
- figures of speech (images that reveal the writer's feelings).

A sample annotation is shown in the following passage on the meaning of color. Read it carefully, noticing the types of markings and annotations that were made.

COLOR AND EMOTIONS

the issue or question

The research in color preference led to a spin-off area of research, that of color and emotional response or moods. Researchers asked whether a reliable mood-color association exists and whether color could influence one's emotional state. Well-controlled

would like reference to these studies

research studies have shown that a definite color-mood tone association exists, although the color-mood association differed widely among people participating in the study. In fact, the studies showed all colors to be associated with all moods in varying degrees of strength. Although certain colors are more strongly associated with

does not state nature and strength of evidence
What evidence? describe?

a given mood or emotion, there was evidence to suggest a one-to-one relationship between a given color and a given emotion. What seemed to make the difference was how strongly a person associated a particular color with a particular mood or emotion.

Colors have been stereotyped by the public when it comes to emotions. In spite of physical evidence to the contrary, most people continue to equate red tones with excitement and activity and blue tones with passivity and tranquillity in color-mood association research. This is a learned behavior. From the time we are very young we learn to associate red with fire engines, stop lights, and danger signals that cause us to form an alert or danger association with red. Further, the red, orange, and yellow tones in fire further cause association between those colors and heat and kinetic energy. We have seen how cultural biases that are a part of our language further support the red equals excitement myth. These subconscious messages clearly affect the response to red. Blue tones, being associated with cool streams, the sky, and the ocean, continue to be equated with calm and tranquillity. This, too, is a learned response with which we are subtly sur-

What are the biological ones?

rounded from early childhood. In understanding color, it is important to differentiate between these culturally learned color associations and true biological responses.

How?

Research on the emotional aspects of color has for the most part resulted in a gross oversimplification of a very involved process. Unfortunately, this oversimplifica-

Clothing design? interior design? building design? —which one?

tion has been promoted heavily in the popular press. The design community too has jumped on the bandwagon, often making sweeping statements about color that are totally unsupported by anything but myth or personal belief. For example, one book refers to blue as "communicating cool, comfort, protective, calming, although may

Could be expert opinion, depending on qualifications of author

Summary

be slightly depressing if other colors are dark; associated with bad taste." There is of course no basis for these statements except as the personal opinion of the author, but too often these <u>personal opinions</u> become accepted as fact.

Colors do not contain any inherent emotional triggers. Rather, it is more likely that our changing moods and emotions caused by our own physiological and psychological makeup at the moment interact with color to create preferences and associations that we then link to the color-emotion response itself.

—Fehrman and Fehrman, *Color: The Secret Influence,* pp. 82–83

EXERCISE 4-17   *Review and write annotations for "Trash Troubles," which appears on page 115.*

■ Synthesize Your Ideas

After you have read (and perhaps reread) a piece of writing and made annotations, the final steps are to review your annotations and arrive at some conclusions and final impressions of the work. This is a creative as well as a logical process that involves looking for patterns and trends, noticing contrasts, thinking about the author's intentions, analyzing the effects of stylistic features, and determining the significance of the work. You might think of it as a process similar to evaluating a film after you have seen it or discussing a controversial television documentary. Your overall purpose is analysis: to arrive at an overall interpretation and evaluation of the work.

When analyzing a work, it may be helpful to write lists of words, issues, problems, and questions to discover patterns and evaluate the author's bias. Use the following questions to guide your analysis:

- What did the author intend to accomplish?
- How effectively did he or she accomplish this?
- What questions does the work raise and answer?
- What questions are ignored or left unanswered?
- What contributions to your course content and objectives does this work make?
- How does this work fit with your course textbook?
- How worthwhile is the material? What are its strengths and weaknesses?

EXERCISE 4-18   *Preview, read, and annotate the following essay titled "The Barbarity of Meat." Assume it is one of several articles your health and nutrition instructor assigned for a class discussion on vegetarianism. Pose several guide questions to focus your reading. Annotate as you read. Then analyze and evaluate the reading using the questions listed on page 120.*

THE BARBARITY OF MEAT

The food industry downplays the connection between steak and cows.

If, as some authors suggest, eating meat is indeed an important statement of human power, it might seem strange that we are apparently becoming progressively more uncomfortable with reminders of its animal origins. Consumer attitudes today are in a state of flux, not least for this reason. Whereas once it was sufficient simply to display whole animals and pieces of meat, the packing of the product is now a more delicate task. Most of us prefer not to think too directly about where our meat has come from, and unwelcome reminders can be distinctly off-putting. As one consumer put it, "I don't like it when you see . . . veins and things coming out of the meat . . . because it always reminds me of my own insides in a funny sort of a way. I suppose it's the idea of, like, blood flowing [that] makes you realize that this slab of meat was once a bit of functioning body, a bit like your own."

Meat marketing has responded accordingly, to assuage customers' sensitivity to the nature of the product. Nowadays, the consumer need never encounter animal flesh in its vulgar, undressed state. Instead it will come cooked and reshaped, in a sesame bun or an exotically flavored sauce, as a turkey roll or as chicken nuggets, in a crumb coating or a vacuum package, with not a hint of blood in sight. More and more butchers' windows sport fresh green vegetables, fragrant herbs, and perhaps a stir-fry mixture. A deliberate process of disguising the source of animal foods has gained momentum in the 20th century, reacting to our evident unease with the idea of eating dead animals: Said one butcher, "I deplore deliveries being carried into the front of my shop on the neck of a van driver—especially if they are not wrapped. . . . I can think of little more guaranteed to turn pedestrians off buying meat than the sight of pigs' heads flopping about as he struggles past them with the carcass."

The number of independent butchers' shops has declined considerably in recent years. Supermarkets have clearly derived particular competitive advantage from presenting meat in conspicuously hygienic conditions with all preparation completed out of sight. Often only the best cuts are displayed; bones, guts, and skin are nowhere to be seen. The hermetically sealed package is effectively dissociated from the animal to which its contents once belonged, a service that is clearly winning customers.

The names we give to the flesh of the main meat animals are another device whereby we reduce the unpleasant impact of having to acknowledge their identity. We do not eat cow, we eat beef; we do not eat pig, we eat pork; we do not eat deer, we eat venison. It is as if we cannot bear to utter the name of the beast whose death we have ordained.

To some, our willingness to consume meat as well as the many other assorted products of the animal industry, but apparent unwillingness to slaughter the beasts for ourselves or even to acknowledge our complicity in that process, is a matter for moral reproof. Said one critic, "I think the meat industry is very dishonest. The people are not allowed to be aware of what's going on. To them meat is wrapped up in cellophane in supermarkets; it's very divorced from the animal that it's coming from. . . . People don't go down on the factory farm to see what's really going on down there. I think if a lot of people did do that or [went] to the slaughterhouse to see how the meat is produced, then a lot of them would become vegetarians."

There is some evidence to support this belief. Many first-generation vegetarians and semivegetarians directly trace their abstinence to occasions when, for one reason or another, they were brought face to face with the connection between the meat on their plate and once-living animals. The particular incident related by any individual—be it the sight of carcasses being carried into a butcher's shop, or an encounter with vegetarian polemicism, or a visit to a slaughterhouse on daily business, or merely an unusually vivid flight of imagination—is of minor importance. What matters is that many people, when confronted with this ethical perplexity, seemingly prefer to forgo meat altogether rather than to condone the treatment of animals on their path from birth to plate. And equally important, perhaps, is how new this rebellion is, or rather how rapid its development has been in recent history.

—Fiddes, *Meat: A Natural Symbol,* pp. 100–101

1. Does the author establish his authority on the subject of vegetarianism?
2. Is the article primarily fact or opinion? Justify your answer.
3. What is the author's purpose? How effectively does he accomplish it?
4. Summarize the evidence the author offers in support of his main points.
5. Does the author anticipate and address objections to his argument? If so, what are the objections and how does he refute them?
6. What questions might be raised during a class discussion of this essay?

Self-Test Summary

1. What does critical reading involve?	It involves interpreting, evaluating, and reacting to ideas.
2. What is an inference?	An inference is a reasoned guess about what you do not know based on what you do know.
3. What are the things you must do while you read in order to make inferences?	Know the literal meaning of the stated ideas and facts; notice details; add up the facts; be alert for clues; verify your inference.
4. What are the questions you should ask in order to assess an author's ideas?	<ul><li>Is the author a qualified expert?</li><li>Which are the facts and which are the opinions?</li><li>What is the author's purpose?</li><li>Is the author biased?</li><li>How strong are the data and evidence?</li></ul>
5. What is meant by "tone"?	Tone refers to how writers sound to their readers and how writers feel about their topics.
6. What are two techniques an author uses to convey tone?	An author conveys tone primarily through choice of words and use of stylistic features.
7. Explain what annotating involves.	Annotating involves writing down your reactions during and after reading, and when you have finished, reviewing your notes and evaluating the writer's ideas.
8. What does is mean to synthesize?	Synthesizing involves analyzing, interpreting, or evaluating a reading following a review of the material and all your annotations.
9. What are the questions you should ask during and after a reading in order to annotate, synthesize, and react to an author's ideas?	<ul><li>What did the author intend to accomplish?</li><li>How effectively did he or she accomplish this?</li><li>What questions does the work ask and answer?</li><li>What questions are ignored or left unanswered?</li><li>What contributions to your course content and objectives does the work make?</li><li>How does the work fit with your course textbook?</li><li>How worthwhile is the material? What are its weaknesses and strengths?</li></ul>

ECOLOGY/ENVIRONMENTAL STUDIES

Reading 1

How Soon Will World's Oil Supplies Peak?
John Dillin

Prereading Questions

1.   Why is the world's oil supply an issue?
2.   What could happen when oil supplies can no longer meet demand?

1   THE QUESTION provokes hot debate among experts, as concerns rise that America isn't prepared for a dropoff.

2   If world crude-oil production hits its peak and then falls within the next five to 10 years, would America be ready? The answer is, almost certainly not.

3   A debate unlike anything seen since the oil embargoes of the 1970s has erupted over the future of world petroleum supplies. A chorus of experts claims that the peak in production may be approaching, and that the impact of a peak and subsequent dropoff would be devastating to the world's economies. Others insist that moment is still distant.

4   Some nations, including China, already appear to be taking steps to lock in future oil supplies from the Middle East, Africa, Central Asia, Canada, and South America. The risks of future oil shortages are huge. As if to illustrate that point, the temporary ripple in supplies after hurricane Katrina sent gasoline prices in the U.S. to record levels.

5   Experts' views on future oil supplies are divided into two major groups—the optimists and the pessimists, David Greene of Oak Ridge National Laboratory said at a recent oil-supply workshop sponsored by the National Academies. On this topic, he said, "the only unbiased opinion is an uninformed opinion."

6   Pessimists predict the world's output of conventional oil will top out within the next few years at about 100 million barrels a day (m.b.d.) and then decline—perhaps by as much as 8 percent a year. Optimists contend that there is plenty of oil, particularly in the Middle East, and output will meet worldwide demand through at least 2030.

7   All sides agree that oil is a finite resource, and that it is vital to know which side is right. But the lack of public data makes that assessment difficult.

8   At the meeting here, dozens of energy analysts from federal agencies, big and small oil companies, universities, and the Organization of Petroleum Exporting Countries (OPEC) debated salient points concerning the world oil outlook:

  • The exact time of a worldwide oil peak is unpredictable, but could happen soon. Once production peaks and begins to fall, it could precipitate a global depression, wide-spread starvation, high unemployment, and even war.

  • If nations are not prepared, prices for crude oil after a peak could rise to hundreds of dollars a barrel, and gasoline could climb to $10 or more a gallon.

  • Mitigating the effects of an oil peak would take decades, even for advanced societies like the United States, Japan, and the European Union. Standards of living could plunge.

- Undeveloped nations could be devastated as heating oil, fertilizer, gasoline, and other petroleum products became unaffordable. More than 1 billion people could be put at risk.

Participants emphasized that repercussions from a downturn in production would last decades.

9   One point of general agreement is that oil output in non-OPEC countries is likely to peak soon after 2010. If this occurs, OPEC's control over supply and price would rise.

10   Ultimately, other liquid fuels to replace oil could be produced from unconventional sources, such as coal, natural gas, shale oil, tar sands, extra heavy oil, and biomass (corn, soybeans, sugar cane). But making the multibillion-dollar investments in alternative-fuel facilities—such as those needed to convert coal to gasoline—could take 20 to 30 years, said David Gray, director of energy systems analysis at Mitretek Systems, a nonprofit scientific-research corporation headquartered in Falls Church, Va.

11   Nor can conservation efforts—such as gas-electric hybrid cars—save the day, said John Heywood, director of Sloan Automotive Laboratory at the Massachusetts Institute of Technology. Autos and trucks last an average of 15 years, so it would take more than a decade to bring down fuel consumption on a large scale with new technology.

12   A representative of ExxonMobil, the world's largest petroleum company, countered these cautionary reports. ExxonMobil contends that its proprietary studies show that oil output will continue to grow to well over 100 m.b.d. worldwide at least through 2030. At ExxonMobil, they are "believers in technology" to boost oil production over time, said Scott Nauman, manager of energy and economics at the firm's corporate planning department. ExxonMobil also sees ways to ultimately control demand through technology such as hybrid autos.

13   Similar assurances came from Adnan Shihab-Eldin, acting secretary-general of OPEC. Dr. Shihab sees 12 m.b.d. of new crude-oil capacity coming on line in the next five years—more than enough to meet the 7 m.b.d. rise in world demand that OPEC forecasts over that period. More than 100 new projects are under way worldwide to add supply, he said.

14   Yet these assurances leave some analysts unsatisfied. Both ExxonMobil and OPEC rely on Middle Eastern geological data that are private, and so not independently verified. No one outside OPEC, for instance, has seen the latest information on Saudi Arabia's oil reserves.

15   "By their nature, the people who explore for oil [like ExxonMobil] are optimists. They have to be," said Robert Hirsch, senior energy program adviser at SAIC, a research and engineering firm with headquarters in San Diego. "But we are betting our [American] civilization on the assumption that they are right."

16   Another critical factor is that OPEC's role will become far more important than it is now after about 2010 because overall oil output in non-OPEC countries—such as the U.S., Mexico, Norway, and Nigeria—is expected (even by ExxonMobil) to peak about that time. After that, OPEC, with 78 percent of the world's proven oil reserves, will hold greater sway over prices and supplies.

17   Trying to pinpoint the date when oil production peaks has become something of a guessing game of late. There have been at least seven predictions that the peak could come within five years. A U.S. Department of Energy analysis in 2000 studied 12 scenarios for peaking, with the mean peak coming in 2016. If true, that gives the U.S. 10 years to prepare—too little time to avoid dislocations.

18   Several experts say it is time for Congress and the president to pay closer attention to the peaking issue, and to take steps soon enough to protect America's energy future.

Writing About the Reading

CHECKING YOUR VOCABULARY

1. For each of the words listed below, use context; prefixes, roots, and suffixes (see Chapter 3); and/or a dictionary to write a brief definition or synonym of the word as it is used in the reading.

   a. embargoes (para. 3) _____

   b. subsequent (para. 3) _____

   c. finite (para. 7) _____

   d. salient (para. 8) _____

   e. precipitate (para. 8) _____

   f. mitigating (para. 8) _____

   g. repercussions (para. 8) _____

   h. proprietary (para. 12) _____

2. Underline new, specialized terms introduced in the reading (see Chapter 3).

3. Draw a word map of one of the words in the reading.

CHECKING YOUR COMPREHENSION

1. What are the two views presented in the reading about the future of oil supplies?
2. What does everyone agree on regarding oil supplies?
3. What are some of the effects of an oil peak?
4. Name some other fuels that could replace oil. What problems are there with using these?
5. Describe the problem with conservation efforts.
6. How do ExxonMobil and OPEC envision the oil supply situation? What is the difficulty with the information that they provide?
7. Who is responsible for helping our country deal with an energy crisis?

THINKING CRITICALLY

1. What is the purpose of this essay?
2. List the author's main points and describe the data used to support these points.
3. What is the author's tone? How is it conveyed?
4. List two facts and two opinions presented in the article. Is there a balance between fact and opinion in the reading? Explain your answer.
5. What conclusions can you draw from the evidence presented by the author? How did you arrive at these conclusions?

LEARNING/STUDY STRATEGY

Annotate the reading by highlighting the various companies, places, and organizations that are mentioned. Indicate their significance to the reading.

ECOLOGY/ENVIRONMENTAL STUDIES

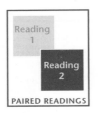

Reading 2

On Oil Supply, Opinions Aren't Scarce

Joseph Nocera

Prereading Questions

1. Are you worried about an energy crisis? Why or why not?
2. How expensive would a gallon of gasoline need to be in order for you to change your consumption of gasoline or petroleum products?

1   "We're halfway through the hydrocarbon era," my old friend T. Boone Pickens has been saying for the last couple of years. You may remember Mr. Pickens as the most famous corporate raider of the 1980's, but he has spent his life in the oil patch. A geologist by training, Mr. Pickens founded Mesa Petroleum at the age of 26 and ran it for the next 40 years. Now, at 77, he works the oil patch in a different way, running a pair of energy-oriented hedge funds in Dallas.

2   A folksy line like Mr. Pickens's—it sticks with you. But I hadn't realized until recently that it also meant Mr. Pickens had taken sides in a surprisingly heated debate. He subscribes to what is being called the peak oil hypothesis, which holds that there simply isn't very much new oil left to be found in the world. As a result, we are currently in the gradual process of draining the more than a trillion barrels of proven reserves that are still in the ground. And when it's gone, it's gone.

3   The best-known "peakist" these days is Matthew R. Simmons, who runs Simmons & Company, an investment bank and consulting firm in Houston specializing in energy companies. Mr. Simmons's essential belief, he told me recently, is that energy demand is about to exceed supply significantly. And that was pre-Hurricane Katrina—before the storm damaged refineries, pipelines and offshore rigs all along the Gulf Coast. "I would argue that we are in a serious energy crisis," Mr. Simmons added. He forecasts increasing oil prices.

4   There is a second group of forecasters, though, who argue with equal vehemence that the world is not in an energy crisis and it probably won't face one for a very long time. The best-known proponent of this view is Daniel Yergin, author of "The Prize: The Epic Quest for Oil, Money and Power," a history of oil that won the 1992 Pulitzer Prize, and the founder of a rather sizable consulting firm, Cambridge Energy Research Associates.

5   "This is the fifth time that we're supposedly running out of oil," Mr. Yergin said. But, he added, each time new technologies made it possible for oil companies to find new sources of oil and extract new oil from old sources. His firm released a survey a few months ago that says from 2004 to 2010, world oil supplies will have increased by as much as 16 million barrels a day, "outstripping the likely demand increase." Most of those who hold this view say that oil prices will eventually drift down.

6   Does it surprise you to learn that when it comes to one of most vital resources known to man, there could be such an incredible divergence of opinion? It sure surprised me.

Even some of the oil majors are on opposites sides, with Chevron taking the peakist view, and Exxon Mobil more aligned with the Yergin camp.

7   There are three reasons for this lack of consensus. First, because oil is buried underground, it is hard to measure. So basic "facts"—like how much oil remains, and how much can be ultimately extracted—are as much the product of guesswork as science. Second, the world of oil can be shrouded in secrecy. As an article in *The New York Times Magazine* recently pointed out, Saudi Arabia, the biggest producer of them all, won't even allow its reserve and production data to be audited.

8   Finally, though, the fact that this enormous divergence has developed speaks volumes about the very different way each camp views the world. "It's the geologists on one side and the economists on the other side," was the way the energy analyst Seth Kleinman of PFC Energy in Washington put it recently. That's an overgeneralization, of course, but one that contains plenty of truth.

9   The two sides do agree on one thing: the recent run-up in oil prices, which began well before Hurricane Katrina, has come about because demand for oil has caught up with supply. The enormous burst of economic activity in China, the generally good economic conditions in the United States and the rest of the West—these and other factors have led to a surge in oil demand.

10   "The world produces about 85 million barrels a day," Mr. Pickens said. "That's where demand is now, too. And I've seen forecasts that demand is going to be higher than that by the end of the year."

11   What's more, Mr. Pickens added, pre-Hurricane Katrina refining capacity was already at the breaking point, which is another point that is pretty unarguable. "Refineries were operating at 96 percent," he said. "You can't operate anything at 96 percent. It'll start breaking down."

12   That last paragraph, though, encapsulates the world view of the peakists: all the easy deals have been done. One reason refineries are operating at such high capacity is that no new refineries have been built in the United States for some 30 years, which Mr. Simmons believes can be attributed to the shortsightedness of the industry. "My theory was that if the industry didn't expand like crazy the U.S. would find itself running short of energy." It didn't, and we are.

13   Even more troubling, the pessimists believe that it is going to be increasingly difficult to replace the oil that we're now using up. "Let me give you a number that is pretty shocking when you hear it," Mr. Pickens said. "The world uses 30 billion barrels of oil a year. There is no way we're replacing 30 billion barrels of oil. Just a million barrels a day is 1,000 wells producing 1,000 barrels. That's big."

14   How do the economists counter the geologists' arguments? They don't deny that it is hard to find new oil. But they believe that whenever tight supplies push up the price of oil, the rising price itself becomes our salvation. For one thing, higher prices temper demand as people begin to change their energy habits. (Mr. Pickens believes this as well.) Surprisingly, this has not yet happened even as gasoline at the pump has more than doubled in the last year or so. But inevitably, there will come a point when it will change behaviors.

15   Secondly, they believe higher prices spur innovation. Oil that couldn't be extracted profitably at, say, $15 a barrel, can be enormously profitable at $60 a barrel. In the view of Mr. Yergin and his allies, in fact, this is exactly what has been happening. They point to new oil that is coming out of the Caspian Sea, deepwater drilling in Brazil and the oil sands in northern Alberta as examples. The 16 million barrels a day of new oil Mr. Yergin expects to

see by 2010, he told me, "is predicated on $25-to-$30 oil." If oil stays higher than that, then there will be even more investment, and not just in ways to extract oil, but in new refineries and pipelines and other infrastructure.

16   If you mention this theory to a hard-core peakist like Mr. Simmons, you'd better be ready for an earful. "These economists are so smug," he said derisively. "All they talk about is the magic of the free market. They don't seem to understand that this is incredibly capital intensive."

17   He pointed to those Canadian oil sands—where, he said, Shell Canada recently announced it was going to raise its investment to $7.3 billion from $4 billion to produce an additional 100,000 barrels a day. "Just think about that; $3.3 billion for just 100,000 barrels," he said. "Doesn't that tell you something?"

18   Of course the economists can be just as dismissive of the peakists. "I've gone from disagreeing with them to debunking them," scoffed the energy consultant Michael C. Lynch. "I believe the world will expand the reserve base. If you put a road in the middle of the jungle, that can wind up expanding the resource base."

19   "By most estimates," he added, "total global resources is eight trillion barrels of oil. They are saying only a small percentage of that is recoverable, and you can't do anything about it. We are saying the amount that is recoverable expands over time."

20   I wish I had the confidence to make my own forecast, but in this case, I don't. What I do know—what we all know—is that oil is a finite resource. Surely, the peakists are right about that. What I also know is historically, the economists have generally been right about how the price of oil has wound up fixing the problem.

21   As Gary N. Ross, the chief executive of the PIRA Energy Group, puts it: "Price is the only thing that matters. The new threshold of price will do its magic on the supply-and-demand side."

22   After all, it always has before. And it will again. Until it doesn't.

Writing About the Reading
CHECKING YOUR VOCABULARY

1. For each of the words listed below, use context; prefixes, roots, and suffixes (see Chapter 3); and/or a dictionary to write a brief definition or synonym of the word as it is used in the reading.

    a. vehemence (para. 4) _____

    b. proponent (para. 4) _____

    c. divergence (para. 6) _____

    d. encapsulates (para. 12) _____

    e. temper (para. 14) _____

    f. derisively (para. 16) _____

    g. dismissive (para. 18) _____

    h. debunking (para. 18) _____

2. Underline new, specialized terms introduced in the reading (see Chapter 3).
3. Draw a word map of one of the words in the reading.

CHECKING YOUR COMPREHENSION

1. Who is T. Boone Pickens and what does he have to say about oil supplies? Why are his thoughts included in the reading?
2. What effect did Hurricane Katrina have on oil supplies and prices?
3. What is Daniel Yergin's view of the oil supply situation?
4. What are the three reasons why experts cannot agree on the future of oil supplies?
5. Explain what both sides of the debate agree upon.
6. Where do economists and geologists fit into the debate on oil supplies?
7. How can oil supplies be extended to meet increasing demand?

THINKING CRITICALLY

1. What is the author's purpose in writing this essay?
2. What are the two basic positions the author presents?
3. Describe the data and evidence presented by the author. How does this support these positions?
4. Which side do you think the author agrees with? Justify your answer.
5. Does the author convince you of any opinion about the future of oil? Why or why not?

LEARNING/STUDY STRATEGY

Annotate the reading by underlining statistics that support the main ideas. Describe how these statistics are relevant.

Thinking About the Paired Readings
INTEGRATING IDEAS

1. Do the authors have the same purpose in writing these articles? Explain your answer.
2. Compare the tones of the two readings.
3. Which reading presents more opinion? How do these opinions contribute to the arguments?
4. Which contains more convincing data? Explain your answer.
5. Where would you go to find more information about the facts presented in these articles?

GENERATING NEW IDEAS

1. Write a letter to your congressional representative urging action on the potential oil shortage.
2. Write an essay that proposes at least one solution to the potential oil shortage.

ADDITIONAL PRACTICE

MULTIMEDIA ACTIVITIES

1. **"Fact or Opinion" Quizzes**

   http://cuip.uchicago.edu/www4teach/97/jlyman/default/quiz/factopquiz.html
   http://dhp.com/~laflemm/RfT/Tut2.htm

   Try these online quizzes. Pay attention to what you hear during the day and try to keep track of the facts and opinions. When do you hear more of one than the other?

2. **Universal Intellectual Standards**

   http://www.criticalthinking.org/about/nationalCouncil.shtml#Universal

   Carefully read the standards on this Web site from the Foundation for Critical Thinking. Then find an article from a newspaper or magazine about a national issue. Write down specific questions you have about that issue based on these standards.

MYREADINGLAB

If your instructor has asked you to use Reading Road Trip, be sure to visit the "The Great Lakes Region," "American Southwest," and "The Getty Museum" modules for multimedia tutorials, exercises, and tests on inference, critical thinking, purpose, and tone.

Evaluating the Author's Techniques

✦To identify connotative
  language

✦To understand
  figurative language

✦To recognize bias

✦To discover missing
  information

✦To evaluate
  generalizations

✦To identify assumptions

✦To recognize
  manipulative language

Think About It!

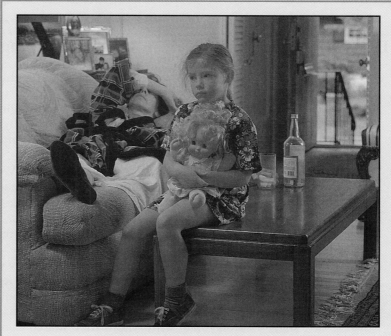

This photograph appears in a health textbook, *Health the Basics*, in a chapter on substance abuse. What point does this photograph make? Although words are not used, the message conveyed by this photograph is clear. How did the photographer accomplish this?

When reading an article or essay, you should ask a similar question: How did the writer achieve his or her results? In other words, ask what techniques (methods) the writer used to communicate the message. How did the writer make you feel sympathetic to her cause? How did the writer make you want to take a particular action? How did the writer change your opinion on an issue? Understanding a writer's techniques will help you think critically about the author's message and form reasonable judgments about the author and his or her message.

In this chapter we will examine the various techniques that writers use to express their ideas and manipulate their readers. We will study connotative and figurative language and examine how writers reveal bias, mislead through omission, and make generalizations and assumptions. We will also examine how writers use language to manipulate ideas using clichés, jargon, allusions, euphemisms, double-speak, and hyperbole. Each topic will be addressed in the form of a question to guide your critical analysis.

■ Does the Writer Use Connotative Language?

If you were wearing a jacket that looked like leather but was made out of man-made fibers, would you prefer it be called *fake* or *synthetic?* Would you rather be part of a *crowd* or a *mob?* Would you rather be called *thin* or *skinny?*

Each of the pairs of words above has basically the same meaning. A *crowd* and a *mob* are both groups of people. Both *fake* and *synthetic* refer to something manmade. If the words have similar meanings, why did you choose *crowd* rather than *mob* and *synthetic* rather than *fake?* While the pairs of words have similar primary meanings, they carry different shades of meaning; each creates a different image or association in your mind. This section explores these shades of meaning, called connotative meanings.

All words have one or more standard meanings. These meanings are called **denotative meanings.** Think of them as those meanings listed in the dictionary. They tell us what the word names. Many words also have connotative meanings. **Connotative meanings** include the feelings and associations that may accompany a word. For example, the denotative meaning of *sister* is a female sibling. However, the word carries many connotations. For some, *sister* suggests a playmate with whom they shared their childhood. For others the term may suggest an older sibling who watched over them. Let us take another example, the word *dinner*. Its denotative meaning is "an evening meal," but its connotative meaning to many suggests a relaxed time to share food and conversation with family or friends.

Connotations can vary from individual to individual. The denotative meaning for the word *flag* is a piece of cloth used as a national emblem. To many, the American flag is a symbol of patriotism and love of one's country. To some people, though, it may mean an interesting decoration to place on their clothing. The word *dog* to dog lovers suggests a loyal and loving companion. To those who are allergic to dogs, however, the word *dog* connotes discomfort and avoidance—itchy eyes, a runny nose, and so forth.

Writers and speakers use connotative meanings to stir your emotions or to bring to mind positive or negative associations. Suppose a writer is describing how someone drinks. The writer could choose words such as *gulp, sip, slurp,* or *guzzle.* Each creates a different image of the person. Connotative meanings, then, are powerful tools of language. When you read, be alert for meanings suggested by the author's word choice. When writing or speaking, be sure to choose words with appropriate connotations.

EXERCISE 5-1

For each of the following pairs of words, underline the word with the more positive connotation.

1.	dimple	dent
2.	bold	sassy
3.	cheap	frugal
4.	displease	repel
5.	tipsy	drunk
6.	ache	agony
7.	untidy	grubby
8.	haughty	proud
9.	deckhand	sailor
10.	job	chore

EXERCISE 5-2

For each word listed, write a word that has a similar denotative meaning but a negative connotation. Then write a word that has a positive or neutral connotation.

WORD	NEGATIVE CONNOTATION	POSITIVE or NEUTRAL CONNOTATION
Example: costly	extravagant	expensive
1. leisurely	_____	_____
2. small	_____	_____
3. take	_____	_____
4. talk	_____	_____
5. satirize	_____	_____
6. farmer	_____	_____
7. choosy	_____	_____
8. delay	_____	_____
9. desire	_____	_____
10. famous	_____	_____

EXERCISE 5-3   *Discuss the differences in connotative meaning of each of the following sets of words. Consult a dictionary, if necessary.*

1. painful: hurtful—sore—excruciating
2. aware: familiar—alert—privy
3. room: chamber—study—cubicle
4. someone who travels: globe-trotter—tourist—pilgrim
5. understanding: mastery—insight—comprehension
6. harmony: agreement—conformity—order
7. education: literacy—schooling—learned
8. proper: correct—appropriate—demure
9. seclusion: isolation—privacy—withdrawal
10. lovable: adorable—attractive—winning

■ Does the Writer Use Figurative Language?

Figurative language makes a comparison between two unlike things that share one common characteristic. If you say that your apartment looked as if it had been struck by a tornado, you are comparing two unlike things—your apartment and the effects of a tornado. Figurative language makes sense creatively or imaginatively, but not literally. You mean that the apartment is messy and disheveled. Figurative language is a powerful tool that allows writers to create images or paint pictures in the reader's mind. We all know the devastation caused by a tornado and have a visual picture of it. Figurative language also allows writers to suggest an idea without directly stating it. If you say the councilman bellowed like a bear, you are suggesting that the councilman was animal-like, loud, and forceful, but you have not said so directly. By planting the image of bear-like behavior, you have communicated your message to your reader.

There are three primary types of figurative language—similes, metaphors, and personification. A **simile** uses the words *like* or *as* to make the comparison:

The computer hums like a beehive.

After 5:00 P.M. our downtown is as quiet as a ghost town.

A **metaphor** states or implies the relationship between the two unlike items. Metaphors often use the word *is*.

The computer lab is a beehive.

After 5:00 P.M. our downtown is a ghost town.

Personification compares humans and nonhumans according to one characteristic, attributing human characteristics to ideas or objects. If you say "the wind screamed its angry message," you are giving the wind the humanlike characteristics of screaming, being angry, and communicating a message. Here are two more examples:

The sun mocked us with its relentless stare.

After two days of writer's block, her pen started dancing across the page.

Because figurative language is a powerful tool, be sure to analyze the author's motive for using it. Often, a writer uses figurative language as a way of describing rather than telling. A writer could say "The woman blushed" (telling) or "The woman's cheeks filled with the glow of a fire" (describing). Other times, however, figurative language is a means of suggesting ideas or creating impressions without directly stating them. When evaluating figurative language, ask the following questions:

- **Why did the writer make the comparison?**
- **What is the basis of the comparison, that is, the shared characteristic?**
- **Is the comparison accurate?**
- **What images do you have in your mind? How do these images make you feel?**
- **Is the comparison positive or negative?**
- **Are several different interpretations possible?**

EXERCISE 5-4   *Explain the comparison in each of the following examples of figurative language.*

1. The view from the summit was like a painting.
2. Her memory was a blank tablet.
3. The library renovation project was an uncontrollable beast.
4. During the morning commute, the lanes of cars were snarled like a nest of snakes.
5. As the tide rolled in, the waves roared at her to escape quickly.

EXERCISE 5-5   *Discuss how the writer of each of the following passages uses figurative language to create a specific impression.*

1.   As a vacation port of call, Southern California has got it all. It's like a giant geographic theme park. Want to lap up glistening waves and bury your feet in the sand? The beach beckons. How about thick forests with fir- and pine-covered mountains? The majestic Angeles National Forest is a quick drive from Los Angeles. I prefer to use Dante's "Inferno" as my Baedeker [a guidebook for travelers]. Every summer, whenever I get the itch for a little rest and relaxation, I venture deep into the inner circle of hell—otherwise known as Palm Springs.

       —Mark Weingarten, from "Palm Springs in August: The Ducks Use Sunblock,"
The New York Times, August 9, 2002. Copyright © 2002 by
The New York Times Co. Reprinted with permission.

2.   Thick as a truck at its base, the Brazil-nut tree rises 10 stories to an opulent crown, lord of the Amazon jungle. It takes the tree a century to grow to maturity; it takes a man with a chain saw an hour to cut it down. "It's a beautiful thing," nods Acelino Cardoso da Silva, a 57-year-old farmer. "But I have six hungry people at home. If the lumberman turns up, I'll sell."

       —Margolis, "A Plot of Their Own," *Newsweek*

3.   If parenting is like an endurance race, senior year should be the section where parents triumphantly glide toward the finish line with a smiling graduate-to-be alongside. Instead, it's often more like heartbreak hill at the 20-mile mark of the Boston marathon, the bump that leaves parents exhausted and wondering what they were thinking 17 years ago.

       —Dunnewind, "Launching Kids to Independence," *Seattle Times*

| EXERCISE 5-6 | *Convert each of the following statements to an expression of figurative language.* |

Example: I am nervous. I feel as if I have a thousand butterflies fluttering in my stomach.

1. He was hungry. _____

2. The clouds were beautiful. _____

3. Everyone argued. _____

4. The test was hard. _____

5. My friend laughed. _____

■ Is the Author Fair or Biased?

Think of a television commercial you have seen recently, perhaps for a particular model of car. The ad tells you the car's advantages—why you want to buy it—but does it tell you its disadvantages? Does it describe ways in which the model compares unfavorably with competitors? Certainly not. Do you feel the ad writer is being unfair? Now let us say you know nothing about e-book readers and want to learn about them. You find an article titled, "What you need to know about e-book readers." If the author of this article told you all the advantages of e-book readers, but none of its disadvantages, would you consider the article unfair? We expect advertisers to present a one-sided view of their products. We expect other forms of writing, however, to be honest and forthright. If a writer is explaining instant messaging, he or she should explain it fully, revealing both strengths and weaknesses. To do otherwise is to present a biased point of view. You can think of bias as a writer's prejudice. If an author is biased, then, he or she is partial to one point of view or one side of a controversial issue. The author's language and selection of facts provide clues about his or her bias.

In the following excerpt from a biology text, the author's choice of words (see underlining) and sarcastic comment in parentheses reveal his attitude toward seal hunters.

Greenpeace is an organization dedicated to the preservation of the sea and its great mammals, notably whales, dolphins, and seals. Its ethic is <u>nonviolent</u> but its <u>aggressiveness</u> in protecting our oceans and the life in them is becoming legendary.

Greenpeace volunteers routinely place their lives in <u>danger</u> in many ways, such as by riding along the backs of whales in inflatable zodiacs, keeping themselves between the animal and the harpoons of ships giving <u>chase</u>. They have pulled alongside Dutch ships to stop the <u>dumping</u> of <u>dangerous toxins</u> into the sea. They have placed their zodiacs directly in the paths of ships <u>disrupting delicate</u> breeding grounds of the sea with soundings and have forced some to turn away or even abandon their efforts. They have confronted hostile sealers on northern ice floes to try to stop them from <u>bludgeoning</u> the baby seals in the birthing grounds, skinning them on the spot, and leaving the mother sniffing at the <u>glistening red corpse</u> of her baby as its skin is <u>stacked</u>

aboard the ship on the way to warm the <u>backs of very fashionable people</u> who gather where the bartender knows their favorite drink. (The mother seal would be <u>proud</u> to know that her dead baby had nearly impressed some bartender.) They have petitioned the International Whaling Commission to establish rules and enact bans.

—Wallace, *Biology: The World of Life*, p. 754

To detect bias, ask the following questions:

- Is the author acting as a reporter—presenting facts—or as salesperson—providing only favorable information?
- Does the author feel strongly about or favor one side of the issue?
- Does the author use connotative or figurative language to create a positive or negative image?
- Does the author seem emotional about the issue?
- Are there other views toward the subject that the writer does not recognize or discuss?

EXERCISE 5-7   *Read each of the following statements, and place a checkmark in front of each that reveals bias.*

_____   1. Cities should be designed for the pedestrian, not the automobile.

_____   2. There are more channels than ever before on cable television.

_____   3. The current system of voter registration is a sham.

_____   4. Professional sports have become elitist.

_____   5. Space exploration costs millions of dollars each year.

EXERCISE 5-8   *Describe the author's bias in each of the following statements.*

1.   The greatest immediate danger to the future of our firearm rights is the media hype typified in a *Washington Times* headline, "Gun Control Drops Off the Screen." Don't for one second buy into it. The goal of the anti-gun-rights crowd this election year is power—total control of the national legislature, and they will try to get it by lulling gun owners into thinking the threat has passed. They want gun owners to stay home election day.

—LaPierre, "Standing Guard," *American Rifleman*

2.   I have expressed in the past that police officers should refrain from enforcing immigration laws so that police departments can maintain good relations with Hispanics. If Latinos fear that police will report them or their family members to the immigration service, they might fear coming forward to help solve crimes.

—Salinas, "Will All Hispanic Men Be Suspect?" *Seattle Post-Intelligencer*

3.   Parents trust their children less and less these days. Convinced beyond a doubt that violent video games will turn their sons and daughters into criminals, parents go to the extreme by banning all forms of electronic entertainment from their homes. Instead of seizing the opportunity to teach a child about limits, self-

regulation, and good taste, moms and dads all over America are unwittingly increasing the desire for taboo entertainment. Today's kids are not being allowed to experiment and test themselves while under their parents' supervision. This parental disservice can only lead to a backlash in the future when young men and women experiment with risky behaviors as soon as they leave their parents' tight hold.

4.   Those clamoring to shut down the farmers, however, should look hard at the prospect of a prairie full of subdivisions and suburban pollution: car exhaust, lawn and garden fertilizers, wood stoves, sewage. Certainly, the smoke from field burning is an annoyance, particularly to the hard-hit Sandpoint area, and to some it's a health hazard. But the benefits the sturdy farmers produce 50 weeks of the year shouldn't be dismissed casually.

—Oliveria, "Burning Will Go; That's Not All Good," *Spokesman Review*

5.   Money doesn't grow on trees, but some trees might as well be pure gold. The world's voracious (and growing) appetite for wood, paper, and other forest products is driving a stampede to mow down forests. Much of this logging is illegal.

—Haugen, "Logging Illogic," *World Watch*

■ What Isn't the Author Telling Me?

Writers mislead by omission. Writers may omit essential details, ignore contradictory evidence, or selectively include only details that favor their position. They may also make incomplete comparisons, use the passive voice, or use unspecified nouns and pronouns.

Suppose, in describing homeschooling, an author states "Many children find homeschooling rewarding." But what is the author not telling us? If the author does not tell us that some children find homeschooling lonely and feel isolated from their peers, the author is not presenting a fair description of homeschooling. The writer has deliberately omitted essential details that a reader needs to understand homeschooling.

Suppose the same writer describes a research study that concludes that homeschooled children excel academically. The writer, to be fair, should also report that other studies have demonstrated that homeschooled children do not differ in academic achievement from traditionally educated students. In this case the writer has ignored contradictory evidence, reporting only evidence that he or she wants the reader to know.

In describing a homeschool environment, suppose the writer reports that "the home environment is ideal" and goes on to describe features such as comfortable home surroundings, flexible scheduling, and supportive parental mentoring. To be fair, the writer should also point out what the home environment lacks. A home environment may lack a library of instructional software, collaborative learning activities with classmates, or the services of learning support specialists. The writer, then, selectively reported details, telling us what was positive and omitting negative details.

Suppose the writer concludes his or her article on homeschooling by saying, "Homeschooling is the better route to follow to produce a well educated child."

What the writer has not told us is what route homeschooling is better than. Is it better than a private school? Is it better than a public school? Is it better than hiring a private tutor? The writer has made an incomplete comparison.

One way writers avoid revealing information is to use a particular sentence structure that does not identify who performed a specified action. In the sentence *The cup broke* you do not know who broke the cup. In the sentence *The bill was paid* you do not know who paid the bill. This sentence pattern is called the passive voice. Here are a few more examples of the passive voice. In each, notice what information is missing.

The tax reform bill was defeated.

The accounting procedures were found to be questionable.

The oil spill was contained.

Another way writers avoid revealing information is to use nouns and pronouns that do not refer to a specific person or thing. The sentence *They said it would rain by noon* does not reveal who predicted rain. The sentence *It always happens to me* does not indicate what always happens to the writer. Here are a few more examples:

They say the enemy is preparing to attack.

Anyone can get rich with this plan; many people have already.

Politicians don't care about people.

To be sure you are getting full and complete information, ask the following questions:

- **What important information is omitted? (What have you not told me?)**
- **What contradictory evidence is not reported?**
- **Has the author selectively reported details to further his or her cause?**
- **Does the author explain incomplete comparisons?**
- **What else do I need to know?**

To answer these questions, it may be necessary to do additional reading or research, either on the Internet or in your college library. Try to locate another article on the same topic and notice what additional information is included.

EXERCISE 5-9   *For each of the following statements, indicate what information is missing.*

1. Our neighborhood was ruined by the water treatment plant.
2. They raised test scores in that state.
3. People were hurt by welfare reform.
4. Some animal testing has been banned in other countries.
5. Athletes are overpaid.
6. They say the Columbia River has too many dams.
7. Anyone can get on the Internet.
8. They filed charges.
9. Orchestras in many cities have gone out of business.
10. The check was probably forged.

■ Does the Author Make and Support Generalizations?

Suppose you are reading an article that states that "Musicians are temperamental people." Do you think that every musician who ever wrote or performed a song or played a musical instrument is temperamental? Can you think of exceptions? This statement is an example of a generalization. A **generalization** is a reasoned statement about an entire group (musicians) based on known information about part of the group (musicians the writer has met or observed). A generalization requires a leap from what is known to a conclusion about what is unknown. Generalizations may be expressed using words such as *all, always, none,* or *never.* Some statements may imply but not directly state that the writer is referring to the entire group or class. The statement "Musicians are temperamental people" suggests but does not directly state that all musicians are temperamental. Here are a few more generalizations:

Rich people are snobs.

Chinese food is never filling.

Pets are always troublesome.

The key to evaluating generalizations is to evaluate the type, quality, and amount of evidence given to support them. Here are a few more generalizations. What type of evidence would you need to convince you that each is or is not true?

College students are undecided about future career goals.

Fast food lacks nutritional value.

Foreign cars outperform similar American models.

For the generalization about college students, you might need to see research studies about college students' career goals, for example. And, then, even if studies did conclude that many college students are undecided, it would not be fair to conclude that every single student is undecided. If no evidence is given, then the generalization is not trustworthy and should be questioned.

You can also evaluate a generalization by seeing whether the author provides specifics about the generalization. For the statement "Pets are always troublesome," ask what kind of pets the author is referring to—a pet potbellied pig, an iguana, or a cat? Then ask what is meant by troublesome—does it mean the animal is time consuming, requires special care, or behaves poorly?

Another way to evaluate a generalization is to try to think of exceptions. For the generalization *Medical doctors are aloof and inaccessible,* can you think of a doctor you have met or heard about who was caring and available to his or her patients? If so, the generalization is not accurate in all cases.

EXERCISE 5-10   *Read each of the following statements and place a checkmark before each generalization.*

_____ 1. The Internet is changing America.

_____ 2. Influenza causes severe epidemics every two years.

_____ 3. Most drug cases start with busts of small, local dealers and move to a search of their suppliers.

_____ 4. Attending college is essential for economic success and advancement.

_____ 5. Colds are caused by viruses, not bacteria, not cold weather, and not improper diet.

EXERCISE 5-11   *Read each of the following paragraphs and underline each generalization.*

1. Child care workers are undereducated in relation to the importance of their jobs. A whole generation of children is being left day after day in the hands of women with little more than high-school-level education. These children will suffer in the future for our inattention to the child care employment pool.
2. Americans have had enough of libraries providing Internet pornography to children. They want filtering on all computers or computers out of libraries. When will librarians listen to their customers (who also pay their salaries)?
3. For the past few years, drivers have been getting worse. Especially guilty of poor driving are the oldest and youngest drivers. There should be stricter tests and more classes for new drivers and yearly eye exams and road tests for drivers once they hit age 60. This is the only way to ensure the safety of our roads.

EXERCISE 5-12   *For each of the following generalizations, indicate what questions you would ask and what types of information you would need to evaluate the generalization.*

1. Vegetarians are pacifists and they do not own guns.
2. Most crimes are committed by high school dropouts.
3. It always rains in Seattle.
4. Private school students get a better education than public school students.
5. Scientists don't believe in any kind of higher power.

■ What Assumptions Is the Author Making?

Suppose a friend asked you, "Have you stopped cheating on your girlfriend?" This person, perhaps not a friend after all, is making an assumption. He or she is assuming that you already have been cheating. An **assumption** is an idea or principle the writer accepts as true and makes no effort to prove or substantiate. Usually, it is a beginning or premise on which he or she bases the remainder of the statement. Assumptions often use words such as *since, if,* or *when.* Here are a few more examples:

- You're going to make that mistake again, are you? (The assumption is that you have already made the mistake at least once.)

- When you're mature, you'll realize you made a mistake. (The assumption is that you are not mature now.)
- You are as arrogant as your sister. (The assumption is that your sister is arrogant.)
- My dog is angry. (The assumption is that dogs have and can express emotions.)

Each of the statements above makes no attempt to prove or support the hidden assumption; it is assumed to be true.

Writers often make assumptions and make no effort to prove or support them. For example, an author may assume that television encourages violent behavior in children and proceed to argue for restrictions on TV viewing. Or a writer may assume that abortion is morally wrong and suggest legal restrictions on how and when abortions are performed. If a writer's assumption is wrong or unsubstantiated, then the statements that follow from the assumption should be questioned. If television does not encourage violent behavior, for example, then the suggestion to restrict viewing should not be accepted unless other reasons are offered.

EXERCISE 5-13   *Read each of the following statements and then place a checkmark before those choices that are assumptions made by the writer of the statement.*

1. Cosmetics should not be tested on animals, since they may cause pain, injury, or even death.

    _____ a. Animals have the right to avoid pain and suffering.

    _____ b. Cosmetics should be tested on people.

    _____ c. Animals should be anesthetized before research is conducted.

2. Teacher's aides lack advanced college degrees: therefore, they are unable to teach children effectively.

    _____ a. Teacher's aides should obtain advanced degrees.

    _____ b. Advanced college degrees are needed in order to teach effectively.

    _____ c. Teachers who hold advanced degrees are not necessarily effective teachers.

3. Border states in the United States must take action to curb illegal immigration; otherwise, state funds will be quickly exhausted.

    _____ a. The writer opposes using state funds to help illegal immigrants.

    _____ b. Illegal immigrants must enter the United States legally to receive state aid.

    _____ c. State funding guidelines should be revised.

EXERCISE 5-14   *For each statement listed below, identify at least one assumption.*

1. Grocery stores should reduce the number of weekly sale items and lower overall prices.
2. Eliminating essay exams from psychology courses would diminish students' writing abilities.
3. More public transit should be added to our cities to reduce traffic and pollution.
4. Endangered species should be bred in captivity to ensure their survival.
5. Artists do not need grants from the government because they sell their works for such high prices.
6. Hunters serve their communities by keeping down the deer population.
7. Lobbyists hinder the work of our elected officials; these groups should be banned from Washington, DC.
8. Doing away with unions would increase productivity in our country.
9. Learning a foreign language is a waste of time; Americans can get by anywhere.
10. Violence in sports affects everyone. Such brutality corrupts play, a form of free expression.

EXERCISE 5-15   *Identify the assumption(s) in each of the following passages.*

1. Most kids, of course, listen barely if at all to what adults say. Instead they watch what adults do. And, for better or worse, there may be no lesson we impart to them so efficiently as how we adults react to events that upset us, from a fender-bender to a threatening new era of conflict.

    —Editorial, "Raising the Sept. 11 Generation," *Chicago Tribune*

2. Speaking from developments in my own family, there are way too many young students out there whose focus centers on partying, dress competition, music, souped-up cars and sex. Goal-setting and accomplishment in their studies as they prepare themselves for what is a highly competitive world do not figure too prominently in their day-to-day lives.

    —Editorial, "School's First Week Provides a Few Bright Exceptions," *Toronto Star*

3. Most products—from cigarette lighters to medicine bottles—have to be designed to protect against foreseeable misuse. But there is no regulator to help the plaintiffs: guns and tobacco are the only products that the Consumer Product Safety Commission does not oversee. And even though lawsuits have often helped push up safety standards elsewhere, there are plenty of conservative judges who do not think it is the courts' job to create gun laws.

    —Editorial, "From the hip; Gun control," *The Economist* (U.S.)

4. In the meantime, a disturbing message is being sent to the guys and girls in the little leagues. Practice hard, work out, eat nutritiously—and sneak illegal steroids because, after all, winning and setting records are everything. And besides, if you make it big, you'll have enough money to care for your broken body.

    —Editorial, "Steroids Should Be Tagged Out," *San Jose Mercury News*

> 5.   Britain on Wednesday marked the 150th anniversary of its public toilets. This reminds us of the barbaric lack of such facilities in the United States. Along with an increasingly chaotic and unfair health system, sparse public transportation and a paucity of neighborhood parks, the absence of public loos here evokes America's depressing distance from the perfect place that pathological patriots assert that it is.
> —Editorial, "Sign of Civilization," *Providence Journal*

■ Does the Author Use Manipulative Language?

Writers can shape their readers' thinking and response to their message by the language they choose to express it. Writers use a variety of language manipulation techniques to achieve a particular effect, to communicate their message in a particular way, and to appeal to specific groups of people. These techniques include clichés, jargon, allusions, euphemisms, doublespeak, and hyperbole.

Clichés

A **cliché** is a tired, overused expression. Here are a few examples:

Curiosity killed the cat.

Bigger is better.

Absence makes the heart grow fonder.

He is as blind as a bat.

These everyday expressions have been overused; they are so commonly used that they no longer carry a specific meaning. They have become pat expressions, used by writers without much thought or creativity. Because the expressions are so common, many readers tend to accept them at face value rather than to evaluate their meaning and appropriateness. When you recognize a cliché, ask yourself the following questions:

- Why did the writer use the cliché?
- Why did the writer not use a fresh expression instead?

Numerous clichés used throughout a piece of writing may suggest that the writer has not thought in depth about the topic or has not made the effort to express his or her ideas in an interesting and unique way.

- **Is the writer trying to gloss over or skip over details by using a cliché?** Clichés often oversimplify a situation that is complex. In trying to decide which courses to register for, a student may say, "Don't put off till tomorrow what you can do today." Actually the student *could* register today, but it may be better to wait until he or she has had time to think, do research, and talk to others about course selection.
- **Is the writer trying to avoid directly stating an unpopular or unpleasant idea?** Suppose you are reading an article on controlling world terrorism. After describing recent acts of terrorism, the writer concludes the article with the cliché, "What will be, will be." What does this cliché really say? The expression is a common one and is commonly

accepted. However, in this context, the cliché suggests (but does not directly state) that nothing can be done about terrorism, an unpopular viewpoint that would receive criticism if directly expressed.

- **Is the cliché fitting and appropriate?** Suppose in writing an article on college financial aid, the writer admonishes students not to spend their financial aid loan before they receive it, by saying, "Don't count your chickens before they are hatched." The writer's audience would be better served if the writer, instead, had offered more detail, explaining that loan checks are often delayed, and that spending money before it is received may cause serious financial problems.
- **What does the use of clichés reveal about the author?** Use of clichés may signal that a writer is not fully aware of his or her audience or interested in accommodating them. A writer who packs an article full of clichés is not aware that his or her readers prefer fresh, descriptive information, rather than standard clichés.

EXERCISE 5-16

For each of the following clichés, explain its meaning and then think of a situation in which it would be untrue or inappropriate.

Example:

Cliché: Don't change horses in midstream.

Meaning: You should not try to change something once you have begun.

Situation: If you realize you have made a poor decision and there is a way to correct it, you should correct it. For example, if you realize you are registered for the wrong level math course, try to drop the course or change to the appropriate level course.

1. Better late than never.
2. Opportunity doesn't knock twice.
3. Good fences make good neighbors.
4. Money makes the world go round.
5. If you don't have anything nice to say, don't say anything at all.

EXERCISE 5-17

Replace each of the following clichés with more specific information that fits the context.

Example: The university president did not want to "toot his own horn," but he enumerated all his accomplishments of the past year.

Replacement: The university president didn't want to brag . . .

1. My older sister turned 40 this year. She is over the hill.
2. The mayor and the governor are like two peas in a pod.
3. Not sure of his itinerary, the salesman decided to play it by ear.
4. The students made sure to read the fine print on their new lease.
5. Our new senator rubs me the wrong way.

Jargon

Jargon refers to words, phrases, and specialized terms used by a particular academic field or special interest group that is not readily understood by the general public. Librarians speak jargon when communicating with each other, for example:

> We are considering several different solutions for the aggregation question that will allow our patrons more targeted periodical database searching.

Doctors use specialized language when communicating treatments to other medical professionals, for example:

> During the technique for nursemaid's elbow reduction, put your thumb in the antecubital fossa, then apply longitudinal traction.

Computer users who communicate through e-mail and instant messaging use words and symbols that carry specialized meaning to other users, for example:

> GTG . . . TTYL = got to go . . . talk to you later

Jargon, when read by people who are not a member of the group that uses it, tends to confuse, isolate, or exclude those readers. A writer may use jargon to appear more knowledgeable or even superior to his or her readers. Unknowing, noncritical readers may accept ideas simply because they are defended by jargon, assuming that the writer must be knowledgeable in order to use complex, unfamiliar terminology.

If a writer uses jargon you do not understand, you may not be the writer's intended audience. This may be the case in reading a medical journal such as the *Journal of the American Medical Association*, which is intended for medical doctors who understand the jargon being used. If you are the intended audience, the writer may be purposely trying to manipulate you. Writers may intentionally use jargon to assume a position of authority. As another example, a writer of a general interest article on organ transplants may use obtuse medical terminology to present facts that, if presented in layman's terms, may be unpleasant or objectionable.

EXERCISE 5-18

Underline the jargon in each of the following statements and discuss how appropriate the language is for you. Can you use context to figure out new terms? Would you continue reading the rest of the article? Is the jargon confusing or manipulative?

1.   Place-based education, which draws from local culture, history, and geography to create a meaningful curriculum, can occur in any type of setting, but it holds particular promise for rural homeschooling. Place-based educators use local particulars to teach universal concepts, engage students in community life, and involve people and resources unique to the home community.

     —Jaycox, "Rural Homeschooling and Place-Based Education," *ERIC Digest*

2.   Extinction is actually a normal process in the course of evolution. Throughout geological time, many more species have become extinct than exist today. These species slowly disappeared because of climatic changes and the inability to adapt to such conditions as competition and predation.

     —"Endangered Species," *Funk & Wagnalls New World Encyclopedia*

3.   Russian air-launched weapons manufacturer Bazalt has begun to develop a family of low-cost precision-guided munitions in the wake of its air force's combat experience in Chechnya, and from watching the U.S. shift to precision-guided air-launched ordnance in its recent combat operations. Work is underway on the development of a glide-bomb wing-kit and terminal-guidance seekers intended to provide the Russian air force with a low-cost short-range standoff attack weapon based around its existing iron bomb inventory. The system is called the FAB-500MPK.

—Barrie, "Russia's Bazalt Working On Standoff Bomb Kit,"
Aviation Week & Space Technology

Allusions

Allusions are references to well-known religious, literary, artistic, or historical works or sources. A writer may refer to a biblical verse, a character in a famous poem or novel, a line in a well-known song, or a historical figure such as Napoleon or George Washington. An allusion makes a connection or points to similarities between the writer's subject and the reference. Writers usually assume that educated readers will recognize and understand their allusions. Here are a few examples of allusions:

- A writer describes a person as having the patience of Job. In the Bible, Job is a righteous man whose faith was tested by God.
- An article on parental relationships with children refers to the Oedipus complex. Oedipus was a figure in Greek mythology who unknowingly killed his father and married his mother. He blinded himself when he discovered what he had done. The Oedipus complex is controversial but refers to a child's tendency to seek sexual fulfillment from a parent of the opposite sex.

If you encounter an allusion you do not understand, check it on the Internet using a search engine such as Google (www.google.com) by typing in the key words of the allusion. The following reference sources may also be helpful:

Merriam-Webster's Dictionary of Allusions

Dictionary of Historical Allusions and Eponyms

The Facts on File Encyclopedia of Word and Phrase Origins

Writers may include numerous literary or scholarly allusions to give their writing the appearance of scholarship. Do not be overly impressed by a writer's use of allusions, particularly obscure ones. A writer may use allusions to divert readers' attention from the lack of substantive detail or support. When evaluating a writer's use of allusions, ask the following questions:

- What does the allusion mean?
- Why did the writer include the allusion?
- What does the allusion contribute to the overall meaning of the work?

EXERCISE 5-19

For each of the following statements, explain the meaning of the allusion.

1. The mayor looked around the hurricane-ravaged city and pondered the Herculean task that lay ahead in rebuilding the lives and homes destroyed.
2. Emily's mother hoped her new regimen of yoga and raw foods would be her fountain of youth.
3. "Whoa, Twilight Zone," the two new friends said to each other when they realized how many coincidences linked them.
4. Her grandparents finally came out of the Dark Ages and bought an answering machine and cordless phone.
5. The campaign manager sought to discover and exploit the opponent's Achilles' heel.
6. Many small business people find themselves in a catch-22 when they realize they must compete in a world of e-commerce but cannot afford to create an e-commerce Web site.
7. When she realized her best friend had joined in with others to betray her, she muttered, "Et tu, Brute?"
8. With a grin like the Cheshire Cat, the defendant sat waiting for the jury's verdict.
9. He awoke from a Kafkaesque dream feeling anxious and lonely, frightened of what his day would bring.
10. The little boy likened himself to George Washington as he confessed to breaking the neighbor's window with his baseball.

Euphemisms

What do these sentences have in common?

> He suffered combat fatigue.

> The company is downsizing.

> Capital punishment is controversial.

Each uses an expression called a euphemism. A **euphemism** is a word or phrase that is used in place of a word that is unpleasant, embarrassing, or otherwise objectionable. The expression *combat fatigue* is a pleasant way to refer to the psychological problems of veterans caused by their experiences in war, *downsizing* replaces the word *firing*, and *capital punishment* is a substitute for *death penalty*.

The word *euphemism* comes from the Greek roots *eu-*, meaning "sounding good," and *-pheme*, meaning "speech." Euphemisms have a long history going back to ancient languages and cultures. Ancient people thought of names as an extension of things themselves. To know and say the name of a person or object gave power over the person or thing. Thus, calling certain things by their names was avoided, even forbidden. God, Satan, deceased relatives, and hunted animals would often be referred to indirectly. For example, in one culture God was called The Kindly One; the bear was called The Grandfather. Today, many euphemisms are widely used in both spoken and written language. Here are a few more examples:

The foreign spy was put out of circulation. (the spy was killed)

He was hit by friendly fire. (accidentally shot by a member of his own country)

My brother works as a sanitation engineer. (janitor or garbage collector)

Euphemisms tend to minimize or downplay something's importance or seriousness. They are often used in politics and advertising. They can be used to camouflage actions or events that may be unacceptable to readers or listeners if bluntly explained. For example, the term *casualties of war* may be used instead of the phrase *dead soldiers* to lessen the impact of the attack. To say that a politician's statement was *at variance with the truth* has less impact and is less forceful than to say that the politician lied.

A writer may use a euphemism to alter your perception of a situation by lessening its harshness, ugliness, severity, or seriousness. When a writer uses a euphemism, substitute the everyday meaning of the euphemism and notice whether the writer's message changes.

EXERCISE 5-20   *For each of the underlined euphemisms, write a substitution that does not minimize or avoid the basic meaning of the term.*

Example: The theater had only one <u>ladies' room</u>.

<u>The theater had only one women's bathroom.</u>

1. The councilman has entered a <u>substance abuse</u> program.
2. <u>Body counts</u> started out high, but then were revised to lower numbers.
3. Reporters are not required to reveal their <u>confidential sources</u>.
4. The high school teacher found her senior English students to be <u>unmotivated</u>.
5. A new <u>correctional facility</u> will be built near Deer Run housing development.
6. You may experience <u>precipitation</u> over the holiday weekend.
7. My midwife says I might feel <u>under the weather</u> during the first trimester of my pregnancy.
8. Richard's parents were surprised to see just how <u>cozy</u> his apartment was.
9. Several countries considered a <u>preemptive strike</u> against the uncooperative nation.
10. Everyone wondered how Aurora would make ends meet now that she was <u>between jobs</u>.

Doublespeak

Doublespeak is deliberately unclear or evasive language. Often, it exaggerates or overstates information that could be expressed simply. William Lutz, an expert on doublespeak, defines it as "language that pretends to communicate but does not," in his book *Beyond Nineteen Eighty-Four*. Here is an example: "the letter from the air force colonel in charge of safety said that rocket boosters weighing more than 300,000 pounds 'have an explosive force upon surface impact that is sufficient to exceed the accepted overpressure threshold of physiological damage for the exposed personnel.'" What does the colonel's state-ment mean in simple words? If a 300,000-pound rocket falls on a person, it will kill him or her. The language the colonel used is an example of doublespeak.

Here is a humorous example of the use of doublespeak, attributed to Everett Dirksen, former U.S. senator:

> I am reminded of the man who filled in an application for an insurance policy. One of the questions he had to answer was, "How old was your father when he died and of what did he die?" Well, his father had been hanged, but he did not want to put that on his application. He puzzled it out for a while. He finally wrote, "My father was 65 when he died. He came to his end while participating in a public function when the platform gave way."
>
> —Grazian, "How Much Do Words Really Matter?" *Public Relations Quarterly*

Here are a few more examples, along with their everyday meanings:

detainees—prisoners

downsizing the company—firing employees

vertically deployed antipersonnel devices—bombs

Doublespeak uses euphemisms, but it tangles language in other ways as well that are intended to confuse or overwhelm the listener or reader. Doublespeak also may use technical language (jargon) that is likely to be unfa-miliar to the audience. Doublespeak also may use inflated language—words that tend to make something seem more important or complex than it really is. Doublespeak also may use long, polysyllabic words. It may scramble the order of words in a sentence to create confusion or avoid giving complete informa-tion. For example, writers may use the passive voice to avoid saying who per-formed an action. In the sentence "The bombs were released, injuring many civilians," we do not know who released the bombs.

When reading doublespeak, be suspicious of the writer's motives. Ask your-self:

- Why is the writer being purposefully evasive or unclear?
- What is he or she trying to hide?

EXERCISE 5-21

Untangle each of the following examples of doublespeak and write a translation in simple English.

Example: Most hospitals are reluctant to publicize negative patient care outcomes.

Hospitals are reluctant to publicize patient deaths.

1. Jessamyn's advisor suggested she try a course in human kinetics, figuring that the outcomes from this class would cause an upward development in the calculation of her GPA.
2. The positive economic adjustments at our most-liked eating establish-ment were meant to counter the recent negative contributions to profit.
3. My female sibling went on a caloric reduction program two seasons prior to her nuptials.

4. More than several students have forgone cowhide back-mounted equipment for those of the vegetarian variety.
5. The drug enterprise leader was apprehended following his deployment of an intrusion detection device.
6. Large amounts of previously owned parts were strewn about the public waste reception center.
7. How much time do our education users spend on task or attending to their learning facilitators?
8. My personal manual database indicates I must procure a social expression product for my chronologically gifted neighbor.
9. In the event of a nonroutine operation, follow the relocation drill.
10. Preliminary reports show a negative gain in test scores in the state's public schools.

Hyperbole

Hyperbole is a deliberate, excessive, and obvious exaggeration. If you say, "I could eat a ton of those chocolate chip cookies!" you are obviously exaggerating. Hyperbole is used for special effect, and it is a way of creating emphasis. It also may be a way of suggesting meaning without directly stating it. If, for instance, a writer, in describing a person's appearance, states that *he could pass for a clown in the circus*, the writer is suggesting, but not directly stating, that the person is comical, gaudy, overstated, and out of place. Here are a few more examples:

> An exasperated commuter exclaimed, "You can't get anywhere in this city during rush hour!"

> The European immigrant bricklayers built our city.

To evaluate the use of hyperbole, ask the following questions:

- What was the hyperbole?
- What is suggested but not directly stated?

EXERCISE 5-22   *Explain what each of the following examples of hyperbole suggests but does not directly state.*

1. No one understands Stephen Hawking's books.
2. The Internet holds the answers to all your questions.
3. I have a mountain of homework papers to correct.
4. The major car companies control the transportation habits of all Americans.
5. Snow never stops falling here; winter will never end.

Self-Test Summary

1. What is the connotative meaning of a word?	The connotative meaning of a word includes the feelings and associations that may accompany it, not just its literal meaning (or denotation).
2. What is figurative language?	Writers use figurative language to create vivid images in a reader's mind by comparing two dissimilar things that share a common characteristic.
3. Define three types of figurative language.	• A simile makes a comparison between two unlike things using the words *as* or *like*. • A metaphor states or implies the relationship between two unlike items, usually using the word "is." • Personification compares humans to things by attributing human characteristics to ideas or objects.
4. What is bias?	Bias is a writer's prejudice, a one-sided viewpoint on a topic or issue.
5. How do writers mislead by omission?	Writers mislead by omission by leaving out, ignoring, or selectively choosing details; by making incomplete comparisons; by using the passive voice; or by using unspecified nouns and pronouns.
6. What is a generalization?	A generalization is a statement about an entire group, based on information known about only part of that group. It is a leap from what is known to a conclusion about what is not known.
7. What is an assumption?	An assumption is an idea or principle a writer accepts as true but makes no effort to prove or substantiate.
8. Why do authors use manipulative language?	Authors use manipulative language to achieve a particular effect, to communicate their message in a particular way, or to appeal to specific groups.
9. Define six commonly used kinds of manipulative language.	• Clichés are tired, overused expressions. • Jargon is the specialized or technical language of a particular field, profession, or group. • Allusions are indirect references to well-known religious, literary, artistic, or historical works or sources. • Euphemisms are words or phrases used in place of ones that are considered unpleasant or objectionable. • Doublespeak is the deliberate use of unclear or evasive language. • Hyperbole is deliberate, excessive, and obvious exaggeration used for emphasis or effect.

POLITICAL SCIENCE

Be Very Afraid!
Sara Ahmed

Prereading Questions

1. What fears are widespread in our nation today?
2. How concerned are you about terrorism?

1   I ARRIVE in New York, clutching my British passport. I hand it over. He looks at me, and then looks at my passport. I know what questions will follow.

2   "Where are you from?" My passport indicates my place of birth. "Britain," I say. I feel like adding, "Can't you read I was born in Salford?" But I stop myself. He looks down at my passport, not at me.

3   "Where is your father from?" It was the same last time. The question seems to locate what is suspect not in my body, but that which has been passed down the family line, almost like a bad inheritance. "Pakistan," I say, slowly.

4   "Do you have a Pakistani passport?" "No," I say.

5   "Do you have any other passports?" "Yes," I say, "an Australian one."

6   "Where is it?" I left it behind. Eventually, he lets me through.

7   The name "Ahmed," a Muslim name, slows me down. It blocks my passage, even if only temporarily. When I fly out of New York later that week, I am held up again. This time it is a friendlier encounter. I find out I am now on the "no-fly list," and they have to ring to get permission to let me through. It takes time, of course. "Don't worry," he says, "my mother is on it too." I feel some strange comradeship with his mother. I know what he is saying: he means "anyone" could be on this list, almost as if to say "even my mother," whose innocence of course would be beyond doubt. I know it's a way of saying "It's not about you. Don't take it personally." It isn't about me, of course. But my name names me, after all. It might not be personal, but that does not make it about just "anyone."

The Impact of Fear

8   Fear is considered a largely negative emotion that anticipates a future threat. Yet fear can have very "present" consequences. Fear may prepare your body for flight. Or it might stop you in your tracks. Fear also binds. It can be crucial to how groups "stick together." Fear can make people consent to what they might otherwise resist. The events of 9/11 remind us how a traumatic memory can become a political weapon. It induces mind-numbing terror over a potential repeat. Frightened people cling together, "adhering" to the nation and its rulers. Adherence in this sense means both to "stick to" and to give one's allegiance. If fear acts as a glue, we need to ask—why do some people "get stuck" while others don't?

9   In my encounter at the borders of New York City, my Muslim name was enough to hold me up. Despite the "right" kind of passports, such names are treated with suspicion. A

Muslim name means a suspect genealogy; you are marked as a threat. And their suspicion becomes your fright. Each time you cross a border, you get stuck, held up. Measures that treat you as a security threat are measures that in turn threaten your security. Simply put, being feared creates fear. Frantz Fanon brilliantly describes this dynamic in his classic book *Black Skin, White Masks.* Fanon sees the "Black man" as the object of collective fears. To be such an object is to become afraid oneself, afraid of what that collective fear will do: "hate stares," name-calling or other forms of verbal abuse, physical harassment, violence, or even murder. Fear circulates and accumulates. It sticks to particular bodies—slowing them down, blocking them, containing them.

Freedom and War

10   When George Bush articulates the imperative "We must wage war on terror," he evokes our fear to suit his purpose. In his 2001 address to a joint session of the U.S. Congress, he suggested "freedom and fear are at war." He has repeated this phrase many times, most recently during his victory speech after the 2004 elections. "We," of course, are on the side of freedom in such a war. There is an irony here for anyone who cares to look. Bush's "national security" involves the restriction of the most basic civil liberties. Not new restrictions, for sure, but 9/11 has allowed such restrictions to be extended and redescribed as a matter of life and death. Such political rhetoric would have it that, to be free, we must give freedom up. The "trusted" state becomes the agent to defend us against others, those threatening our freedom with their fear.

11   But what kind of freedom is Bush evoking? Primarily he uses a negative model of freedom: freedom from fear. Fear is seen as stopping people from expressing their freedom—a kind of blockage or restraint to meaningful human action. But a positive definition of freedom is implied here as well: a freedom to. But freedom to do what? Freedom in this positive sense is of a particular and restricted type: a freedom "to do" some things and exist in some ways, but not in others. Freedom to "go about your daily business," freedom to travel, freedom to consume: these are all freedoms that "support" the mobilities required by global capitalism. Positive freedom in this sense is reduced simply to the "freedom to move."

Suspicion and Prejudice

12   The politics of fear, then, involves the containment of movement. The events of 9/11 are used to justify the detention of "anyone" suspected of being a terrorist. An amendment to Britain's Terrorism Act 2000 says that the secretary of State may issue a certificate if he or she believes that a person's presence is a risk to national security or if he or she suspects a person is an international terrorist. Many other countries have enacted similar provisions. Risk assessment becomes a matter of belief or just prejudice. Suspicion alone is grounds for detention. This extension of the powers of detention does not relate merely to the detention of terrorists. Because "anybody could be a terrorist," we have extended the power of detention so that it can apply to all of us.

13   But this extension does not mean that everyone is affected in the same way. Certain "types" of people have been detained despite very weak links with terrorist networks. Imagined links are based on similar origins or names, on shared places of work or residence. As law professor Muneer Ahmad describes, after 9/11 there was "an unrelenting, multi-valent

assault on the bodies, psyches and rights of Arab, Muslim and South Asian immigrants."[1] Leti Volpp, another legal expert, suggests that the responses to 9/11 facilitated "a new identity category that groups together people who appear 'Middle Eastern, Arab or Muslim.'"[2] The word "terrorism" sticks to such people. Assertions that "this is not a war against Islam" coexist with constant repetition of the phrase "Islamic terrorists," which works to re-stick the words together, despite the official denials.

Fear without End

14   The story of fear involves movement for some and the containment of others. The containment is not always successful. Fear is usually directed toward an object that approaches us. But we become even more afraid when the object passes us by. We can no longer see it. It could be anywhere! Bodies engender even more anxiety if they cannot be held in place. The terrorist "hides in the shadows." It is this fearful invisible terrorist that justifies the expansion of forms of intelligence, surveillance, and detention. The threat of "could-be terrorists" and the "inevitable" impending attack are what establish the politics of security as a permanent feature of the political landscape. The politics of security demand insecurity. The border is policed because it is perpetually "under threat." The terrorists, who are on the edge of our horizon, are almost, but not quite, within sight.

15   This is not to say we have to invent terrorists. Attacks do happen, as we know, and the conditions for the emergence of even more terrorism are all too real. But even if fear politics does not invent terrorism, it is still inventive. It sees only some forms of violence as terrorism. Indeed, it only sees some forms of violence as violence. Violence is what is directed against "us" by terrorists, who could be "anyone," although we already suspect some more than others. We have to watch out for terrorists, to protect "life as we know it." Being on guard is a perpetual task. The economy of fear works to contain the bodies of "could-be terrorists." But such containment can never totally succeed. It must always keep open the grounds for further fear.

—Ahmad, "Be Very Afraid!" *New Internationalist*

---

[1] Muneer Ahmad, "Homeland Insecurities: Racial Violence the Day After September 11," *Social Text 72*, 2002, p. 101.

[2] Leti Volpp, "The Citizen and the Terrorist," *UCLA Law Review 49*(5), 2002, p. 1575.

Writing About the Reading
CHECKING YOUR VOCABULARY

1. For each of the words listed below, use context; prefixes, roots, and suffixes (see Chapter 3); and/or a dictionary to write a brief definition or synonym of the word as it is used in the reading.

    a. comradeship (para. 7) _____

    b. consent (para. 8) _____

    c. induces (para. 8) _____

    d. allegiance (para. 8) _____

e. genealogy (para. 9) _____

f. accumulates (para. 9) _____

g. imperative (para. 10) _____

h. capitalism (para. 11) _____

i. unrelenting (para. 13) _____

j. multi-valent (para. 13) _____

k. assertions (para. 13) _____

l. engender (para. 14) _____

m. perpetual (para. 15) _____

2. Highlight new, specialized terms introduced in the reading (see Chapter 3).

3. Draw a word map of one of the words in the reading.

CHECKING YOUR COMPREHENSION

1. What was the author's experience with flying in and out of New York City? What was her reaction to these situations?
2. How does the author define the word "fear"?
3. How does the author see fear affecting freedom?
4. In what way does the author relate George Bush to fear?
5. What are the author's thoughts on freedom of movement?
6. According to the author, how are the events of 9/11 used to keep us fearful?

THINKING CRITICALLY

1. Why do you think the author wrote this essay?
2. Underline several examples of connotative language.
3. What biases does the author exhibit?
4. Identify at least three generalizations made by the author.
5. In what parts of the essay do you think more information is needed?
6. What assumptions does the author make?
7. Does the author use manipulative language?
8. Explain the figurative expression used at the end of paragraph 8.

LEARNING/STUDY STRATEGY

Annotate the reading in preparation for a class discussion of the reading.

POLITICAL SCIENCE

Reading 1
Reading 2
PAIRED READINGS

Profiles in Pointlessness
Jonah Goldberg

Prereading Questions

1. Do you think national security suffers when the authorities have to worry about being politically correct?
2. What security measures do you think should be enforced in our airports and subways?

1   THERE'S a great scene in one of the *Airplane!* movies in which one gun-toting terrorist after another walks through a metal detector at the airport. The detector buzzer keeps buzzing as security ignores a long line of cigar-chomping bad guys carrying bazookas and the like. But then, suddenly, a tiny little old lady walks through and when the buzzer goes off, security swarms all over her, with one guard taking her down with a full body tackle.

2   It's not so funny anymore.

3   In New York City, Mayor Michael Bloomberg seems more terrified of violating the rules of political correctness than he is of terrorists. In the wake of the London subway bombings, he announced that occasional searches of bags will take place in pre-announced locations, only with the permission of those searched, and only at random. Ideally, four young Middle Eastern Muslims with heavy clothes and backpacks will go by without so much as a nod from the police; but the fifth person, a one-armed Amish octogenarian grandmother, will be examined by the vigilant constables to make sure that the lady fingers she's carrying aren't made out of Semtex.

4   Of course, that won't happen, because at the end of the day New York police aren't as stupid as the policies they're supposed to enforce. But it is amazing how ideological the opposition to the use of racial profiling has become. It's odd how, as a group, leftists are so fond of talking about how the Right has become "blinded" by ideology—when their own preferred policy is to cover their eyes whenever reality becomes inconvenient. Shortly after 9/11, the FBI redrafted its "Most Wanted" list to reflect the fact that a bunch of people had successfully orchestrated the greatest mass-murder of Americans in our history, i.e., it put a bunch of Arabs on the list. "Why pick on Arabs?" responded a leading Muslim intellectual. "Are there no South Americans, Irish, Serbs, Japanese among the most wanted?" An expert from Cambridge University lamented, "All of the indicators, the simplifiers—the head dress, the beards, the appearance—all indicate a particular group, associated with a particular culture."

5   Funny how that works.

6   Other opponents of profiling go the other way, claiming it's ineffective. Law professor David Harris told NPR that by using a racial or ethnic profile even as just one of many factors in making their decisions on whom to stop, police take the focus off behavior, thus making security screens less accurate. This is a variant of the dreaded Tim McVeigh exception, which seems to hold that you shouldn't look for the color brown while hunting grizzly bears because, after all, there are some albino grizzlies you might miss. Harris claims that when Israelis focused on Arab-looking men, the terrorists (occasionally)

switched to men dressed like Jews or to women or whatever. True enough. But what Harris fails to acknowledge is that the terrorists had to change their tactics because the scrutiny on Arab men made things more difficult.

7   Of course, relying solely on race, ethnicity, or gender would be a waste of time. But surely it would be an even bigger waste of time to corner randomly every fifth creature in the forest on the assumption that a suspicious-looking titmouse just might be a bear.

—Jonah Goldberg, "Profiles in Pointlessness," *National Review*

Writing About the Reading
CHECKING YOUR VOCABULARY

1. For each of the words listed below, use context; prefixes, roots, and suffixes (see Chapter 3); and/or a dictionary to write a brief definition or synonym of the word as it is used in the reading.

   a. bazookas (para. 1) _____

   b. octogenarian (para. 3) _____

   c. vigilant (para. 3) _____

   d. constables (para. 3) _____

   e. ideological (para. 4) _____

   f. lamented (para. 4) _____

   g. scrutiny (para. 6) _____

2. Highlight new, specialized terms introduced in the reading (see Chapter 3).

3. Draw a word map of one of the words in the reading.

CHECKING YOUR COMPREHENSION

1. Describe one of the security check situations that the author presents.
2. What does the author think Mayor Bloomberg fears? How does this fear relate to the way in which the author thinks New York City police officers will provide security?
3. Does the author think the FBI was wrong in putting Arabs on the "Most Wanted" list? Explain your answer.
4. Explain the reference to Tim McVeigh.
5. Why do opponents of profiling think it is "ineffective"?
6. What is the author's final conclusion about profiling?

THINKING CRITICALLY

1. What is the author's purpose in writing this essay?
2. Highlight words with a strong positive or negative connotative meaning.
3. What words or phrases does the author use that show bias?
4. What does the author mean by the phrase "reality becomes inconvenient"?
5. Why does the author use quotes from an "intellectual," an "expert," and a professor?

6. Evaluate the reference to the movie *Airplane!* Why does the author include this?
7. Explain the figurative expression used in the last paragraph.

LEARNING/STUDY STRATEGY

Annotate the reading by recording your reactions to the author's ideas.

Thinking About the Paired Readings
INTEGRATING IDEAS

1. How do the authors' purposes differ in these two readings?
2. Compare the attitude of the two authors.
3. In what ways do the authors support their arguments? Is one way more effective?
4. Which reading is more persuasive? Explain your answer.

GENERATING NEW IDEAS

1. Write a response to one of the essays. Your audience is the author of the essay.
2. Compose a letter to a friend arguing for or against racial profiling when used for national security.

ADDITIONAL PRACTICE

MULTIMEDIA ACTIVITIES

1. **Similes and Metaphors**

   http://www.newi.ac.uk/englishresources/workunits/ks3/langmedia/all/simandmet1.pdf

   Print out this list of similes and metaphors from the North East Wales Institute of Higher Education.

   Write down what you think each expression means. Compare your thoughts with your classmates.

2. **Writing for Advertising**

   http://facstaff.elon.edu/gibson/jcm327/Handouts/Writing_Advertising_Copy.html

   Read over this information about writing ads. Then come up with a product and write some advertising copy for it. Use the guidelines to analyze current ads on television and in magazines.

MYREADINGLAB

If your instructor has asked you to use Reading Road Trip, be sure to visit the "American Southwest" module for multimedia tutorials, exercises, and tests on critical thinking.

6 Reading and Evaluating Arguments

LEARNING OBJECTIVES

✦ To recognize the elements of an argument

✦ To recognize types of arguments

✦ To evaluate arguments

✦ To recognize errors in logical reasoning

Think About It!

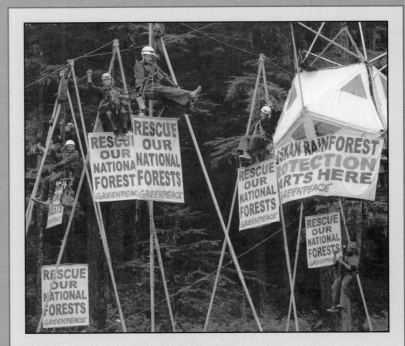

Study the photo above that shows a group of students participating in a demonstration. The signs the demonstrators hold take a position on an issue: Rescue Our National Forests. All that is lacking is evidence or reasons to convince us that our national forests should be saved. The photograph, then, presents the beginnings of an argument.

An argument always presents logical reasons and evidence to support a viewpoint. In a government course, you might read arguments for or against free speech; in a literature class, you may read a piece of literary criticism that argues for or against the value of a particular poem, debates its significance, or rejects a particular interpretation.

■ What Is an Argument?

Here is a brief argument. As you read, notice that the argument offers reasons to support the viewpoint that life without parole is an alternative to the death penalty.

DEATH PENALTY DEBATE FINALLY PRODUCES USEFUL RESULTS

For the past half century, the nation has been locked—deadlocked might be a better word—in a bitter debate over the death penalty. But what if there is a middle ground? With little fanfare, a compromise has been gaining favor for more than a decade, drawing support as DNA evidence has exonerated inmates on death row. Last week, it reached a milestone. Texas, site of one in three executions, gave juries the option to sentence defendants in capital cases to life without parole rather than death.

All but one death-penalty state, New Mexico, now offers that choice, a marked change from the era when life sentences were a meaningless illusion. But why stop at making life without parole just an optional alternative to execution? It is a fitting replacement, assuring severe punishment for the worst of crimes but with a safety valve to protect those falsely accused or wrongly sentenced.

Evidence of the need pours in weekly now. Five times in the past seven months, the Supreme Court has had to rein in state courts that mishandled death penalty cases. On Monday, the court ordered a new sentencing trial in a Pennsylvania case involving shoddy work by the lawyer for an accused murderer. Last week, the court sent back cases from Texas and California that reeked of racial discrimination in jury selection. Earlier, the court ruled against Texas (again) and Missouri (twice) in cases of excluding relevant evidence, making defendants appear in shackles and executing juveniles.

Just last week at the state level:

- An Oklahoma appeals court ordered a new trial for a man sentenced to death in a 1982 murder on the basis of testimony from a police chemist who has since been fired for poor and unreliable lab work.
- An Illinois man jailed for eight months and facing the death penalty in his daughter's death was released when a long-overdue DNA test finally came back—negative.
- A former North Carolina judge urged the state legislature to impose a two-year moratorium on executions.

Against this backdrop, the rate of executions has dropped 40% from its one-time high.

Since the death penalty was reinstated in 1976, the Supreme Court has tried to make clear that it is to be applied carefully and evenhandedly. Nevertheless, cases of incompetent lawyering, suppression of evidence, local prejudice and other affronts to justice keep appearing. The result is evident in the numbers who narrowly escaped execution: While 972 people have been put to death since the 1970s, at least 119 have been taken off death row because of evidence they were wrongly convicted or sentenced.

According to a Gallup Poll in May, 74% of the public supports the death penalty, but backing for capital punishment drops to 56% when respondents are given the alternative of life without parole. Even in Texas, a Scripps-Howard poll last October found that while 75% supported the death penalty, 78% favored the option of life without parole.

Already, life without the death penalty is the norm in a growing number of states. In addition to the 12 that don't allow it, five others have had no executions in more than 30 years; six have used it only once in that time. Abolishing the death penalty and using life without parole instead can't fix all the injustices exposed in courts across the nation. But at least no one would be executed as a result.

—*USA Today,* June 22, 2005

■ Parts of an Argument

An argument has three essential parts. First, an argument must address an **issue**—a problem or controversy about which people disagree. Abortion, gun control, animal rights, and drug legalization are all examples of issues. Second, an argument must take a position on an issue. This position is called a **claim.** An argument may claim that handguns should be outlawed or that medical use of marijuana should be legalized. Finally, an argument offers **support** for the claim. Support consists of reasons and evidence that the claim is reasonable and should be accepted. An argument may also include a fourth part—a **refutation.** A refutation considers opposing viewpoints and may attempt to disprove or discredit them.

In the argument above, the issue is the death penalty. Notice that the title and first paragraph of the argument clearly identify the issue. The author's claim is that life without parole is a viable alternative to the death penalty. The author builds the argument by offering reasons why life without parole is more a justifiable replacement for the death penalty. Life without parole is a safety valve for errors that may occur in the criminal justice system. The author provides evidence about errors that have been made in death penalty cases and statistics about the number of people wrongly convicted. The author also quotes the Gallup Poll results that show that the American public supports life without parole.

In the argument, the author does not refute objections to the claim. An opposing viewpoint may state that the errors in the criminal justice system are legal technicalities that result in guilty people being freed. To refute this opposing viewpoint, the author would need to provide evidence of cases in which new evidence did indeed prove an individual convicted of a capital crime to be innocent.

Types of Claims

The claim is the position or stand the writer takes on the issue. You might think of it as his or her viewpoint. Here are a few sample claims on the issue of animal rights:

> Animals should have none of the rights that humans do.

> Animals have limited rights: freedom from pain and suffering.

> Animals should be afforded the same rights as humans.

There are three common types of claims. A **claim of fact** is a statement that can be proven or verified by observation or research, as in the following example:

> Within ten years, destruction of rain forests will cause hundreds of plant and animal species to become extinct.

A **claim of value** states that one thing or idea is better or more desirable than another. Issues of right versus wrong or acceptable versus unacceptable lead to claims of value. The argument about baseball players' use of steroids is a claim of value. The author argues that steroid use is not acceptable because it is harmful to both the players and the game of baseball.

Here is another example. The following claim of value asserts that mandatory community service is appropriate.

> Requiring community service in high school will produce more community-aware graduates.

A **claim of policy** suggests what should or ought to be done to solve a problem. The following claim of policy suggests action to be taken to combat school violence.

> To reduce school violence, more gun and metal detectors should be installed in public schools.

EXERCISE 6-1

Identify whether each of the following is a claim of fact (F), a claim of value (V), or claim of policy (P), and label each.

_____ 1. Mandatory jail sentences should be imposed for drivers convicted of more than one drunk driving violation.

_____ 2. Student government elections were largely ignored by the student body due to student satisfaction with current policies and leadership.

_____ 3. Marijuana use and abuse continue to escalate in American society.

_____ 4. A mandatory dress code should be implemented in public schools.

_____ 5. Killing deer and other large animals for sport is wrong.

EXERCISE 6-2

For two of the following issues, write two claims about the issue. For each issue, try to write two different types of claims.

1. same-sex marriages
2. violence in schools
3. privacy on the Internet
4. drug testing in the workplace

Types of Support

Three common types of support are reasons, evidence, and emotional appeals. A **reason** is a general statement that supports a claim. It explains why the writer's viewpoint is reasonable and should be accepted. In "Death Penalty Debate Finally Produces Useful Results," the author states two primary reasons why life without parole should replace the death penalty: it protects us against errors and the Ameircan public favors it.

Evidence consists of facts, statistics, experiences, comparisons, and examples that demonstrate why the claim is valid. The author of "Death Penalty Finally Produces Useful Results" offers examples of cases in which errors may have been made. The author also offers Gallup Poll and Scripps-Howard Poll statistics as evidence.

Emotional appeals are ideas that are targeted toward needs or values that readers are likely to care about. Needs include physiological needs (food, drink, shelter) and psychological needs (sense of belonging, sense of accomplishment, sense of self-worth, sense of competency). An argument favoring gun control, for example, may appeal to a reader's need for safety, while an argument favoring restrictions on sharing personal or financial information may appeal to a reader's need for privacy and financial security. In the life without parole essay, the author appeals to the reader's sense of fairness and justice.

EXERCISE 6-3

Identify the type(s) of evidence used to support each of the following brief arguments.

1. Many students have part-time jobs that require them to work late afternoons and evenings during the week. These students are unable to use the library during the week. Therefore, library hours should be extended to weekends.
2. Because parents have the right to determine their children's sexual attitudes, sex education should take place in the home, not at school.
3. No one should be forced to inhale unpleasant or harmful substances. That's why the ban on cigarette smoking in public places was put into effect in our state. Why shouldn't there be a law to prevent people from wearing strong colognes or perfumes, especially in restaurants, since the sense of smell is important to taste?

■ Inductive and Deductive Arguments

Two types of arguments—inductive and deductive—are common. An **inductive argument** reaches a general conclusion from observed specifics. For example, by observing the performance of a large number of athletes, you could conclude that athletes possess physical stamina. A **deductive argument**, on the other hand, begins with a general statement, known as a major premise, and moves toward a more specific statement, known as the minor premise. For example, from the major premise that "Athletes possess physical stamina," you can reason that because Anthony is an athlete (the minor premise), he must possess physical stamina.

Both types of arguments begin with statements that are assumed to be correct. Basically, both follow a general pattern of "If that is so, then this is so . . ." At times, an argument may be more complex, involving several steps—"If that is so, and this happens, then this should be done." You can visualize each type of argument as shown in Figure 6-1.

EXERCISE 6-4   *For each of the following inductive arguments, supply the missing pieces.*

1. Evidence: Prof. Hong wears jeans and flannel shirts to class.

    Evidence: Prof. Hutchinson wears khaki pants and running shoes when he lectures.

    Evidence: _____

    Conclusion: Professors on this campus dress casually for class.

2. Evidence: Many people walk down the street talking on their cellular phones.

FIGURE 6-1   Inductive and Deductive Arguments

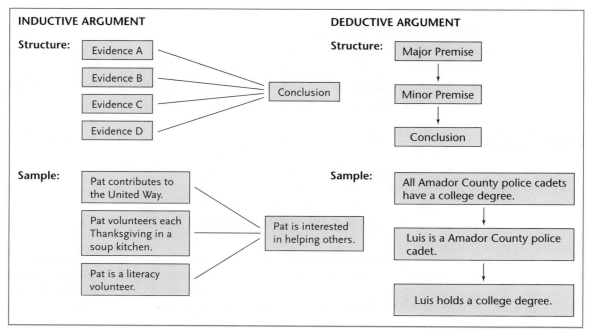

Evidence: Most families own at least two cellular phones.

Evidence: In restaurants and in shopping malls people can be observed using their cellular phones.

Conclusion: _____

EXERCISE 6-5   *For each of the following deductive arguments, supply the conclusion.*

1. Major Premise: All students with yearly averages above 3.5 are offered a summer internship.

   Minor Premise: Jacqueline has a yearly average of 3.7.

   Conclusion: _____

2. Major Premise: Most elementary school children's absences from school are due to illness.

   Minor Premise: Quinne, a fifth grade student, was absent yesterday.

   Conclusion: _____

■ Strategies for Reading an Argument

Arguments need to be read slowly and carefully. Count on reading an argument more than once. The first time you read it, try to get an overview of its three essential elements: issue, claim, and support. Then reread it more carefully to closely follow the author's line of reasoning and to identify and evaluate the evidence provided.

Think Before You Read

1. **What does the title suggest?** Before you read, preview the essay (see p. 165) and ask yourself what the title suggests about the issue and claim or support. The title of the *USA Today* argument on the death penalty (p. 159), for example, suggests the author's position on the issue.

EXERCISE 6-6   *For each of the following titles, predict the issue and claim the essay addresses.*

1. "A Former Smoker Cheers New Legislation"
2. "Overflowing, Overcrowded Jails: New Solutions"
3. "The Right to Die My Way"
4. "The Effects of Unchecked Immigration"
5. "Indecent Proposal: Internet Censorship"

2. **Who is the author, and what are his or her qualifications?** Check to see if you recognize the author, and if so, evaluate whether he or she is qualified to write about the issue. For example, an article written by professional golfer Tiger Woods would be an authoritative source on the issue of

ethics in professional golf. If the same argument were written by a state senator or a medical doctor, it would have less credibility. The specific qualifications of the author have a bearing on the worth of the evidence provided.

3. **What is the date of publication?** Checking the date will prompt you to consider whether new, even possibly contradictory, evidence has recently developed.

4. **What do I already know about the issue?** Try brainstorming using a two-column list. Label one column "pro" and the other "con," and list as many ideas as you can in each. By thinking about the issue on your own, you are less likely to be swayed by the writer's appeals and more likely to think and evaluate the reasons and evidence objectively.

EXERCISE 6-7   *Preview but do not read the following argument. (For previewing guidelines, see Chapter 1, p. 30.) Complete the activities that follow. Read the argument after you have finished the next section, "Read Actively."*

NO MORE JUNK TOYS

Rethinking Children's Gifts

One night, not long after Christmas, my pacifist friends Jay Levy and Su Zuniga quietly crept down to the basement with a hammer while their three-year-old daughter, Samantha, slept. There, they methodically banged on the belly of her brand-new mechanical dog until it stopped yapping. Another friend's daughter received a Victorian makeup table for her fourth birthday. "It's plastic, it's ugly, and it's huge. It's totally inappropriate for a four year old. Not to mention that my daughter is a tomboy," the mother said. When asked about the fate of the gift, she replied firmly, "It is going to 'disappear' very soon."

Some parents are creative in their disposal of "junk toys," as my husband calls them. "The worst toy our daughter ever received," notes one mom, "was a hard-plastic, realistic, talking doll. She purported to be your child's 'best friend' by using a set of prerecorded diskettes that get inserted into her back. We were saddened to think there might be some lonely children out there for whom this doll might actually be enriching. The doll stands in the center of our peace garden as our scarecrow."

Making gifts "disappear" is a last resort for parents whose kids receive junk toys—i.e., toys out of line with their values or taste. Like junk food, junk toys can be fun but are devoid of nutrition. Buying them requires little forethought. They are excessively commercial and are often linked to cross-marketing schemes. They excite children at first, but that initial flicker doesn't endure. Also like junk food, junk toys have hidden environmental and social costs for which the consumers pay.

When we buy a Barbie doll, the relatively low price belies the full cost of her petroleum-intensive plastic manufacturing process, her plastic and paper packaging, and transporting her and her billions of accessories from Southeast Asia to the U.S. These hidden costs, what economists call "externalities," are paid (or more commonly unpaid) not by individual consumers or corporate producers but by collective society at large. We don't — and probably can't — pay enough for the product and its manufacturing, packaging, and shipping to justify the damage caused by these processes.

The vast majority of plastic commercial toys are made by children themselves, working in overseas sweatshops. Girls as young as 13, some working the night shift, stitch Barbie's dresses.[1] In Thailand in 1993, hundreds of workers, including child laborers, died in a fire while stuffing Cabbage Patch dolls for Hasbro, Inc.[2] The Asia Monitor Resource Center and the Coalition for the Charter on the Safe Production of Toys reported that Vietnamese workers making McDonald's Happy Meal toys for as little as six cents an hour had been poisoned by acetone, a chemical solvent used to manufacture plastic.[3] All of this so that I can pull up to the drive-through window and toss my child a Happy Meal figurine? No, thanks.

Then there are the social costs of marketing. Marketers broadcast programming designed to hypnotize toddlers into "cradle-to-grave brand loyalty to these toys."[4] Marketing professionals cross-reference, cross-market, and cross-pollinate products and entertainment. By intentionally blurring the distinctions between products, entertainment, school curricula, and advertisements, marketers readily capitalize on young children's limited ability to differentiate between them. It's no accident that in the children's section of Barnes and Noble, the books starring such television-based characters as Blue, Arthur, and Clifford are displayed most prominently, while the classics get the cheap seats.

North Americans have come to rely on commercial institutions to furnish our stories, heroes, icons, and expectations. The old traditions and rites of passage have been eclipsed by a boy's first Nintendo, a girl's first Barbie, a computer, a first toy gun.

Julie Convisser, a movement therapist and mother of two small boys, worries about the messages kids get from commercial culture. "I feel like they are being groomed to be materialists, to buy into an evil-versus-good world paradigm, and to ignore the spiritual heart of life and the bounty of nature." She buffers the influence of commercial culture as much as possible by limiting her boys' TV viewing and being picky about videos, avoiding media-promotion toys, and sending her older son to a school at which the other children's parents share her values.

Others argue that children should be exposed to commercial culture to avoid becoming victims of it. In fact, direct experience can be a fast way for kids to learn the ropes of misleading ad campaigns. Karin Purdy, mother of three, says, "I let my kids watch TV, and I let them buy some of the products they see. They are usually quite disappointed when they get them and find they aren't as great as they thought. They get smarter as they get older."

Whatever their individual approaches, many parents work hard all year long to protect children from pervasive and cloying commercialism. But despite our best efforts, holidays and birthdays can become gift-crazed free-for-alls. Why allow our

---

[1] Sarah Cox, "The Secret Life of Toys," www.maquilasolidarity.org/campaigns/toy/scox.htm.

[2] Ibid.

[3] Ibid.

[4] Gary Ruskin, "Why They Whine," *Mothering*, No. 97 (November–December 1999): 40–50.

friends and relatives to fall into the trap of giving meaningless gifts when a simple, genuine gesture can mean so much more to the children? "Disappearing" junk toys only compounds the environmental and cultural costs; it's up to us to stop the charade and transform the culture of gift-giving.

—Rubin and Zuniga, *Mothering*

1. What does the title suggest about the issue, claim, or evidence?
2. What do you already know about the issue? Brainstorm a two-column "Pro–Con" list.

Read Actively

When reading arguments, it is especially important to read actively. For general suggestions on active reading, see Chapter 1. Use the following specific strategies for reading arguments:

1. **Read once for an initial impression.** Do not focus on specifics; instead, try to get a general feel for the argument.

2. **Read the argument several more times.** First identify the specific claim the writer is making and start to identify the reasons and evidence that support it. Read the argument again to examine whether the writer acknowledges or refutes opposing viewpoints.

3. **Annotate as you read.** Record your thoughts; note ideas you agree with, those you disagree with, questions that come to mind, additional reasons or evidence overlooked by the author, and the counterarguments not addressed by the author.

4. **Highlight key terms.** Often, an argument depends on how certain terms are defined. In an argument on the destruction of forests, for example, what does "destruction" mean? Does it mean building homes within a forest, or does it refer to clearing the land for timber or to create a housing subdivision? Highlight both the key terms and the definitions the author provides.

5. **Diagram or map to analyze structure.** Because many arguments are complex, you may find it helpful to diagram or map them. By mapping the argument, you may discover unsubstantiated ideas, reasons for which evidence is not provided, or an imbalance between reasons and emotional appeals. Use the format shown in Figure 6-2 (p. 168) to help you analyze an argument's structure. Figure 6-3 on page 169 shows you how the argument presented in "No More Junk Toys" on pages 165–167 is mapped.

■ Strategies for Evaluating Arguments

Once you have understood the article by identifying what is asserted and how it is asserted, the next step is to evaluate the soundness, correctness, and worth of the argument. Specifically, you must evaluate evidence (both type and relevancy), definitions of terms, cause–effect relationships, value systems, and counterarguments, as well as recognize emotional appeals.

FIGURE 6-2   The Structure of an Argument

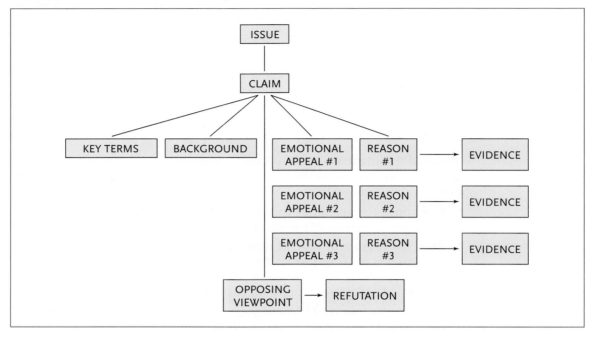

Types of Evidence

The validity of an inductive argument rests, in part, on the soundness and correctness of the evidence provided to draw the conclusion. The validity of a deductive argument, on the other hand, rests on the accuracy and correctness of the premises on which the argument is based. Evaluating each type of argument involves assessing the accuracy and correctness of statements on which the argument is based. Often, writers provide evidence to substantiate their observations or premises. As a critical reader, your task is to assess whether the evidence is sufficient to support the claim. Here are some suggestions for evaluating each type of evidence.

Personal Experience   Writers often substantiate their ideas through experience and observation. Although a writer's personal account of a situation may provide an interesting perspective on an issue, personal experience should not be accepted as proof. The observer may be biased or may have exaggerated or incorrectly perceived a situation.

Examples   Examples are descriptions of particular situations that are used to illustrate or explain a principle, concept, or idea. To explain what aggressive behavior is, your psychology instructor may offer several examples: fighting, punching, and kicking. Examples should not be used by themselves to prove the concept or idea they illustrate, as is done in the following sample:

FIGURE 6–3 A Map of an Argument

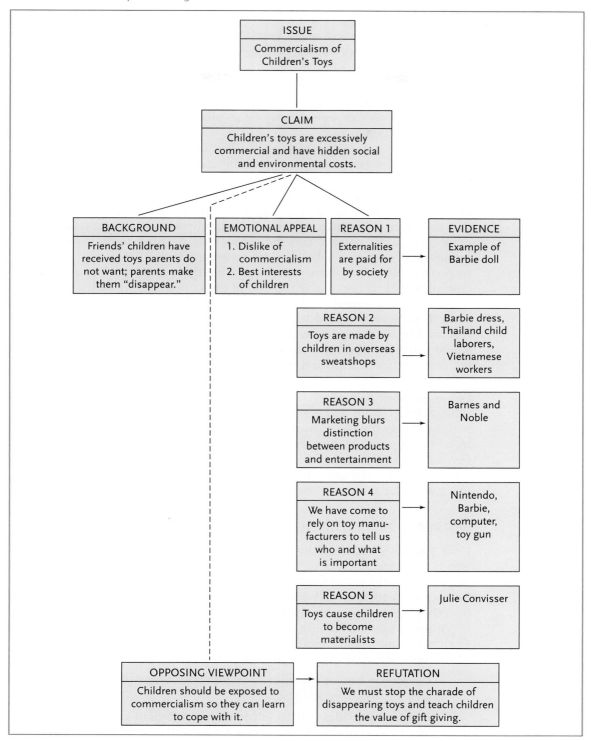

> The American judicial system treats those who are called for jury duty unfairly. It is clear from my sister's experience that the system has little regard for the needs of those called as jurors. My sister was required to report for jury duty the week she was on vacation. She spent the entire week in a crowded, stuffy room waiting to be called to sit on a jury and never was called.

The writer's sister's experience may be atypical, or not representative, of what most jurors experience.

Statistics   Many people are impressed by statistics—the reporting of figures, percentages, averages, and so forth—and assume they are irrefutable proof. Actually, statistics can be misused, misinterpreted, or used selectively to give other than the most objective, accurate picture of a situation. Suppose you read that magazine X has increased its readership by 50 percent while magazine Y made only a 10 percent increase. From this statistic, some readers might assume that magazine X has a wider readership than Y. However, if provided with complete information, you can see that this is not true. The missing, but crucial, statistic is the total readership of each magazine before the increase. If magazine X distributed 20,000 copies, and increased its circulation by 50 percent, its readership would total 30,000. However, if magazine Y's circulation was already 50,000, a 10 percent increase (bringing the new total to 55,000) would still give it the larger readership despite the fact that it made the smaller increase. Approach statistical evidence with a critical, questioning attitude.

Comparisons and Analogies   Comparisons or analogies (extended comparisons) serve as illustrations and are often used in argument. Their reliability depends on how closely the comparison corresponds or how similar it is to the situation to which it is being compared. For example, Martin Luther King, Jr., in his famous letter from the Birmingham jail, compared nonviolent protesters to a robbed man. To evaluate this comparison, you would need to consider how the two are similar and how they are different.

Relevancy and Sufficiency of Evidence

Once you have identified the evidence used to support an argument, the next step is to decide whether there is enough of the right kind of evidence to lead you to accept the writer's claim. This is always a matter of judgment; there are no easy rules to follow. You must determine whether the evidence provided directly supports the claim and whether sufficient evidence has been provided.

Suppose you are reading an article in your campus newspaper that states Freshman Composition should not be required of all students at your college. As evidence, the writer includes the following:

> Composition does not prepare us for the job market. Besides, the reading assignments have no relevancy to modern times.

This reason provides neither adequate nor sufficient evidence. The writer does nothing to substantiate his statements about the irrelevancy of the course to the job market or modern times. For the argument to be regarded seriously, the writer would need to provide facts, statistics, expert opinion, or other forms of documentation.

EXERCISE 6-8 *Reread the argument "No More Junk Toys" on page 165, paying particular attention to the type(s) of evidence used. Then answer the questions that follow.*

1. What type(s) of evidence is/are used?
2. Is the evidence convincing?
3. Is there sufficient evidence?
4. What other types of evidence could have been used to strengthen the argument?

Definition of Terms

A clear and effective argument carefully defines key terms and uses them consistently. For example, an essay arguing for or against animal rights should state what is meant by the term, describe or define those rights, and use that definition through the entire argument.

The following two paragraphs are taken from two different argumentative essays on pornography. Notice how in the first paragraph the author carefully defines what he means by pornography before proceeding with his argument, whereas in the second the term is not clearly defined.

Paragraph 1—Careful Definition

There is unquestionably more pornography available today than 15 years ago. However, is it legitimate to assume that more is worse? Pornography is speech, words, and pictures about sexuality. No one would consider an increase in the level of speech about religion or politics to be a completely negative development. What makes speech about sexuality different?

—Lynn, "Pornography's Many Forms: Not All Bad," *Los Angeles Times*

Paragraph 2—Vague Definition

If we are not talking about writing laws, defining pornography doesn't pose as serious a problem. We do have different tastes. Maybe some of mine come from my middle-class background (my mother wouldn't think so!). I don't like bodies presented without heads, particularly female bodies. The motive may sometimes be the protection of the individual, but the impression is decapitation, and I also happen to be someone who is attracted to people's faces. This is a matter of taste.

—Rule, "Pornography Is a Social Disease," *The Body Politic*

Cause–Effect Relationships

Arguments are often built around the assumption of a cause–effect relationship. For example, an argument supporting gun control legislation may claim that ready availability of guns contributes to an increased number of shootings. This argument implies that availability of guns causes increased use. If the writer provides no evidence that this cause–effect relationship exists, you should question the accuracy of the statement.

Implied or Stated Value System

An argument often implies or rests on a value system (a structure of what the writer feels is right, wrong, worthwhile, and important). However, everyone possesses a personal value system, and although our culture promotes many major points of agreement (murder is wrong, human life is worthwhile, and so forth), it also allows points of departure. One person may think telling lies is always wrong; another person may say it depends on the circumstances. Some people have a value system based on religious beliefs; others may not share those beliefs.

In evaluating an argument, look for value judgments and then decide whether the judgments are consistent with and acceptable to your personal value system. Here are a few examples of value-judgment statements:

Abortion is wrong.

Financial aid for college should be available to everyone regardless of income.

Capital punishment violates human rights.

Recognizing and Refuting Opposing Viewpoints

Many arguments recognize opposing viewpoints. For example, the author of "No More Junk Toys" recognizes that some people argue that children should be exposed to commercial culture in order to avoid becoming victims of it.

Many arguments also attempt to refute opposing viewpoints (explain why they are wrong, flawed, or unacceptable). Basically, the author finds weaknesses in the opponent's argument. One way to do this is to question the accuracy, relevancy, or sufficiency of the opponent's evidence. Another way is to disagree with the opponent's reasons. She refutes this viewpoints by suggesting that parents instead should consider the impact of the gift they give to children.

When reading arguments that address opposing viewpoints, ask yourself the following questions:

- Does the author address opposing viewpoints clearly and fairly?
- Does the author refute the opposing viewpoint with logic and relevant evidence?

Unfair Emotional Appeals

Emotional appeals attempt to involve or excite readers by appealing to their emotions, thereby controlling the reader's attitude toward the subject. Several types of emotional appeals are described below.

1. **Emotionally charged or biased language.** By using words that create an emotional response, writers establish positive or negative feelings. For example, an advertisement for a new line of fragrances promises to "indulge," "refresh," "nourish," and "pamper" the user. An ad for an automobile uses phrases such as "limousine comfort," "European styling," and "animal sleekness" to interest and excite readers.

2. **False authority.** False authority involves using the opinion or action of a well-known or famous person. We have all seen athletes endorsing underwear or movie stars selling shampoo. This type of appeal works on the notion that people admire celebrities and strive to be like them, respect their opinions, and are willing to accept their viewpoints.

3. **Association.** An emotional appeal also is made by associating a product, idea, or position with others that are already accepted or highly regarded. Patriotism is valued, so to call a product All-American in an advertisement is an appeal to the emotions. A car named a Cougar reminds you of a fast, sleek animal. A cigarette ad picturing a scenic waterfall or a speaker standing in front of an American flag are other examples.

4. **Appeal to "common folk."** Some people distrust those who are well educated, wealthy, highly artistic, or in other ways distinctly different from the average person. An emotional appeal to this group is made by selling a product or idea by indicating that it is originated from, held by, or bought by ordinary citizens. A commercial may advertise a product by showing its use in an average household. A politician may describe her background and education to suggest that she is like everyone else; a salesperson may dress in styles similar to his clients.

5. *Ad hominem.* An argument that attacks the holder of an opposing viewpoint, rather than the viewpoint itself, is known as *ad hominem*, or an attack on the man. For example, the statement, "How could a woman who does not even hold a college degree criticize a judicial decision?" attacks the woman's level of education, not her viewpoint.

6. **"Join the crowd" appeal.** The appeal to do, believe, or buy what everyone else is doing, believing, or buying is known as crowd appeal or the bandwagon effect. Commercials that proclaim their product as the "#1 best-selling car in America" are appealing to this motive. Essays that cite opinion polls on a controversial issue in support of a position—"68 percent of Americans favor capital punishment"—are also using this appeal.

■ Errors in Logical Reasoning

Errors in reasoning, often called logical fallacies, are common in arguments. These errors invalidate the argument or render it flawed. Several common errors in logic are described next.

Circular Reasoning

Also known as begging the question, this error involves using part of the conclusion as evidence to support it. Here are two examples.

> Cruel medical experimentation on defenseless animals is inhumane.

> Female police officers should not be sent to crime scenes because apprehending criminals is a man's job.

In circular reasoning, because no evidence is given to support the claim, there is no reason to accept the conclusion.

Hasty Generalization

This fallacy means that the conclusion has been derived from insufficient evidence. Here is one example: you taste three tangerines and each is sour, so you conclude that all tangerines are sour. Here is another: by observing one performance of a musical group, you conclude the group is unfit to perform.

Non Sequitur ("It Does Not Follow")

The false establishment of cause–effect is known as a non sequitur. To say, for example, that "Because my doctor is young, I'm sure she'll be a good doctor" is a non sequitur because youth does not ensure good medical practices. Here is another example: "Arturio Alvarez is the best choice for state senator because he is an ordinary citizen." Being an ordinary citizen will not necessarily make someone an effective state senator.

False Cause

The false cause fallacy is the incorrect assumption that two events that follow each other in time are causally related. Suppose you opened an umbrella and then tripped on an uneven sidewalk. If you said you tripped because you opened the umbrella, you would be assuming false cause.

Either–Or Fallacy

This fallacy assumes that an issue is only two sided, or that there are only two choices or alternatives for a particular situation. In other words, there is no middle ground. Consider the issue of censorship of violence on television. An either–or fallacy is to assume that violence on TV must be either allowed or banned. This fallacy does not recognize other alternatives such as limiting access through viewing hours, restricting certain types of violence, and so forth.

EXERCISE 6-9   *Identify the logical fallacy in each of the following statements.*

1. All African American students in my biology class earned A grades, so African Americans must excel in life sciences.
2. If you are not for nuclear arms control, then you're against protecting our future.
3. My sister cannot do mathematical computations or balance her checkbook because she has math anxiety.
4. A well-known mayor, noting a decline in the crime rate in the four largest cities in his state, quickly announced that his new "get-tough on criminals" publicity campaign was successful and took credit for the decline.
5. I always order a fruit pastry for dessert because I am allergic to chocolate.

EXERCISE 6-10 *Read the following pair of arguments that appeared in* USA Today, *and answer the questions that follow.*

Argument 1
MISSTEP ON VIDEO VIOLENCE

In the booming world of video games, there are more than a few dark corners: Murder and mayhem. Blood and gore. Explicit sex and abuse of women. In one of the best-selling series, Grand Theft Auto, car stealing is accompanied by drug use, shootouts that kill police and bystanders, and simulated sex with comely prostitutes who are beaten with baseball bats afterward.

Small wonder some parents are concerned over what game-crazed teens may be up to. And small wonder, too, that legislators in several states are playing to these concerns by trying to outlaw the sale of violent and sexually explicit games to minors. A bill banning the sale of such games to anyone younger than 18 is awaiting the governor's signature in Illinois. A similar proposal is moving in the Michigan Legislature. The issue has been raised this year in at least nine other states and the District of Columbia. But to what useful end?

This is the latest chapter in a very old story. When teenage entertainment offends adult sensibilities—think Elvis Presley's pulsating hips or the arrival on newsstands of Hugh Hefner's Playboy—the first response is to see the new phenomenon as a threat to social order. The second is to attempt to ban it. Parents—former teenagers all—seem to forget history's lesson: The bans never work. And they're probably not constitutional, anyway. Courts have ruled that today's sophisticated video games are protected as creative expression. If communities want to limit access, they must show overriding evidence that the games pose a public threat. That evidence does not exist.

Lawmakers and activist groups assert that the thrill of engaging in virtual criminal activity will spur teens to try the real thing. But the violent crime rate has gone down nearly 30% since the first bloody shoot-'em-up games debuted in the early 1990s. Youth crime rates have dropped even more. And a Federal Trade Commission survey found parents already involved in 83% of video-game purchases and rentals for minors.

Judges have repeatedly rejected as flawed the studies that advocates say show a link between fantasy violence and anti-social behavior. To the extent there is a threat, it is mainly to the individual, vulnerable teenager, and it can be addressed only by parents.

Unknown to many parents, they're getting some help. The game industry's rating system classifies games in six categories from "early childhood" to "adults only" and requires detailed content descriptions. Also, newer models of popular games include parental controls that can block their use for age-inappropriate games. Manufacturers have announced an expanded ratings-education program, and major retailers are tightening their restrictions on sales to minors.

There will always be a market for the dark, tasteless, even the outrageous, and parents ought to keep kids away from it. But even with the best intentions of legislators, the problem is beyond their reach. New laws are likely to give parents only the false impression that someone else is solving that problem for them.

—USA Today, June 6, 2005

Argument 2

PARENTS NEED OUR HELP

Rod Blagojevich

When I was growing up, my parents used to worry if I was hanging out with the wrong kids in the neighborhood. Today, parents have even more to worry about: instead of playing basketball at the schoolyard, our children are spending their afternoons at the controls of a Sony PlayStation simulating acts of murder, dismemberment, decapitation and sexual seduction.

Games such as Grand Theft Auto and Halo 2 use the same techniques the U.S. military uses to train our soldiers to kill the enemy. Another game, JFK Reloaded, re-enacts the assassination of the late president. As a parent, this is the last thing I want my 8-year-old exposed to.

But the truth is that 92% of children between the ages of 2 and 17 are playing video games—and it's taking a toll on them.

A recent study at Iowa State University tied playing video games with an area of the brain directly linked to extreme behavioral disorders. Another study found that kids who play violent games have lower test scores. As one parent told me, we're "competing with video games for the minds and souls of our children." From what I can tell, the video games are winning.

That's why—as both a parent and a governor—I was delighted we passed legislation last week making Illinois the first state in the nation to prohibit the sale or rental of excessively violent or sexually explicit video games to children under 18.

We don't let our kids buy cigarettes. We don't let them buy alcohol. We don't let children purchase pornography. So why should we let them purchase video games that we know can cause them long-term harm?

Many retailers will argue that they don't sell these kinds of games to kids. But a study by the Federal Trade Commission found that 69% of teenage boys were able to purchase violent and sexually explicit games without permission from their parents. I don't believe we should ever put profits ahead of what's best for our children.

I know that some interest groups don't like the idea of limiting anything. But when it comes to our children and their well-being, how about a little common sense? Telling kids they can purchase violent and sexually explicit video games sends the wrong message and reinforces the wrong values.

Parents deserve a fighting chance. It's our responsibility to give it to them.

—*USA Today,* June 6, 2005

For each argument:

1. Identify the claim.
2. Outline the primary reasons used to support the claim.
3. What types of evidence are used?
4. Evaluate the adequacy and sufficiency of the evidence.
5. What emotional appeals are used?
6. Does the author recognize or refute counterarguments?

Compare the arguments:

1. Compare the types of evidence used.
2. Which argument did you find more convincing? Why?
3. What further information would be useful in assessing the issue?

Self-Test Summary

1. What are the three essential parts of an argument?	The three essential parts of an argument are: • the issue—a problem or controversy about which people disagree. • the claim—the position the writer takes on the issue. • the support—the reasons and evidence that suggest the claim is reasonable and should be accepted.
2. What is a refutation?	A refutation is the part of an argument that considers opposing viewpoints and attempts to disprove or discredit them.
3. What is a claim of fact?	A claim of fact is one that can be verified through observation or research.
4. What is a claim of value?	A claim of value states that one thing or idea is better or more desirable than another.
5. What is a claim of policy?	A claim of policy suggests what should or ought to be done to solve a problem.
6. What are the three common types of support?	Three common types of support are reasons, evidence, and emotional appeals.
7. What is an inductive argument?	An inductive argument reaches a general conclusion from observed specifics.
8. What is a deductive argument?	A deductive argument begins with a general statement (major premise), moves toward a more specific statement (minor premise), then reaches a conclusion.
9. What are six types of emotional appeals writers use?	Types of emotional appeals include emotionally charged language, false authority, association, appeal to "common folk," *ad hominem*, and "join the crowd."
10. What are five common errors in logical reasoning?	Common errors in logical reasoning include circular reasoning, hasty generalization, non sequitur, false cause, and either–or fallacy.

ENVIRONMENTAL STUDIES

Reading 1

Permitting Limited Trade in Ivory Will Help Protect Elephants

Michael De Alessi

Prereading Questions

1. What is an endangered species?
2. What has ivory been used for and how does it endanger elephants?

1   What is the best way to protect endangered species? Is it better to try to devalue those species by banning trade in products derived from them, or is it better to embrace markets and property rights that create positive incentives for stewardship? Every couple of years the debate surrounding this question crystallizes around elephant protection and the international ivory trade. Lately, markets, not mandates, seem to be gaining as the best approach to protect elephants, as well as the human populations that need natural resources to raise their quality of life. The reality is that in much of the world the desperation generated by poverty poses the greatest threat to endangered species survival.

2   The UN-sponsored Convention on International Trade in Endangered Species, or CITES, has been around since 1973, and a ban on trade in elephant ivory was adopted by the Convention in 1989. The ivory ban did succeed in reducing the demand for ivory in Western countries, but not in Asia. So poaching has continued.

3   Ironically, by succeeding in the West, the ivory ban failed in a different manner. CITES started out as an effort to regulate trade, but quickly moved on to outright trade bans on the premise that destroying the economic value of species will aid in their survival. Despite much evidence to the contrary, non-governmental organizations (NGOs) in Kenya and in wealthy Western countries like the U.S. and Europe have promoted this view. But especially in poor countries where many of the world's endangered species live, those species that do not pay their way will be quickly replaced by something else that does, such as agriculture.

Conservation and Commerce

4   These realities don't stop radical environmentalists from having a field day whenever illegal products are found for sale, which they inevitably are (has any prohibition really been successful?). For example, the World Society for the Protection of Animals (WSPA) recently published a report that claimed that its own operatives "easily obtained illegal bear bile products from China at 67 percent of Chinese medicine shops surveyed in Montreal, Toronto, and Vancouver." The report offers an opportunity for the requisite hand-wringing over "putting a price on the head of every living bear"—a nice sound bite which does little to help the bears, since the only result of stricter enforcement would be higher prices.

5   But even the "moral victories" of endangered species trade bans are wearing thin, as southern African states with growing elephant populations and rampant poverty have sought revenues from their stockpiles of elephant ivory (mostly from natural deaths or conservation-minded culls) to plow back into conservation and rural development. Some African nations do have depleted elephant populations, but many, especially in southern Africa, have the opposite problem. In Zimbabwe, for example, the estimated carrying capacity of the elephant population is around 30,000 animals; the current population is over three times that number, resulting in serious environmental degradation.

6   Still, for many people, the announcement [in 2002] that some southern African nations would be allowed to sell a limited amount of elephant ivory surely evoked anachronistic images of gruff, mustachioed colonials from the heydays of hunting. In 2003, however, nothing could be further from the truth. The reality is that combining conservation and commerce offers the greatest hope for improving the lot of both people and wildlife in the developing world.

The CITES Proposal

7   The vote to allow some ivory sales (but not others) that took place at the November 2002 CITES meeting in Santiago, Chile, was bolstered by both Canadian and U.S. support, something past ivory proposals have not had. The United States has traditionally been one of the staunchest opponents of any and all international trade in elephant ivory, and Canada has not been far behind. Even the European Parliament, which passed a resolution urging its CITES negotiators to reject the African proposals, eventually abstained from the elephant votes. The change of heart seems to indicate an important shift in international conservation efforts, toward positive incentives for species and habitat conservation and away from prohibitions on trade in wildlife that have been the norm for the last 20 years.

8   Specifically, Botswana, Namibia, and South Africa will be allowed one-off ivory sales of 20 metric tons (mt), 10mt, and 30mt respectively. This is the second time that CITES has permitted such a one-off sale. In 1999, Botswana, Namibia, and Zimbabwe sold almost 50 metric tons of ivory to Japan for about $5 million. Zimbabwe had another proposal this time as well, but chaos and corruption in that country left international observers unconvinced that the sales could be properly monitored.

9   Even if CITES succeeded in destroying the positive value of species such as elephants, then all that would be left would be their negative value. Poor Africans most often bear the brunt of Western conservation initiatives, which focus on protecting elephants rather than elephant habitat, a far more important factor in ensuring elephant survival. And so, despite trampling crops and humans, knocking houses over, and generally wreaking havoc, elephants are rarely viewed in Western countries as a nuisance to the people who live around them.

10   The idea that wildlife will be better off without any economic value may have some merit for species survival in a national park setting, but on communal lands or on private property it has the opposite effect. This points to another fatal flaw of the CITES ban approach. The best hope for the protection of wildlife, and especially endangered species, is the alleviation of poverty and the reform of domestic institutions that have encouraged poaching and habitat conversion—an area that CITES has no real jurisdiction over.

Turning Toward Sustainable Development

11   A number of southern African countries have moved to devolve control over wildlife to local, rural communities. The idea is to recognize that people will protect and conserve

what they value. Despite corruption, it has been a tremendous step in the right direction. Community conservation programs have led to fierce local protection of wildlife, and the view that wildlife habitat has value far beyond simply being potential farmland.

12   Some CITES officials have also started to recognize the importance of making life better for both people and wildlife. "CITES seeks to promote a healthier and more sustainable relationship between people and wildlife," said CITES Secretary-General Willem Wijnstekers. In addition, Linda Maltby, deputy head of the Canadian CITES delegation in Chile, said, "We support the idea of sustainable livelihoods." Good news if this means that Canada intends to support sustainable conservation through commerce.

13   While the move to support the limited sale of ivory is a welcome one, it remains to be seen whether there has really been any sea change in policy. After all, ivory imports into the United States will continue to be prohibited under both the Endangered Species Act and the African Elephant Conservation Act. Canada, for its part, has the even-more-incongruous-sounding Wild Animal and Plant Protection and Regulation of International and Interprovincial Trade Act (WAPPRIITA).

14   Still, the move to sell some elephant ivory could be the first step towards an acknowledgement that trade bans are detrimental to elephants and other species, and that conservation based on incentives, decentralization, and ownership is better for both people and elephants.

—Opposing Viewpoints Series, 2005

Writing About the Reading
CHECKING YOUR VOCABULARY

1. For each of the words listed below, use context; prefixes, roots, and suffixes (see Chapter 3); and/or a dictionary to write a brief definition or synonym of the word as it is used in the reading.

   a. stewardship (para. 1) _____

   b. crystallizes (para. 1) _____

   c. operatives (para. 4) _____

   d. requisite (para. 4) _____

   e. rampant (para. 5) _____

   f. culls (para. 5) _____

   g. anachronistic (para. 6) _____

   h. staunchest (para. 7) _____

   i. wreaking (para. 9) _____

   j. devolve (para. 11) _____

2. Underline new, specialized terms introduced in the reading (see Chapter 3).

3. Draw a word map of one of the words in the reading.

CHECKING YOUR COMPREHENSION

1. According to the author, what poses the greatest threat to endangered animals?
2. What is CITES? What is its significance?
3. How does conservation relate to the selling of stockpiled ivory?
4. In what way does poverty relate to the conservation of endangered species?
5. What is sustainable development? How does this idea relate to the ivory trade?
6. Are ivory imports into the United States and Canada legal? Why or why not?

THINKING CRITICALLY

1. Re-state the author's basic argument.
2. What emotional appeals does the author make? What effect does this have?
3. What opposing viewpoints does the author recognize? How does he refute them?
4. What type of evidence does the author use? How convincing is this evidence? Explain your answer.
5. What is the author's conclusion?

LEARNING/STUDY STRATEGY

Using the model shown in Figure 6-2 on page 168, diagram the structure of the argument.

ENVIRONMENTAL STUDIES

PAIRED READINGS

Permitting Trade in Ivory Will Harm Elephants

Humane Society of the United States

Prereading Questions

1. How could the ivory trade harm elephants?
2. Why do people want animal products that come from endangered species?

1   Confirming the worst fears of many animal protectionists, greed has won out over good judgment in the southern African nations of Botswana, Namibia, South Africa, Zambia, and Zimbabwe. These nations [have] made it clear to the international community that they value the money from the ivory trade more than they value the survival of already dwindling populations of elephants.

2   The five nations have submitted proposals to the Convention on International Trade in Endangered Species of Wild Fauna and Flora (CITES), asking to reduce international protections given to elephants within their borders and to trade internationally in stock-piled ivory. If the proposals are approved at the CITES meeting in November [2002] in Chile, elephant poaching could increase.[1]

3   The five nations are requesting permission to sell off their stockpiled ivory. They want to export a total of 87 metric tons of ivory at first, representing about 11,000 dead elephants. In addition, they want to export an additional 13 metric tons annually, equaling an additional 1,500 dead elephants each year. Moreover, they want to be able to export an unlimited number of tourist souvenirs each year.

A Catastrophic Proposal

4   Experts see no good coming from approving these proposals. "If the proposals are approved, it will make an already bad situation worse by confusing consumers as to the legality of ivory and by feeding the demand for ivory," says Dr. Teresa Telecky, director of The HSUS's [Humane Society of the United States] Wildlife Trade Program. "As we've already seen, an increased demand for ivory will, in turn, spur an increase in elephant poaching in African and Asian countries that are ill-equipped to fend off poachers."

5   Any legal international trade in ivory could result in the kind of catastrophe seen before the 1989 ivory ban. Prior to 1989, all African elephant populations were listed on CITES Appendix II, which allowed a regulated trade. The ivory trade regulation scheme failed. At that time, over 90% of ivory in trade was from poached elephants. "If we've

[1] In November 2002 the Convention on International Trade in Endangered Species (CITES) partially lifted the ban and permitted South Africa, Namibia, and Botswana to sell sixty tons of stockpiled tusks.

come to understand one thing, it's that international trade in ivory cannot be controlled, and that allowing any international trade, even on a one-time basis, has disastrous results for elephants," says Dr. Telecky.

6   To ban the trade in ivory, the Parties to CITES placed all elephants—African and Asian—on Appendix I. In 1997, CITES agreed to move the elephant populations of Botswana, Namibia, and Zimbabwe back to Appendix II and to allow a one-time export of their stockpiles to Japan, which took place in 1999. Inspired by this turn of events, South Africa fought (and won) to have its elephants downlisted at the 2000 CITES meeting. But opposition from the majority of African countries put the lid on any further ivory trade.

A Surge in Illegal Activities

7   As soon as the first downlisting was allowed, both poaching and illegal trade in ivory surged, though neither has yet reached pre-ban levels. Between January 1, 2000, and May 21, 2002, more than 5.9 metric tons of ivory, 2,542 tusks, and 14,648 pieces of ivory have been seized worldwide—representing more than 2,000 dead elephants. During the same period, a minimum of 965 African elephants and 39 Asian elephants have been poached and their ivory tusks removed. Furthermore, unconfirmed reports indicate that as many as 200 elephants were killed in the Central African Republic in 2001.

8   It isn't only the elephant populations with decreased CITES protection that are targeted by poachers. Kenya's and India's elephants are listed in Appendix I, but they face threats from poaching whenever restrictions on the sale of ivory are eased. "Poachers in many countries increase activity whenever CITES ivory trade proposals are announced in order to stockpile ivory in anticipation that the international ivory trade will soon resume," Dr. Telecky says.

9   This means that nations that shortsightedly choose to make money off the corpses of their elephants jeopardize the success of those nations that choose to profit from live elephants. The money at stake for those nations in the latter category is considerable: In 1989, Kenya's elephants were worth an estimated $25 million in annual tourism revenue. Kenya and India, which have kept their elephants on Appendix I, report high elephant poaching levels in recent years. They have submitted a joint proposal for the CITES meeting that would return all African elephant populations to Appendix I.

10   Ivory markets are flourishing. A recent investigation of South and Southeast Asian ivory markets, by researchers Esmond Martin and Dan Stiles for Save the Elephants, found more than 105,000 ivory items for sale in 521 retail shops in the 17 towns and cities in eight countries surveyed. Tourists and business travelers—including those from Europe, the United States, and Asia—are the main customers. Over 85% of the items on sale were jewelry, which is relatively cheap and easy to smuggle. Ivory products sold in Asian markets are made from the ivory of both Asian and African elephants.

—Opposing Viewpoints Series, 2005

Writing About the Reading
CHECKING YOUR VOCABULARY

1. For each of the words listed below, use context; prefixes, roots, and suffixes (see Chapter 3); and/or a dictionary to write a brief definition or synonym of the word as it is used in the reading.

a. protectionists (para. 1) _____

b. dwindling (para. 1) _____

c. stockpiled (para. 2) _____

d. poaching (para. 2) _____

e. spur (para. 4) _____

f. scheme (para. 5) _____

g. downlisted (para. 6) _____

h. shortsightedly (para. 9) _____

i. flourishing (para. 10) _____

2. Underline new, specialized terms introduced in the reading (see Chapter 3).
3. Draw a word map of one of the words in the reading.

CHECKING YOUR COMPREHENSION

1. The ivory trade of which five nations is criticized in the reading? Why?
2. What will result from an increased demand for ivory?
3. Why is regulated ivory trade unsuccessful?
4. About how many elephants were killed for their ivory from January 1, 2000, to May 21, 2002?
5. How would allowing trade in ivory affect Kenya?

THINKING CRITICALLY

1. What is the basic claim that the author makes? How is this claim supported?
2. What is the author's tone? How is it conveyed?
3. How effective is the author's use of statistics?
4. Identify some of the emotional language that the author uses. How does it contribute to the argument?
5. What assumptions does the author make?
6. Do you agree with the author's conclusion? Why or why not?

LEARNING/STUDY STRATEGY

Using the model shown in Figure 6-2 on page 168, diagram the structure of the argument.

Thinking About the Paired Readings
INTEGRATING IDEAS

1. Compare the purposes of the two authors in writing these essays.
2. Which argument is better stated and supported? Explain your answer.

3. Which contains more convincing data? Explain your answer.
4. What further information would you need in order to take a position on this issue? Where could you find that information?

GENERATING NEW IDEAS

1. Write an essay about the use of animals or animal products for pleasure and enjoyment. Take a position and develop an argument. Limit your argument by choosing one specific use such as wearing furs or hunting game.
2. Write a letter to the delegates of the Convention on International Trade in Endangered Species (CITES) urging them to either lift or re-enforce the ban on ivory trading.

ADDITIONAL PRACTICE

MULTIMEDIA ACTIVITIES

1. **Identifying the Argument of the Essay**

   http://commhum.mccneb.edu/argument/summary.htm

   Try this online tutorial in critical reasoning from Metropolitan Community College in Nebraska. Make notes about the new concepts you learn.

2. **Logic in Argumentative Writing**

   http://owl.english.purdue.edu/handouts/general/gl_argpers.html

   Review the common terms and concepts used in reasoning, and try the online exercises at this site from Purdue University. Use some of these ideas to analyze the conversations you have with your friends or discussions you hear on TV or the radio. Apply them to editorials in the newspaper or political speeches.

MYREADINGLAB

If your instructor has asked you to use Reading Road Trip, be sure to visit the "American Southwest" module for multimedia tutorials, exercises, and tests on critical thinking.

CHAPTER

7

Patterns of Academic Thought

LEARNING OBJECTIVES

✦ To recognize common academic thought patterns

✦ To use thought patterns to focus your reading

Think About It!

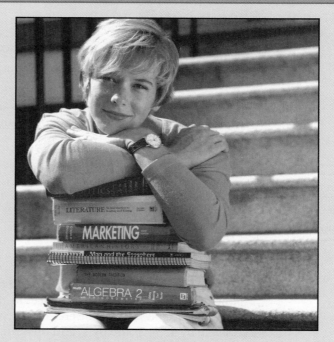

Like the student above, you probably are taking courses in several different disciplines. You may study marketing, anatomy and physiology, mathematics, and English composition all in one semester. During one day, you may read a poem, solve math problems, and study early developments in psychology. These diverse tasks seem difficult to master because you treat each course differently from every other. Consequently, you are forced to shift gears for each course, developing new approaches and strategies.

What few students realize is that a biologist and a psychologist, for example, think about and approach their subject matter in similar ways. Both carefully define terms, examine causes and effects, study similarities and differences, describe sequences of events, classify information, solve problems, and enumerate characteristics. The subject matter and language they use differ, but their approaches to the material are basically the same. Regardless of their field of expertise, researchers, textbook authors, and your professors use standard approaches, or patterns of thought, to organize and express their ideas. The more familiar you become with these patterns, the easier your reading assignments will be.

■ Patterns: A Focus for Reading

Let's begin by trying a few learning experiments.

Experiment 1. Supply the missing numbers in the following numeric sequence:

1, 5, 7, 8, 12, 14, 15, _____, _____, _____

Experiment 2. Study each of the following drawings briefly, and then continue reading.

Next, close the book and quickly sketch each of the drawings you studied.

Now let's analyze your performance. In the first experiment, the last three digits are 19, 21, and 22. If you were correct, you realized the numbers increased successively by 4, by 2, and by 1, and then the pattern repeated. Now supply the next three numbers. Did you get 26, 28, and 29? It is an easy task now that you know the pattern. Reconstructing the entire sequence from memory also is a simple task now that you know the pattern.

For the second experiment, you probably sketched some or all of drawings 1, 2, 4, and 5 correctly. But did you get drawing 3 correct? Probably not. Why? Drawing 3 is irregular and has no pattern.

From these experiments, you can see that patterns make certain tasks easier to complete and that they facilitate your memory and recall. Patterns exist for ideas as well; we will refer to them as **thought patterns.**

Familiarity with these basic thought patterns will enable you to approach all of your courses more effectively. You will find textbook chapters easier to read if you can identify the thought pattern(s) by which they are organized. The same patterns also are used by your professors as they lecture. Lectures will be easier to follow and your notes will be better organized if you can identify these patterns.

Commonly used academic thought patterns include:

- **definition**
- **classification**
- **order or sequence**
- **cause and effect**
- **comparison and contrast**
- **listing/enumeration**

These patterns can work for you in several ways.

1. **Patterns provide a focus for reading by enabling you to anticipate the author's thought development.** For example, from a heading or topic sentence alone, you often can predict the thought pattern that the section or paragraph will follow. When you encounter "Types of Government Spending," you might expect to read about how government spending is divided or classified. Or suppose you read the following topic sentence: "Vaporization, or evaporation as it is also called, is the change from a liquid to a gas." Here, you would anticipate vaporization to be further defined in the paragraph. If your professor announced, "Today we'll consider the impact of stress upon health," then you could expect the speaker to use a cause-and-effect pattern of development.

2. **Patterns help you remember and recall what you read.** Information that is grouped, chunked, or organized is easier to store than single, unrelated bits of information. Also, the manner in which information is stored in memory influences the ease with which it is retrieved. Thought patterns provide a vehicle for organizing information, and they function as retrieval clues for subsequent recall.

3. **Patterns are useful in your own writing;** they help you organize and express your ideas in a more coherent, comprehensible form. As you write essay exam answers, class assignments, or term papers, thought patterns will provide a base or structure around which you can effectively develop ideas.

The following section describes each thought pattern listed above. In subsequent chapters, you will see how these patterns are used in specific academic disciplines.

■ Academic Thought Patterns

Definition

Each academic discipline has its own specialized vocabulary (see Chapter 3). One of the primary purposes of introductory textbooks is to introduce students to this new language. Consequently, definition is a commonly used pattern throughout most introductory-level texts.

Suppose you were asked to define the word *comedian* for someone unfamiliar with the term. First, you would probably say that a comedian is a person who entertains. Then you might distinguish a comedian from other types of entertainers by saying that a comedian is an entertainer who tells jokes and makes others laugh. Finally, you might mention, by way of example, the names of several well-known comedians who have appeared on television. Although you may have presented it informally, your definition would have followed the standard, classic pattern. The first part of your definition tells what general class or group the term belongs to (entertainers). The second part tells what distinguishes the term from other items in the same class or category. The third part includes further explanation, characteristics, examples, or applications.

Here are two additional examples:

TERM	GENERAL CLASS	DISTINGUISHING CHARACTERISTICS
Stress	Physiological reaction	A response to a perceived threat
Mutant	Organism	Carries a gene that has undergone a change

See how the term *genetics* is defined in the following paragraph, and notice how the term and the general class are presented in the first sentence. The remainder of the paragraph presents the distinguishing characteristics.

Genetics is the scientific study of heredity, the transmission of characteristics from parents to offspring. Genetics explains why offspring resemble their parents and also why they are not identical to them. Genetics is a subject that has considerable economic, medical, and social significance and is partly the basis for the modern theory of evolution. Because of its importance, genetics has been a topic of central interest in the study of life for centuries. Modern concepts in genetics are fundamentally different, however, from earlier ones.

—Mix et al., *Biology: The Network of Life,* p. 262

Writers often provide clues that signal the thought pattern being used. These signals may occur within single sentences or as transitions or connections between sentences. Examples of transitional words or phrases used for the definition pattern are shown below. (Transitional words that occur in phrases are italicized here to help you spot them.)

TRANSITIONAL WORDS

genetics *is* . . .

bureaucracy *means* . . .

patronage *refers to* . . .

aggression *can be defined as* . . .

deficit is *another term* that . . .

balance of power *also means* . . .

EXERCISE 7-1   *Read the following paragraphs and answer the questions that follow.*

A. The French satirist and social reformer Voltaire (1694–1778) once defined the family as a "group of people who cannot stand the sight of each other but are forced to live under the same roof." The American poet Robert Frost (1875–1963) in his narrative poem *Death of the Hired Man* has one character observe, "Home is the place where, when you have to go there, They have to take you in." Whether home and family prove burdensome depends upon one's maturity level, emotional stability, and willingness to work on the difficulties which arise from close relationships. Most would agree, however, that there are few households which glide serenely along on a perpetually even keel.

—Janaro and Altshuler, *The Art of Being Human,* p. 334–35

1. What is the definition of family as used in this paragraph?
2. How is home defined?
3. What transitional word(s) is/are used with family?
4. What transitional word(s) is/are used with home?
5. What general class do both home and family belong to according to this paragraph?

B. The integumentary system is the external covering of the body, or the skin. It waterproofs the body and cushions and protects the deeper tissues from injury. It also excretes salts and urea in perspiration and helps regulate body temperature. Temperature, pressure, and pain receptors located in the skin alert us to what is happening at the body surface.

—Mareib, *Essentials of Human Anatomy and Physiology,* p. 3

1. What is the definition of the integumentary system?
2. What transitional word is used in this paragraph?
3. List three things the integumentary system does.
4. How does the skin alert us to what is happening at the body surface?
5. What does the integumentary system excrete?

C. Given that Congress designated the 1990s as "the decade of the brain," it is not surprising that one of the emerging specialties in psychology is concerned with brain functioning. Neuropsychologists are trained to diagnose disorders of the brain. Using various tests, they try to identify specific brain areas that may be malfunctioning. They often conduct research to identify early symptoms that predict the development of disorders such as Huntington's disease. They also devise rehabilitation programs to help patients regain as much of their abilities as possible after suffering brain damage, strokes, or traumatic brain injury.

—Davis and Palladino, *Psychology,* p. 40

1. What general class do neuropsychologists belong to?
2. What is a distinguishing characteristic of neuropsychologists?
3. How do neuropsychologists identify specific brain areas that may be malfunctioning?
4. What kind of research do neuropsychologists often perform?
5. Why do neuropsychologists devise rehabilitation programs?

EXERCISE 7-2   *Read the following passage about polarization and answer the questions that follow.*

Another way in which language can obscure differences is in its preponderance of extreme terms and its relative lack of middle terms, a system that often leads to polarization. **Polarization** is the tendency to look at the world in terms of opposites and to describe it in extremes—good or bad, positive or negative, healthy or sick, intelligent or stupid. It's often referred to as the fallacy of "either-or" or "black or white." Most people exist somewhere between the extremes. Yet there's a strong tendency to view only the extremes and to categorize people, objects, and events in terms of these polar opposites.

Problems are created when opposites are used in inappropriate situations. For example, "The politician is either for us or against us." The politician may be for us in some things and against us in other things, or may be neutral.

In correcting this tendency to polarize, be aware of implying (and believing) that two extreme classes include all possible classes—that an individual must be one or the other, with no alternatives ("Are you pro-choice or pro-life?"). Most people, most events, most qualities exist between polar extremes. When others imply that there are only two sides or alternatives, look for the middle ground.

—DeVito, *Human Communication,* p. 124

1. What is the purpose of the passage?
2. Highlight the topic sentence of each paragraph. If there is no stated main idea, write a sentence expressing the main idea.
3. Highlight all transitional words.
4. What is the definition of polarization?
5. Why is polarization often a problem?
6. What are some examples of polarized opposites?
7. What do polarized opposites exclude?
8. What is the solution to the problem of polarization?

EXERCISE 7-3

Using the definition pattern described above, work with a classmate to write a two-part definition for each of the following terms.

1. robot
2. age discrimination
3. fiction
4. adolescence
5. phobia

Classification

If you were asked to describe types of computers, you might mention desktop, laptop, and notebook computers. By dividing a broad topic into its major categories, you are using a pattern known as **classification.**

This pattern is widely used in many academic subjects. For example, a psychology text might explain human needs by classifying them into two categories: primary and secondary. In a chemistry textbook, various compounds may be grouped and discussed according to common characteristics, such as the presence of hydrogen or oxygen. The classification pattern divides a topic into parts on the basis of common or shared characteristics.

Here are a few examples of topics and the classifications or categories into which each might be divided:

movies: comedy, horror, mystery

motives: achievement, power, affiliation, competency

plant: leaves, stem, roots

Note how the following paragraph classifies the various types of cancers:

> The name of the cancer is derived from the type of tissue in which it develops. Carcinoma (carc = cancer; omo = tumor) refers to a malignant tumor consisting of epithelial cells. A tumor that develops from a gland is called an adenosarcoma (adeno = gland). Sarcoma is a general term for any cancer arising from connective tissue. Osteogenic sarcomas (osteo = bone; genic = origin), the most frequent type of childhood cancer, destroy normal bone tissue and eventually spread to other areas of the body. Myelomas (myelos = marrow) are malignant tumors, occurring in middle-aged and older people, that interfere with the blood-cell-producing function of bone marrow and cause anemia. Chondrosarcomas (chondro = cartilage) are cancerous growths of cartilage.
>
> —Tortora, *Introduction to the Human Body,* p. 56

Examples of transitional words and phrases that indicate the classification pattern follow.

TRANSITIONAL WORDS

there are *several kinds of* chemical bonding . . .

there are *numerous types of* . . .

reproduction can be *classified as* . . .

the human skeleton is *composed of* . . .

muscles *comprise* . . .

one type of communication . . .

another type of communication . . .

finally, there is . . .

EXERCISE 7-4   *Read the following paragraphs and answer the questions that follow.*

A. The reptiles made one of the most spectacular adaptive radiations in all of Earth history. One group, the pterosaurs, took to the air. These "dragons of the sky" possessed huge membranous wings that allowed them rudimentary flight. Another group of reptiles, exemplified by the fossil *Archaeopteryx,* led to more successful flyers: the birds. Whereas some reptiles took to the skies, others returned to the sea, including fish-eating plesiosaurs and ichthyosaurs. These reptiles became proficient swimmers, but retained their reptilian teeth and breathed by means of lungs.

—Tarbuck and Lutgens, *Earth Science,* p. 309

1. List the classifications of reptiles included in this paragraph.
2. Highlight the transitional words in this paragraph that signal the classification pattern.
3. Which classification does *Archaeopteryx* belong to?
4. Which classification of reptiles could swim proficiently?
5. What is another name for pterosaurs?

B. From the hundreds of billions of galaxies, several basic types have been identified: spiral, elliptical, and irregular. The Milky Way and the Great Galaxy in Andromeda are examples of fairly large spiral galaxies. Typically, spiral galaxies are disk-shaped with a somewhat greater concentration of stars near their centers, but there are numerous variations. Viewed broadside, arms are often seen extending from the central nucleus and sweeping gracefully away. One type of spiral galaxy, however, has the stars arranged in the shape of a bar, which rotates as a rigid system. This requires that the outer stars move faster than the inner ones, a fact not easy for astronomers to reconcile with the laws of motion. Attached to each end of these bars are curved spiral arms. These have become known as barred spiral galaxies. The most abundant group, making up 60 percent of the total is the elliptical galaxies. These are generally smaller than spiral galaxies. Some are so much smaller, in fact, that the term dwarf has been applied. Because these dwarf galaxies are not visible at great distances, a survey of the sky reveals more of the conspicuous large spiral galaxies. As their name implies, elliptical galaxies have an ellipsoidal shape that ranges to nearly spherical, and they lack spiral arms. Only 10 percent of the known galaxies lack symmetry and are classified as irregular galaxies. The best-known irregular galaxies, the Large and Small Magellanic Clouds in the Southern Hemisphere, are easily visible with the unaided eye.

—Tarbuck and Lutgens, *Earth Science*, pp. 620–21

1. What are the three primary classifications of galaxies?
2. What determines how a galaxy is classified?
3. Highlight the transitional words that signal the classification pattern.
4. How can the types of spiral galaxies be classified?
5. What is another name for elliptical galaxies?

EXERCISE 7-5   *Read the following passages and answer the questions that follow.*

Passage A
TYPES OF BONES

The bones of the body may be classified into four principal types on the basis of shape: long, short, flat, and irregular. **Long bones** have greater length than width and consist of a shaft and extremities (ends). They are slightly curved for strength. Long bones consist mostly of compact bone (dense bone with few spaces) but also contain considerable amounts of spongy bone (bone with large spaces). The details of compact and spongy bone are discussed shortly. Long bones include bones of the thighs, legs, toes, arms, forearms, and fingers.

Short bones are somewhat cube-shaped and nearly equal in length and width. They are spongy except at the surface where there is a thin layer of compact bone. Short bones include the wrist and ankle bones.

Flat bones are generally thin and composed of two more or less parallel plates of compact bone enclosing a layer of spongy bone. Flat bones afford considerable protection and provide extensive areas for muscle attachment. Flat bones include the cranial bones, the sternum (breastbone), ribs, and the scapulas (shoulder blades).

Irregular bones have complex shapes and cannot be grouped into any of the three categories just described. They also vary in the amount of spongy and compact bone present. Such bones include the vertebrae (backbones) and certain facial bones.

—Tortora, *Introduction to the Human Body,* p. 100

1. What is the purpose of this passage?
2. Highlight the topic sentence of each paragraph. If there is no stated main idea, write a sentence expressing the main idea.
3. Highlight transitional words that signal the classification pattern.
4. What are the four principal types of bones?
5. What is the basis of classification (how are they divided)?
6. How can long bones be classified?
7. Why are irregular bones a separate classification?

Passage B
TYPES OF FOSSILS

Fossils are of many types. The remains of relatively recent organisms may not have been altered at all. Such objects as teeth, bones, and shells are common examples. Far less common are entire animals, flesh included, that have been preserved because of rather unusual circumstances. Remains of prehistoric elephants called mammoths that were frozen in the Arctic tundra of Siberia and Alaska are examples, as are the mummified remains of sloths preserved in a dry cave in Nevada.

Given enough time, the remains of an organism are likely to be modified. Often fossils become *petrified* (literally, "turned into stone"), meaning that the small internal cavities and pores of the original structure are filled with precipitated mineral matter. In other instances *replacement* may occur. Here the cell walls and other solid material are removed and replaced with mineral matter. Sometimes the microscopic details of the replaced structure are faithfully retained.

Molds and casts constitute another common class of fossils. When a shell or other structure is buried in sediment and then dissolved by underground water, a *mold* is created. The mold faithfully reflects only the shape and surface marking of the organism; it does not reveal any information concerning its internal structure. If these hollow spaces are subsequently filled with mineral matter, *casts* are created.

A type of fossilization called *carbonization* is particularly effective in preserving leaves and delicate animal forms. It occurs when fine sediment encases the remains of an organism. As time passes, pressure squeezes out the liquid and gaseous components and leaves behind a thin residue of carbon. Black shales deposited as organic-rich mud in oxygen-poor environments often contain abundant carbonized remains. If the film of carbon is lost from a fossil preserved in fine-grained sediment, a replica of the surface, called an *impression,* may still show considerable detail.

—Tarbuck and Lutgens, *Earth Science,* pp. 278–79

1. What is the purpose of the passage?
2. Highlight the topic sentence of each paragraph. If there is no stated main idea, write a sentence expressing the main idea.
3. Highlight all transitional words.
4. What are the three main classifications of fossils?
5. What are the two types of modified fossils?
6. How are molds and casts distinguished?
7. Which type of fossilization is most effective for leaves?

EXERCISE 7-6   *Divide each of the topics listed below into several groups or categories.*

1. foods _____

2. cars _____

3. arts _____

4. laws _____

5. pollutants _____

Order or Sequence

If you were asked to summarize what you did today, you probably would mention key events in the order in which they occurred. In describing how to write a particular computer program, you would detail the process step by step. If asked to list what you feel are your accomplishments so far this week, you might present them in order of importance, listing your most important accomplishment first. In each case, you are presenting information in a particular sequence or order. Each of these examples illustrates a form of the thought pattern known as **order**, or **sequence**. Let us look at several types of order.

Chronology   **Chronological order** refers to the sequence in which events occur in time. This pattern is essential in the academic disciplines concerned with the interpretation of events in the past. History, government, and anthropology are prime examples. In various forms of literature, chronological order is evident; the narrative form, used in novels, short stories, and narrative essays, relies on chronological order.

The following paragraph uses chronology to describe how full-scale intervention in Vietnam began.

> The pretext for full-scale intervention in Vietnam came in late July 1964. On July 30, South Vietnamese PT (patrol torpedo) boats attacked bases in the Gulf of Tonkin inside North Vietnamese waters. Simultaneously, the *Maddox,* an American destroyer, steamed into the area to disrupt North Vietnamese communication facilities. On August 2, possibly seeing the two separate missions as a combined maneuver against them, the North Vietnamese sent out several PT boats to attack the destroyer. The *Maddox* fired, sinking one of the attackers, then radioed the news to Washington. Johnson ordered another ship into the bay. On August 3 both

destroyers reported another attack, although somewhat later, the commander of the *Maddox* radioed that he was not sure. Nonetheless, the president ordered American planes to retaliate by bombing inside North Vietnam.

—Wilson et al., *The Pursuit of Liberty: A History of the American People,* p. 492–93

Examples of transitional words and phrases that indicate chronological order include the following.

TRANSITIONAL WORDS

in ancient times . . .

at the start of the battle . . .

on September 12 . . .

the *first* primate species . . .

later efforts . . .

Other clue words are:

then, before, during, by the time, while, afterward, as, after, thereafter, meanwhile, at that point

---

Process   In disciplines that focus on procedures, steps, or stages by which actions are accomplished, writers often employ the **process** pattern. These subjects include mathematics, natural and life sciences, computer science, and engineering. The pattern is similar to chronology, in that the steps or stages follow each other in time. Transitional words often used in conjunction with this pattern are similar to those used for chronological order.

Note how this pattern is used in a paragraph explaining what occurs in the brain during sleep.

Let us track your brain waves through the night. As you prepare to go to bed, an EEG records that your brain waves are moving along at a rate of about 14 cycles per second (cps). Once you are comfortably in bed, you begin to relax and your brain waves slow down to a rate of about 8 to 12 cps. When you fall asleep, you enter your *sleep cycle,* each of whose stages shows a distinct EEG pattern. In Stage 1 sleep, the EEG shows brain waves of about 3 to 7 cps. During Stage 2, the EEG is characterized by *sleep spindles,* minute bursts of electrical activity of 12 to 16 cps. In the next two stages (3 and 4) of sleep, you enter into a very deep state of relaxed sleep. Your brain waves slow to about 1 to 2 cps, and your breathing and heart rate decrease. In a final stage, the electrical activity of your brain increases; your EEG looks very similar to those recorded during stages 1 and 2. It is during this stage that you will experience REM sleep, and you will begin to dream.

—Zimbardo and Gerrig, *Psychology and Life,* p. 115

Order of Importance   This pattern of ideas sometimes expresses order of priority or preference. Ideas are arranged in one of two ways: from most to least important, or from least to most important. In the following paragraph, the causes of the downward trend in the standard of living are arranged in order of importance.

The United States' downward trend in standard of living has many different causes, of which only a few major ones can be identified here. Most important is probably dein-dustrialization, the massive loss of manufacturing jobs as many U.S. corporations move their production to poor, labor-cheap countries. But deindustrialization hurts mostly low-skilled manufacturing workers. Most of the well-educated, high-skilled employees in service industries are left unscathed. Deindustrialization alone is therefore not enough to explain the economic decline. Another major factor is the great increase in con-sumption and decrease in savings. Like their government, people spend more than they earn and become deeply in debt. Those who do practice thrift still have an average rate of savings significantly lower than in countries with fast-growing economies. The habits of high consumption and low saving may have resulted from the great affluence after the Second World War up until the early 1970s (Harrison, 1992).

—Thio, *Sociology,* p. 255

Order of importance is used in almost every field of study. Commonly used clues that suggest this pattern are:

TRANSITIONAL WORDS

is *less* essential than . . .

more revealing is . . .

of *primary* interest is . . .

Other clue words are:

first, next, last, most important, primarily, secondarily

Spatial Order   Information organized according to its physical location, or posi-tion or order in space, exhibits a pattern known as **spatial order.** Spatial order is used in academic disciplines in which physical descriptions are important. These include numerous technical fields, engineering, and the biological sciences.

You can see how the following description of a particular type of blood cir-culation relies on spatial relationships.

Pulmonary circulation conducts blood between the heart and the lungs. Oxygen-poor, CO_2-laden blood returns through two large veins (venae cavae) from tissues within the body, enters the right atrium, and is then moved into the right ventricle of the heart. From there, it is pumped into the pulmonary artery, which divides into two branches, each leading to one of the lungs. In the lung, the arteries undergo extensive branching, giving rise to vast networks of capillaries where gas exchange takes place, with blood becoming oxygenated while CO_2 is discharged. Oxygen-rich blood then returns to the heart via the pulmonary veins.

—Mix et al., *Biology: The Network of Life,* pp. 663–64

Diagramming is of the utmost importance in working with this pattern; often, a diagram accompanies text material. For example, a diagram makes the functions of the various parts of the human brain easier to understand. Lecturers often refer to a visual aid or chalkboard drawing when providing spatial descriptions. Examples of transitional words and phrases that indicate spatial order follow.

TRANSITIONAL WORDS

the *left side* of the brain . . .

the *lower* portion . . .

the *outer* covering . . .

beneath the surface . . .

Other transitional words are:

next to, beside, to the left,
in the center, externally

EXERCISE 7-7   *Read the following paragraphs and answer the questions that follow.*

A. *The following paragraph uses the spatial pattern.*

> **Skeletal muscle tissue** is named for its location—attached to bones. Skeletal muscle tissue is also *voluntary* because it can be made to contract by conscious control. A single skeletal muscle fiber (cell) is cylindrical and appears *striated* (striped) under a microscope; when organized in a tissue, the fibers are parallel to each other. Each muscle fiber has a plasma membrane, the **sarcolemma**, surrounding the cytoplasm, or **sarcoplasm**. Skeletal muscle fibers are multinucleate (more than one nucleus), and the nuclei are near the sarcolemma.
>
> —Tortora, *Introduction to the Human Body,* p. 77

1. Briefly describe skeletal muscle tissue.
2. Highlight the transitional words used to indicate the spatial pattern.
3. How are skeletal muscle fibers or cells arranged in a tissue?
4. Where can the sarcolemma (or plasma membrane) be found in muscle fibers?
5. Where are the nuclei in skeletal muscle fibers located?

B. *The following paragraph uses the chronology pattern.*

> Only two presidents have been impeached. The House impeached Andrew Johnson, Lincoln's successor, in 1868 on charges stemming from his disagreement with radical Republicans. He narrowly escaped conviction. Richard Nixon came as close to impeachment as anyone since. On July 31, 1974, the House Judiciary Committee voted to recommend his impeachment to the full House as a result of the **Watergate** scandal. Nixon escaped a certain vote for impeachment by resigning. In 1998, the House voted two articles of impeachment against President Clinton on party-line votes. The public clearly opposed the idea, however, and the Senate voted to acquit the president on both counts in 1999.
>
> —Edwards, *Government in America,* p. 416

1. How many events are described in this paragraph?
2. Highlight the transitional words that are used to indicate the chronology pattern.
3. Which event occurred most recently?
4. When was Andrew Johnson impeached?
5. Whose impeachment episode occurred in 1974?

C. *The following paragraph uses the process pattern.*

BMI [body mass index] is an index of the relationship of height and weight. It is one of the most accurate indicators of a person's health risk due to excessive weight, rather than "fatness" per se. Although many people recoil in fright when they see they have to convert pounds to kilograms and inches to meters to calculate BMI, it really is not as difficult as it may seem. To get your kilogram weight, just divide your weight in pounds (without shoes or clothing) by 2.2. To convert your height to meters squared, divide your height in inches (without shoes) by 39.4, then square this result. Sounds pretty easy and it actually is. Once you have these basic values, calculating your BMI involves dividing your weight in kilograms by your height in meters squared.

$$BMI = \frac{\text{Weight (in lbs)} \div 2.2 \text{ (to determine weight in kg)}}{(\text{Height [in inches]} \div 39.4)^2 \text{ (to determine height in meters squared)}}$$

Healthy weights have been defined as those associated with BMIs of 19 to 25, the range of the lowest statistical health risk. A BMI greater than 25 indicates overweight and potentially significant health risks. The desirable range for females is between 21 and 23; for males, it is between 22 and 24. A body mass index of over 30 is considered obese. Many experts believe this number is too high, particularly for younger adults.

—Donatelle, *Access to Health*, p. 264

1. What process is being described in this paragraph?
2. Highlight the transitional words that are used to signal the process pattern.
3. What is the first step in the process?
4. Is a BMI of 23 considered healthy?
5. How do you convert height to meters squared?

D. *The following paragraph uses the spatial order pattern.*

The nucleus is bound by a double membrane barrier called the **nuclear membrane** or **nuclear envelope**. Between the two membranes is a fluid-filled "moat," or space. At various points, the two layers of the nuclear membrane approach each other and fuse, and nuclear pores penetrate through the fused regions. Like other cellular membranes, the nuclear membrane is selectively permeable, but passage of substances through it is much freer than elsewhere because of its relatively large pores. The nuclear membrane encloses a jellylike fluid called **nucleoplasm** in which the nucleoli and chromatin are suspended.

—Mareib, *Essentials of Human Anatomy and Physiology*, p. 55

1. What is being described in this paragraph?
2. Highlight the transitional words that are used to signal the spatial order pattern.
3. What is between the two outer membranes of a nucleus?
4. What is inside the nucleoplasm?
5. If you read this description in a textbook, what would you expect to accompany it?

E. The following paragraph uses the order of importance pattern.

Media resources are being reassembled in a new pattern, with three main parts. The first is the traditional mass media that will continue to be for a long time the most important element in the pattern in terms of their reach and influence. The second consists of the advanced electronic mass media, operating primarily within the new information utility, and competing increasingly with older media services. Finally, there are newer forms of personal electronic media, formed by clusters of like-minded people to fulfill their own professional or individual information needs. Internet chat rooms and personalized Web pages are fast-expanding examples of this development. Each of these parts of the evolving mass-communications pattern deserves separate scrutiny.

–Dizard, *Old Media, New Media,* p. 179

1. What does this paragraph describe?
2. Highlight the transitional words that are used to signal the pattern.
3. Why is traditional mass media the most important type of resource?
4. Which type of media resource competes the most with the traditional mass media?
5. What are some examples of personal electronic media?

EXERCISE 7-8   *Read the following passages and answer the questions that follow.*

Passage A

The shape of a state may affect its ability to consolidate its territory and control circulation across its borders. A circle would be the most efficient shape on an isotropic plain because a circular state would have the shortest possible border in relation to its territory, and that shape would allow all places to be reached from the center with the least travel. States with shapes closest to this model are sometimes called *compact states.* Bulgaria, Poland, and Zimbabwe are examples. *Prorupted states* are nearly compact, but they have at least one narrow extension of territory. Namibia and Thailand are examples. If these extensions reach out to navigable waterways, the extensions are called *corridors. Elongated states* are long and thin, such as Chile or Norway, and *fragmented states* consist of several isolated bits of territory. *Archipelago states,* made up of several strings of islands, such as Japan or the Philippines, are fragmented states. Still other states, called *perforated states*, are interrupted by the territory of another state enclosed entirely within them. South Africa, for example, is perforated by Lesotho, and Italy is perforated by the Vatican and by San Marino.

The shape of a state's territory may influence the government's ability to organize that territory, but this is not always true. A topographic barrier such as a mountain chain may effectively divide even a compact state. Bolivia and Switzerland, for example, are compact in shape, but mountain chains disrupt their interiors. For some of their regions, trade across international borders is easier than trade with other regions of their own country. The people throughout an archipelago state, by contrast, may be successfully linked by shipping.

Before drawing any conclusions about political control from the shape of a state alone, one must consider the distribution of topographic features, the state's population and resources, and whether any centrifugal forces such as economic or cultural ties straddle the state's borders.

—Bergman and Renwick, *Introduction to Geography,* pp. 442–43

1. What is the purpose of the passage?
2. Highlight the topic sentence of each paragraph. If there is no stated main idea, write a sentence expressing the main idea.
3. Highlight all transitional words.
4. What kind of study aid would help you understand this passage?
5. What is a state that is nearly circular in shape called?
6. What is a corridor?
7. What is a perforated state?

Passage B

The first American daily newspaper was printed in Philadelphia in 1783, but such papers did not proliferate until the technological advances of the mid-nineteenth century. The ratification of the First Amendment in 1791, guaranteeing freedom of speech, gave even the earliest American newspapers freedom to print whatever they saw fit. This has given the media a unique ability to display the government's dirty linen, a propensity that continues to distinguish the American press today.

Rapid printing and cheap paper made possible the "penny press," which could be bought for a penny and read at home. In 1841, Horace Greeley's *New York Tribune* was founded, and in 1851, the *New York Times* started up. By the 1840s, the telegraph permitted a primitive "wire service," which relayed news stories from city to city faster than ever before. The Associated Press, founded in 1849, depended heavily on this new technology.

At the turn of the century, newspaper magnates Joseph Pulitzer and William Randolph Hearst ushered in the era of "yellow journalism." This sensational style of reporting focused on violence, corruption, wars, and gossip, often with a less than scrupulous regard for the truth. On a visit to the United States at that time, young Winston Churchill said that "the essence of American journalism is vulgarity divested of truth." In the midst of the Spanish-American conflict over Cuba, Hearst once boasted of his power over public opinion by telling a news artist "You furnish the pictures and I'll furnish the war."

Newspapers consolidated into **chains** during the early part of the twentieth century. Today's massive media conglomerates (Gannet, Knight-Ridder, and Newhouse are the largest) control newspapers with 78 percent of the nation's daily circulation. Thus, three of four Americans now read a newspaper owned not by a fearless local editor but by a corporation headquartered elsewhere. Often these chains control television and radio stations as well.

—Edwards, *Government in America,* pp. 223–24

1. What is the purpose of the passage?
2. Highlight the topic sentence of each paragraph. If there is no stated main idea, write a sentence expressing the main idea.
3. Highlight all transitional words.
4. How did the American print media begin?

5. When was the *New York Times* founded?
6. What era began at the turn of the century?
7. How are most newspapers owned today?

Passage C
DEATH FROM INFECTIOUS DISEASES

The single leading communicable cause of death in the world today is the human immunodeficiency virus (HIV), which causes AIDS. It was responsible for 2.7 million deaths in 1999, almost 5 percent of all deaths. Acquired immune-deficiency syndrome (AIDS) is a viral disease that destroys the body's ability to fight infections. It is believed that the AIDS virus emerged in Africa in the 1950s; by 2000 about 35 million people worldwide had contracted the AIDS virus, and 15,000 new infections were occurring each day. India was probably the country with the greatest number of infected people (about 3.5 million), but two-thirds of all people infected were in sub-Saharan Africa. In several African countries, AIDS-related illnesses were the leading cause of adult death. AIDS has shortened life expectancy 17 to 20 years in Botswana, Zimbabwe, and Zambia. AIDS causes massive human suffering, and it also has a pernicious economic impact.

The second leading communicable cause of death is diarrheal diseases, responsible for about 4 percent of all deaths. The most important of these is cholera. New strains of cholera appear regularly, and they are spread through contaminated water and poor sanitation. Cholera periodically surges out of Asia.

Tuberculosis is the third leading communicable cause of death, causing about 3 percent of the total. Approximately one-third of the human population carries TB bacilli in their bodies, but in the vast majority of cases the disease is latent and cannot be transmitted. New strains of drug-resistant tuberculosis, however, are multiplying, and the war against this disease continues.

—Bergman and Renwick, *Introduction to Geography*, pp. 182–83

1. What is the purpose of the passage?
2. Highlight the topic sentence of each paragraph. If there is no stated main idea, write a sentence expressing the main idea.
3. Highlight all transitional words.
4. What is AIDS?
5. What is the most important type of diarrheal disease?
6. What is the leading cause of adult death in several African countries?
7. What percent of deaths is caused by tuberculosis?
8. What standard is used to place these diseases in order of importance?

Passage D

Even before you take your first bite of pizza, your body has already begun a series of complex digestive responses. Your mouth prepares for the food by increasing production of **saliva**. Saliva contains mostly water, which aids in chewing and swallowing, but it also contains important enzymes that begin the process of food breakdown, including amylase, which begins to break down carbohydrates. Enzymes are protein compounds that facilitate chemical reactions but are not altered in the process. From the mouth, the food passes down the **esophagus**, a 9-to 10-inch tube that connects the mouth and stomach. A series of contractions and relaxations by the muscles lining the esophagus gently move food to the next digestive organ, the **stomach**. Here food mixes with enzymes and stomach acids. Hydrochloric acid begins to work in combination with pepsin, an enzyme, to break down proteins. In most people, the stomach secretes enough mucus to protect the stomach lining from these harsh digestive juices.

Further digestive activity takes place in the **small intestine**, a 20-foot coiled tube containing three sections: the *duodenum,* the *jejunum,* and the *ileum.* Each section secretes digestive enzymes that, when combined with enzymes from the liver and the pancreas, further contribute to the breakdown of proteins, fats and carbohydrates. Once broken down, these nutrients are absorbed in the bloodstream to supply body cells with energy. The liver is the major organ that determines whether nutrients are stored, sent to cells or organs, or excreted. Solid wastes consisting of fiber, water, and salts are dumped into the large intestine, where most of the water and salts are reabsorbed into the system and the fiber is passed out the anus. The entire digestive process takes approximately 24 hours.

—Donatelle, *Access to Health*, pp. 223–24

1. What is the purpose of the passage?
2. Highlight the topic sentence of each paragraph. If there is no stated main idea, write a sentence expressing the main idea.
3. Highlight all transitional words.
4. What pattern is used to describe digestion?
5. How does food travel from the mouth to the stomach?
6. What role does the liver play?
7. What happens in the stomach?

EXERCISE 7-9   *Read each of the following opening sentences from a textbook reading assignment, and anticipate whether the material will be developed using chronology, process, order of importance, or spatial order. Then underline the portion(s) of the sentence that suggest(s) the pattern you choose.*

1. Several statistical procedures are used to track the changes in the divorce rate.

   _____

2. The immune system's ability to defend against an almost infinite variety of antigens depends on a process called clonal selection.[1]

   _____

3. We have no idea how many individuals comprised the human species in our earliest days, and we don't know much more about our numbers in recent times.[2]

   _____

4. There are sources of information about corporations that might help an investor evaluate them. One of the most useful is the *Value Line Investment Survey.*

---

5. Human development begins at conception, when the father's sperm cell unites with the mother's ovum.[3]

---

6. In the human digestive system, the breakdown of food particles begins in the mouth, where chewing breaks food apart and increases the surface area on which enzymes can act.[4]

---

7. The two atrioventricular (AV) valves, one located at each atrial-ventricular junction, prevent backflow into the atria when the ventricles are contracting.[5]

---

8. One of the most significant benefits of family therapy is the strengthening of the family unit.

---

9. The spinal cord is located within the spinal column; it looks like a section of rope or twine.

---

10. The transition from medieval to modern societies occurred from approximately 1400 to 1800.

Cause and Effect

The **cause-and-effect** pattern expresses a relationship between two or more actions, events, or occurrences that are connected in time. The relationship differs, however, from chronological order in that one event leads to another by *causing* it. Information that is organized in terms of the cause-and-effect pattern may:

- explain causes, sources, reasons, motives, and action
- explain the effect, result, or consequence of a particular action
- explain both causes and effects

Cause and effect is clearly illustrated by the following passage, which gives the sources of fashions or the reasons why fashions occur.

> Why do fashions occur in the first place? One reason is that some cultures, like ours, *value change:* what is new is good, what is newer is even better. Thus, in many

modern societies clothing styles change yearly, while people in traditional societies may wear the same style for generations. A second reason is that many industries promote quick changes in fashion to increase sales. A third reason is that fashions usually trickle down from the top. A new style may occasionally originate from lower-status groups, as blue jeans did. But most fashions come from upper-class people who like to adopt some style or artifact as a badge of their status. But they cannot monopolize most status symbols for long. Their style is adopted by the middle class, maybe copied or modified for use by lower-status groups, offering many people the prestige of possessing a high-status symbol.

—Thio, *Sociology,* p. 534

The cause-and-effect pattern is used extensively in many academic fields. All disciplines that ask the question "Why" employ the cause-and-effect thought pattern. It is widely used in the sciences, technologies, and social sciences.

Many statements expressing cause-and-effect relationships appear in direct order, with the cause stated first and the effect following: "When demand for a product increases, prices rise." However, reverse order is sometimes used, as in the following statement: "Prices rise when a product's demand increases."

EXERCISE 7-10   *Identify the cause and the effect in each of the following statements. Circle the cause and underline the effect.*

1. Most nutritionists agree that long-term weight loss involves a combination of moderate dieting (say, eating 200 to 500 fewer calories a day than your body requires) and moderate exercise, both of which usually involve some behavior modification.[6]
2. When the body loses fluids, the kidneys stimulate the production of a hormone that activates the thirst drive.
3. Anorexia nervosa—a type of self-starvation—may be caused, in part, by our culture's emphasis on thinness.
4. The decrease in tensions between the former Soviet Union and the Western world has made it possible for the UN to become much more active than in the past.[7]
5. A computer program is easy or difficult to run, depending in part on the data entry system you choose.

The cause-and-effect pattern is not limited to an expression of a simple one-cause, one-effect relationship. There may be multiple causes, or multiple effects, or both multiple causes and multiple effects. For example, both slippery road conditions and your failure to buy snow tires (causes) may contribute to your car's sliding into the ditch (effect).

In other instances, a chain of causes or effects may occur. For instance, failing to set your alarm clock may force you to miss your 8:00 A.M. class, which in turn may cause you not to submit your term paper on time, which may result in a grade penalty. Transitional words or phrases that suggest the cause-and-effect pattern follow.

> **TRANSITIONAL WORDS**
>
> stress *causes* . . .
>
> aggression *creates* . . .
>
> depression *leads to* . . .
>
> forethought *yields* . . .
>
> mental retardation *stems from* . . .
>
> life changes *produce* . . .
>
> hostility *breeds* . . .
>
> avoidance *results in* . . .
>
> Other transitional words are:
>
> therefore, consequently, hence, for this reason, since

EXERCISE 7-11

Determine whether each of the following statements expresses single or multiple causes and single or multiple effects. Circle each cause; underline each effect.

1. Heavy drinking (three drinks or more per day) significantly increases the chance of having smaller babies with retarded physical growth, poor coordination, poor muscle tone, intellectual retardation, and other problems, collectively referred to as fetal alcohol syndrome (FAS).[8]

   _____

2. Psychogenic amnesia—a severe and often permanent memory loss—results in disorientation and the inability to draw on past experiences.

   _____

3. Social loafing, the tendency to work less when part of larger groups, may account for declining worker productivity and corporate profits in rapidly expanding businesses.

   _____

4. The world price of an internationally traded product may be influenced greatly, or only slightly, by the demand and supply coming from any one country.[9]

   _____

5. Insulin's main effect is to lower blood sugar levels, but it also influences protein and fat metabolism.[10]

   _____

EXERCISE 7-12

The following paragraphs are organized using the cause-and-effect pattern. Read them and answer the questions that follow.

Paragraph A

All objects continually radiate energy. Why, then, doesn't the temperature of all objects continually decrease? The answer is that all objects also continually absorb radiant energy. If an object is radiating more energy than it is absorbing, its temperature does decrease; but if an object is absorbing more energy than it is emitting, its temperature increases. An object that is warmer than its surroundings emits more energy than it receives, and therefore it cools; an object colder than its surroundings is a net gainer of energy, and its temperature therefore increases. An object whose temperature is constant, then, emits as much radiant energy as it receives. If it receives none, it will radiate away all its available energy, and its temperature will approach absolute zero.

—Hewitt, *Conceptual Physics,* p. 272

1. Explain why not all objects that radiate energy drop in temperature.
2. What happens to an object that radiates energy but does not absorb any?
3. Highlight the transitional words that signal the cause-and-effect pattern.
4. What causes an object's temperature to remain constant?
5. What is the effect of an object radiating away all of its available energy?

Paragraph B

It's the end of the term and you have dutifully typed the last of several papers. After hours of nonstop typing, you find that your hands are numb, and you feel an intense, burning pain that makes the thought of typing one more word almost unbearable. If you are like one of the thousands of students and workers who every year must quit a particular task due to pain, you may be suffering from a **repetitive stress injury (RSI)**. These are injuries to nerves, soft tissue or joints that result from the physical stress of repeated motions. One of the most common RSIs is **carpal tunnel syndrome**, a product of both the information age and the age of technology in general. Hours spent typing at the computer, flipping groceries through computerized scanners, or other jobs "made simpler" by technology can result in irritation to the median nerve in the wrist, causing numbness, tingling, and pain in the fingers and hands.

—Donatelle, *Access to Health,* p. 516

1. What is the cause of RSIs?
2. Highlight the transitional words that are used in this paragraph.
3. What kind of damage causes carpal tunnel syndrome?
4. What do students often do that can be a cause of RSIs?
5. What kinds of symptoms can result from RSI?

Paragraph C
CAUSES OF FITNESS-RELATED INJURIES

There are two types of injuries stemming from participation in fitness-related activities: overuse and traumatic. **Overuse injuries** occur because of cumulative, day-after-day stresses placed on tendons, bones, and ligaments during exercise. The forces that occur normally during physical activity are not enough to cause a ligament sprain or muscle strain, but when these forces are applied on a daily basis for weeks or months, they can result in an injury. Common sites of overuse injuries are the leg, knee, shoulder, and elbow joints. **Traumatic injuries**, which occur suddenly and violently, typically by accident, are the second major type of fitness-related injuries. Typical traumatic injuries are broken bones, torn ligaments and muscles, contusions, and lacerations. Most traumatic injuries are unavoidable—for example, spraining your ankle by landing on another person's foot after jumping up for a rebound in basketball. If your traumatic injury causes a noticeable loss of function and immediate pain or pain that does not go away after 30 minutes, you should have a physician examine it.

—Donatelle, *Access to Health,* p. 300

1. What is the cause of overuse injuries?
2. Highlight the transitional words that are used in this paragraph to signal the cause-and-effect pattern.
3. How do traumatic injuries often occur?
4. What kinds of injuries are typical traumatic injuries?
5. When should you have a traumatic injury examined?

EXERCISE 7-13   *Read the following passage about alcohol and answer the questions that follow.*

IMMEDIATE EFFECTS OF ALCOHOL

The most dramatic effects produced by ethanol occur within the central nervous system (CNS). The primary action of the drug is to reduce the frequency of nerve transmissions and impulses at synaptic junctions. This reduction of nerve transmissions results in a significant depression of CNS functions, with resulting decreases in respiratory rate, pulse rate, and blood pressure. As CNS depression deepens, vital functions become noticeably depressed. In extreme cases, coma and death can result.

Alcohol is a diuretic, causing increased urinary output. Although this effect might be expected to lead to automatic **dehydration** (loss of water), the body actually retains water, most of it in the muscles or in the cerebral tissues. This is because water is usually pulled out of the **cerebrospinal** fluid (fluid within the brain and spinal cord), leading to what is known as mitochondrial dehydration at the cell level within the nervous system. Mitochondria are miniature organs within the cells that are responsible for specific functions. They rely heavily upon fluid balance. When mitochondrial dehydration occurs from drinking, the mitochondria cannot carry out their normal functions, resulting in symptoms that include the "morning-after" headaches suffered by some drinkers.

Alcohol irritates the gastrointestinal system and may cause indigestion and heartburn if taken on an empty stomach. Long-term use of alcohol causes repeated irritation that has been linked to cancers of the esophagus and stomach. In addition, people who engage in brief drinking sprees during which they consume unusually high amounts of alcohol put themselves at risk for irregular heartbeat or even total loss of heart rhythm, which can cause disruption in blood flow and possible damage to the heart muscle.

—Donatelle, *Access to Health,* pp. 337–38

1. What is the purpose of the passage?
2. Highlight the topic sentence of each paragraph. If there is no stated main idea, write a sentence expressing the main idea.
3. Highlight all transitional words.
4. What does the reduction of nerve transmissions result in?
5. What is the result of the diuretic effect of alcohol?
6. Why does drinking alcohol sometimes result in indigestion and heartburn?
7. If alcohol causes irregular heartbeat or loss of heart rhythm, what can result?

Comparison and Contrast

The **comparison** thought pattern is used to emphasize or discuss similarities between or among ideas, theories, concepts, or events, whereas the **contrast** pattern emphasizes differences. When a speaker or writer is concerned with both similarities and differences, a combination pattern is used. The comparison-and-contrast pattern is widely used in the social sciences, where different groups, societies, cultures, or behaviors are studied. Literature courses may require comparisons among poets, among literary works, or among stylistic features. A business course may examine various management styles, compare organizational structures, or contrast retailing plans.

A contrast is shown in the following paragraph, which describes the purchasing processes of small and large businesses.

> Small businesses are likely to have less formal purchasing processes. A small retail grocer might, for example, purchase a computer system after visiting a few suppliers to compare prices and features, while a large grocery store chain might collect bids from a specified number of vendors and then evaluate those bids on pre-established criteria. Usually, fewer individuals are involved in the decision-making process for a small business. The owner of the small business, for example, may make all decisions, and a larger business may operate with a buying committee of several people.
> —Kinnear et al., *Principles of Marketing,* p. 218

Depending on whether a speaker or writer is concerned with similarities, differences, or both similarities and differences, the pattern might be organized in different ways. Suppose a professor of American literature is comparing two American poets, Whitman and Frost. Each of the following organizations is possible:

1. **Compare and then contrast the two.** That is, first discuss how Frost's poetry and Whitman's poetry are similar, and then discuss how they are different.

2. **Discuss by author.** For example, discuss the characteristics of Whitman's poetry; then discuss the characteristics of Frost's poetry; then summarize their similarities and differences.

3. **Discuss by characteristic.** For example, first discuss the two poets' use of metaphor; next discuss their use of rhyme, and then discuss their common themes.

Examples of transitional words and phrases that reflect these patterns follow.

TRANSITIONAL WORDS: CONTRAST

unlike Whitman, Frost . . .

less wordy than Whitman . . .

contrasted with Whitman, Frost . . .

Frost *differs from* . . .

Other contrast transitional words are:

> in contrast, however, on the other hand, as opposed to, whereas

TRANSITIONAL WORDS: COMPARISON

similarities between Frost and Whitman . . .

Frost is *as* powerful *as* . . .

like Frost, Whitman . . .

both Frost and Whitman . . .

Frost *resembles* Whitman in that . . .

Other comparison transitional words are:

> in a like manner, similarly, likewise, correspondingly, in the same way

---

EXERCISE 7-14   *Read the following paragraphs and answer the questions that follow.*

A. When considering the relationship of Congress and the president, the basic differences of the two branches must be kept in mind. Members of Congress are elected from narrower constituencies than is the president. The people usually expect the president to address general concerns such as foreign policy and economic prosperity, while Congresspersons are asked to solve individual problems. There are structural differences as well. Congress is a body composed of hundreds of independent people, each with a different power base, and it is divided along partisan lines. Thus, it is difficult for Congress to act quickly or to project unity and clear policy statements.

—Baradat, *Understanding American Democracy,* p. 300

1. What two branches of the government are discussed?
2. Explain how these two branches are similar and/or different.
3. Highlight the transitional words that signal the comparison-and-contrast pattern.
4. Does this paragraph mainly use comparison, contrast, or both?
5. Why is it difficult for Congress to act quickly?

B. What are the main characteristics of this new postindustrial society? Unlike the industrial society from which we are emerging, its hallmark is not raw materials and manufacturing. Rather, its basic component is *information*. Teachers pass on knowledge to students, while lawyers, physicians, bankers, pilots, and interior decorators sell their specialized knowledge of law, the body, money, aerodynamics, and color schemes to clients. Unlike the factory workers in an industrial society, these workers don't *produce* anything. Rather, they transmit or use information to provide services that others are willing to pay for.

—Henslin, *Social Problems,* p. 154

1. What two things are being compared or contrasted?
2. Highlight the transitional words used to indicate the comparison–contrast pattern.
3. What is the postindustrial society based upon?
4. What did most workers in industrial society do at their jobs?
5. How is information connected to money in a postindustrial society?

C. You have already seen that homosexuality is more common among males than females, a finding that is supported by all researchers who have reported on this matter. Let's see what other differences they have found. One of the most significant is that lesbians are more likely to seek lasting relationships, place a premium on emotional commitment and mutual fidelity, and shun the bar scene. Consequently, while most male homosexuals have "cruised" (sought impersonal sex with strangers), fewer than 20 percent of lesbians have done so. As a result, lesbians tend to have fewer sexual partners than do male homosexuals. Psychologist Alan Bell and sociologist Martin Weinberg interviewed about 1500 homosexuals. They found that almost half the white and one third the African-American homosexual males had at least 500 different sexual partners. About 28 percent of the white sample had more than 1000 different partners. Although their sample is large, it is not representative of homosexuals, because their research focused heavily on bars and steam baths. Bell's and Weinberg's findings do, however, support other studies indicating promiscuity among male homosexuals.

—Henslin, *Social Problems,* p. 74

1. What are two differences between lesbians and gay males?
2. Highlight the transitional words that are used to indicate the comparison–contrast pattern?
3. Why is the research cited in this paragraph not representative of all homosexuals?
4. What does it mean to "cruise"?
5. What percent of white homosexual males had more than 1000 partners?

EXERCISE 7-15   *Read the following passage about behavior and answer the questions that follow.*

MODELS OF ABNORMAL BEHAVIOR

In their efforts to identify and explain abnormal behaviors, psychologists often adopt models, or general views of what causes those behaviors. Models help by pointing out which symptoms are most important, directing attention to their likely causes and suggesting possible treatments.

The Medical Model

Near the end of the eighteenth century, physicians began to document their patients' symptoms and to note which ones occurred together. The occurrence of groups of symptoms, called *syndromes,* helped physicians identify underlying diseases and develop treatments. Approaching abnormal behaviors just as one would approach medical illnesses is known as the **medical model**.

Psychiatrist Thomas Szasz (1993) argues for limiting the medical model to conditions resulting from actual brain dysfunctions. In his opinion, this model has been expanded to cover behaviors that are perhaps annoying or inappropriate but do not constitute diseases of the brain. For example, the list of proposed or recognized diseases includes shoplifting, pathological gambling, and nicotine dependence. According to Szasz, applying the medical model to such behaviors does not advance our understanding of the causes of the problems and allows people to avoid taking responsibility for their problems by attributing them to a disease process.

Accumulating evidence shows that a number of psychological disorders are related to elevated or reduced levels of certain neurotransmitters or structural abnormalities in the brain. What's more, evidence is increasing that heredity plays a significant role in the development of some psychological disorders.

The Psychological Models

In contrast to the medical model, various *psychological models* emphasize the importance of mental functioning, social experiences and learning histories in trying to explain the causes of abnormal behaviors. Sigmund Freud's **psychodynamic model** focuses on unconscious conflicts involving the id, ego and superego or fixations at an early stage of psychosexual development. For example, anxiety is seen as a warning that the ego is about to be overwhelmed by conflict. The **behavioral model**, by contrast, focuses on environmental factors that mold human and animal behaviors. Behavioral theorists such as John B. Watson and B. F. Skinner propose that we learn both normal and abnormal behaviors through the principles of classical conditioning, operant conditioning, and modeling. In contrast to the behavioral model, the cognitive model focuses on understanding the content and processes of human thought. Cognitive psychologists claim that to understand human behavior, we must look beyond actual events to understand how people interpret those events.

—Davis and Palladino, *Psychology,* pp. 535–36

1. What is the purpose of the passage?
2. Highlight the topic sentence of each paragraph. If there is no stated main idea, write a sentence expressing the main idea.
3. Highlight all transitional words.
4. What is the medical model of approaching abnormal behavior?
5. How do psychological models contrast with the medical model?
6. Which psychological model relies on understanding the content and processes of human thought?
7. Why does Szasz argue for limiting the use of the medical model?

EXERCISE 7-16   *Read each of the following opening sentences from a textbook reading assignment and predict whether a comparison, contrast, or combination pattern will be used.*

1. In Rembrandt's *Self-Portrait* and Frank Auerbach's *Head of Michael Podro,* the artists' responsiveness to both the reality of their subjects and the physical nature of paint and painting is clearly visible.[11]

2. The Enlightenment celebrated the power of reason; however, an opposite reaction, Romanticism, soon followed.[12]

_____

3. The small group develops in much the same way that a conversation develops.[13]

_____

4. Think of the hardware in a computer system as the kitchen in a short-order restaurant: It's equipped to produce whatever output a customer (user) requests, but it sits idle until an order (command) is placed.[14]

_____

5. One important conceptual issue that arises frequently in economics is the distinction between stock and flow variables.[15]

_____

EXERCISE 7–17

Write five sentences that express either a comparison or a contrast relationship. Exchange your sentences with a classmate, asking him or her to identify the pattern used.

Listing/Enumeration

If asked to evaluate a film you saw, you might describe the characters, plot, and technical effects. These details about the film could be arranged in any order; each detail provides further information about the film, but they have no specific relationship to one another. This arrangement of ideas is known as **listing** or **enumeration**—giving bits of information on a topic by stating them one after the other. Often, there is no particular method of arrangement for those details.

The following list of managers' difficulties in problem solving could have been presented in any order without altering the meaning of the paragraph.

> Although accurate identification of a problem is essential before the problem can be solved, this stage of decision making creates many difficulties for managers. Sometimes managers' preconceptions of the problem prevent them from seeing the situation as it actually is. They produce an answer before the proper question has ever been asked. In other cases, managers overlook truly significant issues by focusing on unimportant matters. Also, managers may mistakenly analyze problems in terms of symptoms rather than underlying causes.
>
> —Pride et al., *Business,* p. 189

This pattern is widely used in college textbooks in most academic disciplines. In its loosest form, the pattern may be simply a list of items: factors that influence light emission, characteristics of a particular poet, a description of an atom, a list of characteristics that define poverty.

Somewhat tighter is the use of listing to explain, support, or provide evidence. Support may be in the form of facts, statistics, or examples. For instance, the statement "The incidence of white collar crime has dramatically increased over the past 10 years" would be followed by facts and statistics documenting the increase. The transitional words or phrases used for this pattern include the following.

TRANSITIONAL WORDS

one aspect of relativity . . .

a second feature of relativity . . .

also, relativity . . .

there are *several* characteristics of . . .

(1) . . . , *(2)* . . . , and *(3)* . . .

(a) . . . , *(b)* . . . , and *(c)* . . .

Other transitional words are:

in addition, first, second, third, finally, another

EXERCISE 7-18

Read the following paragraphs and answer the questions that follow.

A. By far the most important committees in Congress are the standing committees. Currently 16 standing committees in the Senate and 22 in the House receive the bills that are introduced in Congress. The standing committees are assigned subject-matter jurisdiction by the rules of their respective house, and their titles reflect their general area of expertise. Hence, we have the Senate Finance Committee, the House Agriculture Committee, the Senate Budget Committee, the House Judiciary Committee, and so on. The authority of the standing committees includes the power to study legislation, to subpoena witnesses or information, to remand bills to subcommittees, to vote bills dead, to table bills (putting them aside, thus allowing them to die quietly at the end of the congressional term), to amend bills, to write bills (amending a bill or writing an entirely new version of a bill is called **marking-up**), or to report the bill to the floor.

—Baradat, *Understanding American Democracy,* p. 202

1. What is the topic of the paragraph?
2. What types of information does this paragraph list?
3. Highlight the transitional words used in this paragraph to indicate the listing pattern.
4. What is the purpose of standing committees in general?
5. List two powers of standing committees.

B. Minorities come into existence, then, when, due to expanded political boundaries or migration, people with different customs, languages, values or physical characteristics come under control of the same state organization. There, some groups who share physical and cultural traits discriminate against those with different traits. The losers in this power struggle are forced into minority group status; the winners enjoy the higher status and greater privileges that their dominance brings. Wagley and Harris noted that all minorities share these five characteristics: (1) They are treated unequally by the dominant group. (2) Their physical or cultural traits are held in low esteem by the dominant group. (3) They tend to feel strong group solidarity because of their physical or cultural traits—and the disabilities these traits bring. (4) Their membership in a minority group is not voluntary but comes through birth. (5) They tend to marry within their group. Sharing cultural or physical traits, having similar experiences of discrimination, and marrying within their own group create a shared identity—sometimes even a sense of common destiny. These shared experiences, however, do not mean that all minority groups have the same goals.

—Henslin, *Social Problems,* p. 252

1. How do minorities come into existence?
2. Highlight the transitional words used to indicate the listing pattern.
3. How does minority status impact marriage?
4. At what stage of life does a person enter an already existing minority group?
5. How is a shared identity or destiny created among minorities?

C. Voters make two basic decisions at election time. The first is whether to vote. Americans' right to vote is well established, but in order to do so citizens must go through the registration process. America's unique registration system is one major reason why turnout in American elections is much lower than in most other democracies. The 1996 election was another in a long string of low-turnout elections. Second, those who choose to vote must decide for whom to cast their ballots. Over a generation of research on voting behavior has helped political scientists understand the dominant role played by three factors in voters' choices: party identification, candidate evaluations, and policy positions.

—Edwards, *Government in America,* p. 330

1. What two categories are listed or enumerated in this paragraph?
2. What transitional words are used to indicate the listing or enumeration pattern?
3. What is a major reason why voter turnout is low in America?
4. List the factors involved in voters' choices.
5. What is the first decision a voter must make in an election?

EXERCISE 7-19   *Read the following passage about economics and answer the questions that follow.*

FOUR ECONOMIC PROBLEMS FACING THE UNITED STATES

Capitalism provides the setting for understanding problems of social inequality in the United States. Within this broad context of wealth and poverty are more specific issues that affect the future direction of the U.S. economy. Let's look at four of the problems that spell future trouble.

The first is a decline in people's **real income** (income in constant dollars, that is, adjusted for inflation). For 25 years, from the end of World War II until 1970, the real income of U.S. workers rose steadily. For the past 30 years, however, real income has declined. The situation is deceptive, for workers have more dollars in their paychecks than they used to, but those dollars don't go as far. In spite of fat raises, *each five-year period since 1970 has brought a decline in purchasing power.* Workers don't just *feel* poorer—they *are.*

The second major problem is taxes. Someone coined the term *Tax Freedom Day* to refer to the day when the average American has earned enough to pay his or her annual taxes. Politicians keep promising tax cuts, but because they never deliver on their promise Tax Freedom Day has been pushed forward relentlessly. It now falls on May 6 (Keating 1998). On average, each of us must work for the government for more than four months before we have a cent for our own needs!

The third major problem is that the U.S. savings rate has dropped to a low not seen even during the Great Depression of the 1930s. Americans save less than people in all other industrialized nations—just one-sixth of what the Japanese save. The significance of our drop in savings is that we have less money to invest in new plants and equipment, which may undermine our ability to compete in international trade or to increase our living standard.

Fourth, we import foreign goods at such a frenzied pace that the United States has become the largest debtor nation in the world. Each year, the amount that we spend on products we buy from other nations amounts to almost $200 billion more than the amount we get from selling to them. These mountains of debt cannot keep piling up indefinitely. Just as individuals must repay what they borrow or else get into financial trouble, so it is with nations. To finance **national debt** (the total amount the U.S. government owes), we must pay $250 billion a year in interest (*Statistical Abstract* 1998: Table 538). This is money that we cannot use to build schools and colleges, hire teachers, rebuild our cities, pay for medical services for the poor, operate Head Start programs, or pay for any other services to help improve our quality of life.

—Henslin, *Social Problems,* pp. 216–18

1. What is the purpose of the passage?
2. Highlight the topic sentence of each paragraph. If there is no stated main idea, write a sentence expressing the main idea.
3. Highlight all transitional words.
4. What is real income?
5. Why are taxes a problem for the U.S. economy?
6. How much do Americans save in comparison to the Japanese?
7. How does importing goods negatively affect the U.S. economy?

EXERCISE 7-20 *Identify and circle the topics listed below that might be developed by using the listing pattern.*

1. The Impact of Budget on Crime Prevention
2. The Aims of Legal Punishment
3. America: A Drugged Society?
4. Varieties of Theft
5. Homicide and Assault: The Current Picture

Mixed Patterns

Thought patterns are often combined. In describing a process, a writer may also give reasons why each step must be followed in the prescribed order. A lecturer may define a concept by comparing it to something similar or familiar. Suppose an essay in your political science textbook opens by stating, "The distinction between 'power' and 'power potential' is an important one in considering the balance of power." You might expect a definition pattern (where the two terms are defined), but you also might anticipate that the essay would discuss the difference between the two terms (contrast pattern).

In the passage below, the author uses both definition and listing to explain child abuse.

CHILD ABUSE

Children raised in families in which domestic violence and/or sexual abuse occur are at great risk for damage to personal health and well-being. The effects of such violent acts are powerful and can be very long-lasting. **Child abuse** refers to the systematic harm of a child by a caregiver, generally a parent. The abuse may be sexual, psychological, physical, or any combination of these. Although exact figures are lacking, many experts believe that over 2 million cases of child abuse occur every year in the United States, involving severe injury, permanent disability, or death. Child abusers exist in all gender, social, ethnic, religious, and racial groups.

Certain personal characteristics tend to be common among child abusers: having been abused as a child, having a poor self-image, feelings of isolation, extreme frustration with life, higher stress or anxiety levels than normal, a tendency to abuse drugs and/or alcohol, and unrealistic expectations of the child. It is also estimated that from one half to three quarters of men who batter their female partners also batter children. In fact, spouse abuse is the single most identifiable risk factor for predicting child abuse. Finally, children with handicaps or other "differences" are more likely to be abused.

—Donatelle, *Access to Health,* p. 107

EXERCISE 7-21

The following paragraph describes the beginnings of Earth's atmosphere. Read the paragraph and answer the questions that follow.

Earth's very earliest atmosphere probably was swept into space by the *solar wind,* a vast stream of particles emitted by the Sun. As Earth slowly cooled, a more enduring atmosphere formed. The molten surface solidified into a crust, and gases that had been dissolved in the molten rock were gradually released, a process called **outgassing**. Outgassing continues today from hundreds of active volcanoes worldwide. Thus, geologists hypothesize that Earth's original atmosphere was made up of gases similar to those released in volcanic emissions today: water vapor, carbon dioxide, nitrogen, and several trace gases.

—Tarbuck and Lutgens, *Earth Science,* p. 298

1. Which patterns are used in this paragraph?
2. Highlight the transitional words used to indicate the patterns.
3. What happened to the first atmosphere the Earth had?
4. How does outgassing occur?
5. What was the original atmosphere probably composed of?

EXERCISE 7-22

The following passage uses mixed patterns. Read the passage and answer the questions that follow.

WEATHERING

All materials are susceptible to weathering. Consider, for example, the synthetic rock we call concrete, which closely resembles the sedimentary rock called conglomerate. A newly poured concrete sidewalk has a smooth, fresh look. However, not many years later, the same sidewalk will appear chipped, cracked, and rough, with pebbles exposed at the surface. If a tree is nearby, its roots may grow under the concrete, heaving and buckling it. The same natural processes that eventually break apart a concrete sidewalk also act to disintegrate natural rocks, regardless of their type or strength.

Why does rock weather? Simply, weathering is the response of Earth materials to a changing environment. For instance, after millions of years of uplift and erosion, the rocks overlying a large body of intrusive igneous rock may be removed. This exposes the rock to a whole new environment at the surface. The mass of crystalline rock, which formed deep below ground where temperatures and pressures are much greater than at the surface, is now subjected to very different and comparatively hostile surface conditions. In response, this rock mass will gradually change until it is once again in equilibrium, or balance, with its new environment. Such transformation of rock is what we call *weathering*.

There are two kinds of weathering—mechanical and chemical. Mechanical weathering is the physical breaking up of rocks into smaller pieces. Chemical weathering actually alters a rock's chemistry, changing it into different substances. Although we will consider these two processes separately, keep in mind that they usually work simultaneously in nature.

—Tarbuck and Lutgens, *Earth Science*, p. 61

1. What is the purpose of the passage?
2. Highlight the topic sentence of each paragraph. If there is no stated main idea, write a sentence expressing the main idea.
3. Highlight all transitional words.
4. Which patterns are utilized in this passage?
5. Why do rocks weather?
6. What is the difference between mechanical and chemical weathering?
7. What kind of rock is concrete similar to?

EXERCISE 7–23

For each of the following topic sentences, anticipate what thought pattern(s) the paragraph is likely to exhibit. Record your prediction in the space provided. Underline the word(s) that suggest the pattern(s) you chose.

1. Another form of learning that does not fit neatly into the mold of classical or operant conditioning is learning through insight.

   _____

2. GNP (gross national product) is an economic measure that considers the total value of goods and services that a country produces during a given year.

   _____

3. Diseases of the heart and blood vessels—cardiovascular diseases—are the leading cause of death in the United States today.[16]

4. Impulse conduction in neurons has been compared to electrical impulses in, say, a copper wire, but the analogy is not a good one.[17]

5. The body's first line of defense against infection consists of several kinds of nonspecific resistance, so named because they do not distinguish one invader from another.[18]

6. Research suggests that obsessive-compulsive disorder has a biological basis.[19]

7. Nervous systems consist of two major types of cells: neurons (nerve cells), which are specialized for carrying signals from one location in the body to another, and supporting cells, which protect, insulate, and reinforce neurons.[20]

8. Both Neoclassicism and Romanticism had their beginnings in rebellion.[21]

9. Some astute observers have noted that when we find ourselves in an energy crunch, as when Iraq invaded Kuwait and threatened the Saudi oil fields in 1990, the first response of our national leaders is to act to insure our continued access to Middle East oil.[22]

10. Before the twentieth century, most of the population of Latin America resembled the populations of antiquity, with high birthrates offset by high death rates.[23]

EXERCISE 7-24

Choose a one- or two-page section of one of your textbooks and determine the pattern of each major paragraph. Then identify the overall pattern of the section as a whole.

EXERCISE 7-25

Turn to the table of contents of this text. Predict the thought pattern(s) that any five of the readings will follow. Ask a classmate to confirm or disagree with the patterns you identified.

Other Useful Patterns of Organization

The patterns presented in the previous section are the most common. Table 7-1 presents a brief review of those patterns and their corresponding transitional words. However, writers do not limit themselves to these six patterns. Especially in academic writing, you may find one or more of the patterns listed in Table 7-2 (p. 222), as well. Here is a brief overview of each of these additional patterns.

Statement and Clarification Many writers make a statement of fact and then proceed to clarify or explain that statement. For instance, a writer may open a paragraph by stating that "The best education for you may not be the best education for someone else." The remainder of the paragraph would then discuss that statement and make its meaning clear by explaining how educational needs are individual and based on one's talents, skills, and goals. Transitional words associated with this pattern are listed in Table 7-2.

TABLE 7–1   A Review of Patterns and Transitional Words

PATTERN	CHARACTERISTICS	TRANSITIONAL WORDS
Definition	Explains the meaning of a word or phrase	is, refers to, can be defined as, means, consists of, involves, is a term that, is called, is characterized by, occurs when, are those that, entails, corresponds to, is literally
Classification	Divides a topic into parts based on shared characteristics	classified as, comprises, is composed of, several varieties of, different stages of, different groups that, includes, one, first, second, another, finally, last
Order or Sequence	Describes events, processes, procedures, spatial relationships, and order of importance	first, second, later, before, next, as soon as, after, then, finally, meanwhile, following, last, during, in, on, when, until
Cause–Effect	Describes how one or more things cause or are related to another	*Causes:* because, because of, for, since, stems from, one cause is, one reason is, leads to, causes, creates, yields, produces, due to, breeds, for this reason *Effects:* consequently, results in, one result is, therefore, thus, as a result, hence
Comparison–Contrast	Discusses similarities and/or differences among ideas, theories, concepts, objects, or persons	*Similarities:* both, also, similarly, like, likewise, too, as well as, resembles, correspondingly, in the same way, to compare, in comparison, share *Differences:* unlike, differs from, in contrast, on the other hand, instead, despite, nevertheless, however, in spite of, whereas, as opposed to
Listing/Enumeration	Organizes lists of information, characteristics	the following, several, for example, for instance, one, another, also, too, in other words, first, second

TABLE 7–2 A Review of Additional Patterns and Transitional Words		
PATTERN	**CHARACTERISTICS**	**TRANSITIONAL WORDS**
Statement and Clarification	Indicates that information explaining an idea or concept will follow the topic sentence	in fact, in other words, clearly, evidently, obviously
Summary	Indicates that a condensed review of an idea or piece of writing will be given	in summary, in conclusion, in brief, to summarize, to sum up, in short, on the whole
Generalization and Example	Provides examples that clarify a broad, general statement	for example, for instance, that is, to illustrate, thus
Addition	Indicates that additional information will follow the topic sentence	furthermore, additionally, also, besides, further, in addition, moreover, again

In the following paragraph about sex ratios, the writer uses statement and clarification.

> Sex ratios in the poor countries do not show a consistent pattern. In some poor countries men outnumber women, but in others, in tropical Africa, for example, women outnumber men. In fact, variations in sex ratios can be explained only by a combination of national economic and cultural factors. In the countries of North America and Europe and in Japan, women may suffer many kinds of discrimination, but they are not generally discriminated against when it comes to access to medical care.
>
> —Bergman and Renwick, *Introduction to Geography,* p. 185

Notice that the writer begins with the statement about sex ratios in poor countries and then goes on to clarify this fact. The author uses the transitional words "in fact."

Summary   A summary is a condensed statement that provides the key points of a larger idea or piece of writing. The summaries at the end of each chapter of this text provide a quick review of the chapter's contents. Often writers summarize what they have already said or what someone else has said. For example, in a psychology textbook you will find many summaries of research. Instead of asking you to read an entire research study, the textbook author will summarize the study's findings. Other times a writer may repeat in condensed form what he or she has already said as a means of emphasis or clarification. Transitional words associated with this pattern are listed in Table 7-2.

In the following paragraph about the magazine industry, the author uses the summary method of organization.

> In summary, the magazine industry is adapting to the new world of electronic multimedia information and entertainment, with formats that will be quite different from the familiar ones. Computer-generated publishing has become the norm in the magazine business, expanding beyond its uses in producing newsletters and

other specialized publications. Most general circulation magazines already rely heavily on desktop computers, interacting with other electronic equipment to produce high-quality, graphics-filled products.

—Dizard, *Old, Media, New Media,* p. 169

Notice that the writer summarizes many facts about how the magazine industry uses electronic multimedia information and that the transitional words "in summary" are used.

Generalization and Example   Examples are one of the best ways to explain something that is unfamiliar or unknown. Examples are specific instances or situations that illustrate a concept or idea. Often writers may present a general statement, or generalization, and then explain it by giving examples to make its meaning clear. In a social problems textbook, you might find the following generalization: Computer theft by employees is on the increase. The section might then go on to offer examples from specific companies in which employees insert fictitious information into the company's computer program and steal company funds. Transitional words associated with this pattern are listed in Table 7-2.

In the following paragraph about dreams, the writer uses generalization and example.

Different cultures place varying emphases on dreams and support different beliefs concerning dreams. For example, many people in the United States view dreams as irrelevant fantasy with no connection to everyday life. By contrast, people in other cultures view dreams as key sources of information about the future, the spiritual world, and the dreamer. Such cultural views can influence the probability of dream recall. In many modern Western cultures, people rarely remember their dreams upon awakening. The Parintintin of South America, however, typically remember several dreams every night (Kraeke, 1993) and the Senoi of Malaysia discuss their dreams with family members in the morning (Hennager, 1993).

—Davis and Palladino, *Psychology,* p. 210

Notice that the writer begins with the generalization that different cultures place different emphases on dreams and then goes on to give examples of the way specific cultures treat dreams. Note the use of the transitional words "for example."

Addition   Writers often introduce an idea or make a statement and then supply additional information about that idea or statement. For instance, an education textbook might introduce the concept of homeschooling and then provide in-depth information about its benefits. This pattern is often used to expand, elaborate on, or discuss an idea in greater detail. Transitional words associated with this pattern are listed in Table 7-2.

In the following paragraph about pathogens, the writer uses addition.

Some pathogens [disease-causing organisms] evolve and mutate naturally. Also, patients who fail to complete the full portion of their antibiotic prescriptions allow drug-resistant pathogens to multiply. The use of antibiotics in animal feed and sprayed on fruits and vegetables during food processing increases opportunities for resistant organisms to evolve and thrive. Furthermore, there is evidence that the disruption of Earth's natural habitats can trigger the evolution of new pathogens.

—Bergman and Renwick, *Introduction to Geography,* p. 182

Notice that the writer states that some pathogens mutate naturally and then goes on to add that they also mutate as a result of human activities. Note the use of the transitional words "also" and "furthermore."

EXERCISE 7-26

For each of the following statements, identify the pattern that is evident and write its name in the space provided. Choose from among the following patterns: statement and clarification, summary, generalization and example, and addition.

1. _____ In short, physical anthropologists are still waiting to locate the remains that will connect present day humans with early hominids.

2. _____ Humans have been using pictures to communicate and make sense of their environment since they first evolved. Cave paintings and the creation of constellation figures are just a few examples.

3. _____ Anthrax is a strain of bacteria that is spread through inhalation. Anthrax can also be contracted cutaneously, through contact with the skin.

4. _____ Pedophiles (criminals who molest children) generally cannot be rehabilitated. In fact, many types of therapy have been tried without success.

5. _____ Internet bulletin boards and listservs make it possible for people to casually meet other people that they would not otherwise come into contact with. For instance, a popular listserv made up of tea enthusiasts comprises members from all over the globe.

6. _____ Frogs are able to breathe underwater by absorbing oxygen from the water through their skin. Besides breathing underwater, frogs are also able to breathe while in air, but their skin must be wet in order to absorb oxygen from the air.

7. _____ The Moro reflex in human infants is best summed up as a holdover from life in the trees. When the infant perceives the feeling of falling, it spreads its arms and hands in an attempt to prevent a fall from the branches.

8. _____ What is considered as instinct in animals is often the manifestation of a highly developed sense. As a case in point, salmon are able to return to their spawning stream using a highly developed sense of smell.

9. _____ Crustaceans have exoskeletons instead of internal skeletons. To illustrate this, think of how a lobster has a shell on the outside that can be removed and that once inside the shell, there is only meat.

10. _____ Circulation numbers are crucial in increasing ad revenues for magazines. In fact, many magazines give free or very low cost subscriptions in order to boost their circulation numbers and support increases in ad revenues.

EXERCISE 7-27 *Read each of the following paragraphs and identify the predominant organizational pattern used. Write the name of the pattern in the space provided. Choose from among the following patterns: statement and clarification, summary, generalization and example, and addition.*

1. **Managing Emotional Responses**

Have you have gotten all worked up about something you thought was happening only to find that your perceptions were totally wrong or that a communication problem had caused a misrepresentation of events? If you're like most of us, you probably have. We often get upset not by realities but by our faulty perceptions. For example, suppose you found out that everyone except you is invited to a party. You might easily begin to wonder why you were excluded. Does someone dislike you? Have you offended someone? Such thoughts are typical. However, the reality of the situation may have absolutely nothing to do with your being liked or disliked. Perhaps you were sent an invitation and it didn't get to you.

—Donatelle, *Access to Health,* p. 81

Pattern: _____

2. A serious problem with some drugs is **addiction**, or **drug dependence**. That is, people come to depend on the regular consumption of a drug in order to make it through the day. When people think of **drug addiction**, they are likely to think of addicts huddled in slum doorways, the dregs of society who seldom venture into daylight—unless it is to rob someone. They don't associate addiction with "good," middle-class neighborhoods and "solid citizens." But let's look at drug addiction a little more closely. Although most people may think of heroin as the prime example of an addictive drug, I suggest that nicotine is the better case to consider. I remember a next-door neighbor who stood in his backyard, a lit cigarette in his hand, and told me about the operation in which one of his lungs was removed. I say "I remember," because soon after our conversation he died from his addiction.

—Henslin, *Social Problems,* p. 93

Pattern: _____

3. **The Challenges of Cable TV**

The more immediate challenge to the Big Three television networks, however, came from cable television. The networks were at a structural disadvantage in their attempts to match cable's appeal. They had only one channel with which to reach the home audiences that advertisers wanted. Moreover, network program costs rose as advertising revenues fell. This was especially true of the more popular programs networks had to offer in order to keep what was left of their competitive prime-time edge.

—Dizard, *Old Media, New Media,* p. 87

Pattern: _____

4. Like previous major wars, Vietnam profoundly affected the lives of mainly African Americans. For black soldiers who served in Vietnam, the war offered an opportunity to demonstrate once again that they were prepared to fight for freedom on many fronts. However, controversies in the United States over civil rights and black power reverberated in Vietnam, while at the same time disagreements concerning American intervention in Vietnam affected the civil rights and black power movements. On both the home front and the battlefields, the backdrop of violence shaped the way racial issues were viewed and discussed. Daily newscasts brought the war to the television sets of civilians; some called it the "living room war." The brief tours of duty—no more than a year in Vietnam for most soldiers—reduced the isolation of soldiers. Moreover, as King pointed out in his antiwar speech at Riverside Church, the war affected domestic racial policies by diverting federal funds that might otherwise be spent on the war on poverty and other Great Society social programs.

— Carson et al., *African American Lives*, pp. 490–91.

Pattern: _____

5. In summary, the publishing industry is undergoing major changes, brought on by demographic shifts, financial upheavals, and the pressure of new technologies. Instability and reassessment are common to all parts of the industry—newspapers, magazines, and books—but the situation in each sector is distinct enough to warrant examining them separately.

—Dizard, *Old Media, New Media*, p. 157

Pattern: _____

6. For each American who commits suicide, about ten attempt it. Although many more women than men attempt suicide, more men than women succeed at it. This is likely because the women's attempts are more a "cry for help," while the men are more serious about accomplishing the act. In addition, men tend to choose methods that allow less intervention, such as guns, while women are more likely to use pills. Also guns provide less time to change one's mind or to allow someone to intervene.

—Henslin, *Social Problems*, p. 336

Pattern: _____

7. Be careful not to evaluate negatively the cultural differences you perceive. Be careful that you don't fall into the trap of ethnocentric thinking, evaluating your culture positively and other cultures negatively. For example, many Americans of Northern European descent evaluate negatively the tendency of many Hispanics and Southern Europeans to use the street for a gathering place, for playing Dominoes, and for just sitting on a cool evening. Whether you like or dislike using the street in this way, recognize that neither attitude is logically correct or incorrect. This street behavior is simply adequate or inadequate for *members of the culture*.

—DeVito, *Human Communication*, p. 103

Pattern: _____

8. In short, the view that a drug is good or bad depends not on objective conditions but on subjective concerns. It is a matter of how people define matters. People's definitions, in turn, influence how they use and abuse drugs, whether or not a drug will be legal or illegal, and what social policies they want to adopt. This is the central sociological aspect of drug use and abuse, one that we shall stress over and over in this chapter.

—Henslin, *Social Problems*, p. 91

Pattern: _____

9. Human migration has by no means come to an end. Large-scale migrations still make daily news. The United Nations' Universal Declaration of Human Rights affirms anyone's right to leave his or her homeland to seek a better life elsewhere, but it cannot guarantee that there will be anyplace willing to take anyone. As in the past, the major push and pull factors behind contemporary migration are economic and political. Also, people are trying to move from the poor countries to the rich countries and from the politically repressed countries to more democratic countries. In addition, millions of people are fleeing civil and international warfare. Pressures for migration are growing, and in coming years they may constitute the world's greatest political and economic problem.

—Bergman and Renwick, *Introduction to Geography*, p. 197

Pattern: _____

10. "I'll lose my job if they find out what I sent you." Most companies keep copies of all e-mail that is sent and received, and most do spot checks of the contents. When the above statement was discovered among an employee's outgoing messages, a company security officer wondered whether she had uncovered corporate espionage. Was the message sender giving away—or perhaps selling—company secrets? In this case it was easy to find out: The security officer simply extracted the attachment that had been sent with the message. It turned out to be pornographic material—and the employee did indeed lose his job over this incident.

—Capron and Johnson, *Computers: Tools for an Information Age*, p. 328

Pattern: _____

■ Applying Academic Thought Patterns

Now that you are familiar with the basic thought patterns, you are ready to use these valuable structures to organize your learning and shape your thinking. Patterns give ideas shape or form, thereby making them more readily comprehensible. Look for these patterns as you read, listen for them in lectures, and use them in completing assignments and writing papers.

Subsequent chapters in this text will demonstrate the use of patterns in specific learning situations and in specific academic disciplines. Although it is not within the scope of this text, you also will discover that academic thought patterns are useful in organizing and answering essay questions and writing term papers.

Self-Test Summary

1. What are six common thought patterns used by authors to aid a reader's comprehension?	The patterns are definition, classification, order or sequence, cause and effect, comparison and contrast, and listing/enumeration.
2. What are the three parts of a definition?	The three parts are the term, the general class, and the distinguishing characteristics.
3. What is classification?	Classification breaks a broad topic into its major categories.
4. What are four ways order and sequence can be arranged?	The four ways are chronology, process, order of importance, and spatial arrangement.
5. Define cause and effect.	Cause and effect examines the relationship between two or more actions, events, or occurrences that are connected in time, with one being the direct result of the other.
6. What is the difference between comparison and contrast?	Comparison is used to emphasize similarities, while contrast emphasizes differences in ideas, theories, concepts, or events.
7. Describe the pattern called "listing/enumeration."	Listing/enumeration is a means of presenting supporting details that have no specific relationship to one another.
8. Besides the six common thought patterns you were asked to identify in the first question, what are some other patterns that are often used?	The patterns are: • statement and clarification. • summary. • generalization and example. • addition.

BIOLOGY

The Human Brain
Robert A. Wallace

Prereading Questions

1. What thought pattern(s) do you anticipate this reading will use?
2. What do you already know about right-brain and left-brain dominance?

1   Now we come to the rather interesting notion of the human brain talking about itself. Perhaps it is because of this strange twist that we encounter so many endless accolades about this great organ. Let's begin with some basic descriptions.

2   The human brain is divided into three parts: the hindbrain, the midbrain, and the forebrain. The **hindbrain** consists of the medulla, the cerebellum, and the pons. The hindbrain is sometimes called the "old brain" because it evolved first. These structures still dominate the brain of some animals, as we have seen. The **midbrain**, logically enough, is the area between the forebrain and hindbrain and connects the two. The **forebrain**, or "new brain," consists of the two cerebral hemispheres and certain internal structures.

The Hindbrain
The Medulla

3   As a rough generality, the more subconscious, or mechanical, processes are directed by the more posterior parts of the brain. For example, the hindmost part, the **medulla**, is specialized as a control center for such basic functions as breathing, digestion, and heartbeat. In addition, it is an important center of control for certain charming activities such as swallowing, vomiting, and sneezing. As we have already seen, it connects the spinal cord and the more anterior parts of the brain.

The Cerebellum and Pons

4   Above the medulla and more toward the back of the head is the **cerebellum**, which is concerned with balance, equilibrium, and coordination. Do you suppose there might be differences between athletes and nonathletes in this part of the brain? (Apparently there are, but the differences are slight.) Do you think this "lower" center of the brain is subject to modification through learning? (Can you improve your coordination through practice?) The **pons**, which is the portion of the brainstem just above the medulla, acts as a bridge connecting certain parts of the brain. For instance, it connects the cerebellum and the cerebral cortex, accenting the relationship between the cerebellar part of the hindbrain and the more "conscious" centers of the forebrain.

The Midbrain

5   The **midbrain** connects the hindbrain and forebrain by numerous tracts. In addition, certain parts of the midbrain receive sensory input from the eyes and ears. In vertebrates,

FIGURE A   The human brain in surface view (1) and in sagittal section (2). Note that there is so much regularity in the convolutions that some have been named.

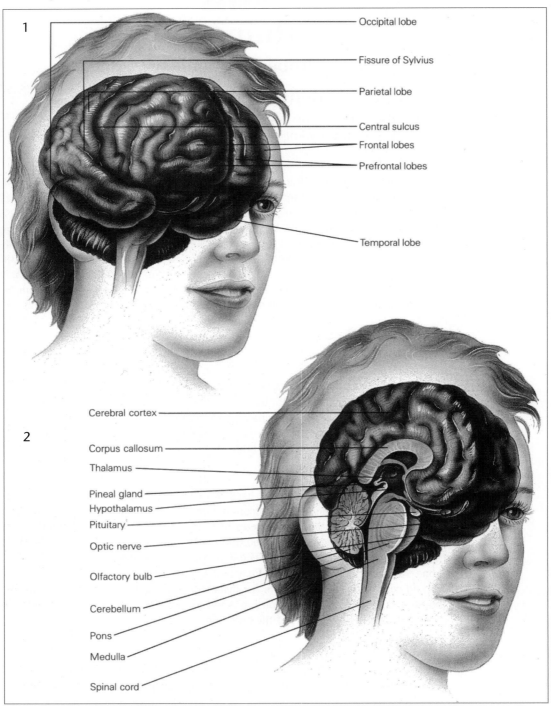

sound is processed here before being sent to the forebrain. The midbrain has a more complex role in fishes and amphibians than in reptiles, birds, and mammals because in the latter group, many of its functions are taken over by the forebrain.

The Forebrain
The Thalamus and Reticular System

6   The thalamus and hypothalamus are located at the base of the forebrain. The **thalamus** is rather unpoetically called the "great relay station" of the brain. It consists of densely packed clusters of nervous cells that presumably connect the various parts of the brain—between the forebrain and the hindbrain, between different parts of the forebrain, and between parts of the sensory system and the cerebral cortex.

7   The thalamus contains a peculiar neural structure called the **reticular system,** an area of interconnected neurons that are almost feltlike in appearance. The reticular system runs through the medulla, pons, and thalamus and extends upward to the cerebral cortex. The role of the reticular system is still a bit mysterious, but several interesting facts are known about it. For example, it bugs your brain. Every afferent and efferent pathway to and from the brain sends side branches to the reticular system as it passes through the thalamus. So all the brain's incoming and outgoing communications are "trapped." Also, these reticular neurons are rather unspecific. That is, the same neuron may respond to stimuli from, say, the hand, foot, ear, or eye. It has been suggested that the reticular system serves to activate the appropriate parts of the brain upon receiving a stimulus. In other words, the reticular system activates the part of the brain that is needed for the particular task at hand. If there is no incoming stimulus—no need for conscious activity—the system sends fewer signals, quieting the brain. You may have noticed it is much easier to fall asleep lying on a soft bed in a quiet, darkened room than on a pool table in a disco. With the quietness, the reticular system receives fewer messages and the brain is lulled rather than aroused. On those nights when you have the "big eye" and just can't sleep, the cause may be continued (possibly spontaneous) firing of reticular neurons.

8   The reticular system may also regulate which impulses are allowed to register in your brain. When you are engrossed in a television program, you may not notice that someone has entered the room. But when you are engaged in even more absorbing activities, it might take a general stimulus on the order of an earthquake to distract you. Such filtering and selective depression of stimuli apparently takes place in the reticular system.

The Hypothalamus

9   The **hypothalamus** is a small body, densely packed with cells. It helps regulate the internal environment as well as some aspects of behavior. For example, the hypothalamus helps to control heart rate, blood pressure, and body temperature. It also plays a part in the regulation of the pituitary gland, as we learned earlier. And it controls such basic drives as hunger, thirst, and sex. So now you know what to blame for all your problems. Experimental electrical stimulation of various centers in the hypothalamus can cause a cat to act hungry, angry, cold, hot, benign, or horny.

The Cerebrum

10   For many people the word *brain* conjures up an image of two large, deeply convoluted gray lobes. What they have in mind, of course, is the outside layer of the two cerebral

hemispheres, the dominant physical aspect of the human brain. The **cerebrum** is present in all vertebrates, but it assumes particular importance in humans. In some animals, it is essentially an elaborate refinement that implements behavior that could be performed to some degree without it. It has a far greater importance in other animals.

Hemispheres and Lobes

11   The human cerebrum consists of two hemispheres, the left and the right, each of these being divided into four lobes. At the back is the **occipital lobe**, which receives and analyzes visual information.

12   The **temporal lobe** is at the side of the brain. It roughly resembles the thumb on a boxing glove, and it is bounded anteriorly by the fissure of Sylvius. The temporal lobe shares in the processing of visual information, but its main function is auditory reception.

13   The **frontal lobe** is right where you would expect to find it—at the front of the cerebrum, just behind the forehead. This is the part that people hit with the heel of the palm when they suddenly remember what they forgot. One part of the frontal lobe is the center for the regulation of precise voluntary movement. Another part functions importantly in the use of language, and damage here results in speech impairment.

14   The area at the very front of the frontal lobe is called the **prefron area**, if you follow that. Whereas it was once believed that this area was the seat of intellect, it is now apparent that its principal function is sorting out information and ordering stimuli. In other words, it places information and stimuli into their proper context. The gentle touch of a mate or the sight of a hand protruding from the bathtub drain might both serve as stimuli, but they would be sorted differently by the prefrontal area. Up until a few years ago, parts of the frontal lobe were surgically removed in efforts to bring the behavior of certain aberrant individuals more into line with what psychologists had decided was the norm. The operation was called a frontal lobotomy, and it resulted in passive and unimaginative individuals. Fortunately, the practice has been largely discontinued, largely because chemical treatments now meet the same objectives.

15   The **parietal lobe** lies directly behind the frontal lobe and is separated from it by the central sulcus. This lobe receives stimuli from the skin receptors, and it helps to process information regarding bodily position. Even if you can't see your feet right now, you have some idea of where they are thanks to neurons in the parietal lobe. Damage to the parietal lobe may produce numbness and may cause a person to perceive his or her own body as wildly distorted and to be unable to perceive spatial relationships in the environment.

Two Brains, Two Minds?

16   The best way to begin a banal conversation a few years ago was, "What sign are you?" Today, though, sophisticates may lead with, "Are you right-brained or left-brained?" Some of the findings of one of the most fascinating branches of neural research have indeed filtered into the public consciousness.

17   The question is based on information that has been accumulating since the middle of the last century when A. L. Wigam, a British physician, performed autopsies on men who had led somewhat normal lives with only half a brain. That is, one hemisphere had been destroyed by accident or other trauma. The question then arose, since we only need half a

brain, then why do we have two? At first it was assumed that this was another case where nature had built in redundancy, or backup, in a critical system.

18   Brain research has revealed a fascinating fact: the hemispheres are not duplicates at all, but structures with quite different specializations. To oversimplify, the left hemisphere is the center of logical, stepwise reasoning, of mathematics and language. It processes information in a fragmentary, sequential manner, sorting out the parts of questions and dealing with each quite rationally. (*Star Trek's* Spock was definitely left-brained.) The right brain, on the other hand, is the center of awareness for music and art. Imagination swells from this lobe and it sees things in their entirety (holistically), often solving problems through insight, as it compares relationships.

19   The flexibility of the two hemispheres has been shown when one is damaged and the other takes over its role. Such flexibility, by the way, may be greater in left-handers than in right-handers. It seems that the brain centers of south-paws are generally more diffuse, less localized, with functions more equally dispersed between the two hemispheres. Brain damage to left-handers may produce different symptoms than right-handers with similar injuries.

20   The two halves of the brain are connected by a great, broad tract of nerve fibers, about 4 inches wide, called the **corpus callosum**. Information from each half can be communicated to the other half via the corpus callosum. Thus, special abilities of the two parts of the brain can be integrated and allow us to solve problems, perform tasks, and appreciate life's offerings by a grand union of complex and differing abilities.

21   Or maybe not. Evidence indicates that usually one hemisphere is dominant and inordinately influences how we approach life. Furthermore, some researchers argue that the hemispheres compete with each other for our attention. Such arguments, at this point, quickly extend beyond science and enter the realm of philosophy.

—Wallace, *Biology: The World of Life*, pp. 604–14

Writing About the Reading
CHECKING YOUR VOCABULARY

1. For each of the words listed below, use context; prefixes, roots, and suffixes (see Chapter 3); and/or a dictionary to write a brief definition or synonym of the word as it is used in the reading.

   a. afferent (para. 7) _____

   b. efferent (para. 7) _____

   c. banal (para. 16) _____

   d. redundancy (para. 17) _____

   e. specializations (para. 18) _____

   f. fragmentary (para. 18) _____

   g. realm (para. 21) _____

2. Underline new, specialized terms introduced in the reading (see Chapter 3).
3. Draw a word map of one of the words in the reading.

CHECKING YOUR COMPREHENSION

1. Which area of the brain is responsible for each of the following functions?

   a. balance and coordination _____

   b. regulation of heart rate _____

   c. vision _____

   d. hearing _____

   e. sorting out information _____

2. Describe the specializations of the right brain and of the left brain.
3. Explain what happens when one brain hemisphere is damaged.
4. Why do left-handed people have more flexibility between hemispheres than right-handed people?
5. Identify the overall thought pattern(s) used in this reading.
6. Underline transitional words that signal the overall pattern(s).

THINKING CRITICALLY

1. If the author of the reading were present, what questions would you like to ask him about right-brain or left-brain dominance or brain functioning?
2. Why does the author defer the argument in paragraph 21 to a philosopher?
3. Are you right- or left-brained? That is, which hemisphere dominates your thinking and behavior?

LEARNING/STUDY STRATEGY

Draw a sketch of the brain. Label its parts.

PSYCHOLOGY

Reading 1
Reading 2
PAIRED READINGS

Are There "His" and "Hers" Brains?

Carole Wade and Carol Tavris

Prereading Questions

1. Do men and women think differently? How?
2. How are male and female brains different?

1   A second stubborn issue concerns the existence of sex differences in the brain. Historically, findings on male-female brain differences have often flip-flopped in a most suspicious manner, a result of the biases of the observers rather than the biology of the brain (Shields, 1975). For example, in the 1960s, scientists speculated that women were more "right-brained" and men were more "left-brained," which supposedly explained why men were "rational" and women "intuitive." Then, when the virtues of the right hemisphere were discovered, such as creativity and ability in art and music, some researchers decided that *men* were more right-brained. But it is now clear that the abilities popularly associated with the two sexes do not fall neatly into the two hemispheres of the brain. The left side is more verbal (presumably a "female" trait), but it is also more mathematical (presumably a "male" trait). The right side is more intuitive ("female"), but it is also more spatially talented ("male").

2   To evaluate the issue of sex differences in the brain intelligently, we need to ask two questions: Do male and female brains differ physically? And if so, what, if anything, do these differences have to do with behavior?

3   Let's consider the first question. Many anatomical and biochemical sex differences have been found in animal brains, especially in areas related to reproduction, such as the hypothalamus (McEwen, 1983). Human sex differences, however, have been more elusive. Of course, we would expect to find male-female brain differences that are related to the regulation of sex hormones and other aspects of reproduction. But many researchers want to know whether there are differences that affect how men and women think or behave—and here, the picture is murkier.

4   For example, in 1982, two anthropologists autopsied 14 human brains and reported an average sex difference in the size and shape of the *splenium,* a small section at the end of the corpus callosum, the bundle of fibers dividing the cerebral hemispheres (de Lacoste-Utamsing & Holloway, 1982). The researchers concluded that women's brains are less lateralized for certain tasks than men's are—that men rely more heavily on one or the other side of the brain, whereas women tend to use both sides. This conclusion quickly made its way into newspapers, magazines, and even textbooks as a verified sex difference.

5   Today, however, the picture has changed. In a review of the available studies, neuroscientist William Byne (1993) found that only the 1982 study reported the splenium to be larger in women. Two very early studies (in 1906 and 1909) found that it was larger in men, and 21 later studies found no sex differences between the two sexes, differences

that paled in comparison with the huge individual variations *within* each sex (Bishop & Wahlsten, 1997). Most people are unaware of these findings because studies that find no differences rarely make headlines.

6   Researchers are now looking for other sex differences in the brain, such as in the density of neurons in specific areas. One team, examining nine brains from autopsied bodies, found that the women had an average of 11 percent more cells in areas of the cortex associated with the processing of auditory information; all of the women had more of these cells than did any of the men (Witelson, Glazer, & Kigar, 1994).

7   Other researchers are searching for sex differences in the brain areas that are active when people work on a particular task. In one study (Shaywitz et al., 1995), 19 men and 19 women were asked to say whether pairs of nonsense words rhymed, a task that required them to process and compare sounds. MRI scans showed that in both sexes an area at the front of the left hemisphere was activated. But in 11 of the women and none of the men, the corresponding area in the right hemisphere was also active. These findings are further evidence for a sex difference in lateralization, at least for this one type of language function. Such a difference could help explain why left-hemisphere damage is less likely to cause language problems in women than in men after a stroke (Inglis & Lawson, 1981; McGlone, 1978).

8   Over the next few years, research may reveal additional anatomical and information processing differences in the brains of males and females. But even if such differences exist, we must then ask our second question: *What do the differences mean for the behavior of men and women in real life?*

9   Some popular writers have been quick to assume that brain differences explain, among other things, women's allegedly superior intuition, women's love of talking about feelings and men's love of talking about sports, women's greater verbal ability, men's edge in math ability, and why men won't ask for directions when they are lost. But there are at least three problems with these conclusions:

10   1 *These supposed gender differences in behavior are stereotypes;* the overlap between the sexes is greater than the difference between them. Although some differences may be statistically significant, most are small in practical terms.

11   2 *A biological difference does not necessarily have behavioral implications.* In the rhyme-judgment study, for example, men and women performed equally well, despite the differences in their MRIs—so what do those brain differences actually mean in practical terms? When it comes to explaining how brain differences are related to more general abilities, speculations are as plentiful as ants at a picnic, but at present they remain just that—speculations (Blum, 1997; Hoptman & Davidson, 1994). To know whether sex differences in the brain translate into significant behavioral differences, we would need to know much more about how brain organization and chemistry affect human abilities and traits.

12   3 *Sex differences in the brain could be the result rather than the cause of behavioral differences.* Remember that experiences in life are constantly sculpting the circuitry of the brain, affecting the way brains are organized and how they function—and males and females often have different experiences.

13   Thus, the answer to our second question, whether physical differences are linked to behavior, is "No one really knows." It is important to keep an open mind about new findings on sex differences in the brain, but because the practical significance of these findings (if any) is not clear, it is also important to be cautious and aware of how such results might be exaggerated and misused.

—Wade and Tavris, *Psychology,* pp. 130–32

Writing About the Reading
CHECKING YOUR VOCABULARY

1. For each of the words listed below, use context; prefixes, roots, and suffixes (see Chapter 3); and/or a dictionary to write a brief definition or synonym of the word as it is used in the reading.

   a. existence (para. 1) _____

   b. biases (para. 1) _____

   c. intuitive (para. 1) _____

   d. hemispheres (para. 1) _____

   e. spatially (para. 1) _____

   f. elusive (para. 3) _____

   g. hypothalamus (para. 3) _____

   h. splenium (para. 4) _____

   i. lateralized (para. 4) _____

   j. speculations (para. 11) _____

2. Underline new, specialized terms introduced in the reading (see Chapter 3).

3. Draw a word map of one of the words in the reading.

CHECKING YOUR COMPREHENSION

1. What did researchers decide about the brain once the right hemisphere abilities were discovered?
2. What questions need to be asked to evaluate if sex is responsible for brain differences?
3. How do male and female brains differ in physical makeup?
4. Why are the differences between male and female brains not as significant as they might seem?
5. What do scientists need to know to determine if sex differences in the brain are related to general abilities?
6. Explain how sex differences in the brain might actually be the result and not the cause of behavioral differences.
7. Why is it important to keep an open mind about sex differences in the brain?
8. What is the overall thought pattern used throughout the reading?

THINKING CRITICALLY

1. How might the findings about sex differences in the brain be misused?
2. Why do you think the author characterizes some traits as "male" and some as "female"? Is this an accurate characterization? Can you name some other traits that are considered typically male or typically female?
3. Why do you think it is important to understand how male and female brains are different? What possible uses could there be for this information?
4. Why do scientists study which areas of the brain are used for different tasks?

5. Are you convinced by this selection that there are significant differences in male and female brains? Why or why not?
6. Describe other types of physical differences between men and women that impact behavior.

LEARNING/STUDY STRATEGY

Write a summary of this selection.

Thinking About the Paired Readings
INTEGRATING IDEAS

1. What is the purpose of each reading?
2. In what ways are these readings similar, and how are they different?
3. Which reading was easier to read? Explain your reasons.
4. Assume you are preparing for an essay exam. How would you study each reading? How would your strategies differ?

GENERATING NEW IDEAS

1. Identify one famous historical figure and write a one-page paper describing whether and how that person is left- or right-brained or how you could argue both ways.
2. Based on the reading "Are There 'His' and 'Hers' Brains?" summarize a short story you could write describing a world in which sex differences in the brain are fully understood and accounted for.

ADDITIONAL PRACTICE
MULTIMEDIA ACTIVITIES

1. **Rhetorical Patterns for Organizing Documents**
   http://www.ecf.utoronto.ca/~writing/handbook-rhetoric.html

   The University of Toronto presents this site, which reviews the ways information is organized. Choose some objects and activities you experience in your daily life. Write about them according to the appropriate guidelines presented here.

2. **Logic Patterns**
   http://www.learner.org/teacherslab/math/patterns/logic.html#activities

   Try these online logic pattern activities from The Teacher's Lab, the Annenberg/CPB Math and Science Project. Observe patterns in your daily life. When do you find yourself sorting and classifying?

MYREADINGLAB

If your instructor has asked you to use Reading Road Trip, be sure to visit the "Ellis Island and the Statue of Liberty" module for multimedia tutorials, exercises, and tests on academic thought patterns.

8 Learning from Textbooks

LEARNING OBJECTIVES

✦ To become familiar with standard textbook format

✦ To use textbook features to facilitate learning

✦ To devise systematic approaches for textbook study

✦ To learn systematic retention and recall techniques

Think About It!

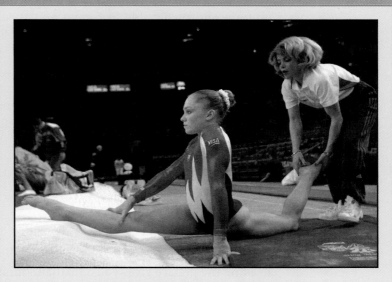

Imagine you have just started training to become a gymnast. The first time the coach tells you to go from a kip to a pike, you have no idea how to do it. But once the coach defines the terms, demonstrates the move, breaks it down into its component parts, and guides you through it a few times, you become comfortable performing it.

Learning a subject is not so different. Instead of a coach, however, you have a textbook. In many college courses, the textbook is your primary source of information. Each term you will spend hours reading, reviewing, and studying textbooks. Class lectures are often coordinated with reading assignments in the course text, written assignments require you to apply or evaluate ideas and concepts presented in the textbook, and term papers explore topics introduced in the text.

This chapter presents strategies for using textbooks as efficiently as possible. It describes the standard format, identifies features that aid learning, discusses systematic approaches to textbook study, and presents recall and retention strategies.

■ Textbook Format

When you first examine a textbook, it may seem like an overwhelming collection of facts and ideas. However, textbooks are highly organized, well-structured sources of information. They follow specific patterns of organization and are uniform and predictable in format and style. Once you become familiar with these structures, you will come to regard textbooks as easy-to-use resources and valuable guides to learning.

Preface

A textbook usually begins with an opening statement called a preface, in which the author describes the text. The preface often specifies the

- structure or organization of the book.
- major points of emphasis.
- distinctive features.
- author's reasons for writing the text.
- intended audience.
- special learning features.
- author's qualifications.
- references or authorities consulted when writing.

Reading the preface gives you a firsthand impression of the author and his or her attitudes toward the text. Think of it as a chance to get a glimpse of the author as a person.

Some authors include, instead of or in addition to a preface, an introduction titled "To the Student." Written specifically for you, it contains information similar to that in a preface. The author may also include an introduction directed "To the Instructor." Although it may often be quite technical, discussing teaching methodologies and theoretical issues, it may contain some material of interest to students as well. Figure 8-1 shows an excerpt from the preface of a computer science text. Marginal annotation and underlining have been added to call your attention to its contents.

EXERCISE 8-1

Read or reread the preface in Academic Reading *and in one of your other textbooks. Using the list above as a guide, list on your own paper the types of information each preface provides.*

FIGURE 8-1   Excerpt from a Preface

What Is Computer Confluence?

book is part of a multimedia package

Computer Confluence is more than a textbook; it's <u>the confluence of three information sources:</u> an illustrated textbook, a multimedia CD-ROM, and a timely World Wide Web site on the Internet. This integrated learning package takes advantage of the unique strengths of three media types:

advantages of textbooks

- *Computer Confluence,* the text. In spite of the talk about a paperless future, a <u>book's user interface still has many advantages:</u> You can read it under a tree or on the subway, you can bend the corners and scribble in the margins, you can study the words and pictures for hours without suffering from eyestrain or backache. A well-written text can serve as a learning tool, a reference work, a study guide, and even a source of motivation and inspiration. A textbook is no substitute for a good teacher, but a good textbook can almost always make a good teacher better. This book, which started out as *Computer Currents* in 1994, has served as an information-age guidebook for thousands of students through its first two editions.

CD-ROM uses

- *Computer Confluence,* the CD-ROM. A CD-ROM may not be as warm and friendly as a good book, but it <u>can deliver video, audio, animation, and other dynamic media that can't be printed on paper.</u> A well-designed CD-ROM can encourage exploration through interactivity. The *Computer Confluence* CD-ROM supplements and reinforces the material in the book with state-of-the-art 3-D animation, audio, and video. It also includes a software sampler for hands-on experimentation and interactive study materials that provide student feedback.

Web site uses

- *Computer Confluence,* the Web site (<u>http://www.computerconfluence.com</u>). The information in computer books and CD-ROMs has a short shelf life. The Internet makes it possible to publish <u>up-to-the-minute news</u> and information regularly and <u>link that information to other sources around the world.</u> The Internet can also serve as a <u>communication conduit for on-line discussion and research.</u> An extensive collection of timely, media-rich Web pages keeps the information in *Computer Confluence* current. The pages include late-breaking news, multimedia tidbits, and links to the most important computer and information technology sites, all organized by chapter and topic. The Web site also includes discussion areas where students, instructors, and authors can meet on-line. Students can also visit the Web site to take practice quizzes and submit answers to on-line exercises.

Computer Confluence presents computers and information technology on three levels:

levels of thinking on which the book focuses

- <u>Explanations:</u> *Computer Confluence* clearly explains what a computer is and what it can (and can't) do; it explains the basics of information technology clearly and concisely.

- <u>Applications:</u> *Computer Confluence* clearly illustrates how computers and networks can be used as practical tools to accomplish a wide variety of tasks and solve a wide variety of problems.

- <u>Implications:</u> *Computer Confluence* puts computers in a human context, illustrating how information technology affects our lives, our world, and our future.

Who Is Computer Confluence For?

intended audience

Computer Confluence: Exploring Tomorrow's Technology is designed especially for the introductory computer class for both nonmajors and majors. *Computer Confluence* is also appropriate for introductory computer science classes, discipline-specific computer courses offered through other departments, high school courses, and adult education courses. *Computer Confluence* can also serve as a self-study guide for anyone who's motivated to understand the changing technological landscape. . . .

How Is Computer Confluence Organized?

The book consists of 16 chapters organized into five broad sections:

overall organization: 5 key topics

1. *Approaching Computers: Hardware and Software Fundamentals*

2. *Using Computers: Essential Applications*

3. *Exploring with Computers: Networks and Gateways*

4. *Mastering Computers: Issues, Algorithms, and Intelligence*

5. *Living with Computers: Information Age Implications*

(continued)

content review
of each part

  Part 1 provides the basics: a brief historical perspective, a nontechnical discussion of computer and Internet basics, and an overview of hardware and software options. These chapters quickly introduce key concepts that recur throughout the book, putting the student on solid ground for understanding future chapters. Part 2 covers the most important and widely used computer applications, including word processing, spreadsheets, graphics, multimedia tools, and databases. These applications, like those in Parts 3 and 4, are presented in terms of concepts and trends rather than keystrokes. Part 3 explores the world of networks, from simple interoffice LANs to the massive global infrastructure that's evolving from the Internet. Part 4 begins with a discussion of information technology risks and related ethical issues; it then explores the process and the problems of creating software, including the curious field of computer science known as artificial intelligence. Part 5 explores the far-reaching impact of computers on our work, our schools, our homes, our society, and our future.

focus of
the text

  Throughout the five parts, the book's focus gradually flows from the concrete to the controversial and from the present to the future. Individual chapters have a similarly expanding focus. After a brief introduction, each chapter flows from concrete concepts that provide grounding for beginners toward abstract, future-oriented questions and ideas.

instructional
aids

  Each chapter includes instructional aids to help students master the material quickly. Key terms are highlighted in boldface type for quick reference; secondary terms are italicized. Terms are defined in context, in a glossary at the end of the text, and in the CD-ROM's hypertext glossary. Each chapter begins with a list of objectives and ends with a chapter summary; a list of key terms; collections of review questions, discussion questions, and projects; and an annotated list of sources and resources for students who want more information or intellectual stimulation.

SOURCE: Beekman, *Computer Confluence*, pp. xix–xxi

Table of Contents

The table of contents is one of the first things a professor looks at to evaluate a book. It is also one of the first things you should look at after you have purchased a textbook. The table of contents is an outline of the textbook's main topics and subtopics. It shows the organization of the text and indicates the interrelations among the topics. You can easily identify predominant thought patterns used throughout the text.

  Besides using the table of contents to preview a text's overall content and organization, be sure to refer to it before reading particular chapters. Although chapters are organized as separate units, they are related. To understand a given chapter, note what topics immediately precede and follow it.

  Recent textbooks may include a brief table of contents listing only unit and chapter titles, followed by a complete table of contents that lists subheadings and various learning aids contained within each chapter. The brief table of contents is most useful for assessing the overall content and structure of the entire text, whereas the complete one is more helpful when you are studying individual chapters.

  Figure 8-2 (p. 243) shows a brief table of contents excerpted from a sociology textbook. You can see that the text approaches the study of sociology by examining first the sociological perspective, followed by the basic concepts of the social framework. It then considers how people are differentiated and treated unequally, the institutions that society creates, and, finally, the causes and results of social change. The thought pattern used to organize the textbook's contents is *classification*.

  Figure 8-3 (p. 244) is an excerpt from the detailed table of contents that appears in the same textbook. The chapter discusses how socialization occurs.

The predominant thought pattern is evident: *order* and *sequence*. Both process and chronological sequence patterns are evident in individual chapter sections, as marked on the figure.

FIGURE 8–2   Brief Table of Contents

Brief Contents

SOURCE: DeVito, *Human Communication,* p. iii

FIGURE 8–3   Detailed Table of Contents

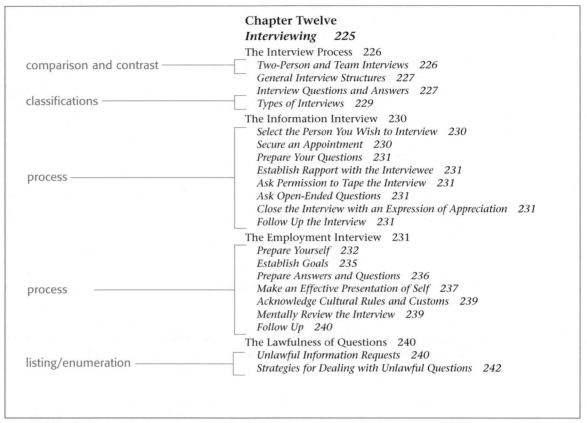

Source: DeVito, *Human Communication*, p. vi

EXERCISE 8-2

Turn to the table of contents of one of your textbooks. Choose a unit or part that you have not read but that will be assigned soon. Predict and list the thought pattern(s) of as many sections of the chapters as possible. Then, when you read the chapter, confirm or reject each of your predictions.

Appendix

The appendix of a textbook contains supplementary information that does not fit within the framework of the chapters. Often, the appendix offers valuable aids. For example, one physics text contains five appendixes:

    Appendix A. Systems of Measurement
    Appendix B. More About Motion
    Appendix C. Graphing
    Appendix D. More About Vectors
    Appendix E. Exponential Growth and Doubling Time

The textbook includes these appendixes for the reader's convenience, and the text refers to each one frequently.

Glossary

A **glossary** is an alphabetical listing of new vocabulary words that are used in the text. The meaning of each word is also included. Located in the back of the text, the glossary serves as a mini-dictionary. To make it even more convenient to use, take some paper clips and attach one to the first page of the glossary in each of your texts. The paper clips will enable you to turn directly to the glossary without hunting and fumbling.

The glossary is easier to use than a regular dictionary. As you know, many words have several meanings, and regular dictionaries list all of the most common meanings. To find the meaning of a word in a dictionary, you have to sort through all the meanings until you find one that suits the way the word is used in the text. A glossary, on the other hand, lists only one meaning—the meaning intended by the author of your text.

The glossary can serve as a useful study aid, particularly at the end of a course when you have completed the text. The glossary is actually a list of words that you should have learned. The easiest way to check whether you have learned these new terms is to go through each column of the glossary, covering up the meanings with an index card or folded sheet of paper. Read each word and try to write a definition for it or just make up the definition mentally. Then uncover the meaning and see whether you were correct. Keep track of the terms you miss, and study them later.

Index

At the end of most texts, you will find an alphabetical subject index that lists topics covered in the text, along with page references. Although its primary function is to enable you to locate information on a specific topic, it can also be used as a study aid for final exams. If you have covered most or all of the chapters in the text, then you should be familiar with each topic indexed. For example, suppose the index of an economics textbook includes the following.

Saving, 487

desired, equilibrium national income and, 497–499

domestic, economic development and, 751

marginal propensity to save and, 490–491

national, 518–519

private, 511

public, 511–512

short- and long-run effects of, 728–729

To review for an exam, you can look at each index entry and test your recall. In the economics textbook example you would ask yourself, "What is the equilib-

FIGURE 8-4   Textbook Checklist

Preface

- ■ States the purpose of the text
- ■ Indicates intended audience
- ■ Explains book organization
- ■ Includes author's credentials
- ■ Describes distinctive features
- ■ Discusses major points of emphasis
- ■ Describes learning aids

Table of Contents

- ■ Includes brief table of contents
- ■ Groups chapters into parts or sections
- ■ Indicates thought pattern(s) throughout the text

Appendix

- ■ Offers useful tables and charts
- ■ Includes supplementary documents
- ■ Describes background or reference material

Glossary

- ■ Includes definitions of special terms
- ■ Provides pronunciation guide, as well as word meanings

Index

- ■ Includes subject index
- ■ Offers separate name index

---

rium national income? How does it relate to desired saving? What is the difference between national and public saving? What are the effects of saving?" and so forth.

Some texts also include a name index that enables you to locate references to individuals mentioned in the text.

The checklist in Figure 8-4 is provided to help you quickly assess a textbook's content and organization.

EXERCISE 8-3

Use the checklist in Figure 8-4 to analyze the content and organization of one of your textbooks. Check each item that describes your textbook.

■ Textbook Learning Features

Most college textbooks are written by professors who are experienced teachers. They understand how students learn, and they know which topics and concepts usually cause students difficulty. Their purpose in writing is not only to present information but also to help students learn actively. Consequently, most textbooks contain numerous learning aids: chapter previews, marginal notes, special-interest boxes or inserts, review questions, lists of key terms, summaries, and references. A textbook is a guide to learning—a source that directs your attention, shows you what is important, and enables you to read actively. Learning will be easier if you use the textbook's learning aids to best advantage.

Chapter Preview

Research indicates that if readers have some knowledge of the content and organization of material *before* they begin to read it, their comprehension and recall increase. Consequently, numerous textbooks begin each chapter with some kind of preview. There are several common forms.

Chapter Objectives   Some texts list the objectives of each chapter beneath the chapter title, as is done in this book. The objectives help to focus your attention on important ideas and concepts. They usually are listed in the order in which the topics appear in the chapter, presenting an abbreviated outline of the main topics.

Chapter Outline   Other texts provide a brief outline of each chapter's contents. Formed from the headings and subheadings used throughout the chapter, the outline reflects both the content and the organization of the chapter. A sample outline from a psychology text is shown in Figure 8-5. As you study a chapter

FIGURE 8-5   Chapter Outline

CHAPTERTHIRTEEN

Development over the Life Span

From Conception to the First Year
Prenatal Development
The Infant's World

Cognitive Development
The Ability to Think
The Ability to Speak

Gender Development

Moral Development
Moral Judgments: Reasoning About Morality
Moral Emotions: Acquiring Empathy, Guilt, and Shame
Moral Action: Learning to Behave Morally

Adolescence
The Physiology of Adolescence
The Psychology of Adolescence

Adulthood
The Biological Clock
The Social Clock

Are Adults Prisoners of Childhood?

Think About It: Puzzles of Psychology
How Long Should We Prolong Life?

Taking Psychology with You
Bringing Up Baby

SOURCE: Wade and Tavris, *Psychology*, p. 491

outline, pay attention to the sequence and progression of topics and look for thought patterns.

Chapter Overview   Some textbook authors provide a preview section in which they state what the chapter is about, explain why certain topics are important, focus the reader's attention on key issues, or indicate how the chapter is related to other chapters in the book. Overviews may be labeled "Chapter Preview," "Overview," a less obvious title such as "Memo," or, as in the sample shown in Figure 8-6 (taken from a biology text), with no title at all, but presented on the opening page of the chapter following the objectives.

Each type of preview can be used to activate and monitor your learning before you begin, while you are reading, and after you finish the chapter.

Before Reading
- Use the chapter preview to activate your prior knowledge of the subject. Recall what you already know about the subject by trying to anticipate the chapter's main points.
- Use chapter previews to predict the predominant thought patterns.
- Use previews to anticipate which portions or sections of the chapter will be the most difficult or challenging.

While Reading
- Use the preview as a guide to what is important to learn.
- Mark or underline key information mentioned in the preview.

After Reading
- Use the preview to monitor your comprehension.
- Test your ability to recall key information.
- Immediately review any material you were unable to recall.

FIGURE 8-6   Chapter Overview

All the known field mice in the universe must live on whatever this planet can provide for them. They run little risk of depleting their planet's resources, however, because their needs are few—a warm hole, a little food, and a little social acceptance. It's a good thing for them that their requirements are so few, because they have only the resources that their planet can provide. Should they deplete or foul those resources, they would be in a bit of a fix, because *that's all there is*. The point is not too subtle, is it? We share the planet with the field mice. And our resources, too, are limited. But their gentle touch on the great, delicate globe is far from our sledgehammer impact.

In this chapter, we will review the state of some of the resources and energy necessary to life and try to see just how our impact is influenced by something very ephemeral and hard to pin down—our values. We will approach the question of whether our behavior and values could or should be based on our access to the Earth's resources and energy. And how have we treated our heritage?

We will consider the Earth's resources to be in one of two categories, renewable and nonrenewable. **Renewable resources** are those that do not exist in set amounts—they can be reused or replenished at least as fast as we use them. If we cut a pine tree, we can grow another one (assuming that the topsoil didn't wash away because we cut the first one). **Nonrenewable resources** are those that exist in set amounts on the planet and cannot be replenished. Once used, they are gone, or they are changed so much that they are difficult to recover in their original form. The two gallons of gasoline your auto consumed on your date last night is an example.

SOURCE: Wallace, *Biology: The World of Life*, p. 535

EXERCISE 8-4 *Refer to the chapter outline in Figure 8-5 to answer the following questions.*

1. What predominant thought pattern(s) do you predict the chapter will use? Why?

   _____

2. Which section do you feel will be the most difficult to read and learn? Justify your choice.

   _____

3. What guide questions could you ask to guide your reading?

   _____

EXERCISE 8-5 *Refer to the chapter overview in Figure 8-6 to answer the following questions.*

1. What do you know about the connections between resources, energy, and human life? Activate your prior knowledge by listing several issues or problems associated with this topic.

   _____

2. What predominant thought pattern(s) do you predict the chapter will use?

   _____

3. Besides listing the topics that will be covered in this chapter, what does the author do to focus attention on the key issues?

   _____

Marginal Notations

Textbooks used to have wide, empty margins that were useful to students for jotting notes. Recently, some textbook authors have taken advantage of this available space to offer comments on the text; pose questions based on the text; provide illustrations, examples, and drawings; or identify key vocabulary. Figure 8-7 (p. 250), excerpted from an economics text, illustrates one type of marginal notation.

In the excerpt, brief definitions of key terms are given in the margin next to the sentences in which the terms are first introduced.

Refer to marginal notes once you have read the text to which they correspond. Use them to review and monitor your comprehension, as well. If the marginal notes are in the form of questions, then you should go through the chapter, section by section, answering each question. Test your ability to define each term in your own words.

EXERCISE 8-6 *Read the excerpt and marginal notations in Figure 8-7. Monitor your comprehension by writing your own definitions of* inflation *and* deflation *without reference to the figure. Compare your definitions with those given in the notations.*

FIGURE 8-7 Marginal Notations

Inflation and Deflation

Inflation
The situation in which the average of all prices of goods and services in an economy is rising.

Deflation
The situation in which the average of all prices of goods and services in an economy is falling.

During World War II, you could buy bread for 8 to 10 cents a loaf and have milk delivered fresh to your door for about 25 cents a half gallon. The average price of a new car was less than $700, and the average house cost less than $3,000. Today bread, milk, cars, and houses all cost more—a lot more. Prices are more than 10 times what they were in 1940. Clearly, this country has experienced quite a bit of *inflation* since then. We define **inflation** as an upward movement in the average level of prices. The opposite of inflation is **deflation,** defined as a downward movement in the average level of prices. Notice that these definitions depend on the *average* level of prices. This means that even during a period of inflation, some prices can be falling if other prices are rising at a faster rate. The prices of electronic equipment have dropped dramatically since the 1960s, even though there has been general inflation.

Source: Miller, *Economics Today,* p. 153

Special-Interest Inserts

Many textbooks contain, within or at the end of the chapter, brief articles, essays, or commentaries that provide a practical perspective or an application of the topic under discussion. Typically, these inserts are set apart from the text by using boxes or shaded or colored print. Usually, too, the insert titles suggest their function. They might be called "Focus," "Counterpoint," or "Today's Problems." In a chapter on drug abuse, a sociology textbook might include a vivid narrative of the life of a drug addict. An economics text might describe

FIGURE 8-8 Special-Interest Insert

Learning from Business Blunders

Oops: Toyota thought it had a clever ad slogan that played off the Chinese proverb, "When you get to the foot of the mountain, a road will appear." The Japanese automaker launched an advertising campaign with the slogan, "Wherever there is a road, there is a Toyota." Not precisely true, to be sure, but it's the sort of advertising-speak that consumers are used to just about everywhere in the world. Not in China, however. Government authorities accused Toyota of false advertising.

What You Can Learn: Most advertisers wouldn't think twice about saying things like "Wherever there is a road, there is a Toyota," but the Chinese government has strict rules about truth in advertising and, after all, there really isn't a Toyota on every road—in China or anywhere else. The message: Don't assume anything when you're doing business in another country; research is vital.

—Bovée and Thill, *Business in Action,* Third Edition

specific situations in which key concepts are applied. Figure 8-8 on page 250 hows an insert from an introductory business textbook. Each chapter contains one or more "Learning from Business Blunders." The one shown in Figure 8-8 appeared in a chapter on competing in the global economy and extends chapter content by showing a mistake one company made. When reading and studying chapters that offer article inserts, try the following approach:

- Read the insert *after* you have read the text material on the page.
- Determine the purpose of the insert, and mark in the margin the concept or principle to which the insert refers.
- When reviewing for exams, especially essay exams, quickly review the chapter inserts, especially if your instructor has emphasized them.

EXERCISE 8-7   *Read the insert below, which is taken from a psychology textbook chapter on the cognitive development of children. Then answer the following questions.*

1. What cognitive tasks does this boxed insert investigate?
2. Summarize the information presented in this box.
3. How useful do you feel this information would be in studying the chapter?
4. What did you learn about children's thought processes from this box?

PSYCHOLOGY LENDS A HAND

Why Knowing How Children Think Is Important—and Useful

As we have seen, research on how children think (including how they make moral judgments) indicates that they are *not* miniature adults. While they are able to carry out many cognitive tasks at a younger age than psychologists once believed, they are definitely not capable of thinking, reasoning, or making decisions in the same way as adults. Does this fact have any practical applications? Definitely. Here are some of the most important:

- **Education should take account of children's cognitive abilities.** At what age should children begin learning a second or third language? At what age should teachers try to get them to reason deductively? When should training designed to help them avoid various cognitive errors begin? Answering these questions has important implications for what goes on in classrooms, so knowing *when* children can handle various cognitive tasks is useful from the point of view of designing effective educational programs.
- **What should parents expect from their children—and when?** Suppose that a four-year-old boy "operates" on his aunt's goldfish in order to find out what makes it swim. When she discovers this deed, should she try to explain that what the child did was bad because life is precious and destroying it is evil? Certainly, she could try, but at age four, the child probably can't understand the abstract principles involved, so her effort is probably doomed to fail. The moral? Parents should speak to children in terms they will understand. Expecting them to reason like adults or to fully understand others' perspectives can usually only lead to disappointment on the part of the parents, and confusion on the part of the children.
- **But don't *underestimate* children's understanding either!** While parents and teachers should be careful not to expect too much from children, they should also take care to avoid expecting too little. True, children can't reason like

adults, and have an incomplete theory of mind: They don't really understand their own mental processes or those of others. But they *can* do quite a lot: Even at young ages they understand something about causality, can appreciate the fact that other people have intentions and goals, and can tell the difference between actions that are "good" and ones that are "bad." If parents and teachers ignore these facts, they run the risk of assuming that children understand less than they really do. This can lead them to say or do things in the children's presence that, they assume, will go right "over their heads," and so will have no impact on the children. In fact, this may not be true. Not only do "little pitchers have big ears," a lot goes on between the ears. Parents who overlook this fact may leave their children with messages they don't really want to transmit. Our overall conclusion: Anyone who deals with children regularly (teachers, parents) should definitely have a basic understanding of their cognitive abilities—and the best place to find it is modern psychology.

—Baron and Kalsher, *Psychology: From Science to Practice*

Review Questions

Some textbook chapters conclude with a set of review questions. Read through these questions *before* you read the chapter. They serve as a list of what is important in the chapter. Usually, the questions are listed in the order in which they appear in the chapter, forming an outline of important topics. As you read and locate answers to the questions in the text, be sure to underline or mark them. Read the review questions again *after* you finish the chapter and use them to test your recall.

Be aware that review questions are a useful—but by no means sufficient—review. These questions often test only factual recall of specific information. They seldom require you to pull together ideas and compare them, assess causes, or react to the information presented.

Lists of Key Terms

Lists of key terms are often found at the end of each chapter. Usually, only specialized terms that are introduced for the first time in that chapter are included. Glancing through the list before reading the chapter will familiarize you with these terms and make reading go more smoothly.

Chapter Summaries

The end-of-chapter summary is useful both before and after you read a chapter. Before reading, the summary familiarizes you with the chapter's basic organization and content. After reading the chapter, it provides an excellent review and helps you to tie together, or consolidate, the major points.

Suggested Readings or References

Many authors provide a list of suggested readings at the end of each chapter or section. This list refers you to additional sources that provide more information on topics discussed in the chapter. References given in this list provide a useful starting point when you are researching a topic discussed in the chapter.

The evaluation list shown in Figure 8-9 will enable you to quickly assess the learning aids that a chapter provides.

Texts Without Learning Features

Instructors are always careful to select textbooks that help their students learn. However, not all textbooks have all the features described in this section. For instance, one of your texts may not include a list of key terms, and another may lack marginal notations. When a text lacks a feature that you find particularly helpful, construct the feature yourself. Prepare your own list of key terms; write your own marginal notations. If your text lacks special-interest boxes that discuss how the material can be applied, take a few moments to think of your own applications. You will find that writing your own features will be at least as helpful as using those supplied by the textbook author.

EXERCISE 8-8

Use the evaluation list shown in Figure 8-9 to analyze how the author of one of your current textbooks guides your learning. Write a brief critique of the textbook, including both strengths and weaknesses.

FIGURE 8-9   Evaluation List

Chapter Preview
- Are thought patterns evident?
- How could the preview be used for review?

Marginal Notes
- How can the notes be used for study and review?

Special-interest Inserts
- How are inserts related to chapter content?
- How much emphasis should be given to the inserts?

Review Questions
- Do the questions provide an outline of chapter content? (Compare them with chapter headings.)
- What types of thinking do the questions require? Are they primarily factual, or do they require critical thinking?

Key Terms
- How many words are already familiar?
- How difficult do you predict the chapter will be?

Chapter Summary
- Does the summary list the main topics the chapter will cover?
- Is a thought pattern evident?

Suggested Readings
- What types of sources are listed?
- To which topics do they refer?

■ Systematic Approaches to Textbook Reading

Throughout this text, you have learned numerous strategies and techniques to improve your textbook reading skills, and you may ask how you can combine them most effectively. Several systems have been developed that integrate these techniques into a step-by-step procedure for learning as you read. In this book, we focus on one particularly useful system.

The SQ3R Reading/Study System

Developed in the 1940s, the SQ3R system has been used successfully for many years and has proved effective in increasing retention of information. It is especially useful for textbooks and other highly factual, well-organized materials. Basically, SQ3R is a way of learning as you read. Its name is taken from the first letter of each step. What follows is a summary of the steps.

Steps in the SQ3R System

Survey Become familiar with the overall content and organization of the material. You already have learned this technique and know it as previewing.

Question Formulate questions about the material that you expect to be able to answer as you read. As you read each successive heading, turn it into a question. This step is similar to establishing guide questions, a topic discussed in Chapter 1.

Read As you read each section, actively search for the answers to your guide questions. When you find the answers, underline or mark the portions of the text that concisely state the information.

Recite Probably the most important part of the system, "recite" means that after each section or after each major heading, you should stop, look away from the page, and try to remember the answer to your question. If you are unable to remember, look back at the page and reread the material. Then test yourself again by looking away from the page and "reciting" the answer to your question. This step is a form of comprehension and retention assessment that enables you to catch and correct weak or incomplete comprehension or recall. Here, you are operating primarily at the knowledge and understanding levels of thinking.

Review Immediately after you have finished reading, go back through the material again, reading titles, introductions, summaries, headings, and graphic material. As you read each heading, recall your question and test yourself to see whether you still can remember the answer. If you cannot, reread that section. Once you are satisfied that you have understood and recalled key information, move toward the higher-level thinking skills. Consider applications, analyze, synthesize, and evaluate the material. Ask questions. Some students like to add a fourth "R" step—for "React."

Now, to get a clear picture of how the steps in the SQ3R method work together to produce an efficient approach to reading/study, let's apply the method to a textbook reading. Suppose you have been assigned the article on the next page on nonverbal communication for a communications class. Follow each of the SQ3R steps in reading this section.

Apply each step, as described below, to the following excerpt, "Types of Nonverbal Cues."

Survey   Preview the article, noting introductions, headings, first sentences, and typographical clues. Refer to Chapter 1, page 29, for more information on previewing. From this prereading, you should have a good idea of what information this article will convey and should know the general conclusions the authors draw about the subject.

Question   Now, using the headings as a starting point, develop several questions to which you expect to find answers in the article. Think of these as guide questions (see Chapter 1, page 35). You might ask such questions as:

What are the major types of nonverbal cues?

What are spatial cues?

What messages are communicated at each of the four distances?

Read   Now read the selection through. Keep your questions in mind. Stop at the end of each major section and proceed to the next step.

Recite   After each section, stop reading and check to see whether you can recall the answer to the corresponding question.

Review   When you have finished reading the entire article, take a few minutes to reread the headings, recall your questions, and write answers to your questions to see how well you can remember the answers.

TYPES OF NONVERBAL CUES

You now have a definition of nonverbal communication, you know how much nonverbal communication counts, you understand the characteristics most nonverbal cues share, and you know the functions and forms, so it is time to examine the types of nonverbal cues. In this section, spatial cues, visual cues, vocal cues, touch, time, and silence will be discussed.

Spatial Cues

Spatial cues are the distances we choose to stand or sit from others. Each of us carries with us something called informal space. We might think of this as a bubble; we occupy the center of the bubble. This bubble expands or contracts depending on varying conditions and circumstances such as these:

- Age and sex of those involved.
- Cultural and ethnic background of the participants.
- Topic or subject matter.
- Setting for the interaction.
- Physical characteristics of the participants (size or shape).

- Attitudinal and emotional orientation of partners.
- Characteristics of the interpersonal relationship (like friendship).
- Personality characteristics of those involved.

In his book *The Silent Language,* Edward T. Hall, a cultural anthropologist, identifies the distances that people assume when they talk with others. He calls these distances intimate, personal, social, and public. In many cases, the adjustments that occur in these distances result from some of the factors listed above.

Intimate distance. At an **intimate distance** (0 to 18 inches), you often use a soft or barely audible whisper to share intimate or confidential information. Physical contact becomes easy at this distance. This is the distance we use for physical comforting, lovemaking, and physical fighting, among other things.

Personal distance. Hall identified the range of 18 inches to 4 feet as **personal distance.** When you disclose yourself to someone, you are likely to do it within this distance. The topics you discuss at this range may be somewhat confidential and usually are personal and mutually involving. At personal distance you are still able to touch another if you want to. This is likely to be the distance between people conversing at a party, between classmates in a casual conversation, or within many work relationships. This distance assumes a well-established acquaintanceship. It is probably the most comfortable distance for free exchange of feedback.

Social distance. When you are talking at a normal level with another person, sharing concerns that are not of a personal nature, you usually use the **social distance** (4 to 12 feet). Many of your on-the-job conversations take place at this distance. Seating arrangements in living rooms may be based on "conversation groups" of chairs placed at a distance of 4 to 7 feet from each other. Hall calls 4 to 7 feet the close phase of social distance; from 7 to 12 feet is the far phase of social distance.

The greater the distance, the more formal the business or social discourse conducted is likely to be. Often, the desks of important people are broad enough to hold visitors at a distance of 7 to 12 feet. Eye contact at this distance becomes more important to the flow of communication; without visual contact one party is likely to feel shut out and the conversation may come to a halt.

Public distance. **Public distance** (12 feet and farther) is well outside the range for close involvement with another person. It is impractical for interpersonal communication. You are limited to what you can see and hear at that distance; topics for conversation are relatively impersonal and formal; and most of the communication that occurs is in the public-speaking style, with subjects planned in advance and limited opportunities for feedback.

—Weaver, *Understanding Interpersonal Communications,* pp. 215–18

How SQ3R Improves Your Reading Efficiency

The SQ3R system improves your reading efficiency in three ways. It increases your comprehension, it enhances your recall, and it saves you valuable time by encouraging you to learn as you read.

Your comprehension is most directly improved by the Survey and Question steps. By surveying or prereading, you acquire an overview of the material that serves as an outline to follow as you read. In the Question step, you are focusing your attention and identifying what is important to look for as you read.

Your recall of the material is improved through the Recite and Review steps. By testing yourself while reading and immediately after you finish, you build a systematic review pattern that provides the repetition needed to promote learning and recall.

Finally, because you are learning as you are reading, you will save time later when you are ready to study the material for an exam. Since you already have learned the material through recitation and review, you will find that you need much less time to prepare for an exam. Instead of learning the material for the first time, you can spend the time reviewing. You also will have time to consider applications, to pull the material together, to analyze it, and to evaluate its usefulness.

Adapting the SQ3R System

To make the best use of SQ3R, you must adapt the procedure to fit the material you are studying. You also must adjust the system to suit how you learn and to fit the kind of learning that is expected.

Adapting SQ3R to Suit the Material   Your texts and other required readings vary greatly from course to course. To accommodate this variation, use the SQ3R system as a base or model. Then add, vary, or rearrange the steps to fit the material.

For example, when working with a mathematics text, you might add a Study the Sample Problems step in which you analyze the problem-solving process. When reading an essay, short story, or poem for a literature class, add a React step in which you analyze various features of the writing, including the writer's style, tone, purpose, and point of view (see Chapter 15). For textbooks with a great deal of factual information to learn, you might add Underline, Take Notes, or Outline steps.

Adapting SQ3R to Suit Your Learning Style   Throughout your school experience, you probably have found that some learning techniques work better for you than others. Just as everyone's personality is unique, so is everyone's learning style. Refer to the Learning Style Questionnaire discussed in Chapter 1, page 18.

Try to use knowledge of your learning style to develop your own reading/study system. Experiment with various study methods and adapt the SQ3R system accordingly. For instance, if writing outlines helps you recall information, then replace the Recite step with an Outline step, and make the Review step a Review of Outline step. Or if you have discovered that you learn well by listening, replace the Recite and Review steps with Tape Record and Listen steps, in which you dictate and record information to be learned and review by listening to the tape.

There are numerous possibilities for developing your own reading/study system. The best approach is to test variations until you find the most effective system.

EXERCISE 8-9

Get together with other students taking the same course (or courses within the same discipline or department). Discuss and prepare a list of modifications to the SQ3R system that would be appropriate for your course's content and learning requirements.

EXERCISE 8-10 *Use the SQ3R system to read one of the readings included in this text. Write your questions on a separate sheet, and underline your answers in the reading selection.*

EXERCISE 8-11 *Apply the SQ3R system to a chapter in one of your other textbooks. List your questions on a separate sheet, and underline the answers in your textbook. Evaluate the effectiveness of your approach and decide on any modifications needed.*

■ Retention and Recall Strategies

Although the SQ3R system is an effective means of improving both comprehension and recall, it cannot ensure complete retention by itself. Periodic review, pattern recognition, association, visualization, mnemonic devices, and the use of writing also are helpful in learning and retaining the text material.

Periodic Review

Immediate review is effective and increases your ability to recall information, but it is not sufficient for remembering material for long periods of time. To remember facts and ideas permanently, you will need to review them periodically, going back and refreshing your recall on a regular basis. For example, suppose you are reading a chapter on criminal behavior in your sociology text, and a midterm exam is scheduled in four weeks. If you read the chapter, reviewed it immediately afterward, and then did nothing with it until the exam a month later, you would not remember enough to score well. To achieve a good grade, you need to review the chapter periodically. You might review the chapter once several days after reading it, again a week later, and once again a week before the exam. Then, when the time comes to study the chapter for the exam, you will find that you are still basically familiar with the chapter's content and you will not need to spend valuable study time becoming reacquainted with the material. Instead, studying will be a matter of learning specifics and organizing particular information into a format that will be easily remembered during the exam. You also will have time to consider how to apply what you have learned—a higher-level thinking skill.

Pattern Recognition

When you read about academic thought patterns in Chapter 7, you learned that it is easier to remember information that has a pattern or structure than it is to remember material that is randomly arranged. Now that you are familiar with the six basic academic thought patterns, you can learn to use these patterns to help you organize ideas.

In some chapters, the patterns will be clearly evident. In others, as well as in articles and essays, a pattern may not be as obvious. You may find it necessary to outline the material or rearrange it into a more meaningful pattern. Chapter 9 describes techniques for organizing information.

Association of Ideas

Association is a useful way to remember new facts and ideas. It involves connecting information that is new and unfamiliar to facts and ideas you already know. For instance, if you are reading a management text for a business class and are trying to remember a list of the characteristics of successful entrepreneurs, you might try to associate each characteristic with a person you know who exhibits that trait.

Using association involves stretching your memory to see what the new information has in common with what you already know. When you find a connection between the known and the unknown, you can retrieve from your memory the new information along with the old.

Visualization

Visualizing, or creating a mental picture of what you have read, often aids recall. The effectiveness of this technique definitely depends on the type of material you are reading. When you are reading descriptive writing in which the writer intends to create a mental picture, visualization is an easy task. When you are reading about events, people, processes, or procedures, visualization is again relatively simple. However, visualization of abstract ideas, theories, philosophies, and concepts may not be possible. Instead, you may need to create in your mind, or on paper, a visual picture of the *relationship* between ideas. For example, suppose you are reading about the invasion of privacy and learn that there are arguments for and against the storage of personal data on each citizen in large computer banks. You might create a visual image of two lists: advantages and disadvantages.

Mnemonic Devices

Memory tricks and devices, often called mnemonics, are useful in helping you recall lists of factual information. You might use a rhyme, such as "Thirty days hath September, April, June, and November . . ." Another device involves making up a word or phrase in which each letter represents an item you are trying to remember. If you remember the name Roy G. Biv, for example, you will be able to recall the colors in the light spectrum: *r*ed, *o*range, *y*ellow, *g*reen, *b*lue, *i*ndigo, *v*iolet.

Use of Writing to Enhance Learning

Your senses of sight, hearing, and touch all can be used to help you remember what you read. Most of the time, you use just one sense—sight—as you read. However, if you are able to use more than one sense, you will find that recall is easier. Activities such as underlining, highlighting, note taking, and outlining involve your sense of touch and enable you to reinforce your learning. These activities also force you to organize and consolidate information. Chapter 9 discusses each of these techniques in detail.

EXERCISE 8-12

Five study/learning situations follow. Decide which of the aids to retention described in this section—periodic review, pattern recognition, association, visualization, mnemonic devices, and the use of writing—might be useful in each situation, and list the aids after each item. Explain why each would be helpful.

1. In a sociology course, you are assigned to read about and remember the causes of child abuse.

   _____

2. You are learning to simplify radicals in a mathematics class.

   _____

3. You are studying mitosis, the multistage process of cell division, in a biology class.

   _____

4. In economics, you are studying the law of demand. The law states, "The price of a product and the amount purchased are inversely related: if the price rises, the quantity demanded falls; if the price falls, the quantity demanded increases."

   _____

5. You are studying the similarities and differences between plant and animal cells for a biology class.

   _____

Self-Test Summary

1. What is a preface and what does it contain?	A preface is an opening statement that specifies the structure or organization of the book and the major points of emphasis.
2. Explain the importance of the table of contents.	A table of contents is an outline of a book's main topics and subtopics. It shows the organization of the text and indicates the interrelations among the topics.
3. What is an appendix?	An appendix contains supplementary information that does not fit within the framework of the chapters, but which offers valuable aids to learning.
4. What is a glossary?	A glossary is an alphabetical listing of new vocabulary words, with their meanings, that are used in a text.
5. What is an index?	An index is an alphabetical subject list that appears at the end of a text.
6. Identify some of the numerous learning aids featured within a textbook chapter.	Learning aids include chapter previews, marginal notes, special-interest inserts, review questions, lists of key terms, and references.
7. What are the five steps in the SQ3R system?	The steps are survey, question, read, recite, and review.
8. What are additional strategies to ensure retention and recall of material you have read?	Additional recall and retention strategies include periodic review, pattern recognition, association, visualization, use of mnemonic devices, and use of writing.
9. What is a mnemonic device?	A mnemonic device is a memory trick, useful for helping in the recall of factual information.

BIOLOGY

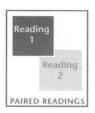

Reading 1

Do Animals Think?

Michael C. Mix, Paul Farber, and Keith I. King

Prereading Questions

1. How would you define thinking?
2. Do you believe animals can think?

1   Scientists have investigated the human organism from a mechanistic viewpoint for over a century. Their underlying assumption has been that humans could be viewed as elegant chemical machines that follow predictable natural laws. This approach has had stunning success. We know a great deal about the human body, we can design drugs to alleviate various ailments, and we can counter numerous conditions that cause suffering or death. Although science can tell us a great deal about our physical condition by treating the human body as a machine, no one doubts that humans, unlike machines, are conscious creatures. Our own consciousness is evident. What about animals?

2   To those of us who have pets, such as dogs or cats, it is difficult to think of them as machines without self-awareness—as entities more akin to our washing machines, personal computers, and blow-dryers than to our family members and friends (see Figure A). Can it be that our clever dog, Cassie, that "comforts" us when we are down, leaps with "joy" when we return from work, and has "outsmarted" the neighbor's dog that used to "steal" her food, is simply a genetically programmed automaton? Or that ZiZi, our neighbor's cat, that would seemingly "favor" starvation to dry cat food and that, if not a connoisseur of lasagna, is known to "prefer"—very definitely—smoked salmon to canned tuna, is, in her behavior, just reflecting an idiosyncratic program rather than expressing a conscious preference?

3   Until shortly after World War I, it seemed obvious to scientists that animals had feelings and that they could think. Charles Darwin believed that female birds showed aesthetic preferences in their choice of mates and that sexual selection was strongly influenced by it.

4   Many writings done in the late nineteenth century on the animal mind, however, were uncritical and highly anthropomorphic. Human desires, fears, and attitudes were attributed to animals, and numerous stories were accepted without any careful attempts at verification. It is not surprising, then, that when we read this literature today, much of it seems comical.

5   Psychologists in the 1920s reacted strongly to this uncritical literature and took the position that it was not possible to verify whether or not animals could think. They concluded that the question of animals' thinking was not a meaningful topic for science because it could not be tested experimentally. Instead, psychologists focused on the observable behavior of animals. They argued that in establishing a scientific psychology, it was irrelevant whether animals thought. They intended to establish scientific laws about how animals learn and behave that could be verified by other scientists. To psychologists like James Watson or B. F. Skinner, the private mind of the animal, if it existed, was closed to human investigation.

6   Ethologists who studied animal behavior, for the most part, were equally dismissive about probing the inner world of animals. A few workers were interested in how the world might "look" to animals, which have different sense organs than humans, but the primary thrust of ethology was in documenting repeatable patterns of behavior and in comparing these patterns with the object of establishing evolutionary connections.

7   Modern animal behavior draws on knowledge derived from psychology, ethology, and an ever-growing body of research in the fields of genetics, ecology, neurophysiology, and neuroanatomy. Until recently, all of these areas of research had been far removed from discussions of animal thought or animal awareness.

8   A well-known investigator of animal behavior, Donald Griffin of Rockefeller University, argues that neglecting animal awareness and thinking is not only an overreaction to the naive acceptance of undocumented animal stories but also a blind spot that retards advances in the scientific understanding of animal behavior. Griffin believes that mental experiences in animals could have an adaptive value—the better an animal understands its environment, the better it can adjust its behavior to survive and reproduce in it. He is also interested in animal communication, which he feels can sometimes be used to convey information about objects or events that are distant in time or space. This form of information may suggest awareness.

9   In support of his ideas, Griffin cites various behaviors that seem to involve accurate evaluation in complex environments. For example, he refers to a classic study on the prey selection of wagtails, a type of bird found in southern England. These birds feed on fly eggs and on a number of small insects. Each day they must make several choices on where to hunt, when to move on to hunt in another area, and whether to join a flock or hunt alone. Scientists who study these wagtails have shown that they hunt with great proficiency.

FIGURE A   (1) Can this animal think?   (2) Do pet tricks reflect thinking ability?

Although proficiency is not necessarily an indicator of awareness, Griffin argues that in cases where accurate evaluation of a changing and complex environment occurs, it is reasonable to consider that the animal is consciously thinking about what it is doing. Cooperative hunting by lions and the cultural transmission of behavior such as the potato washing done by Japanese macaques . . . are other examples of behaviors that suggest to Griffin and others that animals are aware and can think.

10   At present, Griffin and analysts who agree with him are in the minority in the scientific community. How can the question of animal thinking be resolved? One way is to attempt to design experiments that might give an indication one way or the other. Psychologists in the early twentieth century were very outspoken in their rejection of animal consciousness, claiming that testing for it was impossible. Griffin has proposed that some tests may be possible and that evidence can be gathered to support his position. He argues that once we have a better understanding of the electrical signals that are correlated with conscious thinking in humans, we could search for equivalents in animals. If none were found, that would suggest that his hypothesis of animal awareness is false. The strongest supporting evidence of Griffith's hypothesis involves cases in which animal communication is active and specialized, information is exchanged, and the receiving animal responds interactively. To Griffin, such cases are compelling examples of conscious and intentional acts.

11   It is too early to tell what researchers of animal behavior will conclude about animal awareness. Further research on interesting phenomena, such as animal communication, will ultimately provide the results necessary for formulating a scientific conclusion. Until then, we are confident that people will continue to discuss the world with their dogs and cats.

—Mix et al., *Biology: The Network of Life*, pp. 551–52

Writing About the Reading
CHECKING YOUR VOCABULARY

1. For each of the words listed below, use context; prefixes, roots, and suffixes (see Chapter 3); and/or a dictionary to write a brief definition or synonym of the word as it is used in the reading.

   a. entities (para. 2) _____

   b. connoisseur (para. 2) _____

   c. anthropomorphic (para. 4) _____

   d. ethologists (para. 6) _____

   e. dismissive (para. 6) _____

2. Underline new, specialized terms introduced in the reading.

3. Draw a word map of one of the words in the reading.

CHECKING YOUR COMPREHENSION

1. Why did psychologists in the 1920s declare that the question of animal thinking was not meaningful?

2. How do ethologists approach the study of animal behavior?

3. What evidence does Donald Griffin offer in support of animals' ability to think?
4. Explain what Griffin means by "adaptive value" (para. 8).
5. What types of additional evidence are needed to change the opinion of the scientific community?
6. What learning features does this excerpt include?

THINKING CRITICALLY

1. What does the last sentence of the reading suggest about humans?
2. Does the reading contain any clues about the author's answer to the question of whether animals can think?
3. Evaluate the evidence offered by Griffin. Do you feel it is sufficient and convincing?

LEARNING/STUDY STRATEGIES

1. Write a brief set of notes for the reading. (Refer to Chapter 9 pages 275–276 for suggestions on note taking.)
2. What thought pattern(s) is (are) evident in the reading?
3. What retention or recall strategies would be helpful in learning this material?
4. Did you use SQ3R when reading the material? If so, how did you find it helpful?

BIOLOGY

Wild Gorillas Handy with a Stick

Liza Gros

Prereading Questions

1. Do you think wild animals are capable of making and using tools?
2. What thinking skills do making and using tools illustrate?

1   When chimpanzees were first seen using tools in Liberia in 1951, little was known about great ape behavior in the wild. The sighting was published as a short note by Harry Beatty in the Journal of Mammalogy (recounted by primatologist Frans de Waal in The Ape and the Sushi Master). After spotting a shell mound, Beatty saw a chimp "come ambling round a bend bearing an armful of dried palm nuts," sit down beside a rock, select a nut, place it on a flat rock surface, and pound it with another rock to extract the meat. Thirty years passed before primatologists would describe the same behavior in chimps in Guinea. By then it was clear that nonhuman primates used objects for many tasks, from intimidating rivals and predators to taking leaf sponge baths and processing food. Still, the notion that tool use was not the sole province of human intelligence was difficult for some to accept.

2   Though chimps, bonobos, orangutans, and gorillas all use tools in captivity, often imitating behaviors of their keepers, tool use had not been observed for gorillas in the wild. (Chimps famously use sticks to fish for termites and rocks to crack nuts in the wild; orangutans use sticks to extract seeds from the spiny, sharp husk of Neesia fruits in the wild, and bonobos use various tools, including moss as sponges and leafy twigs to swat away bees.) That no one has ever observed wild gorillas using tools—despite decades of intensive study—prompted scientists to speculate that gorillas lost the skill because they didn't need it. The largest of the great apes, gorillas can gnash nuts between their teeth and simply smash termite mounds to release their denizens.

3   But now, as part of an ongoing study of western gorillas in Nouabalé-Ndoki National Park in the Republic of Congo, Thomas Breuer, Mireille Ndoundou-Hockemba, and Vicki Fishlock reveal that gorillas are just as resourceful as the other great apes. From an observation platform at Mbeli Bai, a swampy forest clearing that gorillas frequently visit to forage, Breuer et al. observed an adult female gorilla named Leah (a member of a long-studied gorilla group) at the edge of a pool of water, "looking intently at the water in front of her." Leah walked upright into the water, but stopped and returned to the edge when the water reached her waist. She then walked back into the water, grabbed a branch in front of her, detached it, and, grasping it firmly, repeatedly jabbed the water in front of her with the end of the branch, "apparently using it to test the water depth or substrate stability." She continued walking across the pool, branch in hand, "using it as a walking stick for postural support."

4   In a separate incident, a second adult female named Efi (who belonged to a different group) emerged from the forest and broke off the thin, long trunk from a dead shrub with

both hands. She then jammed the trunk into the ground and grasped it with her left hand while manipulating food with her right hand. Efi then placed the trunk on the swampy ground in front of her, and, walking upright, used it as a bridge to cross the muck.

5   That tool use was seen in lowland gorillas and not mountain gorillas—the most intensively studied gorillas—may reflect the different ecological challenges facing the two populations, supporting the notion that ecology influences the evolution of novel tool use. Though Mbeli Bai gorillas often use intact branches to help them get around, the authors explain, these are the first observations of wild gorillas using detached objects as tools. However the gorillas acquired their skills, these observations suggest that the intelligence required for tool use evolved before the gorilla lineage split off from humans and the other great apes—providing further evidence that intelligence is not unique to humans.

Writing About the Reading
CHECKING YOUR VOCABULARY

1. For each of the words listed below, use context; prefixes, roots, and suffixes (see Chapter 3); and/or a dictionary to write a brief definition or synonym of the word as it is used in the reading.

   a. mammalogy (para. 1) _____

   b. primatologist (para. 1) _____

   c. province (para. 1) _____

   d. denizens (para. 2) _____

   e. forage (para. 3) _____

   f. substrate (para. 3) _____

   g. postural (para. 3) _____

   h. novel (para. 5) _____

2. Underline new, specialized terms introduced in the reading (see Chapter 3).
3. Draw a word map of one of the words in the reading.

CHECKING YOUR COMPREHENSION

1. What was the first sighting of a primate in the wild using a tool?
2. Why are some people uncomfortable with the idea that wild animals could possess intelligence?
3. Why is it common for primates in captivity to use tools?
4. List the reasons that scientists had for the lack of tool use in wild gorillas.
5. Describe what researchers have recently discovered about wild gorillas in the Republic of Congo.
6. How do ecological conditions affect evolutionary adaptations such as tool use as explained in the reading?

THINKING CRITICALLY

1. Why has the author written this article?
2. What is the importance of the examples used in the reading?
3. Do you think the reading is well organized? Explain your answer.

4. The author begins with background information. What does this contribute to your understanding of the article as a whole?
5. What further research needs to be done to evaluate primates' intellectual abilities?

LEARNING/STUDY STRATEGY

Explain what thought pattern(s) is used throughout this article.

Thinking about the Paired Readings
INTEGRATING IDEAS

1. Compare the position each reading takes on what animals are capable of.
2. Compare the organization of the two readings.
3. Compare the purpose of each reading. What is each intended to accomplish?

GENERATING NEW IDEAS

1. Design an experiment that would evaluate whether an animal could think. Explain what you would have the animal do and how you would determine whether thought occurred.
2. If you were to write a research paper on animal intelligence, what further information would you need? Explain what sources you would consult and what information you would need.

ADDITIONAL PRACTICE
MULTIMEDIA ACTIVITIES

1. **Academic Success: Reading Textbooks**

   http://www.dartmouth.edu/~acskills/success/reading.html

   Dartmouth College offers several online handouts designed to help students read textbooks more effectively and efficiently. Two featured documents are "Six Reading Myths" and "Harvard Report on Reading." Read them over and discuss with your classmates how these documents apply to your current experiences. Offer each other suggestions for improving your reading skills.

2. **Mnemonics: Memory Techniques**

   http://www.bucks.edu/~specpop/mnemonics.htm

   Some easy-to-use memory techniques are presented in chart form on this site from Bucks County Community College. Try out each of these techniques over the next few days. Keep track of which ones work best for you.

MYREADINGLAB

If your instructor has asked you to use Reading Road Trip, be sure to visit the "Grand Canyon" module for multimedia tutorials, exercises, and tests on reading textbooks.

Using Writing to Learn

LEARNING OBJECTIVES

✦ To use writing to monitor your comprehension

✦ To use highlighting to improve textbook reading

✦ To use note taking to organize, synthesize, and retain ideas

✦ To use mapping to show relationships

✦ To use summaries to condense information

✦ To use writing as a discovery process

Think About It!

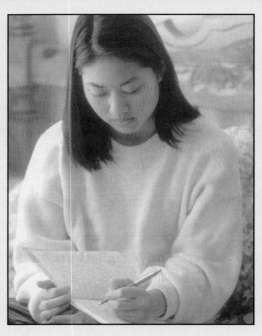

This photo, taken from a college psychology textbook, displays one of the values of writing. The text accompanying the photo explains that research has documented the benefits of writing to relieve stress and trauma. Writing can also be a means of exploring and consolidating one's own ideas. In an English class, for example, you may keep a writing journal, or in an art history class, you may keep a journal of your response to art you have viewed.

Writing, is not just something you do for others, like, writing essay exams and term papers, for example. Writing is a vehicle of expression; it is also a very effective way to learn. You can use it to organize your ideas, pull information together, discover what you think about an issue, or make a difficult reading assignment understandable.

Research studies indicate that you learn information more easily if you elaborate upon it. *Elaboration,* which means "building upon," is a process of expanding your thinking. It involves the multilevel thinking skills discussed in Chapter 1: building connections, developing associations, seeing relationships, and considering applications. Elaboration makes information meaningful and, therefore, easier to recall. Writing is one way to help you elaborate. It forces you to think about the material, to make connections, and to consider applications. This chapter discusses ways to use writing to strengthen comprehension and offers numerous writing strategies that facilitate learning. Not all strategies work equally well for everyone. Experiment to discover which work well for you.

■ Writing to Assess and Strengthen Comprehension

Writing is an excellent means of assessing your comprehension. Let us suppose you are reading a difficult assignment in your political science text. You realize you are not understanding much of it, so you need to try a new approach. One effective technique is to test yourself as you read. After each paragraph, write the main point of the paragraph in your own words. Your writing could take any number of different forms: a summary sentence, an outline, or a list. If you cannot do this, then you know you have not fully understood the paragraph and you need to reread it.

Try the same kind of self-test when you finish a section. Finally, when you have completed the assignment, write a review of key points. Any time you cannot state or recall key points, you need to do more work.

Not only is writing a good way to test whether you are understanding what you read, but it also will improve your comprehension of difficult or complicated material. When you are reading a complex argument for a logic course, you can improve your understanding by writing a list of the argument's main points. Writing each point forces you to think about each one, so connections and relationships become more apparent. Writing also forces you to spend enough time with the material to understand it fully.

Similarly, when you are solving math problems, writing will increase your understanding of the process. Listing the steps used to solve the problem makes the process "real" and more manageable. Writing makes problem solving practical rather than theoretical. There are many other situations in which writing strengthens comprehension. You can use writing to summarize case studies, explain how a process works, or describe similarities and differences among readings.

EXERCISE 9-1

Suppose you have been assigned three chapters to read in your psychology textbook. The next exam in psychology will emphasize these three chapters. Because of time limitations, your instructor will not discuss the chapters in class. Form groups of three or four students, and discuss the following issues.

1. How you would learn the chapters' content
2. What writing strategies you would use
3. How you would know when you were adequately prepared for the exam

■ Highlighting and Annotating Textbooks

Highlighting and annotating are excellent means of improving your comprehension and recall of textbook assignments. Highlighting forces you to decide what is important and to sort the key information from less important material. Sorting ideas this way improves both comprehension and recall. To decide what to highlight, you must think about and evaluate the relative importance of each idea. Highlighting has the following added benefits:

- Highlighting keeps you physically active as you read.
- The physical activity focuses your attention and improves your concentration.
- Highlighting helps you discover how ideas are related.
- Highlighting is a good test of whether you understand what you are reading. If you have difficulty deciding what to highlight, it indicates that you are not comprehending the material.

How to Highlight

To highlight textbook material most effectively, apply these guidelines:

1. **Analyze the assignment.** Preview the assignment, and define what type of learning is required. This will help you determine how much and what type of information you need to highlight.

2. **Assess your familiarity with the subject.** Depending on your background knowledge, you may need to highlight only a little or a great deal. Do not waste time highlighting what you already know. In chemistry, for example, if you already have learned the definition of a mole, then do not highlight it.

3. **Read first, then highlight.** Finish a paragraph or self-contained section before you highlight. As you read, look for signals to academic thought patterns. Each idea may seem important as you first encounter it, but you must see how it fits in with the others before you can judge its relative importance.

4. **Use the boldface headings.** Headings are labels that indicate the overall topic of a section. These headings serve as indicators of what is important to highlight. For example, under the heading "Objectives of Economic Growth," you should be certain to highlight each objective.

5. **Highlight main ideas and only key supporting details.** Try to keep academic thought patterns in mind.

6. **Avoid highlighting complete sentences.** Highlight only enough so that your highlighting makes sense when you reread it. In the following selection, note that only key words and phrases are highlighted. Now read only the highlighted words. Can you grasp the key idea of each paragraph?

BIOMES

By using imagination, we can divide the Earth's land into several kinds of regions called biomes, areas of the earth that support specific assemblages of plants. As would be expected, certain kinds of animals occupy each type of biome, since different species of animals are dependent on different sorts of plant communities for food, shelter, building materials, and hiding places. . . .

Tropical rain forests are found mainly in the Amazon and Congo Basins and in Southeast Asia. The temperature in this biome doesn't vary much throughout the year. Instead, the seasons are marked by variation in the amount of rainfall throughout the year. In some areas, there may be pronounced rainy seasons. These forests support many species of plants. Trees grow throughout the year and reach tremendous heights, with their branches forming a massive canopy overhead. The forest floor, which can be quite open and easy to travel over, may be dark and steamy. Forests literally swarm with insects and birds. Animals may breed throughout the year as a result of the continual availability of food. Competition is generally considered to be very keen in such areas because of the abundance of species.

—Wallace, *Biology: The World of Life,* pp. 708, 710

7. **Move quickly through the document as you highlight.** If you have understood a paragraph or section, then your highlighting should be fast and efficient.

8. **Develop a consistent system of highlighting.** Decide, for example, how you will mark main ideas, how you will distinguish main ideas from details, and how you will highlight new terminology. Some students use a system of symbols such as brackets, asterisks, and circles to distinguish various types of information; others use different colors of highlighters to make distinctions. The specific coding system you devise is unimportant; what is important is that you devise some consistent approach to highlighting. At first, you will need to experiment, testing various systems. However, once you have settled on an effective system, use it regularly.

9. **Use the 15–25 percent rule of thumb.** Although the amount you will highlight will vary from course to course, try to highlight no more than 15 to 25 percent of any given page. If you exceed this figure, it often means that you are not sorting ideas as efficiently as possible. Other times, it may mean that you should choose a different strategy for reviewing the material. Remember, the more you highlight, the smaller your time-saving dividends will be as you review. The first paragraph of the following excerpt provides an example of effective highlighting.

BIOMES (CONT'D)

Temperate deciduous forests once covered most of the eastern United States and all of Central Europe. The dominant trees in these forests are hardwoods. The areas characterized by such plants are subject to harsh winters, times when the trees shed their leaves, and warm summers that mark periods of rapid growth and rejuvenation. Before the new leaves begin to shade the forest floor in the spring, a variety of herbaceous (nonwoody) flowering plants may appear. These wildflowers are usually perennials, plants that live and produce flowers year after year. In the early spring, they don't have time to manufacture the food needed to grow and bloom suddenly. Instead, they draw on food produced and stored in underground parts during the previous year. Rainfall may average 75 to 130 centimeters or more each year in these forests and is rather evenly distributed throughout the year.

People who live in temperate deciduous biomes often consider the seasonal changes as both moving and fascinating. They describe a certain joy that swells within them each spring and a secret pensiveness that overcomes them in the fall as the days darken and the forests become more silent. (Perhaps we are exceeding technical descriptions here, but these are my favorite places.)

Taiga (pronounced "tie-gah") is quite unmistakable; there is nothing else like it. It is confined almost exclusively to the Northern Hemisphere and is identified by the great coniferous forests of pine, spruce, fir, and hemlock that extend across North America, Europe, and Asia. Some of these trees are the largest living things on earth.

Taiga is marked by long, cold, wet winters and short summer growing seasons. The forest is interrupted here and there by extensive bogs, or muskegs, which are the remains of large ponds. The forest floor is usually covered by a carpet of needles. In the dim light at ground level, there may be mosses, ferns, and a few flowering plants. One may move silently on the muffling needles through the Canadian taiga observing a host of mammals, including porcupines, moose, bear, rodents, hares, and wolverines.

Tundra is the northernmost land biome. It is covered throughout most of the year by ice and snow. This biome is most prevalent in the far north (arctic tundra), but it may also appear at high elevations in other parts of the world (alpine tundra). For example, in the United States, it may be seen in the high Rocky Mountains. Tundra appears in places where summer usually lasts two to four months, just long enough to thaw a few feet of the soil above the permafrost, or permanently frozen soil. Thaw brings soggy ground, and ponds and bogs appear in the depressions. The plant life consists mostly of lichens, herbs, mosses, and low-lying shrubs and grasses, as well as a few kinds of trees, such as dwarf willows and birches. Such plants obviously must be hardy, but their hardiness disguises their fragility. Once disturbed, these areas take very long periods to restore themselves.

—Wallace, *Biology: The World of Life*, pp. 712–13

EXERCISE 9-2   *Finish highlighting the preceding passage.*

Evaluating Your Highlighting

As with any learning strategy, you must ask the question "Is it working?" Your final answer, of course, will come when you take your first major examination. If you were able to review the material within a reasonable time and you earn an acceptable grade, you will know your system was effective.

There are two common mistakes you can make when you are highlighting.

Highlighting too much. Using the tired, worn-out "rather safe than sorry" rule, you may tend to highlight almost every idea on the page. Highlighting nearly everything is about as effective as highlighting nothing because no sorting occurs: key ideas are not distinguished from other, less important, ones. Highlighting too much can become a way of escaping or postponing the real issue: deciding what to learn.

Highlighting too little. If you find you are highlighting less than 10 percent per page, this often is a signal that you are having difficulty understanding the material. If you cannot explain the content of a given section in your own words, then you have not understood it. If, however, you understand what you read but are highlighting very little, then you may need to redefine your purpose for reading.

Evaluate your own highlighting by:

- **Selecting a sample page, highlighting it, and rereading only your highlighting.** Then ask yourself the following questions: "Does my highlighting convey the key ideas of the passage?" "Can I follow the author's train of thought and his or her progression of ideas by reading only my highlighting?" "Is the highlighting appropriate for my purposes?"
- **Compare your highlighting with that of another student.** Although there will be individual differences, both sets of highlighting should emphasize the same key ideas.

EXERCISE 9-3 *Evaluate your highlighting in Exercise 9-2 by using one of the preceding suggestions.*

Marginal Annotation

In many situations, highlighting alone is not a sufficient means of identifying what to learn. It does not separate the main ideas from the examples, and each of these from new terminology. Nor does it give you any opportunity to comment on or react to the material. Therefore, it is often necessary to make marginal annotations as well as to highlight.

Annotating is an active reading process. It forces you to monitor your comprehension as well as react to ideas. Table 9-1 (p. 274) suggests various types of annotation used in marking a political science textbook chapter.

Annotation as a means of analysis and evaluation is discussed on page 116 in Chapter 4. Review this section now for additional suggestions on how to annotate effectively.

EXERCISE 9-4

Add annotations to the excerpt that you highlighted in Exercise 9-2 and compare them with those of another student.

EXERCISE 9-5

Select a two- to three-page excerpt from one of your textbooks. Read, highlight, and annotate the selection. Do you feel the combination of processes is more effective than highlighting alone? Why or why not?

TABLE 9-1   Marginal Annotation

Type of Annotation	Example
Circling unknown words	...redressing the apparent (asymmetry) of their relationship
Marking definitions	*def* ⎡ To say that the balance of power favors one party over another is to introduce a disequilibrium.
Marking examples	*ex* ⎡ ...concessions may include negative sanctions, trade agreements...
Numbering lists of ideas, causes, reasons, or events	components of power include ① self-image, ② population, ③ natural resources, and geography ④
Placing asterisks next to important passages	* ⎡ Power comes from three primary sources...
Putting question marks next to confusing passages	? → war prevention occurs through institutionalization of mediation...
Making notes to yourself	Check def in soc text — power is the ability of an actor on the international stage to...
Marking possible test items	T There are several key features in the relationship...
Drawing arrows to show relationships	...natural resources..., ...control of industrial manufacture capacity
Writing comments, noting disagreements and similarities	Can terrorism be prevented through similar balance? — war prevention through balance of power is...
Marking summary statements	*sum* ⎡ the greater the degree of conflict, the more intricate will be...

EXERCISE 9-6

Working with another student in the class, choose one of the end-of-chapter readings in this text. Assume it is a reading assignment for one of your courses. Each of you should read, highlight, and annotate the selection. Then discuss similarities and differences in your work and evaluate each other's annotations.

EXERCISE 9-7

Choose a two- or three-page section from one of your textbooks and highlight it, using the guidelines suggested in this chapter. Then evaluate the effectiveness of your highlighting in preparation for an objective exam on the material.

■ Note Taking to Organize Ideas

Note taking is a writing strategy that can assist you in organizing information and pulling ideas together. It is also an effective way to pull together information from two or more sources—your textbook and class lectures, for example. Finally, note taking is a way to assess your comprehension and strengthen your recall. Use the following tips to take good notes:

1. **Read an entire section and then jot down notes.** Do not try to write notes while you are reading the material for the first time.

2. **As you read, be alert for academic thought patterns.** These patterns will help you organize your notes.

3. **Record all of the most important ideas in the briefest possible form.**

4. **Think of your notes as a list of the main ideas and supporting details of a selection.** Organize them to show how the ideas are related or to reflect the organization of the material.

5. **Use words and short phrases to summarize ideas.** Do not write in complete sentences.

6. **Write in your own words; do not copy sentences or parts of sentences from the selection.**

7. **Be highly selective.** Unless you are sure that a fact or idea is important to remember, do not include it. If you are not selective, you will find that your notes are nearly as long as the selection itself and you will save little time when you review the material.

8. **Use an outline system of indentation to separate main ideas and details.** As a general rule, the greater the importance of an idea, the closer it is placed to the left margin. Ideas of lesser importance are indented and appear closer to the center of the page. Your notes might follow a format such as this:

```
I. TOPIC
      A. Main Idea
            1. Supporting detail
                  a. fact
                  b. fact
            2. Supporting detail
      B. Main Idea
            1. Supporting detail
            2. Supporting detail
                  a. fact
                  b. fact

II. TOPIC
```

As a further illustration of the techniques of note taking, study the notes shown in Figure 9-1. They are based on a portion of the excerpt on biomes that appears earlier in this chapter.

EXERCISE 9-8   *Write a brief set of notes for the reading selection "Body Adornment: The Use of Cosmetics" at the end of this chapter. Working with a classmate, compare, discuss, and revise your notes.*

EXERCISE 9-9   *Select a three- to four-page section from one of your textbooks. Write a brief set of notes, including the key ideas.*

■ Mapping to Show Relationships

Mapping is a way of drawing a diagram to describe how a topic and its related ideas are connected. It organizes and consolidates information, often emphasizing a particular thought pattern. Mapping is a visual means of learning by writing.

This section discusses four types of maps: conceptual maps, process diagrams, part and function diagrams, and time lines. Each uses one of the thought patterns discussed in Chapter 7.

Conceptual Maps

A conceptual map is a form of outline that presents ideas spatially rather than in list form. It is a "picture" of how ideas are related. Use the following steps to construct a conceptual map:

FIGURE 9-1   Sample Notes

Biomes

- Regions of Earth's land
- Each has own plants and animals

Tropical Rain Forests

- Amazon & Congo Basins and Southeast Asia
- Seasons vary according to rainfall amount
- Trees grow throughout year
    - branches form canopy, forest floor dark, steamy
- Animals breed throughout year
    - keen competition

1. **Identify the topic and write it in the center of the page.**
2. **Identify ideas, aspects, parts, and definitions that are related to the topic.** Draw each one on a line radiating from the topic.
3. **As you discover details that further explain an idea already recorded, draw new lines branching from the idea that the details explain.**

A map of Chapter 8 is shown in Figure 9-2. Take a moment now to refer to Chapter 8 before studying the map.

Process Diagrams

In the technologies and the natural sciences, as well as in many other courses, *processes* are an important part of the course content. A diagram that visually describes the steps, variables, or parts of a process will simplify learning. For example, the diagram in Figure 9-3 on page 278 visually describes the steps in the search process for using electronic sources.

the diagram in Figure 9-3 on page 278

EXERCISE 9-10 *Draw a conceptual map of Chapter 3 of this book.*

FIGURE 9-2 Sample Conceptual Map of Chapter 8

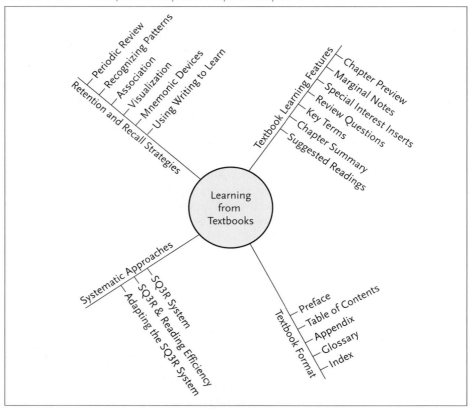

FIGURE 9–3 Sample Process Diagram

The Search Process Using Electronic Sources

Online Encyclopedia	E-Books	Periodical Databases	Specialized Websites
overview of topic	basic information	detailed information; current information	specialized & specific information

EXERCISE 9–11 *Draw a conceptual map of the reading titled "Body Adornment: The Use of Cosmetics" at the end of this chapter.*

EXERCISE 9–12 *The following paragraph describes the sequential effects of taking the psychedelic drug LSD. Read the paragraph and then draw a process diagram that describes this response sequence. Compare your diagram with those of several other students.*

Psychedelics are . . . a group of drugs that produce hallucinations and various other phenomena that very closely mimic certain mental disorders. These drugs include lysergic acid diethylamide (LSD), mescaline, peyote, psilocybin, and various commercial preparations such as Sernyl and Ditran.

Of these, LSD is probably the best known, although its use has apparently diminished since its heyday in the late 1960s. LSD is synthesized from lysergic acid produced by a fungus (ergot) that is parasitic on cereal grains such as rye. It usually produces responses in a particular sequence. The initial reactions may include weakness, dizziness and nausea. These symptoms are followed by a distortion of time and space. The senses may become intensified and strangely intertwined—that is, sounds can be "seen" and colors "heard." Finally, there may be changes in mood, a feeling of separation of the self from the framework of time and space, and changes in the perception of the self. The sensations experienced under the influence of psychedelics are unlike anything encountered within the normal range of experiences. The descriptions of users therefore can only be puzzling to nonusers. Some users experience bad trips or "bummers," which have been known to produce long-term effects. Bad trips can be terrifying experiences and can occur in experienced users for no apparent reason.

—Wallace, *Biology: The World of Life,* pp. 632–33

Part and Function Diagrams: Classification

In courses that deal with the use and description or classification of physical objects, labeled drawings are an important learning tool. In a human anatomy and physiology course, for example, the easiest way to learn the parts and functions of the brain is to draw it. To study, sketch the brain and test your recall of each part and its function. A sample part diagram of the brain appears at the end of Chapter 7 on page 230.

EXERCISE 9-13   *The following paragraph describes the outer layers of the Earth. Read the paragraph, and then draw a diagram that will help you to visualize how the Earth is structured.*

OUTER LAYERS OF THE EARTH

The Earth's crust and the uppermost part of the mantle are known as the *lithosphere.* This is a fairly rigid zone that extends about 100 km below the Earth's surface. The crust extends some 60 km or so under continents, but only about 10 km below the ocean floor. The continental crust has a lower density than the oceanic crust. It is primarily a light granitic rock rich in the silicates of aluminum, iron, and magnesium. In a simplified view, the continental crust can be thought of as layered: On top of a layer of igneous rock (molten rock that has hardened, such as granite) lies a thin layer of sedimentary rocks (rocks formed by sediment and fragments that water deposited, such as limestone and sandstone); there is also a soil layer deposited during past ages in the parts of continents that have had no recent volcanic activity or mountain building.

Sandwiched between the lithosphere and the lower mantle is the partially molten material known as the *asthenosphere,* about 150 km thick. It consists primarily of iron and magnesium silicates that readily deform and flow under pressure.

—Berman and Evans, *Exploring the Cosmos,* p. 145

Time Lines

When you are studying a topic in which the sequence or order of events is a central focus, a time line is a helpful way to organize the information. Time lines are especially useful in history courses. To map a sequence of events, draw a single line and mark it off in year intervals, just as a ruler is marked off in inches. Then write each event next to the corresponding year. For example, the time line in Figure 9-4 on page 280 displays major events during the presidency of Franklin D. Roosevelt. The time line shows the sequence of events and helps you to visualize them more clearly.

EXERCISE 9-14   *The following passage reviews the chronology of events in public school desegregation. Read the selection, and then draw a time line that will help you to visualize these historical events.*

DESEGREGATING THE SCHOOLS

The nation's schools soon became the primary target of civil-rights advocates. The NAACP concentrated first on universities, successfully waging an intensive legal battle to win admission for qualified blacks to graduate and professional schools. Led by Thurgood Marshall, NAACP lawyers then took on the broader issue of segregation in the country's public schools. Challenging the 1896 Supreme Court decision (*Plessy v. Ferguson*) which upheld the constitutionality of separate but equal public facilities, Marshall argued that even substantially equal but separate schools did profound psychological damage to black children and thus violated the Fourteenth Amendment.

FIGURE 9-4   Sample Time Line

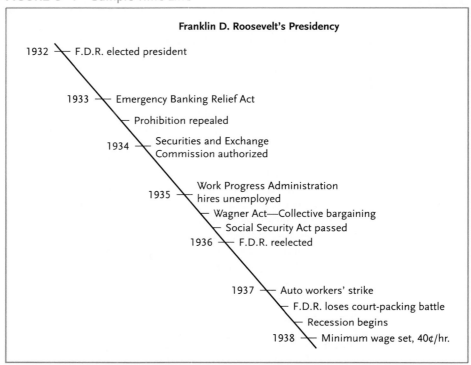

Franklin D. Roosevelt's Presidency

1932 — F.D.R. elected president

1933 — Emergency Banking Relief Act

— Prohibition repealed

1934 — Securities and Exchange Commission authorized

1935 — Work Progress Administration hires unemployed

— Wagner Act—Collective bargaining

— Social Security Act passed

1936 — F.D.R. reelected

1937 — Auto workers' strike

— F.D.R. loses court-packing battle

— Recession begins

1938 — Minimum wage set, 40¢/hr.

A unanimous Supreme Court agreed in its 1954 decision in the case of *Brown v. Board of Education of Topeka.* Chief Justice Earl Warren, recently appointed by President Eisenhower, wrote the landmark opinion which flatly declared that "separate educational facilities are inherently unequal." To divide grade-school children "solely because of their race," Warren argued, "generates a feeling of inferiority as to their status in the community that may affect their hearts and minds in a way unlikely ever to be undone." Despite this sweeping language, Warren realized that it would be difficult to change historic patterns of segregation quickly. Accordingly, in 1955 the Court ruled that implementation should proceed "with all deliberate speed" and left the details to the lower federal courts.

The process of desegregating the schools proved to be agonizingly slow. Officials in the border states quickly complied with the Court's ruling, but states deeper in the South responded with a policy of massive resistance. Local White Citizen's Councils organized to fight for retention of racial separation; 101 congressmen and senators signed a Southern Manifesto in 1956 which denounced the *Brown* decision as "a clear abuse of judicial power." School boards, encouraged by this show of defiance, found a variety of ways to evade the Court's ruling. The most successful was the passage of pupil-placement laws. . . .

Southern leaders mistook Ike's silence for tacit support of segregation. In 1957, Governor Orville Faubus of Arkansas called out the national guard to prevent the integration of Little Rock's Central High School on grounds of a threat to public order. . . .

Despite the snail's pace of school desegregation, the *Brown* decision led to other advances. In 1957, the Eisenhower administration proposed the first general civil-rights legislation since Reconstruction. Strong southern resistance and compromise by both the administration and Senate Democratic leader Lyndon B. Johnson of Texas weakened the bill considerably. The final act, however, did create a permanent Commission for Civil Rights, one of Truman's original goals. It also provided for federal efforts aimed at "securing and protecting the right to vote." A second civil-rights act in 1960 slightly strengthened the voting-rights section.

—Divine et al., *America Past and Present,* pp. 890–91

■ Summarizing to Condense Ideas

Like note taking, summarizing is an excellent way to learn from your reading and to increase recall. A summary is a brief statement that reviews the key points of what you have read. It condenses an author's ideas or arguments into sentences written in your own words. A summary contains only the gist of the text, with limited explanation, background information, or supporting detail. Writing a summary is a step beyond recording the author's ideas; a summary must pull together the writer's ideas by condensing and grouping them. Writing a summary is a useful strategy when an overview of the material is needed, as in the following situations:

- Answering an essay question
- Reviewing a film or videotape
- Writing a term paper
- Recording results of a laboratory experiment or demonstration
- Summarizing the plot of a short story
- Quickly reviewing large amounts of information

Before writing a summary, be sure that you understand the material and that you have identified the writer's major points. Then use the following suggestions.

1. **As a first step, highlight or write brief notes for the material.**

2. **Write one sentence that states the writer's overall concern or most important idea.** To do this, ask yourself what one topic the material is about. Then ask what point the writer is trying to make about that topic. This sentence will be the topic sentence of your summary.

3. **Be sure to paraphrase, using your own words rather than those of the author.**

4. **Next, review the major supporting information that the author gives to explain the major idea.**

5. **The amount of detail you include, if any, depends on your purpose for writing the summary.** For example, if you are writing a summary of a television documentary for a research paper, it might be more detailed than if you were writing it to jog your memory for a class discussion.

FIGURE 9-5 Sample Summary

> The earth is divided into regions called biomes. Each biome has its own species of plants and animals. Tropical rain forests have consistent temperatures but seasonal variation in rainfall. Trees grow throughout the year and animals breed year round. Both plants and animals are abundant in forests. Temperate deciduous forests have seasonal change in temperature; rainfall is evenly distributed. Tiaga, an area of coniferous pine forests, has long wet winters and short summers. Tundra refers to land covered by ice and snow most of the year. Plant life is limited to hardy lichens, herbs, mosses, low-lying shrubs, and dwarf trees.

6. **Normally, present ideas in the summary in the same order in which they appear in the original material.**

7. **If the writer presents a clear opinion or expresses an attitude toward the subject matter, include it in your summary.**

8. **If the summary is for your own use only and is not to be submitted as an assignment, do not worry about sentence structure.** Some students prefer to write summaries using words and phrases rather than complete sentences.

A sample summary of the article on biomes that appears earlier in this chapter is shown in Figure 9-5.

EXERCISE 9-15

Write a summary of one of the end-of-chapter readings that you have already read. Working with a classmate, compare, discuss, and revise your summaries.

EXERCISE 9-16

Select a five- to six-page section from one of your textbooks. Write a brief summary of the section, using the guidelines suggested above.

■ Brainstorming to Discover Ideas

Brainstorming is a writing and thinking exercise that is particularly effective for generating ideas. It works like this: Suppose you are trying to think of a topic for a three-minute informative speech for your speech class. Begin by making a list of any topics that come into your mind. Write continuously. Do not be concerned about whether you are writing in complete sentences or whether the topics are practical or connected to one another. Write continuously for a set period—two or three minutes. When you have finished, reread what you have written. You will be surprised at the number of different topics you have discovered. Highlight those topics that are worth further exploration.

Brainstorming is also a way to get interested in a topic before beginning to read about it. Suppose you must read several lengthy research articles on the psychological effects of color. Before you start, brainstorm. List every possible effect of color and ways to measure its effects. Then read to confirm what you knew and to find out what you did not know.

EXERCISE 9-17   *Assume you will be reading several journal articles on drug testing in schools for a sociology class. Brainstorm for three minutes to discover what you already know about the issue.*

EXERCISE 9-18   *For each of the following statements, suggest one or more writing strategies that would enhance learning.*

1. Some math students are having difficulty because they confuse several similar types of problems and choose incorrect solutions.

   _____

2. A political science class does not have a standard textbook. Instead, the instructor assigns weekly library readings on which she bases class discussions and lectures.

   _____

3. An anthropology student is preparing for an essay exam. She plans to predict possible questions and answer them.

   _____

4. A student in a computer literacy course must learn procedures for merging files using word processing software.

   _____

5. For an English literature class, a student must write a paper comparing two poems by the same poet.

   _____

Self–Test Summary

1. What is a good way to assess and strengthen your reading comprehension?	Self-testing is an effective way to assess and strengthen comprehension. As you read an assignment, write down the main points and write a review of key points when you finish.
2. How can writing help you understand difficult or complex material?	Writing forces you to think about what you read. It helps you to make connections and see the relationships between the main points.
3. Name five writing strategies and describe how each is useful.	Five writing strategies are: • Highlighting and annotating; they help to distinguish what is important to learn and remember. • Note taking; it organizes information and helps pull ideas together. • Mapping; it describes how a topic and its related ideas are connected, helping to organize and consolidate information. • Summarizing; it condenses ideas and provides a review of key points. • Brainstorming; it enables you to discover and clarify ideas, as well as generate interest in a reading assignment.
4. What is a conceptual map?	A conceptual map presents ideas spatially rather than in list form.
5. What is a process diagram?	A process diagram visually describes the steps, variables, or parts of a process.
6. What is a part and function diagram?	A part and function diagram shows labeled parts that aid in the description or classification of physical objects.
7. What is a time line?	A time line is a map showing the sequence in which events occurred.

CULTURAL ANTHROPOLOGY

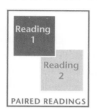

Reading 1

Body Adornment: The Use of Cosmetics

David Hicks and Margaret A. Gwynne

Prereading Questions

1. How could you define the term *cosmetics?*
2. Does the manner in which cosmetics are used vary from society to society?

1   One way in which people adorn their bodies is by temporarily decorating their skin with cosmetics, the general term for preparations designed to improve the appearance of the body, or part of it, by directly but temporarily applying them to the skin. In Western society, cosmetics take the form of various mass-produced, petroleum-based, colored creams, oils, or powders. These are usually applied to the face, and are much more frequently used by females than by males. In other societies, the term *cosmetics* may refer to body as well as face paints, usually made by combining animal or vegetable oils with colored powders made from naturally occurring minerals.

2   The extent to which cosmetics are used in human societies, from the remote jungles of South America to the high-fashion capitals of western Europe, suggests that the notion of adorning or enhancing the surface of the body, like the idea of covering it with clothing,

Cosmetics are universally used to beautify people, protect them from harm, express their social status, or identify them as members of particular groups. In Liberia, a Bassa girl being initiated into the Sande, an all-female secret society, is covered with a chalky white clay.

comes close to being a human universal. There are differences of placement, emphasis, and extent among various traditions of cosmetic use, but the reasons for wearing cosmetics are similar.

3   In every society with a cosmetic tradition, including Western society, one reason bodies are decorated is to enhance them—to make them appear more perfectly in accord with society's ideals of beauty (although what is considered attractive varies widely from society to society). But in some societies, the use of cosmetics quite consciously provides other benefits as well. Cosmetics may protect people from harm, express their social status, or identify them as members of particular classes or families. Benefits of this kind are probably part of the reason behind Western cosmetic use also, although Western cosmetics users may not be aware of it.

4   If Westerners differ little from members of other societies in their primary motivations for applying cosmetics, they do differ from some in the relatively modest extent to which they decorate themselves. Cosmetic use in some societies is so extensive it would make the heavy-handed application of cosmetics to a female American screen star by a Hollywood makeup artist seem moderate.

5   A well-turned-out Nuba male from Kordofan Province in the Sudan of northern Africa is literally painted from head to foot. Among the Nuba, body painting begins in infancy, when a baby's scalp is decorated with either red or yellow paint, depending on its family membership (Faris 1972:30). Thereafter, body painting is used to suggest one's social and physical status as well as to beautify, and it becomes more and more complex with advancing age. A young Nuba boy, for example, wears simple, inconspicuous, red and greyish white decorations on his scalp, gradually earning the right to use increasingly elaborate, colorful, and extensive designs as he matures. Each change of age and status means a new kind of decoration for the boy, as with advancing years he earns the right to use more products in a wider range of colors and designs. (Westerners, too, sometimes use cosmetics as an age marker, as when an American girl is forbidden by her parents to wear lipstick until she has reached a certain age.)

6   The scalp, face, chest, back, arms, and legs of a young adult Nuba male may literally be covered with colorful designs (Faris 1972:18–19, 62), both purely decorative (straight and curved lines, dots, triangles, crosshatching) and representational (animals, airplanes, lightning, stars—even English words, which may or may not be intelligible to the Nuba). Often these designs are asymmetrically placed on the face or body and are strikingly modern looking. They may take up to an hour to apply and may be redone daily.

7   Decorating the body as well as the face with cosmetics is by no means limited to rural or small-scale societies. Some modern, urban girls and women in North Africa, the Middle East, and South Asia decorate their skin with henna, an orange-red dye made from leaves. Urban Moroccan women, for example, may be decorated on suitable occasions with fine lines and dots forming intricate designs. These are typically applied to the hands and feet, which then look as if they are clad in lace gloves or stockings. Henna is applied at a "henna party," to which the girl or woman to be decorated invites her friends, a professional henna artist, and sometimes professional musicians or other entertainers. During the long and careful process of decorating, the guests eat, sing songs, tell jokes, and dance around the woman being decorated (Messina 1988).

8   Moroccan women who use henna say they apply it for a variety of reasons. A girl or woman may be decorated in preparation for a religious festival or her wedding, to cheer her up in late pregnancy, to soften her skin, to prevent spirits called *jinni* from causing illness or misfortune, or to calm her nerves. Whatever the reason, applying henna is cause for celebration; a

henna party provides a "lively departure" from formal Islamic expectations of proper female behavior (Messina 1988:46). People from different regions admire different designs, and styles of decoration change constantly, but the designs themselves have no explicit meanings.

—Hicks and Gwynne, *Cultural Anthropology,* pp. 378–80

Writing About the Reading
CHECKING YOUR VOCABULARY

1. For each of the words listed below, use context; prefixes, roots, and suffixes (see Chapter 3); and/or a dictionary to write a brief definition or synonym of the word as it is used in the reading.

   a. status (para. 3) _____

   b. inconspicuous (para. 5) _____

   c. elaborate (para. 5) _____

   d. representational (para. 6) _____

   e. asymmetrically (para. 6) _____

   f. explicit (para. 8) _____

2. Highlight new, specialized terms introduced in the reading (see Chapter 3).
3. Draw a word map of one of the words in the reading.

CHECKING YOUR COMPREHENSION

1. What main point about the use of cosmetics does this reading make?
2. How does the use of cosmetics differ between Western and other societies?
3. For what single purpose do all societies use cosmetics?
4. Explain how cosmetics are used by males in the Nuba society.
5. How do Moroccan women use henna?

THINKING CRITICALLY

1. What is the author's purpose for writing?
2. What generalizations do the authors make about the use of cosmetics? What types of evidence do the authors give to support their generalizations?
3. Discuss the use of cosmetics in Western society. For what purposes are they used? How does their use vary from subgroup to subgroup?

LEARNING/STUDY STRATEGIES

1. Draw a map that shows the key ideas of this reading.
2. Assume you have to write a short paper for a sociology class explaining why Western women use cosmetics. Review the reading, and make annotations that would help you develop ideas for your paper.

CULTURAL ANTHROPOLOGY

Reading 2

The Decorated Body
France Borel

Prereading Questions

1. In what ways do people decorate their bodies?
2. Do you think most people are comfortable with their bodies? Why?

1   Human nakedness, according to social custom, is unacceptable, unbearable, and dangerous. From the moment of birth, society takes charge, managing, dressing, forming, and deforming the child—sometimes even with a certain degree of violence. Aside from the most elementary caretaking concerns—the very diversity of which shows how subjective the motivation is—an unfathomably deep and universal tendency pushes families, clans, and tribes to rapidly modify a person's physical appearance.

2   One's genuine physical makeup, one's given anatomy, is always felt to be unacceptable. Flesh, in its raw state, seems both intolerable and threatening. In its naked state, body and skin have no possible existence. The organism is acceptable only when it is transformed, covered with signs. The body only speaks if it is dressed in artifice.

3   For millennia, in the four quarters of the globe, mothers have molded the shape of their newborn babies' skulls to give them silhouettes conforming to prevalent criteria of beauty. In the nineteenth century, western children were tightly swaddled to keep their limbs straight. In the so-called primitive world, children were scarred or tattooed at a very early age in rituals which were repeated at all the most important steps of their lives. At a very young age, children were fitted with belts, necklaces, or bracelets; their lips, ears, or noses were pierced or stretched.

4   Some cultures have designed sophisticated appliances to alter physical structure and appearance. American Indian cradleboards crushed the skull to flatten it; the Mangbetus of Africa wrapped knotted rope made of bark around the child's head to elongate it into a sugarloaf shape, which was considered to be aesthetically pleasing. The feet of very young Chinese girls were bound and spliced, intentionally and irreversibly deforming them, because this was seen to guarantee the girls' eventual amorous and matrimonial success.

5   Claude Levi-Strauss said about the Caduveo of Brazil: "In order to be a man, one had to be painted; whoever remained in a natural state was no different from the beasts." In Polynesia, unless a girl was tattooed, she would not find a husband. An unornamented hand could not cook, nor dip into the communal food bowl. Pink lips were despicable and ugly. Anyone who refused the test of the tattoo was seen to be marginal and suspect.

6   Among the Tivs of Nigeria, women called attention to their legs by means of elaborate scarification and the use of pearl leg bands; the best decorated calves were known for miles around. Tribal incisions behind the ears of Chad men rendered the skin "as smooth and stretched as that of a drum." The women would laugh at any man lacking these incisions, and they would never accept him as a husband. Men would subject themselves willingly to this custom, hoping for scars deep enough to leave marks on their skulls after death.

7   At the beginning of the eighteenth century, Father Laurent de Lucques noted that any young girl of the Congo who was not able to bear the pain of scarification and who

cried so loudly that the operation had to be stopped was considered "good for nothing." That is why, before marriage, men would check to see if the pattern traced on the belly of their intended bride was beautiful and well-detailed.

8   The fact that such motivations and pretexts depend on aesthetic, erotic, hygienic, or even medical considerations has no influence on the result, which is always in the direction of transforming the appearance of the body. Such a transformation is wished for, whether or not it is effective.

9   The body is a supple, malleable, and transformable prime material, a kind of modelling clay, easily molded by social will and wish. Human skin is an ideal subject for inscription, a surface for all sorts of marks which make it possible to differentiate the human from the animal. The physical body offers itself willingly for tattooing or scarring so that, visibly and recognizably, it becomes a social entity.

10   The absolutely naked body is considered as brutish, reduced to the level of nature where no distinction is made between man and beast. The decorated body, on the other hand, dressed (if even only in a belt), tattooed, or mutilated, publicly exhibits humanity and membership in an established group. As Theophile Gautier said, "The ideal disturbs even the roughest nature, and the taste for ornamentation distinguishes the intelligent being from the beast more exactly than anything else. Indeed, dogs have never dreamed of putting on earrings."

11   So, it is by their categorical refusal of nakedness that human beings are distinguished from nature. The "mark makes unremarkable"—it creates an interval between what is biologically and brutally given in the animal realm and what is won in the cultural realm. The body is tamed continuously; social custom demands, at any price—including pain, constraint, or discomfort—that wildness be abandoned. Each civilization chooses—through a network of elective relationships which are difficult to determine—which areas of the body deserve transformation. These areas are as difficult to define and as shifting as those of eroticism or modesty. An individual alone eludes bodily modifications; they are the expression of a homogeneous collectivity which, at a chosen moment, comes to a tacit agreement to attack one or another part of the anatomy.

12   Whatever the choices, options, or differences may be, that which remains constant is the transformation of appearance. In spite of our contemporary western belief that the body is perfect as it is, we are constantly changing it: clothing it in musculature, suntan, or makeup; dying its head hair or pulling out its bodily hair. The seemingly most innocent gestures for taking care of the body very often hide a persistent and disguised tendency to make it adhere to the strictest of norms, reclothing it in a veil of civilization. The total nudity offered at birth does not exist in any region of the world. Man puts his stamp on man. The body is not a product of nature, but of culture.

—Borel, "The Decorated Body," *Parabola*, Vol. 19, No. 3 (Fall 1994), p. 74

Writing About the Reading
CHECKING YOUR VOCABULARY

1. For each of the words listed below, use context; prefixes, roots, and suffixes (see Chapter 3); and/or a dictionary to write a brief definition or synonym of the word as it is used in the reading.

   a. diversity (para. 1) _____

   b. subjective (para. 1) _____

   c. prevalent (para. 3) _____

d. swaddled (para. 3) _____

e. aesthetically (para. 4) _____

f. spliced (para. 4) _____

g. marginal (para. 5) _____

h. scarification (para. 6) _____

i. pretexts (para. 8) _____

j. erotic (para. 8) _____

k. inscription (para. 9) _____

l. interval (para. 11) _____

m. tacit (para. 11) _____

2. Highlight new, specialized terms introduced in the reading (see Chapter 3).
3. Draw a word map of one of the words in the reading.

CHECKING YOUR COMPREHENSION

1. What is the author's view of human nakedness?
2. How did the Mangbetus of Africa change the heads of children?
3. What was done to Chinese girls to alter their appearance? Why was this done?
4. Why did the men of the Congo check the stomachs of their brides before marrying them?
5. Describe how the Tiv women of Nigeria treated their legs.

THINKING CRITICALLY

1. What is the author's purpose in writing this article?
2. What can you conclude about human beauty from this reading?
3. In Polynesia, a girl without a tattoo would not be considered for marriage. Why do you think that was?
4. How do young men and women in American culture decorate their bodies today?
5. The author states that humans decorate their bodies to designate their membership in an established group. In what other ways do humans signal group membership?

LEARNING/STUDY STRATEGY

Create a chart that lists the cultures referred to in this reading and describes the type of body decoration each used.

Thinking About the Paired Readings
INTEGRATING IDEAS

1. In what ways do the authors agree on the purposes for body decoration, and in what ways do they differ?

2. How do the two readings differ in content?
3. What do you think would be the best way to learn the information in these readings in light of what you have learned in this chapter?
4. If you were writing a ten-page research paper on the purposes and types of body decoration, what further information would you need?
5. What aspects of both readings apply to people in the United States today?
6. Of the two readings, which do you think was more difficult to read and remember? Why?

GENERATING NEW IDEAS

1. Take ten minutes to brainstorm ideas about body adornment in order to narrow a topic for a two-page paper.
2. Suppose you have a friend or relative who lives in a foreign country and is unfamiliar with western forms of body decoration. Your friend is planning to visit the United States soon. Write a letter to that person describing what unusual decorations he or she might expect to see.

ADDITIONAL PRACTICE

MULTIMEDIA ACTIVITIES

1. PBS Timelines:

http://www.pbs.org/deepspace/timeline/index.html
http://www.pbs.org/kera/usmexicanwar/timeline/index.html
http://www.pbs.org/wgbh/amex/telephone/timeline/
http://www.pbs.org/wnet/pharaohs/timeline1.html
http://www.pbs.org/wgbh/amex/eleanor/timeline/index.html

Many of the programs on PBS have accompanying Web sites with time lines. Visit the Internet pages above and evaluate their design and content. How well do they clarify the sequence of events and their importance? Write down your thoughts about the concept of time. Explain how you organize the passage of time in your own mind.

2. Visual Organizers

http://www.bucks.edu/~specpop/visual-org.htm

Explanations and examples of various ways to represent information graphically are presented here at this site created by Bucks County Community College. Create several of your own visual organizers centered around your life. Try topics such as your schedule, family history, future plans, friends, or ideas for a novel/movie/art project.

MYREADINGLAB

If your instructor has asked you to use Reading Road Trip, be sure to visit the "Spring Break! Florida" and "Seattle" modules for multimedia tutorials; exercises; and tests on outlining, summarizing, notetaking, and highlighting.

10 Reading Graphics and Visuals

LEARNING OBJECTIVES

✦To develop reading strategies for graphics

✦To learn to read different types of graphics

Think About It!

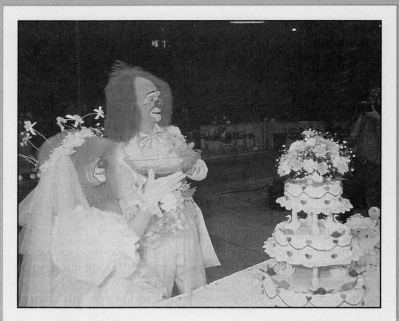

Study the photo above. Why was it included in a sociology text-book chapter that discusses deviance and conformity? What point does the photograph make? In what ways are the bride and groom conforming to society's norms? In what ways are they deviating from them?

■ How to Read Graphics

Many college textbooks include graphics and visuals such as maps, diagrams, charts, tables, graphs, photographs, and cartoons. Some students find graphics intimidating, mainly because they have not learned how to approach them. All graphic devices serve the same primary functions. Graphics summarize and condense written information, and make it easier to comprehend and retain. In this respect, graphics actually save you time by eliminating lengthy written explanations. To illustrate, first study the table in Figure 10-1 below. Then read the paragraph that begins to present the factual information contained in the table.

FIGURE 10-1 Sample Graphic

Co-occurrence of Three Serious Problem Behaviors Among Adolescent Girls and Boys

NUMBER OF SERIOUS PROBLEM BEHAVIORS	FEMALES	MALES
None	57.4%	21.9%
One		
Sex	15.5	26.6
Substance use	7.9	2.8
Total	23.4	29.4
Two		
Sex/substance use	14.0	27.0
Substance use/assault	2.6	2.5
Total	16.6	29.5
Three		
Sex/substance use/assault	2.6	19.1

Paragraph:

57.4 percent of females exhibited no serious problem behaviors, 23.4 percent engaged in one (sex or substance use), 16.6 percent reported serious engagement in two problem behaviors, and 2.6 percent had been involved in all three. The males in the sample were more generally involved than females in problem behaviors, but 21.9 percent had not engaged seriously in any of the three problem behaviors. About 29 percent of the males had engaged seriously in one problem behavior (primarily sex), nearly 30 percent had engaged in two (primarily sex combined with substance use), and 19.1 percent had engaged in all three.

SOURCE: Conger and Galambos, *Adolescence and Youth*, pp. 296–97

Which would you rather read, the table or the paragraph? The paragraph is dull, routine reading, whereas the table presents the same information concisely and in a more interesting format. The table also makes it easier to understand the relationship between individual bits of information. A glance at the table tells you that 19.1 percent of adolescent boys engaged in three problem behaviors, compared to 2.6 percent of girls. (Locating this information would be much more difficult if it were presented only in paragraph form.) By providing a visual picture of the information, graphics also make relationships, trends, and patterns easier to grasp.

It is tempting to skip over the graphic and visual aids included in textbooks. Stopping to study a graph, photograph, or chart takes time and may seem to interrupt your flow of reading. Because graphics do not present information in words (there are no statements to underline or remember), you may think they are unimportant. Actually, graphics often are more important than the paragraphs that surround them. They are included to call your attention to, emphasize, and concisely describe a relationship.

Here are some general suggestions that will help you get the most out of graphic elements in the material you read.

1. **Read the title or caption.** The title tells you what situation or relationship is being described.
2. **Determine how the graphic is organized.** If you are working with a table, note the column headings. For a graph, note what is marked on the vertical and horizontal axes.
3. **Note any symbols and abbreviations used.**
4. **Determine the scale or unit of measurement.** Note how the variables are measured. For example, does a graph show expenditures in dollars, thousands of dollars, or millions of dollars?
5. **Identify the trend(s), pattern(s), or relationship(s) the graphic is intended to show.** The following sections will discuss this step in greater detail.
6. **Read any footnotes.** Footnotes, printed at the bottom of a graph or chart, indicate how the data were collected, explain what certain numbers or headings mean, or describe the statistical procedures used.
7. **Check the source.** The source of data is usually cited at the bottom of the graph or chart. Unless the information was collected by the author, you are likely to find listed a research journal or publication from which the data were taken. Identifying the source is helpful in assessing the reliability of the data.

■ Types of Graphics

All graphics describe some type of relationship. Not coincidentally, these relationships correspond to the thought patterns we examined in Chapter 7.

Tables: Comparison and Classification of Information

Sociologists, psychologists, scientists, economists, and business analysts frequently use tables to organize and present statistical evidence. A table is an organized display of factual information, usually numbers or statistics. Its purpose is to classify information so that comparisons can be made between or among data.

Take a few minutes now to study Figure 10-2, using the suggestions listed above. Then use the following steps to analyze the table.

1. **Determine how the data are classified, or divided.** This table classifies sources of sound according to level of intensity. Note that the relative sound intensity and the effects of prolonged exposure are also included.

2. **Make comparisons and look for trends.** This step involves surveying the rows and columns, noting how each entry compares with the others. Be sure to compare columns and rows, noting both similarities and differences and focusing on trends. In Figure 10-2, you might compare the relative intensities of several common sounds to which you are exposed.

3. **Draw conclusions.** Decide what the data show. You can conclude from Figure 10-2 that prolonged exposure to some sounds is dangerous. Often you will find clues, and sometimes direct statements, in the paragraphs that correspond to the table. The portion of the text that refers you to the table often makes a general statement about what the table is intended to highlight.

FIGURE 10-2   Interpreting a Table

The Intensity of Some Common Sounds

SOUND SOURCE EXPOSURE	DECIBELS (dbA)	RELATIVE SOUND INTENSITY	EFFECT ON HEARING (PROLONGED EXPOSURE)
	0*	1	Audibility threshold
Breathing	10	10	
Whisper, rustling leaves	20	100	Very quiet
Quiet rural nighttime	30	1000	
Library, soft music	40	10,000	
Normal conversation	50	100,000	Quiet
Average office	60	1,000,000	
Vacuum cleaner	70	10,000,000	Annoying
Garbage disposal	80	100,000,000	Possible hearing damage
City traffic, diesel truck	90	1,000,000,000	Hearing damage (8 hours or more exposure)
Garbage truck, chain saw	100	10,000,000,000	Serious hearing damage (8 hours or more exposure)
Live rock band; portable stereo held close to ear	110	100,000,000,000	
Siren (close range); jet takeoff (200 yds)	120	1,000,000,000,000	Hearing pain threshold
Crack of gunfire	130	10,000,000,000,000	
Aircraft carrier deck	140	100,000,000,000,000	Eardrum ruptures
Jet takeoff (close range)	150	1,000,000,000,000,000	

*The threshold of hearing is 0 decibels because the scale is logarithmic, and the logarithm of 1 is 0.

SOURCE: Byer and Shainberg, *Living Well: Health in Your Hands,* p. 788

Once you have drawn your conclusions, stop, think, and react. For example, you might consider what the data in Figure 10-2 suggest about your daily activities.

| EXERCISE 10-1 |

Study the table shown in Figure 10-3, and answer the following questions.

1. What is the subject of the table? _____

2. Describe how the data are organized. _____

3. Overall, which age group spends the most total time getting news? Which age group spends the least? _____

4. Which age group has the largest percent of people who did not get any news yesterday? _____

5. Which news source is used most often by all groups combined? _____

6. What overall trends does this table suggest? _____

Graphs: Relationships Among Variables

Graphs depict the relationship between two or more variables such as price and demand or expenditures over time. Put simply, they are pictures of relationships between two or more sets of information. As you read and study in various academic disciplines, you will encounter many variations of a few basic types of graphs.

FIGURE 10–3   Interpreting a Table

SPENDING TIME WITH THE NEWS

The PEW Research Center asked a representative sample of the population how much time they spent during an average day getting the news from TV, newspapers, and radio. The table below shows the results, broken down by age.

	Spending Time with the News (Avg. Minutes Yesterday*)				
	Total	Paper	TV	Radio	No News Yesterday
All	66	18	31	17	14%
18–24	48	9	26	13	25%
25–29	50	11	23	16	17%
30–34	54	11	24	19	15%
35–49	63	16	28	19	14%
50–64	71	21	34	16	14%
65+	96	33	44	19	6%

*All averages are estimated.
SOURCE: Reprinted by permission of the PEW Research Center for the People & Press from their Web site: http://www.people-press.org/medsec3.htm.

SOURCE: Edwards, Wattenburg, and Lineberry, *Government in America*, p. 226

Linear Graphs   In linear graphs, information is plotted along a vertical and a horizontal axis, with one or more variables plotted on each. The resulting graph makes it easy to see the relationship between the variables. A sample linear graph is shown in Figure 10-4. The line graph compares population statistics and change for four racial/ethnic groups in the United States. What trends does the graph reveal?

In addition to the comparison, the graph also allows you to see changes in population within each group throughout the years. The graph enables you to determine the general trend or pattern among the variables. Generally, this graph shows a steady decrease in the White, non-Hispanic population and a steady increase in the Hispanic population

A graph can show one of three general relationships: positive, inverse, or independent. Each of these is shown in Figure 10-5 on the next page.

1. **Positive relationships.** When both variables increase or decrease simultaneously, the relationship is positive and is shown on a graph by an upwardly sloping line. In Figure 10-5, Graph A shows the relation between

FIGURE 10–4   A Sample Linear Graph

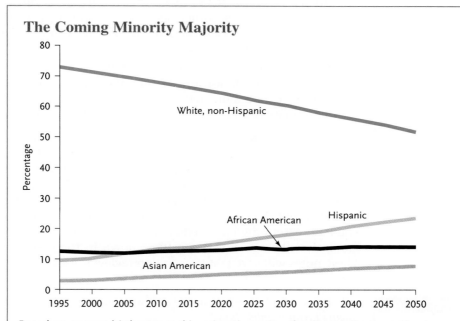

The Coming Minority Majority

Based on current birthrates and immigration rates, the Census Bureau estimates that the demographics of the country should change as shown in the accompanying graph. Extend the lines a bit beyond the year 2050, and it is clear that the minority groups will soon be in the majority nationwide. Of course, should the rates of birth and immigration change, so will these estimates. But already there are 65 congressional districts with a minority majority, about 85 percent of which are represented in the House by an African American, a Hispanic, or an Asian American.

Source: Edwards et al., *Government in America,* Twelfth Edition

FIGURE 10-5   Relationships Shown by Graphs

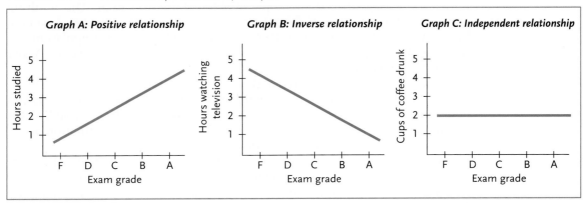

how long a student studied and his or her exam grade. As the study time increases, so does the exam grade.

2. **Inverse relationships.** Inverse relationships occur when one variable increases while the other decreases, as shown in Graph B. Here, as the exam grade increases, the amount of time spent watching TV decreases. The inverse relationship is shown by the line or curve that slopes downward and to the right of the point of origin.

3. **Independent relationships.** When the variables have no effect on or relationship to one another, the graph looks like Graph C. There, you can see that the amount of coffee drunk while studying has no effect on exam grades.

From these three relationships, you can see that linear graphs may suggest a cause-and-effect relationship between the variables. However, do not assume that simply because two variables both change, one is acting on the other. Two events may occur at the same time but have no relation to one another. For example, your grades may improve during a semester in which you modify your diet, but the change in diet did not cause your grades to improve. Once you have determined the trend and the nature of the relationship that a linear graph describes, be sure to jot these down in the margin next to the graph. These notes will save you time as you review the chapter.

| EXERCISE 10-2 | *What type of relationship (positive, inverse, or independent) would each of the following linear graphs show?* |

1. In a graph that plots the way effective use of study time is related to semester grade point average, what type of relationship would you expect?

_____

_____

2. In a graph that plots the way time spent reading is related to time spent playing tennis, what relationship would you predict?

_____

_____

3. What type of relationship would be shown by a graph that plots the way time checking a dictionary for unknown words is related to reading speed?

_____

_____

EXERCISE 10-3   *Study the graph shown in Figure 10-6, and answer the following questions.*

FIGURE 10-6   Interpreting a Linear Graph

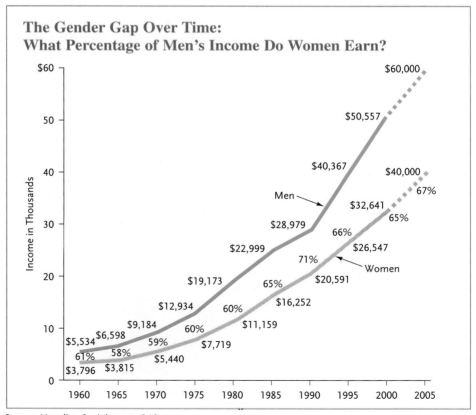

The Gender Gap Over Time:
What Percentage of Men's Income Do Women Earn?

Source: Henslin, *Sociology,* p. 240

1. What is the purpose of this graph?

   _____

2. What type of relationship (positive, inverse, or independent) does this graph show?

   _____

3. What trend does this graph reveal about the gender income gap?

   _____

4. In what year was the gap the smallest?

   _____

5. Have men's income and women's income risen at nearly the same or a quite different rate?

   _____

6. What overall trend does this graph reveal about the gender income gap?

   _____

Circle Graphs   A circle graph, also called a pie chart, is used to show the relationships of parts to the whole or to show how given parts of a unit have been divided or classified. Figure 10-7 is a circle graph that shows the sources of payment of medical costs. In this graph, payments are divided into six categories. Notice that private insurance covers only about one-third of health care costs and that government sources (Medicare and Medicaid combined with other government sources) pay for nearly half.

FIGURE 10-7   Sample Circle Graph

The Nation's Health Care Dollar: Who Pays?

Source: Edwards et al., *Government in America*, p. 593

Circle graphs often are used to emphasize proportions or to show the relative size or importance of various parts. You can see from this graph that private insurance is the greatest source of medical payments, and that other private sources make up the smallest identified source.

EXERCISE 10-4   *Study the circle graphs shown in Figure 10-8, and answer the following questions.*

1. What are these circle graphs intended to show?

   _____

2. Which country uses the most freshwater for agriculture?

   _____

3. Which country reports no agricultural use?

   _____

FIGURE 10-8   Comparing Circle Graphs

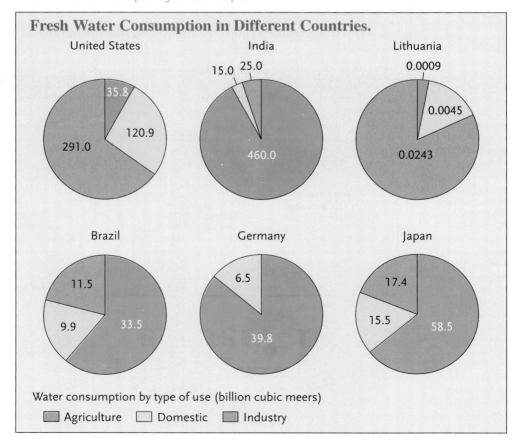

Fresh Water Consumption in Different Countries.

United States — 35.8, 120.9, 291.0

India — 15.0, 25.0, 460.0

Lithuania — 0.0009, 0.0045, 0.0243

Brazil — 11.5, 9.9, 33.5

Germany — 6.5, 39.8

Japan — 17.4, 15.5, 58.5

Water consumption by type of use (billion cubic meers)

☐ Agriculture   ☐ Domestic   ☐ Industry

Source: Brennan & Wittgott, *Environment: The Science Behind the Stories,* p. 428

4. Which two countries use the most freshwater for industry? Which one uses the least?

_____

5. What country's usage is most dramatically different from the other five?

_____

Bar Graphs   A bar graph is often used to make comparisons between quantities or amounts. The horizontal scale often measures time and the vertical scale quantity. A sample bar graph is shown in Figure 10-9. It depicts trends in aging from 1950 to 2050.

EXERCISE 10-5

Study the bar graph shown in Figure 10-9, and answer the questions below.

1. What is the purpose of the graph? _____

_____

2. In what year will the population over age 65 be the greatest in size?

_____

3. Which age group is projected to increase the most in size from 1990 to 2050? _____

4. What overall trends does this bar graph suggest? _____

_____

FIGURE 10-9   Sample Bar Graph

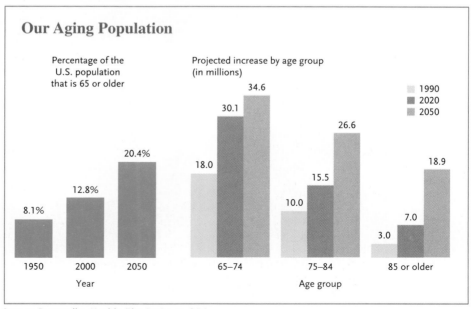

Source: Donatelle, *Health: The Basics*, p. 354

Diagrams: Explanations of Processes

Diagrams are often included in technical and scientific as well as business and economic texts to explain processes. Diagrams are intended to help you see relationships between parts and understand sequences. Figure 10-10, which is taken from a geography textbook, shows how the food chain works. It shows how plant-eating animals, called herbivores, begin the food chain by eating plants, how carnivores (meat-eating animals) consume herbivores, and how animal bodily wastes return nutrients to the soil. These nutrients may be used for new plant growth, thus creating a cyclical relationship.

Reading diagrams differs from reading other types of graphics in that diagrams often correspond to fairly large segments of text. This means you have to switch back and forth frequently between the text and the diagram to determine what part of the process each paragraph is discussing.

Because diagrams of processes and the corresponding text are often difficult, complicated, or highly technical, plan to read these sections more than once. Use the first reading to grasp the overall process. In subsequent readings, focus on the details of the process, examining each step and understanding how the process unfolds.

FIGURE 10–10   Sample Diagram

SOURCE: McKnight, *Physical Geography: A Landscape Appreciation*, p. 148

One of the best ways to study a diagram is to redraw it without referring to the original, including as much detail as possible. Redrawing is a true test of whether you understand the process you have diagrammed. Alternatively, you can test your understanding and recall of the process illustrated in a diagram by explaining it step by step in writing, using your own words.

EXERCISE 10-6

Study the diagram in Figure 10-11 on the next page, which shows how the AIDS virus spreads in the bloodstream. Then answer the following questions.

1. What type of cell does the AIDS virus attack?

   _____

2. Why doesn't the host cell reject the AIDS virus?

   _____

   _____

   _____

3. Explain how the AIDS virus spreads beyond the first cell it attacks.

   _____

   _____

   _____

Maps: Physical Relationships

Maps describe relationships and provide information about location and direction. They are commonly found in geography and history texts, and they also appear in ecology, biology, and anthropology texts. Most of us think of maps as describing distances and locations, but maps are also used to describe placement of geographical and ecological features such as areas of pollution, areas of population density, or political data (voting districts).

When reading maps, use the following steps:

1. **Read the caption.** This identifies the subject of the map.
2. **Use the legend or key to identify the symbols or codes used.**
3. **Note distance scales.**
4. **Study the map, looking for trends or key points.** Often, the text that accompanies the map states the key points that the map illustrates.
5. **Try to visualize, or create a mental picture of, the map.**
6. **As a learning and study aid, write, in your own words, a statement of what the map shows.**

Now refer to the map shown in Figure 10-12 on page 306, which is taken from a biology textbook.

FIGURE 10–11   Sample Diagram

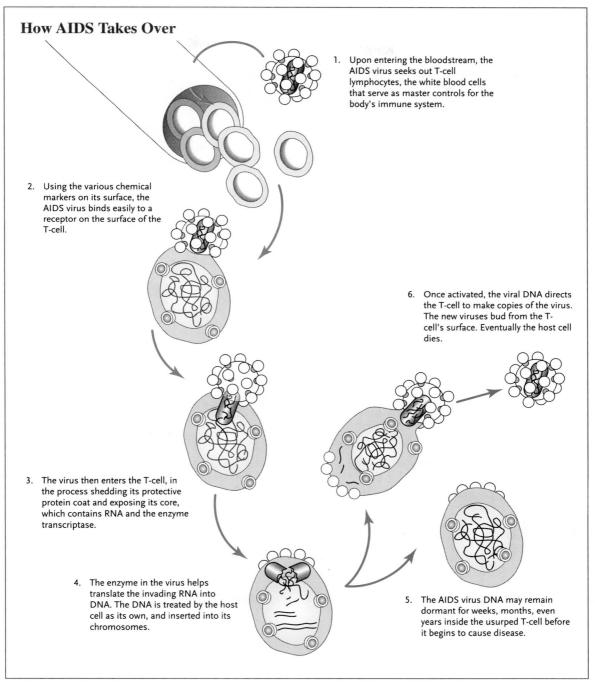

How AIDS Takes Over

1. Upon entering the bloodstream, the AIDS virus seeks out T-cell lymphocytes, the white blood cells that serve as master controls for the body's immune system.

2. Using the various chemical markers on its surface, the AIDS virus binds easily to a receptor on the surface of the T-cell.

6. Once activated, the viral DNA directs the T-cell to make copies of the virus. The new viruses bud from the T-cell's surface. Eventually the host cell dies.

3. The virus then enters the T-cell, in the process shedding its protective protein coat and exposing its core, which contains RNA and the enzyme transcriptase.

4. The enzyme in the virus helps translate the invading RNA into DNA. The DNA is treated by the host cell as its own, and inserted into its chromosomes.

5. The AIDS virus DNA may remain dormant for weeks, months, even years inside the usurped T-cell before it begins to cause disease.

SOURCE: Wallace, *Biology: The World of Life,* p. 567

305

FIGURE 10–12 Sample Map

Tree Species in North America

Tree species diversity in North America decreases from east to west and from south to north. Along transect A, the change in species diversity is primarily associated with increasing longitude, whereas along transect B, species diversity decreases with increasing latitude. The lines delineate areas, each labeled with the number of species that grow there.

SOURCE: Mix et al., *Biology: The Network of Life,* p. 128

This map shows the number of different species of trees located in North America. The caption notes trends and explains that diversity is affected by changes in longitude and latitude.

EXERCISE 10-7 *Study the map shown in Figure 10-13 (p. 307), and answer the following questions.*

1. What is the purpose of the map? _____

_____

2. What area has the lowest incidence of HIV/AIDS infection? _____

_____

3. In what area is the largest number of people infected with HIV/AIDS?

_____

4. How does the number of HIV/AIDS-infected people in North America compare with that of the other areas represented in this map?

_____

FIGURE 10-13   Sample Map

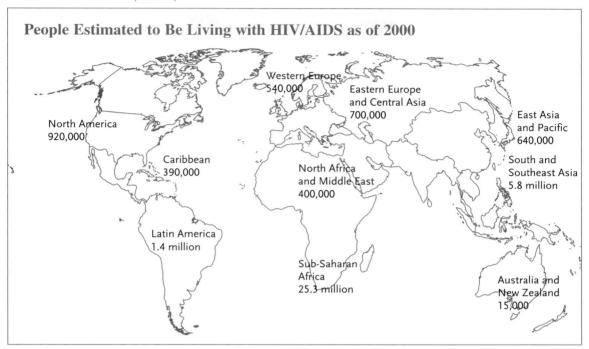

People Estimated to Be Living with HIV/AIDS as of 2000

Western Europe
540,000

Eastern Europe
and Central Asia
700,000

East Asia
and Pacific
640,000

North America
920,000

Caribbean
390,000

North Africa
and Middle East
400,000

South and
Southeast Asia
5.8 million

Latin America
1.4 million

Sub-Saharan
Africa
25.3 million

Australia and
New Zealand
15,000

Source: Powers and Dodd, *Total Fitness and Wellness,* p. 320

EXERCISE 10-8   *Use the following statistics to construct a graphic that organizes some or all of this information on world population growth. Exchange your creation with a classmate, and offer each other ideas for improvement.*

1. In 1970, the world population was 3,632 million.
2. In 1990, the world population was 5,320 million.
3. In 2000, the world population was 6,080 million.
4. In 1970, the population of Africa was 344 million.
5. In 1990, the population of Africa was 660 million.
6. In 2000, the population of Africa was 805 million.
7. In 1970, the population of Asia was 2,045 million.
8. In 1990, the population of Asia was 3,111 million.
9. In 2000, the population of Asia was 3,688 million.
10. In 1970, the population of Europe was 462 million.
11. In 1990, the population of Europe was 499 million.
12. In 2000, the population of Europe was 729 million.

EXERCISE 10-9   *Select two different graphic devices used in a textbook chapter you have read recently, and answer the following questions about each.*

1. What is the subject of the graphic?
2. What is its purpose?

3. If it presents data, how is it organized? If it is a diagram or photo, how does it achieve its purpose?
4. What is its source, and how recent is it?

■ Understanding Visuals

Many textbooks contain numerous cartoons and photographs, always related in some way to chapter content. Be sure to study both cartoons and photographs closely to determine why they were included.

Cartoons

Cartoons are a visual feature included in textbooks to make a point quickly or simply to lighten the text by adding a touch of humor about the topic at hand. Cartoons usually appear without a title or legend, and there is usually no reference within the text to the cartoon.

Cartoons can make abstract ideas and concepts concrete and real. Pay close attention to cartoons, especially if you are a visually oriented learner. They may help you recall ideas easily by serving as a recall clue that triggers your memory of related material. The cartoon in Figure 10-14 appears in the same sociology textbook chapter and on the same page as the photograph shown in the chapter opener, "Think About It!" on page 292. Notice that it humorously illustrates the concept of conformity and deviance.

Photographs: A Visual Impression

Photographs are often considered an art form, but they serve some of the same purposes as other graphics: they are used in textbooks in place of verbal descriptions to present information. Photographs are also used to spark your interest and, often, to draw out an emotional response or impression. Study the photograph shown in Figure 10-15 on the next page.

FIGURE 10–14

Source: Tribune Media Services, Inc. All Rights Reserved. Reprinted with permission.

FIGURE 10-15   Sample Photograph

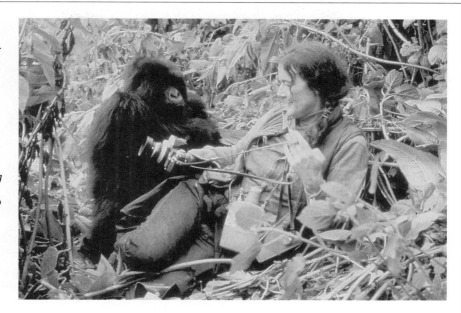

Much of what we know in science is due to simple observation. Dian Fossey told us a great deal about mountain gorillas by being able to move among them. The arrogant, tough, and dedicated Fossey was instrumental in protecting these shy beasts from poachers (who sell gorilla hands to wealthy Europeans to be used for ashtrays) until she was killed by an assailant in her mountain cabin.

Source: Wallace, *Biology: The World of Life,* p. 38 (text); Peter Weit, Corbis/Sygma (photo)

This photograph appears on a page of a biology textbook chapter titled "Resources, Energy and Human Life." The photograph of Dian Fossey, a scientist who studied gorilla behavior, reveals the trusting relationship she established with gorillas. Use the following steps to understand photographs:

1. **Read the caption to discover the subject and context of the photograph.**
2. **If the photo is referred to in the text, read the text before studying the photograph.** What details are emphasized? What conclusions are drawn?
3. **Study the photograph.** What is your first overall impression? What details did you notice first? Answering these questions will lead you to discover the purpose of the photograph.

EXERCISE 10-10   *Study the photograph shown in Figure 10-16 (p. 310). Then answer the questions below.*

1. What emotional reaction does this photograph elicit?

   _____

   _____

2. Why would it be included in a sociology textbook chapter titled "Third World Problems"?

   _____

   _____

FIGURE 10–16 Interpreting a Photograph

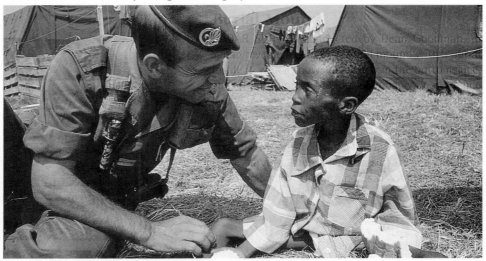

Source: Charles Caratini, Corbis/Sygma

Self–Test Summary

1. What are the functions of graphics?	Graphics summarize and condense information and emphasize or clarify relationships.
2. What is it important to do when reading graphics?	It is important to read the caption; determine the organization of the graphic; note symbols, abbreviations, and/or scales; identify trends or patterns; study footnotes; and check the source of information.
3. Name three different types of graphs and explain how they work.	Linear graphs plot information along a vertical and horizontal axis, with one or more variables on each; circle graphs, or pie charts, show the relationships of parts to the whole; and bar graphs make comparisons between quantities or amounts.
4. Describe the following types of graphics in terms of how they supply information: 　Tables 　Graphs 　Diagrams	• Tables are used to compare and classify data or information. • Graphs depict relationships among variables. • Diagrams present visual representations of processes or sequences.
5. Describe the function of each of the following graphics: 　Cartoons 　Maps 　Photographs	• Cartoons make abstract ideas concrete and real, or may be used to add a touch of humor. • Maps are used to describe physical relationships. • Photographs provide visual impressions and often provoke an emotional response.

BIOLOGY

Reading
1

Reading
2

PAIRED READINGS

Reading 1

Biodiversity Loss
and Species Extinction

Scott Brennan and Jay Withgott

Prereading Questions

1. What is biodiversity?
2. What species are considered endangered or extinct?

1   Biodiversity at all levels is being lost to human impact, most irretrievably in the extinction of species, which, once vanished, can never return. Extinction occurs when the last member of a species dies and the species ceases to exist. In contrast, the extinction of a particular population from a given area, but not the entire species globally, is called **extirpation.** The tiger has been extirpated from most of its historic range, but it is not yet extinct. Although a species that is extirpated from one place may still exist in others, extirpation is an erosive process that can, over time, lead to extinction.

Extinction Is "Natural"

2   Extirpation and extinction are natural processes. If organisms did not naturally go extinct, we would be up to our ears in dinosaurs, trilobites, ammonites, and the millions of other types of organisms that vanished from Earth long before humans appeared. Paleontologists estimate that roughly 99% of all species that have ever lived are already extinct; that is, the wealth of species on our planet today comprises only about 1% of all the species that ever lived. Most extinctions preceding the appearance of humans have occurred one by one, at a rate that paleontologists refer to as the **background rate of extinction.** For example, the fossil record indicates that for both birds and mammals, one species in the world typically became extinct every 500–1,000 years.

The Earth Has Experienced Five
Previous Mass Extinction Episodes

3   Extinction rated have risen far above this background rate during several mass extinction events of Earth's history. In the last 440 million years, there have been five major episodes of mass extinction (Figure A), each of which has taken more than one-fifth of life's families and at least half its species (Table B). The most severe episode occurred at the end of the Permian period, approximately 248 million years ago, when close to 54% of all families, 90% of all species, and 95% of marine species became extinct. The best-known episode occurred at the end of the Cretaceous period, 65 million years ago, when an apparent asteroid impact brought an end to the dinosaurs and many other groups. In addition, there is evidence for further mass extinctions in the Cambrian period and earlier, more than half a billion years ago.

4   If current trends continue, the modern era, also known as the Quaternary period, may see the extinction of more than half of all species. Although similar in scale to previous

FIGURE A

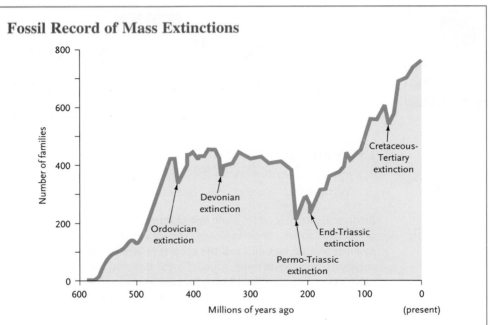

Figure A   The fossil record shows evidence of five episodes of mass extinction during the past half-billion years of Earth history. At the end of the Ordovician, the end of the Devonian, the end of the Permian, the end of the Triassic, and the end of the Cretaceous, 50%–95% of the world's species appear to have gone extinct. Each time, biodiversity has later rebounded to equal or higher levels, but the rebound has taken millions of years in each case. Data from David M. Raup and J. John Sepkoski, Mass Extinctions in the Marine Fossil Record, *Science,* March 19, 1982.

mass extinctions, today's ongoing mass extinction is different in two primary respects. First, humans are causing it. Second, humans will suffer as a result of it.

Humans Set the Sixth Mass Extinction in Motion Years Ago

5   In our written history, we have recorded many instances of human-induced species extinction over the past few hundred years. Sailors documented the extinction of the dodo on the Indian Ocean island of Mauritius in the 17th century, for example, and we still have a few of the dodo's body parts in museums. Among North American birds in the past two centuries, we have lost the passenger pigeon, Carolina parakeet, great auk, Labrador duck, and probably the Bachman's warbler and ivory-billed woodpecker. Several more species, including the whooping crane, California condor, and Kirtland's warbler, teeter on the brink of extinction.

6   However, species extinctions caused by humans likely precede written history; people may have been hunting species to extinction for thousands of years. Scientists have inferred this from archaeological evidence in areas of the world that humans have colonized relatively recently. In case after case, a wave of extinctions has seemingly followed close on the heels of human arrival (Figure C). After Polynesians reached Hawaii, for instance, many birds went extinct, and evidence of an extinction

TABLE B   Mass Extinctions

EVENT	DATE (MYA: MILLIONS OF YEARS AGO)	CAUSE	TYPES OF LIFE MOST AFFECTED	PERCENT OF LIFE DEPLETED
Ordovician	440 mya	unknown	marine organisms; but terrestial record unknown	>20% of families
Devonian	370 mya	unknown	marine organisms; but terrestial record unknown	>20% of families
Permo-Triassic (P-T)	250 mya	possibly volcanism	marine organisms; but terrestial record less known	>50% of families; 80–95% of species
end-Triassic	202 mya	unknown	marine organisms; but terrestial record less known	20% of families; 50% of genera
Cretaceous-Teritary (K-T)	65 mya	asteroid impact	marine and terrestial organisms, including dinosaurs	15% of families; >50% of species
Current	Beginning 0.01 mya	human impact *via* habitat destruction, land and resource use, hunting, and promoting invasive species	large animals, specialized organisms, island organisms, organisms hunted or harvested by humans	ongoing

wave also exists from larger island nations, such as New Zealand and Madagascar. The pattern also holds for at least two continents; large vertebrates died off in Australia after Aborigines arrived roughly 50,000 years ago, and North America lost 35 genera of large mammals after humans arrived in the continent at least 10,000–13,000 years ago. Although some scientists hold that climate variation instead of hunting may be responsible for the North American extinctions, the fact that human arrival co-occurs with extinction waves independently in several regions at different times in history is certainly strongly suggestive.

Current Extinction Rates Are Much Higher Than Normal

7   Humans have raised the rate of extinction above the background rate for centuries now. However, today species loss is proceeding at a still more accelerated pace as our population growth and resource consumption put ever-increasing strain on habitats and wildlife.

8   In late 1995, 1,500 of the world's leading scientists reported to the United Nations that the current global extinction rate was more than 1,000 times greater than it would have been without human destruction of habitat. The scientists went on to report in their Global Biodiversity Assessment that more than 30,000 plant and animal species face extinction and that in the preceding 400 years, 484 animals and 654 plant species were known to have become extinct. The scientists also reported that mammals—like the tiger—were becoming extinct 40 times faster than ever before. Independent estimates by UNEP in 2002 reported that extinction is occurring 50–100 times faster than the back-

FIGURE C

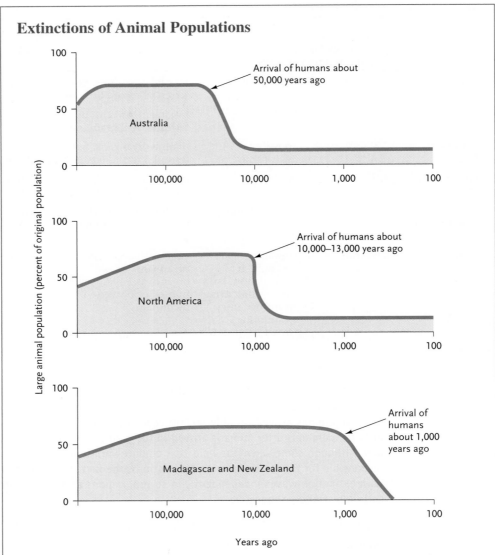

Extinctions of Animal Populations

Figure C Shortly after humans arrived in Australia, North America, Madagascar, and New Zealand a large number of species of large mammals and flightless birds became extinct. It is thought that this did not occur in Africa because humans and other animals evolved together there for many millions of years. Data from E. O. Wilson, *The Diversity of Life,* Belknap Press, 1999.

ground rate and that 45% of Earth's forests, 50% of its mangrove ecosystems, and 10% of its coral reefs had been destroyed by recent human activity.

9   To keep track of the current status of endangered species, the World Conservation Union (IUCN, the acronym derived from the name in which the organization was founded—

the International Union for Conservation of Nature and Natural Resources (1956)) maintains the Red List, an updated list of species facing unusually high risks of extinction. The 2003 Red List reported that 24% (1,130) of mammal species and 12% (1,194) of bird species are threatened with extinction. Among other major groups (for which assessments are not fully complete), estimates of the percentage of species threatened ranged from 39% to 89%. From 1996 to 2003, the total number of vertebrate animals listed as threatened climbed by 6%, from 3,314 to 3,524. Since 1970, at least 58 fish species, 9 bird species, and 1 mammal species have become extinct, and in the United States alone over the past 500 years, 236 animals and 17 plants are confirmed to have gone extinct. For all of these figures, the *actual* numbers of species extinct and threatened, like the actual number of total species in the world, are doubtless greater than the *known* numbers.

10   Among the 1,130 mammals facing possible extinction on the IUCN's Red List is the tiger, which despite—or perhaps because of—its tremendous size and reputation as a fierce predator, is one of the most endangered large animals on the planet. In 1950 eight tiger subspecies existed. Today three are extinct. The Bali tiger, *Panthera tigris balica*, went extinct in the 1940s; the Caspian tiger, *Panthera tigris virgata*, during the 1970s; and the Javan tiger, *Panthera tigris sondaica*, during the 1980s. In each case, overhunting and habitat alteration were responsible.

The Major Causes of Species Loss Spell "HIPPO"

11   The overharvesting that decimated Siberian tiger populations in the early 20th century is only one form of human activity that has reduced the populations of many species. Overexploitation provides the "O" in HIPPO, an acronym scientists have coined to denote the five primary causes of species decline and extinction: Habitat alteration, Invasive species, Pollution, Population growth, and Overexploitation. The most prevalent and powerful of these five causes is habitat alteration.

Writing About the Reading
CHECKING YOUR VOCABULARY

1. For each of the words listed below, use context; prefixes, roots, and suffixes (see Chapter 3); and/or a dictionary to write a brief definition or synonym of the word as it is used in the reading.

    a. irretrievably (para. 1) _____

    b. paleontologists (para. 2) _____

    c. episodes (para. 3) _____

    d. colonized (para. 6) _____

    e. vertebrates (para. 6) _____

    f. co-occurs (para. 6) _____

    g. consumption (para. 7) _____

    h. ecosystems (para. 8) _____

    i. overexploitation (para. 11) _____

2. Underline new, specialized terms introduced in the reading (see Chapter 3).

3. Draw a word map of one of the words in the reading.

CHECKING YOUR COMPREHENSION

1. What is *extirpation?*
2. Explain what is meant by the "background rate of extinction."
3. Give two reasons why today's period of mass extinctions differs from previous mass extinctions.
4. What is the Red List?
5. What are the five primary causes of species decline and extinction, as denoted by the acronym HIPPO? Which is the most prevalent and powerful of these causes?

THINKING CRITICALLY

1. Using Figure A, list the five mass extinction episodes that have taken place in the last 500 million years and note the approximate number of families in each episode.
2. According to Table B, which period experienced the most severe episode of mass extinction? What may have caused the episode?
3. According to Figure C, when did humans arrive in Madagascar and New Zealand?
4. What pattern of extinction is depicted in Figure C?
5. What kind of graphic would you use to depict the information about endangered species given in paragraphs 9 and 10? Explain why.
6. According to the reading, some scientists believe that climate variation, not hunting, is responsible for the extinctions in North America. What is your opinion, based on what you have learned from this article and on your previous knowledge?
7. Explain the statement, "For all of these figures, the *actual* numbers of species extinct and threatened, like the actual number of total species in the world, are doubtless greater than the *known* numbers" (para. 9).

LEARNING/STUDY STRATEGY

Predict an essay question that might be based on this reading.

Reading 2

Biodiversity and Its Decline
Richard T. Wright

Prereading Questions

1. Why does it matter if species become extinct?
2. What causes species to become extinct?

1   Biodiversity was defined as simply *the variety of life on earth*. The dimensions of biodiversity include the genetic diversity within species, as well as the diversity of ecosystems and habitats. The main focus of biodiversity, however, is the species. Recall that, over time, natural selection leads to speciation—the creation of new species—as well as extinction—the disappearance of species. Over geological time, the net balance of these processes has favored the gradual accumulation of more and more species—in other words, an increase in biodiversity.

2   *How Many Species?*   How much biodiversity of species is there? Estimates range widely, and the fact is, no one knows. Today, the only two certainties are that 1.75 million species have been described and many more than that exist. Most people are completely unaware of the great diversity of species within any given taxonomic category. Groups especially rich in species are the flowering plants (270,000 species) and the insects (950,000 species), but even less diverse groups, such as birds or ferns are rich with species that are unknown to most people (Fig. A). Taxonomists are aware that their work in finding and describing new species is incomplete. Groups that are conspicuous or commercially important, such as birds, mammals, fish, and trees, are much more fully explored and described than, say, insects, very small invertebrates like mites, and soil nematodes, fungi, and bacteria. Trained researchers who can identify major groups of organisms are few, and the task of fully exploring the diversity of life would require a major sustained effort in systematic biology.

3   Estimates of the number of species on Earth today are based on recent work in the tropical rain forests, which hold more living species than all other habitats combined. Costa Rica, less than half the size of New York State, is estimated to contain at least 5% of all living species. The upper boundary of the estimate keeps rising as taxonomists explore the rain forests more and more. Some (enthusiastic?) estimates place the high end at 112 million species. Whatever the number, the planet's biodiversity represents an amazing and diverse storehouse of biological wealth.

The Decline of Biodiversity

4   *North America.*   The biota of the United States is as well known as any. At least 500 species native to the United States are known to have become extinct since the early days of colonization. Over 100 of these are vertebrates. At least 200,000 species of plants, animals, and microbes are estimated to live in the nation, but not much is known about most of them. An inventory of 20,897 wild plant and animal species in the 50 states, carried out in the late

FIGURE A Known and Estimated Species on Earth

TAXONOMIC GROUP	NUMBER OF KNOWN SPECIES	ESTIMATED NUMBERS			ACCURACY
		HIGH	LOW	WORKING	
Viruses	4,000	1,000,000	50,000	400,000	Very poor
Bacteria	4,000	3,000,000	50,000	1,000,000	Very poor
Fungi	72,000	2,700,000	200,000	1,500,000	Moderate
Protozoa	40,000	200,000	60,000	200,000	Very poor
Algae	40,000	1,000,000	150,000	400,000	Very poor
Plants	270,000	500,000	300,000	320,000	Good
Nematodes	25,000	1,000,000	100,000	400,000	Poor
Anthropods:					
Crustaceans	40,000	200,000	75,000	150,000	Moderate
Arachnids	75,000	1,000,000	300,000	750,000	Moderate
Insects	950,000	100,000,000	2,000,000	8,000,000	Moderate
Mollusks	70,000	200,000	100,000	200,000	Moderate
Chordates	45,000	55,000	50,000	50,000	Good
Others	115,000	800,000	200,000	250,000	Moderate
Total	**1,750,000**	**111,655,000**	**3,635,000**	**13,620,000**	**Very poor**

Source: United Nations Environment Programme, "Global Biodiversity Assessment" (Cambridge, U.K.: Cambridge University Press, 1995): 118, Table 3.1–1

1990s by a team of biologists from the Nature Conservancy and the National Heritage Network and more recently amplified by a new conservation network, NatureServe, concluded that one-third are vulnerable, imperiled, or already extinct (Fig. B). Mussels, crayfish, fishes, and amphibians—all species that depend on freshwater habitats—are most at risk. Flowering plants are also of great concern, with one-third of their numbers in trouble.

5   It is fair to say that species *populations* are a more important element of biodiversity than just the species' *existence*. It is the populations that occupy different habitats and ranges and that contribute to biological wealth as they provide goods and services important in ecosystems. Across North America, general population declines of well-studied wild species are also occurring. Commercial landings of many species of fish are down, puzzling reductions in amphibian populations are occurring in North America and other parts of the world, and many North American songbird species, such as the Kentucky warbler, wood thrush, and scarlet tanager, have been declining and have disappeared entirely from some local regions. These birds are Neotropical migrants; that is, they winter in the neotropics of Central and South America and breed in temperate North America. According to a report from the National Audubon Society, more than one-fourth of North American birds are already declining or are in danger of doing so.

FIGURE B   The State of U.S. Species

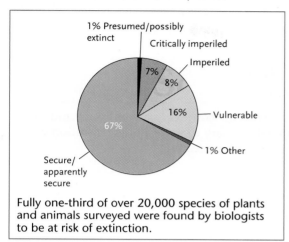

1% Presumed/possibly extinct

Critically imperiled

Imperiled

7%

8%

16%

Vulnerable

67%

1% Other

Secure/apparently secure

Fully one-third of over 20,000 species of plants and animals surveyed were found by biologists to be at risk of extinction.

SOURCE: Data from the Nature Conservancy and NatureServe

FIGURE C   Known Causes of Animal Extinctions Since 1600

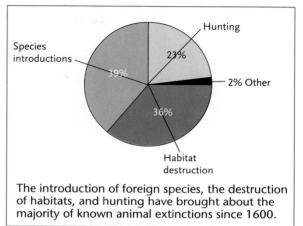

Species introductions

Hunting

23%

39%

2% Other

36%

Habitat destruction

The introduction of foreign species, the destruction of habitats, and hunting have brought about the majority of known animal extinctions since 1600.

SOURCE: Data from World Conservation Monitoring Centre

6   *Global Outlook.*   Worldwide, the loss of biodiversity is even more disturbing. The known causes of animal extinctions, recently assessed by the World Conservation Union, are shown in Figure C. At least 726 animal species and 90 plant species have become extinct since 1500. Most of the known extinctions of the past several hundred years have occurred on oceanic islands, where small landmasses limit the size of populations and human intrusions are most severe. The extinction rate for mammals and birds has been 20 to 25 species per hundred years. This rate can be compared with the "background extinction rate" seen in the fossil record of one bird or mammal species every 400 and 800 years, respectively.

7   The *Global Biodiversity Outlook,* published in 2001 by UNEP to provide information for the Convention on Biological Diversity, estimates that some 24% of mammal (1,130) and 12% of bird species (1,183) are globally threatened. These two groups have been thoroughly studied. The status of all other groups of organisms is much less well known. A recent study compared historic and present-day ranges for 173 larger terrestrial mammal species. The research showed that the species collectively have lost two-thirds of their historic ranges due to human activities. Again, this represents a significant loss of ecosystem capital, as well as a loss of biodiversity.

8   Biodiversity is richest in the tropical forests—a richness that is almost unimaginable. Biologist E. O. Wilson identified 43 species of ants on a single tree in a Peruvian rain forest, a level of diversity equal to the entire ant fauna of the British Isles. Other scientists found 300 species of trees in a single 2.5-acre (1-ha) plot and as many as 10,000 species of insects on a single tree in Peru. Unfortunately, the same tropical forests that hold such high biodiversity are also experiencing the highest rate of deforestation. Because the inventory of species in these ecosystems is so poorly known, it is virtually impossible to assess extinction rates in such forests. Some scientists have tried, though, with estimates ranging from 4,000 to 17,000 species lost per year. Not all scientists agree with these calculations, however, because the estimates are based on many assumptions. Regardless of

the exact rates, numerous species are in decline and some are becoming extinct. No one knows how many, but the loss is real, and it represents a continuing depletion of the biological wealth of our planet.

Writing About the Reading
CHECKING YOUR VOCABULARY

1. For each of the words listed below, use context; prefixes, roots, and suffixes (see Chapter 3); and/or a dictionary to write a brief definition or synonym of the word as it is used in the reading.

   a. accumulation (para. 1) _____

   b. taxonomists (para. 2) _____

   c. conspicuous (para. 2) _____

   d. biota (para. 4) _____

   e. intrusions (para. 6) _____

   f. terrestrial (para. 7) _____

   g. collectively (para. 7) _____

   h. fauna (para. 8) _____

   i. deforestation (para. 8) _____

2. Underline new, specialized terms introduced in the reading (see Chapter 3).

3. Draw a word map of one of the words in the reading.

CHECKING YOUR COMPREHENSION

1. Explain the following terms: biodiversity, speciation, and extinction.
2. Why are estimates of the number of species on Earth today based on research in the tropical rain forests?
3. How many species are estimated to live in the United States?
4. How many species have become extinct since the early days of colonization of the United States?
5. Name the four species that are most at risk. What do these species have in common?
6. Where have most of the known extinctions of the past several hundred years occurred, and why?

THINKING CRITICALLY

1. Based on Figure A, what is the total number of known species?
2. Based on Figure A, what two taxonomic groups provide the most accurate estimates?

3. According to Figure B, what percentage of plant and animal species are secure or apparently secure? What percentage are vulnerable, imperiled, or already extinct?
4. According to Figure C, what are the three major causes of animal extinctions?
5. Why are species *populations* a more important element of biodiversity than the species' *existence?*
6. What do you think is the best way to address the causes of species' extinctions?
7. Explain why certain groups, such as birds and mammals, have been thoroughly studied while the status of all other groups is much less well known.

LEARNING/STUDY STRATEGY

Create a chart or study sheet that includes evidence of biodiversity decline and its effects.

Thinking About the Paired Readings
INTEGRATING IDEAS

1. Compare the purpose of each of the readings. What is each intended to accomplish?
2. The two readings contain a total of six graphics. Which one was the most useful to you? Which one was most interesting? Explain your answers.
3. Imagine that you have been chosen to address a group of college students about the loss of biodiversity in North America. What information from each reading would you use? What points would you choose to emphasize in your speech?

GENERATING NEW IDEAS

1. Consider the following statement: "If current trends continue, the modern era . . . may see the extinction of more than half of all species." Do you think current trends can be altered? How? Brainstorm a list of actions that you can take (such as recycling, conserving water, or volunteering to help restore habitats in your area) to make a positive impact on Earth's species.
2. According to the World Conservation Union, the tiger is one of the most endangered large animals on the planet, with three tiger subspecies going extinct since 1950 because of overhunting and habitat alteration. Why is it important to prevent the extinction of the tiger? Write an essay explaining your answer.
3. The tropical rain forests contain the greatest amount of biodiversity on Earth, but they also experience the highest rate of deforestation. Choose one of the following questions—or think of another issue related to deforestation—and discuss your response:

- Do you think "outsiders" have the right to tell people who live in rain forest countries how to use their forests? Why or why not?
- Can you support progress (better roads, jobs, etc.) in a rain forest country if it causes damage to the rain forest? Why or why not?
- What political, economic, and social factors may be involved in the preservation of rain forests?

LEARNING/STUDY STRATEGY

1. Write a summary stating reasons for the decline of biodiversity.

ADDITIONAL PRACTICE

MULTIMEDIA ACTIVITIES

1. **Charts and Graphs**

   http://www.kcmetro.cc.mo.us/longview/ctac/GRAPHS.HTM

   The Critical Thinking Across the Curriculum Project from Longview Community College invites you to analyze the way statistical information is represented visually. Look through some newspapers and magazines with a friend to locate charts and graphs. Analyze their reliability based on the information presented on this site. What is your perception of the media's use of statistics?

2. **Gallery of Data Visualization**

   http://www.math.yorku.ca/SCS?Gallery

   Visit this Web site and click on "Darts" to discover how graphics can be misleading. Make a list of things to watch for as you read and study graphics.

MYREADINGLAB

If your instructor has asked you to use Reading Road Trip, be sure to visit the "Wall Street, New York City" module for multimedia tutorials, exercises, and tests on graphics and visual aids.

CHAPTER

11 Reading and Evaluating Electronic Sources

LEARNING OBJECTIVES

✦ To locate electronic sources more effectively

✦ To evaluate Internet sources

✦ To read electronic text

✦ To develop new reading and thinking strategies for reading electronic sources

Think About It!

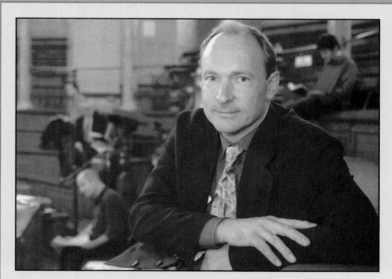

Study the photograph above. Who is this man? His work has probably influenced your life. Take a guess, taking into account the title of this chapter.

His name is Tim Berners-Lee and he is the original Webmaster. He developed the coding that created the World Wide Web, the worldwide network through which computers communicate over the Internet. Now that you know who he is, you can begin to think of how the World Wide Web has influenced your life.

As a college student, you will find the Internet to be a valuable and useful resource. The Internet is a worldwide network of computers through which you can access a wide variety of information and services. Through the Internet, you can access the **World Wide Web** (WWW), a system of Internet servers that allows exchange of information of specially formatted documents. It connects a vast array of resources (documents, graphics, and audio and video files) and allows users to move between and among them easily and rapidly. Many instructors use the Internet and have begun requiring their students to do so. In this chapter, you will learn to read and study electronic sources differently than you do print sources.

Although in most courses your textbook is still your primary source of information, more and more instructors expect their students to use the Internet to supplement their textbook or obtain additional, more current information by visiting Web sites on the Internet. (Textbooks, no matter how up to date they may be, often do not contain information learned within the year of their publication.)

Other instructors expect their students to consult Internet sources in researching a topic for a research paper. Many students, too, are finding valuable information on personal or special interests on the Internet.

For example, Maria Valquez, a student majoring in liberal arts, over the course of a week conducted the following activities using electronic sources:

- Visited an online writing center, http://www.purdue.edu, for help with an English paper.
- Searched for Web sites on the topic of tattooing for a sociology research paper.
- Sent and received e-mail from friends.
- Checked the weather in her hometown in anticipation of a weekend trip.
- Visited a Latino student Web site for ideas for organizing a Latino student group on her campus.
- Ordered a music CD from Amazon.com, an online book and music store.

Electronic sources are becoming increasingly important in many students' academic and personal lives. Therefore, it is important to know how Web sites are structured, how to locate useful sources, how to evaluate the sources you locate, how to understand differences from print sources, and how to navigate through them in an efficient way.

Although this chapter focuses on using electronic sources, you should realize that the Internet is not always the best source of information. Sometimes it is easier and quicker to find a piece of information in a book or other traditional sources.

■ Locating Electronic Sources on the Web

Begin by gaining access to the Internet. In addition to a computer, you will need a modem and a browser, such as Microsoft Explorer or Netscape Navigator. You will also need an Internet service provider (ISP) to connect your computer to the Internet. Your college's computer center, your telephone or cable company, or a commercial service provider such as America Online can connect you. You will need a name you use online, called a username, and a password. If you need help getting started, check with the staff in your college's computer lab.

Identifying Keywords

To search for information on a topic, you need to come up with a group of specific words that describe your topic; these are known as **keywords.** It is often necessary to narrow your topic in order to identify specific keywords. For example, if you searched the topic homeschooling, you would find thousands of sources. However, if you narrowed your topic to homeschooling of primary grade children in California, you would identify far fewer sources.

There are three basic groups of search tools you can use to locate information: subject directories, search engines, and meta-search engines.

Using Subject Directories

Subject directories classify Web resources by categories and subcategories. Some offer reviews or evaluations of sites. Use a subject directory when you want to browse the Web using general topics or when you are conducting a broad search. A subject directory would be helpful if you were looking for sites about parenting issues or wanted to find a list of organizations for animal welfare. Two useful subject directories are INFOMINE http://infomine.ucr.edu and Yahoo! http://www.yahoo.com.

Using a Search Engine

A **search engine** is a computer program that helps you locate information on a topic. A search engine searches for keywords and provides connections to documents that contain the keywords you instruct it to search for. Depending on your topic, some search engines are more useful than others. In addition, each search engine may require a different way of entering the keywords. For example, some may require you to place quotation marks around a phrase ("capital punishment"). Other times, you may need to use plus signs (+) between keywords ("homeschooling" + "primary grades" + "California"). The quotation marks around "primary grades" will create a search for those words used as a phrase, rather than as single terms. Be sure to use the "help" feature when you use a new search engine to discover the best way to enter keywords.

Using Meta-Search Engines

You can use a number of search engines at the same time and combine all the results in a single listing using a **meta-search engine.** Use these types of engines when you are searching for a very specific or obscure topic or one for which you are having trouble finding information. Table 11-1 (p. 326) describes several popular search and meta-search engines.

TABLE 11-1   Useful Search and Meta-Search Engines

NAME	URL	DESCRIPTION
Google	http://www.google.com	An extensive and very popular tool. Has basic and advanced (menu-based) searching. Many extra features such as translation, domain/file type searches, and filtering. Online help provided.
Exalead	http://www.exalead.com/	Features special navigation and design. Offers related terms and categories. Includes a thumbnail of the Web sites in the results list and opens the site in a viewing frame.
Yahoo!	http://www.yahoo.com	Pages are organized in a searchable directory. A few advanced features available. Internet portal and site recommendations.
Infomine	http://infomine.ucr.edu/	Academic and research sites compiled, organized, and annotated by college and university librarians. Basic and advanced searching (tips provided). Users can submit sites for inclusion.
Ixquick	www.ixquick.com	A meta-search engine covering at least nine other search tools. Features music, picture, and news searches. Search results are rated.
Kartoo	http://www.kartoo.com/	A metasearch engine that features a unique results list. The hits are arranged visually in concept-map format.

EXERCISE 11-1

Use one of the search tools listed earlier to locate three sources on one of the following topics. Then use a different tool or different search engine to search the same topic again. Compare your results. Which engine was easier to use? Which produced more sources?

1. The Baseball Hall of Fame
2. Telecommuting
3. Oil drilling in Alaska
4. Parenting issues

■ Evaluating Internet Sources

Although the Internet contains a great deal of valuable information and resources, it also contains rumor, gossip, hoaxes, and misinformation. In other words, not all Internet sources are trustworthy. You must evaluate a source before accepting it. Here are some guidelines to follow when evaluating Internet sources.

Discover the Purpose of Web Sites

There are thousands of Web sites, and they vary widely in purpose. Table 11-2 on page 327 summarizes five primary types of Web sites.

TABLE 11-2   Types of Web Sites

TYPE	PURPOSE AND DESCRIPTION	DOMAIN	SAMPLE SITES
Informational	To present facts, information, and research data. May contain reports, statistical data, results of research studies, and reference materials.	.edu or .gov	http://www.haskins.yale.edu/ http://www.census.gov/
News	To provide current information on local, national, and international news. Often supplements print newspapers, periodicals, and television news programs.	.com or .org	http://news.yahoo.com/ http://www.theheart.org/ index.cfm
Advocacy	To promote a particular cause or point of view. Usually concerned with a controversial issue; often sponsored by nonprofit groups	.com or .org	http://www.goveg.com/ http://www.bradycampaign.org/
Personal	To provide information about an individual and his/her interests and accomplishments. May list publications or include the individual's resume.	Varies. May contain .com, .org, .biz, .edu, .info. May contain a tilde (~).	http://www.jessamyn.com/ http://www.srmi.biz/ resumeJohn.html http://www.maryrussell.info/ http://www.plu.edu/~chasega/
Commercial	To promote goods or services. May provide news and information related to products.	.com, .biz, .info	http://www.nmgroup.biz/ http://www.alhemer.com/ http://www.vintageradio.info/

EXERCISE 11-2   *Determine the purpose of each of the following Web sites using the information in Table 11-2. Some sites may have more than one purpose. Be sure to investigate the whole site carefully and explain your choices.*

1. College Finder: http://www.college-finder.info/
2. Israel—A Country Study: http://lcweb2.loc.gov/frd/cs/iltoc.html
3. Senator Chuck Schumer: http://schumer.senate.gov/
4. Center for Science in the Public Interest: http://www.cspinet.org/
5. Meridian: http://www.ncsu.edu/meridian/
6. Professor Hunt's Dog Page: http://www.cofc.edu/~huntc/dogpage.html

Evaluate the Content of a Web Site

When evaluating the content of a Web site, evaluate its appropriateness, its source, its level of technical detail, its presentation, its completeness, and its links.

Evaluate Appropriateness To be worthwhile a Web site should contain the information you need. It should answer one or more of your search questions. If the site touches upon answers to your questions but does not address them in detail, check the links on the site to see if they lead you to more detailed information. If they do not, search for another, more useful site.

Evaluate the Source Another important step in evaluating a Web site is to determine its source. Ask yourself "Who is the sponsor?" and "Why was this site put up on the Web?" The sponsor of a Web site is the person or organization that paid for it to be created and placed on the Web. The sponsor often suggests the purpose of a Web site. For example, a Web site sponsored by Nike is designed to promote its products, while a site sponsored by a university library is designed to help students use its resources more effectively.

If you are uncertain of who sponsors a Web site, check its URL, its copyright, and the links it offers. The ending of the URL often suggests the type of sponsorship, as shown in Table 11-2. The copyright indicates the owner of the site. Links may also reveal the sponsor. Some links may lead to commercial advertising; others may lead to sites sponsored by nonprofit groups, for example.

Another way to check the ownership of a Web site is to try to locate the site's home page. You can do this by using only the first part of its URL—up to the first slash (/) mark. For example, suppose you found information on Medicare on the Internet at the URL http://www.phaa.net.au/friends_of_medicare/factsheet1.html. This page deals with Medicare, but it begins by talking about Australia. If you wanted to track its source, you could go back in the URL to http://www.phaa.net.au and discover that the sponsoring organization is the Public Health Association of Australia.

Evaluate the Level of Technical Detail A Web site should contain the level of detail that is suited to your purpose. Some sites may provide information that is too sketchy for your search purposes; others assume a level of background knowledge or technical sophistication that you lack. For example, if you are writing a short, introductory-level paper on global warming, information on the University of New Hampshire's NASA Earth Observing System site (http://www.eos-ids.sr.unh.edu/) may be too technical and contain more information than you need, unless you have some previous knowledge in that field.

Evaluate the Presentation Information on a Web site should be presented clearly; it should be well written. If you find a site that is not clear and well written, you should be suspicious of it. If the author did not take time to present ideas clearly and correctly, he or she may not have taken time to collect accurate information, either.

Evaluate Completeness Determine whether the site provides complete information on its topic. Does it address all aspects of the topic that you feel it should? For example, if a Web site on important twentieth-century American poets does not mention Robert Frost, then the site is incomplete. If you discover that a site is incomplete, search for sites that present a more thorough treatment of the topic.

Evaluate the Links   Many reputable sites supply links to related sites. Make sure that the links work and are current. Also check to see if the sites to which you are sent are reliable sources of information. If the links do not work or the sources appear unreliable, you should question the reliability of the site itself. Also determine whether the links provided are comprehensive or present only a representative sample. Either is acceptable, but the site should make clear the nature of the links it is providing.

EXERCISE 11-3   *Evaluate the content of two of the following sites. Explain why you would either trust or distrust each site for reliable content.*

1. http://www.circleofpoets.com
2. http://www.earlham.edu/~peters/knotlink.htm
3. http://www.age-of-the-sage.org/psychology/

Evaluate the Accuracy of a Web Site

When using information on a Web site for an academic paper, it is important to be sure that you have found accurate information. One way to determine the accuracy of a Web site is to compare it with print sources (periodicals and books) on the same topic. If you find a wide discrepancy between the Web site and the printed sources, do not trust the Web site. Another way to determine the accuracy of a site's information is to compare it with other Web sites that address the same topic. If discrepancies exist, further research is needed to determine which site is more accurate.

The site itself will also provide clues about the accuracy of its information. Ask yourself the following questions:

- **Are the author's name and credentials provided?** A well-known writer with established credentials is likely to author only reliable, accurate information. If no author is given, you should question whether the information is accurate.
- **Is contact information for the author included on the site?** Often, sites provide an e-mail address where the author may be contacted.
- **Is the information complete or in summary form?** If it is a summary, use the site to find the original source. Original information has less chance of error and is usually preferred in academic papers.
- **If opinions are offered, are they presented clearly as opinions?** Authors who disguise their opinions as facts are not trustworthy (see Distinguishing Between Fact and Opinion, Chapter 4, p. 105).
- **Does the writer make unsubstantiated assumptions or base his or her ideas on misconceptions?** If so, the information presented may not be accurate.
- **Does the site provide a list of works cited?** As with any form of research, sources used to put information up on a Web site must be documented. If sources are not credited, you should question the accuracy of the Web site.

It may be helpful to determine whether the information is available in print form. If it is, try to obtain the print version. Errors may occur when the article or essay is put up on the Web. Web sites move, change, and delete information, so it may be difficult for a reader of an academic paper to locate the Web site that you used in writing it. Also, page numbers are easier to cite in print sources than in electronic ones.

EXERCISE 11–4   *Evaluate the accuracy of two of the following Web sites.*

1. http://www.idausa.org/facts/pg.html
2. http://www.smokingsection.com/issues1.html#smoke
3. http://www.fairus.org/site/PageServer/pagename=iic_immigrationissuecenters6ce3

Evaluate the Timeliness of a Web Site

Although the Web is well known for providing up-to-the-minute information, not all Web sites are current. Evaluate the timeliness by checking

- The date on which the Web site was mounted (put on the Web).
- The date when the document you are using was added.
- The date when the site was last revised.
- The date when the links were last checked.

This information is usually provided at the end of the site's home page or at the end of the document you are using.

EXERCISE 11–5   *Evaluate the timeliness of two of the following Web sites, using the directions given above.*

1. http://www.rmc.sierraclub.org/ipg/curriss.htm
2. http://www.mhric.org/mozart/index2.html
3. http://www.epa.gov/oam/main/text.old#SPECIAL

EXERCISE 11–6   *Evaluate each of the sites you examined for Exercise 11-2. Assign a rating of 1–5 (1 = low reliability; 5 = high reliability). Be prepared to discuss your ratings.*

EXERCISE 11–7   *Visit a Web site and become familiar with its organization and content. Evaluate it using the suggested criteria. Then write a brief paragraph explaining why the Web site is or is not a reliable source.*

■ Reading Electronic Text

Reading electronic text (also called hypertext) is very different from reading traditional printed text such as textbooks or magazines or newspaper articles. The term electronic text, as used in this chapter, refers to information presented on a Web site. It does not refer to articles and essays that can be downloaded from Searchbank or from an e-journal, for example. Because Web sites are unique, they require a different mind-set and different reading strategies. If electronic text is new or unfamiliar to you, you need to change the way you read and the way you think when approaching Web sites. If you attempt to read Web sites the same way you read traditional text, you may lose focus or perspective, miss important information, or become generally disoriented. Text on Web sites is different in the following ways from traditional print text:

- **Reading Web sites involves paying attention to sound, graphics, and movement, as well as words.** Your senses, then, may pull you in several different directions simultaneously. Banner advertisements, flashing graphics, and colorful drawings or photos may distract you. Some Web sites are available in two formats—graphical and text-only. This is most common for academic sites. If you are distracted by the sound and graphics, check to see if a text-only version of the site is available.
- **Text on Web sites comes in brief, independent screenfuls, sometimes called nodes.** These screenfuls tend to be brief, condensed pieces of information. Unlike traditional text, they are not set within a context, and background information is often not supplied. They do not depend on other pages for meaning either. In traditional print text, paragraphs and pages are dependent—you often must have read and understood a previous one in order to comprehend the one that follows it. Electronic pages are often intended to stand alone.
- **Text on Web sites may not follow the traditional main idea–supporting details organization of traditional paragraphs.** Instead, the screen may appear as a group of topic sentences without detail.
- **Web sites are multidirectional and unique; traditional text progresses in a single direction.** When reading traditional text, a reader usually follows a single direction, working through the text from beginning to end as the author has written it. Web site text is multidirectional; each electronic reader creates his or her own unique text, by following or ignoring different paths. Two readers of the same Web site may read entirely different material, or the same material in a different order. For example, one user of the National Library of Medicine site shown in Figure 11-1 (p. 332) might begin by reading "Current Health News"; another user might start by looking for information using MEDLINEplus; a third might begin by clicking on the NIH link for upcoming exhibits.
- **Web site text requires readers to make decisions.** Because screens have menus and links, electronic readers must always make choices. They can focus on one aspect of the topic and ignore all others, for example, by following a path of links. Readers of print text, however, have far fewer choices to make.
- **Web sites allow readers the flexibility to choose the order in which to receive the information.** Partly due to learning style, people prefer to acquire information in different sequences. Some may prefer to begin with details and then come to understand underlying rules or principles. Others may prefer to begin in the opposite way. Electronic sources allow readers to approach the text in any manner compatible with their learning style. A pragmatic learner may prefer to move through a site systematically, either clicking or ignoring links as they appear on the screen from top to bottom, for example.
- **Web sites use new symbol systems.** Electronic texts introduce new and sometimes unfamiliar symbols. A flashing or blinking light may suggest a new feature on the site, or an underlined word or a word in a different color may suggest a link.

FIGURE 11-1   Web Sites Are Multidirectional

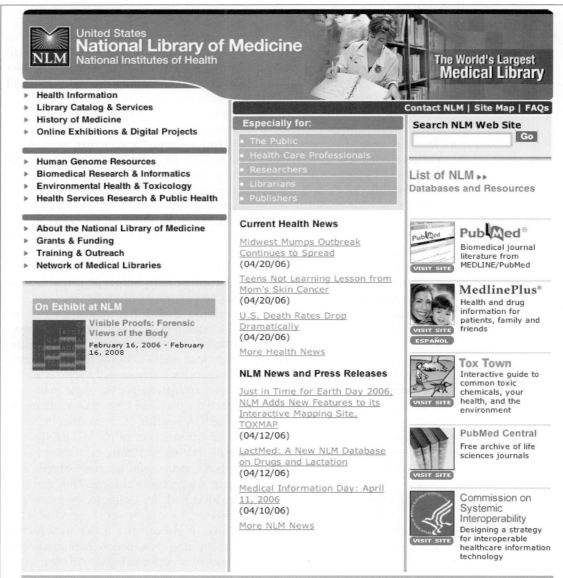

Source: The National Library of Medicine (http://www.nlm.nih.gov/)

EXERCISE 11-8   *Locate a Web site on a topic related to one of the end-of-chapter readings in this text. Write a list of characteristics that distinguish the site from the print readings.*

Changing Your Reading Strategies for Reading Electronic Text

Reading electronic text is relatively new to the current generation of college students. This will no doubt change with the upcoming generations who, as children, will learn to read both print and electronic text. Most current college students and teachers first learned to read using print text. We have read print text for many more years than electronic text; consequently, our brains have developed numerous strategies or "work orders" for reading traditional texts. Our work orders, however, are less fully developed for electronic text. Electronic texts have a wider variety of formats and more variables to cope with than traditional texts. A textbook page is usually made up of headings, paragraphs, and an occasional photo or graphic. Web sites have vibrant color, animation, sound, and music as well as words.

Reading is not only different, but it also tends to be slower on the computer screen than on print sources. Your eyes can see the layout of two full pages in a book. From the two pages, you can see headings, division of ideas, and subtopics. By glancing at a print page, you get an initial assessment of what it contains. You can tell, for example, if a page is heavily statistical (your eye will see numbers, dates, symbols) or is anecdotal (your eye will see capitalized proper names, quotation marks, and numerous indented paragraphs for dialogue, for example). Because you have a sense of what the page contains and how it is organized, you can read somewhat faster. Because a screen holds fewer words, you get far less feedback by previewing.

■ Developing New Ways of Thinking and Reading

Reading of electronic sources demands a different type of thinking than print sources. A print source is linear—it goes in a straight line from idea to idea. Electronic sources, due to the presence of links, tend to be multidirectional and let you follow numerous paths (see illustration).

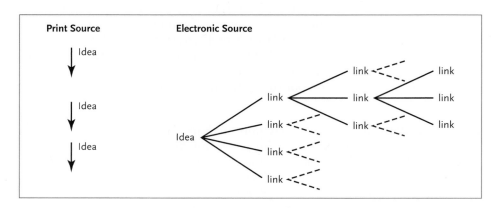

Reading electronic text also requires new strategies. The first steps to reading electronic text easily and effectively are to understand how it is different (see preceding section) and realize that you must change and adapt how you read. Some specific suggestions follow.

Focus on Your Purpose

Focus clearly on your purpose for visiting the site. What information do you need? Because you must create your own path through the site, unless you fix in mind what you are looking for, you may wander aimlessly, wasting valuable time, or even become lost, following numerous links that lead you farther and farther away from the site at which you began.

Get Used to the Site's Design and Layout

Each Web site has unique features and arranges information differently.

1. **When you reach a new site, spend a few minutes getting used to it and discovering how it is organized.** Scroll through it quickly to determine how it is organized and what information is available. Ask yourself the following questions:
   - What information is available?
   - How is it arranged on the screen?
2. **Expect the first screen to grab your attention and make a main point.** (Web site authors know that many people [up to 90 percent] who read a Web page do not scroll down to see the next page.)
3. **Get used to the colors, flashing images, and sounds before you attempt to obtain information from the site.** Your eye may have a tendency to focus on color or movement, rather than on print. Because Web sites are highly visual, they require visual as well as verbal thinking. The owner of the Web site intends for you to respond to photos, graphics, and animation.
4. **Consider both the focus and limitations of your learning style.** Are you a spatial learner? If so, you may have a tendency to focus too heavily on the graphic elements on the screen. If, on the other hand, you are a verbal learner, you may ignore important visual elements or signals. If you focus *only* on the words and ignore color and graphics on a particular screen, you will probably miss information or may not move through the site in the most efficient way. Review your learning style (p. 18), and consider both your strengths and limitations as they apply to electronic text.

EXERCISE 11-9

In groups of two or three students, consider at least two aspects of learning style. For each, discuss the tendencies, limitations, and implications these particular learning styles may have for reading electronic text. For example, consider how a visual learner would approach a Web site with numerous links and buttons. Then consider how a creative learner's approach might differ.

EXERCISE 11-10 *Locate two Web sites that you think are interesting and appealing. Then answer the following questions.*

1. How does each use color?
2. How does each use graphics?
3. Do the sites use sound or motion? If so, how?

Pay Attention to How Information Is Organized

Because you can navigate through a Web site in many different ways, it is important to have the right expectations about how information is organized on the site and to make several decisions before you begin.

Some Web sites are much better organized than others. Some have clear headings and labels that make it easy to discover how to proceed; others do not and will require more thought before beginning. For example, if you are reading an article with 10–15 underlined words (links), these links are not categorized in any way.

Use the following suggestions to grasp a site's organization.

1. **Use the site map, if provided, to discover what information is available and how it is organized.** A sample site map from the Web site of the Better Business Bureau is shown in Figure 11-2. Notice that the links are categorized by subject: File a Complaint, National Programs/Services. Go To Local BBB, and so forth.

FIGURE 11-2   A Web Site Map with Links

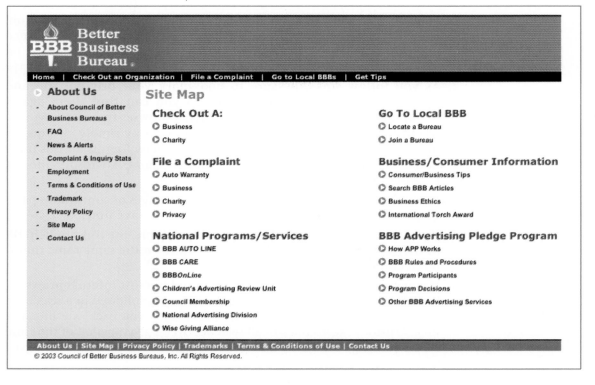

2. **Consider the order in which you want to take in information.** Choose an order in which to explore links; avoid randomly clicking on link buttons. Doing so is somewhat like randomly choosing pages to read out of a reference book. Do you need definitions first? Do you want historical background first? Your decision will be partly influenced by your learning style.

3. **Consider writing brief notes to yourself as you explore a complicated Web site.** Alternatively, you could print the site's home page and jot notes on it.

4. **Expect shorter, less detailed sentences and paragraphs.** Much online communication tends to be briefer and more concise than in traditional sources. As a result, you may have to fill in transitions mentally and make inferences about relationships among ideas. For example, you may have to infer similarities and differences or recognize cause-and-effect connections.

Visit two Web sites on the same topic. Write a few sentences comparing and contrasting the sites' organization and design.

Use Links to Find the Information You Need

Links are unique to electronic text. Here's how to use them:

1. **Plan on exploring links to find complete and detailed information.** Links—both remote links (those that take you to another site) and related links within a site—are intended to provide more detailed information on topics introduced on the home page.

2. **As you follow links, be sure to bookmark your original site and other useful sites you come across so you can find them again. Bookmarking** is a feature on your Internet browser that allows you to record Web site addresses and access them later by simply clicking on the site name. Different search engines use different terms for this function. Netscape and Safari use the term *Bookmarks;* Microsoft Internet Explorer calls it *Favorites.*

3. **If you use a site or a link that provides many pages of continuous paragraphs, print the material and read it offline to save time.**

4. **If you find you need more background on a topic, use links to help fill in the gaps or search for a different Web site on the same topic that is less technical.**

5. **If you get lost, use the history feature found in most Internet browsers.** It allows you to backtrack or retrace the links you followed in a search. In Netscape, for example, clicking on "Back" takes you back one link at a time; "History" keeps track of all searches over a given period of time and allows you to go directly to a chosen site, rather than backtracking step by step.

| EXERCISE 11-13 | *For one of the Web sites you visited earlier in the chapter or on a new site of your choice, follow at least three links and then answer the following questions.* |

1. What type of information did each site contain?
2. Was each source reliable? How do you know?
3. Which was the easiest to read and follow? Why?

■ Avoiding Cyberplagiarism When Conducting Research on the Web

As you write papers for college classes, you will probably use electronic sources to locate the information you need. As you read and take notes, and later, as you write the paper, you need to know the rules for indicating that you have taken information or ideas from the work of other people. You identify your sources in order to help readers find a source if they want to look further into the ideas of that author, as well as to give credit to the person who originally wrote the material or thought of the idea. *Plagiarism* means borrowing someone else's ideas or exact wording without giving that person credit. If you take information on Frank Lloyd Wright's architecture from a reference source, but do not indicate where you found it, you have plagiarized. If you take the six-word phrase "Martinez, the vengeful, despicable drug czar" from an online news article on the war on drugs without putting quotation marks around it and noting the source, you have plagiarized. Plagiarism is intellectually dishonest because you are taking someone else's ideas or wording and passing it off as your own. There are academic penalties for plagiarism. You may receive a failing grade on your paper or you may fail the entire course. At some institutions you can even be academically dismissed.

Cyberplagiarism is a special type of plagiarism; it involves borrowing information from the Internet without giving credit to the source posting the information. It is also called *cut and paste plagiarism*, referring to the ease with which a person can copy something from an Internet document and paste it into his or her own paper. Numerous Web sites offer student papers for sale on the Internet. *Cyberplagiarism* also refers to using these papers and submitting them as one's own.

What Constitutes Plagiarism

Plagiarism can be intentional (planned) or unintentional (done by accident or oversight). Either way it carries the same academic penalty. If you buy a paper from an Internet site or deliberately copy and paste a section of an article from a Web site into your paper, your plagiarism is intentional. If you take notes from a source and copy exact wording, forget to enclose the wording in quotation marks, and later use that exact wording in your paper, your plagiarism is unintentional, but it is still dishonest. Here are some guidelines that will help you understand exactly what is considered plagiarism:

- Plagiarism is the use of another person's words without giving credit to that person.

- Plagiarism uses another person's theory, opinion, or idea without listing where the information was taken from.
- Plagiarism results when another person's exact words are not placed inside quotation marks. Both the quotation marks and a citation (reference) to the original source are required.
- Paraphrasing (rewording) another person's words without giving credit to that person is plagiarism.
- Using facts, data, graphs, charts, and so on without stating where they were taken from is plagiarism.
- Using commonly known facts or information is not plagiarism and you need not give a source for your information. For example, the fact that Neil Armstrong set foot on the moon in 1969 is widely known and so does not require documentation.

Avoiding Cyberplagiarism

Use the following suggestions to avoid unintentional plagiarism:

- If you copy exact words from any source, put them in quotation marks in your notes, along with the publication information: the author, title, publisher, date of publication, and page number of the source, or, for Web sites, the author, the name of the site or page, its date of publication, the date you access the Web site, and its URL. Be sure to consult a style manual for details on how to indicate in your paper which material is borrowed and how to set up a list of the works you used in your paper.
- List sources for all the information you include in your notes regardless of whether the information takes the form of direct quotations, paraphrases, or summaries of someone else's ideas.
- Never copy and paste directly from a Web site into your paper without enclosing the words in quotation marks and listing their source.
- When paraphrasing someone else's words, phrase the information in your own words. Try not to follow the exact same organization of information. Credit from where the information came.
- Write paraphrases without looking at the original text so you will rephrase it in your own words.

EXERCISE 11-14

Read the following passage from Sociology for the Twenty-First Century *by Tim Curry, Robert Jiobu, and Kent Schwirian. Place a checkmark next to each statement that is an example of plagiarism.*

Mexican Americans. Currently, Mexican Americans are the second-largest racial or ethnic minority in the United States, but by early in the next century they will be the largest group. Their numbers will swell as a result of continual immigration from Mexico and the relatively high Mexican birth rate. Mexican Americans are one of the oldest racial-ethnic groups in the United States. Under the terms of the treaty ending the Mexican-

American War in 1848, Mexicans living in territories acquired by the United States could remain there and were to be treated as American citizens. Those that did stay became known as "Californios," "Tejanos," or "Hispanos."

_____ a. Mexican Americans are the second-largest minority in the United States. Their number grows as more people immigrate from Mexico.

_____ b. After the Mexican-American War, those Mexicans living in territories owned by the U.S. became American citizens and were called "Californios," "Tejanos," and "Hispanos" (Curry, Jiobu, and Schwirian, 207).

_____ c. "Mexican Americans are one of the oldest racial-ethnic groups in the United States."

_____ d. The Mexican-American War ended in 1848.

Self-Test Summary

1. Name and describe the two tools you need to use in order to locate sources of information on the World Wide Web.	Keywords, specific words that describe the topic; and search engines, computer programs that help locate information on a topic.
2. What factors should you take into consideration when evaluating a Web site?	To evaluate a Web site consider content (appropriateness, source or sponsor, level of technical detail, presentation, completeness, links), accuracy, and timeliness.
3. Describe the ways in which Web sites differ from print sources of information.	Web sites involve more graphics, sound, color, and animation; language on Web sites tends to be briefer. Screens are often independent of one another; Web sites are multidirectional, require decision making, and allow flexibility when searching.
4. What should you do when you read electronic text?	• Identify the purpose of the site. • Familiarize yourself with the site's design and layout. • Pay attention to how the information is organized. • Use links to find additional information.
5. What are plagiarism and cyberplagiarism?	Plagiarism is presenting someone else's work or ideas as your own. Cyberplagiarism refers to borrowing information, ideas, or papers found on the Internet and presenting them as your own.

ARCHAEOLOGY

PAIRED READINGS

Reading 1

Slices of the Past
Alan Hall

Prereading Questions

1. How do archaeologists know there might be an important artifact buried under the earth?
2. What can artifacts reveal about the past?

Field Work *Conyers and his team have set up their radar base station at a site near Bluff, Utah, believed to conceal a ceremonial room, or kiva, of the ancient Anasazi people.*

1   When archaeologists suspect than an important find lies buried beneath the earth, they reach for their shovels, hoping to hit some clue of a buried city or important burial site; sometimes they even call in backhoes and trenching machines. But now, a University of Denver anthropology professor has come up with a ground-breaking alternative that may turn traditional archaeology upside down.

2   Lawrence B. Conyers and his colleague, Dean Goodman, have adapted a technology known as "ground penetrating radar" to pioneer a new era of "non-invasive" archaeology. By pumping radar pulses into the ground and creating images of the radar reflections on a computer, they can obtain detailed pictures of a potentially important site before the first shovel of dirt is lifted. Then, the researchers can decide whether to dig—and where to dig—while doing the least damage to important artifacts.

3   "Archaeologists tend to be very low-tech people," Conyers says. "They have a tendency to be more comfortable digging in the dirt than working with computers. But this radar can help to locate sites and objects that you can't see on the surface. It can help us save sites that could be destroyed with traditional excavation techniques."

4   Ground-penetrating radar has been used for decades for everything from locating buried family treasures hidden from the Nazis to finding the engines of the ValuJet that crashed in the Everglades. Conyers has used the technology, and the software written by Goodman, to: map a Mayan village buried under 15 feet of volcanic ash in Ceren, El Salvador; create images of a Mayan ceremonial center buried in a sugar cane field in Coatzalmaguapa, Guatemala; locate 1,700-year-old kiln sites and a large village buried in wind-blown sand between two ceremonial pyramids in Peru; and disclose details of ancient burial sites in Japan.

Series of radar images *probe beneath an alfalfa field (top) in Japan to reveal the long-buried circular moat of an ancient burial mound (bottom).*

5   Closer to his home base in Denver, Conyers has employed the new technique to reveal the history of the ancient Anasazi people of the American West. Because of their sacred nature, the issue of whether to disturb these sites is crucial to their descendants. Near Bluff, Utah, Conyers and his colleagues pinpointed a subterranean kiva, used in ceremonial rites by the Anasazi people. "Even though the people that constructed this kiva have been dead for more than 900 years, these sites are still very sacred," says Conyers. "So radar was a method that we could use to first image what was there and then adjust our excavation procedures to dig only in certain spots to test our scientific ideas."

Fragments of pottery *litter the ground at a site near Bluff, Utah, where Conyers and his colleagues located a village of Anasazi "pit houses." The broken ceramics were dated about A.D. 1100.*

6   Nearby, Conyers and his colleagues also found a field littered with shards of pottery that dated to 1100 A.D. By searching the area with radar, they located a village of Anasazi "pit houses." Archaeologists usually use this type of evidence to locate sites, but of course have no idea where they are under the ground, says Conyers. "The typical way of finding the buried houses of this sort is to randomly dig test pits or drill auger holes—or, even worse, use backhoe trenchers that really destroy the site."

7   Mapping these sites using traditional excavation methods would have cost millions of dollars and taken many years. Conyers, using ground-penetrating radar and 3-D imaging software developed by Goodman, can map a site for a fraction of the cost in as little as three weeks. Many buried sites would not have been discovered without the ground-penetrating radar technology and would be potentially at risk from construction and erosion.

8   The next step for Conyers is the creation of moving 3-D images that will allow people to take video "tours" of archaeological sites that have not been unearthed. Maybe those people who Conyers refers to as "dirt archaeologists" will soon retire their shovels.

Related Reading

"Ground-penetrating Radar: An Introduction for Archaeologists," by Lawrence B. Conyers and Dean Goodman, Altamira Press, Walnut Creek, California, 1997.

—Hall, "Slices of the Past," *Scientific American—Exhibit: Radar Archaeology* (June 22, 1998) (http://www.sciam.com)

[By clicking on the "burial mound" link, the following site was located.]

Burial Mound

9   RADAR SURVEY, conducted by Dean Goodman, in Japan revealed a circular burial mound with a burial inside it, which shows up clearly in the bottom slice. The straight line at the left is probably an old fence line when the area was used for horse corrals about 500–600 years ago (Edo Period). The burial moat is much older, probably at least 1100 years old (Kofun Period). The surface is an alfalfa field. "As is usual in these surveys, there were no surface indicators of what was below the ground," says Conyers.

10   IMAGE is a 3-dimensional cutaway of a burial chamber that was found by Dean Goodman on a mound on the Island of Kyushu in Japan. It contained the remains of a warrior with a variety of artifacts, including bronze swords. This is a 3-D cutaway image of this chamber. It reveals a main chamber and a vertical shaft that leads to an offering below the burial.

Images: Lawrence B. Conyers and Dean Goodman, from "Ground-penetrating Radar: An Introduction for Archaeologists," Altamira Press, Walnut Creek, California, 1997.

Back to Slices of the Past

—"Burial Mound," *Scientific American—Exhibit: Radar Archaeology* (June 22, 1998) (http://www.sciam.com)

Writing About the Reading

CHECKING YOUR VOCABULARY

1. For each of the words listed below, use context; prefixes, roots, and suffixes (see Chapter 3); and/or a dictionary to write a brief definition or synonym of the word as it is used in the reading.

   a. alternative (para. 1) _____

   b. potentially (para. 2) _____

   c. artifacts (para. 2) _____

   d. excavation (para. 3) _____

   e. disclose (para. 4) _____

   f. subterranean (para. 5) _____

   g. shards (para. 6) _____

2. Underline new, specialized terms introduced in the reading.

3. Draw a word map of one of the words in the reading.

CHECKING YOUR COMPREHENSION

1. Why is the radar procedure referred to as noninvasive?
2. Name two important advantages of using the ground-penetrating radar.
3. What is the usual way of finding buried artifacts?
4. Why do archaeologists not like to use backhoe trenchers?
5. Why was it important to use radar to examine the subterranean kivas built by the Anasazi people?
6. How long does it take to map a site using this new radar technique, compared with traditional excavation?
7. What did the radar survey conducted by Dean Goodman reveal?

THINKING CRITICALLY

1. What would you do if you wanted to know more about Lawrence B. Conyers?
2. What does Conyers mean by the term *dirt archaeologists?*
3. For what other nonarchaeological situation can you imagine using ground-penetrating radar?
4. Do you think archaeologists should be permitted to dig up sacred sites? Explain.
5. How did this Web site differ from a textbook?
6. How useful did you find the link to "burial mound"?

LEARNING/STUDY STRATEGY

Design a study sheet explaining the different types of remote sensing.

ARCHAEOLOGY

PAIRED READINGS

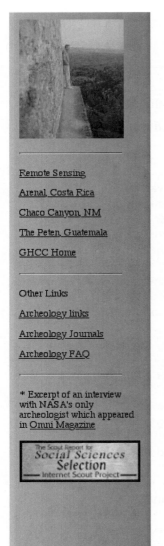

Remote Sensing

Arenal, Costa Rica

Chaco Canyon, NM

The Peten, Guatemala

GHCC Home

_____

Other Links

Archeology links

Archeology Journals

Archeology FAQ

_____

* Excerpt of an interview
with NASA's only
archeologist which appeared
in Omni Magazine

The Scout Report for
Social Sciences
Selection
Internet Scout Project

Reading 2

Archaeology
Tom Sever

Prereading Questions

1. Why is the study of archaeology important?
2. What is remote sensing?

1   Much of human history can be traced through the impacts of human actions upon the environment. The use of remote sensing technology offers the archaeologist the opportunity to detect these impacts which are often invisible to the naked eye. This information can be used to address issues in human settlement, environmental interaction, and climate change. Archaeologists want to know how ancient people successfully adapted to their environment and what factors may have led to their collapse or disappearance.

Did they over-extend the capacity of their landscape, causing destructive environmental effects which led to their demise? Can this information be applied to modern day societies so that the mistakes of the past are not repeated?

2   Remote sensing can be used as a methodological procedure for detecting, inventorying, and prioritizing surface and shallow-depth archaeological information in a rapid, accurate, and quantified manner. Man is a tropical creature who has invaded every environment on earth successfully; now we are ready to explore, and eventually colonize, the delicate environments of Space. Understanding how ancient man successfully managed Earth is important for the success of current and future societies.

3   "The stereotype has archaeologists just digging up spearheads and pottery and anthropologists just writing down the words of primitive tribes. But we're examining how people adapted to their environment throughout

time, how they experienced environmental shift, why cultures come and go. Soils associated with artifacts are as important as the artifacts themselves—probably more relevant to us than the actual objects. Now more than ever, archaeological research is interdisciplinary: botany, forestry, soil science, hydrology—all of which contribute to a more complete understanding of the earth, climatic shifts, and how people adapt to large regions. This understanding is critical to future decision making affecting the planet.

4   In Costa Rica, the culture survived repeated volcanic explosions that repeatedly destroyed the environment, explosions equal to the force of a nuclear blast. Other cultures, like the advanced Maya societies, did not survive or recover from similar eruptions. Did it have to do with the size and violence of the eruption, the way they farmed their land over time, or territorial and political struggle?"

> We have not inherited the earth from our fathers,
> we are borrowing it from our children
> Amish Farmer

—Sever, "Archaeology," Global Hydrology and Climate Center, NASA/Marshall Space Flight Center Web site (http://www.msfc.nasa.gov)

[By clicking on the "Remote Sensing" link, the following site was located.]

Archaeological Remote Sensing

Remote Sensing

Remote Sensing

Arenal, Costa Rica

Chaco Canyon, NM

The Petén, Guatemala

Archeology Home

GHCC Home

Other Links

Remote Sensing Tutorial

5   Now more than ever, archaeological research is interdisciplinary: botany, forestry, soil science, hydrology—all of which contribute to a more complete understanding of the Earth, climatic shifts, and how people adapt to large regions.

6   As a species, we've been literally blind to the universe around us. If the known electromagnetic spectrum were scaled up to stretch around the Earth's circumference, the human eye would see a portion equal to the diameter of a pencil. Our ability to build detectors that see for us where we can't see, and computers that bring the invisible information back to our eyesight, will ultimately contribute to our survival on Earth and in space.

7   The spectrum of sunlight reflected by the Earth's surface contains information about the composition of the surface, and it may reveal traces of past human activities, such as agriculture. Since sand, cultivated soil, vegetation, and all kinds of rocks each have distinctive temperatures and emit heat at different rates, sensors can "see" things beyond ordinary vision or cameras. Differences in soil texture are revealed by fractional temperature variations. So it is possible to identify loose soil that had been prehistoric agricultural fields, or was covering buried remains. The Maya causeway was detected through emissions of infrared radiation at a different wavelength from

surrounding vegetation. More advanced versions of such multi-spectral scanner (Visible & IR) can detect irrigation ditches filled with sediment because they hold more moisture and thus have a temperature different from other soil. The ground above a buried stone wall, for instance, may be a touch hotter than the surrounding terrain because the stone absorbs more heat. Radar can penetrate darkness, cloud cover, thick jungle canopies, and even the ground.

8   Remote sensing can be a discovery technique, since the computer can be programmed to look for distinctive "signatures" of energy emitted by a known site or feature in areas where surveys have not been conducted. Such "signatures" serve as recognition features or fingerprints. Such characteristics as elevation, distance from water, distance between sites or cities, corridors, and transportation routes can help to predict the location of potential archaeological sites.

Computational Techniques Used to Analyze Data

1. sun-angle correction
2. density slicing
3. band ratioing
4. edge enhancement
5. synthetic color assignment
6. filtering
7. multichannel analysis

Remote Sensing Instruments

10   Aerial Photography:
Many features which are difficult or impossible to see standing on the ground become very clear when seen from the air. But, black and white photography only records about twenty-two perceptible shades of gray in the visible spectrum. Also, optical sources have certain liabilities; they must operate in daylight, during clear weather, on days with minimal atmospheric haze.

11   Color Infrared Film (CIR):
Detects longer wavelengths somewhat beyond the red end of the light spectrum. CIR film was initially employed during World War II to differentiate objects that had been artificially camouflaged. Infrared photography has the same problems that conventional photography has; you need light and clear skies. Even so, CIR is sensitive to very slight differences in vegetation. Because buried archaeological features can affect how plants grow above them, such features become visible in color infrared photography.

12   Thermal Infrared Multispectral Scanner (TIMS):
A six-channel scanner that measures the thermal radiation given off by the ground, with accuracy to 0.1 degree centigrade. The pixel (picture element) is the square area being sensed, and the size of the pixel is directly proportional to sensor height. For example, pixels from Landsat satellites are about 100 feet (30 m) on a side, and thus have limited archaeological applications. However, pixels in TIMS data measure only a few feet on a side and as such can be used for archaeological research. TIMS data were used to detect ancient Anasazi roads in Chaco Canyon, NM.

13   Airborne Oceanographic Lidar (ADI):
A laser device that makes "profiles" of the earth's surface. The laser beam pulses to the ground 400 times per second, striking the surface every three and a half inches, and

bounces back to its source. In most cases, the beam bounces off the top of the vegetation cover and off the ground surface; the difference between the two gives information on forest height, or even the height of grass in pastures. As the lidar passes over an eroded footpath that still affects the topography, the pathway's indentation is recorded by the laser beam. The lidar data can be processed to reveal tree height as well as elevation, slope, aspect, and slope length of ground features. Lidar can also be used to penetrate water to measure the morphology of coastal water, detect oil forms, fluorescent dye traces, water clarity, and organic pigments including chlorophyll. In this case, part of the pulse is reflected off the water surface, while the rest travels to the water bottom and is reflected. The time elapsed between the received impulses allows for a determination of water depth and subsurface topography.

14   Synthetic Aperture Radar (SAR):

SAR beams energy waves to the ground and records the energy reflected. Radar is sensitive to linear and geometric features on the ground, particularly when different radar wavelengths and different combinations of the horizontal and vertical data are employed. Different wavelengths are sensitive to vegetation or to ground surface phenomena. In dry, porous soils, radar can penetrate the surface. In 1982, radar from the space shuttle penetrated the sand of the Sudanese desert and revealed ancient watercourses. Using airborne radar in Costa Rica, prehistoric footpaths have been found.

15   Microwave Radar:

Beaming radar pulses into the ground and measuring the echo is a good way of finding buried artifacts in arid regions (water absorbs microwaves). Man-made objects tend to reflect the microwaves, giving one a "picture" of what is underground without disturbing the site.

Selected Papers

"Remote Sensing Methods," In *Advances in Science and Technology for Historic Preservation,* edited by Ray Williamson, Plenum Press. (In Press).

"Remote Sensing," In *American Journal of Archaeology,* 99:83–84, 1995.

"Applications of Ecological Concepts and Remote Sensing Technologies in Archaeological Site Reconnaissance," with F. Miller and D. Lee. (In *Applications of Space-Age Technology in Anthropology,* edited by Clifford Behrens and Thomas Sever. NASA, Stennis Space Center, MS, 1991.)

"Remote Sensing," Chapter 14 of *Benchmarks In Time and Culture: Introductory Essays in the Methodology of Syro-Palestinian Archaeology.* Scholars Press. March, 1988.

"Cultural and Ecological Applications of Remote Sensing." Final Report of a Conference Sponsored by the National Science Foundation. With Daniel Gross and Paul Shankman. University of Boulder Colorado, Boulder. April, 1988.

"Conference on Remote Sensing: Potential for the Future." NASA, Stennis Space Center, Science and Technology Laboratory, SSC, MS., January, 1985.

—Global Hydrology and Climate Center, NASA/Marshall Space
Flight Center Web site (http://www.msfc.nasa.gov)

Writing About the Reading

CHECKING YOUR VOCABULARY

1. For each of the words listed below, use context; prefixes, roots, and suffixes (see Chapter 3); and/or a dictionary to write a brief definition or synonym of the word as it is used in the reading.

   a. impacts (para. 1) _____

   b. demise (para. 1) _____

   c. methodological (para. 2) _____

   d. prioritizing (para. 2) _____

   e. quantified (para. 2) _____

   f. emit (para. 7) _____

   g. infrared (para. 7) _____

   h. perceptible (para. 10) _____

   i. optical (para. 10) _____

   j. camouflaged (para. 11) _____

   k. eroded (para. 13) _____

   l. morphology (para. 13) _____

   m. porous (para. 14) _____

2. Underline new, specialized terms introduced in the reading.

3. Draw a word map of one of the words in the reading.

CHECKING YOUR COMPREHENSION

1. Why do archaeologists need remote sensing?
2. What is the value of research that allows archaeologists to uncover previously invisible information?
3. Describe one archaeological discovery that was made using remote sensing.
4. What characteristics can predict the potential of an archaeological site?
5. Why might the ground above a buried stone wall be a little warmer than the ground surrounding it?
6. Name and briefly describe one remote sensing instrument.

THINKING CRITICALLY

1. If you did not understand the term *remote sensing*, what would you do?
2. What is the purpose of the quotation given in paragraphs 3–4?
3. Which of the remote sensing instruments might be useful in environmental preservation and conservation of wetland and coastal areas?

4. Name two advantages of reading material electronically (as opposed to a print source) that this electronic reading provided.
5. If you wanted additional information on synthetic aperture radar, how would you go about finding it?
6. Evaluate this Web site using the criteria suggested in the chapter.

LEARNING/STUDY STRATEGIES

1. Locate at least three additional electronic articles on ground-penetrating radar.
2. Evaluate each source you identify.

Thinking About the Paired Readings
INTEGRATING IDEAS

1. Which of the two readings do you think offers the most information?
2. Compare the author's purpose in both readings.
3. How do the readings differ?
4. Which of the two readings offers a more scientifically based definition of radar as used in the study of archaeology? Explain your answer.
5. If you came across these two readings online, which one would you find more "user friendly" and why?

GENERATING NEW IDEAS

1. Visit one or both of the Web sites from which these readings were taken. Search for updated information on research tools in archaeology. Write a brief summary of your findings.
2. Write a cause-and-effect essay explaining how technology has affected and changed the field of archaeology.

ADDITIONAL PRACTICE
MULTIMEDIA ACTIVITIES

1. **Worst of the Web/Best of the Web**

   http://www.worstoftheweb.com/
   http://www.webbyawards.com/webbys/current.php

   Explore some links from these sites and try to determine why they were given their respective "awards." Do you have sites that you return to over and over? What about them appeals to you? What types of sites do you avoid? Why?

2. **Web Site Evaluation Worksheet**

   http://www.pace.edu/library/instruct/webevalworksheet.htm

   Print this worksheet from the Pace University Library and use it to evaluate the Web sites that you visit on a regular basis.

CHAPTER

12

Reading in the Social Sciences

LEARNING OBJECTIVES

✦ To learn why social sciences are "sciences"

✦ To discover specialized reading techniques for the social sciences

✦ To learn what common thought patterns to anticipate

✦ To adapt your study techniques for social science courses

Think About It!

"To cherish the life of the world"

In 1928, after spending a year on the island of Ta'u, anthropologist Margaret Mead published her most important work, *Coming of Age in Samoa*. In it, she concluded that the passage from childhood to adulthood—adolescence—in Samoa was smooth, not the emotionally and psychologically tumultuous transition it is in the United States. While some doubts have arisen about her conclusions, Margaret Mead remains one of the most respected and influential social scientists of the twentieth century.

The social sciences are concerned with the study of people, their development, and how they function together and interact. These disciplines deal with the political, economic, social, cultural, and behavioral aspects of human beings. The social sciences include psychology, anthropology, sociology, political science, and economics. History, which is sometimes considered one of the humanities, and geography, which is sometimes treated as a physical science, are included among the social sciences for the purposes of this book. During your college career, you probably will take at least two or three social science courses; many students take more.

As you select these courses, it is helpful to understand the basic focus and approach of each discipline. Each one of the social sciences focuses on selected aspects of human behavior, social relationships, or social systems and the laws or principles that govern them. Table 12-1 provides an overview of each discipline and shows how they differ by giving examples of the questions each discipline would ask about a particular topic—in this case, an accident on an oil tanker in the Gulf of Mexico resulting in a major oil spill.

TABLE 12-1   The Social Science Disciplines Topic: Oil Spill

DISCIPLINE	OVERVIEW	QUESTIONS
Anthropology	Examines concepts, customs, and rules in different societies and cultures	Does each country involved view the spill the same way? What rules and customs must be followed?
Economics	Studies how goods, services, and wealth are produced, consumed, and distributed within societies	How will environmental damage affect the economy of each country?
Geography	Focuses on the surface of the earth, its divisions, climate, inhabitants, and resources	What environmental damage has occurred? How will the spill affect the ecology of each area involved?
History	Provides a chronological record of past events; tells story of people's past	What other oil spills have occurred? How is this spill similar to and different from others?
Political science	Studies political power, governments, processes	How will each country be compensated for environmental damage? Who will decide the amount of compensation?
Psychology	Focuses on human mental processes and behavior	How will the pilot and crew of the tanker cope with the accident and its effects?
Sociology	Deals with human relationships, social systems, and societies	What leadership patterns emerged on the tanker after the accident? How were the cleanup efforts organized? What groups were most active?

Why Study the Social Sciences?

On many campuses, courses in the social sciences are among the most popular. Because social science courses focus on how people develop, behave, and interact, students find they learn a great deal about themselves and those around them. They also learn answers to many questions they have always wondered about: Why do some people commit violent crimes? Why and how do people fall in love? What can we learn from events of the past? Why is religion important in our lives, and how did it evolve? What factors determine how many jobs are available in a given city?

Social science courses are required courses for many college degrees because social science links to many other fields. If you plan to become a nurse, interacting with patients is important. If you plan to work in business, your success often depends on understanding people and the economy in which you are working. If you plan to work as a commercial Web site designer, you have to understand what motivates people to purchase goods and services. You can see, then, that social science courses are valuable in the workplace because all jobs require you to interact with people to some degree.

The Social Sciences: A Scientific Approach

Although each social science focuses on a different aspect of human life, they have much in common. Each is interested in general laws, principles, and generalizations that describe how events, facts, and observations are related. The author of your social science textbook and your course instructor are both social scientists, and their approach to problems and the way they organize ideas are similar and predictable. Once you are familiar with this approach, you'll find social science courses much easier to handle.

Textbooks in the social sciences share several characteristics.

1. **The emphasis is on facts.** Especially in introductory courses, an instructor's first task often is to acquaint you with what has already been discovered—known principles, rules, and facts—so that you can use this information to approach new problems and situations. Consequently, you must comprehend and retain large amounts of factual information. Refer to "Locating Main Ideas and Supporting Details" in Chapter 2 and "Retention and Recall Strategies" in Chapter 8 for specific suggestions.

2. **Many new terms are introduced.** Each social science has developed an extensive terminology to make its broad topics as objective and as quantifiable as possible.

3. **Graphics are important.** Refer to Chapter 10, "Reading Graphics and Visuals," for specific suggestions on reading and interpreting charts, tables, and graphs.

4. **Research references are stressed.** Many texts present research studies as supporting evidence. In introductory courses, the outcome of the research and what it proves or suggests usually are most important.

A Sociology Professor . . .

**Robert A. Schwegler, PhD,
Professor of Writing,
University of Rhode Island**

Talks About This Chapter

"In general, the chapter covers the reading
and study skills for the discipline, and it does
so very well. It addresses most of the key
points of writing in the social sciences, especially those that prove difficult for under-
graduate readers. It also looks at specific
reading strategies that undermine student
success in sociology and psychology courses
and in other courses in the social sciences,
and it suggests concrete strategies to replace
the ineffective ones. I like this approach."

Offers Advice to
Social Science Students

1. Students need to "concentrate on identifying
   and remembering terms and understanding
   their implications and relationships."

2. "My students have trouble recognizing the
   cues that identify a summary of a theoretical
   approach or research findings. They often
   read the summaries as statements of fact,
   not as reports of someone's work, even
   though they realize that not everything in a
   textbook or article is fact. I think the problem
   is that they miss the cues that say, 'This is X's
   work' etc. . . . Students [need to] identify the
   formal cues, recognize summaries, and deal
   with the summarized information as the
   interpretations or conclusions of specific
   scholars."

5. **Theories and their creators are emphasized.** Often, the social scientists
   who have developed important theories are discussed at length.

Now that you are familiar with the scientific method, you will understand how
social scientists approach their subject matter and how you will be expected to
think and analyze information in social science courses. You will have a competitive advantage over other students who mistakenly regard social science
courses as subjective or unscientific.

■ Specialized Reading Techniques

Especially in introductory-level social science courses, you will need to learn a
large volume of information. Use the following suggestions to read social science materials and retain as much information as possible.

Identify Key Terms

The key to mastering any new discipline is to learn its language: specialized and
technical terms unique to the discipline. The social sciences use precise terminology to describe observations as well as processes. Terminology in the social

sciences includes everyday words with specialized meanings, as well as new words not used elsewhere. Instructors recognize the importance of learning terminology; consequently, they often include items on their exams to test your knowledge of key terms. Refer to Chapter 3 for specific suggestions for learning specialized terminology.

In social science courses, it is particularly important to learn

- Terms that describe general behavior and organizational patterns.
  Examples: denial, power, aggression, primary/secondary groups, free trade
- Names of stages and processes.
  Examples: Piaget's stages of cognitive development, Maslow's hierarchy of needs
- Laws, principles, theories, and models.
  Examples: figure-ground principles, income/expenditures model, models of attention, Keynesian theory
- Names of important researchers and theorists.
  Examples: Marx, Freud, Skinner, Durkheim, Mead

Understand Theories

An important part of most social science courses is the study of theories that explain various behaviors. A theory is a set of propositions that explains a certain phenomenon or occurrence. You might, for example, develop a theory to explain why your roommate cannot fall asleep without music or why your history professor always opens class with the same comment. A theory is a reasoned explanation of an observable occurrence. Theories are often tested using the scientific method. In sociology, you may study exchange theory, which explains social behavior as a series of exchanges or trade-offs involving rewards (benefits) and costs. In economics, you may study the natural rate hypothesis that states that workers do not immediately react to changes in wages.

When studying theories, read to find the following information:

- What is the theory? What is its name?
- Who proposed the theory?
- When was it proposed? (Is it recent or historical?)
- What behavior or occurrence does it explain?
- What evidence or rationale is offered that the theory is correct?
- What use or application does the theory have?

Read the following excerpt from a sociology text. Note how the text has been marked to indicate the answers to each of the questions listed above.

CONFLICT THEORY

behavior ——— *Conflict* theory also had its origins in early sociology, especially in the work of
origin — Marx. Among its more recent proponents are such people as Mills, Coser, and
recent proponents — Dahrendorf. They share the view that society is best understood and analyzed in
statement of theory — terms of conflict and power.

rationale

Karl Marx began with a very simple assumption: the structure of society is determined by economic organization, particularly the ownership of property. Religious dogmas, cultural values, personal beliefs, institutional arrangements, class structures—all are basically reflections of the economic organization of a society. Inherent in any economic system that supports inequality are forces that generate revolutionary class conflict, according to Marx. The exploited classes eventually recognize their submissive and inferior status and revolt against the dominant class of property owners and employers. The story of history, then, is the story of class struggle between the owners and workers, the dominators and the dominated, the powerful and the powerless.

applications

Contemporary conflict theorists assume that conflict is a permanent feature of social life and that as a result societies are in a state of constant change. Unlike Marx, however, these theorists rarely assume that conflict is always based on class or that it always reflects economic organization and ownership. Conflicts are assumed to involve a broad range of groups or interests: young against old, male against female, or one racial group against another, as well as workers against employers. These conflicts result because things like power, wealth, and prestige are not available to everyone—they are limited commodities, and the demand exceeds the supply. Conflict theory also assumes that those who have or control desirable goods and services will defend and protect their own interests at the expense of others.

—Eshleman et al., *Sociology: An Introduction,* p. 46

In some texts, you may find several theories presented to explain a single phenomenon. Often, these theories are not compatible, and they may even be contradictory. In this case, first make certain that you understand each theory; then examine how they differ and consider the evidence offered in support of each.

EXERCISE 12-1

Write a summary of the conflict theory described above. Refer to page 281 for suggestions on writing summaries. Compare your summary with those of several classmates.

EXERCISE 12-2

Read this excerpt from a psychology textbook, and answer the questions that follow.

KOHLBERG'S THEORY OF MORAL DEVELOPMENT

How children learn to reason about and make judgments about what is right and wrong is an aspect of cognitive development that has received considerable attention (Darley & Schultz, 1990; Vitz, 1990). Piaget included the study of moral development in his theory, arguing that morality is related to cognitive awareness, and that children are unable to make moral judgments until they are at least 3 or 4 years old (Piaget, 1932/1948).

Lawrence Kohlberg (1963, 1969, 1981, 1985) has offered a theory that focuses on moral development. Like Piaget's approach, Kohlberg's is a theory of stages, of moving from one stage to another in an orderly fashion. Kohlberg's database comes from the responses made by young boys who were asked questions about stories that involve a moral dilemma. A commonly cited example concerns whether a man should steal a drug in order to save his wife's life after the pharmacist who invented the drug refuses to sell it to him. Should the man steal the drug; why or why not?

On the basis of responses to such dilemmas, Kohlberg proposed three levels of moral development, with two stages (or "orientations") at each level. The result is the six stages of moral development. . . . For example, a child who says that the man should not steal the drug because "he'll get caught and be put in jail" is at the first, *preconventional*, level of reasoning because the prime interest of the child is simply with the punishment that comes from breaking a rule. A child who says that the man should steal the drug because "it will make his wife happy, and probably most people would do it anyway" is reflecting a type of reasoning at the second, *conventional*, level because the judgment is based on an accepted social convention, and social approval matters as much as or more than anything else. The argument that "no, he shouldn't steal the drug for a basically selfish reason, which in the long run would just promote more stealing in the society in general" is an example of moral reasoning at the third, *postconventional*, level because it reflects complex, internalized standards. Notice that what matters most is not the choice the child makes, but the reasoning behind the choice.

—Gerow, *Psychology: An Introduction*, p. 290

1. Who proposed the theory?
2. What is it intended to explain?
3. Explain the three levels in your own words.
4. How did Kohlberg arrive at the theory?
5. What practical uses can you see for the theory?
6. Underline terminology in the passage that is important to learn.
7. Construct a story about a moral dilemma, and indicate responses at each of the three levels.

Read Research Reports

Because the social sciences rely heavily on observation, research, and experimentation based on the scientific method, textbooks often include brief descriptions of, or references to, research studies. Writers in the social sciences often give clues rather than directly state that they are about to summarize research. Here are two ways writers tell you that a summary of research is to follow:

- Use of researcher's name.
  Example: Margaret's Mead's (1935) classic study of sex and temperament . . .
  Example: According to Turner (2005), teenage gangs . . .

- Use of parentheses to include author's name and date of research.
  Example: Children who have been read to at home have fewer reading problems in school (Thompson 2003).

When reading reports about research, keep these guidelines in mind:

- Determine who conducted the research.
- Identify its purpose.
- Read reviews of current research in the field of study.
- Find out how the research was done.

- Understand the results of the research.
- Find out what theory the results support or what conclusion was drawn.
- Discover the implications and applications of the research. Ask "Why is it important?"

The following excerpt from a sociology textbook describes research on masculine and feminine behavior. See how the marked passages reflect the guidelines given above.

Although biologically men are men and women are women, roles—that is, definitions of masculine and feminine behavior—differ widely from one culture to another. The discovery of cross-cultural variation in gender was one of the earliest kinds of evidence against the idea that each sex has a "natural" temperament and set of interests. In American culture, for example, it is considered "feminine" to be artistic and emotional, but in other cultures men are supposed to be more emotionally expressive and artistic than women. Margaret Mead's (1935) classic study of sex and temperament in three cultures was the earliest <u>study of the variability of gender patterning.</u> In one of the New Guinea tribes, the Arapesh, both men and women were found to be cooperative, unaggressive, and gentle. In contrast, the Mundugumor prescribed what would be a masculine temperament in our culture for both sexes—ruthlessness, aggressiveness, and severity. Neither the Arapesh nor the Mundugumor emphasized a contrast between the sexes. In a third New Guinea tribe, the Tchambuli, however, there was such a contrast, but it was the reverse of sex-role temperament in our culture. Tchambuli women tended to be aggressive, domineering, and managerial, whereas the men tended to be dependent, artistic, and sensitive. In short, the study concludes that sex differences are arbitrary and do not reflect any underlying predisposition.

—Skolnick, *The Intimate Environment: Exploring Marriage and the Family,* pp. 193–94

Purpose

Results

Conclusion

Not all research in the social sciences involves experiments with numerical results. Some disciplines use more subjective research. These results may be reported as a narrative (story). These include case studies, ethnographies (description of ethnic groups), memoirs, and field studies or reports. When reading these, be sure to focus on the findings and their significance and application to the topics you are studying.

EXERCISE 12-3

Read the following excerpt from a psychology textbook, and answer the questions that follow.

Researchers have looked at the relationship between adolescent drug use and psychological health (Shedler & Block, 1990). Participants in this investigation were 18-year-olds who had been under study since they were 3 years old. Based on their level of drug use, they were divided into one of three groups: (1) *abstainers* (N = 29), who had never tried any drug; (2) *experimenters* (N = 36), who had used marijuana "once or twice, or a few times" and who tried no more than one other drug; and (3) *frequent users* (N = 20), who used marijuana frequently and tried at least one other drug. There were no socioeconomic or IQ differences among the groups.

The researchers found that *frequent users* were generally maladjusted, alienated, deficient in impulse control, and "manifestly" distressed. The *abstainers* were overly anxious, "emotionally constricted," and lacking in social skills. These same results were apparent when the researchers examined records from when the same subjects were 7 and 11 years old. Generally, the *experimenters* were better adjusted and psychologically "healthier" than either of the other two groups. The authors of this study are concerned that their data may be misinterpreted—that their data might be taken to indicate "that drug use might somehow improve an adolescent's psychological health." Clearly, this interpretation would be in error. You recognize these as correlational data from which no conclusion regarding cause and effect is justified.

While drug use among adolescents is a matter of great concern, there is evidence that we need not get hysterical about infrequent drug use among teenagers.

—Gerow, *Psychology: An Introduction,* pp. 305–06

1. Who conducted the research?
2. What was its purpose?
3. What methods were used?
4. What were the results?
5. What did the results demonstrate?
6. What is the practical value of the research?
7. Why did the author feel compelled to caution against misinterpretation?

Read to Make Comparisons and Connections

In the social sciences, the ability to see relationships among different ideas and concepts is a necessary skill. Often neither your instructor nor your textbook will make explicit, direct comparisons, yet you will be expected to compare or contrast ideas and concepts. Suppose you are reading about three forms of imperfect economic competition: monopoly, oligopoly, and monopolistic competition. You would, of course, be expected to understand each form. However, you must also know how they are similar, how they are different, and in what economic situation each is found.

When making comparisons, keep the following question in mind: "What does what I am reading have to do with other topics in the chapter?" Then spend a few minutes thinking about how the topics and ideas in the chapter are connected to one another. Begin by reviewing the chapter using the steps you used to preview it (see Chapter 1). Then study your text's detailed table of contents and review the lecture notes that correspond to the chapter. For example, one student connected the forms of imperfect competition to other market variables she had learned in economics: number of sellers, ease of entry, product type, price influence, and price level. Then she drew the chart shown in Table 12-2 (p. 360) to compare the three forms according to the market variables that she identified.

In addition to charts, you can organize comparisons by making outlines or lists or by drawing maps that summarize similarities and differences (refer to Chapter 9).

TABLE 12-2   Sample Comparison Chart

| | FORMS OF IMPERFECT COMPETITION | | |
	MONOPOLY	OLIGOPOLY	MONOPOLISTIC COMPETITION
Number of sellers	One	Several	Many
Entry	Difficult	Less difficult	Easy
Product	Unique	Homogeneous or differentiated	Differentiated
Price influence	Price makers	Price makers	Limited price makers
Price level	Higher price, lower quantity than competition	Somewhat higher price and lower quantity than competition	Slightly higher price than competition and frequently higher production costs

EXERCISE 12-4

Read the following excerpt from a sociology textbook chapter titled "Religious Groups and Systems," and make comparisons between Hinduism and Buddhism by listing, charting, or mapping. Compare your work with the work of other students, discussing its relative effectiveness.

Hinduism

The great majority of Hindus in the world live in India and Pakistan. In India, approximately 85 percent of the population is Hindu. Hinduism has evolved over about 4000 years and comprises an enormous variety of beliefs and practices. It hardly corresponds to most Western conceptions of religion because organization is minimal, and there is no religious hierarchy.

Hinduism is so closely intertwined with other aspects of the society that it is difficult to describe it clearly, especially in regard to castes. . . . Hindus sometimes refer to the ideal way of life as fulfilling the duties of one's class and station, which means obeying the rules of the four great castes of India: the Brahmins, or priests; the Kshatriyas, warriors and rulers; the Vaisyas, merchants and farmers; and the Sudras, peasants and laborers. A fifth class, the Untouchables, includes those whose occupations require them to handle "unclean objects."

These classes encompass males only. The position of women is ambiguous. In some respects, they are treated as symbols of the divine, yet in other ways, they are considered inferior beings. Traditionally, women have been expected to serve their husbands and to have no independent interests, but this is rapidly changing.

Although caste is a powerful influence in Hindu religious behavior, a person's village community and family are important as well. Every village has gods and goddesses who ward off epidemics and drought. Hindu belief holds that the universe is populated by a multitude of gods (polytheism) who behave much as humans do, and worship of these gods takes many forms. Some are thought to require sacrifices, others are worshipped at shrines or temples, and shrines devoted to several gods associated with a family deity are often erected in private homes.

To Hindus, the word *dharma* means the cosmos, or the social order. Hindus practice rituals that uphold the great cosmic order. They believe that to be righteous, a person must strive to behave in accordance with the way things are. In a sense, the Hindu sees life as a ritual. The world is regarded as a great dance determined by one's karma, or personal destiny, and the final goal of the believer is liberation from this cosmic dance. Hindus also believe in *transmigration of souls:* After an individual dies, that individual's soul is born again in another form, as either a higher or lower being, depending on whether the person was righteous or evil in the previous life. If an individual becomes righteous enough, the soul will be liberated and will cease to be reborn into an earthly form and will exist only as spirit.

A fundamental principle of Hinduism is that our perceptions of the external world are limitations. When we think about one thing, we are cut off from the infinite number of things we are not thinking about but could be. If we think of nothing, we become in tune with the universe and freed of these limitations. One means of doing this is through meditation.

The actual belief systems of India are extremely confusing to Westerners, because so many different tribal religions have been assimilated into Hinduism, but the basic nature of polytheism in general and of Hinduism in particular permits new gods to be admitted.

Buddhism

It is impossible to precisely determine the number of Buddhists because many people accept Buddhist beliefs and engage in Buddhist rites while practicing other religions such as Shintoism, Confucianism, Taoism, or Hinduism.

Buddhism is thought to have originated as a reaction against the Brahminic tradition of Hinduism in the fifth century B.C. At this time, a prince named Siddhartha Gautama was born in northern India to a prosperous ruling family. As he grew older, he was distressed by the suffering he witnessed among the people. At the age of 29, he left his wife and family to go on a religious quest. One day, sitting under a giant fig tree, he passed through several stages of awareness and became the Buddha, the enlightened one. He decided to share his experience with others and became a wandering teacher, preaching his doctrine of the "Four Noble Truths": (1) this life is suffering and pain; (2) the source of suffering is desire and craving; (3) suffering can cease; and (4) the practice of an "eightfold path" can end suffering. The eightfold path consisted of right views, right intentions, right speech, right conduct, right livelihood, right effort, right mindfulness, and right concentration. It combined ethical and disciplinary practices, training in concentration and meditation, and the development of enlightened wisdom. This doctrine was Buddha's message until the age of 80, when he passed into final nirvana, a state of transcendence forever free from the cycle of suffering and rebirth.

After Buddha's death, legends of his great deeds and supernatural powers emerged. Stories were told of his heroism in past lives, and speculations arose about his true nature. Some groups viewed him as a historical figure, whereas others placed him in a succession of several Buddhas of the past and a Buddha yet to come. Differing views eventually led to a diversity of Buddhist sects in different countries. Some remained householders who set up Buddha images and established many holy sites that became centers of pilgrimage. Others became monks, living in monastic communities and depending on the laity for food and material support. Many monks became beggars, and in several Southeast Asian countries, they still go on daily alms rounds. They spend their days in rituals, devotions, meditation, study, and preaching. Flowers, incense, and praise are offered to the image of the Buddha. These acts are thought to ensure that the monks will be reborn in one of the heavens or in a better place in life, from which they may be able to attain the goal of enlightenment.

In every society where Buddhism is widespread, people combine Buddhist thought with a native religion, supporting the monks and paying for rituals in the temples. These societies are also organized around other religions, however.

Today, the integration of Buddhism into many cultures has resulted in different interpretations of the way to Buddhahood. Yet we can supposedly reach Nirvana by seeing with complete detachment, by seeing things as they really are without being attached to any theoretical concept or doctrine.

—Eshleman et al., *Sociology: An Introduction,* pp. 356–58

Pay Attention to Visual Information

Social science textbooks include a great deal of visual information in the form of photographs, diagrams, and other graphics. Be sure to "read" these to learn why the author included them and what information about the topic they convey. For example, say to yourself, "Here is a photograph from a _____ book, included in a chapter on _____. It was included because it_____."

Read to Make Practical Applications

In many courses, instructors want students to apply what they learn to everyday, practical situations. Consequently, instructors expect and encourage students to use their reasoning skills to go beyond what is stated in the text and consider practical applications of textbook information. For example, your psychology instructor may ask this question on a midterm exam:

Five-year-old Sammy tells his grandmother that three dinosaurs are hiding in his closet. Knowing this is not true, his grandmother spanks Sammy. Grandmother should be

a. encouraged to be consistent, spanking Sammy whenever he talks about dinosaurs.

b. reminded that children of this age often confuse fantasy and reality.

c. thanked for acting as a good role model for Sammy.

d. told that her authoritarian response will improve his ability to relate to adults.

Or, in your American government class, the following question might appear on an essay exam:

Project the key political issues that will be involved in the next presidential election.

To be prepared for questions such as these, consider the practical applications of what you read. Try to relate each idea to a real-life situation, and, if possible, connect the material to your own experience.

Focus on Large Ideas

Because many social science courses present a great deal of factual information, it is easy to become convinced that the facts are all you need to learn. Actually, factual information is only a starting point, a base from which to approach the real content of a course. Most social science instructors expect you to go beyond facts to analysis—to consider the meaning of facts and details. Many students fail to understand the overriding concepts of their courses because they are too concerned with memorizing information. They fail to ask, "Why do I need to know this? Why is this important? What principle or trend does this illustrate? What is its significance?" Table 12-3 gives examples of details from a course in American history and the more important trends, concepts, or principles they represent.

Be certain you stay focused on major ideas; after you preview a chapter, write a list of key topics and concepts you expect to read about. After you have read about each one, check it off on your list. Before you continue, review what you have learned. After completing an assignment, return again to your list to reestablish what is important and recheck your recall. Restate each idea in your own words; if you can do so, you can be confident that you understand the ideas, rather than just recall the author's words.

TABLE 12-3   Identifying Key Concepts

TOPICS	FACTS	SIGNIFICANCE
The slavery controversy	On May 22, 1856, Representative Brooks from South Carolina approached Senator Sumner of Massachusetts (who had recently given a speech condemning the South for trying to extend slavery) on the floor of the Senate and beat him with a cane until he was near death.	The antagonism between the North and South had become bitter and violent by 1856.
Annexation of territories to the United States	Texas was annexed in 1845. In 1845 and 1846 a great controversy arose over the Oregon territory. The Democrats wanted to make all of the Oregon territory (stretching north above today's border into British Columbia) part of the United States. The British also claimed this land. A war over the territory was barely avoided.	In the late 1840s a belief called *Manifest Destiny* was widespread. People felt it was the destiny of the United States to spread from the Atlantic Ocean to the Pacific Ocean and eventually take over the entire continent.
Industry	Henry Ford perfected the Model T for manufacture in 1914, and by 1924 more than 40,000 workers were working in the first mass-production, assembly-line factory.	This began the trend toward mass production, which led to the second Industrial Revolution.

■ Thought Patterns in the Social Sciences

Four thought patterns that predominate in the social sciences are comparison and contrast, cause and effect, listing, and definition. Table 12-4 describes the uses of each pattern and includes several examples from a specific discipline.

EXERCISE 12-5

Figure 12-1 on page 365 is a chapter outline from a sociology textbook. Read the headings and subheadings and identify the thought pattern of each shaded section. For some headings, more than one pattern may be identified. Refer to Chapter 7 for a review of thought patterns.

EXERCISE 12-6

Form groups of three students, and have each student bring a social science textbook to class. Each group should select one text and, using the table of contents, work together to agree on a list of patterns likely to appear in the first five chapters.

TABLE 12–4   Thought Patterns in the Social Sciences

PATTERN	USES	TOPICAL EXAMPLES
Comparison and contrast	To evaluate two sides of an issue; to compare and contrast theories, groups, behaviors, events	*Anthropology* Limbic and nonlimbic communication Theories of aggression Anatomical comparison: archaic and modern Relative versus chronometric dating methods
Cause and effect	To study behavior and motivation; to examine connections between events, actions, behaviors	*Economics* Price determination Factors affecting individual's demand curve Aggregate effects of taxes Factors influencing consumption and saving
Listing	To present facts, illustrations, or examples; to list research findings	*Sociology* Ways children learn Three sociological research methods Myths about old age Agencies of socialization
Definition	To label and describe behaviors, social systems, laws, cycles, etc.	*Political Science* Coercive power Utilitarian power Capitalism Conservatism

FIGURE 12-1   Chapter Outline

Socialization

Nature Versus Nurture

Becoming Human

The Effects of Social Isolation

Personality Development: A Psychological View

Developing a Concept of Self:

A Sociological Approach

Socialization and the Life Course

Childhood Socialization

Adult Socialization

Resocialization

Major Agents of Socialization

The Family

Schools

Religion

Peers

The Workplace

The Mass Media

Socialization: Future Directions

Box 4.1 Sociological Focus:

Nature Versus Nurture:

The Case of Willie Bosket Jr.

Box 4.2 Applied Sociology:

Resocialization in a Marine Corps Boot Camp

Source: Thompson and Hickey, *Society in Focus: An Introduction to Sociology,* p. 81

■ Adapting Your Study Techniques

Use the following suggestions in adapting your study methods to the social science field:

1. **Schedule several two- to three-hour blocks of time per week for reading, review, and study.** Avoid last-minute cramming. Study that is distributed over several periods is more effective than one marathon session.

2. **Recognize that understanding is not the same as learning and recall.** Do not assume that because you have read an assignment, you have learned it. To ensure learning, use writing to organize the information. Refer to Chapter 9 for specific strategies.

3. **Use the SQ3R system, or your own adaptation of it, to learn the material.** Review this system in Chapter 8. Writing is useful in the recitation step because it allows for greater retention of information through multiple sensory stimulation.

4. **Review frequently.** Review each assignment immediately after you have read it and again the next day. Add periodic reviews to your regular study sessions.

5. **Make connections between topics and chapters.** Each topic is an essential part of the discipline, as is every chapter. Information gained in one chapter should be used and applied in subsequent chapters.

6. **Use the study guide.** Many social science textbooks have a study guide that may be purchased separately. These guides contain useful reviews, sample test questions, and additional practice materials.

7. **Keep a log of total hours studied per week.** The log will help you maintain your motivation and enable you to see how the grades you are earning are related to the amount of time you spend studying.

Test–Taking Tips
Preparing for Exams in the Social Sciences

Many exams you will take in social science courses will be objective: multiple choice, true-false, matching, or fill-in-the-blank. Your task in these types of questions is to recognize correct answers. To prepare for objective exams, use the following suggestions:

1. Attend review classes if your instructor conducts them.

2. **Prepare study sheets.** Organize and summarize important information from your notes and your text on topics you expect the exam to cover.

3. **Use index cards to record factual information that you must learn** (names, dates, definitions, theories, research findings). Record the name, date, name of theory, and so forth on the front of the card, and record what the person is noted for, the event, or the theory itself on the back. Test yourself by reading the front of the card and trying to recall what is on the back. Shuffle the pack of cards so that you do not learn the material in a fixed order.

4. **Review previous exams and quizzes.** Look for patterns of errors, and identify kinds of questions you missed (knowledge or critical thinking), as well as topics that you need to review.

Self-Test Summary

1. What is the primary concern of the social sciences?	The social sciences focus on the study of people, their development, and how they function and interact, as well as human behavior, social relationships, or social systems and the laws or principles that govern them.
2. What are some of the disciplines included in the social sciences?	Disciplines include psychology, anthropology, sociology, political science, geography, history, and economics.
3. What is a theory?	A theory is a set of propositions that explains a certain phenomenon or occurrence.
4. What are some guidelines for reading in the social sciences?	The guidelines for reading research are • identify key terms. • understand theories. • read research reports. • read to make comparisons and connections. • read to make practical applications. • focus on large ideas.
5. What are the guidelines for reading research material?	The guidelines for reading research material are • determine who conducted the research. • identify its purpose. • read the reviews of current research in the field of study. • find out how the research was done. • understand the results. • identify the conclusion. • discover the implications and applications.
6. How can you organize information to make comparisons?	Use comparison charts, outlines, lists, or maps.
7. What are the four thought patterns that predominate in the social sciences?	The patterns are comparison and contrast, cause and effect, listing, and definition.

SOCIOLOGY

Crowd Behavior

J. Ross Eshleman, Barbara J. Cashion, and Laurence A. Basirico

Prereading Questions

1.   What is a crowd?
2.   How is one crowd different from another?

Characteristics of Crowds

1   A **spatially proximate collective** exists when people are geographically close and physically visible to one another. The most common type of spatially proximate collective is the **crowd**, a temporary group of people in face-to-face contact who share a common interest or focus of attention. This common interest may be unexpected and unusual, but it is not necessarily so. Although people in a crowd interact a good deal, the crowd as a whole is organized poorly if at all. According to Turner (1985), crowds have four features that make them a unique area for study: anonymity, suggestibility, contagion, and emotional arousability.

2   Most types of collective behavior involve *anonymity.* People who do not know those around them may behave in ways that they would consider unacceptable if they were alone or with their family or neighbors. During a riot, the anonymity of crowd members makes it easier for people to loot and steal. In a lynch mob, brutal acts can be committed without feelings of shame or responsibility. Whatever the type of crowd, the anonymity of the individuals involved shifts the responsibility to the crowd as a whole.

Crowds exist when many people are in face-to-face contact and share a common interest. Some crowds, such as at a sporting event or outdoor concert, may behave collectively by shouting, clapping, jumping, or waving when the performers engage in a particular activity: a home run or touchdown, a hit song, an emotionally charged speech, and so forth.

3   Because crowds are relatively unstructured and often unpredictable, crowd members are often highly *suggestible*. People who are seeking direction in an uncertain situation are highly responsive to the suggestions of others and become very willing to do what a leader or group of individuals suggests, especially given the crowd's anonymity.

4   The characteristic of *contagion* is closely linked to anonymity and suggestibility. Turner (1985) defines this aspect of crowd behavior as "interactional amplification." As people interact, the crowd's response to the common event or situation increases in intensity. If they are clapping or screaming, their behavior is likely to move others to clap or scream, and contagion increases when people are packed close together. An alert evangelist, comedian, or rock singer will try to get the audience to move close to one another to increase the likelihood of contagion and to encourage the listeners to get caught up in the mood, spirit, and activity of the crowd.

5   A fourth characteristic is *emotional arousal*. Anonymity, suggestibility, and contagion tend to arouse emotions. Inhibitions are forgotten, and people become emotionally charged to act. In some cases, their emotional involvement encourages them to act in uncharacteristic ways. During the Beatles concerts in the early 1960s, for example, teenage girls who were presumably quite conventional most of the time tried to rush on stage and had to be carried away by police. The combination of the four characteristics of crowds makes their behavior extremely volatile and frightening.

6   Although these four aspects of crowd behavior may be seen in almost any crowd, their intensity varies. Some crowds permit greater anonymity than others, and some have higher levels of suggestibility and contagion, yet one or more of these characteristics may not appear at all. The presence or absence of certain crowd features can be used to organize crowds into different categories.

Types of Crowds

7   All crowds are spatially proximate and temporary, and every crowd shares a common focus. However, some crowds are very low in emotional arousal and are highly unstructured, whereas others are quite emotional, aggressive, and even dangerous to one's safety.

8   The literature on collective behavior, following the lead of Herbert Blumer (1939), tends to label the nonemotional, unstructured crowd as a **casual crowd**. People who stop to look at an animated holiday display or who gather to watch a street musician would be of this type. Another type of crowd, sometimes called a **conventional crowd**, is more highly structured and occurs, for example, when spectators gather at a baseball game, attend a concert, or ride on an airplane. Although the participants are generally unknown to one another (anonymous), they have a specific goal or common purpose and are expected to follow established norms and procedures. At symphony concerts, for example, people applaud at the end of the music (an established procedure). When the music is being played, however, they do not run up and down the aisles or call out to a friend at the opposite side of the concert hall (not an established procedure).

9   The . . . crowds that attract the most public attention are called **acting crowds**, the behavior of which is centered around and typifies aroused impulses. The two most dramatic forms of acting crowds are mobs and riots.

10   **Mobs** are groups that are emotionally aroused and ready to engage in violent behavior. They are generally short-lived and highly unstable. Their violent actions often stem from strong dissatisfaction with existing government policies or social circumstances; extreme discontentment with prevailing conditions is used to justify immediate and direct action. Disdainful of regular institutional channels and legal approaches, mobs take matters into their own hands.

11   Most mobs are predisposed to violence before their actions are triggered by a specific event. When feelings of frustration and hostility are widespread, leaders can easily recruit and command members. With aggressive leadership, an angry, frustrated mob in an atmosphere of hostility can be readily motivated to riot, commit lynchings, throw fire-bombs, hang people in effigy, or engage in destructive orgies.

12   Mob violence has erupted in many different circumstances. During the French Revolution of the 1780s and 1790s, angry mobs stormed through Paris, breaking into the Bastille prison for arms and calling for the execution of Louis XVI. In nineteenth-century England, enraged workers burned the factories in which they worked. Lynchings of blacks in the United States for real or imagined offenses continued into the twentieth century, often with little or no opposition from the formal agencies of control—police, courts, and public officials. Although lynch mobs are uncommon today, occasional instances of mob behavior take place over civil rights issues such as busing or housing, during political conventions and rallies, and among student or labor groups angry about perceived injustices. In 1987, for example, mob violence erupted in all-white Forsyth County, Georgia, when a white mob disrupted a march by whites and blacks protesting discriminatory antiblack housing policy.

13   **Riots** are collective actions involving mass violence and mob actions. The targets of their hostility and violence are less specific than those of mobs, and the groups involved are more diffuse. Most riots result from an intense hatred of a particular group with no specific person or property in mind. Destruction, burning, or looting may be indiscriminate, and unfocused anger can lead to violent acts against any object or person who happens to be in the wrong area at the wrong time. Like mobs, rioters take actions into their own hands when they feel that institutional reaction to their concerns about war, poverty, racial injustices, or other problems is inadequate.

—Eshleman et al., *Sociology: An Introduction*, pp. 487–90

Writing About the Reading
CHECKING YOUR VOCABULARY

1. For each of the words listed below, use context; prefixes, roots, and suffixes (see Chapter 3); and/or a dictionary to write a brief definition or synonym of the word as it is used in the reading.

   a. anonymity (para. 1, 2) _____

   b. suggestible (para. 3) _____

   c. contagion (para. 1, 4) _____

   d. arousal (para. 5) _____

   e. evangelist (para. 4) _____

   f. uncharacteristic (para. 5) _____

   g. volatile (para. 5) _____

   h. typifies (para. 9) _____

   i. disdainful (para. 10) _____

   j. channels (para. 10) _____

k. predisposed (para. 11) _____

l. effigy (para. 11) _____

m. orgies (para. 11) _____

n. diffuse (para. 13) _____

o. indiscriminate (para. 13) _____

2. Underline new, specialized terms introduced in the reading.

3. Draw a word map of one of the words in the reading.

CHECKING YOUR COMPREHENSION

1. Identify and explain the four features of a crowd.
2. Name two characteristics that all crowds have in common.
3. Describe the difference between a "casual" crowd and a "conventional" crowd.
4. What are two forms of acting crowds?
5. Describe a mob and give an example of one.
6. How do mobs and riots differ from one another?

THINKING CRITICALLY

1. Explain how school pep rallies make use of the four features of a crowd to engage the spectators.
2. How can we use our knowledge of crowds to prevent crowd violence?
3. Give a specific example of a persuasive leader inciting a crowd to violence.
4. Explain why the right of people to assemble is often the first right restricted by leaders who gain governmental control forcibly.

LEARNING/STUDY STRATEGIES

1. Review the section on "Characteristics of Crowds" by completing the following study chart on features of crowds and how they support unacceptable behaviors by individuals within the crowd.
2. What is the overall thought pattern used in this reading?

FEATURE	SUPPORTS UNACCEPTABLE BEHAVIOR BY:
1.	
2.	
3.	
4.	

ONLINE RESEARCH: CROWD BEHAVIOR*

Sociology, like the other social sciences, has many practical applications. For example, examine these sites on the Internet that describe two different types of crowd management. Then answer the questions that follow.

1. Go to http://crowdsafe.com/taskrpt/chpt1.html to access "Crowd Management," part of a report on managing crowd behavior at public events such as concerts. In the second section, "Crowd Behavior," sociologist Dr. Irving Goldaber is quoted as saying that various "sociological signals" received by people attending an event can influence their behavior. What specific examples of these signals does the report give?
2. Go to http://www.animationartist.com/2002/07_jul/features/digitalcrowds.htm. Read over the first page of the article, "Digital Crowds." Discuss how crowd behavior and management is important to filmmakers and video game creators.

ADDITIONAL PRACTICE

THE SOCIAL SCIENCES ON THE INTERNET

The Internet has numerous resources available for research in the social sciences, including directories and Web guides to help you find material relevant to your studies, journals and databases, references works, and government resources. Here is a list of useful academic Web sites to get you started.

Directories/Web Guides

The Virtual Library: Social Sciences
http://vlib.org/SocialSciences.html

Yahoo! Social Science
http://dir.yahoo.com/Social_Science/

Open Directory Project: Social Sciences
http://dmoz.org/Science/Social_Sciences/

Journals/Indexes/Databases

Social Sciences Electronic Journals
http://www.dialogical.net/socialsciences/journals.html

References

The Internet Public Library: Social Sciences Resources
http://www.ipl.org/ref/RR/static/soc00.00.00.html
http://sosig.esrc.bris.ac.uk/welcome.html

---

*If either of these sites is unavailable, use a search engine to locate a new Web site on the same topic.

Government Resources

National Center for Education Statistics
http://nces.ed.gov/

USGS National Mapping Information
http://mapping.usgs.gov/

Professional Organizations

American Psychological Association
http:www.apa.org

American Sociological Association
http://www.asanet.org

MULTIMEDIA ACTIVITIES

Practice your reading and research skills on the Web.

1. **University of Pennsylvania Museum of Archaeology and Anthropology**

   http://www.upenn.edu/museum/Collections/ourgalleries.html

   Write down some questions about different cultures that you would expect to be answered at this Web site. Include questions that stem from the thought patterns of the social sciences. Then view one of the galleries featured on the Web site and find the answers to your questions. Review the information and write a short essay or teach a friend about what you learned.

2. **American Psychological Society: Psychological Research on the Net**

   http://psych.hanover.edu/Research/exponnet.html

   Take part in some online experiments and contribute to important research. A special September 11 section consists of studies that ask questions about your thoughts, feelings, and actions since the terrorist attacks.

13 Reading in Business

Think About It!

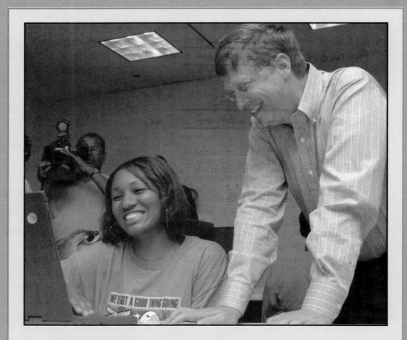

This photo is of Bill Gates working with a student. He is the CEO of Microsoft, is one of the most successful and wealthiest people in business in the world, and has contributed millions of dollars to education. He once said, "Your most unhappy customers are your greatest source of learning."

Bill Gates has a sense of business savvy. He understands that you learn from your mistakes. What else does Bill Gates probably know about running a business? What does the field of business involve? What does it take to be successful in business courses that will lead to a career in business or business-related fields? Read this chapter to find out.

Business is a diverse field that includes business management, information systems, accounting, finance, statistics, retailing, organizational behavior, and corporate strategy. In general, business is concerned with the production and sale of economic goods or services that satisfy people's needs and yield a profit. Because business is a broad field, course work for a degree in business often includes requirements in such related fields as computer science, economics, and communications.

■ Business: A Focus on Organization and Management

Suppose you decided to start a new business that would produce and sell six varieties of gourmet desserts throughout the country. Now suppose you hired 200 employees and that all you told your workers was that their job was to make and sell these desserts. Your business would probably be a dismal failure; none of your employees would know what to do or how to do it. Your business lacked two essential ingredients: organization and management. These ingredients also are a key to your success in getting the most from your business courses.

Organization is a system or structure, and management is a process by which all parts of the system—employees, technology, job responsibilities, and resources—are combined and coordinated. In business courses, you study how businesses are set up and how they are made to operate effectively. These two key aspects, however, encompass numerous other areas: product development, communication, marketing, labor relations, retailing, advertising, financing, banking, accounting, computer systems, legal aspects, and international trade.

Business courses are practical, then. They deal with aspects of creating or operating a business. Business courses are interrelated. Business economics courses use concepts from accounting; marketing courses use concepts from management courses, and so on. Math is also an important part of some business courses. For advice on reading mathematics, see Chapter 15.

Why Study Business?

All of us are in contact with businesses on a daily basis. When you stop for gas, buy a sandwich, or pick up the telephone, you are involved in a business transaction. The world of business surrounds us. Business courses have a number of advantages, as follows:

- **Business courses can make you a savvy, better-informed consumer.** You discover how to make better-informed buying decisions and how to spend your money wisely.
- **Business courses will help you make career decisions.** You will discover a wide range of employment opportunities.

A Business Professor . . .

John Ribezzo, MS,
Professor of Business,
Community College of
Rhode Island

Talks About This Chapter

"I believe this chapter would improve the
performance of weak students, as well as
strong students, because it gives them the
tools necessary to better comprehend material in the area of business. I would describe
the chapter . . . as one that provides students
with techniques and methods they can use to
improve their reading and study skills to perform better in a business curriculum."

Offers Advice on Studying Business

"Whatever your major concentration of study
is, success at the college level is dependent
upon several factors, including attending class
on a regular basis, being prepared for class,
and participating in class discussions.
Students in the area of business should not
only be concerned with subject content, but
should take advantage of the college experience to sharpen their so-called soft skills.
Employers are particularly interested in the
prospective employee's ability to think critically, communicate orally and in writing, work
in teams, lead, and have an overall understanding of how an organization operates."

- **Business courses will help you become a successful employee.** Getting a job is only the first step to a successful career; you must be proficient at your job. By learning how businesses operate, you will be able to contribute effectively to your company.
- **Business courses will help you start your own business.** If you plan to start your own business, business courses will give you the knowledge and skills to make your business a success.

Current Hot Topics in Business

Whenever you take a course, you should always try to discover the trends, issues, and themes that are emphasized. Identifying these "hot topics" will help you predict essay exam questions, choose worthwhile topics for papers and assignments, and make valuable contributions to class discussions.

In business courses, there are at least five current topics:

- **Globalization of Business.** Growing numbers of U.S. companies are doing business with firms in other countries. United States businesses compete in foreign markets, and the number of international trade agreements continues to grow. Consequently, it is important to recognize business as an international venture and understand the role of the United States in the world market.
- **Role of Technology.** As technology continues to develop and change, so must businesses change and adapt to keep pace. The Internet, telecommunications, computers, and robotics all have an impact on business. For

example, growing numbers of businesses have Web sites; increasing numbers of employees are telecommuting (working at home); and small robots are used increasingly in manufacturing. Awareness of technology will keep you on the cutting edge of business growth and change.

- **Importance of Diversity.** Today's workforce consists of individuals from a variety of cultural and ethnic groups. A wider range of interests, social customs, and value systems is represented. Diversity can be a strong advantage for a company by offering a variety of resources and perspectives.
- **Growth and Role of Small Businesses.** Increasingly, small businesses are a major source of employment. A report to the president on the state of small businesses estimates that nearly 71 percent of future employment is likely to come from small businesses. Besides providing employment, small businesses provide competition and are responsible for change and innovation. Many people mistakenly think of businesses as only large corporations. By recognizing the role and importance of small businesses, you will approach business courses with a broadened perspective.
- **Importance of Ethical Decisions and Social Responsibility.** There is an increasing emphasis in business on making ethical decisions and demonstrating social responsibility. Business ethics refers to the application of moral standards to business situations. Ethical issues include fairness and honesty, conflict of interest (between personal and business interests), and communication. Using misleading advertising, falsifying information, taking bribes, and endangering a consumer's health are examples of ethical problems that companies should strive to avoid.
- **Accountability and Open Financial Reporting.** There is an increasing emphasis in business on accountability, internal auditing, and financial disclosure. The Sarbanes-Oxley Act of 2002 specifies accounting and auditing procedures. In light of recent large corporate scandals like Enron, reporting and disclosure guidelines are of growing importance.

■ Specialized Reading Techniques

Business courses often require you to read and work with models, case studies, and specialized graphics. The following sections describe these features and offer strategies for reading each one.

Reading Models

Because business courses focus on organization and management, many texts include models to describe these structures and processes. A model is an overall plan or representation that describes how something is designed, how it functions, or why it occurs.

Models contain general features or characteristics that pertain to many situations. For example, you could construct a model that describes the enrollment/advisement/registration process at your college. It would describe the procedures most students follow from the time they apply for college admission to the time they first attend classes.

Models also may function as explanations of complex processes. For example, you may study models of decision making, information processing, or leadership. These models contain all the pertinent variables, factors, and characteristics that control how something works or explain why it occurs. Diagrams often accompany text descriptions of a model.

The excerpt below and model in Figure A (p. 379) are taken from a business text. They describe how a company develops short-term financial plans. The remainder of the chapter from which this introduction was taken provides detailed information about the process. The excerpt has been annotated to indicate the types of information to look for as you read models.

SHORT-TERM (OPERATING) FINANCIAL PLANS

purpose/function

time frame

key parts

reference to diagram

Short-term (operating) financial plans specify short-term financial actions and the anticipated impact of those actions. These plans most often cover a 1- to 2-year period. Key inputs include the sales forecast and various forms of operating and financial data. Key outputs include a number of operating budgets, the cash budget, and pro forma [document prepared in advance] financial statements. The entire short-term financial planning process is outlined in the flow diagram of Figure A.

summary of model

Short-term financial planning begins with the sales forecast. From it production plans are developed that take into account lead (preparation) times and include estimates of the required types and quantities of raw materials. Using the production plans, the firm can estimate direct labor requirements, factory overhead outlays, and operating expenses. Once these estimates have been made, the firm's pro forma income statement and cash budget can be prepared. With the basic inputs—pro forma income statement, cash budget, fixed asset outlay plan, long-term financing plan, and current period balance sheet—the pro forma balance sheet can finally be developed. Throughout the remainder of this chapter, we will concentrate on the key outputs of the short-term financial planning process: the cash budget, the pro forma income statement, and the pro forma balance sheet.

—Gitman, *Principles of Managerial Finance,* pp. 580–81

When reading and studying models, be sure to:

1. **Find out what the model represents and why it is considered a model.** In the example above, the model explains the short-term financial planning process and factors that affect it. You should also know who developed the model and when it was developed. A model often is named after the person who proposed it.

2. **Determine how the model was derived.** Was it developed through study and research (theory), or by observing and working with the actual process (practice)? (In the previous excerpt, the author does not include information on the development of the model under discussion.)

3. **Analyze the model closely.** Identify each stage or step, and understand the relationship between the parts or steps. If a diagram such as the one shown in the preceding excerpt is not included, try to draw one.

FIGURE A   The Short-Term (Operating) Financial Planning Process

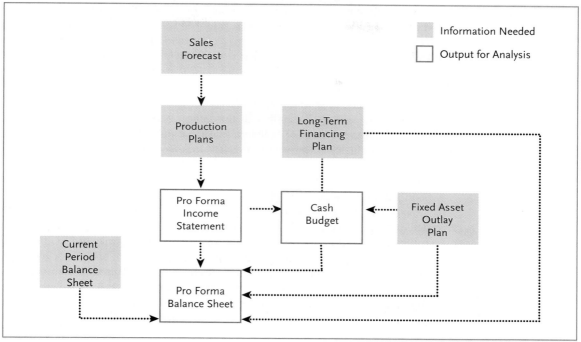

4. **Summarize the model in your own words, including its key features.** This will test your understanding and strengthen your recall.

5. **Examine the model critically.** Does it account for all aspects or variations of the process? What are its limitations?

6. **Determine the usefulness or application of the model.** How and when can you use it? To what practical situations will it apply? The author may suggest applications or this task may be left to the reader.

7. **If more than one model is presented for a given process, focus on their similarities and differences.**

EXERCISE 13-1

The following excerpt presents a model of group collaboration—the process whereby members of a group work together toward a common goal. Study the model and answer the accompanying questions.

CHARACTERISTICS OF GROUP COLLABORATION

Group collaboration has several characteristics. One characteristic is *when* the collaboration takes place and another is *where* it takes place. This section examines these characteristics to provide a basis for understanding workgroup information systems.

Time and Place of Collaboration

Two of the basic characteristics of group collaboration are *time* and *place*—the "when" and "where" of collaboration. Figure B, titled "Time and Place of Group Collaboration," shows these characteristics in two dimensions. If two or more people collaborate, they may do so at the same time or at different times. To work together at the same time, they could be in a room together or talk by telephone. To collaborate at different times, they could leave voice messages, send faxes, use overnight delivery, or send regular mail.

People may also work together at the same place or at different places. They may be in the same room or building, making it possible for them to have direct contact. Alternatively, they may be at widely separated locations, in which case they cannot have direct contact without extensive travel.

The figure shows four possible combinations of these characteristics. People working at the same time and place can collaborate directly. A face-to-face meeting is an example of this type of collaboration. People working at the same time but in different places often use the telephone for collaboration. Conference calls also are common in this situation. When people work at different times but at the same place, they collaborate by leaving messages, either on the telephone or by paper notes. Putting written messages in mailboxes in staff mail rooms is a common way of communicating in this situation. The most complex situation is when people working at different times and places need to collaborate. Voice messages, faxes, overnight deliveries, and regular mail are used in this situation.

FIGURE B   Time and Place of Group Collaboration

Form of Communication

Another way of characterizing group collaboration is by the *form* that the communication between people takes—the "what" of collaboration. Figure C, titled "Forms of Communication in Group Collaboration," summarizes some of the forms taken. Perhaps the most often used form of communication in business is *audio communication;* people talk to each other, either in person or on the telephone. Audio communication is not only what is said, but also how it is said. Tone, inflection, and other characteristics of speech often express information. In addition to live, verbal communication, recorded sound is used in group collaboration. Voice mail, taped sound, and other recorded sound are part of audio communication.

A second form of communication in group collaboration is *visual communication,* specifically sights of people or other real things. When groups meet in person, the

FIGURE C   Forms of Communication in Group Collaboration

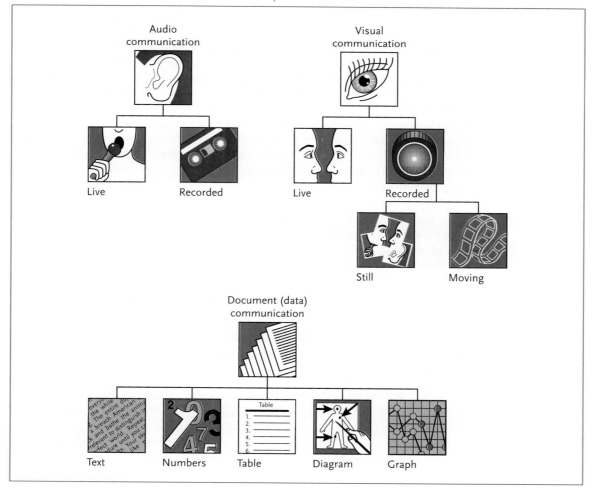

members of the group can see each other. Their facial expressions and body language give visual clues that provide information about what they are saying and thinking. Recorded sights also are used in some collaborative situations. Still pictures or moving images on video tape may be shown to groups for discussion.

A final form of communication used in group collaboration is *document* (or *data*) *communication*. Documents may contain text, numbers, table, diagrams, graphs, and other written representations of information. Examples are a report sent to members of a team, a table of data examined by committee members, a diagram of a design examined by several people, and a graph of data discussed by a group.

—Nickerson, *Business and Information Systems,* pp. 263–65

1. What is the model intended to show?
2. Summarize the process described in the model.
3. Evaluate the model. Does the model account for all possibilities? What are its limitations?
4. Of what practical use is the model? When might you use it?

Reading Case Studies

Case studies often are included in business texts. Case studies are reports of single incidents or evaluations of a particular individual, firm, or transaction. They describe how a particular business is organized or how it manages a particular problem or process. They may be intended to introduce a concept, illustrate a principle, describe a situation, or provoke discussion and evaluation. Case studies also give you insights into and experience with actual problems or situations you may face on the job. In some texts, case studies are referred to as "business profiles" or simply as "cases." Other texts include a short case study, known as a "vignette," that provides a brief insight into a particular problem or issue.

The brief case study that follows appears in a marketing text. As you read it, try to discover why it was included in a chapter titled "Managing the Business Enterprise." The excerpt has been annotated to indicate the kinds of information presented.

This case study describes how a small company, Maine Roasters, has faced competition from Starbucks. The case was included to provide an example of how a small business operates and copes with competition.

When reading a case study, keep the following questions in mind:

1. **What is the problem the case study addresses?**
2. **What alternative solutions are proposed or considered, if any?**
3. **How do the alternatives compare**? What are the pros and cons of each?
4. **What alternative or solution was selected?** What was the outcome?
5. **What is the case study intended to demonstrate?** For example, does it illustrate practical problems? Discuss limitations? Point out advantages or disadvantages? Demonstrate a process? Describe a management strategy? Demonstrate a particular philosophy or approach?

GROUNDS FOR THE DEFENSE

Maine Roasters versus Starbucks

In some ways it's like David and Goliath—a small upstart New England coffee retailer called Maine Roasters going toe-to-toe with Starbucks, www.starbucks.com, the fastest-growing and, arguably, the highest-profile food and beverage company in the United States. To understand the competitive dynamics of this situation, let's first find out how Starbucks became the big kid on the block. It was started in Seattle in 1971 by three coffee aficionados. Their primary business at the time was buying premium coffee beans, roasting them, and then selling the coffee by the pound. The business performed modestly well and soon grew to nine stores, all in the Seattle area. When they thought their business growth had stalled in 1987, the three partners sold Starbucks to a former employee named Howard Schultz. Schultz promptly reoriented, trading in bulk coffee sales for retail coffee sales through the firm's coffee bars.

background about Starbucks

Starbucks' status today

Today Starbucks is not only the country's largest coffee importer and roaster of specialty beans but also the largest specialty coffee bean retailer in the United States. There are more than 2,100 Starbucks locations in the United States. The firm has revenues of over $1.7 billion a year, annual profits of almost $102 million, and a workforce of more than 37,000 employees.

Starbucks in competition with Maine Roasters

Given the enormous marketing and financial muscle that a company like Starbucks brings to the table, imagine how Rand Smith, the owner of Maine Roasters www.maineroasters.qpg.com, a small coffee shop in Portland, Maine, reacted when he heard that the coffee Goliah was coming to town. "It's Maine versus the national giant," said Smith, who decided to load whatever slingshot he could find.

Maine Roasters' strategy

Smith's strategy was grounded in the passion and loyalty that exist among Maine residents for the sanctity of their home state. He has mounted a finely tuned plan for portraying Starbucks as a big bully from the "outside" and his own upstart operation as the homespun underdog. To promote this image, every morning he dispatches a team of his employees to stand outside the Starbucks restaurant closest to his own store to pass out chocolate drops and to encourage Starbucks customers to "Support a Maine-owned-and-operated company." So far, his efforts are paying off. The local paper, for example, has editorialized against corporate heavyweights, community groups have picketed Starbucks, and there has even been a spate of vandalism against Starbucks, usually involving broken store windows. Smith does not condone such tactics, but he no doubt privately sees each stone being thrown through a Starbucks window as a metaphor for the stone with which David felled Goliath in an earlier time.

local support

Outcome

So far, Maine Roasters is holding its own in its hometown of Portland, Maine. Rand Smith's strategy of pitching his small company as a David to Starbucks' Goliath has attracted considerable local sympathy. But Smith faces some other problems, too. For one thing, even as he pitches his business as a local, down-home operation, his original business plan called for more than 30 stores spread throughout New England. (As of yet, only a handful have been opened.) Smith openly acknowledges the inherent contradiction in his portrayal of Starbucks and his own vision. He also sees the day when he might very well be interested in selling his company—and thinks Starbucks might be

Additional problem

Starbucks'
effect
on sales
the most logical buyer. In an especially ironic twist, he actually credits Starbucks with boosting sales at his coffee shops by educating consumers about specialty coffees and, thus, broadening the local market.

—Ebert and Griffen, *Business Essentials,* pp. 114–15, 134–35

EXERCISE 13-2   *Read the following brief case study taken from a business textbook chapter titled "An Overview of Marketing," and answer the questions that follow.*

CAMPBELL SOUP SERVES UP VARIETY

Over 120 years ago, the Campbell Soup Company introduced canned condensed soup and gave the world its first convenience food. Since then, those well-known red and white labels and the sigh "Mmmm, mmmm, good" have become symbols of American culture. However, today's increasingly health-conscious consumers often spurn canned soup in favor of those made with fresh ingredients. Although sales of the popular brand total $1.1 billion, earning the line 48.9 percent of the canned soup market, Campbell faces declining domestic sales. Turning to global markets, the company's executives hope that by the year 2000, more than half of the firm's profits will come from sales outside the United States.

Experts caution that strong cultural and regional tastes and preferences make food more difficult to translate to foreign markets than soda or laundry detergent. The editor of *Food and Drink Daily* recently stressed the importance of recognizing the unique characteristics of individual global market segments. Just because Americans love to ladle out clam chowder and tomato soup by the bowl full doesn't mean those same flavors appeal to customers around the world. Marketers at Campbell know that demographics, lifestyle, and geography influence customer choices, with diet especially sensitive to local fancies. To avoid potential pitfalls that differences often create, Campbell conducts extensive research in specific consumer segments before generating and marketing brands.

All over the globe, Campbell's research and taste tests are resulting in new, locally pleasing recipes. In Argentina, consumers don't take to the enduring American favorite, chicken noodle soup, but they do like split pea with ham. Emphasizing *Sopa de Campbell's* fresh ingredients, regional ads proclaim it "the real soup." Polish soup lovers, who eat an average of five bowls each week, can choose from eight varieties of Campbell's *zupa,* including *flaki*—tripe soup spiced with lots of pepper. To please Mexican palates, Campbell came up with hot and spicy Cream of Chile Poblano.

To become a major player in the global market, Campbell will face stiff competition. British consumers, for example, have known and preferred Heinz canned soup for many years. To attract more British shoppers, Campbell is creating new products developed specifically to meet English tastes. To expand its Japanese distribution from Tokyo and Osaka to include all of Japan, the soupmaker recently entered a joint venture with Nakano Vinegar Company of Japan.

Is the world ready for Campbell's soup? The company's CEO believes the answer is a resounding yes. His considerable international experience—as a former marketing executive with Colgate-Palmolive in South Africa and with Parke-Davis in Hong Kong—tells him that responding to consumer preferences leads to increased sales.

—Pride et al., *Business,* pp. 386–87

1. What is the problem the case study addresses?
2. What solution did Campell pursue?
3. What is this case study intended to demonstrate about global marketing?
4. What does this study tell you about the problems of global marketing?
5. What factors influence consumer choice of soups?

Graphics: Reading Organization Charts

Because the focus in the field of business is on organization and process, business texts frequently include graphs, charts, and tables to synthesize and/or summarize text material that describes those structures and processes. Chapter 10 offers general techniques for reading each of these graphic aids.

Particularly common in the field of business is the organization chart. Organization charts often are used to reflect structure or to define relationships; they may, for example, show levels of responsibility, roles, or functions. The chart shown in Figure 13-1 on page 386 describes the organization of a corporation, emphasizing its financial structure.

Organization charts also may be used to describe group behaviors or define employee responsibilities. The impact of decisions or marketing strategies, and the classification of markets, also may be shown on an organization chart.

When reading organization charts, keep in mind the following tips:

1. **Read the text that accompanies the chart.** It should establish the context and provide details about the chart.

2. **Read the caption or title of the chart.** Note the key, abbreviations, or coding.

3. **Study the chart carefully.** Determine how the chart is organized. Charts often use a vertical or horizontal structure, moving from top to bottom or left to right in diminishing degrees of authority, importance, or responsibility. In Figure 13-1, the chart is organized vertically, with the positions of highest authority at the top.

4. **Decide how the items are related.** In Figure 13-1, each position on the same horizontal line is of equal importance.

5. **Determine what pattern, principle, or concept the chart describes.** Figure 13-1 describes the financial functions within a corporation.

EXERCISE 13-3   *Study the organization chart shown in Figure 13-2 on page 387, and answer the questions that follow.*

1. What is the chart intended to show?
2. Describe how the chart is organized and how the items are related.

EXERCISE 13-4   *Construct an organization chart that describes the structure of an organization (college, church, club, or business) with which you are familiar.*

Graphics: Reading Flowcharts

A flowchart is a specialized diagram that shows how a process or procedure works. Lines or arrows are used to show the direction (route or routes) through

FIGURE 13-1   Organization Chart

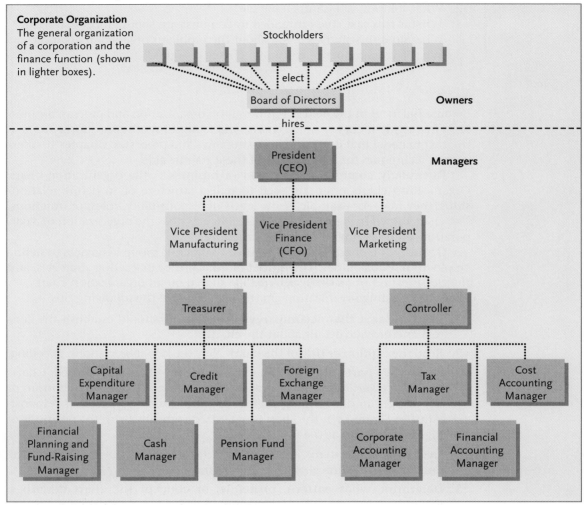

Corporate Organization
The general organization of a corporation and the finance function (shown in lighter boxes).

Stockholders

elect

Board of Directors   **Owners**

hires

President (CEO)   **Managers**

Vice President Manufacturing   Vice President Finance (CFO)   Vice President Marketing

Treasurer   Controller

Capital Expenditure Manager   Credit Manager   Foreign Exchange Manager   Tax Manager   Cost Accounting Manager

Financial Planning and Fund-Raising Manager   Cash Manager   Pension Fund Manager   Corporate Accounting Manager   Financial Accounting Manager

SOURCE: Gitman, *Principles of Managerial Finance,* p. 8

the procedure. Various shapes (boxes, circles, rectangles) enclose what is done at each stage or step. You could, for example, draw a flowchart to describe how to apply for and obtain a student loan or how to locate a malfunction in your car's electrical system.

A sample flowchart, taken from a business and information systems text, is shown in Figure 13-3 (p. 388); it describes the information flow related to sales.

To read flowcharts effectively, use the following suggestions:

1. **Figure out what process the flowchart illustrates.** Figure 13-3 shows the process by which information flows from a sale.

2. **Next, follow the arrows, and read each step in the chart.**

FIGURE 13-2   Organization Chart

The Divisional Design

SOURCE: Van Fleet, *Contemporary Management,* p. 251

3. **When you have finished, summarize the process in your own words.** For example, you might write "When a customer places an order, the order information is transmitted to the sales department. The sales department sends sales information to the shipping department; the shipping department sends shipping information to the billing department, which sends billing information to the customer and to the accounts receivable department. Customer payment is sent to the accounts receivable department, which also sends reminders to customers." Then try to draw the chart from memory without referring to the text. Compare your drawing with the chart, and note any discrepancies.

EXERCISE 13-5   *The flowchart shown in Figure 13-4 (p. 389), taken from a business text, describes a process for human resource planning. Study the chart and then, without referring to it, list the steps or sketch your own flowchart.*

■ Thought Patterns in Business

The three most common thought patterns you will find in business courses are classification, process, and enumeration, although others may be used as well. Refer to Chapter 7 for a complete discussion of these patterns.

FIGURE 13–3   Sample Flowchart

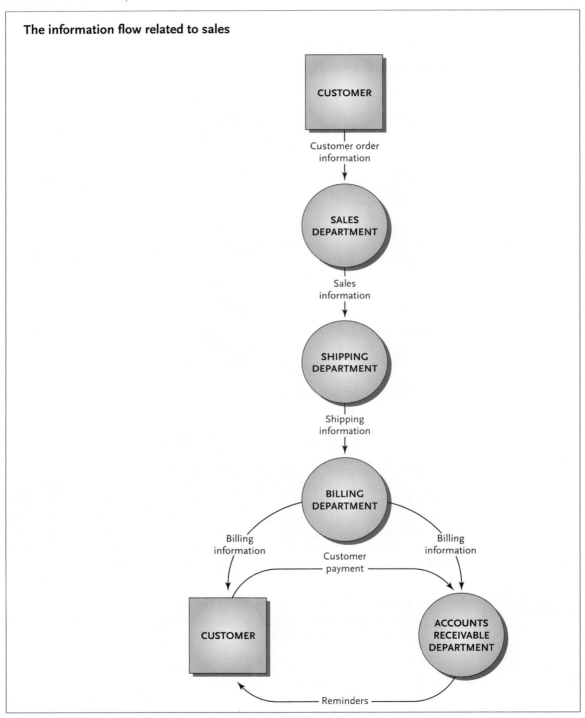

The information flow related to sales

CUSTOMER

Customer order
information

SALES
DEPARTMENT

Sales
information

SHIPPING
DEPARTMENT

Shipping
information

BILLING
DEPARTMENT

Billing
information

Customer
payment

Billing
information

CUSTOMER

ACCOUNTS
RECEIVABLE
DEPARTMENT

Reminders

Sᴏᴜʀᴄᴇ: Nickerson, *Business and Information Systems*, p. 40

FIGURE 13-4   Flowchart

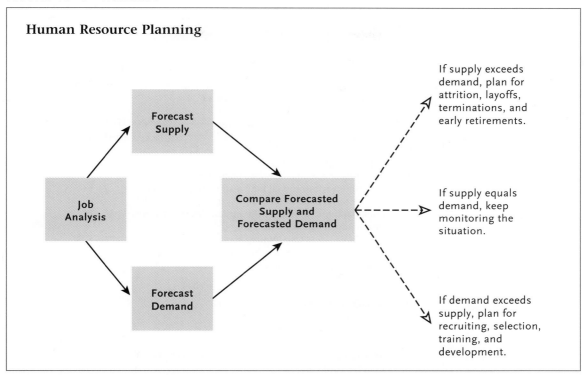

Human Resource Planning

Forecast Supply

Job Analysis

Compare Forecasted Supply and Forecasted Demand

Forecast Demand

If supply exceeds demand, plan for attrition, layoffs, terminations, and early retirements.

If supply equals demand, keep monitoring the situation.

If demand exceeds supply, plan for recruiting, selection, training, and development.

SOURCE: Van Fleet, *Contemporary Management,* p. 270

Classification—subdividing a topic into its parts—is commonly encountered because it is an effective means of describing the components of management. Process—the study of how events occur—is used frequently because of the focus on *how* a business operates and is managed. Enumeration, or listing, is a commonly used pattern because much information in the business field is descriptive: listings of characteristics, factors, principles, and theories that affect a business's organization and management. A sample page from the table of contents of a business marketing text is shown in Figure 13-5 (p. 390). The figure is marked to indicate the patterns you should anticipate. As you can see, process, enumeration, and classification patterns appear, as well as definition and comparison–contrast.

■ Adapting Your Study Techniques

Because the field of business is diverse and includes courses in a wide range of topics, it is especially important to adapt your study techniques to suit each course you are taking. What follows are a few suggestions for handling your course load:

FIGURE 13-5   Table of Contents

SOURCE: Nickerson, *Business and Information Systems,* p. xvii

1. **Begin each class by analyzing course content.** Study course objectives, pay close attention to the course syllabus, and analyze your textbook's preface and individual chapter learning objectives for additional clues. Then select reading and study strategies for each course. Figure out what types of reading are required and what level of recall is demanded; then identify appropriate reading strategies to use. Refer to Chapter 2 for a discussion of adjusting your reading rate. Also select appropriate learning and review strategies and decide how writing could help you with each course. (Refer to Chapter 9 for a review of various strategies.)

2. **Take time to shift gears.** It is important to "shift gears" as you move from studying one course to studying another. Do this by taking a 10- to 15-minute break between study periods. As you begin working on the next course, spend a minute or two focusing your attention on it. You can do this easily by reviewing a previous assignment, your last set of lecture notes, or the last homework assignment you completed. Finally, preview

your current assignment, define your goals, and set a time limit to complete the task. Monitor your comprehension as you work, by using the suggestions in Chapter 1.

3. **Use available text supplements.** Some business texts have accompanying study guides, problem sets, exercise books, or simulations. If they are recommended by your instructor, they will guide you in applying chapter content. These guides also will introduce you to the type of questions you may be asked on exams. Some of these materials are available on computer diskettes or CDs as well as in printed form.

4. **Use chapter aids.** Business textbook chapters typically contain numerous features that supplement and enhance basic chapter content. These include learning objectives, lists of keywords, chapter outlines, special-interest material, summaries, and review exercises. These features are intended to make the chapter easier to understand, study, and learn. Chapter 8 describes how to use each of these features effectively.

5. **Learn formulas and problem-solving strategies.** Some courses, such as accounting, investment, and finance, rely heavily on learning formulas and solving problems. For reading and study strategies useful in these courses, refer to Chapter 15, "Reading Mathematics."

Test-Taking Tips
Objective Exams

Exams in business are often objective. Refer to the test-taking tips in Chapter 12 for suggestions on preparing for objective exams. When taking exams, keep the following suggestions in mind:

1. **Be sure to arrive at the exam on time.** Sit in the front of the room; you will avoid distractions and be able to concentrate more easily.

2. **Preread the exam.** Look through the whole exam before beginning. Then plan your time: decide how much time to spend on each part.

3. **Read the directions carefully.**

4. **Leave nothing blank.** Guess if you are not sure of an answer; circle the question number so you can return to it later if you have time.

5. **Be sure to read all choices before answering a multiple-choice question.** Often, the directions require you to select the "best" choice.

6. **If you are uncertain about a multiple-choice item, eliminate obviously wrong choices.** Then analyze those that remain. When two choices seem similar, analyze how they differ.

7. **Express similar or confusing choices in your own words.** Often, this process will help you discover the right answer.

Self-Test Summary

1. What, in general, is the focus of business courses?	Business courses focus on all aspects of creating and operating a business.
2. What are some of the diverse areas included in the broad field of business?	Areas include business management, information systems, accounting, finance, statistics, retailing, advertising, organizational behavior, and corporate strategy.
3. Identify some current "hot topics" or trends in business.	Current hot topics include globalization, the role of technology, diversity, the growth and role of small business, and the importance of ethical decisions and social responsibility in business.
4. In business, what is meant by a "model"?	A model is an overall plan or representation that describes how something is designed, how it functions, or why it occurs.
5. What is a case study? What questions should you ask when reading and evaluating a case study?	A case study is a report of a single company, firm, or individual's business problem, transaction, profit, or decision-making. The steps in reading and evaluating a case study are • identify the problem. • determine alternative solutions. • analyze and compare alternatives. • evaluate the alternative selected. • determine what the case study is intended to demonstrate.
6. What is the purpose of an organizational chart?	An organizational chart reflects structure or defines relationships.
7. What is the purpose of a flowchart?	A flowchart shows how a process or procedure works.
8. What three thought patterns predominate in business texts? Define each.	The three thought patterns are • classification: subdividing a topic into its parts. • process: the study of how events occur. • enumeration: listing of information, such as business characteristics, factors, principles, and theories.

MARKETING

Marketing Throughout the Product Life Cycle

Michael R. Solomon and Elnora W. Stuart

Prereading Questions

1. What is a product life cycle?
2. What factors influence how long a product's life cycle will last?

1   The zipper is an example of a humble, low-tech product that has managed to live an exceptionally long life. Invented in the 1800s, the zipper was not used in men's clothing until the 1930s. These "hookless fasteners," as they were once called, were originally intended for use on high-buttoned shoes. It took time to be used in men's trousers because competitors argued that this "newfangled gadget" could result in serious injuries (ouch!). In 1936 the Prince of Wales adopted the zipper and was the first monarch to "sit on a throne bezippered."

product life cycle
Concept that explains how products go through four distinct stages from birth to death: introduction, growth, maturity, and decline.

2   In fact, many products have very long lives. The **product life cycle** is a useful way to explain how product features change over the life of a product. We have talked about how marketers go about introducing new products, but launching a product is only the beginning. Product marketing strategies must evolve and change as they continue through the product life cycle.

3   The concept of the product life cycle does not relate to a single brand but to the generic product. Thus, we talk about the life cycle of personal computers, not Compaq computers, of automobiles, not Mustangs. Some individual brands may have short life expectancies. Who remembers the Nash car, or Evening in Paris perfume? Others seem almost immortal: A Boston Consulting Group study found that 27 or 30 brands that were number one in 1930 are still number one today. These brands include Ivory soap, Campbell's soup, and Gold Medal flour.

The Introduction Stage

introduction
The first stage of the product life cycle in which slow growth follows the introduction of a new product in the marketplace.

4   We can divide the life of a product into four separate stages. The first stage of the product life cycle, shown in Figure A (p. 394), is **introduction** when customers get their first chance to purchase the good or service. During this early stage, a single company usually produces the product. If the product is accepted and profitable, competitors will follow with their own versions.

5   During the introduction stage, the goal is to get first-time buyers to try the product. Sales (hopefully) increase at a steady but slow pace. Also evident in Figure A, the company does not make a profit during this stage. Why? Two reasons: research and development (R&D) costs and heavy spending for advertising and other promotional costs.

6   During the introduction stage, pricing may be high to recover the research and development costs (demand permitting) or low to attract large numbers of consumers. For example, the Panasonic digital Palmcorder has a suggested retail price that's about

FIGURE A   The Product Life Cycle

double that of Panasonic's nondigital Palmcorders and is designed to appeal to consumers who are willing to pay dearly for the latest technological advances. The high cost helps Panasonic recover its R&D costs.

7   How long does the introduction stage last? How long the introduction stage lasts depends on a number of factors, including marketplace acceptance and producer willingness to support the product during its start-up. In the case of the microwave, sales in countries such as Japan were much stronger, which supported the product through its long introduction stage.

8   Not all products make it past the introduction stage. For a new product to be successful, consumers must first know about it. Then they must believe that the product is something they need. Thus, marketing during this stage often focuses on informing consumers about the product, how to use it, and its benefits. Overall, 38 percent of all new products fail.

9   One of the most noted examples of products that never got past the introduction stage is the Ford Edsel automobile. Introduced in 1957 and named after the only son of Ford's founder, the Edsel was designed to compete with such cars as the Chrysler New Yorker. It boasted high horsepower, tail fins, three-tone paint jobs, wraparound windshields, a "horsecollar" grille, and a push-button gearshift. The problem was that consumers didn't like the Edsel (many considered it just plain ugly) and only 110,847 Edsels were made before Ford abandoned the car, making the word *Edsel* synonymous with failure.

growth stage
The second stage in the product life cycle during which the product is accepted and sales rapidly increase.

The Growth Stage

10   The second stage in the product life cycle, the **growth stage**, sees a rapid increase in sales while profits increase and peak. Marketing's goal here is to encourage brand loyalty by

convincing the market that this brand is superior to others in the categroy. In this stage marketing strategies may include the introduction of product variations to attract market segments and grow market share. When competitors appear, markets must use heavy advertising and other types of promotion. Price competition may develop, driving profits down. Some firms may seek to capture a particular segment of the market by positioning their product to appeal to a certain group.

The Maturity Stage

maturity stage
The third and longest stage in the product life cycle in which sales peak and profit margins narrow.

11 The **maturity stage** of the product life cycle is usually the longest. Sales peak and then begin to level off and even decline while profit margins narrow. Competition grows intense when remaining competitors fight for a piece of a shrinking pie. Because most customers have already accepted the product, sales are often to replace a "worn-out" item or to take advantage of product improvements. For example, almost everyone owns a television so companies typically sell new TVs when consumers' sets die. During the maturity stage, firms will try to sell their product through all suitable retailers because product availability is crucial in a very competitive market. Consumers will not go far to find one brand when others are closer at hand.

12 To remain competitive and maintain market share during the maturity stage, firms may tinker with the marketing mix. Competitors may add new "bells and whistles" to their products' features, as when producers of potato chips and other snack foods modify their products. When consumers turned from high-fat snacks, chip makers gave them baked, "low-fat" products. In 1998 Frito-Lay introduced its WOW! Line of fat-free chips. And television manufacturers are hoping to invigorate sales with new flat-screen TVs.

13 Attracting new users of the product is another strategy used in the maturity stage. Market development, means introducing an existing product to a market that doesn't currently use it. Many U.S. firms are finding new markets in Eastern Europe for products whose domestic sales are lagging. For example, in the early 1990s, when IBM personal computers lost popularity in the United States, the company was able to capture a large percentage of the exploding Eastern European computer market.

The Decline Stage

decline stage
The final stage in the product life cycle in which sales decrease as customer needs change.

14 The **decline stage** of the product life cycle is characterized by a decrease in product category sales. Often this is because new technology has made the product obsolete, as when computers caused the decline of the typewriter. Although a single firm may still be profitable, the market as a whole begins to shrink, profits decline, and suppliers pull out. In this stage, there are usually many competitors with no one having a distinct advantage.

15 A firm's major product decision in the decline stage is whether or not to keep the product. Once the product is no longer profitable, it drains resources from the firm—resources that could help develop new products. If the decision is to drop the product, elimination may be handled in two ways: phase it out by cutting production in stages and letting existing stocks run out, or simply drop the product immediately. If the established market leader anticipates that there will be some residual demand for the product for a long time, it may make sense to keep the product on the market. The idea is to sell a limited quantity of the product with little or no support from sales, merchandising, advertising, and distribution and just let it "wither on the vine." Some classic products have been able to hang in there with little or no marketing support, such as the Pilot Stapler, which has been on the market for 70 years.

—Solomon and Stuart, *Marketing: Real People, Real Choices,* pp. 266–69

Writing About the Reading
CHECKING YOUR VOCABULARY

1. For each of the words listed below, use context; prefixes, roots, and suffixes (see Chapter 3); and/or a dictionary to write a brief definition or synonym for the word as it is used in the reading.

   a. competitors (para. 1) _____

   b. generic (para. 3) _____

   c. expectancies (para. 3) _____

   d. profitable (para. 4) _____

   e. synonymous (para. 9) _____

   f. variations (para. 10) _____

   g. elimination (para. 15) _____

   h. residual (para. 15) _____

2. Underline new, specialized terms introduced in the reading (see Chapter 3).

3. Draw a word map of one of the words in the reading.

CHECKING YOUR COMPREHENSION

1. Why is a product life cycle considered only for generic products?
2. Name the four stages of a product life cycle.
3. Why doesn't the company make a profit during the introductory stage?
4. What two things need to happen for consumers to buy a product during the introductory stage?
5. What happens when price competition develops during the growth stage?
6. Why do most customers make purchases during the maturity stage?
7. If a product is phased out in the decline stage, what methods of elimination are used?
8. What is market development?

THINKING CRITICALLY

1. Give an example of a product you feel will be phased out and why.
2. If you wanted to increase the life cycle of a product, what steps could you take?
3. Give an example of a product not discussed in the selection that did not make it past the introductory stage. Why do you think this happened?
4. What kids of products would you expect to have long life cycles and why?
5. Name a product that is a favorite of yours that has had a long life cycle with little or no advertising support. Why do you think this product has lasted?

LEARNING/STUDY STRATEGY

Draw a chart that summarizes the factors that influence product life span. Use the following format.

Stage	Definition	Goal	Profits/Sales
1. Introduction			
2. Growth			
3. Maturity			
4. Decline			

ONLINE RESEARCH: PRODUCT LIFE CYCLE*

A large part of pushing a product through its life cycle is advertising. Visit these sites on the Internet that provide more information on advertising, and answer the questions that follow.

1. Explore the timeline from Advertising Age (http://www.adage.com/century/TIMELINE/). What are the different techniques used in advertising? How do these techniques reflect the stages of a product's life cyle?
2. Advertising has become almost part of our daily existence. Read the scenarios at BadAds.org (http://www.badads.org/misc.shtml). Make a list of all the places you see advertising, and indicate whether you think these places are appropriate.
3. Read about product positioning at AdCracker.com (http://www.adcracker.com/position/). Make a list of memorable slogans. Have any of these influenced your buying habits?

ADDITIONAL PRACTICE

BUSINESS ON THE INTERNET

The Internet has numerous resources available for research in the field of business, including directories and Web guides to help you find material relevant to your studies, journals and databases, references works, and government resources. Here is a list of useful Web sites to get you started.

Directories/Web Guides

Researching Companies Online
http://www.learnwebskills.com/company/index.html

*If either of these sites is unavailable, use a search engine to locate a new Web site on the same topic.

Yahoo! Business and Economy
http://dir.yahoo.com/business_and_economy/

Journals/Indexes/Databases

The Internet Public Library: Business and Economics Serials
http://www.ipl.org/cgi-bin/reading/serials.out.pl?ty=long&id=bus00.00.00

Web-Ec List of Economics Journals
http://netec.wustl.edu/WebEc/journals.html

Business News and Electronic Journals
http://www.lib.washington.edu/subject/busecon/busnews/

References

Business Statistics
http://www.lib.washington.edu/subject/BusinessStats/

Hoover's Online
http://www.hoovers.com

Government Resources

U.S. Securities and Exchange Commission
http://www.sec.gov/

Small Business Administration
http://www.sba.gov/

MULTIMEDIA ACTIVITIES

Practice your reading and research skills on the Web.

1. **2000 State Occupational Employment and Wage Estimates**
   http://stats.bls.gov/oes/2000/oessrcst.htm

   The U.S. Bureau of Labor Statistics maintains a large site containing a great deal of information. Explore this section by picking a state and then an occupation category. View salary data for that occupation. Try comparing the data from different states. How can this information be useful?

2. **Researching Philanthropy—Top 100 U.S. Foundations by Total Giving**
   http://fdncenter.org/research/trends_analysis/top100giving.html

   Examine this chart compiled by the Foundation Center. Are you familiar with many of these organizations? What conclusions can you draw from this information? Find out more about a few of the foundations by following the links to their home pages. How much more information can you discover about their activities?

CHAPTER

14

Reading in the Humanities and Arts

LEARNING OBJECTIVES

- ◆ To learn specialized reading techniques for literature

- ◆ To develop an approach to studying visual arts

- ◆ To learn to read and use criticism

- ◆ To identify predominant thought patterns

- ◆ To adapt your learning skills for the humanities and arts

Think About It!

This is a photograph taken in the Louvre Museum in Paris which houses many famous paintings and sculpture. Why are the paintings here famous and valuable? Why are other paintings and sculpture less valuable? Why are others sold at garage sales for a few dollars? What makes one novel, poem, or short story qualify as literature, while others do not? These are questions that you will examine as you study the humanities and arts.

The humanities and the arts are areas of knowledge concerned with human thought and ideas and their creative expression in written or visual form. They deal with large, global questions such as "What is worthwhile in life?" "What is moral?" "What is beautiful?" This chapter will consider two major branches of study: literature and the visual arts.

A Humanities Professor . . .

Patrick Mathias, MA,
Professor of English, Itasca
Community College

but are forced to take humanities courses."

Talks About This Chapter

"I would describe this chapter as an excellent prep chapter for those just starting in the humanities, those who are less prepared for college lit. courses, and those strong college students who aren't humanities minded

Offers Advice for Humanities Courses

"I've found it very useful to use the Internet to do a quick bio [biography] search of the author. Sometimes it yields insights into the life of the writer, time frame, culture, etc., that really help get a grip on the piece."

■ Literature: A Focus on Ideas

Literature focuses on the search for reasons, values, and interpretation in all areas of human interest and experience. In literature classes, you will examine numerous literary works and will discuss and write about their value and meaning. Literature courses, then, concentrate on the analysis, subjective evaluation, and interpretation of ideas expressed through literary, philosophical, or artistic works. At first, literature courses may seem easier than other courses because most emphasize interpretation rather than factual recall. However, literature courses are demanding: they require critical reading, analysis, and evaluation.

Why Study Literature?

Literature describes human experience. It is a creative record of the thoughts, feelings, emotions, or experiences of other people. By reading literature, you can learn about yourself and understand both painful and joyful experiences without actually going though them yourself. For example, you can read a poem about the birth of a child and come to understand the range of feelings parents share, even though you may not be a parent. In other words, literature allows you to live vicariously, sharing the lives of others without physical participation.

■ Reading and Analyzing Literature

Literature includes poetry, drama, essays, short stories, and novels. Each is a literary form, or *genre,* through which a writer shares his or her view of the world and of humanity. The focus on reading any form of literature is interpretation.

Your goal is to discover what the writer means. You are looking for a statement or message the writer is making about an issue, problem, attitude, or feeling. Use the following suggestions to guide your reading of literature:

- **Read slowly and carefully.** Literature uses language in unique ways that require interpretation and reaction. Consequently, you must read carefully and slowly, paying attention to numerous language features that provide clues to meaning. For example, observe word choice, syntax, and the order and arrangement of ideas.
- **Plan on reading the work several times.** Unlike some other types of material, a single reading is *not* sufficient to understand some literary works adequately. During the first reading, try to become familiar with the work and its literal meaning. On the second and subsequent readings, focus on the writer's message, on the significance of the work, and on literary concerns such as the use of language.
- **Ask questions to establish the literal meaning first; then work on interpretation.** In order to interpret and analyze a literary work, first try to understand it on a literal, or factual, level. An effective approach to reading literature is first to establish "who did what, when, and where." Then ask why the writer wrote the piece and determine the message the writer is conveying.

Who?	Identify the subject or topic.
What is happening?	Describe the basic plot or sequence of events.
When/Where?	Establish the scene, setting, or context (for essays).
Why?	Why did the author write this?
Message?	What is the message the author is conveying and what is its significance?

This approach is shown in the following poem, "Mirror," written by Sylvia Plath.

MIRROR
Sylvia Plath

I am silver and exact. I have no preconceptions.
Whatever I see I swallow immediately
Just as it is, unmisted by love or dislike.
I am not cruel, only truthful—
The eye of a little god, four-cornered.
Most of the time I meditate on the opposite wall.
It is pink, with speckles. I have looked at it so long
I think it is a part of my heart. But it flickers.
Faces and darkness separate us over and over.
Now I am a lake. A woman bends over me,
Searching my reaches for what she really is.

Then she turns to those liars, the candles or the moon.
I see her back, and reflect it faithfully.
She rewards me with tears and an agitation of hands.
I am important to her. She comes and goes.
Each morning it is her face that replaces the darkness.
In me she has drowned a young girl, and in me an old woman
Rises toward her day after day, like a terrible fish.

—*Crossing the Water* by Sylvia Plath

QUESTIONS	RESPONSES
Who or What?	A mirror
What is happening?	Plath describes what the mirror reflects.
When/Where?	The mirror is hanging on a wall facing another wall.
Why?	Plath is using the mirror to comment on life and peoples' desire to know how they appear to others or to see their true selves.
Message?	The mirror is exact, accurate, and truthful. Life, in contrast, is affected, untruthful, and cruel.

1. **Annotate as you read.** To understand the message, jot down your reactions, hunches, insights, feelings, and questions. Mark or underline words, sentences, or sections you feel are important statements, and words and phrases that provide clues to meaning. A sample annotation follows.

MIRROR

Sylvia Plath

consumes — I am silver and exact. I have no <u>preconceptions.</u> — *open—clear view*
reality — Whatever I see I (swallow) immediately
(Just as it is) (unmisted by love or dislike.) — *unemotional, untainted*
I am <u>not cruel,</u> only <u>truthful</u> — *all*
The eye of a little (god,) four-cornered. — *mirror is godlike—all knowing*
reflecting — Most of the time I meditate on the opposite wall.
shows truth (It is pink, with speckles. I have looked at it so long
whatever it is — I think it is a part of my heart. But it flickers.
deep, reflective — Faces and darkness separate us over and over.) *obstacles of life*
Now I am a (lake.) A woman bends over me, *searching for truth*
<u>Searching my reaches for what she really is.</u> — *about herself*
Then she turns to those <u>liars,</u> the (candles or the moon.) *deceptive, not faithful*
not usually thought — I see her back, and <u>reflect it faithfully.</u>
of as rewards — She rewards me with (tears and an agitation of hands.)
I am important to her. She comes and goes.) *she comes and goes through reality*
Each morning it is her face that replaces the darkness.
inescapable — In me she has drowned a young girl, and in me an old woman) *mirror holds the past*
reality of aging — Rises toward (her) day after day, like a terrible fish.

2. **Identify themes and patterns.** After you have read and annotated, the next step is to study your annotations, looking for themes and patterns. Try to discover how ideas work together to suggest themes. Themes are large or universal topics or subjects that are important to nearly everyone. A study of the Plath poem and annotations indicates that her theme is the realities of life. Possible themes in literature are

- questions, issues, problems raised by the story: moral, political, philosophical, religious.
- abstract ideas: love, death, heroism, escapism, honor.
- conflicts: appearance versus reality, freedom versus restraint, poverty versus wealth, men against women, humans against society, humans versus nature.
- common literary topics: self-realization, inescapability of death, fall from innocence, search for the meaning of life.

EXERCISE 14-1

Refer to the multilevel thinking skills discussed in Chapter 1 and predict exam questions that might be asked about the Plath poem. Compare your questions with those of another student.

Understanding the Language of Literature

Literature is unique in its extensive use of descriptive, connotative, and figurative language to express images, attitudes, and feelings. In order to succeed in your literature courses, you need to be able to use and understand the specialized vocabulary of literary works.

Descriptive Language   Writers often use words that create sensory impressions or responses. They are intended to help the reader re-create mentally what the author is describing. For example, in describing a stormy night, a poet may write, "Under the thunder-dark clouds, the storm mounts, flashes, and resounds." These terms give you a feeling about the storm and help you imagine its strength. Instead of saying two characters looked at each other, a novelist may write, "their eyes locked momentarily in a gaze, reflecting the strength of their opposing wills." Now, read the following paragraph. Note, in particular, the underlined words.

> Old men, old women, almost 20 million of them. They constitute 10 percent of the total population, and the percentage is steadily growing. Some of them, like <u>conspirators,</u> walk all <u>bent over, as if hiding some precious secret, filled with self-protection.</u> The body seems to gather itself around those vital parts, <u>folding shoulders,</u> arms, <u>pelvis like a fading rose.</u> Watch and you see how <u>fragile</u> old people come to think they are.
>
> —Curtin, "Aging in the Land of the Young," *Nobody Ever Died of Old Age*

Connotative Language   The connotations of a word are the meanings it commonly suggests or implies beyond its primary, denotative meaning. Thus, the word *dinner* denotes an evening meal but connotes a time of conversation, friendship, and interaction. The word *father* means "male parent" but often connotes a person who guides and directs. A connotative meaning may carry either a positive or a negative impression. For example, all of the following words mean an assembled group of people, but they have very different connotations.

crowd, congregation, mob, gang, audience, class

Read the following paragraph, which is taken from Martin Luther King Jr.'s "Letter from Birmingham Jail." He wrote it after being jailed for leading a civil rights demonstration.

> We have waited for more than 340 years for our constitutional and God-given rights. The nations of Asia and Africa are moving with <u>jetlike</u> speed toward gaining political independence, but we still <u>creep</u> at <u>horse-and-buggy pace</u> toward gaining a cup of coffee at a lunch counter. I guess it is easy for those who have never felt the <u>stinging darts of segregation</u> to say, "Wait." But when you have seen <u>vicious mobs lynch</u> your mothers and fathers at will and drown your sisters and brothers at whim; when you have seen <u>hate-filled</u> policemen <u>curse, kick,</u> and even kill your black brothers and sisters; when you see the vast majority of your 20 million Negro brothers <u>smothering</u> in an airtight <u>cage of poverty</u> in the midst of an affluent society; when you suddenly find your tongue twisted and your speech <u>stammering</u> as you seek to explain to your six-year-old daughter why she can't go to the public amusement park that has just been advertised on television, and see tears <u>welling up</u> in her eyes when she is told that Funtown is closed to colored children, and see <u>ominous clouds of inferiority</u> beginning to form in her little mental sky, and see her beginning to distort her personality by developing an unconscious bitterness toward white people . . . then you will understand why we find it difficult to wait.
>
> —King, "Letter from Birmingham Jail," *Why We Can't Wait,* p. 363

The underlined words reveal King's feeling toward segregation and discrimination. For example, notice that King uses the phrase "vicious mobs lynch" rather than "groups of people kill" and "hate-filled policemen curse, kick," instead of "policemen shout and strike." These choices of words are deliberate. King hopes to create an emotional response in his readers.

Figurative Language   Figurative language is a way of describing something that makes sense on an imaginative level but not on a literal or factual level. Many common expressions are figurative:

The exam was a piece of cake.

Sam eats like a horse.

He walks like a gazelle.

In each of these expressions, two unlike objects are compared on the basis of some quality they have in common. Take, for example, Hamlet's statement "I will speak daggers to her, but use none." Here the writer is comparing the features of daggers (sharp, pointed, dangerous, harmful) with something that can be used like daggers—words.

Figurative language is striking, often surprising, even shocking. This reaction is created by the unlikeness of the two objects being compared. To find the similarity and understand the figurative expression, focus on connotative meanings rather than literal meanings. For example, in reading the lines

> A sea
>
> Harsher than granite

from an Ezra Pound poem, you must think not only of rock or stone but also of the characteristics of granite: hardness, toughness, impermeability. Then you can see that the lines mean that the sea is rough and resistant. Figurative words, which are also called figures of speech, are used to communicate and emphasize relationships that cannot be communicated through literal meaning. For example, the statement by Jonathan Swift, "She wears her clothes as if they were thrown on by a pitchfork," creates a stronger image and conveys a more meaningful description than saying "She dresses sloppily."

The three most common types of figurative expressions are similes, metaphors, and symbols. Similes make the comparison explicit by using the word *like* or *as*. Metaphors, on the other hand, directly equate the two objects. Here are several examples of each.

SIMILES

We lie back to back.
Curtains lift and fall,
like the chest of someone sleeping.

—Kenyon

Life, like a dome of many-colored glass,
stains the white radiance of Eternity.

—Shelley

METAPHORS

My Life has stood—a Loaded Gun—
In Corners—till a Day
The Owner passed—identified—
And carried Me away—

—Emily Dickinson

. . . his hair lengthened into sunbeams . . .

—Gustave Flaubert

For more on figurative language, refer to Chapter 5, page 132.

EXERCISE 14-2

Working with a group of classmates, make a list of figurative expressions you use in everyday speech.

EXERCISE 14-3

Explain the meaning of each of the following figures of speech. Several interpretations are possible.

Shall I compare thee to a summer's day?
Thou art more lovely and more temperate.

—Shakespeare

In plucking the fruit of memory,
one runs the risk of spoiling its bloom.

—Joseph Conrad

The scarlet of the maples can shake me like a cry
Of bugles going by.

—Carman

THE EAGLE

He clasps the crag with crooked hands;
Close to the sun in lonely lands,

Ringed with the azure world, he stands.
The wrinkled sea beneath him crawls;
He watches from his mountain walls,
And like a thunderbolt he falls.

—Tennyson

Symbols also make a comparison, but only one term of the comparison is stated. A symbol suggests more than its literal meaning. In fact, sometimes more than one meaning is suggested. In your everyday life, a flag is a symbol of patriotism; a four-leaf clover stands for good luck. A writer may describe a character dressed in white to symbolize her innocence and purity, but the words *innocence* and *purity* will not be mentioned. It is left to the reader to recognize the symbol and to make the comparison.

Symbols often are crucial to the writer's theme or essential meaning. For example, Hemingway's short story "A Clean, Well-Lighted Place" describes an aging man who visits a café. In this story, the café symbolizes an escape from loneliness, old age, and death. Hemingway's theme is the inevitability and inescapability of aging and death; the café closes, and the man's escape is short-lived. Melville's novel *Moby-Dick* is the story of a white whale given the name Moby Dick. But the novel is about much more than an aquatic mammal; the whale takes on numerous meanings. The novel's characters imply he is the devil. Later, the whale seems to represent the forces of nature or the created universe.

Symbols, then, are usually objects—concrete items, not abstract feelings such as pity or hate. To recognize symbols, look for objects given a particular or unusual emphasis. The object may be mentioned often, or it may even be suggested in the title. The story or poem may open and/or close with reference to the object. Objects that suggest more than one meaning are possible symbols. Perhaps the best way to identify symbols is to look for objects that point to the author's theme.

EXERCISE 14-4   *Reread Sylvia Plath's poem "Mirror" on page 401. Is the mirror a symbol? If so, what does it symbolize?*

EXERCISE 14-5   *Read the following poem by Langston Hughes, and answer the questions that follow.*

THE NEGRO SPEAKS OF RIVERS
Langston Hughes

I've known rivers:
I've known rivers ancient as the world and older than the flow of
human blood in human veins.
My soul has grown deep like the rivers.

I bathed in the Euphrates when dawns were young.
I built my hut near the Congo and it lulled me to sleep.
I looked upon the Nile and raised the pyramids above it.
I heard the singing of the Mississippi when Abe Lincoln went down to
New Orleans, and I've seen its muddy bosom turn all golden in the
sunset.

I've known rivers:
Ancient, dusky rivers.

My soul has grown deep like the rivers.

—Hughes, *The Collected Poems of Langston Hughes*

1. What does the river symbolize?
2. Explain any metaphors or similes the poem contains.

Reading and Analyzing Poetry

Poetry is a form of expression in which ideas are presented in a unique format. Poems are written in verse-lines and stanzas rather than paragraphs. Often, poetry requires more reading time and greater concentration than other types of material. In reading prose, you could skip a word in a paragraph and your comprehension of the whole paragraph would not suffer; poetry, however, is very compact and precise. Each word is important and carries special meaning. You have to pay attention to each word—its sound, its meaning, and its meaning when combined with other words. Here are a few guidelines to help you approach poetry effectively:

1. **Read the poem once straight through, without any defined purpose.** Be open-minded, experiencing the poem as it is written. If you meet an unknown word or confusing reference, keep reading.

2. **Use punctuation to guide your comprehension.** Although poetry is written in lines, do not expect each line to make sense by itself. Meaning often flows on from line to line, eventually forming a sentence. Use the punctuation to guide you, as you do in reading paragraphs. If there is no punctuation at the end of the line, consider it as a slight pause, with an emphasis on the last word.

3. **Read the poem a second time.** Identify and correct any difficulties, such as an unknown word.

4. **Notice the action.** *Who* is doing *what, when,* and *where?*

5. **Analyze the poem's intent.** Decide what it was written to accomplish. Does it describe a feeling or a person, express a memory, present an argument?

6. **Determine who is speaking.** Poems often refer to an unidentified "I" or "we." Try to describe the speaker's viewpoint or feelings.

7. **Establish the speaker's tone.** Is the author serious, challenging, saddened, frustrated? Read aloud; your intonation, your emphasis on certain words, and the rise and fall of your voice may provide clues. You may "hear" a poet's anger, despondency, or elation.

8. **Identify to whom the poem is addressed.** Is it written to a person, to the reader, to an object? Consider the possibility that the poet may be writing to work out a problem or as an emotional outlet.

9. **Reread difficult or confusing sections.** Read them aloud several times. Copying these sections word for word may be helpful. Look up unfamiliar words.

10. **Check unfamiliar references.** A poet may refer to people, objects, or events outside of the poem. These are known as *allusions*. Often, the allusion is important to the overall meaning of the poem. When you see Oedipus mentioned in a poem, you will need to find out who he was. Paperback books on mythology and literary figures are a good investment.

11. **Analyze the language of the poem.** Consider connotative meanings and study figures of speech.

12. **Look for the poet's meaning or the poem's theme.** Paraphrase the poem; express it in your own words and connect it to your own experience. Then put all the ideas together to discover its overall meaning. Ask yourself, "What is the poet trying to tell me?" "What is the message?"

Now read the poem "Dream Deferred," by Langston Hughes, applying the preceding guidelines.

DREAM DEFERRED
Langston Hughes

What happens to a dream deferred?

Does it dry up
like a raisin in the sun?
Or fester like a sore—
And then run?
Does it stink like rotten meat?
Or crust and sugar over—
like a syrupy sweet?
Maybe it just sags.
like a heavy load.

Or does it explode?

—Hughes, *The Collected Poems of Langston Hughes*

One key to understanding the poem is the meaning of the word *deferred*. Here, it means put off or postponed. A dream deferred, then, refers to unfulfilled or postponed hopes. A poet questions what happens to a dream that is deferred and offers six alternatives. Note the connotative meanings of the first four choices: "dry up," "fester, "stink," "crust and sugar over." Each of these suggests some type of decay. The term sags suggests heaviness and inaction. The last alternative, "explode," is active: posing a threat and implying danger. The poet's purpose is to explore the negative consequences of unfulfilled hopes and to suggest that violent outcomes may result.

EXERCISE 14-6

Read the following poem by Emily Dickinson, and use the guidelines for analyzing poetry to help you answer the questions below.

BECAUSE I COULD NOT STOP FOR DEATH
Emily Dickinson

Because I could not stop for Death—
He kindly stopped for me—
The Carriage held but just Ourselves—
And Immortality.

We slowly drove—He knew no haste
And I had put away
My labor and my leisure too,
For His Civility—

We passed the School, where Children strove
At Recess—in the Ring—
We passed the Fields of Gazing Grain—
We passed the Setting Sun—

Or rather—He passed Us—
The Dews drew quivering and chill—
For only Gossamer,[1] my Gown—
My Tippet[2]—only Tulle—

We paused before a House that seemed
A Swelling of the Ground—
The Roof was Scarcely visible—
The Cornice[3]—in the Ground

Since then—'tis Centuries—and yet
Feels shorter than the Day
I first surmised the Horses' Heads
Were toward Eternity—

—*The Poems of Emily Dickinson,* ed. by Thomas H. Johnson

[1]A light, thin cloth
[2]Cape
[3]Section beneath roof

1. Summarize the literal action in the poem. Your summary should include answers to the questions given earlier in this chapter (who, what, where, when, and why).
2. Annotate the poem by marking words and phrases that describe death or the poet's attitude toward it.
3. What message is the author communicating about death?

Reading and Analyzing Short Stories and Novels

A short story is a brief work of prose narrative with an organized plot. It differs from the novel not only in length but also in magnitude: the size and proportion of the story, its scope, its impact, and its effects. A short story may discuss one event that shaped a person's life, whereas a novel describes the numerous actions that contribute to a character's development. However, both the short story and the novel share basic features.

Plot The plot is the basic storyline—the sequence of events as they occur in the work. The plot, however, also consists of the actions through which the work's meaning is expressed. The plot often follows a predictable structure. Frequently, the plot begins by setting the scene, introducing the main characters, and providing background information needed to follow the story. Often, there is a complication or problem that arises. Suspense is built as the problem or conflict unfolds. Near the end of the story, events come to a climax: the point at which the outcome of the conflict will be decided. A conclusion quickly follows as the story ends.

Characterization Characters are the actors in a narrative story. The characters reveal themselves by what they say—the dialog—and by their actions, appearance, thoughts, and feelings. The narrator, or person who tells the story, also may comment on or reveal information about the characters. Sometimes, the narrator is not the author, in which case you need to consider his or her characterization as well. As a critical reader, you need to analyze the characters' traits and motives, analyze their personalities, study their interaction, and examine character changes.

Setting The setting is the time, place, and circumstances in which the action occurs. The setting provides a framework for the actions and establishes an atmosphere in which the characters interact.

Point of View The point of view is the way the story is presented or from whose perspective or outlook the story is told. Often, the author of a story is not the narrator. The story may be told from the perspective of a narrator who is not one of the characters or by one of the characters themselves. In analyzing the point of view, determine the narrator's role and function. Is the narrator accurate and knowledgeable (even all-knowing), or is his or her view limited or restricted? Sometimes the narrator is able to enter the minds of some or all of the characters, knowing their thoughts and understanding their actions and motivations. Other times, a narrator may be naive or innocent, unable to understand the actions or implications of the story.

Tone   The tone of a story suggests the author's attitude. Like tone of voice, tone in a story suggests feelings. Many ingredients contribute to tone, including the author's choice of details, characters, events, and situations. The tone of a story may be amusing, angry, or contemptuous. The author's feelings are not necessarily those of the characters or of the narrator. Instead, it is through the characters' actions and the narrator's description of them that we infer tone. The style in which a work is written often suggests the tone. Style means the way a writer writes, especially his or her use of language.

Theme   The theme of the story is the main point or message it conveys through all of the elements above. It is an insight into life revealed by the story. Themes are often large, universal ideas: life and death, human values, or human existence. To establish the theme, ask yourself, "What is the author trying to say about life by telling the story?" Try to explain it in a single sentence. If you are having difficulty stating the theme, try the following suggestions:

1. **Study the title.** Now that you have read the story, does it take on any new meanings?

2. **Analyze the main character.** Does he or she change? If so, how, and in reaction to what?

3. **Look for broad, general statements that a character or the narrator makes about life or the problems the characters face.**

4. **Look for symbols, figurative expressions, and meaningful names (for example, Mrs. Goodheart), or objects that hint at bigger ideas.**

Read "The Story of an Hour" by Kate Chopin, paying particular attention to each of the features above.

THE STORY OF AN HOUR

Kate Chopin

Knowing that Mrs. Mallard was afflicted with heart trouble, great care was taken to break to her as gently as possible the news of her husband's death.

It was her sister Josephine who told her, in broken sentences; veiled hints that revealed in half concealing. Her husband's friend Richards was there, too, near her. It was he who had been in the newspaper office when intelligence of the railroad disaster was received, with Brently Mallard's name leading the list of "killed." He had only taken the time to assure himself of its truth by a second telegram, and had hastened to forestall any less careful, less tender friend in bearing the sad message.

She did not hear the story as many women have heard the same, with a paralyzed inability to accept its significance. She wept at once, with sudden, wild abandonment, in her sister's arms. When the storm of grief had spent itself she went away to her room alone. She would have no one follow her.

There stood, facing the open window, a comfortable, roomy armchair. Into this she sank, pressed down by a physical exhaustion that haunted her body and seemed to reach into her soul.

She could see in the open square before her house the tops of trees that were all aquiver with the new spring life. The delicious breath of rain was in the air. In the street below a peddler was crying his wares. The notes of a distant song which someone was singing reached her faintly, and countless sparrows were twittering in the eaves.

There were patches of blue sky showing here and there through the clouds that had met and piled one above the other in the west facing her window.

She sat with her head thrown back upon the cushion of the chair, quite motionless, except when a sob came up into her throat and shook her, as a child who has cried itself to sleep continues to sob in its dreams.

She was young, with a fair, calm face, whose lines bespoke repression and even a certain strength. But now there was a dull stare in her eyes, whose gaze was fixed away off yonder on one of those patches of blue sky. It was not a glance of reflection, but rather indicated a suspension of intelligent thought.

There was something coming to her and she was waiting for it, fearfully. What was it? She did not know; it was too subtle and elusive to name. But she felt it, creeping out of the sky, reaching toward her through the sounds, the scents, the color that filled the air.

Now her bosom rose and fell tumultuously. She was beginning to recognize this thing that was approaching to possess her, and she was striving to beat it back with her will—as powerless as her two white slender hands would have been.

When she abandoned herself a little whispered word escaped her slightly parted lips. She said it over and over under her breath: "free, free, free!" The vacant stare and the look of terror that had followed it went from her eyes. They stayed keen and bright. Her pulses beat fast, and the coursing blood warmed and relaxed every inch of her body.

She did not stop to ask if it were or were not a monstrous joy that held her. A clear and exalted perception enabled her to dismiss the suggestion as trivial.

She knew that she would weep again when she saw the kind, tender hands folded in death; the face that had never looked save with love upon her, fixed and gray and dead. But she saw beyond that bitter moment a long procession of years to come that would belong to her absolutely. And she opened and spread her arms out to them in welcome.

There would be no one to live for her during those coming years; she would live for herself. There would be no powerful will bending hers in that blind persistence with which men and women believe they have a right to impose a private will upon a fellow-creature. A kind intention or a cruel intention made the act seem no less a crime as she looked upon it in that brief moment of illumination.

And yet she had loved him—sometimes. Often she had not. What did it matter! What could love, the unresolved mystery, count for in face of this possession of self-assertion which she suddenly recognized as the strongest impulse of her being!

"Free! Body and soul free!" she kept whispering.

Josephine was kneeling before the closed door with her lips to the keyhole, imploring for admission. "Louise, open the door! I beg; open the door—you will make yourself ill. What are you doing, Louise? For heaven's sake open the door."

"Go away. I am not making myself ill." No; she was drinking in a very elixir of life through that open window.

Her fancy was running riot along those days ahead of her. Spring days, and summer days, and all sorts of days that would be her own. She breathed a quick prayer that life might be long. It was only yesterday she had thought with a shudder that life might be long.

She arose at length and opened the door to her sister's importunities. There was a feverish triumph in her eyes, and she carried herself unwittingly like a goddess of Victory. She clasped her sister's waist, and together they descended the stairs. Richards stood waiting for them at the bottom.

Someone was opening the front door with a latchkey. It was Brently Mallard who entered, a little travel-stained, composedly carrying his grip-sack and umbrella. He had been far from the scene of accident, and did not even know there had been one. He stood amazed at Josephine's piercing cry; at Richards' quick motion to screen him from the view of his wife.

But Richards was too late.

When the doctors came they said she had died of heart disease—of joy that kills.

—Chopin, *The Awakening: Selected Stories of Kate Chopin*

The plot of this short story involves a surprise ending: Mrs. Mallard learns that her husband, who she thought had been killed in a railroad disaster, is alive. She ponders his death and relishes the freedom it will bring. Upon discovering that her husband is not dead, Mrs. Mallard suffers a heart attack and dies. The key character is Mrs. Mallard; her thoughts and actions after learning of her husband's supposed death are the crux of the story. The setting is one hour in a time near the present in the Mallards' home. The story is told by a third-person narrator who is knowledgeable and understands the characters' actions and motives. In the story's last line, the narrator tells us that doctors assumed Mrs. Mallard died of "the joy that kills."

EXERCISE 14–7   *Answer the following questions about Chopin's "The Story of an Hour."*

1. When did you first realize that Mrs. Mallard's reaction to her husband's death would be unusual? Underline words and phrases that led you to suspect her response would be unusual.
2. Explain the meaning of the phrase "the joy that kills."
3. What do Mrs. Mallard's response to the news of her husband's death and the surprise ending suggest about life and death and the nature of true happiness?

■ The Visual Arts: Expression Without Words

A work of art, such as a painting or a sculpture, is the visual expression of an idea. The idea is expressed using a medium—a material such as canvas, clay, fiber, stone, or paint. In a poem, the medium is words; in a sculpture, the medium may be marble. The medium is the vehicle through which the idea is expressed.

Why Study Art?

Many people study art because it is beautiful and they enjoy it. Art can arouse emotions and feelings, stimulate our imaginations, and help us think in new ways. It can enrich our lives. Besides providing enjoyment and enrichment, art also can be a form of communication. By studying the stained glass window in a cathedral, for example, you can learn how, during the Middle Ages, religion was taught to an illiterate population. Art may also have a spiritual (religious) value. Cave drawings may have been used by prehistoric humans to depict animals they valued for food or to magically exert control over them. Finally, art may have a functional value. Some works of art were useful in daily life. Intricately dyed or carved rawhide may have been used to transport personal goods, for instance. By studying works of art, we can learn about a society's religious beliefs and daily living habits.

How to Study Art

To study art, you have to think visually. Use the following suggestions to develop your visual thinking skills. As you read through this section, refer to a photograph taken by Dorothea Lange, *Migrant Mother, Nipomo, California, 1936,* shown on the next page.

See as Well as Look   Looking means taking in what is before you in a physical, mechanical way. Your eyes focus on visual images. Seeing is a more active mental, as well as physical, process. It may require conscious effort. The distinction between looking and seeing is similar to that between hearing and listening. When you hear, you take in sound. When you listen, you understand meaning and grasp the speaker's message. When you see a work of art, you take away some meaning or understanding. What do you *see* in Lange's photograph?

Identify the Subject Matter   Decide who or what the work of art depicts or describes. For example, Michelangelo's "The Creation of Adam" describes, as its title suggests, the biblical creation of the first human. An Inuit stone carving may depict an animal valued by Inuit tribes, such as an eagle or bear. In Lange's photograph, the subject is a mother and her children.

Consider the Title   The title often offers clues that will help you construct an interpretation of the work. You should be aware that not all titles were given to the work by the original artist. The title of Lange's photograph is very revealing. We learn that the woman is a migrant worker and can infer that the children are her children. We also learn that the photograph was taken in California and can infer that the woman was a migrant worker there.

Study the Visual Elements   When you look at a painting the first time, you may notice only a face, or when you study a sculpture, you may notice only its shape. Broaden your study to include the common visual elements. They are line, shape, mass, time, motion, light, color, and texture. Not every element exists within every work of art, but some are important in each.

These elements, sometimes referred to as the form, contribute to the meaning. Small details are important. For example, the grain of marble in a sculpture or the kinds of brush strokes in a painting are meaningful. A painting with deep, heavy, sharply angular lines creates a different impression from one with softly flowing lines.

Dorothea Lange, Migrant Mother, Nipomo, California, 1936.

Source: Copyright the Dorothea Lange Collection. The Oakland Museum, City of Oakland. Gift of Paul S. Taylor.

In Lange's photograph, light seems to be shining on the woman's face and hand. You see harsh, strong lines in her face. Her arm is angular, not graceful. The children seem less sharp.

Write Your Reactions As you study a work of art, jot down your responses. Write questions, initial reactions, your emotions, and so forth. Do not worry about the order of your ideas or about expressing them in grammatically correct sentences. Just record your impressions. Together, these may help you develop an interpretation of the work. While studying Lange's photograph, one student wrote the following:

- The photo is disturbing—not pleasing.
- The children's faces are hidden—are they ashamed? or perhaps crying? or afraid?
- The woman seems worried. Her hand is at her mouth.
- The children seem highly dependent on her; they seem emotionally close.

- The woman seems to be thinking, but there is no action or movement in the photograph.
- The family seems poor and disheveled.
- The mother seems in control.
- Are they homeless?

Analyze the Work   Analyzing means dividing something into parts in order to understand it. If you are looking at a statue, for instance, you might examine the pose, size, facial expression, medium, gestures, clothing, and so forth. In Lange's photograph, you might first analyze the woman and then the children. Or you might analyze how each is holding his or her body and then how each is dressed. In Lange's photograph, the woman's facial expression is particularly striking.

Consider the Meaning of the Work   An interpretation is a description of a meaning of the work. Many art historians believe that a work of art can have more than one meaning. One meaning is the meaning that it had for the artist; another is the meaning it had for the first people who looked at it. Still another is the meaning it offers to us today. Other art historians argue that a work has no meaning in itself; its only meaning is that given to it by those who view it. This latter viewpoint is known as reader-response theory.

One meaning that Lange's photograph seems to be depicting is the plight of migrant workers, thus suggesting sympathy. Another meaning may be drawn from the similarity of the pose of the woman and her children to traditional paintings of the Madonna and child, perhaps suggesting that the migrant woman is a universal mother figure. Many women share her worry and concern about their place in life.

EXERCISE 14-8

Study the work of art shown on the next page, and answer the following questions.

1. Describe the subject.
2. Identify striking visual elements. For example, consider the size and balance of the preacher's body parts. Consider, too, the background.
3. Write your reactions.
4. Describe the meaning of the work.

■ Reading Criticism

Criticism discusses, interprets, and evaluates a particular work. Some students erroneously assume that criticism is only negative, or limited to finding fault with a work. Actually, its primary purpose is to analyze and interpret; it may include both positive and negative aspects. Film and book reviews are examples of criticism. Criticism also includes scholarly works that carefully research or closely examine a particular aspect, theme, or approach in literature or art. Often, in order to complete a term paper, you will be required to consult several critical sources. Other times, to understand a work better, you may decide to read several interpretations by critical authorities.

*Charles White,
Preacher, 1952. Ink
on cardboard,
sight; 21⅜ x 29⅜
inches.*
Source: Whitney
Museum of American
Art, New York; 52.25.
Photograph © 2000.
Whitney Museum of
American Art.

Following is a brief excerpt from a critical work discussing Emily Dickinson's poem "Because I Could Not Stop for Death," which appears on page 409 in this chapter. Read the excerpt, and note that it offers an interpretation of the poem's meaning: the poet fears life and escapes this fear through a journey to death.

Naive, blank-faced, repelling thought and emotion, the speaker permits herself to be transported to worlds unknown. The first step is easy. The gentleman-caller she calls Death is kindly, civil. The threesome is cozy, he does what she cannot do, the unexamined space of the carriage arouses no anxiety in her, the journey is a leisured one. . . . She has all the time in the world, and in other worlds besides. Remarking on the presence of a third figure, Immortality, she cannot stop to ask herself what this barely personified abstraction, the shard of a disintegrated religious tradition, signifies. Wholly engrossed as she is by her deceptive double, she cannot afford to question whether beneath the smooth, seductive surface his intentions are equally decorous. What she has done is to yield herself up to the power of a dominant obsession. What this obsession is we do not know absolutely. The poem invokes a reason only to dismiss it: "Because I could not . . . He." Thus, although the idea of suicide is implicit in its denial, so too is the idea of controlling this death-wish by displacing it onto another character who is initially capable of masking the deception motif the poem is designed to reveal. In limited terms, perhaps this obsession may be described as the compulsion to repress the anxiety that the circumstances of her life have aroused in her. In its broadest terms, perhaps this obsession may be described as her fear of mortality itself.

—Pollak, *Dickinson: The Anxiety of Gender*, p. 191

In using critical sources, follow these guidelines.

1. **Read the original work carefully and thoroughly before you consult critical sources.**

2. **Make a preliminary interpretation of the work before reading criticism.** Decide what *you* think the work means and why it was produced. Record these ideas in note form. If you consult sources before forming your own impressions, your judgment will be colored by what you read and you will have difficulty separating your ideas from those you encounter as you read.

3. **Recognize that not all critics agree.** You may encounter three critics who present three different interpretations of Shakespeare's *Hamlet* or Renoir's "The Luncheon of the Boating Party."

4. **Make certain that the interpretations you read are substantiated with references to the original work.**

5. **Although it is perfectly acceptable to revise your own interpretations on the basis of your reading, do not discard your own interpretation as soon as you encounter one that differs.** Look to the original work to develop support for your interpretations.

6. **Make notes on your readings, recording only key points.**

To locate criticism on a particular literary or artistic work, consult one of several reference sources.

The Reader's Guide to Periodical Literature

Essay and General Literature Index

The MLA Bibliography

In many libraries, computerized versions are available.

EXERCISE 14–9 *The following excerpt provides another critical interpretation of Dickinson's poem "Because I Could Not Stop for Death." Read the excerpt, and answer the questions that follow.*

At first reading, the orthodox reassurance against the fear of death appears to be invoked, though with the novelty of a suitor replacing the traditional angel, by emphasizing his compassionate mission in taking her out of the woes of this world into the bliss of the next. 'Death,' usually rude, sudden, and impersonal, has been transformed into a kindly and leisurely gentleman. Although she was aware this is a last ride, since his 'Carriage' can only be a hearse, its terror is subdued by the 'Civility' of the driver who is merely serving the end of 'Immortality.' The loneliness of the journey, with Death on the driver's seat and her body laid out in the coach behind, is dispelled by the presence of her immortal part that rides with her as a co-passenger, this slight personification being justified by the separable concept of the soul. Too occupied with life herself to stop, like all busy mortals, Death 'kindly stopped' for her. But this figure of a gentleman taking a lady for a carriage ride is carefully underplayed and then dropped after two stanzas.

The balanced parallelism of the first stanza is slightly quickened by the alliterating 'labor' and 'leisure' of the second, which encompass vividly all that must be renounced in order to ride 'toward Eternity.' So the deliberate slow-paced action that lies suspended behind the poem is charged with a forward movement by the sound pattern, taking on a kind of inevitability in the insistent reiteration of the following stanza:

> We passed the School, where Children strove
> At Recess—in the Ring—
> We passed the Fields of Gazing Grain—
> We passed the Setting Sun—

Here her intensely conscious leave-taking of the world is rendered with fine economy, and instead of the sentimental grief of parting there is an objectively presented scene. The seemingly disparate parts of this are fused into a vivid re-enactment of the mortal experience. It includes the three stages of youth, maturity, and age, the cycle of day from morning to evening, and even a suggestion of seasonal progression from the year's upspring through ripening to decline. The labor and leisure of life are made concrete in the joyous activity of children contrasted with the passivity of nature and again, by the optical illusion of the sun's setting, in the image of motion that has come to rest. Also the whole range of the earthly life is symbolized, first human nature, then animate, and finally inanimate nature. But, absorbed 'in the Ring' of childhood's games, the players at life do not even stop to look up at the passing carriage of death. And the indifference of nature is given a kind of cold vitality by transferring the stare in the dead traveler's eyes to the 'Gazing Grain.' This simple maneuver in grammar creates an involute paradox, giving the fixity of death to the living corn while the corpse itself passes by on its journey to immortality. Then with the westering sun, traditional symbol of the soul's passing, comes the obliterating darkness of eternity. Finally, the sequence follows the natural route of a funeral train, past the schoolhouse in the village, then the outlying fields, and on to the remote burying ground.

—Anderson, *Emily Dickinson's Poetry: Stairway to Surprise*, pp. 245–46

1. According to this critic, what is the speaker's attitude toward death?
2. Does the criticism enhance your understanding of the poem? If so, how?
3. How does this critic's interpretation compare with that of the earlier interpretation on page 417? Discuss the similarities and differences.
4. Compare this critic's interpretation with your own interpretation.

■ Thought Patterns in the Humanities and Arts

Common thought patterns in the humanities and arts include process, chronological order, cause and effect, and comparison and contrast. Table 14-1 on the next page describes the uses of these patterns and offers examples.

TABLE 14-1   Thought Patterns in the Humanities and Arts

PATTERNS	USES	EXAMPLES
Process	Examining the process through which the writer achieved his or her effect	Studying e.e. cummings's use of space and print size
Chronological order	Sequence of events in fictional works; noting the development of various artists or historical or literary periods	Noting development of Impressionist style of painting
Cause and effect	Examining character motivation, studying effects of various literary and artistic techniques	Evaluating the effect of harsh brush strokes in a painting
Comparison and contrast	Studying two or more artists, works, writers, or schools of thought	Comparing the works of Wordsworth and Coleridge

■ Learning Strategies for Humanities and Art Courses

Humanities and art courses are unique. Grades are often based on papers or essay exams rather than on objective tests or quizzes. Frequently, the focus is on ideas and your interpretation and evaluation of them. Here are several suggestions to help you get the most from these courses:

1. **Learn appropriate terminology.** Learn the names and meanings of literary devices (stream of consciousness, pathos, persona, intrigue). Consult M. L. Abrams's *A Glossary of Literary Terms.*

2. **Learn classifications.** In literature and art history, works and authors are often grouped or classified, and groupings may be chronological (the Romantic period, 1789–1832; the Victorian period, 1832–1901 in literature, for example). Learn these periods (names, inclusive dates, and characteristics) so that you will understand the historical context of a particular work.

3. **Focus on themes and patterns.** Always analyze and evaluate. Focus on a work's significance and literary merit.

4. **Highlight and annotate as you read.** Mark key figures of speech, global statements by characters, and words and phrases that suggest the theme. Mark confusing sections or unknown references as well.

5. **Write for review.** Write plot summaries of short stories. Make brief outlines of essays. Write a statement of your interpretation of a poem or work or art. These statements will be useful as you prepare for exams or select topics for papers.

6. **Predict exam questions.** Exams are usually in essay form or call for short answers. Prepare for this by predicting the questions and drafting outline answers.

7. **Discuss the work with a classmate.** If you are having difficulty with a particular work, consult with your instructor.

Test-Taking Tips
Preparing for Exams in the Humanities and Arts

In many literature classes, you write papers instead of taking exams, although some instructors do give brief objective tests based on the assigned readings. Most final essay assignments require you to analyze and write about a work or works you have read or viewed.

You may be given several types of writing assignments. It is important to know what is expected in each. Use the following tips:

1. **Explication.** An explication is a full, detailed explanation of the meaning of the work. It proceeds through the work line by line or even word by word, explaining meanings and examining word choices, figures of speech, and so forth. Although it is detailed, it is not limited to a discussion of specifics. Larger concerns such as theme and plot are also discussed.

2. **Analysis.** Analysis involves separating the work into components and then examining and explaining closely one or more of the parts. Usually, analyses are limited to one aspect or element, such as Hawthorne's use of symbolism in *The Scarlet Letter* or an analysis of the point of view in Poe's "The Tell-Tale Heart."

3. **Comparison and Contrast.** Writing assignments may ask you to compare two or more works or two or more authors. To do this, you must examine similarities and differences. If you are given a choice of works or authors, choose two that have much in common; you will find you have more to say than if the two are widely divergent. For suggestions on how to compare two works, refer to Chapter 4. When writing a comparison paper, you should generally integrate your discussion of the works rather than discuss each separately. Select several points or aspects that you will discuss for each work, and then organize your paper to proceed from aspect to aspect.

4. **Synopsis.** Some instructors ask students to write a synopsis or summary of a work. This assignment demands a concise description of major features of the work, such as plot, setting, and characterization. Others ask for a card report (a point-by-point description of various elements, usually on an index card). Generally, some form of evaluation of the work is also expected. If you are not certain what aspects to include or what format to use, ask your instructor.

Self-Test Summary

1. What is the focus of literature?	Literature focuses on the search for reasons, values, and interpretations in all areas of human interest and experience.
2. Define the term "genre" and list some examples of different genres.	Genre means a particular type or form of literary, musical, or artistic composition. In literature, examples include poetry, drama, essays, short stories, and novels.
3. What are some of the types of language used in literature?	Literature uses descriptive, connotative, and figurative language to express images, attitudes, and feelings.
4. Give some specific suggestions for reading poetry.	Reread frequently. Note the poem's action, audience, and tone. Analyze the poem's intent, and search for its theme and meaning. Check unfamiliar references.
5. What are the basic features of short stories and novels?	The basic features are plot, characterization, setting, point of view, tone, and theme.
6. What do the visual arts focus on?	Visual arts focus on expressing an idea through a medium, such as canvas, clay, or fiber.
7. How should you study art?	Studying art involves • seeing as well as looking. • identifying the subject matter. • considering the title. • studying the visual elements. • writing reactions. • analyzing the work. • considering meaning.
8. What is criticism?	Criticism is a work that discusses, interprets, or evaluates a piece of art or literature.
9. Name the predominant thought patterns or strategies used when reading literary criticism.	The patterns are process, chronological order, cause and effect, and comparison and contrast.

LITERATURE READING

Leaves

Lloyd Schwartz

Prereading Questions

(Answer after reading the entire poem once.)
1. What is the subject of the poem?
2. Summarize the literal action.

1.

1   Every October it becomes important, no, *necessary*
to see the leaves turning, to be surrounded
by leaves turning: it's not just the symbolism,
to confront in the death of the year your death,
5   one blazing farewell appearance, though the irony
isn't lost on you that nature is most seductive
when it's about to die, flaunting the dazzle of its
incipient exit, an ending that at least so far
the effects of human progress (pollution, acid rain)
10   have not yet frightened you enough to make you believe
is real; that is, you know this ending is a deception
because of course nature is always renewing itself—
    the trees don't *die,* they just pretend,
    go out in style, and return in style: a new style.

2.

15   It is deliberate how far they make you go
especially if you live in the city to get far
enough away from home to see not just trees
but only trees. The boring highways, roadsigns, high
speeds, 10-axle trucks passing you as if they were
20   in an even greater hurry than you to look at leaves:
so you drive in terror for literal hours and it looks
like rain, or *snow,* but it's probably just clouds
(too cloudy to see any color?) and you wonder,
given the poverty of your memory, which road had the
25   most color last year, but it doesn't matter since
you're probably too late anyway, or too early—
    whichever road you take will be the wrong one
    and you've probably come all this way for nothing.

3.

You'll be driving along depressed when suddenly
30   a cloud will move and the sun will muscle through
and ignite the hills. It may not last. Probably

won't last. But for a moment the whole world
comes to. Wakes up. Proves it lives. It lives—
red, yellow, orange, brown, russet, ocher, vermillion,
35 *gold.* Flame and rust. Flame and rust, the permutations
of burning. You're on fire. Your eyes are on fire.
It won't last, you don't want it to last. You
can't stand any more. But you don't want it to stop.
It's what you've come for. It's what you'll
40 come back for. It won't stay with you, but you'll
remember that it felt like nothing else you've felt
or something you've felt that also didn't last.

—Schwartz, "Leaves," *Goodnight, Gracie*

Writing About the Reading
CHECKING YOUR VOCABULARY

1. For each of the words listed below, use context; prefixes, roots, and suffixes (see Chapter 3); and/or a dictionary to write a brief definition or synonym of the word as it is used in the reading.

   a. irony (line 5) _____

   b. seductive (line 6) _____

   c. incipient (line 8) _____

   d. vermillion (line 34) _____

   e. permutations (line 35) _____

2. Draw a word map of one of the words used in the reading.

CHECKING YOUR COMPREHENSION

1. In line 3, Schwartz mentions symbolism. To what symbolism is he referring?
2. What is the poet's attitude toward human progress (line 9)?
3. To whom does the word *they* refer in line 15?
4. Describe the poem's tone.
5. What is the poem's theme?

THINKING CRITICALLY

Why does the author mention pollution and acid rain in line 9?

LEARNING/STUDY STRATEGY

Annotate the poem using the suggestions for analyzing poetry on page 407.

ONLINE RESEARCH: POETRY

Poetry, like other creative arts, depends on the reader, viewer, or listener for interpretation. How would your interpretation of a poem change if you could hear the poet reading the poem, instead of only seeing it on the page? You can hear poets reading their own poems at the second site listed below. Go to both of the sites, and then follow the directions below. (*Note:* You need a program called RealAudio to hear the poems. It can be downloaded from the second site.)

- Visit the Poet's Corner at http://www.theotherpages.org/poems/. Using the subject matter or author index, choose a poem to read.
- Visit The Academy of American Poet's Web site at http://www.poets.org/audio.php.

This site includes a "Listening Booth" that allows you to listen to a poem being read. Choose a poem and listen to it.

1. Discuss the differences between reading and listening to a poem. Which did you prefer? Why?
2. Was your interpretation of the poem that you listened to influenced by the reader? If so, how?

ADDITIONAL PRACTICE

THE HUMANITIES AND ARTS ON THE INTERNET

The Internet has numerous resources available for research in the humanities and arts, including directories and Web guides to help you find material relevant to your studies, journals and databases, references works, and government resources. Here is a list of useful Web sites to get you started.

Directories/Web Guides

Voice of the Shuttle
http://vos.ucsb.edu/

Yahoo! Arts and Humanities
http://dir.yahoo.com/Arts/

ADAM
http://adam.ac.uk/

Journals/Indexes/Databases

The Internet Public Library: Arts and Humanities Serials
http://www.ipl.org/cgi-bin/reading/serials.out.pl?ty=long&id=hum00.00.00

Online Books Page
http://onlinebooks.library.upenn.edu/

Humanities Directories
http://www.lib.washington.edu/subject/Humanities/dr/eldir.html

References

The Cambridge History of English and American Literature
http://www.bartleby.com/cambridge/

ArtLex Art Dictionary
http://www.artlex.com

Government Resources

National Endowment for the Arts: National Initiatives
http://arts.endow.gov/national/index.html

National Endowment for the Humanities Supported Projects
http://www.neh.fed.us/projects/index.html

MULTIMEDIA ACTIVITIES

Practice your reading and research skills on the Web.

1. **Imagination Gallery B: American Treasures of the Library of Congress**
   http://www.loc.gov/exhibits/treasures/tr33b.html#lit

   View these special items from art and literature held by the Library of Congress. Read about their history and significance. Why is it important to preserve these items? Pick one that interests you the most. Teach a friend about it.

2. **Sounds of Harpsichords and Related Instruments**
   http://www-personal.umich.edu/~bpl/hpsi.html#sounds

   Listen to snippets of music played on various instruments. Scroll down to the builder sites and visit some manufacturers' Web sites. What connections can you make between music and other disciplines?

Reading Mathematics

LEARNING OBJECTIVES

✦ To understand the sequential nature of mathematics

✦ To develop a systematic approach for reading mathematics textbooks

✦ To solve word problems in mathematics

✦ To learn common thought patterns used in mathematics

✦ To develop study techniques for mathematics

Think About It!

Which of the professions shown in the above collage rely upon mathematics? If you said all of them, you are correct. Mathematics is the foundation of many academic disciplines. Think of it as an enabler—a discipline that enables all other disciplines, and researchers and workers in that discipline, to function. Here is a list of careers. Think of an example of how mathematics is important in each: nurse, police officer, journalist, salesperson, veterinarian, restaurant owner, and park ranger.

Mathematics is involved in a wide range of careers and academic disciplines because it is concerned with ideas, concepts, measurement, and problem-solving. Mathematics requires logical and critical thinking and the ability to deal with abstractions, relationships, and theoretical ideas. You will find mathematics to be extremely rewarding because you *see* yourself learning and making progress; you can solve a problem today that you could not solve yesterday.

■ Mathematics: A Sequential Thinking Process

Learning mathematics is a sequential process. You solve problems by estimating answers, trying a variety of special techniques, and verifying the results. In mathematics, much of what you learn is based on skills you have learned earlier; it is cumulative. In algebra, you have to understand radicals before you can solve quadratic equations, whose solutions involve radicals. In business math, to use a compound interest schedule, you must understand simple interest.

Because mathematics is sequential and cumulative, it is most important that you begin with a course at the proper level. For example, a calculus course often is required for accounting majors. However, if you have not studied trigonometry, you lack the necessary background for calculus and should take a trigonometry course first. Check the course description in your college catalog for prerequisites, or consult your academic advisor for information on

A Mathematics Professor . . .

Jerry R. Muir, Jr., PhD, Assistant Professor of Mathematics, University of Scranton

Talks About This Chapter

1. "Many of the comments made by the author are things that I have told countless students who are struggling with the transition from high school to college mathematics."

2. "I believe that students would be well served to religiously follow the strategies outlined in this book when it comes to attacking their mathematics classes. They must be made aware that these strategies could seem foreign to them, and may run contrary to their instincts and habits. This adjustment requires discipline and maturity, but will greatly help them adapt to more difficult mathematical topics presented at a more aggressive pace."

Offers Advice to Students

1. "Reading in mathematics will proceed at a much slower pace than reading in other dis-

ciplines. It is a common mistake for students to read a math text as if it were a history or philosophy text. Sometimes a history reading assignment will cover one hundred pages, while a math reading assignment will be as few as ten pages. It shouldn't come as a surprise to students that, if they read for understanding, these assignments could take the same amount of time."

2. "When reading a math text, students should literally go sentence by sentence. After each sentence, they should make sure they understand what they have read. If they do not, they should go back to earlier parts of the section that might need to be reread to understand the new point or turn to scratch paper, as perhaps a side calculation is necessary."

3. "When reading mathematics for understanding, the predominant thought in the student's mind ought to be 'why?' After every sentence is read or after every step in a solution of a sample problem, the student should ask, 'Why is that valid?' or 'Why did the author think to do that?'"

appropriate course placement. If it has been several years since your last math course, your college learning center may offer a placement test to assess your present level of skill.

Mathematics is a process of solving problems—a process of reasoning about situations and understanding the relationships between variables. Too many students learn steps, memorize procedures, and follow rules to solve problems without understanding why they are performing the operations. In mathematics, understanding the meaning of the various operations is essential. Make your learning practical and useful by understanding *how* and *why* the operations work.

Why Study Mathematics?

Mathematics is a required course in many fields of study. It is essential for majors in nursing, accounting, business and finance, technologies, and the natural sciences, for example. Mathematics provides the tools with which to explore relationships and solve problems. In nursing, mathematics allows you to compute and measure dosages of drugs. In accounting, it is mathematics that enables you to calculate profits and losses, for instance.

Besides fulfilling degree requirements, however, mathematics trains you to think logically, quantitatively, and analytically. In some disciplines, you may be required to study advanced mathematics courses, such as calculus, to gain the necessary thinking and reasoning skills for that discipline.

Mathematics can be fun because it is exact and precise; you are either right or wrong in solving a problem. Mathematics can provide the same satisfying, deep concentration that solving a crossword puzzle or playing a game of chess does.

■ Reading Mathematics Textbooks

To learn from mathematics texts, you must allow plenty of time and work at peak concentration. Mathematics texts are concise and to the point; nearly everything is important. Use the following suggestions to develop a systematic approach for reading in mathematics.

Preview Before Reading

Previewing before reading is as important in mathematics as it is in every other discipline. For mathematics texts, however, your preview should include a brief review of your previous chapter assignment. Because learning new skills hinges on remembering what you have learned before, a brief review of previously learned material is valuable.

Understand Mathematical Language

One of the first steps to success with mathematics is learning to understand its language. Mathematics uses a symbolic language in which notations, symbols, numbers, and formulas are used to express ideas and relationships. Working with mathematics requires that you be able to convert mathematical language to everyday language. To understand a formula, for example, $I = prt$, you must translate mathematical language into everyday language: "Interest equals principal times rate times time." To solve a word problem expressed in everyday language, first you must convert it into mathematical language. You might think of equations as mathematical sentences. Just as an English sentence expresses a complete idea, an equation describes a mathematical relationship. Here are a few examples.

SENTENCE	EQUATION
The speed of train A is four times the speed of train B.	$A = 4B$
When I am as old as my mother (m), I shall be five times as old as my daughter (d) is now.	$5d = m$
In a sewing box, there are three times as many pins as needles, and one-third as many buttons as needles; the total number of pins, needles, and buttons is 1,872.	$3n + n + \frac{1}{3}n = 1872$

When you learn a foreign language, it is not sufficient only to learn the new vocabulary; you also must learn the rules of word order, grammar, punctuation, and so forth. To read and understand mathematics, then, you must know not only the signs and symbols (the vocabulary) but also the basic rules for expressing relationships in mathematical form. Figure 15-1 hows five

FIGURE 15-1 Aspects of Mathematical Language

Type	Function	Example
Punctuation marks	Make clear what parts of a statement are or are not separable; distinguish groups within groups	$(0, 1, 2, ...)$ $[3 - (a + b)^2]$
Models (graphs, charts, drawings)	Present a pictorial representation of a relationship or situation	
Numbers	Indicate size, order	$3, 7, 9, 11$
Variables	Represent a number that is unknown or may vary	x, y
Signs for relations	Indicate relationships	$a = b$ (a equals b) $c > d$ (c is greater than b)
Signs for operations	Give instructions	$15 \div 3$ (divide 15 by 3) $a - b$ (subtract b from a)

FIGURE 15-2 Sample Textbook Page

OBJECTIVE ▶ Inequalities can be used to solve applied problems involving phrases that suggest inequality. The chart below gives some of the more common such phrases, along with examples and translations.

Phrase	Example	Inequality
Is more than	A number *is more than* 4	$x > 4$
Is less than	A number *is less than* −12	$x < -12$
Is at least	A number *is at least* 6	$x \geq 6$
Is at most	A number *is at most* 8	$x \leq 8$

Caution
Do not confuse phrases like "5 more than a number" and statements like "5 *is* more than a number." The first of these is expressed as "x + 5" while the second is expressed as "5 > x."

E X A M P L E   8   **Finding an Average Test Score**

Brent has grades of 86, 88, and 78 on his first three tests in geometry. If he wants an average of at least 80 after his fourth test, what score must he make on his fourth test?

   Let *x* represent Brent's score on his fourth test. To find the average of the four scores, add them and find $\frac{1}{4}$ of the sum.

$$\frac{1}{4}(86 + 88 + 78 + x) \geq 80$$

$$4 \cdot \frac{1}{4}(252 + x) \geq 4 \cdot 80 \qquad \text{Multiply by 4.}$$

$$252 + x \geq 320 \qquad \text{Multiply.}$$

$$252 - \mathbf{252} + x \geq 320 - \mathbf{252} \qquad \text{Subtract 252.}$$

$$x \geq 68 \qquad \text{Combine terms.}$$

He must also score 68 or more on the fourth test to have an average of *at least* 80.

SOURCE: Lial et al., *Introductory Algebra,* pp. 163–64

important types of symbols and mathematical language and gives examples of each, taken from introductory algebra.

   Figure 15-2 shows a sample page from an introductory algebra textbook. It has been marked to indicate the types of mathematical language used.

   Much information is packed into small units of mathematical language. Some students find it helpful to translate formulas into words as they read, as is shown in the following equation for a right triangle:

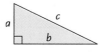

$c^2 = a^2 + b^2$ means the square of the hypotenuse of a right triangle is equal to the sum of the squares of the two remaining sides.

In mathematics, you must know the *exact* meaning of both words and symbols. There are several places to find the definition of a new term. If it is from the current chapter, look at the end-of-chapter material, which often includes key vocabulary. You might also check the index to find page numbers or use the glossary to read a brief definition, if one is included. Use the index card system described in Chapter 3 to help you learn the language of mathematics. Record the term or symbol, its meaning, an example, and a diagram, if possible. Also include a page reference to where the term is used in your textbook. Two sample index cards are shown in Figure 15-3.

EXERCISE 15-1   *Read the excerpt from an algebra text shown in Figure 15-4 on the next page, and underline five examples of mathematical language that the author assumes you know.*

1. Write a definition of each term you have underlined.
2. Write your own definition of the phrase, "evaluating an expression." Include an example to illustrate your definition.

Follow the Chapter Organization

Chapters in most mathematics textbooks contain four essential elements: the presentation or explanation, sample problems, graphs and diagrams, and exercises. Mathematics textbook chapters often use a decimal system for dividing the chapter into sections. For example, Chapter 3 might be numbered 3.1, 3.2, 3.3, and so on. Each number with a decimal is a new section of the chapter.

Reading Chapter Explanations   Each new operation, process, or term is explained in the text. As you read this explanation, focus on *how* and *why* the process works. Discover the reasoning behind the process. If the author refers to a sample problem in the explanation, it is necessary to move back and forth between the

FIGURE 15-3   Sample Index Cards

Front	Back
Median	A measure of central tendency; median is middle-most number: half are above it, half are below it Example: Given scores of 6, 8, 10, 14, 19, 21, 58, the median is *14*
Prime number	A whole number, greater than one, that cannot be divided evenly by any whole number, except one and itself. (0 and 1 are NOT prime numbers.) Examples: 2, 3, 5, 7, 11, 13...

FIGURE 15-4   Excerpt from an Algebra Text

Evaluating an Expression   If you like to fish, you can use an expression (rule) like the one below to find the approximate weight (in pounds) of a fish you catch. Measure the length (in inches) of the fish and then use the correct expression for that type of fish. For a northern pike, the weight expression is shown.

Variable (length of fish) $\longrightarrow \dfrac{l^3}{3600}$

where l is the length of the fish in inches.

To evaluate this expression for a fish that is 43 inches long, follow the rule by calculating

$$\dfrac{43^3}{3600}$$ Replace l with 43, the length of the fish in inches.

In the numerator, you can multiply $43 \cdot 43 \cdot 43$ or use the $\boxed{y^x}$ key on your calculator. Then divide by 3600.

Enter 43 $\boxed{y^x}$ 3 $\boxed{\div}$ 3600 $\boxed{=}$ **Calculator shows 22.08527778**

Base   Exponent

The fish weighs about 22 pounds.

Now evaluate the expression to find the approximate weight of a northern pike that is 37 inches long. (Answer: about 14 pounds.)

Notice that variables are used on your calculator keys. On the $\boxed{y^x}$ key, y represents the base and x represents the exponent. You evaluated y^x by entering 43 as the base and 3 as the exponent for the first fish. Then you evaluated y^x by entering 37 as the base and 3 as the exponent for the second fish.

SOURCE: Lial and Hestwood, *Prealgebra,* p. 87

explanation and the sample problem. Read a sentence or two and then refer to the sample problem to see how the information is applied. Your purpose is to see how the sample problem illustrates the process being described. The steps to follow in computing the total installment cost and finance charge on a credit card are given in Figure 15-5 on page 434. Then the authors give a sample problem and show how it is solved using the steps they have listed.

As you read, refer to previous chapters if an operation is unclear or if unfamiliar terms are used. In mathematics, you should expect to look back frequently because much of the material is sequential.

Reading Sample Problems   Sample problems demonstrate how an operation or process works. It may be tempting to skip over sample problems because they require time to work through or because they lack an accompanying verbal explanation. However, careful study of the sample problems is an essential part of learning in mathematics. Follow these steps in reading sample problems:

1. **Before you read the solution, think of how you would solve the problem, choose a method, and solve the problem.** More than one approach may be possible.

FIGURE 15-5   Problem Solving Step by Step

<table>
<tr><td>

Since the enactment of the **Federal Truth-in-Lending Act** (Regulation Z) in 1969, lenders must report their **finance charge** (the charge for credit) and their **annual percentage rate.** The truth-in-lending law does not regulate interest rates or credit charges but merely requires a standardized and truthful report of what they are. The individual states set the allowable interest rates and charges.
</td><td>back-ground</td></tr>
<tr><td>

Find the annual percentage rate by first finding the **total installment cost** (or the **deferred payment price**) and the finance charge on the loan. Do this with the following steps.
</td><td>overview of process</td></tr>
</table>

Finding total installment cost and finance charge

Step 1.   Find the total installment cost.

> **Total installment cost = Down payment**
>
> **+ (Amount of each payment x Number of payments)**

Step 2.   Find the finance charge.

> **Finance charge = Total installment cost – Cash price**

Step 3.   Finally, find the amount financed.

> **Amount financed = Cash price – Down payment**

(step-by-step procedure)

Example   Diane Phillips bought a motorcycle for $980. She paid $200 down and then made 24 payments of $39.60 each. Find the (a) total installment cost, (b) finance charge, and (c) amount financed.

(Sample problem)

Solution

(a) Find the total installment cost by multiplying the amount of each payment by the number of payments, and adding the down payment.

$$\text{Total installment cost} = \$200 + (\$39.60 \times 24)$$
$$= \$200 + \$950.40$$
$$= \$1150.40$$

(b) The finance charge is the difference between the total installment cost and the cash price.

$$\text{Finance charge} = \$1150.40 - \$980$$
$$= \$170.40$$

Phillips pays an additional $170.40 for the motorcycle because it is bought on credit.

(c) The amount financed is
$$\$980 - \$200 = \$780$$

(Solution)

Source: Miller and Salzman, *Business Mathematics,* p. 373

2. **Read the solution and compare your answer with the textbook's.**

3. **Be sure you understand each step; you should know exactly what calculations were performed and why they were done.**

4. **When you have finished reading the sample problem, explain the steps in your own words.** This will help you remember the method later. The best way to verbalize is to write the process down; this forces you to be clear and precise. Figure 15-6 presents two sample problems and shows how a student verbalized each process.

5. **Test your understanding by covering up the text's solution and solving the problem yourself.** Finally, look over the solution, verifying its reasonableness and reviewing the process once again.

FIGURE 15-6   *Verbalizing a Process*

Problem 1: Find the principal of a loan that gives an interest of $30 at 10% per year for 91 days.

Solution	Verbalization
1. $P = \dfrac{I}{RT}$	1. The formula for computing principal is interest divided by the product of the rate multiplied by the time.
2. $P = \dfrac{30}{.10 \times \dfrac{91}{365}}$	2. The interest is $30. The rate, 10% per year, is converted to a decimal, .10, and the time is expressed as a fraction of a year.
3. $P = \dfrac{30}{.025}$	3. The denominator is simplified.
4. $P = \$1200$	4. The principal is $1200.

Problem 2: $\sqrt{3x + 1} - \sqrt{x + 9} = 2$

Solution	Verbalization
1. $\sqrt{3x + 1} = 2 + \sqrt{x + 9}$	Isolate one radical on one side of the equation.
2. $(-\sqrt{3x + 1})^2 = (2 + \sqrt{x + 9})^2$	Square both sides.
3. $3x + 1 = 4 + 4\sqrt{x + 9} + x + 9$	Use formula $(a + b)^2 = a^2 + 2ab + b^2$.
4. $2x - 12 = 4\sqrt{x + 9}$	Isolate the radical.
5. $x - 6 = 2\sqrt{x + 9}$	Factor out 2 on the left side. Divide the equation by 2.
6. $(x - 6)^2 = (2\sqrt{x + 9})^2$ $x^2 - 12x + 36 = 4(x + 9)$	Square both sides.
7. $x^2 - 12x + 36 = 4x + 36$ $x^2 - 16x = 0$ $x(x - 16) = 0$ $x = 16$	Solve for x.

Ignore the solution $x = 0$ because it will not check in the original equation. Extraneous roots can occur when you square both sides of an equation.

Source: Johnson and Steffensen, *Elementary Algebra,* p. 178

EXERCISE 15-2   *For each of the following problems and solutions, verbalize the process and write each step in your own words. Compare your verbalization with that of another student.*

1. Problem: The sum of two numbers is 21 and their difference is 9. Find the numbers.

    Solution: Let x, y be the two numbers.

$$x + y = 21$$
$$x - y = 9$$
$$2x = 30$$
$$x = 15$$
$$\text{Then, } 15 + y = 21$$
$$\text{so, } y = 21 - 15$$
$$y = 6$$

2. Problem: Solve $x^2 - 6x + 8 = 0$ using the quadratic formula.
   Solution: $a = 1$, $b = -6$, $c = 8$

$$x = \frac{-b \pm \sqrt{b^2 - 4ac}}{2a}$$

$$= \frac{-(-6) \pm \sqrt{(-6)^2 - 4(1)\,(8)}}{2(1)}$$

$$= \frac{6 \pm \sqrt{36 - 32}}{2}$$

$$= \frac{6 \pm \sqrt{4}}{2} = \frac{6 \pm 2}{2}$$

$$x = \frac{6 + 2}{2} = \frac{8}{2} = 4$$

or

$$x = \frac{6 - 2}{2} = \frac{4}{2} = 2$$

$$x = 4, 2$$

Reading and Drawing Graphs, Tables, and Diagrams   Graphs, tables, and diagrams are often included in textbook chapters. These are intended to help you understand processes and concepts by providing a visual representation. Treat these drawings as essential parts of the chapter. Here are a few suggestions on how to use them:

1. **Study each drawing closely, frequently referring to the text that accompanies it.** Test your understanding of the drawing by reconstructing and labeling it without reference to the text drawing; then compare drawings.

2. **Use the drawings in the text as models on which to base your own drawings.** As you solve end-of-chapter problems, create drawings similar to those included in the text. These may be useful as you decide how to solve the problem.

3. **Draw your own diagrams to clarify or explore relationships.** For example, an algebra student drew the following diagram of the trinomial equation:

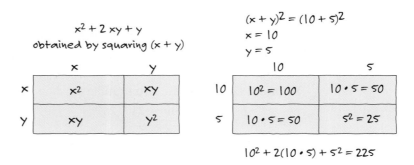

Another student drew the following diagram to explain why the formula for finding the area of a parallelogram is $A = bh$.

Cut off the triangle on
left side of parallelogram.

Move the triangle to create
a rectangle.
Area of rectangle = base • height
so Area of parallelogram also = base • height
$A = bh$

4. **Use tables to organize and categorize large amounts of complicated data.** For example, a student made the following table to solve a frequency distribution problem in statistics, in which she was asked to identify the frequency of female Democrats and male Republicans. She was provided with the following information: Of a sample of 150 people, 62 males and 31 females are Democrats. Thirty-eight males and 19 females are Republicans.

	DEMOCRAT	REPUBLICAN	TOTALS
Male	62	38	100
Female	31	19	50
Totals	93	57	150

Solving Word Problems Most textbook chapters have numerous problem-solving exercises; quizzes and exams also consist primarily of problems. Often, the problems are expressed in words and are not conveniently set up for you in formulas or equations. Solving word problems is a seven-step process. In your textbook, be sure to work through exercises as they occur in the chapter. Do not wait until the end and try to work them all at once. Read the problem once to get an overview of the situation; then use the following steps:

1. **Identify what is asked for.** What are you supposed to find?
2. **Locate the information that is provided to solve the problem.** (Some math problems may include irrelevant information; if so, underline or circle pertinent data.)
3. **Draw a diagram, if possible.** Label the diagram.
4. **Estimate your answer.** If possible, make a guess about what the answer should be. Be sure your guess is reasonable and logical.
5. **Decide on a procedure to solve the problem.** Recall formulas you have learned that are related to the problem, and look for clue words that indicate a particular process. For example, the phrase "how fast" means *rate;* you may be able to use the formula $r = d/t$. If you do not know how to solve a problem, look for similarities between it and sample problems you have studied.
6. **Solve the problem.** Begin by choosing variables to represent the unknown quantities. Then set up an equation.
7. **Verify your answer.** Compare your answer with your estimate. If there is a large discrepancy, this is a signal that you have made an error. There are

three possibilities: (1) the solution is correct, but the estimate was off base, (2) the solution is wrong, but the estimate is good, or (3) both the answer and estimate are wrong. Check to be sure your estimate is reasonable and logical. Then check your problem-solving strategy and your arithmetic.

Figure 15-7 gives an example of how this problem-solving process works.

FIGURE 15-7   Sample Word Problem

Problem: A four-ton passenger paddleboat goes 210 miles down the Mississippi River in the same time it can go 140 miles upriver. The speed of the current is five miles per hour. Find the speed of the boat in still water.

Steps	*Solution*
1. Identify what is asked for.	speed in still water
2. Locate given quantities.	210 miles down 140 miles up
3. Draw a diagram.	

4. Estimate the answer.	Estimate: 20 mph
5. Decide on a procedure; recall formulas.	$d = rt$ (distance = rate x time)
6. Solve the problem.	x = speed in still water time up = time down $d = r \times t$ downstream $210 = (x + 5)t$ upstream $140 = (x - 5)t$
(a) Solve for t.	$d = rt$ $t = d/r$
(b) Determine t values.	$t \text{ (downstream)} = \dfrac{210}{(x + 5)}$ $t \text{ (upstream)} = \dfrac{140}{(x - 5)}$
(c) $t = t$	$\dfrac{210}{(x + 5)} = \dfrac{140}{(x - 5)}$
(d) Multiply both sides by $(x + 5)$ $(x - 5)$.	$(x + 5)(x - 5)\dfrac{210}{(x + 5)} = (x + 5)(x - 5)\dfrac{140}{(x - 5)}$
(e) Solve the equation.	$210 (x - 5) = 140 (x + 5)$ $210x - 1050 = 140x + 700$ $70x = 1750$ $x = 25$
7. Compare with estimate and check arithmetic.	answer 25 mph (estimate was 20 mph)

EXERCISE 15-3   *Complete each of the following problems using the procedure outlined above. Label each step.*

1. Samantha receives an 11% commission on her sales of cosmetics. During one week, her daily sales were $482.10, $379.80, $729.62, $524.24, and $310.40. Find her gross earnings for the week.
2. If a microwave oven costs the retailer $325 and the markup is 35%, find the selling price.
3. Two joggers start jogging from the same point on a highway. One is running north, and the other is running south. One jogs 2 miles per hour faster than the other. They are 24 miles apart after 3 hours. At what rate is each jogging?
4. A collection of nickels and dimes is worth $2.85. If there are 34 coins in the collection, how many of each type of coin are there?
5. One number is 6 larger than another. The square of the larger is 96 more than the square of the smaller. Find the numbers.

EXERCISE 15-4   *Write three sample word problems. Exchange your problems with another student, and solve each other's problems.*

Using End-of-Chapter Material   Many mathematics texts include useful review material at the end of the chapter. Typically, there is a summary of key ideas from the chapter, often with sample worked examples; key terms; review exercises; and a chapter test. Use these materials to test yourself.

Use Writing to Learn

As in most disciplines, reading is not sufficient for learning mathematics. Highlighting and marking are the strategies students generally use to enhance learning; however, these techniques do not work well in mathematics. Mathematics texts are concise; everything is important. Writing, instead of highlighting, is a useful reading and learning strategy in mathematics. Writing in your own words will force you to convert mathematical language to everyday language. It will also demonstrate what you understand and what you do not. The following list suggests a few ways to use writing to increase your understanding and learning in mathematics:

1. **Definitions.** Read the textbook definition; then close the book and write your own. Compare it with the textbook definition, noticing and correcting discrepancies. Rewrite your definition until it is correct and complete.
2. **Class notes.** Rewrite your notes, including more detail and explanation. Focus on process; include reasons and explanations. Include information from the corresponding textbook section.
3. **Questions.** Write lists of questions based on chapter assignments, homework assignments, and your class notes. Seek answers from classmates, your instructor, a review book, or the learning lab or tutorial services.

4. **Problems.** Once you think you understand a particular problem or process, write down what you understand. To test your recall, write several questions based on your written explanation. Put aside both your explanation and your questions for several days. Then take out the question sheet and, without reference to your explanation, try to answer your questions. Compare your answers with your original explanation.

5. **Tests.** When preparing for an exam, construct and answer sample questions and problems. It is also effective to exchange self-constructed problems with a classmate and solve them.

6. **Diagrams.** Draw diagrams of sample problems as you read, and diagram actual problems before you attempt a solution. Describing the situation in visual terms often makes it more understandable.

7. **Review.** Review your course weekly. Write a description of what you have learned in the past week. You might compare your description with those of your classmates. Keep your weekly descriptions; they will be useful as you review for tests and final exams.

EXERCISE 15-5

Read Figure 15-8 on page 441, an excerpt from a basic college mathematics textbook on the Pythagorean Theorem. Then complete each of the following steps.

1. List the terminology that is essential to understand when reading this excerpt.
2. Without referring to the text, write a definition of *hypotenuse*. Make a diagram to illustrate your definition. Compare your definition and diagram with the text excerpt. Revise your definition and diagram, if necessary.
3. Without referring to the text, describe how to use the Pythagorean Theorem to find the unknown length of the hypotenuse in a right triangle. Compare your description with the text excerpt. Revise your description if necessary.
4. Find the unknown length in the following right triangles.

(a)   (b)   (c)

Expect Gradual Understanding

Mathematics is a reasoning process: a process of understanding relationships and seeing similarities and differences. Consequently, mathematics is not an "either you understand it or you don't" discipline. Your understanding will develop by degrees; it grows as you work or "play with" problems. Here is how you can work toward developing your understanding as you read:

1. **Plan on reading, and then reading and solving, and finally re-solving, problems.** As you reread and re-solve problems, you often will come to a new understanding of the process involved. (This is similar to seeing a film

FIGURE 15–8   Pythagorean Theorem

Objective ▸   One place you will use square roots is when working with the *Pythagorean Theorem.* This theorem applies only to *right* triangles (triangles with a 90° angle). The longest side of a right triangle is called the **hypotenuse** (hy-POT-en-oos). It is opposite the right angle. The other two sides are called *legs.* The legs form the right angle.

Examples of right triangles

Pythagorean Theorem

$$(\text{hypotenuse})^2 = (\text{leg})^2 + (\text{leg})^2$$

In other words, square the length of each side. After you have squared all the sides, the sum of the squares of the two legs will equal the square of the hypotenuse.

$$(\text{hypotenuse})^2 = (\text{leg})^2 + (\text{leg})^2$$
$$5^2 = 4^2 + 3^2$$
$$25 = 16 + 9$$
$$25 = 25$$

If you know the lengths of any two sides in a right triangle, you can use the Pythagorean Theorem to find the length of the third side.

Pythagorean Theorem

To find the hypotenuse, use this formula:

$$\text{hypotenuse} = \sqrt{(\text{leg})^2 + (\text{leg})^2}$$

EXAMPLE 2   Finding the Unknown Length in a Right Triangle

Find the unknown length in this right triangle.

The length of the side opposite the right angle is unknown. That side is the hypotenuse, so use this formula.

$\text{hypotenuse} = \sqrt{(\text{leg})^2 + (\text{leg})^2}$	Find the hypotenuse.
$\text{hypotenuse} = \sqrt{(3)^2 + (4)^2}$	Legs are 3 and 4.
$= \sqrt{9 + 16}$	$3 \cdot 3$ is 9 and $4 \cdot 4$ is 16
$= \sqrt{25}$	
$= 5$	

The hypotenuse is 5 ft. long.

Note: You use the Pythagorean Theorem to find the *length* of one side, *not* the area of the triangle. Your answer will be in linear units, such as ft, yd, cm, m, and so on (*not* ft², cm², m²).

Source: Lial et al., *Basic College Mathematics,* pp. 548–49 or reading a novel a second time; you will notice and discover things you did not see the first time.)

2. **Experiment with the chapter's content.** The style of most textbooks is concise, but this does not mean that there is no room for creativity or experimentation. Try various solutions to problems. As you experiment, you will come to a new understanding of the problems and solutions.

3. **Take risks.** Attempt a solution to a problem even if you do not fully understand it. As you work, you may discover more about how to arrive at the correct answer.

4. **Be active.** Active reading (see Chapter 1) is essential in mathematics. Get involved with the ideas, ask questions, and search for applications.

5. **Study mathematics frequently.** Because learning is gradual, it is better to study mathematics frequently rather than in large blocks of time. For example, studying one hour a day for six days is much better than studying three hours on two different days.

■ Thought Patterns in Mathematics

Many students think that memorizing formulas, entire problems, and complete theories is the key to success in mathematics. This does not usually work because one predominant thought pattern in mathematics is *process*. Your goal in many situations is to see *how* a problem is solved or *how* a theory applies. As you make notes on chapters and as you rewrite class notes, explain, in your own words, how and why things work. Include reasons, explain relationships, and state why a particular operation was selected or why one problem-solving strategy was chosen over another.

Problem solving is also a primary pattern in most mathematics courses. Class activities, homework, and exams all require problem solving. Problem solving in mathematics involves creativity and even playfulness. It is not, as many students think, a matter of merely plugging numbers into a preselected formula and completing the necessary computations. Instead, problem solving is the process of assessing a situation (problem) and assembling and applying what you have learned that fits the problem. As you attempt to solve problems, do not immediately reach for a formula. Instead, analyze, think, and experiment while you work. Try several approaches and decide which one works best.

A third common thought pattern evident in many mathematics courses is comparison and contrast. Understanding and solving problems often requires you to see the similarities and differences among problem types and to study variations of sample problems. Often, you must look at a series of examples and detect a pattern (similarities) and then find a way to state this pattern as an equation or formula or rule. As you read and study, then, make notes about similarities and differences as they occur to you. Write, in your own words, how one problem differs from, or is a variation of, a type of problem you have previously learned about.

■ Studying Mathematics

Be certain to attend all classes. Because mathematics is sequential, if you miss one specific skill, that gap in your understanding may cause you trouble all term. Expect regular homework assignments and complete them on time, even if your instructor does not require you to turn them in. Practice is an essential element in all mathematics courses. Never let yourself get behind or skip assignments. Try to study mathematics at least three times a week—more often, if possible. Use the following suggestions to learn mathematics more effectively.

Preparing for Class

1. **Emphasize accuracy and precision.** In mathematics, knowing how to solve the problem is not enough; you must produce the right answer. A small error in arithmetic can produce a wrong answer, even when you know how to solve the problem. Use a calculator if your instructor allows it.

2. **Read the chapter carefully before working on exercises.** Do not worry if you do not understand everything right away. Then, as you work on the problems, refer to the chapter frequently.

3. **Before you begin a new chapter or assignment, always review the preceding one.** If you take a break while working on an assignment, do a brief one-minute review when you resume study.

4. **Read the portion of your textbook that covers the next day's lecture before attending class.** The lecture will be more meaningful if you have some idea of what it is about beforehand.

5. **In your class notes, be sure to record sample problems that your instructor solves in class.** If you get behind in taking notes, leave some blank space; then fill in what is missing later by working with a classmate or asking your instructor. After class, review and organize your notes, rewriting them if necessary. Add your own observations and ideas from your textbook as well.

6. **Rework sample problems solved in class.** This is an excellent means of review.

7. **Find a study group and work together to solve problems immediately after class.** Get the phone numbers of a few people in class whom you can call if you have missed an assignment or are stuck on a problem.

8. **Keep your homework in a special notebook.** Star the problems you have trouble with. Bring this notebook with you when you ask your instructor for help so that you can go immediately to those problems. When you review for a test, study the starred problems.

Preparing Sample Tests

One of the best ways to learn mathematics is to create your own sample tests. Use index cards to write your questions. Try to create three or four test question cards for each section of the chapter as you go along. Write the problem, including the directions, on the front of the card; write the solution and a page number reference to your text on the back. When preparing for a test, shuffle the cards so you are forced to work the problems out of order. Try to simulate test conditions; give yourself a time limit, allow yourself the same equipment (such as a calculator), and so forth.

Building Your Confidence

1. **Approach mathematics confidently.** Both men and women can suffer what has come to be known as "math anxiety." Math anxiety often reflects a negative self-concept: "I'm not good at math." Some students think, incorrectly, that one either has or does not have a mathematical mind. This is a myth. Some people may find the subject easier than others, but the average student can learn mathematics.

2. **If you feel uncomfortable about taking your first math course, consider taking a basic refresher course in which you are likely to be successful.** You may not earn college credit, but you will build your confidence and prove to yourself that you can handle math. Other students find working with computerized review programs helpful when catching up on fundamentals. The machine is nonthreatening, offers no time pressures, and allows you to review a lesson as many times as you want. Many campuses offer workshops on overcoming math anxiety. To find out what help is available, check with your instructor, the learning lab, or the counseling center. A particularly useful book is *Conquering Math Anxiety,* by Cynthia Arem.

Test-Taking Tips
Preparing for Exams in Mathematics

Exams in mathematics usually consist of problems to solve. Use the following tips to prepare for exams in mathematics:

1. When studying for exams, pay attention to what your instructor has emphasized. Predict what will be on the exam, and make a sample test that includes all the important topics, and practice completing it.

2. When studying for an exam, review as many sample problems as possible. Do not just read the problems; practice solving them. Try to anticipate the variations that may appear. For example, a variation of the paddleboat problem shown in Figure 15-7 may give you the rate but ask you to compute the distance.

3. Identify problems that are most characteristic of the techniques presented in the chapter you are studying. Record these on a study sheet, and summarize in your own words how you worked them. Compare your study sheet with that of a friend.

4. As you solve homework problems and review returned exams and quizzes, search for a pattern of errors. Is there one type of problem you frequently have trouble with? Do you make mistakes when setting up the equation, in factoring, or in computation? If you identify such a pattern, pay special attention to correcting these errors.

5. **If you are having trouble with your course, get help immediately.** Once you get behind, it is difficult to catch up. Consult with your instructor during his or her office hours. Check with the learning lab for tutoring or computer-assisted review programs.

6. **If you find you are weak in a particular fundamental such as fractions, correct the problem as soon as possible.** If you do not, it will interfere with your performance.

7. **Obtain additional study aids.** Schaum's *College Outline Series* offers excellent study guides. Check with your instructor for additional references.

8. **When a test is returned, rework the problems on which you lost points to find out exactly what you did wrong.**

Self-Test Summary

1. What is the primary process involved in learning mathematics?	Mathematics is largely sequential and cumulative, with each skill building on—and hinging on—previously learned skills.
2. What are four useful techniques for reading mathematics?	Four useful techniques for reading mathematics are • previewing before reading. • learning mathematical language. • following chapter organization (including explanations, sample problems, diagrams, and graphs). • learning to solve word problems.
3. In mathematics, how are ideas and relationships expressed?	Ideas and relationships are expressed through notations, symbols, numbers, and formulas.
4. List the seven steps used in solving word problems.	Seven steps for resolving word problems are • identifying what is being asked for. • locating the information that is provided to solve the problem. • drawing a diagram, if possible, and labeling it. • estimating your answer. • deciding on a procedure to use to solve the problem. • solving the problem. • verifying the answer.

(continued)

Self–Test Summary   *(continued)*

5. List seven ways to use writing to help you learn mathematics.	Use writing for • writing your own definitions of terms. • rewriting class notes. • writing questions based on assignments and class notes. • recording problem-solving methods. • preparing sample problems for tests. • drawing diagrams as you read. • reviewing your learning.
6. List five techniques that will help you gradually understand mathematics.	To gradually understand mathematics, • plan on rereading and resolving problems. • experiment with chapter content. • take risks. • read actively. • study frequently.
7. What are the three most common thought patterns used in mathematics?	The three patterns are process, problem/solution, and comparison and contrast.
8. List three tips for studying mathematics.	Three tips for studying mathematics are • prepare for class. • prepare sample tests. • build your confidence.

Introduction to Statistics: Mean, Median, and Mode

Margaret L. Lial and Diana L. Hestwood

Prereading Questions

1. Preview this selection. On the basis of your preview, write a sentence describing its contents.
2. How difficult do you predict it will be to complete the exercises at the end of this selection?

1   The word *statistics* originally came from words that mean *state numbers.* State numbers refer to numerical information, or *data,* gathered by the government such as the number of births, deaths, or marriages in a population. Today the word *statistics* has a much broader meaning; data from the fields of economics, social science, science, and business can all be organized and studied under the branch of mathematics called *statistics.*

2   **Objective ▶** Making sense of a long list of numbers can be hard. So when you analyze data, one of the first things to look for is a *measure of central tendency*—a single number that you can use to represent the entire list of numbers. One such measure is the *average* or **mean.** The mean can be found with the following formula.

Finding the Mean (Average)

3
$$\text{mean} = \frac{\text{sum of all values}}{\text{number of all values}}$$

EXAMPLE 1 Finding the Mean

4   David had test scores of 84, 90, 95, 98, and 88. Find his average or mean score. Use the formula for finding mean. Add up all the test scores and then divide by the number of tests.

$$\text{mean} = \frac{84 + 90 + 95 + 98 + 88}{5} \quad \begin{array}{l} \leftarrow \text{Sum of test scores} \\ \leftarrow \text{Number of tests} \end{array}$$

$$= \frac{455}{5} \quad \text{Divide}$$

$$= 91$$

David has a mean score of 91.

5   **Objective ▶** Some items in a list of data might appear more than once. In this case, we find a **weighted mean,** in which each value is "weighted" by multiplying it by the number of times it occurs.

EXAMPLE 2 Understanding the Weighted Mean

6   The following table shows the amount of contribution and the number of times the amount was given (frequency) to a food pantry. Find the weighted mean.

Contribution	
Value	Frequency
$ 3	4
$ 5	2
$ 7	1
$ 8	5
$ 9	3
$10	2
$12	1
$13	2

7   The same amount was given by more than one person: for example, $5 was given twice and $8 was given five times. Other amounts, such as $12, were given once. To find the mean, multiply each contribution value by its frequency. Then add the products. Next, add the numbers in the *frequency* column to find the total number of values.

Value	Frequency	Product
$ 3	4	$(3 \cdot 4) = \$12$
$ 5	2	$(5 \cdot 2) = \$10$
$ 7	1	$(7 \cdot 1) = \$ 7$
$ 8	5	$(8 \cdot 5) = \$40$
$ 9	3	$(9 \cdot 3) = \$27$
$10	2	$(10 \cdot 2) = \$20$
$12	1	$(12 \cdot 1) = \$12$
$13	2	$(13 \cdot 2) = \$26$
Totals	20	$154

Finally, divide the totals.

$$\text{mean} = \frac{\$154}{20} = \$7.70$$

The mean contribution to the food pantry was $7.70.

8   A common use of the weighted mean is to find a student's *grade point average*, as shown by the next example.

EXAMPLE 3 Applying the Weighted Mean

9   Find the grade point average for a student earning the following grades. Assume A = 4, B = 3, C = 2, D = 1, and F = 0. The number of credits determines how many times the grade is counted (the frequency).

Course	Credits	Grade	Credits · Grade
Mathematics	3	A (= 4)	$3 \cdot 4 = 12$
Speech	3	C (= 2)	$3 \cdot 2 = 6$
English	3	B (= 3)	$3 \cdot 3 = 9$
Computer Science	3	A (= 4)	$3 \cdot 4 = 12$
Lab for Computer Science	2	D (= 1)	$2 \cdot 1 = 2$
Totals	14		41

It is common to round grade point averages to the nearest hundredth. So the grade point average for this student is shown below.

$$\frac{41}{14} \approx 2.93$$

10   **Objective ▶** Because it can be affected by extremely high or low numbers, the mean is often a poor indicator of central tendency for a list of numbers. In cases like this, another measure of central tendency, called the **median** (MEE-dee-un), can be used. The *median* divides a group of numbers in half; half the numbers lie above the median, and half lie below the median.

11   Find the median by listing the numbers *in order* from *smallest* to *largest.* If the list contains an *odd* number of items, the median is the *middle number.*

EXAMPLE 4 Using the Median

12   Find the median for the following list of prices.

$$\$7, \$23, \$15, \$6, \$18, \$12, \$24$$

First arrange the numbers in numerical order from smallest to largest.

Smallest → 6, 7, 12, 15, 18, 23, 24 ← Largest

Next, find the middle number in the list.

$$\underbrace{6, 7, 12}, 15, \underbrace{18, 23, 24}$$

Three are below | Three are above

Middle number

The median price is $15.

13   If a list contains an *even* number of items, there is no single middle number. In this case, the median is defined as the mean (average) of the *middle two* numbers.

EXAMPLE 5 Finding the Median

14   Find the median for the following list of ages.

74, 7, 15, 13, 25, 28, 47, 59, 32, 68

First arrange the numbers in numerical order. Then find the middle two numbers.

Smallest → 7, 13, 15, 25, $\underbrace{28, 32,}$ 47, 59, 68, 74 ← Largest

Middle two numbers

The median age is the mean of these two numbers.

$$\text{median} = \frac{28 + 32}{2} = \frac{60}{2} = 30 \text{ years}$$

15   **Objective ▶** The last important statistical measure is the **mode,** the number that occurs most often in a list of numbers. For example, if the test scores for 10 students were

↓   ↓   ↓

74, 81, 39, 74, 82, 80, 100, 92, 74, and 85

then the mode is 74. Three students earned a score of 74, so 74 appears more times on the list than any other score.

16   A list can have two modes; such a list is sometimes called *bimodal.* If no number occurs more frequently than any other number in a list, the list has *no mode.*

Measures of Central Tendency

17   The **mean** is the sum of all the values divided by the number of values. It is the mathematical average.

The **median** is the middle number in a group of values that are listed from smallest to largest. It divides a group of numbers in half.

The **mode** is the value that occurs most often in a group of values.

—Lial and Hestwood, *Prealgebra*, pp. 347–50

Writing About the Reading
CHECKING YOUR VOCABULARY

1. For each of the words listed below, use context; prefixes, roots, and suffixes (see Chapter 3); and/or a dictionary to write a brief definition of the word as it used in the reading.

    a. state numbers (para. 1) _____

    b. data (para. 1) _____

    c. values (para. 3) _____

    d. frequency (para. 6) _____

2. Underline new, specialized terms introduced in the reading.

3. Draw a word map of one of the words in the reading.

CHECKING YOUR COMPREHENSION

1. To assess your comprehension, define each of the following terms in your own words without reference to the reading: *statistics, measure of central*

tendency, mean, median, mode. Verify your definitions by comparing them with the definitions in the reading.

2. What is the difference between a mean and a mode?
3. What is the difference between a mean and a median?

THINKING CRITICALLY

1. List the names and ages of 15 friends or classmates. (Estimate the ages, if necessary.)
   a. Find the mean age and the median age.
   b. Are the mean and median ages similar or different? Why did that happen?
2. List the names and ages of 10 family members or relatives. Try to include one very young person or one very old person (but not both). Estimate the ages, if necessary.
   a. Find the mean age and the median age.
   b. Are the mean age and median ages similar or different? Why did that happen?
3. List the courses you are taking at this time and the number of credits for each course.
   a. List the highest grade you think you will earn in each course. Then find your grade point average.
   b. List the lowest grade you think you will earn in each course. Then find your grade point average.
4. Suppose you own a gift shop. Last summer, you stocked T-shirts in five different sizes, but they took up too much shelf space. This summer, you want to order only one size. Using last summer's sales, should you find the mean size, median size, or mode size? Explain your answer.

LEARNING/STUDY STRATEGIES

1. Write a summary of the process involved in finding
   a. the mean.
   b. the median.
   c. the mode.
2. What overall thought pattern(s) is or are used in the reading?

ONLINE RESEARCH: STATISTICS*

Statistics are used to describe the results of surveys and other research in many different fields. Often, the "raw" data are not given in reports; instead, the researcher has already analyzed the data before presenting it to the public. The sites listed below include instances of both raw data and data that have already been analyzed. The questions, however, focus on raw data that you can analyze yourself.

---

*If either of these sites is unavailable, use a search engine to locate a new Web site on the same topic.

1. The Media Awareness Network maintains statistics about television and other media. Visit their "Media Content: Television" page at http://www.media-awareness.ca/english/resources/researchdocuments/ statistics/advertising/clutterrise.cfm. Find the summary titled "T.V. 'Clutter' On The Rise." Read the summary to find out how much TV broadcasting time is taken up by commercials and other nonprogramming content. List the four time slots mentioned and the amount of time taken in each hour (given in minutes and seconds) for nonprogramming content. What is the mean amount of time for nonprogramming content per hour of TV content overall?

2. The Center for Science in the Public Interest, an organization that seeks to improve the safety and nutritional quality of food, includes an article about soft drinks titled "Liquid Candy" at http://www.cspinet.org/ sodapop/liquidcandy.htm. Scan the article to find Table 2. From the table data, determine the mean ounces per day of soda drunk by all teens (boys and girls together). Then find the median number of ounces per day. Finally, does the list include a mode? If so, what is it?

ADDITIONAL PRACTICE

MATHEMATICS ON THE INTERNET

The Internet has numerous resources available for research in mathematics, including directories and Web guides to help you find material relevant to your studies, journals and databases, references works, and government resources. Here is a list of useful Web sites to get you started.

Directories/Web Guides

Yahoo! Mathematics
http://dir.yahoo.com/Science/Mathematics/

Mathematics WWW Virtual Library
http://www.math.fsu.edu/Science/math.html

Journals/Indexes/Databases

Math on the Web: Mathematical Journals
http://www.ams.org/mathweb/mi-journals.html

Mathematics Journals
http://www.math.psu.edu/MathLists/Journals.html

References

Women Mathematicians
http://www.agnesscott.edu/lriddle/women/women.htm

Math Problems Database
http://endeavor.MACUSA.net/mathprogress/index.htm

Government Resources

MCS Research
http://www-fp.mcs.anl.gov/division/research/

Toward a Metric America
http://www.pueblo.gsa.gov/cic_text/misc/usmetric/metric.htm

MULTIMEDIA ACTIVITIES

Practice your reading and research skills on the Web.

1. **Math in Daily Life**

   http://www.learner.org/exhibits/dailymath/index.html

   Make a list of all the ways you apply math in your daily life. Then compare your list with the situations presented on this site. Do you use more math than you realized?

2. **Math Formula Sheets**

   http://faculty.prairiestate.edu/skifowit/htdocs/sheets/sheets.htm

   Print out these clear formula study sheets. Use memory building techniques to help you memorize them. Make copies and post them where you can see them easily. Try gluing them to index cards and quizzing yourself or a classmate.

16 Reading in the Natural Sciences

- ✦To understand the scientific approach

- ✦To develop specialized reading techniques for the sciences

- ✦To learn to work with process, cause and effect, classification, and problem/solution patterns

- ✦To adapt study strategies for the sciences

Think About It!

Albert

Rachel

Claude

Can you identify these people? Can you pick out the individual who is not a scientist? You probably had difficulty picking out the person who did not belong. Scientists are ordinary people who have chosen to study the natural world around them.

The third photo does not belong. Claude Monet is a famous impressionist painter. The other photos are of Albert Einstein and

Rachel Carson. Einstein is often thought of as the father of modern science; Carson is well-known as a marine scientist.

What does it take to be a scientist? To study the sciences, you have to think and work like a scientist. In this chapter you will learn to read and study the natural sciences.

The natural sciences are divided into two categories: life sciences and physical sciences. The life sciences—biology, botany, zoology, and physiology—are concerned with the study of living organisms: how they grow, develop, function, and reproduce. The physical sciences are concerned with the properties, functions, structure, and composition of matter, substances, and energy. They include physics, chemistry, astronomy, and physical geography and geology.

■ The Sciences: Explaining Natural Phenomena

Science is built on knowledge resulting from scientific investigation. Through a process of asking well-defined, specific questions and searching for answers, science has accumulated a body of knowledge about how our physical and biological worlds function. The goal of science is to explain natural phenomena that affect our daily lives. Scientists ask questions and search for answers about any unexplained event. Consider, for example, the disease called AIDS. In scientific research that is still continuing, scientists have asked questions such as:

What causes it?

Why does it occur?

How is it transmitted?

What is its incubation period?

What are its precise effects on the immune system?

Because the emphasis is on observation and experimentation, most science courses have a required weekly lab in which you are given the opportunity to observe and experiment. The lab gives you direct experience with the scientific method while reinforcing, explaining, or demonstrating theories and principles presented in the course lectures.

Why Study the Sciences?

The field of natural science investigates the physical world around us. Science addresses and attempts to answer many important questions:

Is there extraterrestrial life?

Why do leaves change color in the fall?

Why do I have blue eyes when my parents' eyes are brown?

Science also explores questions essential to our well-being:

A Science Professor . . .

William J. Straits, PhD, Assistant Professor of Science Education, University of California, Long Beach

Talks About This Chapter

"Overall this chapter does do a fine job of describing reading and study skills. . . . I like that the author includes a section on how to study and draw diagrams, as these are of great importance in learning science, particularly learning science from texts."

Offers Advice for Learning in the Sciences

1. "I always encourage my students to ask themselves, 'What concepts would I test about if I was the instructor?' and to then compare their ideas with two or three classmates. I find collectively a small group of students are nearly always able to identify the most important ideas."

2. "Controversy seems to be *the new issue* in science today. Students need to be able to, and need to be open to, reading information about the science related to bio-engineering, evolution, global warming, etc., regardless of their individual beliefs about the appropriateness of these issues in society. . . . Students often get sidetracked in the politicized aspects of an issue; they want to discuss what they 'feel.' In science classes these personal opinions, while important, must be informed by an understanding of what the scientific community 'knows.'"

How can cancer be cured or prevented?

What synthetic substitutes can prevent depletion of our natural resources?

How can water pollution be prevented?

The study of science is fun and rewarding because you come to understand more about yourself and how you interact with the physical world around you.

■ Specialized Reading Techniques

Although most college courses present new concepts and principles, they often cover subjects in the realm of your experience. The social sciences, for example, deal with social groups and physical and emotional needs—all concerns familiar to you. Science courses, on the other hand, sometimes deal with less familiar topics—molecular structure, mutant genes, or radioactive isotopes, for instance. Treatment of these topics may also be detailed and technical, involving a new and extensive vocabulary.

Because of the detailed nature of scientific material, plan to commit more time to reading and studying it than you would to studying other material—generally twice as much. Many students find that scientific study requires much greater time and effort than their other courses. Taking a science course is like taking three courses in one. You are, in a sense, taking a language course, since there is much new terminology to learn. A science course is also like a logic or philosophy course, since you must learn to work flexibly and logically with new ideas. Finally, a science course is like a graphic arts course in which you learn to draw and understand visual representations.

Reading scientific material requires specialized techniques, as does each of your other courses, but once you develop an effective approach, you will find science courses to be interesting and challenging, as well as manageable.

Use the following strategies to strengthen your approach to scientific reading.

Preview Before Reading

Because scientific material is often detailed and unfamiliar, previewing is even more important than in other courses. (Refer to Chapter 1 for a review of previewing techniques.) Your preview should include looking at problems at the end of the chapter and the chapter summary because they will provide clues about principles and formulas emphasized in the chapter.

Adopt a Scientific Mind–Set

To read effectively in a science course, it is essential to adopt a scientific way of thinking. The usual concerns (such as "What is important to learn?" and "How much supporting information do I need to learn?") may be of only secondary importance. Instead, to be successful, you must adopt the scientific mind-set of asking questions and seeking answers, analyzing problems, and looking for solutions or explanations. As you read, continually ask questions such as:

- **What does this mean? What does it *not* mean?**
- **Does this make sense to me?**
- **Why is this so?**
- **How do we know this?**
- **How does this happen?**
- **What does this show?**
- **Are alternative explanations plausible?**
- **What laws govern or affect this?**

To illustrate this process, Figure 16-1 (p. 458) shows the questions a student asked as she read a page of her chemistry textbook.

Sometimes, the questions you ask will be answered as you continue reading. Other times, you may need to seek answers yourself by referring to another chapter, by asking your instructor, or by talking with classmates. Asking and answering these questions will get you involved with the material and direct you toward scientific critical thinking.

EXERCISE 16-1   *Read the following excerpt from a human physiology textbook. What questions could you ask about the excerpt? Write them in the margin.*

FIGURE 16-1   Scientific Thinking

MARS

How far away is it?

Mars is the only planet whose surface features can be seen through Earth-based telescopes. Its distinctive rust-colored hue makes it stand out in the night sky. When Mars is near opposition, even telescopes for home use reveal its seasonal changes. Dark markings on the Martian surface can be seen to vary, and prominent polar caps shrink noticeably during the spring and summer months.

Why?

6-7 Earth-based observations originally suggested that Mars might harbor extraterrestrial life

Is it similar in other ways, as well?

The Dutch physicist Christian Huygens made the first reliable observations of Mars in 1659. Using a telescope of his own design, Huygens identified a prominent, dark surface feature that re-emerged roughly every 24 hours, suggesting a rate of rotation very much like the Earth's. Huygens' observations soon led to speculation about life on Mars because the planet seemed so similar to Earth.

In 1877 Giovanni Virginio Schiaparelli, an Italian astronomer, reported seeing 40 lines crisscrossing the Martian surface. He called these dark features *canali,* an Italian term meaning "water channels." It was soon mistranslated into English as *canals,* implying the existence on Mars of intelligent creatures capable of substantial engineering feats. This speculation led Percival Lowell, who came from a wealthy Boston family, to finance a major new observatory near Flagstaff, Arizona. By the end of the nineteenth century, Lowell had allegedly observed 160 Martian canals.

What evidence did he offer?

Why was it fashionable?
Who did this?

It soon became fashionable to speculate that the Martian canals formed an enormous planetwide irrigation network to transport water from melting polar caps to vegetation near the equator. (The seasonal changes in Mars' dark surface markings can be mistaken for vegetation.) In view of the planet's reddish, desertlike appearance, Mars was thought to be a dying planet whose inhabitants must go to great lengths to irrigate their farmlands. No doubt the Martians would readily abandon their arid ancestral homeland and invade the Earth for its abundant resources. Hundreds of science fiction stories and dozens of monster movies owe their existence to the canali of Schiaparelli.

What causes them?

Source: Kaufmann and Comins, *Discovering the Universe,* pp. 144–45

COLLOIDS IN THE CAFETERIA

The next time you are in a cafeteria, look closely at the colorful gelatin dessert. It appears to be a transparent, wobbly solid, yet it consists primarily of water. The chocolate pudding nearby is also mainly water. Is it a solid or a liquid? When you fill your glass with milk, can you determine whether it is a solution or a mixture? Like most foods, these are *colloids,* suspensions of particles ranging from 20 μm to 100 μm in diameter, in a solvent. Colloidal particles are much larger than most molecules but are too small to be seen with a microscope. Colloids thus are often classified between homogeneous solutions and heterogeneous mixtures. The small particles give the colloid a homogeneous appearance but are large enough to scatter light. The light scattering explains why milk is white, not transparent.

A colloid that is a suspension of solids in a liquid is called a *sol,* and a suspension of one liquid in another is called an *emulsion.* For example, skim milk is a suspension of solids, mainly proteins, in water, so it is a sol; mayonnaise has small droplets of water suspended in oil, so it is an emulsion. When we whip cream, milk rich in butterfat, or beat egg whites to form meringues, we make *foams,* suspensions of a gas in a liquid or solid. When we separate the fat from milk and churn it into butter, we create a *solid emulsion,* a suspension of a liquid, in this case, milk, in a solid, butterfat. Gelatin desserts are a type of solid emulsion called a *gel,* which is soft, but holds its shape.

Aqueous colloids can be classified as hydrophilic or hydrophobic. Suspensions of fat in water, such as milk and mayonnaise, are hydrophobic colloids, because fat molecules have little attraction for water molecules. Gels and puddings are examples of hydrophilic colloids. The macromolecules of the proteins in gelatin and the starch in pudding have many hydrophilic groups that attract water. The giant protein molecules in gelatin uncoil in hot water. Their abundant amide groups form hydrogen bonds with water. When the mixture cools, the protein chains link together again, but now they enclose many water molecules within themselves, as well as molecules of sugar, dye, and flavoring agents. The result is an open network of protein chains that hold the water in a flexible solid structure.

—Atkins and Jones, *Chemistry: Molecules, Matter, and Change,* p. 444

Learn Terminology and Notation

Physics: wave-particle duality, torque, tangential acceleration, $v = dx/dt$

Physiology: hemagglutination, ventricular diastole, myocardial infarction, DNA

Chemistry: NaCl

Astronomy: mass-luminosity relation, eclipsing binaries, bok globules

How many of these terms are familiar? They are only a few of the new terms and notations encountered in each of these courses. As you can see, you will need to spend considerable time and effort learning terminology. You must understand the meaning of specialized and technical words in order to understand the ideas and concepts being presented.

In some courses, such as physics and chemistry, formulas and notation are important as well. Symbols, abbreviations, and formulas are used to represent objects and concepts in abbreviated form. You might think of these as shorthand systems for naming elements and quantities and describing their interaction. As you read and study, avoid memorizing formulas; instead, focus on understanding what they mean and how to apply them.

A course master file, described in Chapter 3, is extremely valuable in science courses. Mapping also works well, especially in the life sciences. Finally, as you learn the meaning of each new term, also learn its correct pronunciation and spelling.

Learn Symbols and Abbreviations

Symbols and abbreviations are frequently used in the sciences. The abbreviation "g" is a shortcut expression for a unit of mass, called a gram. The symbol "g" can also stand for the gravitational constant, 9.8N/kg, for the surface of the

Earth. Textbooks use different kinds of type to distinguish types of quantities. For instance, "*v*" (in italics) means speed while "**v**" (in boldface) means velocity. Watch for clues your textbook provides.

Special Meanings of Everyday Words

Scientists sometimes attach specialized meanings to ordinary words. For example, *power, pressure, force,* and *impulse* are everyday words, but they have very specific meanings to a physicist. Power, for instance, is a measure of how fast work is done or energy is transformed and is represented by the formula:

Power = work ÷ time

Note that its meaning in science is different from its meaning in mathematics, too, where *power* refers to a number multiplied by itself. *Pressure,* another everyday term, in physics means the amount of force per area over which the force is distributed.

Because you are familiar with these words, it is easy to overlook them when studying or to assume you already know them. Be sure to include these terms in your course master file, along with the other specialized terminology and notations.

Learn Common Prefixes, Roots, and Suffixes

As you discovered in Chapter 3, many words in our language contain prefixes, roots, and suffixes. In most science courses, you will discover a common core of these word parts that are used as the basic building blocks of a specialized terminology. In physics, for example, units of measurement take prefixes.

PREFIX	MEANING
micro-	millionth
milli-	thousandth
centi-	hundredth
deci-	tenth
deka-	ten
hecto-	hundred
kilo-	thousand
mega-	million
giga-	billion

In physiology, roots and suffixes unlock the meaning of numerous frequently used terms.

ROOT	SUFFIX	WORD
hem(a)—blood	-logy (study of)	hematology
	-oma (growth, tumor)	hematoma
	-thermal (heat)	hemathermal

Similarly, in chemistry, astronomy, and biology you will find sets of core prefixes, roots, and suffixes. Include these in your master file, as suggested in Chapter 3.

Read Section by Section

Chapters in science texts are usually lengthy. Because the material is so complex, try not to read an entire chapter in one sitting. Instead, divide the chapter into sections and read one portion at a time. Look for end-of-chapter problems or questions that apply to the sections you are reading. Mark them and remember to work them out after you have read the section. Be sure to make connections between sections.

Study Sample Problems

In the physical sciences, sample problems are often included in the text to demonstrate a problem-solving process. Read the sample problems carefully, alternating between the text explanation and the mathematical solution. Next, explain the process in your own words. Doing so will solidify it in your memory. If you are unable to express the process in your own words or if you must refer back frequently to the text, this indicates that you do not fully understand the process. Do not expect to get it all the first time. These are difficult subjects, and understanding may come gradually.

Study and Draw Diagrams

Science texts contain numerous diagrams and drawings of structures and processes. These drawings often clarify a principle or concept; a diagram of a gun firing and recoiling, for example, makes the concept of conservation of momentum clear. Diagrams also are used to show forces, conditions, shapes, directions, processes, or positions. Diagrams provide a visual representation of an object or occurrence, and they increase your ability both to understand and to retain information. Diagrams are also important in answering questions and solving problems. Consult Chapter 10 of this text to learn how to read and study graphics and visuals.

Many students do not pay enough attention to the diagrams included in their texts. Take time to study each drawing as you read. As you review, use the drawings to refresh your recall of key concepts and processes. Test your recall by closing the book and drawing the diagram from memory. Compare your drawing with the one in the text, noting errors, missing parts, or discrepancies. Do not be concerned if your drawings seem poor in comparison to the text; your ability to draw will improve as you practice.

You will also find diagrams useful in laboratory situations. Draw brief sketches of your equipment setup, techniques, and observations. These will help as you write your lab reports.

Brush Up on Math Skills

Mathematics is an integral part of many science courses, especially chemistry and physics. Many instructors assume you have taken algebra, which is often needed to solve equations and problems. If your math background is weak or if it has been a number of years since you studied algebra, you may need to brush up on your skills. You might consider taking a review course, purchasing a skills practice book, or using computer-assisted instructional programs in the learning lab. Talk with your instructor, and ask for recommendations.

■ Thought Patterns in the Natural Sciences

Four thought patterns are common in the sciences: process, cause and effect, classification, and problem/solution.

The Process and Cause-and-Effect Patterns

Many of the sciences are concerned with how and why things happen: how a tadpole turns into a frog, what makes light reflect, how the tides work, how our metabolism functions, and so forth. Process and cause-and-effect patterns are often used to explain natural phenomena. Process and cause-and-effect patterns are logically linked to each other. In a process, the steps may be linked in a cause-and-effect chain. You may find that you need to read process descriptions more than once. Read the description the first time to get an overview; then read it at least once more to understand the steps and the connections between them.

Use the following strategies to read process material:

1. **List the steps.** Either in the text margin or in your notebook, write a step-by-step summary of the process in your own words. Figure 16-2 on page 463 shows the notes a student wrote for a physics textbook chapter on plate tectonics, explaining how islands and mountains are formed.

2. **Draw diagrams or maps.** Diagrams, maps, or flowcharts help you visualize the process and will enhance your recall as well. Chapter 10 describes several types of mapping. Figure 16-3 on page 464 shows a diagram a biology student drew to describe how convection currents stir the air and create winds.

3. **Describe the process aloud.** Assume you are explaining the process to a friend who is not taking the course, or better yet, actually study with a friend. By forcing yourself to explain the process in a nontechnical way, you can test whether you really understand it and are not simply rephrasing the technical language used by the author.

EXERCISE 16-2

LEARNING COLLABORATIVELY

Read the excerpt from a biology textbook on pp. 464–465. Working with a classmate, one student should write a summary of the transpiration process while the other draws a diagram. Exchange your work, and draw a diagram based only on your partner's summary, or write a summary based only on his or her diagram. Then compare the results with the whole excerpt.

FIGURE 16–2   Sample Summary

PLATE TECTONICS

Summary:

1. Earth's crust has approx. 12 large plates = lithosphere. These rest on the asthenosphere.

2. These plates spread and sink (subduction).

3. When a continental plate and an ocean plate collide, a trench and island arc will form.

4. When ocean plates collide, they create a marginal or inland sea.

5. When continental plates collide, folding and faulting of sediment and rock occurs, creating mountain ranges.

Recent ideas concerning seafloor spreading and the origin and evolution of the ocean basins are incorporated into an even more encompassing concept called **plate tectonics.** In plate tectonics theory, Earth's entire crust is composed of about a dozen large plates, up to 160 km (100 miles) thick. These plates make up the lithosphere. Each moves essentially as a rigid block over Earth's surface. The lithosphere rests upon the less rigid part of Earth called the **asthenosphere.**

The plates can be visualized as curved caps covering a large ball, or perhaps as sections of peel on an orange. Boundaries of the individual plates are usually areas of high seismic (earthquake) activity. Deformation, such as faulting, folding, or shearing mainly occurs at the boundaries between the plates. Because the surface area of Earth is essentially constant, spreading in one place must be balanced by sinking or **subduction** somewhere else.

The appearance of the edge of a continent is often influenced by its relation to areas of seafloor spreading or subduction. If a continent's edge is at the boundary of a subducting oceanic plate, a trench will form, and sometimes an **island arc** or coastal mountain range (Figure a). A **trench** is a deep, long narrow depression in the seafloor, with very steep slopes. An island arc is a curved pattern of mainly volcanic islands and a trench. It is

a Ocean/continent

generally curved in a convex direction (bows out) toward the ocean, with the trench on the seaward side. The Aleutian Islands and Aleutian Trench in the north Pacific is a good example of a trench-island arc system.

The subducting plate forms the trench. In the process of submerging beneath the other plate, much of its sediment is scraped off onto the landward side of the trench. This material and the subducting plate may be reheated, perhaps even melted, eventually becoming part of the continental plate and forming a coastal mountain range. These are events that occur when oceanic crust is subducted beneath lighter continental crust. A similar sequence occurs during the collision of two ocean plates. The main difference is that an inland or marginal sea may form behind an island arc (Figure b).

Results can be quite different when two plates of continental composition collide. In this case, both plates are of similar density, so neither easily overrides the other. The result is unusually intense folding and faulting of the sediments and rocks, often leading to the formation of a major mountain range (Figure c). The Himalayan Mountains are still being formed in this manner by the collision of India (continental crust) with Asia (continental crust).

b Ocean/ocean

c Continent/continent

SOURCE: Ross, *Introduction to Oceanography,* pp. 51–52

F!GURE 16-3   Sample Diagram

DIAGRAM

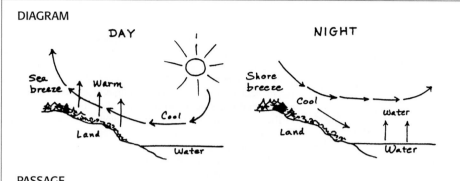

PASSAGE

Convection currents stirring the atmosphere result in winds. Some parts of the Earth's surface absorb heat from the sun more readily than others, and as a result the air near the surface is heated unevenly and convection currents form. This is evident at the seashore. In the daytime the shore warms more easily than the water; air over the shore is pushed up (we say it rises) by cooler air from above the water taking its place. The result is a sea breeze. At night the process reverses because the shore cools off more quickly than the water, and then the warmer air is over the sea. Build a fire on the beach and you'll notice that the smoke sweeps inward during the day and seaward at night.

SOURCE: Hewitt, *Conceptual Physics,* pp. 274–75

CARBON DIOXIDE AND THE GREENHOUSE EFFECT

The possible relationship between carbon dioxide in the atmosphere and climate warming was proposed by Svante Arrhenius, one of the early winners of the Nobel Prize in chemistry (1903). Arrhenius knew a great deal about geology as well as chemistry, and he was familiar with the effects of glaciation on the terrain of his native Sweden. He was also aware of the growing discussion of the causes of glaciations that enlivened many geologists' meetings at the end of the nineteenth century. He reasoned that the small amount of carbon dioxide in the atmosphere (now about 345 ppm) could affect climate because the carbon dioxide molecules strongly absorb heat rays from the Earth.

Here is how it works. The atmosphere is relatively transparent to the incoming visible rays of the Sun. Much of this radiant energy from the Sun is absorbed by the Earth's surface and then reemitted as invisible infrared heat rays. Just as a hot pavement radiates heat as it is warmed by the Sun, the Earth's surface radiates heat back to the atmosphere. The atmosphere, however, is not transparent to these infrared rays, because carbon dioxide and water molecules strongly absorb the infrared instead of allowing it to escape to space. As a result, the atmosphere is heated and radiates heat back to the surface. this is called the *greenhouse effect,* by analogy to the warming of a greenhouse, whose glass lets in visible light but lets little heat escape.

The more carbon dioxide, the warmer the atmosphere; the less carbon dioxide, the colder. Without any greenhouse effect, Earth's surface temperature would be well below freezing and the oceans would be a solid mass of ice. Geologists now have evidence that, aside from glaciations, climates ranged from warm to cool in the geological past. It is likely that some of these changes were related to changes in the amount of carbon dioxide in the atmosphere.

—Press and Siever, *Understanding Earth*, p. 348

The Classification Pattern

In the life sciences, classification is an important pattern. As a means of studying life forms or species, biologists classify them into groups or types based on shared or similar characteristics. Organisms are first divided into three domains. Those domains are subdivided into groups called kingdoms, and then into phyla classes, orders, families, genera, and species.

Other examples of classification include types of cells, methods of reproduction, and types of tissues.

Classification is also used in the physical sciences. In chemistry, elements are grouped and listed by groupings on the periodic table. In physics, matter is classified into gases, liquids, plasmas, and solids.

When reading material written in this pattern, first determine what is being classified and what the types or groups are. Look for a topic or summary sentence that states what is being classified. Next, discover why or on what basis the classification was made. That is, determine what characteristics members of the group share. For example, the following excerpt from a biology textbook describes the classification of animal eggs.

TYPES OF EGGS

The three basic types of animal eggs are roughly categorized according to the amount of *yolk* they have. The amount of yolk is critical since it is the embryo's food supply, at least for a time. In some species, the embryo needs only a small supply of yolk since it soon switches to nutrients derived from the mother's blood, as is the case with humans. We only need enough to last until the embryo has implanted in the wall of the uterus. In contrast, birds leave their mother's body at a very early developmental stage, and they must carry their entire embryonic food supply with them. So, whereas a human egg is smaller than the period at the end of this sentence, it would be hard to hide an ostrich egg with this whole book. Interestingly, both the young and the adults of these two species are about the same size.

Other kinds of animals have a moderate yolk supply. In these, the young must begin to find its own food long before it has reached its final body organization. The frog is an example. The frog egg has just enough yolk to get the developing embryo to the tadpole stage; after that, the tadpole can survive on food stored in its tail for a time, but it must soon begin to eat on its own.

—Wallace, *Biology: The World of Life,* pp. 446–47

In this excerpt, the basis of classification is directly stated in the first sentence: eggs are classified according to the size of the yolk.

EXERCISE 16-3   *Read this excerpt from a physiology textbook, and answer the questions that follow.*

TYPES OF SMOOTH MUSCLE

The smooth muscle in different body organs varies substantially in its (1) fiber arrangement and organization, (2) responsiveness to various stimuli, and (3) innervation. However, for simplicity, smooth muscle is usually categorized into two major types: *single-unit* and *multiunit smooth muscle.*

Single-Unit Smooth Muscle

Single-unit smooth muscle, commonly called **visceral muscle,** is far more common. Its cells (1) contract as a unit and rhythmically, (2) are electrically coupled to one another by *gap junctions,* and (3) often exhibit spontaneous action potentials. All the smooth muscle characteristics described so far pertain to single-unit smooth muscle. Thus, the cells of single-unit smooth muscle are arranged in sheets, exhibit the stress-relaxation response, and so on.

Multiunit Smooth Muscle

The smooth muscles in the large airways to the lungs and in large arteries, the arrector pili muscles attached to hair follicles, and the internal eye muscles that adjust your pupil size and allow you to focus visually are all examples of **multiunit smooth muscle.**

In contrast to what we see in single-unit muscle, gap junctions are rare and spontaneous and synchronous depolarizations infrequent. Multiunit smooth muscle, like skeletal muscle, (1) consists of muscle fibers that are structurally independent of each other; (2) is richly supplied with nerve endings, each of which forms a motor unit with a number of muscle fibers; and (3) responds to neural stimulation with graded contractions. However, while skeletal muscle is served by the somatic (voluntary) division of the nervous system, multiunit smooth muscle (like single-unit smooth muscle) is innervated by the autonomic (involuntary) division and is also responsive to hormonal controls.

—Marieb, *Human Anatomy and Physiology,* p. 294

1. What does this excerpt classify?
2. Describe each type of smooth muscle.
3. On what basis is the classification made?

The Problem/Solution Pattern

Textbook chapters, homework, and exams in the physical sciences often contain problems. To solve these problems, you must apply the concepts, laws, and formulas presented in the chapter. Use the following steps to solve problems:

1. **Read the problem and identify what is given and what is asked for.** In word problems, mark or underline critical information. Next, restate the information using the symbols you will use as you solve the problem. Be certain not to use the same symbol to represent different quantities. For example, if there are two objects in a situation with different masses, do not use m for both masses. Use m_1 and m_2 to distinguish between the two masses.

2. **If possible, make a drawing of the problem.** Label known quantities with the correct symbols; using the symbols may suggest which equation to use in solving the problem, if you are not certain.

3. **State the principle that is related to the problem, and write the general equation that embodies the principle.**

4. **Calculate the solution.** Always write the units after each number (seconds, moles, liters, etc.).

5. **Analyze your answer.** Does it make sense? Compare your solution with similar sample problems and determine whether you followed the correct procedure. Check the units as well as the numerical values.

6. **Review your solution process.** Especially if you had difficulty with the problem, pause after you solve it to figure out what you should have done or known in order to solve it more easily. Did you overlook a step or ignore a key concept? Analyzing your solution process will help you solve similar problems more easily in the future.

Here is an example of the use of this problem-solving procedure:

PROBLEM: A cat steps off a ledge and drops to the ground in ½ second. What is the cat's speed on striking the ground? What is the cat's average speed during the ½ second? How high is the ledge from the ground?

Steps	**Example**
1. Identify what is given and what is asked for.	Given: drops in ½ sec, $t = ½$ sec Asked for: 1. speed (velocity) (v) 2. average speed (average velocity) ($\bar{v}$) 3. height (distance) (d)
2. Draw a diagram.	$t = ½$ sec
3. Determine the principle and formula.	Principle: acceleration and motion of free-falling bodies Formulae: $v = gt, d = \bar{v}t$ $g = 10$ m/s² $\bar{v} = \dfrac{\text{beginning } v + \text{final } v}{2}$
4. Calculate the solution.	$v = gt$ $v = 10$ m/s² $\times$ ½ s $= 5$ m/s $\bar{v} = \dfrac{0\text{m/s} + 5 \text{ m/s}}{2} = 2.5$ m/s
5. Analyze the answer.	$d = \bar{v}t = 2.5$ m/s² $\times$ ½ s $= 1.25$ m
6. Review the solution process.	Had to know acceleration of free-falling bodies is 10 m/s²

—Hewitt, *Conceptual Physics*, p. 30

■ Adapting Your Study Techniques

Because of the unique content of science courses, it is especially important to adapt your study habits. Use the following suggestions for studying in the sciences.

1. **Complete reading assignments before attending lectures.** Because of the unfamiliar subject matter, you can understand lectures better if you know something about the topic. You may not understand everything you read (and it will be necessary to reread after the lecture), but you will have an advantage during the lecture because the terms, concepts, and principles will be more familiar.

2. **Highlight your textbook selectively.** Everything looks important in scientific texts, and it is easy to fall into the habit of over-highlighting. Avoid this pitfall by reading a paragraph or section before highlighting. Then go back and mark only key terms and concepts. Do not try to highlight all useful facts. Refer to Chapter 8 for suggestions on how to highlight effectively.

3. **Use outlining.** Especially in the life sciences, many students find outlining to be an effective study and review technique. Some texts in the life sciences include chapter outlines; even though your text may have one, make your own. It is the process of making the outline that is important. Outlining forces you to decide what information is important and how it is related and then to express the ideas in your own words. Refer to Chapter 9 for specific suggestions on taking outline notes.

4. **Integrate your lab work with the text and lectures.** Most science courses have a required lab. Because the lab is scheduled separately from the lecture and has its own manual, you may fail to see the lab as an integral part of the course. The lab is intended to help you understand and apply principles and research techniques used in your course and provides you with an opportunity to ask pertinent questions. Use the following tips for handling lab work:

   - Be prepared before going to lab. Read the experiment once to understand its overall purpose and a second time to understand the specific procedures. Make notes or underline key information.
   - Ask questions before you make a mistake. Lab procedures can be time-consuming to repeat, so ask questions first.
   - Be sure you understand the purpose of each step before you perform it.
   - Analyze your results and do the lab report as soon as possible. The best time to study your results is while the experiment and procedures are still fresh in your mind. If you finish the lab work early, stay and discuss results and interpretations with other students or your lab instructor.
   - Follow the required format closely when writing your report.

5. **Use chapter problems as guides.** The end-of-chapter problems in your textbook help you determine what it is important to learn. Do the prob-

lems even if they have not been assigned by your instructor. As you read the problems, note the variables (temperature, pressure, volume, etc.) that appear in the problems. Then be certain to learn definitions, concepts, principles, and formulas pertaining to these variables.

6. **Develop a weekly study plan.** Science is best studied on a daily basis. Devise a weekly plan that includes time every day for previewing text assignments, reviewing lecture notes, reading text assignments, preparing for and writing up labs, and—most important—reviewing in such a way as to integrate lectures, the text, and lab sessions.

7. **Prepare for exams.** Exams and quizzes in the sciences require you to learn factual information as well as develop problem-solving ability and apply your learning to practical situations. To be prepared for exams,

- Make lists of types of problems you have studied and key facts about their solution.
- Identify key laws, principles, and concepts.
- Determine where your instructor placed her or his emphasis.
- Prepare a practice test, using problems from your text, and take it as though it were an actual exam.
- Consider forming a study group with classmates.

■ If You Are Having Difficulty

If the sciences are typically a difficult field of study for you, or if you suddenly find yourself not doing well in a science course, try the following survival tactics:

Use available resources. Visit your instructor during office hours to discuss your performance or to get help with particular problems. Check to see whether tutoring is available through the department office or the college's learning center.

Make changes in your learning strategies. If you are a non-science major taking your one or two required science courses, you may feel as strange as if you were in a foreign country. First, you must revise your approaches and strategies. Plan on making the changes already described in this section.

Learn from classmates. Talk with and observe the strategies of students who are doing well in the course. You are likely to pick up new and useful procedures.

Double your study time. If you are having trouble with a course, make a commitment to spend more time on it and to work harder. Use this added time to revise and try out new study strategies. Never spend time using a strategy that is not working.

Use ancillary materials. Many major science texts have study guides or problem-solving guides to accompany them. These may be in print or electronic form. Also check the book's Web site for useful study aids.

Finally, here are some specific tips to help you "pull the course together":

1. **Review your lecture notes and text assignments frequently; discover how they work together and where they seem to be headed.**

2. **As you review, make a list of topics you do understand and a list of those you do not.**

3. **Decide whether you are experiencing difficulty as a result of gaps in your scientific background.** Ask yourself whether the instructor assumes you know things when you do not. If so, consider finding a tutor.

4. **Make a list of specific questions and ask for help from both your classmates and your instructor.**

Test-Taking Tips
Preparing for Exams in the Natural Sciences

Exams in the sciences require you to learn factual information as well as to develop problem-solving ability and apply your learning to practical situations. To be prepared for exams, use the following tips:

1. **Identify key laws, principles, and concepts.** Prepare review sheets on which you summarize important information.

2. **Make lists of types of problems you have studied.** For example, in chemistry, for a chapter on gases, you might identify problem types such as pressure and volume, temperature and pressure, and temperature and volume. For each problem type, list steps in the solution. Practice solving each problem type by using exercises in the text or by constructing your own problems.

3. **Consider forming a study group with classmates.** Quiz each other, and work through sample problems.

4. **Prepare a practice exam using problems or review questions from your text, and take it as though it were an actual exam.**

5. **Do not review by simply rereading your text and notes.** The material will look familiar, and you will think you have learned it. Instead, test yourself: Ask yourself questions and answer them. Use guide questions (see Chapter 1).

Self-Test Summary

1. What do the natural sciences focus on?	The natural sciences focus on asking questions about the physical and biological world and seeking answers to those questions.
2. Into what two categories are the natural sciences divided? Define each category.	The natural sciences are divided into the life sciences (concerned with the study of living organisms) and the physical sciences (concerned with the properties, functions, structure, and composition of matter, substances, and energy).
3. List six specialized techniques for reading in the natural sciences.	The six techniques are • previewing before reading. • adopting a scientific mind-set. • learning terminology and notation. • reading section by section. • studying sample problems. • studying drawings and diagrams. • brushing up on math skills.
4. Identify the four thought patterns that predominate in the natural sciences.	The patterns are process, cause and effect, classification, and problem/solution.
5. List the ways in which you might adapt your usual study techniques to the sciences.	Ways to adapt study techniques are • complete reading assignments before attending lectures. • highlight the textbook selectively. • use outlining. • integrate lab work with the text and lectures. • use chapter problems as guides. • develop a weekly study plan. • prepare for exams.
6. What should you do if you are having difficulty in a science course?	If you are having difficulty, you should • meet with your instructor; check about tutors. • change your learning strategies. • learn from classmates. • double your study time. • use ancillary materials.

Stem-cell Therapy: Promise and Reality

Prereading Questions

1. What are stem cells?
2. Why is federal funding limited for stem-cell research?

1   The potential of stem cells to treat devastating diseases has been hailed as one of the greatest medical breakthroughs of all time. But the rapidly unfolding ability of scientists to manipulate those undifferentiated cells into any type of specialized cell, including the pulsing cells of the heart, the insulin-producing cells of the pancreas, and the nerve cells in the spinal cord and brain, has also aroused controversy.

2   While President Bush has said there's great promise in this research, in August 2001 he announced that federal funding for embryonic stem-cell research would be limited. He cited "profound ethical questions" as the reason for restricting government-funded studies to some 60 embryonic stem-cell lines that were in use when the executive order was signed. Research on adult and animal stem cells was not limited.

3   The combination of high hopes and contention has left many people confused about where those potential treatments stand today, seven years after human embryonic stem cells were isolated and grown in the laboratory. This report separates the hype from the hope and reports on the current state of stem-cell treatments for a wide variety of chronic diseases and disabilities.

Basis of the Therapy

2   All of the 200 specialized cell types in the human body derive from the undifferentiated cells that begin to divide when an egg is fertilized by a sperm. If the ability of those early dividing cells to change into any type of cell could be harnessed, the theory goes, it might someday be possible to replace diseased or defective cells that cause degenerative diseases and disabilities. One day, researchers may even be able to use stem cells to grow entire hearts, livers, or kidneys.

5   Stem cells are found in embryos and in the umbilical-cord blood of newborns. They have also been identified in adults. Adult stem cells have been found in blood, bone marrow, brain, liver, skeletal muscle, skin, and even fat cells. Unlike embryonic stem cells, the ability of adult stem cells to morph into specialized cells and grow appears to be limited.

Sources of Cells Used in Research

6   Federally funded embryonic stem-cell research uses stem-cell lines derived before Aug. 9, 2001, from fertilized eggs donated by infertile couples who underwent in-vitro fertilization procedures. Some people object to such research on fertilized eggs because extracting the stem cells destroys the potential for life.

7   When the fertilized eggs are smaller than a grain of sand, stem cells lining the inner surface of a hollow ball of cells called a blastocyst are taken out. Some researchers cus-

tomize unfertilized eggs by removing their genetic material and replacing it with DNA from the stem-cell recipient. This experimental technique creates an embryonic stem-cell line that is almost genetically identical to the DNA donor, reducing the chance that stem cells transplanted back into the donor would trigger an immune response and cause rejection of the transplanted stem cells.

Treatments Available Today

8   Blood-forming stem cells found in adult bone marrow and the circulatory system develop into the red blood cells that carry oxygen, white blood cells that fight infection, and platelets that help the blood to clot. They are commonly collected from a matched donor and given to cancer patients to replace the bone-marrow cells destroyed by chemotherapy or radiation.

9   Some 45,000 to 50,000 bone marrow transplants are performed worldwide each year for patients with life-threatening diseases who urgently needed stem cells to regenerate their bone marrow.

10   About 4.5 million Americans have registered as volunteer bone marrow donors. In addition, doctors have begun to collect cancer patients' own stem cells, returning them as autologous transplants after treatments have ended and the drugs have washed out of patients' systems. When patients get back their own stem cells, there is no chance of immune mismatch or potentially fatal graft-vs.-host disease. An additional problem is that not all patients who need transplants can find suitably matched donors, and not all diseases can be treated with adult stem cells.

11   Stem-cell treatment is also being used for blood disorders, including aplastic anemia, sickle-cell anemia, and amyloidosis, a rare disease that can damage major organ systems. Some insurance companies will pay for all or part of stem-cell transplants. The federal government announced in March that Medicare is considering covering stem-cell transplants for amyloidosis.

12   Private and public banks are now available for freezing and storing blood left over in the umbilical cord after a child is born. This blood is rich in the stem cells used in the treatment of certain cancers and blood disorders. Private banking of the cord blood for personal use is considered an option for families with a child who has a disease that could someday require a stem-cell transplant. Public cord-blood banks accept donations of umbilical cord blood and make them available to patients who need a transplant, if a close match can be found.

Scientific Barriers to Stem-cell Therapies

13   Many scientific hurdles to stem-cell transplants remain. To use adult stem cells more widely, researchers need to find ways to identify them in the body and grow them in sufficient numbers. For both embryonic and adult stem-cell lines, methods need to be found to enable the cells to differentiate into the desired cell types. Then techniques are needed to transplant the stem cells so that they integrate and survive in the surrounding tissue and function as desired.

14   Investigators would need to somehow modify these cells and the recipient's immune system to help prevent rejection of the stem cells as foreign material. Another concern is the possible risk that transplanted stem cells could turn cancerous if cell division went

out of control. However, encouraging results are beginning to be reported in human clinical studies involving patients with congestive heart failure, and from lab and animal research into other major diseases and disorders.

State Initiatives

15   Last fiscal year, the National Institutes of Health awarded $24 million for embryonic stem-cell research. That's not enough to advance research, say some experts. They worry that this may lead to a brain drain as scientists leave for labs outside the U.S., where there are fewer restrictions and more money for research. California and New Jersey are currently the only states that expressly permit embryonic-stem-cell research, according to the National Conference on State Legislatures. Ten other states are considering such legislation. Last year California voters approved a statewide referendum that earmarks $3 billion in state funding over the next 10 years for studies on embryonic stem cells and, secondarily, umbilical-cord blood and adult stem cells. In New Jersey, a state-funded stem-cell research center will be constructed at Rutgers University. In Massachusetts, seven teaching hospitals have collaborated to form the Harvard Stem Cell Institute to develop therapies from embryonic and adult stem cells.

—*Consumer Reports*, June 2005

Writing About the Reading
CHECKING YOUR VOCABULARY

1. For each of the words listed below, use context; prefixes, roots, and suffixes (see Chapter 3); and/or a dictionary to write a brief definition or synonym of the word as it is used in the reading.

   a. devastating (para. 1) _____

   b. manipulate (para. 1) _____

   c. contention (para. 3) _____

   d. derive (para. 4) _____

   e. morph (para. 5) _____

   f. integrate (para. 13) _____

   g. earmarks (para. 15) _____

   h. collaborated (para. 15) _____

2. Highlight new, specialized terms introduced in the reading.

3. Draw a word map of one of the words in the reading.

CHECKING YOUR COMPREHENSION

1. What is the main point of this selection?
2. Explain how embryonic stem cells differ from adult stem cells.
3. What is controversial about stem-cell research?

4. What are some of the disorders that have been treated successfully using stem cells?
5. Underline the topic sentence of paragraph 13.
6. What are some of the scientific barriers to stem-cell transplants?
7. Which two states expressly permit embryonic-stem-cell research?

THINKING CRITICALLY

1. Do you agree that federal funding for embryonic stem-cell research should be limited? Why or why not?
2. Does the article present a biased or an objective view of stem-cell therapy?
3. According to the article, some insurers will pay for stem-cell transplants, and Medicare is considering covering stem-cell transplants for amyloidosis. Do you think insurers and Medicare should cover such treatments? Why or why not?
4. Consider how this article affected your knowledge of and attitude toward stem-cell therapy. Are you more or less likely to support stem-cell research after reading this?
5. According to the article, some experts fear that a "brain drain" will occur (para. 15). Explain what is meant by this phrase and whether you believe this is a real possibility.

LEARNING/STUDY STRATEGY

Draw a chart that summarizes the uses of and problems with stem cells.

ONLINE RESEARCH: STEM CELLS

Scientists use more than just the written word to present their research and views. Use these sites on stem cells to learn and teach in different ways.

1. Watch this tutorial about stem cells and stem cell therapy at http://www.sumanasinc.com/webcontent/anisamples/generalscience/stemcells.html. After a first viewing, watch it a second time and take notes. Then write a summary based on your notes. Watch the tutorial a third time to make sure your summary is accurate and complete enough. Try to teach someone else about stem cells using your summary and the tutorial. Reflect on how this media enhances or detracts from your learning.
2. Read through this Web page from the University of Utah on current issues in stem cell research at http://gslc.genetics.utah.edu/units/stemcells/scissues/. Pick one of the "Questions to Ponder" and prepare a short talk on your views. Use the reading area, as well as other areas of this Web site, plus any additional resources you might find for your research.

ADDITIONAL PRACTICE

THE NATURAL SCIENCES ON THE INTERNET

The Internet has numerous resources available for research in the natural sciences, including directories and Web guides to help you find material relevant to your studies, journals and databases, references works, and government resources. Here is a list of useful Web sites to get you started.

Directories/Web Guides

The Academy of Natural Sciences Internet Resources
http://www.acnatsci.org/library/link.html

Internet Public Library: Life Sciences
http://www.ipl.org/ref/RR/static/sci36.00.00.html

Journals/Indexes/Databases

Agricola
http://agricola.nal.usda.gov/

PubMed
http://www.ncbi.nlm.nih.gov/entrez/query.fcgi

References

FishBase
http://www.fishbase.org/search.php

MEDLINEplus Medical Encyclopedia
http://www.nlm.nih.gov/medlineplus/encyclopedia.html

Government Resources

Earth Science Enterprise
http://www.earth.nasa.gov/

LLNL Biology and Biotechnology Research Program
http://www-bio.llnl.gov/bbrp/bbrp.homepage.html

MULTIMEDIA ACTIVITIES

Practice your reading and research skills on the Web.

1. Astronomy Magazine

http://www.astronomy.com/home.asp

Explore the "final frontier" with the online version of this classic magazine. Find out what is in the sky tonight or read up on the latest discoveries. Be sure to visit the photo gallery. Write a list of words describing how you feel about the universe and your place in it.

2. Current Earthquake Information

http://earthquake.usgs.gov/recenteqsww/Quakes/quakes_all.html

Research the movement of the Earth at this site from the U.S. Geological Survey. Have there been any earthquakes near you lately? You may be surprised.

17 Reading in Technical and Applied Fields

LEARNING OBJECTIVES

✦To learn what to expect in technical courses

✦To develop specialized reading techniques for technical material

✦To learn processes and develop problem-solving strategies

✦To adapt your study strategies for technical material

Think About It!

The medical personnel above are working with a patient. While working with patients is the most important part of their job, they spend a large portion of it dealing with patient-related services—patient records, test results, referrals, and so forth. They also deal with a large number of technical details, as do students in other career fields.

Our society has become a technological one, in which there is a heavy reliance on automation and computerization. Consequently, more technical knowledge and expertise are required. More students are pursuing degrees in a variety of technical fields, including computer information systems, environmental technology, mechanical and electrical technology, and computer-assisted drafting. Applied fields such as EKG and X-ray technology, air conditioning and refrigeration, food service, and horticulture are other examples.

■ Technical Fields: What to Expect

If you are earning a degree in a technical field, you will take two basic types of courses: the technical courses in your major and required courses in related disciplines. For example, if you are earning an associate's degree in information technology, you will take numerous technical courses in programming, logic, and systems design, but you are also required to complete courses such as English composition, business communication, and physical education. Here is what to expect in each of these categories.

Technical Courses

The goal of many technical courses is to teach specific procedures and techniques that you will use on the job. These courses often present the theory and principles that govern the procedure, as well.

Grading and evaluation in technical courses is often performance-based. In addition to traditional exams and quizzes, instructors use "hands-on" exercises to evaluate your performance. In an air conditioning and refrigeration course, for example, you may be given a broken air conditioner to repair.

Work in technical fields often involves situations that require problem solving: a computer program has a "bug," a lab test produces inconsistent results, a number of landscape plantings die. Consequently, many instructors are careful to include problem-solving tasks in class, during labs, or on exams.

Many fields involve the use of instruments and equipment; others require measurement and recording of data. In either case, procedures must be followed exactly; measurements must be precise.

Although classroom lectures usually are a part of technical courses, most include some practical forms of instruction as well. Their purpose is to provide you with hands-on experience working with the procedures you are learning. As you work through lab assignments, remember that your skills are on display to your instructor just as they will be later to an employer. Develop systematic, organized routines to handle frequently used procedures and processes. Concentrate on following directions carefully. Always check and double-check your work. (Refer to Chapter 16, page 468, for additional suggestions on how to

An Engineering Professor . . .

Jim White, Dean, MeD, Industrial and Engineering Technology, Central Carolina Technical College

Talks About This Chapter

"This text helps students learn how to approach complicated reading material. I like the methodical and simple nature of the chapters I have read."

Offers Advice to Students

1. "Some documentation [manuals, etc.] accompanying equipment or equipment-related software may be difficult to read, as it may have originally been written by people whose native language is not English."

2. "Technology obviously changes at an incredible rate. As a result, the half-life of knowledge learned today is even shorter than 15 to 20 years ago. Students must learn how to approach problem solving step-by-step, or they will be overwhelmed."

prepare and conduct lab work.) Labs also give you an opportunity to find out whether you actually understood the lecture on which the lab is based. Labs will also help you discover whether you like the career you have chosen. If you dislike labs or find them extremely difficult or too routine, you should question the appropriateness of your career choice.

Nontechnical Required Courses

Make a genuine effort to benefit from courses outside your technical field. If you are taking a required introductory psychology course, you may be the only student in the class majoring in nursing; in this case, your psychology professor can do little or nothing to relate the course to your field. As your instructor discusses various topics, you should consider how they can be applied in your field. As you learn about defense mechanisms, for example, you might consider how they might be exhibited by patients. As you study nontechnical courses, be sure to make connections and applications to your field.

■ Reading Technical Material

Textbooks in technical fields are highly factual and packed with information. Compared to other textbooks, technical writing may seem "crowded" and difficult to read. In many technical courses, your instructor requires you to read manuals as well as textbooks. These are even more dense and, on occasion, poorly written. Use the following suggestions to help you read and learn from technical writing.

Read Slowly

Because technical writing is factual and contains numerous illustrations, diagrams, and sample problems, adjust your reading rate accordingly. Plan on spending twice as long reading a technical textbook as you spend on reading other, nontechnical texts.

Reread When Necessary

Do not expect to understand everything the first time you read the assignment. It is helpful to read an assignment once rather quickly to get an overview of the processes and procedures it presents. Reread it to learn the exact steps or details.

Have a Specific Purpose

Reading technical material requires that you have a carefully defined purpose. Unless you know why you are reading and what you are looking for, it is easy to become lost or to lose your concentration. Previewing is particularly helpful in establishing purposes for reading.

Pay Attention to Illustrations and Drawings

Most technical books contain illustrations, diagrams, and drawings, as well as more common graphical aids such as tables, graphs, and charts. (Refer to Chapter 10 for suggestions on reading graphics and visuals). Although graphics can make the text appear more complicated than it really is, they actually are a form of visual explanation designed to make the text easier to understand. Read the following excerpt from a building design and construction textbook describing the framing of roof rafters.

ROOF RAFTERS

Once the ceiling joists are nailed in place, the **roof rafters** can be installed. Common sizes for roof rafters include 2 in. x 6 in., 2 in. x 8 in., or 2 in. x 10 in. members spaced 12 in., 16 in., or 24 in. o.c., depending upon the width of the house and the magnitude of the dead and live loads imposed on the roof.

The rafters from both sides are usually connected at the top to a ridge board (Fig. A). Due to the angle cut in the rafters, the ridge board must be a larger size than the rafter. The ridge board runs the entire length of the roof and helps to distribute the roof load among several rafters. The location where the rafter bears on the exterior wall is notched to form a snug fit. The notch is commonly known as a "bird's mouth." The end of the roof is known as the gable and is the location where the roof and wall join.

Collar beams (i.e., collar ties) are often required when roof spans are long and the slopes are flat. Steeper slopes and shorter spans also may require collar beams, but only between every third rafter pair. Collar beams are usually 1 in. x 6 in. or 2 in. x 4 in. members.

—Willenbrock et al., *Residential Building Design and Construction,* pp. 171–72

FIGURE A   Roof Rafter/Ceiling Joist Roof Framing System

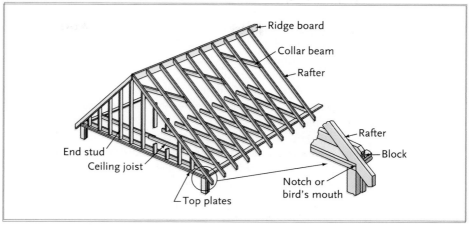

Source: Gerald E. Sherwood and Robert C. Stroh, *Wood Frame House Construction,* p. 81 (Mineola, NY: Dover Publications, Inc. 1989)

Now, study the diagram and reread the passage above. Does the diagram make the passage easier to understand?

Here are a few suggestions on how to read illustrations and diagrams:

1. **Note the type of illustrations or diagrams included in the assignment when you preview the chapter.**

2. **Look over each illustration, and determine its purpose.** The title or caption usually indicates what it is intended to show.

3. **Examine the illustration first.** Alternate between the text and the illustrations; illustrations are intended to be used with the paragraphs that refer to them. You may have to stop reading several times to refer to an illustration. For instance, when collar beams are mentioned in the preceding example, stop reading and find where they are placed in the diagram. You may also have to reread parts of the explanation several times.

4. **Look at each part of the illustration and note how the parts are connected.** Notice any abbreviations, symbols, arrows, or labels.

5. **Test your understanding of illustrations by drawing and labeling an illustration of your own without looking at the one in the text.** Then compare your drawing with the text. Note whether anything is left out. If so, continue drawing and checking until your drawing is complete and correct. Include these drawings in your notebook and use them for review and study.

EXERCISE 17-1   *Read the following excerpt on ignition coils from an automotive technology textbook, and answer the questions that follow.*

IGNITION COILS

The heart of any ignition system is the **ignition coil.** The coil creates a high-voltage spark by electromagnetic induction. Many ignition coils contain two separate but electrically connected windings of copper wire. Other coils are true transformers in which the primary and secondary windings are not electrically connected. See Figure B.

The center of an ignition coil contains a core of laminated soft iron (thin strips of soft iron). This core increases the magnetic strength of the coil. Surrounding the laminated core are approximately 20,000 turns of fine wire (approximately 42-gauge). These windings are called the **secondary** coil windings. Surrounding the secondary winding are approximately 150 turns of heavy wire (approximately 21-gauge). These windings are called the **primary** coil windings. In many coils, these windings are surrounded with a thin metal shield and insulating paper and placed in a metal container. Many coils contain oil to help cool the ignition coil. Other coil designs, such as those used on GM's **high energy ignition (HEI)** systems, use an air-cooled, epoxy-sealed **E coil** named for the *E* shape of the metal laminations inside the coil.

—Halderman and Mitchell, *Automotive Technology:*
Principles, Diagnosis, and Service, pp. 382–83

1. What is the purpose of the illustration?
2. Does the diagram make the text easier to understand? Briefly describe how.
3. Sketch a diagram of an ignition coil without referring to the drawing above.

Use Visualization

Visualization is a process of creating mental pictures or images. As you read, try to visualize the process or procedure that is being described. Make your image as specific and detailed as possible. Visualization will make reading these descriptions easier, as well as improving your ability to recall details. Here are a few examples of how students use visualization:

FIGURE B
Internal construction of an oil-cooled ignition coil. Notice that the primary winding is electrically connected to the secondary winding. The polarity (positive or negative) of a coil is determined by the direction in which the coil is wound.

A nursing student learned the eight family life cycles by visualizing her sister's family at each stage.

A student taking a computer course was studying the two basic methods of organizing data on a magnetic disk: the sector method and the cylinder method. She visualized the sector method as slices of pie and the cylinder method as a stack of dinner plates.

Now read the following description of an optical disk system from a computer science textbook, and try to visualize as you read.

OPTICAL DISKS

Optical technology used with laser disk systems is providing a very high capacity storage medium with the **optical disk,** also called a **videodisk.** Videodisks will open new applications, since they can be used to store data, text, audio, and video images.

Optical disk systems look like magnetic disk systems. Each has a rotating platter and a head mechanism to record information. However, optical systems differ because they use light energy rather than magnetic fields to store data. A high-powered laser beam records data by one of two methods. With the **ablative method,** a hole is burned in the disk surface. With the **bubble method,** the disk surface is heated until a bubble forms.

The laser beam, in a lower power mode, reads the data by sensing the presence or absence of holes or bumps. The light beam will be reflected at different angles from a flat or disfigured surface. A series of mirrors is used to reflect the light beam to a photodiode, which transforms the light energy into an electric signal. The photodiode process works like the automatic doors at your local supermarket. As you walk toward the door, you deflect a light beam, which signals the doors to open.

—Athey et al., *Computers and End-User Software*, pp. 122–23

Did you visualize the disks with tiny holes or bumps?

EXERCISE 17-2

Read the following passage describing a standard bumper jack. As you read, try to visualize the jack. After you have finished, draw a sketch of the jack as it is described in the passage, without looking at the diagram. After you have completed your sketch, compare it with Figure C on page 484.

DESCRIPTION OF A STANDARD BUMPER JACK

Introduction—General Description

The standard bumper jack is a portable mechanism for raising the front or rear of a car through force applied with a lever. This jack enables even a frail person to lift one corner of a 2-ton automobile.

The jack consists of a molded steel base supporting a free-standing, perpendicular notched shaft. Attached to the shaft are a leverage mechanism, a bumper catch, and a cylinder for insertion of the jack handle. Except for the main shaft and leverage mechanism, the jack is made to be dismantled and to fit neatly in the car's trunk.

The jack operates on a leverage principle, with the human hand traveling 18 inches and the car only ⅜ of an inch during a normal jacking stroke. Such a device requires many strokes to raise the car off the ground, but may prove a lifesaver to a motorist on some deserted road.

Five main parts make up the jack: base, notched shaft, leverage mechanism, bumper catch, and handle.

Description of Parts and Their Function

Base

The rectangular base is a molded steel plate that provides support and a point of insertion for the shaft. The base slopes upward to form a platform containing a 1-inch depression that provides a stabilizing well for the shaft. Stability is increased by a 1-inch cuff around the well. As the base rests on its flat surface, the bottom end of the shaft is inserted into its stabilizing well.

FIGURE C   Sample Diagram

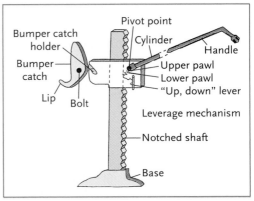

Shaft

The notched shaft is a steel bar (32 inches long) that provides a vertical track for the leverage mechanism. The notches, which hold the mechanism in its position on the shaft, face the operator.

The shaft vertically supports the raised automobile, and attached to it is the leverage mechanism, which rests on individual notches.

Leverage Mechanism

The leverage mechanism provides the mechanical advantage needed for the operator to raise the car. It is made to slide up and down the notched shaft. The main body of this pressed-steel mechanism contains two units: one for transferring the leverage and one for holding the bumper catch.

The leverage unit has four major parts: the cylinder, connecting the handle and a pivot point; a lower pawl (a device that fits into the notches to allow forward and prevent backward motion), connected directly to the cylinder; an upper pawl, connected at the pivot point; and an "up-down" lever, which applies or releases pressure on the upper pawl by means of a spring. Moving the cylinder up and down with the handle causes the alternate release of the pawls, and thus movement up or down the shaft—depending on the setting of the "up-down" lever. The movement is transferred by the metal body of the unit to the bumper-catch holder.

The holder consists of a downsloping groove, partially blocked by a wire spring. The spring is mounted in such a way as to keep the bumper catch in place during operation.

Bumper Catch

The bumper catch is a steel device that attaches the leverage mechanism to the bumper. This 9-inch molded plate is bent to fit the shape of the bumper. Its outer ½ inch is bent up to form a lip, which hooks behind the bumper to hold the catch in place. The two sides of the plate are bent back 90 degrees to leave a 2-inch bumper-contact surface, and a bolt is riveted between them. This bolt slips into the groove in the leverage mechanism and provides the attachment between the leverage unit and the car.

Jack Handle

The jack handle is a steel bar that serves both as lever and lug-bolt remover. This round bar is 22 inches long, ⅝ inch in diameter, and is bent 135 degrees roughly 5 inches from its outer end. Its outer end is a wrench made to fit the wheel's lug bolts. Its inner end is beveled to form a blade-like point for prying the wheel covers and for insertion into the cylinder on the leverage mechanism.

Conclusion and Operating Description

One quickly assembles the jack by inserting the bottom of the notched shaft into the stabilizing well in the base, the bumper catch into the groove on the leverage mechanism, and the beveled end of the jack handle into the cylinder. The bumper catch is then attached to the bumper, with the lever set in the "up" position.

As the operator exerts an up-down pumping motion on the jack handle, the leverage mechanism gradually climbs the vertical notched shaft until the car's wheel is raised above the ground. When the lever is in the "down" position, the same pumping motion causes the leverage mechanism to descend the shaft.

—Lannon, *Technical Writing,* pp. 419–21

Mark and Highlight

You may find your textbooks to be valuable reference sources for lab or on-site experiences; you may also use them when you are employed in your field. Take special care, then, to mark and highlight your textbooks for future reference. Marking will also make previewing for exams easier. Develop a marking system that uses particular symbols or colors of ink to indicate procedures, important formulas, troubleshooting charts, and so forth. Refer to Chapter 9 for additional suggestions on how to highlight effectively.

Learn to Read Technical Manuals

Many technical courses require students to operate equipment or become familiar with computer software. Study of and frequent reference to a specific manual are additional requirements in some technical courses. Unfortunately, many technical manuals are poorly written and organized, so you need to approach them differently from textbooks. Use the following suggestions when reading technical manuals:

1. **Preview the manual to establish how it is arranged and exactly what it contains.** Does it have an index, a troubleshooting section, a section with specific operating instructions? Study the table of contents carefully and mark sections that will be particularly useful.

2. **Do not read the manual from cover to cover.** First, locate and review those sections you identified as particularly useful. Concentrate on the parts that describe the overall operation of the machine: its purpose, capabilities, and functions.

3. **Next, learn the codes, symbols, commands, or terminology used in the manual.** Check to see if the manual provides a list of special terms. Many computer software manuals, for instance, contain a list of symbols, commands, or procedures used throughout the manual. If such a list is not included, begin making your own list on a separate sheet or on the inside cover of the manual.

4. **Begin working with the manual and the equipment simultaneously, applying each step as you read it.**

5. **If the manual does not contain a useful index, make your own by jotting down page numbers of sections you know you will need to refer to frequently.**

6. **If the manual is overly complicated or difficult to read, simplify it by writing your own step-by-step directions in the margin or on a separate sheet.**

■ The Allied Health Fields

Allied health is one of the fastest growing career fields due to a variety of factors including the increasing life expectancy of the U.S. population and ongoing scientific and medical advances and innovations. This section of the chapter offers suggestions for reading, learning, and studying in allied health courses.

Learn Medical Terminology

Medical terminology is the vocabulary of technical terms used in medicine. These terms are used in written and oral communication in all allied health settings including labs, hospitals, doctors' offices, and other treatment facilities. In order to be part of a medical team and to communicate with your team's members, you must be able to "speak the language." This means you must be able to read, write, and speak using medical terminology.

Medical terminology is specialized and precise. Specific words are used to refer to diseases, procedures, equipment, and parts of the body. As medical science advances, new terms are introduced to describe new procedures, diseases, and drugs, thereby expanding the store of medical terminology. Here are a few suggestions for learning this new vocabulary.

Learn Word Parts   The key to understanding medical terminology is to learn the meaning of word parts commonly used in medicine. Think of word parts as the key to unlocking the code of medical terminology. Learning the meaning of word parts, which are used in many words, is a much more efficient way of mastering terminology than memorizing the meaning of each individual word you need to learn. Word parts are discussed in detail in Chapter 3 of this book. Be sure to review this section to help you get started using word parts to decipher unfamiliar medical terms.

An Allied Health Professor . . .

Brad Foley, RN, BSN,
Nursing Instructor,
Minneapolis Community
Technical College

Talks About This Chapter

"The emphasis on terminology is well placed and a must for allied health."

Advice to Students

1. "The goal of classroom work is to allow you to reason out your actions and articulate your reasoning."

2. "Students should learn to re-read sections (probably up to six times). Each re-reading should have a specific goal."

Many long and complicated medical terms can be broken down into parts. The word *bilateral* has three word parts:

bi means two

later means side

al means pertaining to

So you can figure out that *bilateral* refers to something that is two-sided.

To learn a large number of word parts, many students find it effective to use index cards. Record the word part on the front and its meaning on the back. Create packs of cards that pertain to various topics you are studying, such as the various body systems—the skeletal system, the nervous system, and so forth. This index card system is explained in Chapter 3 on page 72.

Learn Eponyms   **Eponyms** are words that are based on a person's name. In medicine, they are often used to describe diseases, drugs, or structures discovered or described by particular individuals. For example, Hodgkin's lymphoma is a type of cancer first described by a physician named William Hodgkin.

Learn Acronyms   **Acronyms** are words created from the first letters of a group of words. CAT scan, for example, stands for computed axial tomography scan. STD stands for sexually transmitted disease, and MRI stands for magnetic resonance imaging.

Develop Your Mathematics Skills

Mathematics skills are vital in allied health fields because making correct measurements, such as medication dosages, are very important. However, mathematics as used in allied health often involves more than simple calculations. Three types of skills are involved in these math-related tasks. First, you have to have knowledge. For example, you need to know what certain drugs are used for, what are safe dosages of them, and how often they can be given to a patient. Second, you need good reasoning skills. You need to be able to make inferences and draw conclusions about different situations. Finally, you need to be able to make simple calculations.

Here is an example of a common math problem that involves these skills:

Sample Problem

According to the manufacturer's recommendations, children 9 to 10 years old should not receive more than 2 grams of acetaminophen in a 24-hour period. If you are using acetaminophen solution containing 160 milligrams in 3.33 milliliters, how many milliliters per day would you give to reach the maximum dose?

In this problem situation, which a nurse may typically encounter, you have to understand what acetaminophen is and what it is used to treat. You also need to be able to reason out how to calculate the number of milliliters you can administer without exceeding the maximum dose for a 24-hour period, and then do the actual calculations.

Pay Attention to Processes and Procedures

Processes and procedures are important in all allied health fields. Processes are particularly complicated to understand when there is more than one option for treatment in a particular situation. As you read your textbooks, be sure to mark or highlight processes and procedures. To learn and remember how processes and procedures work, it may be helpful to construct a diagram or flowchart that details the options and shows what action to take depending on a given situation.

Here is an example of a flowchart that details the procedures to follow when rechecking the temperature of a patient who is suffering from hyperthermia (unusually high body temperature).

FIGURE 17-1 Response to Hyperthermia

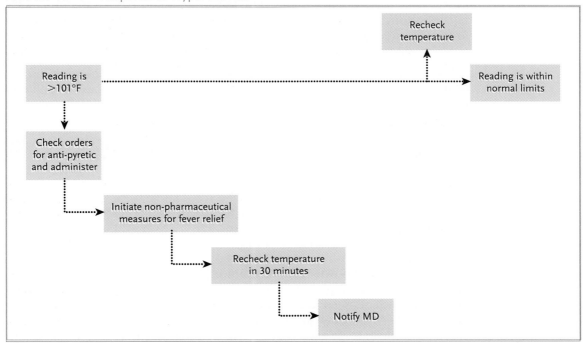

Plan on Rereading Frequently

Plan on rereading your text and other course materials frequently. You cannot expect to grasp everything on a single reading. Read a textbook chapter once to get a general idea of what it is about. Read the chapter again to focus on the chapter's main points. Read it a third time and focus on a specific goal, for example, to learn new terminology, or to learn about the use of medications in treating a particular disease process, or to find out how to perform a specific procedure,

Polish Your Reasoning Skills

Learning in the allied health fields goes far beyond memorizing facts. While it is essential to acquire a solid base of knowledge, that is not all that will be expected of you. Rather, you must use your factual knowledge base to reason out what must be done in specific situations, and be able to explain your reasoning to others. Skills such as making inferences, drawing conclusions, and evaluating data and evidence are essential. (Refer to Chapter 4 of this book for a review of these skills.) For example, if you are working as an ER nurse, you must use your knowledge of what vital signs mean to reason out what immediate action is appropriate for you to take when a patient is first admitted.

Develop Skills in Informatics

Informatics is the use of information and computer technology to support medical diagnosis and treatment, as well as to manage a medical office. Think of informatics as the managing of information and records. All workers in the allied health fields are involved with informatics, since accurate recordkeeping is essential to communication and quality care. Here are a few examples of the types of information nursing care professionals need to manage: documentation of patient care and discharge, computerized patient records, online drug information, and the monitoring of devices that record patient vital signs.

Here is what you can do to be prepared:

- **Polish your computer literacy and keyboarding skills.**
- **Learn medical terminology so you are prepared to "speak the language."**
- **Take any training classes or workshops, either in real time or online, that are available.**
- **Develop an awareness of patient confidentiality.** Patient records are protected by privacy laws, and you must take steps to insure privacy regulations are followed. (The reading at the end of the chapter provides more information on this topic.)

Use Practicum Experiences to Your Advantage

Many allied health fields require practicum experiences. A practicum is a work experience in a medical setting where you learn practical, on-the-job skills and apply the skills and knowledge you have learned in the classroom. Be sure to treat this experience seriously; it is an important part, if not *the* most important part of your training. Here is how to succeed in and use practicum experience to your advantage:

- **Prepare in advance.** Do not just show up on the assigned day. Learn about the facility; consider visiting it before your first day.
- **Take notes during or after each day at work.** Record information that you are expected to know and use; it is annoying to supervisors if you keep asking the same questions. Also, record what you have learned. Many students find keeping a journal helpful. Avoid personal thoughts: instead record your experience in a factual manner.
- **Expect to be evaluated.** Your performance will be evaluated by a supervisor. Ask for and expect feedback on your work. Remember, too, that a positive evaluation may lead to a job offer.
- **Use the practicum to learn about where you would like to work.** Your practicum can provide you with valuable information about the type of patients you enjoy working with, the kind of facility in which you would like to work, and the area of the health field you would like to specialize in.

■ Thought Patterns in Technical Fields

The two thought patterns most commonly used in technical fields are process and problem/solution. Each is used in textbooks and manuals as well as in practical, hands-on situations.

Reading Process Descriptions

Testing procedures, directions, installations, repairs, instructions, and diagnostic checking procedures all follow the process pattern. To read materials written in this pattern, you must not only learn the steps but also learn them in the correct order. To study process material, use the following tips:

1. **Prepare study sheets that summarize each process.** For example, a nursing student learning the steps in venipuncture (taking a blood sample) wrote the summary sheet shown in Figure 17-2 on page 491.
2. **Test your recall by writing out the steps from memory.** Recheck periodically by mentally reviewing each step.
3. **For difficult or lengthy procedures, write each step on a separate index card.** Shuffle the pack and practice putting the cards in the correct order.
4. **Be certain you understand the logic behind the process.** Figure out why each step is performed in the specified order.

EXERCISE 17-3
LEARNING COLLABORATIVELY

Read the following excerpt describing acid rain. After you have read it, write a process summary of each stage of the acid rain process. Compare your process summary with that of a classmate.

FIGURE 17-2   Sample Summary Sheet

<u>Venipuncture</u>

1. Wash hands, explain procedure to patient; assess patient status
2. Assemble equipment
3. Locate puncture site
4. Apply tourniquet, cleanse site
5. Place thumb distal to puncture site
6. Insert needle 30° angle, aspirate desired amount
7. Remove tourniquet, place dry compress on needle tip & withdraw
8. Remove needle from syringe and place specimen in container; label

HOW ACID RAIN DEVELOPS, SPREADS, AND DESTROYS

Introduction

Acid rain is environmentally damaging rainfall that occurs after fossil fuels burn, releasing nitrogen and sulfur oxides into the atmosphere. Acid rain, simply stated, increases the acidity level of waterways because these nitrogen and sulfur oxides combine with the air's normal moisture. The resulting rainfall is far more acidic than normal rainfall. Acid rain is a silent threat because its effects, although slow, are cumulative. This report explains the cause, the distribution cycle, and the effects of acid rain.

Most research shows that power plants burning oil or coal are the primary cause of acid rain. The burnt fuel is not completely expended, and some residue enters the atmosphere. Although this residue contains several potentially toxic elements, sulfur oxide and, to a lesser extent, nitrogen oxide are the major problem, because they are transformed when they combine with moisture. This chemical reaction forms sulfur dioxide and nitric acid, which then rain down to earth.

The major steps explained here are (1) how acid rain develops, (2) how acid rain spreads, and (3) how acid rain destroys.

The Process

How Acid Rain Develops

Once fossil fuels have been burned, their usefulness is over. Unfortunately, it is here that the acid rain problem begins.

Fossil fuels contain a number of elements that are released during combustion. Two of these, sulfur oxide and nitrogen oxide, combine with normal moisture to produce sulfuric acid and nitric acid. (Figure D illustrates how acid rain develops.) The released gases undergo a chemical change as they combine with atmospheric ozone and water vapor. The resulting rain or snowfall is more acid than normal precipitation.

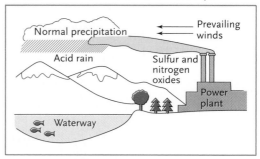

FIGURE D   How Acid Rain Develops

Acid level is measured by pH readings. The pH scale runs from 0 through 14—a pH of 7 is considered neutral. (Distilled water has a pH of 7.) Numbers above 7 indicate increasing degrees of alkalinity. (Household ammonia has a pH of 11.) Numbers below 7 indicate increasing acidity. Movement in either direction on the pH scale, however, means multiplying by 10. Lemon juice, which has a pH value of 2, is 10 times more acidic than apples, which have a pH of 3, and is 1,000 times more acidic than carrots, which have a pH of 5.

Because of carbon dioxide (an acid substance) normally present in air, unaffected rainfall has a pH of 5.6. At this time, the pH of precipitation in the northeastern United States and Canada is between 4.5 and 4. In Massachusetts, rain and snowfall have an average pH reading of 4.1. A pH reading below 5 is considered to be abnormally acidic, and therefore a threat to aquatic populations.

How Acid Rain Spreads

Although it might seem that areas containing power plants would be most severely affected, acid rain can in fact travel thousands of miles from its source. Stack gases escape and drift with the wind currents. The sulfur and nitrogen oxides are thus able to travel great distances before they return to earth as acid rain.

For an average of two to five days, the gases follow the prevailing winds far from the point of origin. For example, estimates show that about 50 percent of the acid rain that affects Canada originates in the United States; at the same time, 15 to 25 percent of the U.S. acid rain problem originates in Canada.

The tendency of stack gases to drift makes acid rain such a widespread menace. More than 200 lakes in the Adirondacks, hundreds of miles from any industrial center, are unable to support life because their water has become so acidic.

How Acid Rain Destroys

Acid rain causes damage wherever it falls. It erodes various types of building rock such as limestone, marble, and mortar, which are gradually eaten away by the constant bathing in acid. Damage to buildings, houses, monuments, statues, and cars is widespread. Some priceless monuments and carvings already have been destroyed, and even trees of some varieties are dying in large numbers.

More important, however, is acid rain damage to waterways in the affected areas. (Figure E illustrates how a typical waterway is infiltrated.) Because of its high acidity, acid rain dramatically lowers the pH of lakes and streams.

Although its effect is not immediate, acid rain can eventually make a waterway so acidic it dies. In areas with natural acid-buffering elements such as limestone, the dilute acid has less effect. The northeastern United States and Canada, however, lack this natural protection, and so are continually vulnerable.

The pH level in an affected waterway drops so low that some species cease to reproduce. In fact, a pH level of 5.1 to 5.4 means that fisheries are threatened; once a waterway reaches a pH level of 4.5, no fish reproduction occurs. Because each creature is part of the overall food chain, loss of one element in the chain disrupts the whole cycle.

FIGURE E How Acid Rain Destroys

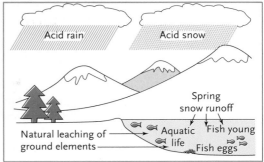

In the northeastern United States and Canada, the acidity problem is compounded by the runoff from acid snow. During the cold winter months, acid snow sits with little melting, so that by spring thaw, the acid released is greatly concentrated. Aluminum and other heavy metals normally present in soil are released by acid rain and runoff. These toxic substances leach into waterways in heavy concentrations, affecting fish in all stages of development.

Summary

Acid rain develops from nitrogen and sulfur oxides emitted by industrial and power plants burning fossil fuels. In the atmosphere, these oxides combine with ozone and water to form acid rain: precipitation with a lower-than-average pH. This acid precipitation returns to earth many miles from its source, severely damaging waterways that lack natural buffering agents. The northeastern United States and Canada are the most severely affected areas in North America.

—Lannon, *Technical Writing*, pp. 452–55

Problem-Solving Strategies

In technical fields, you will encounter hypothetical problems to solve that require you to apply formulas and work with procedures. More important, you will face simulated problems in labs and actual problems throughout your career. A systematic approach is helpful to improve your problem-solving abilities.

It is easy to panic when a piece of equipment fails or a procedure does not produce the expected results. Using a systematic approach to solving problems will help you in these situations. A problem is basically a conflict between "what is" (the present state) and "what should be" or "what is desired" (the goal state). For example, a medical office assistant has a problem when she cannot calm a frightened child in order to take her blood pressure. The following steps can help you attack problem situations:

Step 1: Specify the problem. Do this by evaluating the present state and determining how it differs from what is desired. The more specific you can be, the more likely that you will be able to identify working solutions. For example, if you are faced with a machine that does not function properly, decide what part or feature is malfunctioning. Do not simply say the machine does not work; instead, decide that the robot arm does not remain in position to complete the task. If your patient will not cooperate when you need to take her blood pressure, try to discover why she is unwilling.

Step 2: Analyze the problem. Analysis is a complex critical thinking skill. Begin by learning as much as you can about the problem. For instance, it may be necessary to find out why your young patient is frightened in order to be able to calm her down. To analyze a problem, it may be necessary to look beyond the obvious solution—to stretch your imagination and reach for creative options. For example, you may discover the child is frightened because you are wearing white and the child's dentist, of whom she is frightened, also wears white. When analyzing a problem, use the following suggestions:

- **Be flexible in your analysis.** Do not eliminate possibilities because they seem unlikely or never have happened in the past.
- **Brainstorm about all the possibilities.** Except for problems that must be solved immediately, spend a few minutes listing anything you can think of that is remotely related to your problem. Sort through the list later, preferably the next day. You probably will discover the seeds of a solution.
- **Talk with others about the problem.** By putting the problem into words (to a classmate or your instructor), you may hear yourself say things that will lead to further understanding.
- **Research problems for which you lack complete information.**

Step 3: Formulate a solution path. Identify a possible solution to the problem. For some problems, such as a machine malfunction, there is only one correct solution. For others, such as an uncooperative patient, various solutions may be feasible.

Step 4: Evaluate possible solution paths. If you have identified more than one solution path, the next step is to weigh the advantages and disadvantages of each one. You will need to think through each solution path in detail, considering how, when, and where you could accomplish each. Consider the likelihood of success with each solution, and weigh both short- and long-term effects. Thinking aloud may help you realize why various solutions will not work.

Step 5: Implement the solution. If your solution does not solve the problem, analyze what went wrong and repeat the problem-solving process. A trial-and-error process may be necessary. Be sure to use a logical, systematic approach and keep track of your results for each trial.

EXERCISE 17-4

Form groups of four to five students and discuss and develop a strategy for solving each of the following problems.

1. A microcomputer will not boot the program when the disk is inserted in the second disk drive.
2. A student in a science laboratory technology course gets a different result for his lab experiment than other students conducting the same experiment.

■ Study Techniques for Technical Courses

Use the following suggestions to adapt your study skills to technical courses.

Pronounce and Use Technical Vocabulary

Understanding the technical vocabulary in your discipline is essential. For technical and applied fields, it is especially important to learn to pronounce technical terms and to use them in your speech. To establish yourself as a professional in the field and to communicate effectively with other professionals, it is essential to speak the language. Use the suggestions in Chapter 3 for learning specialized terminology.

Draw Diagrams and Pictures

Although your textbook may include numerous drawings and illustrations, there is not enough space to include drawings for every process. An effective learning strategy is to draw diagrams and pictures whenever possible. These should be fast sketches; be concerned with describing parts or processes, and do not worry about artwork or scale drawings. For example, a student studying air conditioning and refrigeration repair drew a quick sketch of a unit he was to repair in his lab before he began to disassemble it. He then referred to sketches he had drawn in his notebook as he diagnosed the problem.

Reserve Blocks of Time Each Day for Study

Daily study and review are important in technical courses. Many technical courses require large blocks of time (two to three hours) to complete projects, problems, or drawings. Technical students find that taking less time is inefficient because if they leave a project unfinished, they have to spend time rethinking it and reviewing what they have already done when they return to the project.

Focus on Concepts and Principles

Because technical subjects are so detailed, many students focus on these details rather than on the concepts and principles to which they relate. Keep a sheet in the front of your notebook on which you record information to which you need to refer frequently. Include constants, conversions, formulas, metric equivalents, and commonly used abbreviations. Refer to this sheet so you will not interrupt your train of thought in order to search for these pieces of information. Then you can focus on ideas rather than specific details.

Make Use of the Glossary and Index

Because of the large number of technical terms, formulas, and notations you will encounter, often it is necessary to refer to definitions and explanations. Place a paper clip at the beginning of the glossary in your textbook and a second at its index so you can find them easily.

Test-Taking Tips
Preparing for Exams in Technical Courses

Exams in technical courses may consist of objective questions or of problems to solve. (For suggestions on preparing for and taking these types of exams, see the test-taking tips in Chapters 12, 13, and 15.) Other times, exams may take the form of a practicum. A practicum is a simulation, or a rehearsal, of some problem or task you may face on the job. For example, a nursing student may be asked to perform a procedure while a supervisor observes. Or an EKG technologist may be evaluated in administering an EKG to a patient. Use these suggestions to prepare for practicum exams:

1. Identify possible tasks you may be asked to perform.

2. Learn the steps each task involves. Write summary notes, and test your recall by writing or mentally rehearsing them without reference to your notes. Visualize yourself performing the task.

3. If possible, practice performing the task, mentally reviewing the steps you learned as you proceed.

4. Study with another student; test and evaluate each other.

Self-Test Summary

1. What kinds of courses do students in technical or applied fields study?	Students take both technical courses and nontechnical courses in other disciplines.
2. Identify six specific techniques for reading technical writing.	Six techniques for reading technical writing are • reading slowly. • rereading when necessary. • setting a specific purpose for reading. • studying illustrations and drawings. • using visualization. • marking and highlighting.
3. Which two patterns of thought predominate in technical and applied fields?	The two thought patterns are process and problem/solution.
4. List the five steps in the problem-solving process.	The five steps in the problem-solving process are • specify the problem. • analyze the problem. • formulate a solution path. • evaluate the possible solution paths. • implement the solution.
5. How should you adapt your study skills for technical courses?	You can adapt your study skills to read technical material by • pronouncing and using technical vocabulary. • drawing diagrams and pictures. • reserving large blocks of time in which to study. • focusing on concepts and principles, rather than just details. • making use of your textbook's glossary and index.

Information Security and Confidentiality

Prereading Questions

1. What kinds of information should be kept secure and confidential? Why?
2. What concerns do you have about your personal private information in medical settings?

1   The recent implementation of Health Insurance Portability and Accountability Act (HIPAA) regulations heightened awareness about information security and privacy practices. Health care information systems must provide rapid access to accurate and complete client information to legitimate users, while safeguarding client privacy and confidentiality. Electronic records facilitate efficient and effective sharing of information, but the ease with which they can be accessed creates concerns over confidentiality. At the same time, health care administrators must demonstrate measures that protect information to comply with HIPAA requirements and meet accreditation criteria set forth by the Joint Commission on Accreditation of Healthcare Organizations (JCAHO). These criteria continue to evolve. The HIPAA security rule does not specify the utilization of particular technologies; instead it calls for organizations to determine threats and appropriate protective measures for information in all formats. Protection of client privacy and confidentiality requires an understanding of the concepts of privacy, confidentiality, information privacy, and security as well as potential threats within an organization.

Privacy, Confidentiality, and Security

2   While the terms *privacy* and *confidentiality* are often used interchangeably, they are not the same. **Privacy** is a state of mind, a specific place, freedom from intrusion, or control over the exposure of self or of personal information. Privacy includes the right to determine what information is collected, how it is used, and the ability to access collected information to review its security and accuracy. Anonymity may be requested by an individual because they hold public office or are a celebrity. HIPAA regulations now require that clients must be given clear written explanations of how facilities and providers may use and disclose their health information. The movement to protect privacy is consistent with an international trend seen among industrialized nations.

3   **Confidentiality** refers to a situation in which a relationship has been established and private information is shared. Confidentiality is essential for the accurate assessment, diagnosis, and treatment of health problems. Once a client discloses confidential information, control over its redisclosure lies with the persons who access it. Private information should only be shared with parties who require it for client treatment. The ethical duty of confidentiality entails keeping information shared during the course of a professional relationship secure and secret from others. This involves making appropriate security arrangements for storage and transmission of private information, ensuring the equipment used for storage and transmission is secure and that measures are used to prevent the interception of e-mail, instant messages, Faxes, and other correspondence con-

taining private information. Nurses are obligated by the American Nurses' Association Code of Ethics and state practice laws to protect patient privacy. Inappropriate redisclosure can be extremely damaging. For example, insurance companies may deny coverage based on information revealed to them without the client's knowledge or consent. Inappropriate disclosure can also damage reputations and personal relationships or result in loss of employment. Most breaches of confidentiality occur as a result of carelessness and can be avoided by not discussing clients in public areas or with persons who do not have a "need-to-know," and through tight control of client records.

4   **Information privacy** is the right to choose the conditions and extent to which information and beliefs are shared. Informed consent for the release of specific information illustrates information privacy in practice. Information privacy includes the right to ensure accuracy of information collected by an organization. **Information security,** on the other hand, is the protection of information against threats to its integrity, inadvertent disclosure or availability. Information systems can improve protection for client information in some ways and endanger it in others. Unlike the paper record that can be read by anyone, the automated record cannot easily be viewed without an access code. Poorly secured information systems threaten record confidentiality because they may be accessed from multiple sites with immediate dissemination of information. This makes clients highly vulnerable to the redisclosure of sensitive information. The HIPAA Privacy Rule focuses on the protection of the privacy of people who seek care.

5   **Consent** is the process by which an individual authorizes health care personnel to process their information based on an informed understanding of how this information will be used. Obtaining consent should include making the individual aware of any risks that may exist to privacy as well as measures in place to protect privacy.

Handling and Disposal of Confidential Information

6   Although most people recognize the need to keep medical records confidential, many are less attentive to safeguarding information printed from the record or extracted from it electronically for report purposes. All client record information should be treated as confidential and not left out for view by unauthorized persons.

Computer Printouts

7   The primary sources of unauthorized release of information are printing and Faxing. All papers containing personal health information (PHI) such as prescriptions, laboratory specimen labels, identification bracelets, meal descriptions, addressograph plates or any other items that carry a patient's name or address, Social Security number, date of birth, or age must be destroyed. This may entail using shredders or locked receptacles for shredding and incineration later. Shredding onsite may offer better control as well as cost savings. Nurses may also be responsible for erasing computer files from the hard drive containing calendars, surgery schedules, or other daily records that include PHI. Disposal policies for records must be clear and enforced. For tracking purposes, each page of output should have a serial number or other means of identification so that an audit trail is maintained that identifies what each paper record is as well as the date and method for destruction and the identity of individuals witnessing the destruction. Control must be established over the materials that users print or Fax. Some institutions include a header on all printouts such as lab results that display the word "Confidential" in large letters. This reminds staff to dispose of materials appropriately.

Faxes

8   Sound institutional and departmental policies are needed for the use of Fax machines that consider what types of information can be sent, who should receive the transmissions, the location to which transmissions are sent, and verification of receipt. Information should not exceed that requested or required for immediate clinical needs. Legal counsel should review policies for consistency with federal and state law. Clients should sign a release form before Faxing information.

Electronic Files

9   Given that virtually all documents originate in electronic format, the destruction of paper printouts is almost incidental. For this reason, measures must be taken to ensure that confidential information contained on storage media, computers, and hard drives that is no longer needed is also disposed of properly. This method must go beyond the dumpster to include destruction of the storage media or electronically writing over files to ensure that no information can be retrieved from them. This is particularly important as equipment is often moved from one area of an organization to another and may even be donated to outside entities.

E-mail and the Internet

10 Policy should dictate what types of information may be sent via e-mail. E-mail is a great means of disseminating information, such as announcements, to large numbers of people quickly and inexpensively. However, information that is potentially sensitive should not be sent via e-mail unless it is encrypted. Nonencrypted messages can be read and public e-mail password protection of mailboxes can be cracked. When looking at encryption, ask whether your e-mail software encrypts all messages between users, whether messages are encrypted both in transit and when stored in the mailbox, and whether messages remain encrypted when sent between different e-mail packages. Unauthorized, or dormant, mail accounts should be destroyed and firewalls used for additional protection. It is all too easy to inadvertently send out e-mail to the wrong party, attach the wrong document or include persons who do not need the information. Software can be used to monitor network traffic for patterns that represent client information such as lists or Social Security numbers. This same software can detect requests for files, and monitor instant messaging and Web-based mail to determine if requests come from appropriate parties or if there are problems with information going out to unauthorized recipients.

11   Monitoring e-mail is important to avoid legal liability and maintain network security, employee productivity, and the confidentiality of information.

Writing About The Reading
CHECKING YOUR VOCABULARY

1. For each of the words listed below, use context; prefixes, roots, and suffixes (see Chapter 3); and/or a dictionary to write a brief definition or synonym of the word as it is used in the reading.

a. facilitate (para. 1) _____

b. accreditation (para. 1) _____

c. anonymity (para. 2) _____

d. discloses (para. 3) _____

e. breaches (para. 3) _____

f. inadvertent (para. 4) _____

g. dissemination (para. 4) _____

h. entities (para. 9) _____

i. encrypted (para. 10) _____

j. dormant (para. 10) _____

2. Highlight new, specialized terms introduced in the reading.

3. Draw a word map of one of the words in the reading.

CHECKING YOUR COMPREHENSION

1. Define the following terms: privacy, confidentiality, information privacy, and information security.
2. List at least two requirements specified by HIPAA regulations.
3. According to the reading, what are the two primary sources of unauthorized release of information?
4. Describe the proper disposal of confidential information contained on storage media, computers, and hard drives.
5. Why is it important to monitor e-mail?
6. Identify the thought pattern used in paragraphs 2 through 5.

THINKING CRITICALLY

1. In general, do you believe that your health care information is kept confidential? Why or why not? Did this reading change your opinion?
2. Explain the statement, "Information systems can improve protection for client information in some ways and endanger it in others" (para. 4).
3. Discuss the importance of consent. In what situations might it be difficult to establish an "informed understanding"?
4. Who do you think is the primary audience for this reading? Why?
5. How would you prefer to have confidential health information communicated to you (e.g., e-mail, fax, telephone, or regular mail)? Explain your answer.

LEARNING/STUDY STRATEGY

Draw a conceptual map showing the various methods of data transmission.

ONLINE RESEARCH: ALLIED HEALTH FIELDS

In allied health fields of study, privacy of medical information is important. The Internet provides useful information on privacy issues.

1. Visit the government's site for HIPPA at http://www.hhs.gov/ocr/hipaa. Review the fact sheets and comment on their usefulness. Critique their design, clarity, and purpose. What are the limitations to expressing this information in these ways?
2. Find your school's FERPA policy. For example, go to http://www.spu .edu/depts./sas/ferpa.html. How easy was this information to find? Had you seen this information before? Do you find that these policies are carried out on your campus? Discuss your experiences with classmates. Perhaps create and conduct a survey asking other students if they know about FERPA and what is allowed under it.

ADDITIONAL PRACTICE

TECHNICAL AND APPLIED FIELDS ON THE INTERNET

The Internet has numerous resources available for research in the technical and applied fields, including directories and Web guides to help you find material relevant to your studies, journals and databases, references works, and government resources. Here is a list of useful Web sites to get you started.

Directories/Web Guides
Internet Public Library: Engineering
http://www.ipl.org/ref/RR/static/sci15.00.00.html

Journals/Indexes/Databases
Engineering E-journal Search Engine
http://www.eevl.ac.uk/eese/

NIST Virtual Library Electronic Journals
http://srdata.nist.gov/gateway/gateway?dblist=0

References
TechWeb Encyclopedia
http://www.techweb.com/encyclopedia/

Academic Press Dictionary of Science and Technology
http://www.onelook.com/?d=all_tech&v=&sort=&langdf=all

Nursing Portal
http://www.nursing-portal.com/

WEB MED
http://www.webmed.com

Government Resources

National Institutes of Health Nursing Resources
http://nihlibrary.nih.gov/ResearchTools/Nursing.htm

National Science Foundation
http://www.nsf.gov/

MULTIMEDIA ACTIVITIES

Practice your reading and research skills on the Web.

1. **How Things Work**

   http://www.howstuffworks.com/index.htm
   http://howthingswork.virginia.edu/

   Pick some mechanical objects you use every day and find how they do
   what they do. Then learn about something completely new. As you use
   these two sites, compare their design, approach, and usability. Do you
   prefer one site over the other?

2. **F-Secure: Security Information Center**

   http://www.data-fellows.com/virus-info/hoax/

   Find out if that latest virus warning you received is a hoax at this comprehensive computer security site. Refer your e-mail do-gooders to this
   site when they forward something bogus to you. What tone does this site
   take toward Internet security? Write a list of the specific ways you use e-
   mail. Then place these into broader categories. Also record the amount of
   time you spend on each type of message. Evaluate your usage. How does
   it fit in with your overall time management plan?

Credits

Photo Credits

Page 15 Corbis; **41:** Mary Kate Denny/PhotoEdit Inc.; **45:** Jonas Ekstromer/AFP/Getty Images c 2005 AFP; **62:** c 2002 Mark Adams/FPG/Getty Images; **63:** Bob Daemmrich/The Image Works; **65:** Lawrence Migdale/Stone/GettyImages; **68:** c Robert W. Ginn\PhotoEdit, Inc.; **97:** Courtesy of Cesar c/o Almap/BBDO Communicacaoes Ltda.; **99:** Tony Savino/The Image Works; **111:** AP/Wide World Photos; **129:** Richard Hutchings/Photo Researchers, Inc.; **158:** AP/Wide World Photos; **187:** Dennis Degnan/Corbis; **239:** Chris Trotman/NewsSport/Corbis; **262:** both c Michael Mix; **268:** David Young-Wolff/PhotoEdit, Inc.; **285:** c Charles D. Miller III; **292:** c Scott McKiernan/Black Star; **323:** AP/Wide World Photos; **351:** AP/Wide World Photos; **368:** Flip Schulke/Black Star; **374:** AP Photo/Bill Haber; **399:** Owen Franken/Corbis; **427:** Images.com/Corbis; **454:** top left Ruth Orkin/Hulton Archive/GettyImages; **454:** top right Alfred Eisenstaedt/Time & Life Pictures/GettyImages; **454 bottom:** Self-Portrait, Claude Monet.1875. Oil on canvas, 85 x 60.5 cm. Hulton Archive/GettyImages; **477:** AP/WideWorld Photos.

Text Credits

Chapter 1 p. 27: Josh R. Gerow, from *Psychology: An Introduction*, 5th Edition, pp. 217-219. Copyright (c) 1997 by Addison-Wesley Educational Publishers, Inc. Reprinted by permission of Pearson Education, Inc. **28:** Richard L. Weaver II, from *Understanding Interpersonal Communication*, 7th Edition, pp. 423-426. Copyright (c) 1996 by HarperCollins College Publishers, Inc. Reprinted by permission of Pearson Education, Inc. **30:** Bruce E. Gronbeck, Kathleen German, Douglas Ehninger, and Alan H. Monroe, from *Principles of Speech Communication*, 12th Brief Edition, pp. 38-39. Copyright (c) 1995 by HarperCollins College Publishers, Inc. Reprinted by permission of Pearson Education, Inc. **36:** Frank Schmalleger, from *Criminal Justice Today: An Introductory Text for the Twenty-First Century*, 5th Edition, p. xviii. Copyright (c) 1999. Reprinted by permission of Prentice-Hall, Inc., Upper Saddle River, NJ. **37:** Weaver II, *Understanding Interpersonal Communication*, 7th Edition, pp. 226-227. **38:** Jerry A. Nathanson, P. E., *Basic Environmental Technology*, 3rd Edition, p. 351. Upper Saddle River, NJ: Prentice-Hall, 2000. **41:** Josh R. Gerow, from *Psychology: An Introduction*, 3rd Edition, pp. 654-656. Copyright (c) 1992 by HarperCollins College Publishers, Inc. Reprinted by permission of Pearson Education, Inc.

Chapter 2 46: Leon Baradat, from *Understanding American Democracy*, p. 163. Copyright (c) 1992 by HarperCollins Publishers, Inc. Reprinted by permission of Pearson Education, Inc. **47:** William E. Thompson and Joseph V. Hickey, *Society in Focus: An Introduction to Sociology*, 5th Edition, p. 131. Boston: Allyn and Bacon, 2005. **48:** Joseph A. DeVito, from *Human Communication: The Basic Course*, 7th Edition, p. 182. New York: Longman, 1997. **48:** Josh R. Gerow, from *Psychology: An Introduction*, 3rd Edition, p. 700. Copyright (c) 1992 by HarperCollins College Publishers, Inc. Reprinted by permission of Pearson Education, Inc. **48:** Robert A. Wallace, from *Biology:*

The World of Life, 6th Edition, p. 283. Copyright (c) 1992 by HarperCollins Publishers, Inc. Reprinted by permission of Pearson Education, Inc. **49:** James William Coleman and Donald R. Cressey, from *Social Problems*, 6th Edition, p. 277. New York: HarperCollins College Publishers, Inc., 1996. **49:** Jeffrey Bennett et al., *The Cosmic Perspective*, Brief Edition, p. 28. San Francisco: Addison Wesley Longman, 2000. **49:** Gerow, *Psychology: An Introduction*, 3rd Edition, p. 250. **49:** Karen C. Timberlake, from *Chemistry: An Introduction to General, Organic, and Biological Chemistry*, 6th Edition, p. 30. Copyright (c) 1996 by HarperCollins College Publishers, Inc. Reprinted by permission of Pearson Education, Inc. **50:** Michael C. Mix, Paul Farber, and Keith I. King, from *Biology: The Network of Life*, 2nd Edition, p. 532. (c) 1992 by Michael C. Mix, Paul Farber, and Keith I. King. Reprinted by permission of Pearson Education, Inc. **50:** William E. Thompson and Joseph V. Hickey, *Society in Focus: An Introduction to Sociology*, 5th Edition, p. 355 **51:** Gerow, *Psychology: An Introduction*, 3rd Edition, p. 319. **51:** Gerald Audesirk, Teresa Audesirk, and Bruce E. Byers, from *Biology: Life on Earth*, 7th Edition, pp. 2, 4. (c) 2005. Adapted by permission of Pearson Education, Inc., Upper Saddle River, NJ. **53:** Samuel L. Becker, from *Discovering Mass Communication*, 3rd Edition, p. 159. Copyright (c) 1992 by HarperCollins College Publishers, Inc. Reprinted by permission of Pearson Education, Inc. **53:** Philip G. Zimbardo, Ann L. Weber, and Robert L. Johnson, from *Psychology: Core Concepts*, 4th Edition, pp. 381-384. Published by Allyn and Bacon, Boston, MA, Pearson Education. Copyright (c) 2003, 2000 by Philip G. Zimbardo. Reprinted by permission of the publisher. **62:** James M. Henslin, from *Sociology: A Down-To-Earth Approach*, 6th Edition, pp. 482-485, incl. Fig. 16.4. Published by Allyn and Bacon, Boston, MA, Pearson Education. Copyright (c) 2003 by James M. Henslin. Reprinted by permission of the publisher.

Chapter 3 70: Pocket Dictionary, "Dilemma" from Philip D. Morehead, *The New American Webster Handy College Dictionary*, 3rd Edition, p. 197. New York: Signet, a division of Penguin Books USA, Inc., 1995. **70:** Collegiate Dictionary, "Dilemma." Copyright (c) 2000 by Houghton Mifflin Company. Reproduced by permission from *The American Heritage Dictionary of the English Language*, Fourth Edition. **71:** Entry #541.12 "talk about" from *Roget's International Thesaurus*, 5th Edition by Peter Mark Roget and edited by Robert L. Chapman, p. 389. Copyright (c) 1992 by HarperCollins Publishers, Inc. Reprinted by permission of HarperCollins Publishers. **74:** J. Ross Eshleman, Barbara G. Cashion, and Laurence A. Basirico, from *Sociology: An Introduction*, 4th Edition, pp. 34-35. Copyright (c) 1993 by HarperCollins College Publishers. Reprinted by permission of Pearson Education, Inc. **74:** Walter S. Jones, from *The Logic of International Relations*, 7th Edition, p. 379. (c) 1993 by Walter S. Jones. Reprinted by permission of Pearson Education, Inc. **75:** J. Ross Eshleman and Barbara Cashion, from *Sociology: An Introduction*, 2nd Edition, p. 380. Copyright (c) 1985 by HarperCollins College Publishers, Inc. Reprinted by permission of Pearson Education, Inc. **77:** Jack Levin and James L. Spates, from *Starting Sociology*, 4th Edition, pp. 251-252. (c) 1990 by Jack Levin and James L. Spates. Reprinted by permission of Pearson Education, Inc. **84:** Thomas C. Kinnear, Kenneth L. Bernhardt, and Kathleen A.

Krentler, from *Principles of Marketing*, 4th Edition, pp. 57-58. Copyright (c) 1995 by HarperCollins Publishers. Reprinted by permission of Pearson Education, Inc. **85:** Michael C. Howard, from *Contemporary Cultural Anthropology*, 5th Edition, pp. 12-13. Copyright (c) 1996 by HarperCollins College Publishers. Reprinted by permission of Pearson Education, Inc. **92:** Richard L. Weaver II, from *Understanding Interpersonal Communication*, 6th Edition, pp. 230-233. Copyright (c) 1993 by HarperCollins College Publishers. Reprinted by permission of Pearson Education, Inc.

Chapter 4   100: Thomas C. Kinnear, Kenneth L. Bernhardt, and Kathleen A. Krentler, from *Principles of Marketing*, 4th Edition, p. 301. Copyright (c) 1995 by HarperCollins Publishers. Reprinted by permission of Pearson Education, Inc. **103:** Gini Stephens Frings, *Fashion: From Concepts to Consumer*, 6th Edition, p. 11. Upper Saddle River, NJ: Prentice-Hall, Inc., 1999. **104:** Philip G. Zimbardo and Richard J. Gerrig, from *Psychology and Life*, 14th Edition, p. 501. (c) 1996 by Philip G. Zimbardo, Inc. and Richard J. Gerrig. Reprinted by permission of Pearson Education, Inc. **104:** Donald C. Mosley, Paul H. Pietri, and Leon C. Megginson, from *Management: Leadership in Action*, 5th Edition, p. 555. Copyright (c) 1996 by HarperCollins Publishers, Inc. Reprinted by permission of Pearson Education, Inc. **106:** Sources for quotations: Bill Gates: www.microsoft.com/billgates/writing.asp; David Satcher: www.surgeongeneral.gov/news/pressreleases/obesitypressrelease.html; Sir Edmund Hillary: http://teacher.scholastic.com/hillary/hilltran.htm. **106:** Arlene S. Skolnick, from *The Intimate Environment: Exploring Marriage and the Family*, 6th Edition, p. 224. (c) 1996 by Arlene S. Skolnick. Reprinted by permission of Pearson Education, Inc. **106:** Jeffrey Bennett et al., *The Cosmic Perspective*, 2nd Edition, pp. 311-312. San Francisco: Addison-Wesley, 2002. **108:** Rebecca Donatelle and Lorraine Davis, *Access to Health*, 6th Edition, pp. 281, 282, 292. Boston: Allyn and Bacon, 2000. **108:** B.E. Pruitt and Jane Stein, *Health Styles*, 2nd Edition, pp. 572-573. Boston: Allyn and Bacon, 1999. **113:** Stephen Kosslyn and Robin Rosenberg, *Psychology: The Brain, The Person, The World*, p. 162. Boston: Allyn and Bacon, 2001. **113:** X.J. Kennedy and Dana Gioia, *Literature: An Introduction to Fiction, Poetry, and Drama*, 2nd Edition, p. 789. New York: Longman, 2000. **115:** Arthur H. Purcell, "Trash Troubles" from *The World & I*, November 1998, Vol. 3, No. 11. Reprinted with permission from The World & I, a publication of The Washington Times Corporation, Copyright 1998. **117:** Dr. Kenneth R. Fehrman and Cherie Fehrman, from *Color: The Secret Influence*, pp. 82, 83. (c) 2000 by Prentice-Hall, Inc. Reprinted by permission of Prentice-Hall, Inc., Upper Saddle River, NJ. **118:** Nick Fiddes, from *Meat: A Natural Symbol*, pp. 100-101. (c) 1991, Routledge. Reprinted by permission of Taylor & Francis Books UK. **121:** John Dillin, "How Soon Will World's Oil Supply Peak?" from *The Christian Science Monitor*, November 9, 2005. Reprinted by permission of the author. **124:** Joseph Nocera "On Oil Supply, Opinions Aren't Scarce," *The New York Times*, September 10, 2005. Copyright (c) 2005 by The New York Times Co. Reprinted with permission.

Chapter 5   133: Mark Weingarten, from "Palm Springs in August: The Ducks Use Sunblock," *The New York Times*, August 9, 2002. Copyright (c) 2002 by The New York Times Co. Reprinted with permission. **133:** Mac Margolis, "A Plot of Their Own," *Newsweek*, January 21, 2002. **133:** Stephanie Dunnewind, "Launching Kids to Independence," *Seattle Times*, August 17, 2002. **134:** Robert A. Wallace, from *Biology: The World of Life*, 6th Edition, p. 754. Copyright (c) 1992 by HarperCollins Publishers, Inc. Reprinted by permission of Pearson Education, Inc. **135:** Wayne LaPierre, from "Standing Guard," *American Rifleman*, August 2002, Vol. 150, Issue 8, p. 12. Reprinted by permission of the National Rifle Association of America. **135:** Maria Elena Salinas, "Will All Hispanic Men be Suspect," *Seattle Post - Intelligencer*, July 30, 2002. **135:** D.F. Oliveria, "Burning Will Go; That's Not All Good," *Spokesman-Review*, July 24, 2002. **136:** Christine Haugen, "Logging Illogic," *World Watch*, September/October, 2002. **141:** Editorial, "Raising the September 11 Generation," *Chicago Tribune*, September 8, 2002. **141:** Letter to the Editor from Russ O'Hearn, "School's First Week Provides a Few Bright Exceptions," *Toronto Star*, September 6, 2002. **141:** "From the Hip; Gun Control," *The Economist* (US), November 23, 2002. **141:** Editorial, "Steroids Should be Tagged Out," *San Jose Mercury News*, June 3, 2002. **142:** Editorial, "Sign of Civilization," *Providence Journal*, August 15, 2002. **144:** Rebecca Jaycox, "Rural Home Schooling and Place-Based Education," *ERIC Digest*, December 1, 2001. **144:** "Endangered Species," *Funk & Wagnall's New World Encyclopedia*, EBSCO Online Reference System. **145:** Douglas Barrie, "Russia's Bazalt Working On Standoff Bomb Kit," *Aviation Week & Space Technology*, August 5, 2002. **148:** Frank Grazian, "How Much Do Words Really Matter," *Public Relations Quarterly*, Summer 1998, p. 37. **151:** Sara Ahmed, "Be Very Afraid" from the *New Internationalist* magazine, March 2005/Issue 376. Reprinted by kind permission of the New Internationalist. Copyright New Internationalist. www.newint.org. **155:** Jonah Goldberg "Profiles in Pointlessness," *National Review*, August 29, 2005. (c) 2005 by National Review, Inc., 215 Lexington Avenue, New York, NY 10016. Reprinted with permission.

Chapter 6   159: "Death Penalty Debate Finally Produces Results," *USA Today*, June 22, 2005. Copyright (c) USA TODAY, 2005. Reprinted with permission. **165:** Judith L. Rubin, from "No More Junk Toys," *Mothering*, November / December 2003. Reprinted by permission of the author. **171:** Barry W. Lynn, from "Pornography's Many Forms: Not All Bad," *Los Angeles Times*, May 23, 1985. **171:** Jane Rule, from "Pornography Is a Social Disease," *The Body Politic*, January/February 1984. **175:** "Misstep on Video Violence," *USA Today*, June 6, 2005. Copyright (c) USA TODAY, 2005. Reprinted with permission. **176:** Rod Blagojevich, "Parents Need Our Help," *USA Today*, June 6, 2005. Copyright (c) USA TODAY, 2005. Reprinted with permission. **178:** Michael De Alessi, "Elephants, Markets, & Mandates," *Fraser Forum*, April 2003, pp. 9-10. Reprinted by permission of The Fraser Institute. www.fraserinstitute.ca. **182:** "A Deadly Trade: Five South African Nations Bid to Sell Ivory" from *Humane Society International(tm) Newsletter*, Volume 7, July 2002, Issue 2. Reprinted by permission of The Humane Society of the United States/Humane Society International.

Chapter 7   190: Michael C. Mix, Paul Farber, and Keith I. King, from *Biology: The Network of Life*, 2nd Edition, p. 262. (c) 1996 by Michael C. Mix, Paul Farber, and Keith I. King. Reprinted by permission of Pearson Education, Inc. **191:** Richard Paul Janaro and Thelma C. Altshuler, from *The Art of Being Human*, 4th Edition, pp. 334-335. (c)1993 by Paul Janaro and Thelma Altshuler. Reprinted by permission of Pearson Education, Inc. **191:** Elaine Marieb, *Essentials of Human Anatomy and Physiology*, 6th Edition, p. 3. San Francisco: Benjamin Cummings, 2000. **191:** Stephen Davis and Joseph

Palladino, from *Psychology*, 3rd Edition, p. 40. (c) 2000 by Prentice-Hall, Inc. Reprinted by permission of Pearson Education, Inc., Upper Saddle River, NJ. **192:** Joseph A. DeVito, *Human Communication: The Basic Course*, 8th Edition, p. 124. New York: Longman, 2000. **193:** Gerard J. Tortora, from *Introduction to the Human Body: The Essentials of Anatomy and Physiology*, 2nd Edition, p. 56. (c)1991 by Biological Sciences Textbooks, Inc. and A and P Textbooks, Inc. Reprinted by permission of Pearson Education, Inc. **193:** Edward Tarbuck and Frederick Lutgens, from *Earth Science*, 9th Edition, p. 309. (c) 2000 by Prentice-Hall, Inc. Reprinted by permission of Pearson Education, Inc., Upper Saddle River, NJ. **194:** Tarbuck and Lutgens, *Earth Science*, 9th Edition, pp. 620-621. **194:** Gerard J. Tortora, from *Introduction to the Human Body: The Essentials of Anatomy and Physiology*, 3rd Edition, p. 100. (c) 1994 by Biological Sciences Textbooks, Inc. and A and P Textbooks, Inc. Reprinted by permission of Pearson Education, Inc. **195:** Tarbuck and Lutgens, *Earth Science*, 9th Edition, pp. 278-279. **196:** R. Jackson Wilson et al., from *The Pursuit of Liberty: A History of the American People*, Vol. 2, 3rd Edition, pp. 492-493. Copyright (c) 1996 by HarperCollins College Publishers. Reprinted by permission of Pearson Education, Inc. **197:** Philip G. Zimbardo and Richard J. Gerrig, from *Psychology and Life*, 14th Edition, p. 115. (c)1996 by Philip G. Zimbardo and Richard J. Gerrig. Reprinted by permission of Pearson Education, Inc. **198:** Alex Thio, from *Sociology*, 4th Edition, p. 255. Copyright (c) 1996 by HarperCollins College Publishers. Reprinted by permission of Pearson Education, Inc. **198:** Mix, Farber, and King, *Biology: The Network of Life*, 2nd Edition, pp. 663-664. **199:** Tortora, *Introduction to the Human Body: The Essentials of Anatomy and Physiology*, 2nd Edition, p. 77. **199:** George C. Edwards, Martin Wattenberg, and Robert Lineberry, from *Government in America*, 9th Edition, p. 416. Copyright (c) 2000 by Addison-Wesley Educational Publishers, Inc. Reprinted by permission of Pearson Education, Inc. **200:** Rebecca Donatelle, from *Access to Health*, 7th Edition, p. 264. Copyright (c) 2002 Pearson Education, publishing as Benjamin Cummings. Reprinted by permission of Pearson Education, Inc. **200:** Marieb, *Essentials of Human Anatomy and Physiology*, 6th Edition, p. 55. **201:** Wilson Dizard, *Old Media, New Media*, 3rd Edition, p. 179. New York: Longman, 2000. **201:** Edward Bergman and William Renwick, from *Introduction to Geography*, Updated 2nd Edition, pp. 442-443. (c) 2003 by Pearson Education, Inc. Reprinted by permission of Pearson Education, Inc., Upper Saddle River, NJ. **202:** Edwards et al., *Government in America*, 9th Edition, pp. 223-224. **203:** Bergman and Renwick, *Introduction to Geography*, Updated 2nd Edition, pp. 182-183. **203:** Donatelle, *Access to Health*, 7th Edition, pp. 223-224. **204:** Note 1, Neil A. Campbell, Lawrence G. Mitchell, Jane B. Reece, from *Biology: Concepts and Connections*, 2nd Edition, p. 478. Copyright (c) 1997 by The Benjamin/Cummings Publishing Company. Reprinted by permission of Pearson Education, Inc. **204:** Note 2, Robert A. Wallace, from *Biology: The World of Life*, 7th Edition, p. 524. Copyright (c) 1997 by Addison-Wesley Educational Publishers, Inc. Reprinted by permission of Pearson Education, Inc. **205:** Note 3, Josh R. Gerow, from *Psychology: An Introduction*, 5th Edition, p. 276. Copyright (c) 1997 by Addison-Wesley Educational Publishers. Reprinted by permission of Pearson Education, Inc.. **205:** Note 4, Wallace, *Biology: The World of Life*, 7th Edition, p. 378. **205:** Note 5, Elaine Marieb, *Human Anatomy & Physiology*, 4th Edition, p. 663. Menlo Park, CA: The Benjamin/Cummings Publishing Company, Inc., 1998. **205:** Thio, *Sociology*, 4th Edition, p. 534. **206:** Note 6, Wallace, *Biology: The World of Life*, 7th Edition, p.

382. **206:** Note 7, James A. Glynn, C.F. Hohm, E.W. Stewart, *Global Social Problems*, p. 449. New York: HarperCollins College Publishers, 1996. **207:** Note 8, Gerow, *Psychology: An Introduction*, 5th Edition, p. 278. **207:** Note 9, Richard G. Lipsey, Paul N. Courant, and Christopher Ragan, *Economics*, 12th Edition, p. 129. Reading, MA: Addison-Wesley Publishing Company, 1999. **207:** Note 10, Marieb, *Human Anatomy & Physiology*, 4th Edition, p. 614. **208:** Paul G. Hewitt, from *Conceptual Physics*, 7th Edition, p. 272. (c) 1993 by Paul G. Hewitt. Reprinted by permission of Pearson Education, Inc. **208:** Donatelle, *Access to Health*, 7th Edition, p. 516. **208:** Donatelle, *Access to Health*, 7th Edition, p. 300. **209:** Donatelle, *Access to Health*, 7th Edition, pp. 337-338. **210:** Thomas C. Kinnear, Kenneth L. Bernhardt, and Kathleen A. Krentler, from *Principles of Marketing*, 4th Edition, p. 218. Copyright (c) 1995 by HarperCollins College Publishers. Reprinted by permission of Pearson Education, Inc. **211:** Leon Baradat, from *Understanding American Democracy*, p. 300. Copyright (c) 1992 by HarperCollins Publishers, Inc. Reprinted by permission of Pearson Education, Inc. **211:** James M. Henslin, from *Social Problems*, 5th Edition, p. 154. (c) 2000 by James M. Henslin. Reprinted by permission of Pearson Education, Inc., Upper Saddle River, NJ. **212:** Henslin, *Social Problems*, 5th Edition, p. 74. **212:** Davis and Palladino, *Psychology*, 3rd Edition, pp. 535-536. **213:** Note 11, Duane Preble, Sarah Preble, and Patrick Frank, *Artforms: An Introduction to the Visual Arts*, 6th Edition, p. 136. New York: Longman, 1999. **214:** Note 12, Duane Preble et al., *Artforms: An Introduction to the Visual Arts*, 6th Edition, p. 380. **214:** Note 13, Joseph A. DeVito, *Human Communication: The Basic Course*, 7th Edition, p. 300. New York: Longman, 1997. **214:** Note 14, George Beekman, from *Computer Confluence: Exploring Tomorrow's Technology*, 3rd Edition, p. 74. (c) 1999 by Addison Wesley Longman, Inc. Reprinted by permission of Pearson Education, Inc. **214:** Note 15, Lipsey et al., *Economics*, 12th Edition, p. 71. **214:** William M. Pride, Robert J. Hughes, and Jack R. Kapoor, from *Business*, 5th Edition, p. 189. Copyright (c) 1996 by Houghton Mifflin Company. Reprinted with permission. **215:** Baradat, *Understanding American Democracy*, p. 202. **215:** Henslin, *Social Problems*, 5th Edition, p. 252. **216:** Edwards et al., *Government in America*, 9th Edition, p. 330. **216:** Henslin, *Social Problems*, 5th Edition, pp. 216-218. **218:** Donatelle, *Access to Health*, 7th Edition, p. 107. **218:** Tarbuck and Lutgens, *Earth Science*, 9th Edition, p. 298. **219:** Tarbuck and Lutgens, *Earth Science*, 9th Edition, p. 61. **220:** Note 16, Campbell et al., *Biology: Concepts & Connections*, 2nd Edition, p. 460. **220:** Note 17, Wallace, *Biology: The World of Life*, 7th Edition, p. 414. **220:** Note 18, Campbell et al., *Biology: Concepts and Connections*, 2nd Edition, p. 472. **220:** Note 19, Gerow, *Psychology: An Introduction*, 5th Edition, p. 438. **220:** Note 20, Campbell et al., *Biology: Concepts and Connections*, 2nd Edition, p. 552. **220:** Note 21, Duane Preble et al., *Artforms: An Introduction to the Visual Arts*, 6th Edition, p. 384. **220:** Note 22, Wallace, *Biology: The World of Life*, 7th Edition, p. 555. **220:** Note 23, Glynn et al., *Global Social Problems*, p. 139. **222:** Bergman and Renwick, *Introduction to Geography*, Updated 2nd Edition, p. 185. **222:** Dizard, *Old Media, New Media*, 3rd Edition, p. 169. **223:** Davis and Palladino, *Psychology*, 3rd Edition, p. 210. **223:** Bergman and Renwick, *Introduction to Geography*, Updated 2nd Edition, p. 182. **225:** Donatelle, *Access to Health*, 7th Edition, p. 81. **225:** Henslin, *Social Problems*, 5th Edition, p. 93. **225:** Dizard, *Old Media, New Media*, 3rd Edition, p. 87. **226:** Clayborne Carson et al., *African American Lives: The Struggle for Freedom*, pp. 490-491. New York: Longman, 2005. **226:** Dizard, *Old Media, New Media*, 3rd Edition, p. 157. **226:**

INDEX